T0181984

Communications
in Computer and Information Science 1323

More information about this series at http://www.springer.com/series/7899

Irena Koprinska · Michael Kamp ·
Annalisa Appice · Corrado Loglisci ·
Luiza Antonie · Albrecht Zimmermann ·
Riccardo Guidotti · Özlem Özgöbek et al. (Eds.)

ECML PKDD 2020 Workshops

Workshops of the European Conference on Machine
Learning and Knowledge Discovery in Databases
(ECML PKDD 2020): SoGood 2020, PDFL 2020,
MLCS 2020, NFMCP 2020, DINA 2020,
EDML 2020, XKDD 2020 and INRA 2020
Ghent, Belgium, September 14–18, 2020
Proceedings

 Springer

For the full list of editors *see next page*

ISSN 1865-0929 ISSN 1865-0937 (electronic)
Communications in Computer and Information Science
ISBN 978-3-030-65964-6 ISBN 978-3-030-65965-3 (eBook)
https://doi.org/10.1007/978-3-030-65965-3

This Springer imprint is published by the registered company Springer Nature Switzerland AG
The registered company address is: Gewerbestrasse 11, 6330 Cham, Switzerland

Editors

Irena Koprinska (iD)
University of Sydney
Sydney, NSW, Australia

Annalisa Appice (iD)
University of Bari Aldo Moro
Bari, Italy

Luiza Antonie (iD)
University of Guelph
Guelph, ON, Canada

Riccardo Guidotti (iD)
University of Pisa
Pisa, Italy

Rita P. Ribeiro (iD)
University of Porto
Porto, Portugal

João Gama (iD)
University of Porto
Porto, Portugal

Yamuna Krishnamurthy (iD)
Royal Holloway University of London
Egham, UK

Donato Malerba (iD)
University of Bari Aldo Moro
Bari, Italy

Michelangelo Ceci (iD)
University of Bari Aldo Moro
Bari, Italy

Elio Masciari (iD)
University of Naples Federico II
Naples, Italy

Peter Christen (iD)
Australian National University
Canberra, ACT, Australia

Erich Schubert
Technical University of Dortmund
Dortmund, Germany

Anna Monreale (iD)
University of Pisa
Pisa, Italy

Salvatore Rinzivillo (iD)
ISTI-CNR
PISA, Italy

Andreas Lommatzsch
Berlin Institute of Technology
Berlin, Germany

Michael Kamp (iD)
Monash University
Clayton, VIC, Australia

Corrado Loglisci (iD)
University of Bari Aldo Moro
Bari, Italy

Albrecht Zimmermann (iD)
University of Caen Normandy
Caen, France

Özlem Özgöbek
Norwegian University of Science
and Technology
Trondheim, Norway

Ricard Gavaldà (iD)
UPC BarcelonaTech
Barcelona, Spain

Linara Adilova
Fraunhofer IAIS
St. Augustin, Germany

Pedro M. Ferreira (iD)
University of Lisbon
Lisbon, Portugal

Ibéria Medeiros (iD)
University of Lisbon
Lisbon, Portugal

Giuseppe Manco (iD)
ICAR-CNR
Rende, Italy

Zbigniew W. Ras (iD)
University of North Carolina
Charlotte, NC, USA

Eirini Ntoutsi
Leibniz University Hannover
Hannover, Germany

Arthur Zimek (iD)
University of Southern Denmark
Odense, Denmark

Przemyslaw Biecek (iD)
Warsaw University of Technology
Warsaw, Poland

Benjamin Kille (iD)
Berlin Institute of Technology
Berlin, Germany

Jon Atle Gulla
Norwegian University of Science
and Technology
Trondheim, Norway

Preface

The European Conference on Machine Learning and Principles and Practice of Knowledge Discovery in Databases (ECML PKDD 2020) is the premier European conference on machine learning and data mining. ECML PKDD was scheduled to take place in Ghent, Belgium, but due to the COVID-19 pandemic it was held fully virtually during September 14–18, 2020.

The program included workshops on specialized topics held during the first and last day of the conference. This volume includes the proceedings of the following workshops:

1. Fifth Workshop on Data Science for Social Good (SoGood 2020)
2. Workshop on Parallel, Distributed and Federated Learning (PDFL 2020)
3. Second Workshop on Machine Learning for Cybersecurity (MLCS 2020)
4. Ninth International Workshop on New Frontiers in Mining Complex Patterns (NFMCP 2020)
5. Workshop on Data Integration and Applications (DINA 2020)
6. Second Workshop on Evaluation and Experimental Design in Data Mining and Machine Learning (EDML 2020)
7. Second International Workshop on eXplainable Knowledge Discovery in Data Mining (XKDD 2020)
8. Eighth International Workshop on News Recommendation and Analytics (INRA 2020)

Each workshop section contains the papers from the workshop and a preface from the organizers.

We would like to thank all participants and invited speakers, the program committees and reviewers, and the ECML PKDD conference and workshop chairs – thank you for making the workshops a successful event. We are also grateful to Springer for their help in publishing this volume.

October 2020

Irena Koprinska
on behalf of the volume editors

Organization

Workshop Chairs

SoGood 2020

Ricard Gavaldà	UPC BarcelonaTech, Spain
Irena Koprinska	The University of Sydney, Australia
João Gama	University of Porto, Portugal
Rita P. Ribeiro	University of Porto, Portugal

PDFL 2020

Michael Kamp	Monash University, Australia
Linara Adilova	Fraunhofer IAIS, Germany
Yamuna Krishnamurthy	Royal Holloway, University of London, UK

MLCS 2020

Annalisa Appice	University of Bari Aldo Moro, Italy
Pedro M. Ferreira	University of Lisbon, Portugal
Michael Kamp	Monash University, Australia
Donato Malerba	University of Bari Aldo Moro, Italy
Ibéria Medeiros	University of Lisbon, Portugal

NFMCP 2020

Michelangelo Ceci	University of Bari Aldo Moro, Italy
Corrado Loglisci	University of Bari Aldo Moro, Italy
Giuseppe Manco	ICAR-CNR, Italy
Elio Masciari	University of Naples Federico II, Italy
Zbigniew W. Ras	The University of North Carolina at Charlotte, USA

DINA 2020

Luiza Antonie	University of Guelph, Canada
Peter Christen	The Australian National University, Australia
Erhard Rahm	University of Leipzig, Germany
Osmar Zaiane	University of Alberta, Canada

EDML 2020

Eirini Ntoutsi	Leibniz University Hannover, Germany
Erich Schubert	Technical University of Dortmund, Germany
Athur Zimek	University of Southern Denmark, Denmark
Albrecht Zimmermann	University of Caen Normandy, France

XKDD 2020

Riccardo Guidotti	University of Pisa, Italy
Anna Monreale	University of Pisa, Italy
Salvatore Rinzivillo	ISTI-CNR, Italy
Przemyslaw Biecek	Warsaw University of Technology, Poland

INRA 2020

Özlem Özgöbek	Norwegian University of Science and Technology, Norway
Benjamin Kille	Berlin Institute of Technology, Germany
Andreas Lommatzsch	Berlin Institute of Technology, Germany
Jon Atle Gulla	Norwegian University of Science and Technology, Norway

Contents

**Second Workshop on Evaluation and Experimental Design
in Data Mining and Machine Learning (EDML 2020)**

**Second International Workshop on eXplainable Knowledge
Discovery in Data Mining (XKDD 2020)**

**Eighth International Workshop on News Recommendation
and Analytics (INRA 2020)**

Short Paper – DINA 2020

Fifth Workshop on Data Science for Social Good (SoGood 2020)

Workshop on Data Science for Social Good (SoGood 2020)

The *Fifth Workshop on Data Science for Social Good (SoGood 2020)* was held in conjunction with the *European Conference on Machine Learning and Principles and Practice of Knowledge Discovery in Databases (ECML PKDD 2020)* on 18th September 2020. The conference and workshop were scheduled to take place in Ghent, Belgium, but due to the COVID-19 pandemic they were held fully virtually. The previous four editions of the workshop were also held jointly with ECML PKDD in 2016–2019.

The possibilities of using Data Science for contributing to social, common, or public good are often not sufficiently perceived by the public at large. Data Science applications are already helping in serving people at the bottom of the economic pyramid, aiding people with special needs, helping international cooperation, and dealing with environmental problems, disasters, and climate change. In regular conferences and journals, papers on these topics are often scattered among sessions with names that hide their common nature (such as "Social networks", "Predictive models" or the catch-all term "Applications"). Additionally, such forums tend to have a strong bias for papers that are novel in the strictly technical sense (new algorithms, new kinds of data analysis, new technologies) rather than novel in terms of social impact of the application.

This workshop aimed to attract papers presenting applications of Data Science for Social Good (which may or may not require new methods), or applications that take into account social aspects of Data Science methods and techniques. It also aimed to bring together researchers, students and practitioners to share their experience and foster discussion about the possible applications, challenges and open research problems, and to continue building a research community in the area of Data Science for Social Good.

There are numerous application domains; the call for papers included the following non-exclusive list of topics:

- Government transparency and IT against corruption
- Public safety and disaster relief
- Public policies in epidemic growth and related issues
- Access to food, water and utilities
- Efficiency and sustainability
- Data journalism
- Economic, social and personal development
- Transportation
- Energy
- Smart city services
- Education
- Social services, unemployment and homelessness
- Healthcare

- Ethical issues, fairness and accountability
- Topics aligned with the UN Sustainable Development Goals: http://www.un.org/sustainabledevelopment/sustainable-development-goals/

The workshop papers were selected through a peer-reviewed process in which each submitted paper was assigned to three members of the Program Committee. The main selection criteria were the novelty of the application and its social impact. Seven papers were accepted for presentation.

The *SoGood 2020 Best Paper Award* was awarded to Hendrik Santoso Sugiarto and Ee-Peng Lim for their paper "On Modeling Labor Markets for Fine-grained Insights".

The program included two keynotes:

- "Data for Good by Design: Concrete Examples" by Natalia Adler from Pebble Analytics
- "Dealing with Bias and Fairness in Data Science Social Good Projects" by Pedro Saleiro from Feedzai Research

More information about the workshop, including the slides of the keynote talks, can be found on the workshop website: https://sites.google.com/view/ecmlpkddsogood2020/.

Many people contributed to making this workshop a successful event. We would like to thank Natalia Adler and Pedro Saleiro for their excellent talks, the Program Committee members and additional reviewers for their detailed and constructive reviews, the authors for their well-prepared presentations, all workshop attendees for their engagement and participation, and UPC BarcelonaTech for providing partial support for the keynote speakers.

October 2020

Ricard Gavaldà
Irena Koprinska
João Gama
Rita P. Ribeiro

SoGood 2020 Workshop Organization

Workshop Co-chairs

Ricard Gavaldà   UPC BarcelonaTech, Spain, gavalda@cs.upc.edu
Irena Koprinska   University of Sydney, Australia,
                            irena.koprinska@sydney.edu.au
João Gama   University of Porto, Portugal, jgama@fep.up.pt
Rita P. Ribeiro   University of Porto, Portugal, rpribeiro@fc.up.pt

Program Committee

Marta Arias   UPC BarcelonaTech, Spain
Ricardo Cerri   Federal University of São Carlos, Brazil
Calros Ferreira   University of Porto, Portugal
Cèsar Ferri   Technical University of Valencia, Spain
Geoffrey Holmes   University of Waikato, New Zealand
Konstantin Kutzkov   Amalfi Analytics, Spain
Rafael Morales-Bueno   University of Malaga, Spain
Nuno Moniz   University of Porto, Portugal
Ana Nogueira   INESC TEC, Portugal
Panagiotis Papapetrou   University of Stockholm, Sweden
Maria Pedroto   INESC TEC, Portugal
Perdo Saleiro   Feedzai Research, Portugal
Sónia Teixeira   INESC TEC, Portugal
Emma Tonkin   University of Bristol, UK
Alicia Troncoso   University Pablo de Olavide, Spain
Evgueni Smirnov   University of Maastricht, The Netherlands
Kristina Yordanova   University of Rostock, Germany
Martí Zamora   UPC BarcelonaTech, Spain

Additional Reviewers

Joel Costa   Federal University of São Carlos, Brazil
Thiago Miranda   Federal University of São Carlos, Brazil

SoGood 2020 Keynote Talks

Data for Good by Design: Concrete Examples

Natalia Adler

Pebble Analytics

Abstract. In recent years, compelling cases have shown the value of using privately-held data and data science for social good. However, the move beyond ad-hoc projects into sustainable initiatives has proved challenging. This talk starts with an overview of examples of data collaboratives of private-sector data sharing for social good involving large organizations (e.g. UNICEF, Telefonica, Bloomberg, Microsoft). The talk then delves into practical examples of how data for good can be done by design from the start. It showcases the role of market solutions in creating win-win business models and maximizing social impact, while upholding the highest standards of data protection and privacy.

Biography

Natalia Adler is the Co-Founder and CEO of Pebble Analytics (https://pebbleanalytics.com/), a social impact startup that uses data science, technology and market solutions to forecast social risks. She brings over 14 years of experience leveraging innovative solutions for social problems at the United Nations Children's Fund (UNICEF). Natalia conceptualized and ran the Data Collaboratives initiative with New York University's GovLab and with the private sector aimed at using data science to tackle some of the world's most complex challenges, including epidemics, suicides, urban mobility, migration and forced displacement. She has introduced a Human Centered Design approach to support policymaking in Nicaragua, developed a Sustainability Framework for Latin America; fostered the creation of 'entrepreneurial ecosystems' in Central America, and supported equitable and pro-poor spending through Public Finance Management analytics in Mozambique. Natalia holds a Master's in Human Rights from Columbia University and a Bachelor's in French Literature from the University of Pennsylvania, where she graduated summa cum laude and with the highest honors.

Dealing with Bias and Fairness in Data Science Social Good Projects

Pedro Saleiro

Feedzai Research

Abstract. Tackling issues of bias and fairness in AI has received increased attention from the research community in recent years, yet a lot of the research has focused on theoretical aspects and very little extensive empirical work has been done on real-world policy problems. Treating bias and fairness as primary metrics of interest, from project scoping to model building and selection should be a standard practice in data science for social good (DSSG) projects. In this talk we will try to bridge the gap between research and practice, by deep diving into algorithmic fairness, from metrics and definitions to practical case studies in DSSG, including bias audits using the Aequitas toolkit (http://github.com/dssg/aequitas).

Biography

Pedro Saleiro is a senior research manager at Feedzai Research (https://feedzai.com/research/) where he leads the FATE (Fairness, Accountability, Transparency, and Ethics) research group. He is responsible for several initiatives related to improving model explainability in the context of financial crime prevention, bias auditing and algorithmic fairness, experimentation and A/B testing, ML governance and reproducibility. Previously, Pedro was postdoc at the University of Chicago and research data scientist at the Center for Data Science and Public Policy working with Rayid Ghani, developing new methods and open source tools, and doing data science for social good projects with government and non-profit partners in diverse policy areas. Pedro was a data science mentor at the Data Science for Social Good Summer Fellowship 2018.

On Modeling Labor Markets
for Fine-Grained Insights

Hendrik Santoso Sugiarto[✉] and Ee-Peng Lim

Singapore Management University, Singapore, Singapore
{hendriks,eplim}@smu.edu.sg

Abstract. The labor market consists of job seekers looking for jobs, and job openings waiting for applications. Classical labor market models assume that salary is the primary factor explaining why job-seekers select certain jobs. In practice, job seeker behavior is much more complex and there are other factors that should be considered. In this paper, we therefore propose the **Probabilistic Labor Model (PLM)** which considers salary satisfaction, topic preference matching, and accessibility as important criteria for job seekers to decide when they apply for jobs. We also determine the user and job latent variables for each criterion and define a graphical model to link the variables to observed applications. The latent variables learned can be subsequently used in downstream applications including job recommendation, labor market analysis, and others. We evaluate the PLM model against other baseline models using two real-world datasets. Our experiments show that PLM outperforms other baseline models in an application prediction task. We also demonstrate how PLM can be effectively used to analyse gender and age differences in major labor market segments.

Keywords: Labor market · Probabilistic labor market modeling · Labor market analysis

1 Introduction

Motivation. Recent technological advances create new jobs while making many existing ones obsolete. This rapid change not only affects job seekers and employers, but also governments which are tasked to address labor shortage or excess problems in the labor market. It is thus ideal to have the labor market analysed quickly to detect trends and events for intervention. Meanwhile, job portals on the Web bring jobs closer to job seekers at the same time collecting a lot of data about the jobs, job seekers and their application behavior. In some cases, the job portals are so large that they could represent sizeable labor markets. The job portal datasets also open up new possibilities for labor market research which are much more efficient than traditional surveys. Labor market surveys are usually conducted sporadically as they incur significant costs and human efforts. They

© Springer Nature Switzerland AG 2020
I. Koprinska et al. (Eds.): ECML PKDD 2020 Workshops, CCIS 1323, pp. 9–25, 2020.
https://doi.org/10.1007/978-3-030-65965-3_1

are not always able to reflect the pace of change in the labor market. Moreover, traditional research methods could only analyse the labor market at the macro-level, limiting its ability to support interventions with focus targets.

Research Objectives. In this paper, we therefore seek to introduce a new labor market model to conduct fine-grained analysis of jobs and job seekers in a labor market. Instead of a salary-only approach, we consider a rich set of variables to model the salary, topic, and accessibility criteria applicants use to decide which jobs to apply. As offer salary information can be found in almost every job, an applicant can easily compare that with his/her own reserved salary before submitting applications. There are also clusters (or topics) of jobs which different groups of applicants show interest in. There are also factors affecting how easy applicants can access the jobs. For each criterion, we consider a set of relevant latent variables (e.g., reserved salary), observed variables (e.g., offer salary), and the inter-variable relationships so as to construct the full labor market model.

The latent variables learned from the new labor model will benefit different market stakeholders. From the labor researcher's standpoint, this solution approach significantly lowers the barrier of analysing labor markets and their behavior. The model can help job seekers to determine their asking salaries for specific type of jobs. Employers can utilize the model to set appropriate salaries to attract talent. Finally, the analysis from this model can be utilized by policy makers in a targeted manner (e.g., immigration policy [9] and education system [7,24] to counter labor shortage/excess.

Overview of Modeling Approach. We first define the observed labor market data as $D = (U, P, A)$. U denotes a set of job seekers, or simply users; P denotes a set of job posts; and $A = \{A_{i,j}\}$ denote job application matrix of dimension $|U| \times |P|$. Every job p_j is assigned an offer salary range $[w_j^{min}, w_j^{max}]$. $A_{i,j} = 1$ when job seeker u_i applies job p_j, and $= 0$ otherwise.

With the observed labor market data, we develop a model called the *Probabilistic Labor Market (PLM) Model*. This model learns several important user variables, namely: (a) user topics, (b) user reserved salary, (c) user effort level, and (d) user optimism, as well as job variables, namely: (a) job topics, and (b) job visibility. The interactions between these latent variables and observed variables lead to multiple criteria behind users applying for jobs. More details about PLM is given in Sect. 3.

By incorporating all the above criteria, we can jointly learn all the PLM latent variables for all users and jobs in the market. This will then enable us to: (a) analyse the values and distributions of latent user and job variables, determine interesting patterns in their values, and correlate them to explain the observed application behavioral data; (b) derive latent labor market segments for dividing the labor market into smaller sectors that facilitate fine-grained analyses; and (c) predict the missing application which could be used for job recommendation.

Contributions. In the paper, we make the following key contributions:

– We develop a novel probabilistic model PLM for modeling labor markets. To the best of our knowledge, this is the first of its kind using observed job and application data to construct a generative labor market model.
– We evaluate PLM against several baseline models in application prediction task and show that PLM yields the best prediction accuracies.
– We apply PLM on real world job and application datasets. The analysis of the learned user and job variables reveals differences between labor markets, differences between labor market segments, and interesting gender/age differences across labor market segments.

Paper Outline. We will first cover some related works in Sect. 2. We present the PLM model in Sect. 3. Section 4 shows the experiment results using real world data respectively. Finally, we apply PLM to conduct labor market analysis in Sect. 5. Section 6 concludes the paper and highlights future works.

2   Related Works

Much of the past labor market research was derived from the labor economic theory of supply and demand which has been used to determine market equilibrium [3]. Many criticisms have been expressed toward this classical theory because many employers and applicants cannot be matched directly based on this theory and it cannot resolve long-term unemployment [1,10]. Other researchers proposed labor market models to cover wage differentials among similar workers [15]. In recent years, economists have also developed a search theory to study the frictional unemployment [22] and other implications [21].

Nevertheless, classical economics usually only assumes a unified labor market with open competition [6,19]. Alternatively, the theory of labor market segmentation considers partitioning the labor market according to specific criteria such as occupation and location in which participants from one market group cannot easily be included by other market groups [2,8]. In contrast to previous approaches, we propose a model with soft market segmentation based on labor topics. Although our model includes all applicants and jobs in an open competition setting, it distinguishes them by topical groupings and the probability of joining a specific market depends on interest matching between jobs and users.

Furthermore, labor market studies also require extensive experiments or a lot of effort to conduct surveys or census on employers and employees to collect relevant data [4,5,11,12]. In contrast, our proposed probabilistic model utilizes machine learning to learn the labor market situation directly from the interaction between employers and applicants through a job portal. This approach is not only novel but can be built and deployed efficiently. Lately, there are also several studies on labor market from the machine learning perspective. But they are trying to answer different problems. Such as fairness [13], ranking [18], reputation inflation[17], indexing [20], or even data infrastructure [23].

3   Labor Market Modeling

3.1   Probabilistic Labor Market (PLM) Model

In this section, we describe our proposed Probabilistic Labor Market (PLM) Model, the criteria it uses to model the application behavior of users as well as the associated user and job variables. The observed data for learning PLM consists of: (a) a set of users U, (b) a set of jobs P, and (c) a set of applications represented by $A = \{A_{i,j} \in \{0,1\} | u_i \in U, p_j \in P\}$. $A_{i,j} = 1$ when u_i is observed to apply p_j, and $A_{i,j} = 0$ otherwise. In real world settings, we can only observe $A_{i,j} = 1$'s. Each job $p_j \in P$ has an offer salary interval $[w_j^{min}, w_j^{max}]$. While $w_j^{min} < w_j^{max}$ in most cases, it is possible for a job to have $w_j^{min} = w_j^{max}$. As shown in Fig. 1, PLM incorporates salary, topic and accessibility criteria for determining whether a user u_i applies job p_j. The three criteria are represented as the following three probabilities: (a) salary-based probability ($a_{i,j}^s$); topic-based probability ($a_{i,j}^t$); and accessibility-based probability ($a_{i,j}^a$). We then define the probability of u_i applying p_j as $\hat{a}_{i,j} = a_{i,j}^s \cdot a_{i,j}^t \cdot a_{i,j}^a$.

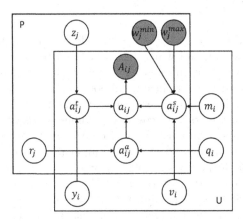

Fig. 1. Probabilistic labor market model

Salary Criteria. The salary criteria is inspired by labor economics. Salary-wise, every user u_i is assumed to have a *reserved salary* v_i. A job p_j is attractive if it offers salary higher than v_i. As each job has an offer salary interval, users may perceive an **effective offer salary** within interval for the purpose of comparison with reserved salary. We thus introduce for each user an optimism variable $m_i \in [0.1]$, to derive effective offer salary $s_{i,j}$ of job p_j with respect to user u_i as follows: $s_{i,j} = m_i \cdot w_j^{max} + (1 - m_i)w_j^{min}$. A user with extreme optimism $m_i = 1$ will use maximum offer salary as effective offer salary, and another user with extreme pessimism $m_i = 0$ will use minimum offer salary instead.

The salary-based probability $a_{i,j}^s$ is then determined by how well the reserved salary v_i is satisfied by the effective offer salary $s_{i,j}$. The more $s_{i,j}$ exceeds v_i, the more likely u_i is interested in job post p_j, which in turns increases $a^s_{i,j}$. We thus define $a^s_{i,j}$ as: $a^s_{i,j} = \sigma(\frac{s_{i,j} - v_i}{S})$. The sigmoid function $\sigma(x) = 1/(1 + e^{-x})$ converts the salary difference into a probability. We apply a simple global scaling S defined by the average difference between maximum and minimum salaries, i.e., $S = \frac{1}{|P|} \sum_{p_j \in P} (w^{max}_j - w^{min}_j)$.

Topic Criteria. Topic-wise, we expect each user to seek jobs matching his or her topical interests. In PLM, we use y_i and z_j to denote topic distributions of user u_i and job p_j respectively. Users should find topic-matching jobs more interesting than non-matching ones. We assume that both users and jobs share the same set of K topics. Probability $a^t_{i,j}$ is then defined by cosine similarity between user and job topic distributions, i.e.: $a^t_{i,j} = cosine(y_i, z_j)$. Cosine similarity is chosen because we want to represent topic matching as a probability (between 0 and 1). Other studies also show that cosine similarity generally performs better than other common measures such as Jansen-Shannon divergence [25].

Accessibility Criteria. Finally, the accessibility-based probability $a^a_{i,j}$ is determined by the effort-level of user u_i in job seeking, denoted by q_i ($q_i \in [0, 1]$) and the visibility of the job j, denoted by r_j ($r_j \in [0, 1]$). If $q_i = 0$, u_i is known to put in zero effort into job seeking resulting in not applying for any jobs that suit him or her. If $q_i = 1$, u_i will apply for all jobs that suit him or her. Mathematically, we define $a^a_{i,j}$ as: $a^a_{i,j} = q_i \cdot r_j$.

As we want to minimize the difference between model predictions and real applications, we define the objective function of PLM as:

$$F(U, P, A) = \sum_{u_i \in U, p_j \in P} (A_{i,j} - \hat{a}_{i,j})^2$$

To learn PLM well, we sample a subset of negative user-job pairs randomly and denote it by D^-. Specifically, for each positive user-item pair (u_i, p_j) with $A_{i,j} = 1$, we randomly select a set of N_{neg} negative user-item pairs, $(u_i, p_{j'})$'s such that $(u_i, p_{j'}) \notin D^+$ and add to D^-. The *positive-negative ratio* refers to $1/N_{neg}$. In our experiments, we have use $1/5$ as the default ratio. Since the user-job matrix is usually sparse, better performance can be achieved by assigning higher ratio. However, higher ratio requires costlier calculation time. This ratio choice allows the model to achieve a reasonable performance within a reasonable time. Combining the negative sampling strategy, the objective function is revised as follows:

$$F(U, P, A) = \sum_{(u_i, p_j) \in D^+} (A_{i,j} - \hat{a}_{i,j})^2 + \sum_{(u_i, p_j) \in D^-} (A_{i,j} - \hat{a}_{i,j})^2$$

3.2   Model Learning

The learning of our model variables $\mathbf{X} = [\mathbf{v}, \mathbf{m}, \mathbf{q}, \mathbf{y}, \mathbf{r}, \mathbf{z}]$ is performed by minimizing the objective function. Specifically, for any model latent variables x, we update it by $x^{next} = x - \gamma \frac{\partial F(x)}{\partial x}$ iteratively. The derivative of F is:

$$\frac{\partial F}{\partial x} = -2 \sum_{(u_i,p_j) \in D^+} (A_{i,j} - \hat{a}_{i,j}) \frac{\partial \hat{a}_{i,j}}{\partial x} - 2 \sum_{(u_i,p_j) \in D^-} (A_{i,j} - \hat{a}_{i,j}) \frac{\partial \hat{a}_{i,j}}{\partial x}$$

By definition, the value of v_i, y_{ik}, z_{jk} should be non-negative. Every time the model updated any of those variables into a negative value, we clip the value back to 0. Similarly, the values of m_i, q_i, and r_j should be between 0 and 1. Therefore we clip the updating of these variables to be between 0 and 1.

The parameter, number of topics (K), has to be empirically determined for every given dataset. In our experiments on real world data, we therefore vary and select an appropriate value for K.

4   Experiments

We obtain two large job application datasets and design experiments to evaluate PLM against other models for the application prediction task.

4.1   Datasets

The main dataset in this paper is taken from the jobs bank of a major Asian city (SJD). This dataset covers job vacancies posted by all registered companies in the city as required by law and applications to these jobs in the year 2015. We acquired this dataset through collaboration with the dataset owner. The dataset consists of three types of data: (a) job posts, (b) applicants, and (c) applications. Every application involves an applicant and the job post he/she applied. The dataset covers jobs from all job sectors and can be accessed by all applicants.

The second dataset is the Wuzzuf Job dataset (WJD) which is available at Kaggle[1]. The jobs and applicants are mainly from Egypt. Similar to SJD, the WJD dataset covers: (a) job posts, (b) applicants, and (c) applications. It is unclear how representative WJD is but its data size is comparable to that of SJD. Most of the jobs in WJD are from the engineering and IT sectors.

Data Pre-processing. We performed the following data pre-processing steps to each dataset. First, we removed job posts and their corresponding applications which involve part-time, internship, and other ad-hoc jobs. Second, we also removed some jobs to ensure the salary information is reliable [14,16]. Those removed involved: (i) empty offer salary information; (ii) $\frac{w_j^{max}}{w_j^{min}} \geq 3$ (unrealistic salary range); (iii) $w_j = \frac{1}{2} \cdot (w_j^{max} + w_j^{min}) < \$500$ (possible hourly/daily/weekly wages); (iv) $|w_j - \mu_w| > 2\sigma_w$ where μ_w and σ_w are mean and standard deviation of w_j's respectively (salary outliers); (v) $w_j < w_o^{Q1} - 1.5 \times IQR_o$ or $w_j > w_o^{Q3} + 1.5 \times IQR_o$ where IQR_o denotes the inter-quartile range of offer salary of jobs sharing the same occupation o as p_j (occupation-specific salary

---

[1] https://www.kaggle.com/WUZZUF/wuzzuf-job-posts.

outliers). Finally, we filter users and jobs with less than 5 applications and a maximum of 300 applications iteratively until all users and jobs have at least 5 applications and maximum 300 applications to get high quality application data for training. The above filtering removed non-active users and non-popular jobs, as well as users who are spammers or testers the job portal. This filtering also removed possible scam jobs that attracted many users. For WJD, we only consider jobs using Egyptian currency in their offer salaries.

After pre-processing, we retain for SJD dataset 68,091 jobs (about 26% of all jobs), 33,866 users (about 41% of all users), and 827,380 applications (about 29% of all applications). For WJD, we retain 16,928 jobs (about 80% of all jobs), 66,734 users (about 21% all users), and 1,216,445 applications (about 66% of all applications).

4.2   Application Prediction Task

Task Definition. In this task, we predict the (user,item) pairs that are likely to have applications. This prediction task involves ranking a set of (user,item) pairs (u_i, p_j)'s by application probabilities a_{ij}'s from highest to lowest. The higher the rank, the more likely user u_i applies for job p_j.

Probabilistic Labor Market Prediction Model (PLM): PLM performs application prediction as follows:

$$a_{i,j}^{PLM} = \sigma((s_{i,j}^{PLM} - \hat{v}_i^{PLM})/S) \cdot cosine(\mathbf{y}_i^{PLM}, \mathbf{z}_j^{PLM}) \cdot q_i^{PLM} \cdot r_j^{PLM}$$

Note that the PLM predicts using all topic, salary and accessibility criteria. The variables $s_{i,j}^{PLM}$, v_i^{PLM}, $\mathbf{y}_i^{PLM}$, $\mathbf{z}_j^{PLM}$, q_i^{PLM}, and r_j^{PLM} are variables under the PLM model defined in Sect. 3.1.

Other PLM Variants: We also introduce several reduced variants of PLM for application prediction. We derive them by dropping one of the salary, topic and accessibility criteria:

- **PLM using Salary and Topic Criteria (PLM(ST)):** This is a PLM variant that assumes that accessibility does not play a part in application decisions. Hence, user efforts and job visibilities are assumed to be identical and set to 1 for all users and jobs respectively.
- **PLM using Salary and Accessibility Criteria (PLM(SA)):** This is a PLM variant that assumes that topical interest does not play a part. Hence, all user and job topic distributions are set to have uniform values $\frac{1}{K}$.
- **PLM using Topic and Accessibility Criteria (PLM(TA)):** This PLM variant assumes that salary is not important and users are always satisfied with any offer salary. Consequently, reserved salaries are set to $0 and optimisms are set to 1.

Non-PLM Baselines: We also include several other baseline models as follows:

- **Optimism-based (Opt):** This method predicts based on the estimated optimism of user u_i to derive the expected salary for the job p_j:

$$a_{i,j}^{RAvg} = \sigma'(\hat{m}_i^{RAvg} \cdot w_j^{max} + (1 - \hat{m}_i^{RAvg})w_j^{min})$$

where

$$\hat{m}_i^{RAvg} = 2 \cdot \sigma'(Avg_{A_{i,j}=1}w_j^{max} - w_j^{min}) - 1$$

In the above equations, we use a sigmoid function, σ', which normalizes the input variable by its average over i, i.e., $\sigma'(x_i) = \sigma(\frac{x_i}{(1/|U|)\Sigma_{i'}x_{i'}})$. Note that if the input variable x_i across all baseline methods is always positive, the function $\sigma'(x_i)$ is bounded between 0.5 and 1 (consequently, $0 \le 2 \cdot \sigma'(x_i) - 1 \le 1$). On the other hand, if input variable x_i across all baseline methods is not always positive, the function $\sigma'(x_i)$ is bounded between 0 and 1.
- **Salary-based (Sal-A):** This method predicts based on the difference between the average of offer salary upper and lower bounds of job p_j and the reserved salary of u_i derived by averaging the salaries of the applied jobs:

$$a_{i,j}^{Avg} = \sigma'(\frac{1}{2}(w_j^{min} + w_j^{max}) - \hat{v}_i^{Avg})$$

where

$$\hat{v}_i^{Avg} = Avg_{\{A_{i,j}=1\}}(w_j^{min} + w_j^{max})/2$$

- **Salary-based (Sal-M):** This method is similar to Sal-A except a different reserved salary definition.

$$a_{i,j}^{Min} = \sigma'(\frac{1}{2}(w_j^{min} + w_j^{max}) - \hat{v}_i^{Min})$$

where

$$\hat{v}_i^{Min} = Min_{\{A_{i,j}=1\}}(w_j^{min} + w_j^{max})/2$$

- **Topic-based (NMF):** This is a NMF-based model with K latent factors.

$$a_{i,j}^{NMF} = \hat{\mathbf{y}}_i^{NMF} \cdot \hat{\mathbf{z}}_j^{NMF}$$

- **Topic-based (LDA):** This is a LDA based model with K topics.

$$a_{ij}^{LDA} = \hat{\mathbf{y}}_i^{LDA} \cdot \hat{\mathbf{z}}_j^{LDA}$$

- **User Effort and Job Visibility-based (EV):**

$$a_{ij}^{Pop} = \hat{q}_i^{Pop-q} \cdot \hat{r}_j^{Pop-r}$$

where q_i^{Pop-q} estimates the effort of user u_i by the total number of applications made by u_i, and r_j^{Pop-r} estimates the job visibility of job p_j as the number of applications on p_j. That is:

$$\hat{q}_i^{Pop-q} = 2 \cdot \sigma'(\Sigma_{p_j \in P}A_{ij}) - 1$$

$$\hat{r}_j^{Pop-r} = 2 \cdot \sigma'(\Sigma_{u_i \in U}A_{ij}) - 1$$

Table 1. Application prediction AUCPRC results (real dataset)

SJD					WJD				
Without topics					Without topics				
Opt	Sal-A	Sal-M	EV	PLM(SA)	Opt	Sal-A	Sal-M	EV	PLM(SA)
0.167	0.151	0.174	0.464	<u>0.482</u>	0.167	0.155	0.176	0.464	<u>0.474</u>
With topics					With topics				
K NMF	LDA	PLM(ST)	PLM(TA)	PLM	NMF	LDA	PLM(ST)	PLM(TA)	PLM
3 0.425	0.474	0.486	0.595	**0.623**	0.580	0.519	0.465	0.624	**0.640**
5 0.560	0.494	0.571	0.664	**0.686**	0.671	0.545	0.568	0.690	**0.702**
10 0.673	0.495	0.705	0.757	**0.771**	0.752	0.629	0.712	0.774	**0.779**
15 0.720	0.481	0.760	0.794	**0.806**	0.787	0.664	0.770	0.809	**0.813**
20 0.758	0.466	0.796	0.817	**0.829**	0.808	0.700	0.799	0.827	**0.831**
25 0.775	0.459	0.820	0.835	**0.845**	0.825	0.709	0.822	0.841	**0.845**
30 0.788	0.438	0.836	0.846	**0.855**	0.838	0.726	0.836	0.851	**0.855**

4.3 Application Prediction Results

We conduct 5-fold cross validation in which 20% of positive and negative samples are withheld for testing, and the remaining 80% are used for model training. We measure the prediction results by Precision@N and Recall@N at different N so as to report the Area Under the Precision-Recall curve (AUCPRC).

Results. The average AUCPRC results over the 5-fold experiments are shown in Table 1. For the SJD dataset, PLM outperforms all other models across different number of topics, and PLM (TA) yields the second best results. NMF yields the best result among the non-PLM models. LDA performance does not increase anymore beyond $K = 10$. In general, topic-aware models outperform all non topic-aware ones, including PLM(SA) (the best non topic-aware model). This suggests that application prediction is less accurate without knowing the user's and job's topic. PLM, PLM(ST), PLM(TA), and NMF improves their AUCPRC as K increases. We however witness a diminishing improvement as K increases. For example, PLM improves by 0.077 from $K = 5$ to $K = 10$, but only 0.01 from $K = 25$ to $K = 30$. $K = 25$ is then used in subsequent analysis.

Similarly, for the WJD dataset, PLM outperforms all other models across different numbers of topics. Again, NMF yields the second best results. All topic-aware models beat all non topic-aware models and the performance results of all topic-aware models improve as K increases. We also observe the improvement diminishing as K increases.

5 Labor Market Analysis Using PLM

In this section we demonstrate how PLM model is used to compare the SJD and WJD labor markets by the learned latent variables, and to analyse job seekers of different gender and age groups across different market segments. For the job seeker analysis, only SJD dataset is used as it covers jobs across wider sectors than the WJD dataset. Furthermore, based on the results of latent variable recovery experiment by using synthetic data (not shown here because of page limitation), PLM also performs significantly better than any other alternative baselines in recovering the latent variables. Therefore, we can confidently utilize the learned latent variables from PLM to analyze the labor market. In the following, we use PLM with 25 topics (i.e., $K = 25$) which yields fairly accurate application prediction results in Sect. 4.

5.1   Market Analysis and Comparison

One of the key objectives of PLM is to learn the latent variables of users and jobs. These include the reserved salary (v_i), optimism (m_i) and effort-level (q_i) of each user u_i, and the visibility (r_j) of job p_j. We now compare these variables between WJD and SJD markets. Note that topics are not included in this comparison because they are separately learned for the two datasets. As the two markets adopt different currencies and the reserved salaries of WJD are generally much lower than that of SJD, we focus on comparing the reserved salary distributions of the two markets relative to their average market offer salary. Therefore, we first scale the reserved salaries by the mean of the maximum offer salary of the market ($\frac{v_i}{Avg_{p_j \in P} w_j^{max}}$). Maximum offer salary is used here instead of mid offer salary since both markets have more applicants with high optimism.

Figure 2 shows the boxplots of these variables. The triangle symbol (▲) indicates the average value. The figure shows that the SJD labor market observes higher normalized reserved salary values than the WJD labor market. SJD also has a more balanced distribution than WJD which has a high concentration of users with low reserved salaries.

For optimism, SJD observes a slightly higher average optimism among its users than WJD. On the other hand, users from WJD put up higher effort level than users from SJD. Above observations together reveal that WJD is a tougher labor market than SJD. Finally, we could not find any obvious differences in job visibility distribution between the two markets.

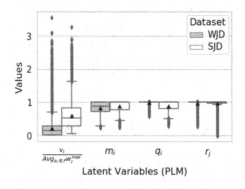

Fig. 2. Distribution of latent variables

5.2   Topic-Specific Labor Segments

We now analyse the topics of SJD dataset being learned by PLM to determine its major labor segments. Each market segment consists of a group of users interested in a cluster of jobs sharing the same topic. These topic-specific labor segments are "soft" as they are not defined by any observable market variable.

For each topic l, we include a user u_i under the topic l labor segment if $cosine(\mathbf{y}_i, \mathbf{t}_l) \geq 0.5$. Similarly, we include a job p_j under the labor segment if $cosine(\mathbf{z}_j, \mathbf{t}_l) \geq 0.5$. Here we use the original definition of PLM, where $cosine(\mathbf{z}_j, \mathbf{t}_l)$ is the degree of matching between job p_j and the topic l ($\mathbf{t}_l$ is a one-hot K dimensional vector for topic l). With this rule, each user or job can also belong to exactly one topic-specific labor segment. We use U_l and P_l to denote the users and jobs in this topic-l labor segment respectively.

While we have $K = 25$ topics, we focus on a few more popular topic-specific labor segments with number of users and jobs $|U_l| + |P_l| > 2000$. Table 2 show the top 13 topic-specific labor segments and their representative jobs. We manually assign for each topic a label to summarize jobs in that segment. Table 2 shows that the major topic-specific labor segments have clear topics. Across these 13 major labor segments, Trading & Investment is the only segment having more users than jobs, i.e., $|U_l| > |P_l|$. The other market segments have a distinctive shortage of supply of manpower as there are more available jobs than suitable applicants who can fill them.

5.3   Labor Segment Level User Analysis

In this section, we analyse reserved salary, optimism and effort-level of users in each of the major topic-specific labor segments of SJD labor market. Figure 3 shows distributions of these variables. The median and average values of each distribution are indicated by line $(-)$ and triangle $(\blacktriangle)$ symbols respectively.

The distributions of optimism and effort-level for all these labor segments are skewed towards high values. This suggests that users have high optimism and high effort. The Financial Management and PM+Design & Architecture labor segments have the most optimistic users, and the Clerical labor segment has the least optimistic users. Effort-level wise, users from the Finance management, Accounting and PM+Design & Architecture segments seem to put in highest efforts in job seeking. On the other hand, users from the Education+Programming segment seems to put in less effort.

The distribution of reserved salary for all these labor segments are skewed towards lower values. It means the majority of people expect lower reserved salaries. Only few people expect very high reserved salaries across different labor segments. The clerical segment has the lowest median and mean reserved salary, while Education + Programming, Information Technology, Project Management + Design & Architecture segments have higher median and mean reserved salaries.

Table 2. Major topic-specific labor segments

Topics (l)	Top dominant jobs	$|U_l|$	$|P_l|$
Clerical	Admin Assistant, Admin Clerk, Receptionist (General), Admin Executive, Administrator, Customer Service Officer, Call Centre Agent, Sales Coordinator	2634	4554
Secretarial & Personal Assistant (PA)	Admin Assistant, Human Resource Executive, Secretary, Human Resource & Admin Officer, Assistant, Personal, Human Resource Asst, Receptionist (General), Admin Exec'	2234	4103
Financial Management	Accountant, Finance Manager, Assistant Finance Manager, Accounts Executive, Analyst, Financial, Controller, Financial, Senior Accountant (General), Accounting Manager	1717	3507
Marketing & Public Relation (PR)	Manager, Marketing, Marketing Executive, Brand Manager, Assistant Marketing Manager, Regional Marketing Manager, Marketing Communications Manager, Marketing Communications Exec, Senior Marketing Exec	1631	2563
Accounting	Accounts Executive, Accounts Assistant, Accountant, Account Executive, Finance Executive, Account Assistant, Accounts Officer, Accountant, Assistant	1152	2939
Human Resource (HR)	HR Executive, HR Manager, HR Business Partner, HR & Admin Officer, Senior HR Executive, HR Assistant, HR & Admin Manager, HR Assistant Manager	1268	1826
Research & Lab	Research Assistant, Research Officer, Clinical research coord, Laboratory Technician, Medical Technologist, Researcher, Chemist, Laboratory Assistant	1216	1645
Project Management + Design & Architecture	IT Project Manager, IT Manager, Designer, Graphic, Project Manager, Svc Delivery Manager, Architectural Designer, Designer, Interior, Architectural Asst	1100	1597
Trading & Investment	Analyst, Associate, Trader, Mgmt Trainee, Invt Analyst, Risk Analyst, Commodities Trader, Business Analyst	1629	975
Supply Chain	Resident Engineer, Purchasing Executive, Purchaser, Buyer, Marine Superintendent, Logistics Executive, Technical Superintendent, Procurement Executive	1001	1572
Business Software	Business Analyst, Application Support Analyst, Information Technology Business Analyst, Associate, Senior Business Analyst, Analyst, System Analyst, Engineer, Software	754	1720
Information Technology	System Administrator, Art Director, IS Engineer, IT Project Manager, IT Manager, Desktop Support Engineer, Compliance Officer, Analyst	844	1512
Education + Programming	Teacher (Int School), Java Dev, Sr Engineer, Software, Sr Java Developer, Project Manager, Engineer, Software, Application Developer, Commercial School Teacher	839	1200

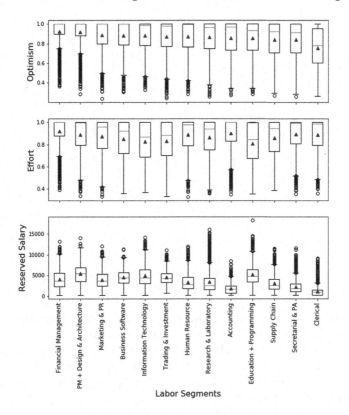

Fig. 3. User variables of labor segments

5.4 User Analysis by Gender and Age

User Analysis by Gender. Next, we study gender differences in the major labor segments as shown in Fig. 4. Female-male applicant proportions across all labor segments is almost equal (49 : 51). This proportion is represented by dotted black line. The bar chart indicates the percentage of female applicants in each labor segment (the rest is filled by male applicants). The labor segments are sorted by increasing female dominance. Labor segments such as Clerical, Secretarial & PA, Accounting and Human Resource are more preferred by female applicants. In contrast, PM + Design & Architecture, Information Technology, and Trading & Investment are dominated by male applicants.

According to the male-female median reserved salary ratios $\frac{v^{male}}{v^{female}}$ indicated by the blue squares, male users enjoy higher median reserved salary than females across all the major labor segments (except for Accounting segment). In particular, for the clerical labor segment which females dominate, male users have overall reserved salary more than 50% higher than that of female users. Female applicants appear to expect less reserved salary than male applicants.

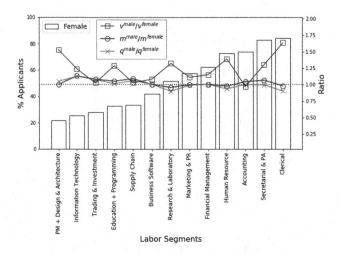

Fig. 4. Gender specific latent variables in major labor segments

Moreover, we also observe that male users have higher optimism (indicated by green circles) and effort (indicated by red crosses) in labor segments such as IT and Supply Chain. On the other hand, female users have higher optimism and effort in other labor segments such as Research & Laboratory and HR. However, the gaps in terms of optimism and effort values between female and male users are not as big as reserved salary.

User Analysis by Age. We now examine the age differences in the major labor segments. Specifically we only focus on the profile differences between users below 30 and above 30 in Fig. 5. The below-30 group accounts for 38% of all applicants as indicated by the black dotted line. Trading & investment, research & laboratory, marketing & PR, clerical, and secretarial & PA labor segments are preferred by younger applicants, or they may be more suited for younger applicants. PM + Design & Architecture, Education + Programming, and several others segments are preferred by older applicants.

We observe that median reserved salary for older users (indicated by blue squares) is generally higher than that of younger applicants across all the major labor segments (except in Accounting and Clerical segments where median reserved salaries are approximately equal). The above observations are reasonable as older applicants usually expect higher salaries. Accounting and clerical segments are likely to be age-neutral.

We also observe that older applicants have higher optimism (shown as green circles) and effort (shown as red crosses) in IT and Supply Chain. On the other hand, younger applicants have higher optimism and effort in other labor segments such as Research & Laboratory.

While the above analysis only involves gender and age, similar analysis can be performed for user groups defined based on other attributes such as race, and education. This allows us to understand differences between other user groups

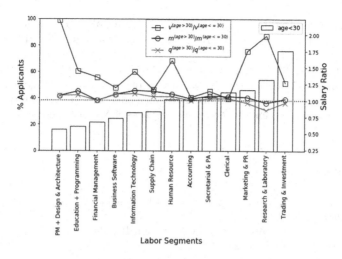

Fig. 5. Age specific latent variables in major labor segments

in the labor market or labor market segments. We shall leave these studies to future work.

6   Conclusion

We have developed a probabilistic model called PLM to study labor market directly using observed data. This model combines salary requirement, topic matching, and job accessibility are the three main criteria for users to select jobs to apply for. PLM also learns user and job factors useful for data science analysis. Our experiments show that PLM outperforms other baseline models in prediction tasks. Moreover, we also demonstrate the strength of the model in analyzing various aspects of the labor market.

The immediate applicability for the social good lies in the learned latent variables. These information can be utilized by a job seeker to compare his/her personal latent variables (e.g. reserved salary, effort, optimism) with his/her competitors'. The employers can also compare their salary competitiveness with their potential applicants' reserved salary. Furthermore, the policy maker can also utilize labor topics analysis to tackle labor shortage or even gender gap in a targeted manner (i.e. specific labor segments).

There are some limitations of this study that can be improved in future work. More advanced versions of the PLM will be developed to cope with the long tailed data distribution. The performance of the model can also be improved by considering different negative sampling strategies. We also plan to extend the model to conduct analysis at the user or job level to generate even more fine-grained insights. Moreover, the learned latent variables from PLM can be utilized and aligned into labor economics problems such as labor supply, demand, elasticity, and the equilibrium state of each market. PLM can also be extended to model the labor segments more accurately using textual features of job descriptions.

Acknowledgment. This research is supported by the National Research Foundation, Singapore under its International Research Centres in Singapore Funding Initiative. Any opinions, findings and conclusions or recommendations expressed in this material are those of the author(s) and do not reflect the views of National Research Foundation, Singapore.

References

1. Arulampalam, W., Booth, A.L., Taylor, M.P.: Unemployment persistence. Oxford Econ. Pap. **52**(1), 24–50 (2000)
2. Bauder, H.: Labor Movement: How Migration Regulates Labor Markets. Oxford University Press, Oxford (2006)
3. Becker, G.S.: Economic Theory. Routledge, Abingdon (2017)
4. Berinsky, A.J., Huber, G.A., Lenz, G.S.: Evaluating online labor markets for experimental research: Amazon.com's mechanical turk. Polit. Anal. **20**(3), 351–368 (2012)
5. Borjas, G.J.: The labor demand curve is downward sloping: reexamining the impact of immigration on the labor market. Q. J. Econ. **118**(4), 1335–1374 (2003)
6. Cain, G.G.: The challenge of segmented labor market theories to orthodox theory: a survey. J. Econ. Lit. **14**(4), 1215–1257 (1976)
7. Cappelli, P.H., Gaps, S., Shortages, S., Mismatches, S.: Evidence and arguments for the United States. ILR Rev. **68**(2), 251–290 (2015)
8. Dickens, W.T., Lang, K.: The reemergence of segmented labor market theory. Am. Econ. Rev. **78**(2), 129–134 (1988)
9. Guzi, M., Kahanec, M., Kurekova, L.M.: How immigration grease is affected by economic, institutional, and policy contexts: evidence from EU labor markets. Kyklos **71**(2), 213–243 (2018)
10. Hall, R.E.: Employment efficiency and sticky wages: evidence from flows in the labor market. Rev. Econ. Stat. **87**(3), 397–407 (2005)
11. Heim, B.T.: The incredible shrinking elasticities: married female labor supply, 1978–2002. J. Hum. Resour. **42**(4), 881–918 (2007)
12. Horton, J.J., Chilton, L.B.: The labor economics of paid crowdsourcing. In: The 11th ACM Conference on Electronic Commerce, pp. 209–218 (2010)
13. Hu, L., Chen, Y.: A short-term intervention for long-term fairness in the labor market. In: The 2018 World Wide Web Conference (2018)
14. Joinson, A.N., Woodley, A., Reips, U.D.: Personalization, authentication and self-disclosure in self-administered internet surveys. Comput. Hum. Behav. **23**(1), 275–285 (2007)
15. Kaufman, B., Hotchkiss, J.: The Economics of Labor Markets. Harcourt College Publishers (1705)
16. Kenthapadi, K., Ambler, S., Zhang, L., Agarwal, D.: Bringing salary transparency to the world: computing robust compensation insights via linkedin salary. In: ACM Conference on Information and Knowledge Management (CIKM) (2017)
17. Kokkodis, M.: Reputation deflation through dynamic expertise assessment in online labor markets. In: The 2019 World Wide Web Conference (2019)

18. Kokkodis, M., Papadimitriou, P., Ipeirotis, P.G.: Hiring behavior models for online labor markets. In: ACM International Conference on Web Search and Data Mining (2015)
19. Machin, S., Manning, A.: A test of competitive labor market theory: the wage structure among care assistants in the south of England. ILR Rev. **57**(3), 371–385 (2004)
20. Maltseva, A.V., Makhnytkina, O.V., Shilkina, N.E., Soshnev, A.N., Evseev, E.A.: A multilevel index model of labor market dysfunction. In: International Conference on Engineering and MIS (2019)
21. Mortensen, D.T., Pissarides, C.A.: Job creation and job destruction in the theory of unemployment. Rev. Econ. Stud. **61**(3), 397–415 (1994)
22. Pissarides, C.A.: Equilibrium in the labor market with search frictions. Am. Econ. Rev. **101**(4), 1092–1105 (2011)
23. Pitts, R.K.: Spatio-temporal labor market analytics: Building a national web-based system. In: 1st International Conference and Exhibition on Computing for Geospatial Research & Application (2010)
24. Waring, P., Vas, C., Bali, A.S.: The challenges of state intervention in Singapore's youth labour market. Equality Diversity Inclusion: Int. J. **37**, 138–150 (2018)
25. Wartena, C.: Distributional similarity of words with different frequencies. In: Dutch-Belgian Information Retrieval Workshop (2013)

Reasoning About Neural Network Activations: An Application in Spatial Animal Behaviour from Camera Trap Classifications

Benjamin C. Evans[1]([✉])[iD], Allan Tucker[1][iD], Oliver R. Wearn[2][iD],
and Chris Carbone[2][iD]

[1] Brunel University London, Uxbridge UB8 3PH, UK
{Benjamin.Evans,Allan.Tucker}@brunel.ac.uk
[2] Institute of Zoology, Zoological Society of London, London NW1 4RY, UK
Oliver.Wearn@gmail.com, Chris.Carbone@ioz.ac.uk

Abstract. Camera traps are a vital tool for ecologists to enable them to monitor wildlife over large areas in order to determine population changes, habitat, and behaviour. As a result, camera-trap datasets are rapidly growing in size. Recent advancements in Artificial Neural Networks (ANN) have emerged in image recognition and detection tasks which are now being applied to automate camera-trap labelling. An ANN designed for species detection will output a set of activations, representing the observation of a particular species (an individual class) at a particular location and time and are often used as a way to calculate population sizes in different regions. Here we go one step further and explore how we can combine ANNs with probabilistic graphical models to reason about animal behaviour using the ANN outputs over different geographical locations. By using the output activations from ANNs as data along with the trap's associated spatial coordinates, we build spatial Bayesian networks to explore species behaviours (how they move and distribute themselves) and interactions (how they distribute in relation to other species). This combination of probabilistic reasoning and deep learning offers many advantages for large camera trap projects as well as potential for other remote sensing datasets that require automated labelling.

Keywords: Animal behavior · Convolutional Neural Networks · Bayesian networks · Activation based reasoning

1 Introduction

Artificial Neural Networks (ANNs), and in particular, Convolutional Neural Networks (CNNs) have superseded traditional statistical methods in a multitude of

Benjamin C. Evans work is funded by NERC (The Natural Environment Research Council).

I. Koprinska et al. (Eds.): ECML PKDD 2020 Workshops, CCIS 1323, pp. 26–37, 2020.
https://doi.org/10.1007/978-3-030-65965-3_2

domains, ranging from speech recognition and synthesis [6], natural language processing [2] as well as image processing, detection and recognition tasks [1].

Recently there has been growing interest by ecologists into the use of machine learning to assist with the growing task of labelling camera trap data [4]. A camera trap consists of an imaging device with an automatic trigger. These triggers are often in the form of a passive infrared sensor or timer which starts off the capture of a series of images, from here on in referred to as a sequence. Ecologists have increasingly used camera trap surveys to monitor and investigate species populations and animal behaviour without the need for physical capture of the animals [7]. With the decrease in the cost of camera technology and storage hardware, we've seen a rapid increase in size and extent of these datasets.

Traditionally an individual researcher, or their team, would process through each image taken during the survey, labelling each with the species seen and any behaviour that may be of interest to the study. As the datasets grew, researchers began to enlist citizen scientists to assist with the endeavour. This, however, still requires vast amounts of human time [4]. Which in turn has led ecologists to investigate alternative means in labelling, in particular, the use of machine learning to assist the endeavour in reducing human dependency and potentially speeding up the process of labelling. Initial work in species classification has utilised CNNs by feeding whole images into the model with individual neuron outputs representing each species occurring in a given image. This has shown promising results but has also identified certain issues with CNNs that are particularly apparent with camera trap data.

One major issue is that of overfitting. Given that each camera trap placed is usually left in the same location for the duration of a study, the background of all images from a single camera is the same. When there is a high density of a single species at one location, CNNs tend to focus on the background rather than the features of the animal within the image. To overcome this issue, Beery et al. have developed an object-detection model called MegaDetector which identifies 'animal', 'human' and 'vehicle' classes along with their predicted bounding box within the given image [1]. These detections can then be cropped in accordance to the predicted bounding box and passed to a species classifier for finer grain prediction, reducing the ability of the species classifier to overfit to the background of the images.

While there is still research to be done on fine-tuning the automation of the labelling process, there is a potential for reasoning about the labelling of images given the uncertainty of the classification to better understand the behaviour of different species. Thus, we propose a framework for reasoning about species behaviour, based on the activations of a CNN trained to identify species in different geographical locations.

Bayesian Networks (BNs) have been successfully used in many areas of research where data is characterised by uncertainty, including in ecology [3,5,11]. There has also been some work exploring the use of spatial Bayesian networks to analyse the movement of species [10]. In this paper, we investigate combining ANNs with BNs so that rather than reasoning about observations made by humans, we can automate the entire process of understanding animal behaviour starting from the image and ending with predictive models that explain complex spatial behaviours.

In the next section, we will firstly describe the BorneoCam dataset that we focus on for this study. Secondly, we shall present the deep-learning-based classifier for automating the labelling of images in the BorneoCam dataset. We then describe how we use these labels (in the form of ANN activations as data) to learn a Bayesian Network allowing us to reason and predict about the species sightings across a number of cameras spread over different geographical locations.

2   Methodology

2.1   Camera Trap Data

The BorneoCam dataset includes camera trap imagery from multiple surveys across northern Borneo which will be made publicly available at a later date. For the following experimentation, we utilise just one subset of the dataset relating to a single survey, identified as 'OG3' as shown in Fig. 1. The region consists of 47 camera locations further split into North, West and East subregions each consisting of 15 to 16 cameras. The images in Fig. 1 show a sample camera trap image along with a sample extraction/detection containing just the animal.

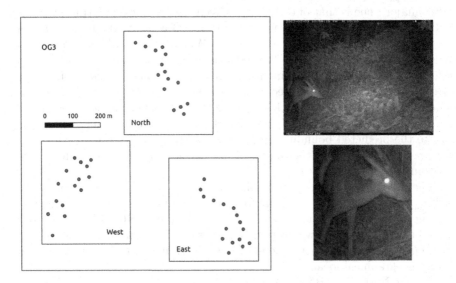

Fig. 1. OG3 Survey Site with Camera Locations from the BorneoCam Dataset, a sample camera trap image and detection extract of a Red muntjac.

2.2   Experiments

Firstly, the MegaDetector is used, an object detection model trained on a variety of datasets from around the world which identifies 'animal', 'human' and 'vehicle' classes along with their associated bounding box [1]. Through qualitative analysis, the results of the model seem reasonable enough to assume some degree of certainty that when an image has a species label and has one detection from the MegaDetector that the bounding box from the detection matches the region of image containing the species identified in the labelled set. With these one-detection, one-label images we are able to build a dataset to train a deep-learning-based classifier just on the region of an image that contains the animal limiting the risk of the classifier to overfit to the background of each location.

In order to demonstrate our approach, we train a CNN species classifier on the six species with the highest image frequencies from the dataset while merging 'Red muntjac' and 'Yellow muntjac' into a singular 'Muntjac' class. This is due to difficulties in classifying these species because of subtle differences in their visual characteristics. This presents us with 'Bearded Pig', 'Long-tailed porcupine', 'Southern pig-tailed macaque', 'Muntjac' and 'Spiny rat' (Fig. 2).

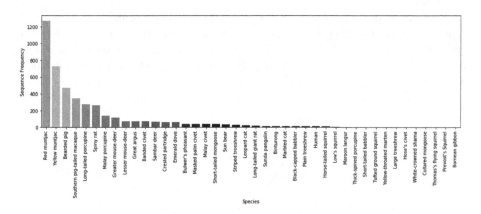

Fig. 2. Visualisation of sequence frequency by species in the OG3 region.

The survey in use from the BorneoCam dataset was set up so that each camera captures a sequence of ten images once the device has been triggered. Often it is found that the first image contains no or a small portion of the animal as the triggers viewing angle is wider than the camera's view. Thus, we take the second image of each sequence to obtain a higher likelihood of the animal in view. The resulting dataset is split based on camera location into 70% training, 5% validation and 25% testing subsets. Splitting based on camera location allows us to test that the model is able to generalise to images taken from previously unseen locations. Once the images are sorted into the relevant sets, the number of images per species is normalised so that each class has a fair representation of samples.

A model is trained based on the ResNet50v2 architecture [12] with a classification head of one average pooling layer followed by a dropout layer of 0.2 and finally a dense layer using softmax activations. The model is trained utilising transfer learning from a model pretrained on the ImageNet dataset [8]. Categorical cross-entropy is used as the loss function and a learning rate of 1e-3 for five epochs is run with only the classification head trainable. Followed by five epochs with a learning rate of 1e-4 where layers above 150 are trainable. The ResNet50v2 architecture has been chosen based on prior experimentation as appears to be less prone to overfitting and provides a reasonable result in accuracy.

In order to build the BN from the activation data, the activations generated from the Resnet are pre-processed into intervals over the duration of the camera trap study. These intervals are derived by considering the highest activation of each predicted image as a sighting of the respective species. This is then recorded as a sighting at the interval the image capture falls within for the relevant camera location and species. The interval size can be determined based upon the idealised granularity ensuring that the interval is greater than the estimated time required for the species of interest to pass by two or more camera locations.

BNs are graphical models that encode the joint distribution of a dataset using a graphical structure to capture independent relations between variables and local conditional probability distributions. See Fig. 3 for an example BN with five nodes where the probability distribution at each node is conditioned upon its parents.

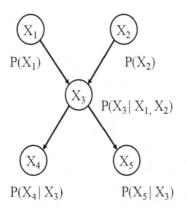

Fig. 3. A Bayesian network with 5 nodes.

BNs can be inferred from data using score and search methods such as hill climbing with the log-likelihood metric, or constraint-based methods such as the PC algorithm [9]. In this paper, these approaches were both explored to infer BN models from a subset of the processed activation data (70% as training data).

Here, each BN node will represent one species at a particular spatial coordinate. The resulting structures were explored for spatial features and specific species interactions. The remaining 30% of activation data was used to test the BNs as predictive models. Prediction was then conducted on a location-by-location basis. It involved using inference where evidence was entered into the BN model based upon the activations of all surrounding locations and the BN model was used to predict the presence of species in each test location (in the form of a posterior probability distribution over all species).

Figure 4 presents an overview process diagram visualising the steps taken in the methodology.

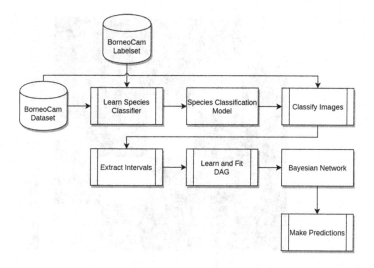

Fig. 4. Process diagram providing an overview of the methodology.

3   Results

First, we look at the ability of the CNN to automatically identify species from the BorneoCam data. Figure 5 shows the learning of the model with 5 epochs training the classification head and the last 5 epochs fine-tuning with layers 150+ trainable. Figure 6 shows the confusion matrices, visualising the difference between the labels and that of the predictions from the ResNet model. We can see that on the whole, the model performs well with relatively high numbers of correct classification (frequencies on the diagonal). The classes that are most confused are that of the long-tailed porcupine and the spiny rat. This could be because both are relatively small, have a long tail and similar body shape. The long-tailed porcupine has a distinctive "brush" on the end of the tail, but this can be missing or difficult to see, so it's unlikely the ANN has learnt this feature.

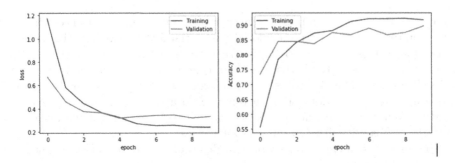

Fig. 5. Training/validation loss and accuracy by epoch.

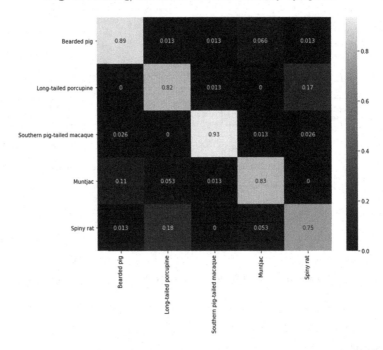

Fig. 6. Confusion matrix of the species classifier.

Now we explore the use of the output activations as data that we want to reason about. To do this, interval pre-processing was used as explained in the methods section. Figure 7 shows the images taken within the OG3 region overtime giving us an overview of the total time period. The size of each circle represents the number of images taken for that location at a particular time. Notice that for a small number of cameras, there is potential malfunction, empty battery or full memory as the images stop recording after a fixed time. These cameras with missing data may need to be removed from further analysis, though if there are enough arcs learnt towards the nodes in the network where we are missing data it may be possible to predict the missing sightings.

Fig. 7. Visualisation of images taken at each camera location over time. Colour relates to the individual cameras/rows. (Color figure online)

Now we turn to the Bayesian network analysis. Table 1 shows the accuracy for each species and each location of a network learnt on the west subregion when tested on the test dataset. It is clear that some species/locations are more easily predicted than others which may infer a stronger relation, be it a higher number of arcs directed to the relevant nodes in the BN or that there is a strong pattern identified in the learning and fitting.

BNs are learnt for individual species and one network incorporating all species as seen in Fig. 8. We can see that when incorporating additional species into the model that links are identified both between the same species at different locations but also between differing species. This in turn provides further information for making predictions and presents avenues of exploration into the underlying variables behind the inter-species behaviour patterns.

Table 1. OG3 west BN prediction statistics

Species	Accuracy	Sensitivity	Specificity	Precision	Recall	F1
Bearded Pig	0.934	0.989	0.204	0.942	0.989	0.965
Long Tailed Porcupine	0.906	0.986	0.15	0.917	0.986	0.95
Muntjac	0.821	0.965	0.262	0.835	0.965	0.895
Southern Pig Tailed Macaque	0.97	0.989	0.45	0.98	0.989	0.985
Spiny Rat	0.915	0.967	0.349	0.941	0.967	0.954

Table 2 and Fig. 9 show the resulting BN structure over all regions for all species. It is clear that there are predictive relationships that span greater dis-

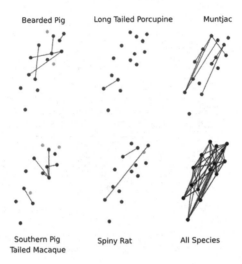

Fig. 8. BNs for each species (Bearded Pig, Long Tailed Porcupine, Muntjac, Southern Pig Tailed Macaque, Spiny Rat) and all species in OG3 West.

tances than the local ones discovered in Fig. 8. These long distance relationships seem to involve all the species which may imply that there are regular activity patterns across the subregions where species are seen or not seen within the same day. This opens up further exploration into the factors at play, such as the time of day or weather conditions impacting behaviour.

Figure 10 shows a detail of the overall network structure that combines multiple species and locations whilst Table 2 summarises all inter-species links. Notice how some species interact far less than others (e.g. spiny rat only seems to have

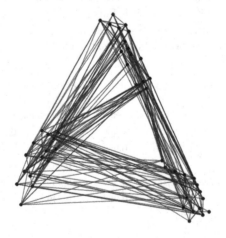

Fig. 9. The discovered BN across all 3 regions for all species.

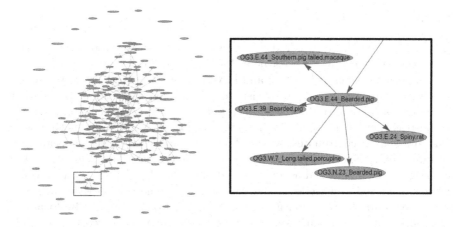

Fig. 10. Species interaction network (and detailed section as discussed).

some loose relationship to Muntjac, and no relationship to spiny rats in other locations), whilst other species interact a great deal with themselves across locations (e.g. SPT Macaques indicating one or more of the species moving between locations) and with other species (SPT Macaques with Bearded Pigs indicating some avoidance or following behaviour).

We can also see in Fig. 10 that the relationships being made can be reasoned about in terms of both species and location. In the zoomed in portion of the network, the center-most Bearded Pig node has the highest frequency of relationships to nodes that are of the same species and the same (East) subregion, highlighting that the BN has learnt what appears to be logical relationships (likely to be the same animals as they move around a localised area).

Table 2. Summary of BN arcs for OG3 with multiple species showing the total number of arcs between species with "from" on the Y axis and "to" on the X axis.

	Bearded pig	Long tailed porcupine	Muntjac	Southern pig tailed macaque	Spiny rat
Bearded Pig	14	10	9	5	10
Long Tailed Porcupine	4	4	16	10	7
Muntjac	11	15	18	11	8
Southern Pig Tailed Macaque	12	3	12	18	4
Spiny Rat	10	9	9	6	7

4 Conclusions

In this paper, we have explored a framework for reasoning about images that have been analysed by deep learners. We have applied a combination of deep learning (for image classification) and Bayesian networks (for spatial reasoning) to camera trap data, used by ecologists to better understand animal populations and behaviour. We have shown, using trap data from BorneoCam, that by treating deep learner label outputs (activations) as data and by combining them with time and spatial coordinates, we can build probabilistic models that can identify and predict specific species' behaviours and interactions. Whilst the deep learning classifier achieved accuracies of 0.92 for labelling species, the Bayesian network achieved accuracies of 0.97 for predicting whether a species would be present at a specific location given other information about nearby locations. This work is still in the early stages and there is a great deal of work that will be followed up including the incorporation of deep learning activations as measures of certainty in a species being present, the exploration of other datasets and the integration of geographical and climate features such as rivers and weather into the models.

References

1. Beery, S., Morris, D., Yang, S.: Efficient pipeline for camera trap image review. arXiv:1907.06772 [cs.CV] (2019). https://arxiv.org/abs/1907.06772
2. Devlin, J., Chang, M.W., Lee, K., Toutanova, K.: Bert: pre-training of deep bidirectional transformers for language understanding. In: Proceedings of the 2019 Conference of the North (2019). https://doi.org/10.18653/v1/n19-1423
3. Franco, C., Hepburn, L.A., Smith, D.J., Nimrod, S., Tucker, A.: A Bayesian belief network to assess rate of changes in coral reef ecosystems. Environ. Model. Softw. **80**, 132–142 (2016). https://doi.org/10.1016/j.envsoft.2016.02.029. http://www.sciencedirect.com/science/article/pii/S1364815216300494
4. Glover-Kapfer, P., Soto-Navarro, C.A., Wearn, O.R.: Camera-trapping version 3.0: current constraints and future priorities for development. Remote Sens. Ecol. Conserv. **5**(3), 209–223 (2019). https://doi.org/10.1002/rse2.106. https://zslpublications.onlinelibrary.wiley.com/doi/abs/10.1002/rse2.106
5. Maldonado, A., Uusitalo, L., Tucker, A., Blenckner, T., Aguilera, P., Salmerón, A.: Prediction of a complex system with few data: evaluation of the effect of model structure and amount of data with dynamic Bayesian network models. Environ. Model. Softw. **118**, 281–297 (2019). https://doi.org/10.1016/j.envsoft.2019.04.011. http://www.sciencedirect.com/science/article/pii/S1364815218310338
6. van den Oord, A., et al.: Wavenet: a generative model for raw audio. arXiv:1609.03499 [cs.SD] (2016). https://arxiv.org/abs/1609.03499
7. Rowcliffe, J.M., Carbone, C.: Surveys using camera traps: are we looking to abrighter future? Anim. Conserv. **11**(3), 185–186 (2008). https://doi.org/10.1111/j.1469-1795.2008.00180.x. https://zslpublications.onlinelibrary.wiley.com/doi/abs/10.1111/j.1469-1795.2008.00180.x
8. Russakovsky, O., et al.: ImageNet large scale visual recognition challenge. Int. J. Comput. Vision **115**(3), 211–252 (2015). https://doi.org/10.1007/s11263-015-0816-y

9. Spirtes, P., Glymour, C., Scheines, R.: Causation, prediction, and search (1993)
10. Trifonova, N., Kenny, A., Maxwell, D., Duplisea, D., Fernandes, J., Tucker, A.: Spatio-temporal Bayesian network models with latent variables for revealingtrophic dynamics and functional networks in fisheries ecology. Ecol. Inf. **30**, 142–158 (2015). https://doi.org/10.1016/j.ecoinf.2015.10.003. http://www.sciencedirect.com/science/article/pii/S1574954115001648
11. Uusitalo, L.: Advantages and challenges of Bayesian networks in environmentalmodelling. Ecol. Model. **203**(3), 312–318 (2007). https://doi.org/10.1016/j.ecolmodel.2006.11.033. http://www.sciencedirect.com/science/article/pii/S0304380006006089
12. Xie, S., Girshick, R., Dollar, P., Tu, Z., He, K.: Aggregated residual transformations for deep neural networks. In: 2017 IEEE Conference on Computer Vision and Pattern Recognition (CVPR), July 2017. https://doi.org/10.1109/cvpr.2017.634

Practical Lessons from Generating Synthetic Healthcare Data with Bayesian Networks

Juan de Benedetti[1], Namir Oues[1], Zhenchen Wang[1], Puja Myles[1],
and Allan Tucker[2(✉)]

[1] Medicine and Health Regulatory Authority, London, UK
[2] Intelligent Data Analysis Group, Brunel University London, Uxbridge, UK
allan.tucker@brunel.ac.uk
http://www.ida-research.net

Abstract. Healthcare data holds huge societal and monetary value. It contains information about how disease manifests within populations over time, and therefore could be used to improve public health dramatically. To the growing AI in health industry, this data offers huge potential in generating markets for new technologies in healthcare. However, primary care data is extremely sensitive. It contains data on individuals that is of a highly personal nature. As a result, many countries are reluctant to release this resource. This paper explores some key issues in the use of synthetic data as a substitute for real primary care data: Handling the complexities of real world data to transparently capture realistic distributions and relationships, modelling time, and minimising the matching of real patients to synthetic datapoints. We show that if the correct modelling approaches are used, then transparency and trust can be ensured in the underlying distributions and relationships of the resulting synthetic datasets. What is more, these datasets offer a strong level of privacy through lower risks of identifying real patients.

Keywords: Synthetic data · HealthCare data · Bayesian Networks

1 Introduction

Health care data encodes vast amounts of individual patients' visits over years of their life. It represents a detailed if noisy and uneven record of an entire population including cases of many different types of disease. If this data were to be freely available it would clearly enrich society with respect to our knowledge of disease and population health. However, there are convincing reasons to protect this data. People are generally very wary of enabling their personal data, including their primary care information, from being made available without any protection. The General Data Protection Regulations, implemented in 2018 [4], aims to protect individuals from their personal data being made public (or being unknowingly released to companies or institutions). As a result, there is

I. Koprinska et al. (Eds.): ECML PKDD 2020 Workshops, CCIS 1323, pp. 38–47, 2020.
https://doi.org/10.1007/978-3-030-65965-3_3

a demand for the generation of synthetic data: data that mirrors many of the characteristics of real Ground Truth (GT) data with similar distributions and relationships but made up of purely simulated patients. These datasets would offer the ability to train and validate many of the state-of-the-art machine learning models that are emerging, which in turn should lead to better detection and managing of many different diseases.

Previously, there have been a number of key approaches to working with synthetic data. The concept of k-anonymisation [10] works with the idea of measuring how likely it is to identify an individual from a small population, e-differential privacy [9] explores how aggregates of data can be released without identifying individuals from multiple requests of samples, generative adversarial networks have been used to build highly parameterised models from large datasets [11,14] whilst PrivBayes highlighted the importance of transparency of the underlying model as well as the concept of adding noise to ensure no individual can be re-identified [7]. We agree that underlying models must be transparent so that there is confidence and trust in the generated data and as a result, we focus on the use of graphical model approaches based on our earlier work [1]. If a GAN is used to generate data where knowledge of the underlying dependencies are not clear, then there are risks that biases, incorrect dependencies or even prejudices can be introduced [15].

In this paper we explore three fundamental questions: Firstly, can probabilistic graphical models be used to capture key distributions and relationships to generate realistic synthetic data? Secondly, can they be extended to longitudinal data such as is common in primary care settings? Finally, does the generated synthetic data protect against the identification of real patients and their sensitive features? In the next section we explore the methods, datasets and results of our experiments that explore these questions, before concluding.

2   Methods and Results

2.1   Datasets

MIMIC: For the first part of this paper we will explore the potential of Bayesian Networks (BNs) for modelling and generating synthetic data on the MIMIC III dataset [2]. MIMIC III is a publicly available dataset that records details of the stay of a patient. It contains general information about the subjects such as the age, religion, ethnicity, type of healthcare insurance. It also contains clinical information, such as the diagnoses which are represented by ICD-9 codes among the stay in the hospital. The dataset has a total number of 47,764 observations with 36,243 different subjects. All numerical data was discretised into 5 states using a frequency based approach ensuring a similar number of each state for all features.

CPRD: In order to demonstrate the ability of probabilistic graphical models to deal with temporal patient data we use the Clinical Practice Research Datalink (CPRD Aurum Database) [3]. CPRD primary care data cover 21% of the UK population and include over 17,400 clinical event types across patients with 25% of the patient data tracing back at least 20 years. We will focus on two key temporal features related to blood pressure, namely the Systolic Blood Pressure (SBP) and Diastolic Blood Pressure (DBP). This will be used to see if the BN modelling methods used on the MIMIC dataset can be extended to generate high-fidelity synthetic data reflecting the temporal characteristics.

2.2   Modelling MIMIC Data with Bayesian Networks

A Bayesian Network (BN) encodes the joint distribution of a dataset using a combination of a graphical structure that represents conditional independence between features and local conditional probability distributions [5] (see Fig. 1a for an example). They facilitate the integration of expert knowledge and data, and can handle missing data naturally. Inference can be used to extract posterior probabilities over sets of features given some observations. This means that they can be used for classification (Fig. 1b) and prediction. They are also generative models and can be used to generate samples of data based on the underlying distributions and independencies. What is more, they can be inferred from data using a number of different approaches including score-and-search methods [12] or contraint based methods [5]. An extension of the BN is the Dynamic Bayesian Network (DBN) which models time-series (Fig. 1c) and the Hidden Markov Model which encodes an unmeasured latent process [6] (Fig. 1d).

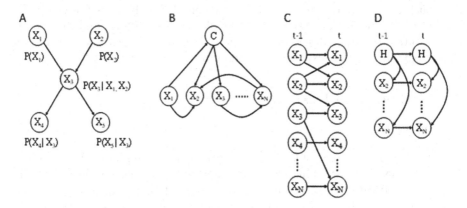

Fig. 1. Example A-Bayesian Network, B- Naive Bayes Classifier, C - Dynamic Bayesian Network and D- Hidden Markov Model

In order to test the BN framework on the MIMIC data, we used a well known BN learning algorithm that can deal with missing data known as Structural Expectation Maximization (SEM) to infer the structure and parameters of the model [13]. A key advantage of the BN is that it models the data in a transparent way where relationships between variables can be hard-coded or removed to influence learning.

Figure 2a shows the resulting structure. Two relationships that were known to exist (between blood disease and infections, and between age and circulatory conditions) were manually added. We then used this parameterised model to generate data synthetic data and compare the correlations (Fig. 2b and c) and distributions (Fig. 3) to the GT data. It can be seen that both the correlations and distributions are extremely similar to the GT data. We applied Kullbaeck Liebler tests and found no significant difference between all distributions. We wanted to see how this modelling technique could be extended to temporal data that is common in many health datasets by using the CPRD data.

2.3   Modelling Time

We exploited a natural extension of the BN known as the Dynamic Bayesian Network (DBN) which allows model structures over discrete time slices. See Fig. 4a for an example DBN that includes a hidden variable. In fact, the Hidden Markov Model (HMM) can be seen as a special case of DBN with fixed structure and a single hidden variable that models an underlying and unobserved process.

We used a hidden variable with 4 hidden states to capture the dynamics of the relationship between SBP and DBP. Figure 4b shows the resulting state transition diagram that has been inferred from the data (again using the SEM algorithm). The plots in Fig. 4c show a number of different characteristic comparisons between the original time-series ground-truth (GT) and the generated synthetic time-series. Firstly, in the top row can be seen a simple comparison of values for each patient for DBP, for SBP, and for the difference between DBP and SBP. All of these have a tight correlation. On the bottom row can be seen comparisons of temporal characteristics, namely the Auto-Correlation (ACF) per patient for DBP and SBP and also the Cross Correlation (CCF) between the two variables per patient. The ACFs show slightly skewed predictions where the synthetic data is often slightly lower than the ground truth, whereas the CCFs show very tight prediction values. These results imply that a realistic time-series of synthetic patient data can be generated using DBNs.

2.4   Risks of Matching Real Patients to Synthetic Data

Synthetic data offers an ideal way to allow the sharing of data that captures many of the characteristics of real patient data but without any of the privacy concerns. However, there is still a risk that synthetic data can be used to match individuals to simlar synthetic data and infer personal information about them. For example, if someone has access to some limited ground truth data about an individual and that information results in the individual being matched to similar outlying synthetic datapoints, then other more personal information may be inferred.

We explored this by looking at outliers in the Ground Truth (GT) data - those GT patients who have a small number of "nearest neighbours" which are significantly separate from the rest of the population of data. We did this by repeatedly sampling data from a mix of GT data (red in top of Fig. 5) and

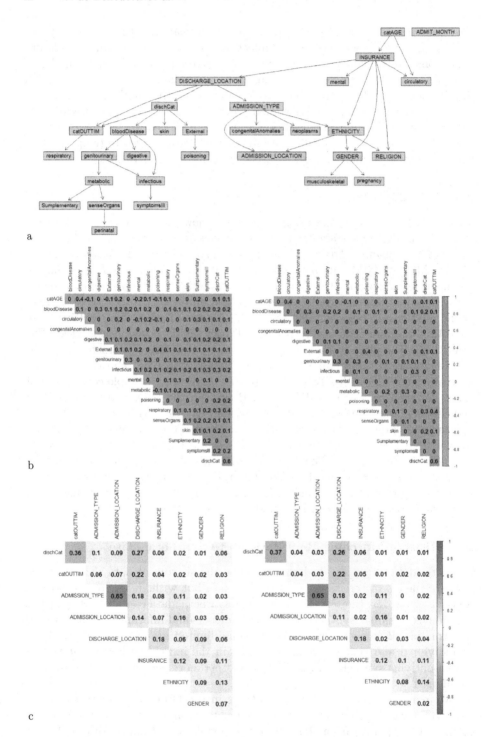

Fig. 2. a) the MIMIC BN and b/c) correlation matrices for ground truth (left) compared to synthetic data (right)

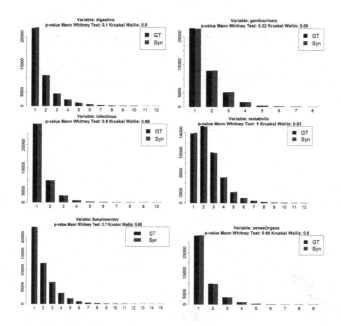

Fig. 3. Synthetic data distributions comparing frequencies for GT in red and synthetic in green (Color figure online)

synthetic data (blue). Synthetic data is generated using the BN methodology described earlier on CPRD data. Outlying ground truth datapoints (see A and B in top of Fig. 5) are then identified and these are used to explore the nearest neighbours that are from the synthetic data.

First we calculated the number of outlying ground truth datapoints that contain a single significant nearest neighbour from the synthetic dataset. This would mean that many of the characteristics of the synthetic datapoint could also be characteristics of the ground truth and risks the inferring of personal information. For example, in Fig. 5 (bottom) we can see how 6 attributes that are known about a real individual can be used to match them to a synthetic datapoint, and therefore infer more attributes that are *mostly* the same.

By running 100 repeated samples to calculate these risks we found the results in Table 1 for 4 different combinations of starting ground truth features. Firstly, notice how the number of GT outliers (first column) only slowly decreases as more GT features are made available. This implies that adding more knowledge of an individual to the attacker does not increase risk greatly. Secondly, notice that as the number of these available GT features increase, the number of single synthetic nearest neighbours decrease (column 3 representing the number of GT outliers with exactly one synthetic nearest neighbour and column 4 represents this as a proportion of all GT datapoints). Remember a very low number here may enable one to infer new personal information about the GT patient by exploring other features in the synthetic datapoint. The observed fall in number

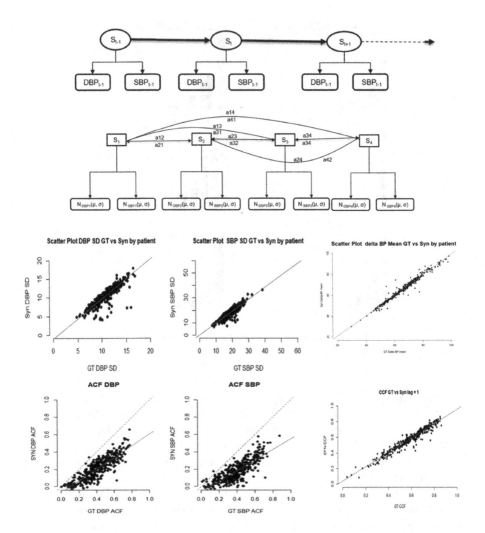

Fig. 4. DBN structure/state transitions and resulting data characteristics

is expected as an attacker can identify more precisely which synthetic data points match our ground truth patients. In our worst case, When we have 12 features known about a GT patient (in the bottom row) then we can identify a single nearest synthetic neighbour in only 43.5 out of 6180 cases on average, which is a real but small risk (0.7%). What is more, in many of these cases, the synthetic datapoint is not identical to the GT patient in semantically substantial ways (such as the example in Fig. 5 where the nearest synthetic datapoint is not a stroke sufferer unlike the GT patient).

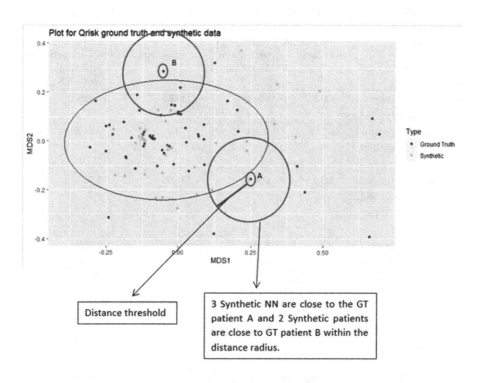

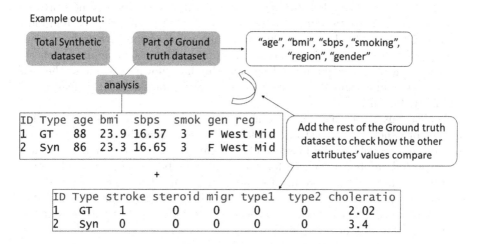

Fig. 5. Simulating attacking synthetic data with limited ground truth info (Color figure online)

Table 1. Statistics for matching similar individuals from synthetic data

GT attributes	Num of GT outliers	Num of GT patients in 10000 sample	Num of *single synth* NN	Proportion of GT outliers with single synth NN
Age, smoking, region, gender, ethnicity, ckidney	396.3	6248	113.8	1.82%
Age, smoking, region, gender, ethnicity, bmi, sbps, ckidney	377	6250	77.7	1.24%
Age, smoking, region, gender, ethnicity, bmi, choleratio, sbp, sbps, ckidney	363.1	6289	48.22	0.76%
Age, smoking, region, gender, ethnicity, bmi, sbps, ckidney, sle, atyantip, type1, streroid	363.4	6180	43.5	0.70%

3   Conclusions

This paper has explored some key issues when attempting to use synthetic data by learning models from sensitive healthcare data. It has carried out an empirical analysis on two real datasets using a probabilistic graphical modelling approach in the form of Bayesian networks for transparently capturing the key characteristics of data and emulating them in generated samples with very positive results. It has also extended this approach using dynamic Bayesian networks to model longitudinal data and has been successful in capturing the key temporal characteristics of blood pressure data. Finally, a set of simulations have been carried out to extract risks of matching ground truth data to similar synthetic data using nearest neighbour analysis and this has shown that whilst the risk is real, it is remote and the ability to infer information on sensitive features is extremely difficult.

Whilst this paper has made some very positive findings there are still a number of issues that need to be explored. For example, the data that is used to train any model may be biased and it is important that transparent models are inspected carefully to check for this. This may be easy on relatively small models such as explored here but for those with many 100s of features this will become far more tricky. We have looked at only two datasets and considerably more experimentation is needed to ascertain proper statistics with confidence bounds for the risks involved in matching real patients to synthetic data.

References

1. Wang, Z., Myles, P., Tucker, A.: Generating and evaluating synthetic UK primary care data: preserving data utility & patient privacy. In: 2019 IEEE 32nd International Symposium on Computer-Based Medical Systems, pp. 126–131 (2019)
2. Johnson, A.E.W., et al.: MIMIC-III, a freely accessible critical care database. Sci. Data (2016). https://doi.org/10.1038/sdata.2016.35
3. Wolf, A., et al.: Data resource profile: clinical practice research datalink (CPRD) aurum. Int. J. Epidemiol. **44**(3), 827–836 (2019)
4. https://gdpr-info.eu/
5. Spirtes, P., Glymour, C., Scheines, R.: Causation, Prediction and Search. Lecture Notes in Statistics, vol. 81. Springer, New York (1993). https://doi.org/10.1007/978-1-4612-2748-9
6. Rabiner, R.: A tutorial on hidden Markov models and selected applications in speech recognition. Proc. IEEE **77**(2), 257–286 (1989)
7. Zhang, J., Cormode, G., Procopiuc, C.M., Srivastava, D., Xiao, X.: PrivBayes: private data release via Bayesian networks. In: SIGMOD 2014, Snowbird, UT, USA, 22–27 June 2014 (2014)
8. Patki, N., Wedge, R., Veeramachaneni, K.: The synthetic data vault. In: IEEE 3rd International Conference on Data Science and Advanced Analytics (DSAA), vol. 1, pp. 399–410 (2016). https://doi.org/10.1109/DSAA.2016.49
9. Snoke, J., Slavkovi, A.: pMSE Mechanism: Differentially Private Synthetic Data with Maximal Distributional Similarity. arXiv:1805.09392v1 (2018)
10. Sweeney, L.: Achieving k-anonymity privacy protection using generalization and suppression. Int. J. Uncertain. Fuzziness Knowl.-Based Syst. **10**(5), 571–588 (2002)
11. Abay, N., Zhou, Y., Kantarcioglu, M., Thuraisingham, B., Sweeney, L.: Privacy Preserving Synthetic Data Release Using Deep Learning, pp. 510–526 (2018). https://doi.org/10.1007/978-3-030-10925-7
12. Cooper, G.F., Herskovits, E.: A Bayesian method for the induction of probabilistic networks from data. Mach. Learn. **9**, 309–347 (1992)
13. Friedman, N.: Learning belief networks in the presence of missing values and hidden variables. In: Proceedings of the 14th International Conference on Machine Learning, pp. 125–133 (1997)
14. Xu, L., et al.: Modeling tabular data using conditional GAN. In: 33rd Conference on Neural Information Processing Systems (2019)
15. Jia, S., Lansdall-Welfare, T., Cristianini, N.: Right for the right reason: training agnostic networks. In: Advances in Intelligent Data Analysis XVII 17th International Symposium, IDA (2018)

Building Trajectories Over Topology with TDA-PTS: An Application in Modelling Temporal Phenotypes of Disease

Seyed Erfan Sajjadi[1]($^{\boxtimes}$), Barbara Draghi[2], Lucia Sacchi[2], Arianna Dagliani[3], John Holmes[4], and Allan Tucker[1]

[1] Brunel University London, Uxbridge, UK
seyed.sajjadi@brunel.ac.uk
[2] University of Pavia, Pavia, Italy
[3] University of Manchester, Manchester, UK
[4] University of Pennsylvania, Philadelphia, USA

Abstract. Being able to better understand the underlying structure of clinical data is a topic of growing importance. Topological data analysis enables data scientists to uncover the "shape" of data by extracting the underlying topological structure which enables distinct regions to be identified. For example, certain regions may be associated with early-stage disease whilst others may represent different advanced disease sub-types. The identification of these regions can help clinicians to better understand specific patients' symptoms based upon where they lie in the disease topology, and therefore to make more targeted interventions. However, these topologies do not capture any sequential or temporal information. Pseudo-time series analysis can generate realistic trajectories through non-time-series data based on a combination of graph theory and the exploitation of expert knowledge (e.g. disease staging information). In this paper, we explore the combination of pseudo time and topological data analysis to build realistic trajectories over disease topologies. Using three different datasets: simulated, diabetes and genomic data, we explore how the combined method can highlight distinct temporal phenotypes in each disease based on the possible trajectories through the disease process.

Keywords: Topological data analysis (TDA) · Pseudo-time series (PTS) · Temporal phenotypes · Trajectory · Topology gene expression

1 Introduction

In the UK the National Health Service states that the 'one size fits all' approach to the care and treatment of patients is ineffective as everyone responds to diseases differently. The need for personalised medicine arises to better manage patients' health and to adapt treatment to the patient's data. Machine learning techniques can be used to help with this. This can be through identifying sub-groups of patients using unsupervised learning or building predictive models tailored to specific subgroups that are able to make better informed decisions based on historic data. Machine learning can also be used for

© Springer Nature Switzerland AG 2020
I. Koprinska et al. (Eds.): ECML PKDD 2020 Workshops, CCIS 1323, pp. 48–61, 2020.
https://doi.org/10.1007/978-3-030-65965-3_4

phenotyping. Phenotyping is used to distinguish clinically expressive information from patient data in order to identify traits or characteristics of patient groups. The research outlined here is to simultaneously identify the *shape* of a disease using topological data analysis and model disease *progression* by building realistic trajectories through the topologies. The aim is to discover temporal characteristics of disease progression for sub-groups of patients in the form of temporal phenotypes [1, 2].

Topological Data Analysis (TDA) is a relatively novel but increasingly popular approach to data analysis. This approach attempts to analyse datasets by studying the shape of the data to either reduce the dimensionality or better understand the underlying structure. This type of analysis can allow clinicians to gain a better understanding of potential sub-groups of patients for personalising interventions [3–5]. Singh, et al. introduced the Mapper algorithm as a geometrical tool to analyse and visualise the topology of datasets [6] in the form of graphical structures. These mappers are used to discover the shape characteristics in the data set by means of specific filter functions [7, 8] and partial clustering of the dataset. A major benefit is that the method does not depend on a specific clustering technique or algorithm and hence, it gives freedom and flexibility for the user to implement any appropriate clustering technique that best suits the data under analysis. The TDA Mapper has been used in many different studies such as the detection of topics in twitter [9], text representation for natural language processing and mining [10–12] and various clinical data such as breast cancer patients [7], spinal cord and brain injury [4], protein interaction networks [13], RNA-sequencing analysis [14] and analysing high and low functioning neuro-phenotypes within fragile X syndrome [15].

One weakness with any resulting topology is that there is no temporal information or ordering over the resulting graphs. For example, knowing that one region in the topology represents early disease and another represents advanced disease would be of great benefit.

Pseudo-time series (PTS) analysis is an effective method to create realistic trajectories through non-time-series data based upon distance metrics and expert knowledge on staging within a process (such as disease state). This can enable the temporal behaviour of measured features to be understood when time series data is not available. Forming an ordering of the patients in the data set, will allow a series of disease states to be determined, which can be used to map trajectories through disease progression. To construct a PTS, firstly a distance matrix is created between all data points and used to construct a weighted graph [16]. This graph is then used to build multiple shortest paths from pre-labelled start points to pre-labelled end points using a combination of resampling and graph theory [17]. Previously PTS and TDA have been compared as methods to analyse and understand clinical data [18].

In this paper, we introduce a new algorithm, TDA-PTS, which combines TDA and PTS techniques so that we can build trajectories over discovered topologies from patients' data. Following TDA and enrichment, we create PTS models from the cross-sectional output of the TDA using overlap between the partial clusters as a measure of similarity and the majority class allocation to each vertex in a topology as a staging label. The trajectories can then be used to create temporal models. [19] have shown that using bootstrapping over the topology to build these trajectories results in more robust PTS models. Furthermore, using the updated method of PTS explored by [20] may give us the ability to identify intermediate stages in a disease process and to visualise subtle differences in symptoms. In the next section we describe our proposed method in detail, In Sect. 3 we document the results on three very different datasets: one simulated dataset, one diabetes dataset, and a combined genomic dataset from 3 cancer studies. In Sect. 4 we draw some conclusions.

2 Method

In this section, we firstly define our TDA-PTS approach. We then introduce the three datasets that we test the approach on. Finally, we describe the empirical analysis.

2.1 TDA-PTS

The dataset, D, illustrated below in Fig. 1, can be defined as a real valued matrix of m by n, where m (columns) is the number of samples that are the patients and n (rows) is the number of variables that are the clinical features in the data. D_i can be defined as the ith column of matrix D. Furthermore, $C = [c_1, c_2, ..., c_m]$ is used as a vector that represents class labels of the dataset, where $c_i \in \{0,1\}$ corresponds to the sample i. Subsequently, $c_i = 1$ and $c_i = 0$ represents the patients in the sample i that are the diseased cases and the healthy cases within the dataset respectively. The classes of the sample i have been determined based upon the diagnosis made by experts or clinicians.

We define a filter function, $F: D \subseteq X \rightarrow Y$, where X is the underlying space of the point cloud data (R_n for some $n \in N$) and Y is the parameter space ($Y \in \mathbb{R}$). We then find the range I of the filter function F restricted to D. We partition the range I into subintervals S so that it creates a cover of D which overlap. This step produces two parameters which can be used to control the resolution, specifically the length of the smaller intervals L, and the overlap percentage between successive intervals O. For every subinterval $S_i \in S$, the following set is created which forms its domain $X_i = \{x \mid F(x) \in S_i\}$. The set $U = \{X_i\}$ forms a cover of D and $D \subseteq U_i X_i$. A suitable metric is used to get the set of all interpoint distances $B_i = \{d(x_a, x_b) \mid x_a, x_b \in X_i\}$. The shortest path or distances is used known as the Euclidean distances between the clusters but other distances such as Minkowski or Manhattan distances can be used based on the needs of the study. Clusters X_{ij} are found for each X_i with the set of distances B_i. Finally, each cluster X_{ij} represents a node or a vertex in the complex and an edge is created between nodes or vertices X_{ij} and X_{rs} if $X_{ij} \cap X_{rs} \neq 0$, which means that the two clusters share a common point. A topology has now been created for the dataset, which is ready to be enriched. This enrichment is conducted so that PTS can be applied to plot trajectories through the cross-sectional data (generated from the TDA) based upon distances between each node or vertex using the prior knowledge of healthy and disease patients (classes, C).

The topology graph $G = (V, E)$, where V is a set of elements known as vertices and E is a set of two-sets of vertices known as edges, produces an adjacency matrix based upon the vertices. This adjacency matrix is defined by a h by h matrix of binary values in which location $(i, j) = 1$ if $(i, j) \in E$ and 0 $otherwise$. Thus, for an undirected graph the matrix is symmetric and 0 along the diagonal. The vertices are linked via edges based on a certain level of overlap, which means that 2 vertices will have common data points. We replace the $(i, j) = 1$ values of the adjacency matrix with the amount of overlap between each corresponding vertex, which defines a weighted distance matrix, W, of the topology, which is represented by a t by t matrix, where t_{ij} is the level of overlap between t_i and t_j. Subsequently, each vertex consists of datapoints from different classes, we determine the majority class within each vertex and calculate the amount of majority. This defines a new vector $M = [m_1, m_2, ..., m_t]$ that represents the weighted majority classes on the vertices in the topology of the dataset. The TDA of the dataset has now been enriched to produce a weighted distance matrix, W, and a weighted class vector, M. The matrix and corresponding vector can be used as the input for building a PTS to plot the trajectories on the topology.

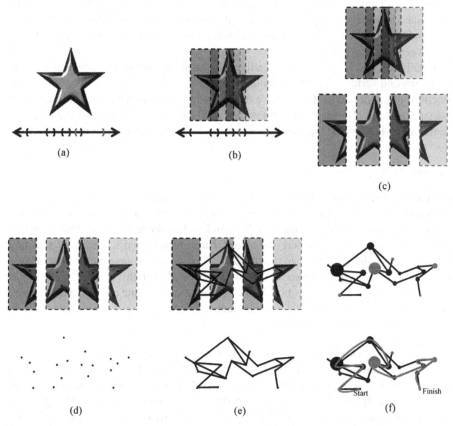

Fig. 1. TDA and PTS on the star shape data cloud: a) First we project the whole data cloud to embedded space (here x-axis). b) Then we partition the embedded space into overlapping bins (here showed as coloured intervals). c) Then we put data into overlapping bins. d) Next we use any clustering algorithm to cluster the points in the cloud data. e) Each cluster of points in every bin represents a vertex of the graph and we draw and edge between two vertices if they share a common data point. f) Then, we enrich the graph so that the vertex sizes represent the density of the cluster and the colours represent the class majority. Finally, we create a PTS model which maps trajectories from one predefined starting vertex to another predefined ending vertex.

We define a set of pseudo time-series indices as $P = \{p_1, p_2, ..., p_k\}$ and every p_i is a t length vector. Subsequently, p_{ij} is defined as the jth element of p_i and each $p_{ij} \in (0, ..., m)$. Now the function $F(pi) = [pi1, ..., pit]$ is defined, where $F(p_i) = W(p_{ij})$ and finally, a PTS can be built by using this operator from each p_i. Also, the corresponding weighted class vector of each PTS produced by the function $F(p_i)$ is given by $G(p_i) = [M(p_{i1}), ..., M(p_{it})]$. We define a set of k PTS with their associated vector M sampled from the matrix W indexed by the elements of p_i. The ordering of the p_i elements is defined based upon randomly indicating a start and end p_i so that the *mstart* is a starting vertex and the *mend* is an ending vertex in the associated topology graph. This procedure should map trajectories from a starting node, which could be a healthy state to an ending node, which should be a diseased state. However, the trajectories might pick up insightful starting and ending nodes between the different classes of disease states. The ordering can now be determined by the shortest path, which is computed from the Floyd–Warshall algorithm [21] and then applied to the minimum spanning tree of the Euclidean distance matrix Z_i between samples in $F(p_i)$ [20].

Finally, we can create a PTS from the TDA to show how the trajectories progress from a starting vertex (e.g. with a healthy state) to an ending vertex (disease state). The benefit of this approach is that we have discovered trajectories not only from healthy to disease states but also revealed multiple potential routes to multiple end states. Using the output of TDA as the input of PTS creates more meaningful trajectories.

2.2 Datasets

Simulated HMM Data: Simulated data was used generated from an autoregressive Hidden Markov Model with 2 variables. This enabled the manipulation of underlying states to direct the topology of the data. We hand-crafted the model to simulate multiple patient time-series with 5 underlying states. These represented a branching structure from a single healthy state to two possible advanced disease states via two intermediate disease states. From 100 time-series that were generated from this process, we sample a single point to mimic a cross-sectional study. Figure 2 shows some sample data generated where each data point represents a single sample from a time-series. This data is freely available from the author's website.

Diabetes Patient Data: Data for this study was previously collected for clinical and management purposes during the MOSAIC project funded by the European Commission under the 7th Framework Program, (Theme Virtual Physiological Human, 2013–2016) [4, 7, 19]. Health records were accumulated from 924 pre-diagnosed T2DM patients, which resulted in 13,623 instances in our data set. Risk factors found to influence T2DM [4] include: body mass index (BMI), systolic blood pressure (SBP), diastolic blood pressure (DBP), high-density lipoprotein (HDL), triglycerides, glycated haemoglobin (HbA1c), total cholesterol and smoking habits. Accordingly with previous studies on the MOSAIC project [4], the experimental results were mined for microvascular comorbidities (diabetic nephropathy, neuropathy, and retinopathy). The following variables were used to build the topology and pseudo time-series: age, smoking habit, HbA1c, BMI, SBP, total cholesterol, and triglycerides. Continuous variables were normalized

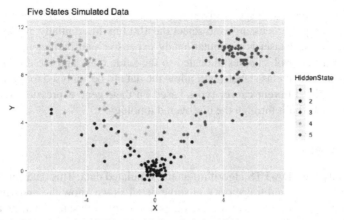

Fig. 2. Sampled data from the ARHMM with 5 underlying hidden states, one representing healthy patients (red), two representing early stage disease (brown and green) and two representing advanced disease states (blue and purple). (Color figure online)

on a -1 to $+1$ scale. While we did not exploit the temporal nature of this data for phenotype identification, we used the fact that many of these patients had varying follow-up measurements to evaluate our trajectories. In particular, we used time-since-first-visit to assess whether the trajectories correctly model patient progression.

Genomic Cancer Data: The genomic cancer dataset combines 3 datasets of lung cancer, pancreatic tumour and renal tumour patients along with their respective control patients.

The 91 human lung tissue samples in the lung cancer dataset (healthy and diseases) were analysed using the Human Genome U133 Plus 2.0 chip from Affymetrix in Hospital Universitario San Cecilio. The aim of the research for this dataset was to determine any correlation between the phenotypic heterogeneity and genetic diversity of lung cancer [22]. However, the data was processed through microarray analysis to generate expressed gene sequence, which is ideal for building trajectories through the topology of the data.

The pancreatic tumour data was collected and processed at the Mayo Clinic in the United States. 52 samples were collected and like the lung cancer data, microarrays were to identify the expression differences of FKBP5 gene between the pancreatic tumour and normal samples. It was discovered that on average normal samples had more FKBP5 expression compared to tumour samples [23]. The data was processed into gene expression data, which can be used along with the lung cancer data.

For the renal tumour data set, which was collected in Erasmus Medical Centre Rotterdam, the Affymetrix microarray was used to establish the gene expression signatures of normal kidneys and different types of renal tumours. This investigating was conducted to identify and evaluate specific molecular markers with the aim of reliable diagnostics and outcome prediction of renal neoplasms [24]. The data was recorded as gene expression data.

The 3 datasets are combined, and the batch effect is removed. Additionally, the class vector is adapted to define $c_i = 1, 2, 3$ representing the lung cancer, pancreatic tumour and renal tumour patients respectively and $c_i = 0$ represents all healthy cases. The next stage of the data pre-processing is to select the 100 top differentially expressed genes as using the entire dataset is computationally expensive and inefficient. The merged dataset, with all control samples allocated to the same class and the different cancer types assigned unique class labels, will allow the data to be analysed to see if there are links between the different cancer types based on their gene expression and whether trajectories can be built through the discovered topology.

2.3 Experiments

First, we apply the TDA-PTS algorithm on the simulated data. This data can be used to explore the topology and trajectories in some detail as we know the underlying states and temporal process. Therefore, we use the positions of each sample within their original time-series to validate if the topology and trajectories are realistic. We should see an ordering of increasing timepoints as a trajectory is traversed. We can also use the underlying hidden states to label the topology and trajectories to confirm that the start, intermediate and end states are appropriately located.

For the Diabetes data we use a similar approach to the simulated data because these have a true time-series that the data was sampled from in the form of time-since diagnosis. We can validate the topologies and trajectories by using the distributions of this time information, as well as plot how real patients' time-series move over the topology.

Finally, for the genomic cancer data we have no temporal information, so we aim to explore the behaviour of the gene expression for several genes to see how they vary from trajectories as they move from control datasets to the three types of cancer.

3 Results

Here is where the results from the three different datasets are explored to see how combined TDA-PTS algorithm performs. As stated before, the data is pre-processed before TDA is applied and subsequently, PTS is applied to map out the trajectories through the topology. The outcome of the TDA-PTS approach is accompanied by the distribution of the datapoints through the trajectory that PTS takes.

Simulated HMM Data
We first investigate the results of applying our combined TDA-PTS algorithm on the simulated data. Firstly, notice in Fig. 3 how the V-shaped topology of the simulated data is preserved within the topology. We enrich the graphs using the hidden state where the initial state is in red and the two end states are in blue and purple with intermediate as green and yellow. The enriched graphs are used along with knowledge from the temporal information to validate the trajectories created. This validation process improves the trajectory robustness. It is clear that the earlier stages of the temporal process are located to the left of the topology and dominated by the first (healthy disease state) with nodes coloured red or orange, whilst the two end states are characterized in the top and bottom right of the topology (in blue and purple).

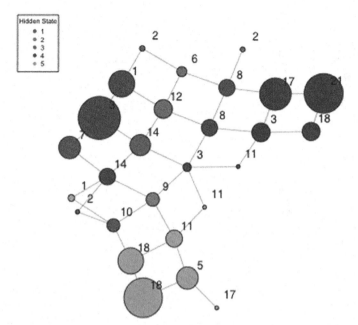

Fig. 3. The TDA learnt from the ARHMM data with colour indicating majority hidden state for data allocated to each vertex, size of vertex represents number of datapoints assigned and labels indicate the position in the original generating ARHMM. (Color figure online)

As these datapoints are sampled from a real temporal process (generated by the ARHMM) we can also label each vertex with the position in the original ARHMM time series. We would, therefore, expect to see lower (earlier) positions in the time-series in the healthy red state and higher (later) positions in the disease states (blue and purple). This is exactly what is observed with the large red vertex (healthy stages) having a mean position in the time-series of 3, and the largest blue (disease stages) having a position of 21 and the purple (disease stages) having 18.

In Fig. 4 we show three types of PTS trajectory (which we refer to as *temporal phenotype*). Notice that the trajectories over the topology capture the two main paths from healthy in red to either disease state in blue or disease state in purple (though sometimes the PTS ends early at an intermediate state as in the final phenotype). The distributions of data over the vertices on the right show that the appropriate trajectory behaviour is captured. For example, X values decrease and Y increase for the first example phenotype (red to blue), whilst both X and Y values increase in the second phenotype (red to purple).

We now explore how the method works on two real datasets.

Diabetes Patient Data

We now explore the Diabetes dataset. Recall for this set that we also have the real underlying time-series in terms of time since diagnosis. This allows us to explore the discovered trajectories to see if they are realistic. Figure 5 on the left shows three types of trajectory (or temporal phenotype discovered by grouping PTS trajectories that move from and

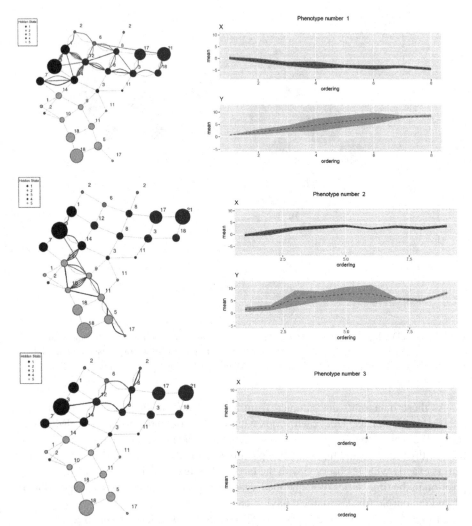

Fig. 4. Sample pseudo time-series over three types of trajectory along with the distributions of the simulated variables for each vertex in the topology ordered along each PTS.

to similar regions). Here, a blue vertex represents data with multiple comorbidities and red represents none. On the right of Fig. 5 are the associated distributions of the key features for that phenotype: glycated haemoglobin (hba1c), body mass index, systolic blood pressure, total cholesterol and triglycerides. In the same way as with the simulated data we enrich the discovered topology with temporal information, here we use an index associated with time since diagnosis. Similar to the simulated date, combining the enriched topology with the temporal information allows us to validate the trajectories. The picture is quite complex with different regions capturing different stages in disease progression. For example, the far right and left has vertices associated with later stage disease (with generally higher values), whilst the centre and bottom regions of the topology capture earlier stages (with lower values). The three phenotypes capture quite distinct behaviours. For example, the first phenotype is characterised by most features decreasing in value over time, whilst the second phenotype shows an increasing trend for haemoglobin and triglycerides but more stable over other features. The third phenotype is characterised by much more variation in the middle stage of the trajectory. In

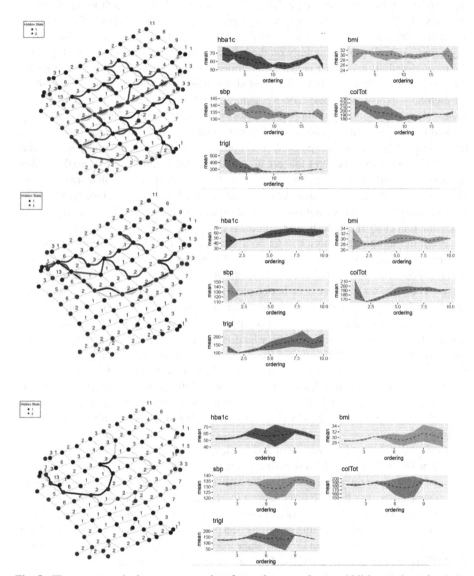

Fig. 5. Three temporal phenotypes moving from absence of comorbidities (red vertices) to the presence of comorbidities (blue). On the right side, the distributions of the main clinical characteristics over the topology ordered along each PTS Trajectory. (Color figure online)

summary the combination of PTS and TDA has enabled complex temporal phenotypes to be characterised over a topology.

Genomic Cancer Data

For the genomic cancer data, we do not have any temporal validation, but we have three types of label based on cancer type: Lung, Pancreatic and Renal, which we can explore in terms of how the gene expression behaviour differs. Figure 6 shows the topology and three sample trajectories with their distribution of classes and gene values for 3 key genes. As well as the topology on the left, we have plotted the majority class with the mean distribution of each vertex as the trajectory progresses (in a lighter colour on the right). Furthermore, we have also plotted the mean distribution of three top-ranked differentially expressed genes: 219787_s_at, 212992_at and 222646_s_at within each vertex along their corresponding trajectories. Notice that the healthy class is neatly located in the top of the topology (in red) and the three cancer types are at the bottom left and right (green, blue and purple). Also notice in the class distribution plots how the trajectories move from vertices that are dominated by the healthy class (state 0) to ones dominated by one cancer type or another (class states 1, 2 and 3). It is interesting that the class distribution starts off with a vertex that are far more uniform in class membership but that shortly after we see a mixture of class states indicating an early warning signal along the trajectory that a particular cancer type is likely further downstream.

From the sample trajectories in 6a-6c it seems that class 3 (renal tumour patients) acts like a transition point for progression to the other two cancer types. This implies that there could be similar genetic mechanisms at play between the cancers in the early stages. The 3 top-ranked gene distribution plots give us an effective visual representation of how each gene progresses through the different trajectories. Figure 6a shows that all three genes generally increase as the trajectory progresses. Gene 219787_s_at starts very low at the beginning of the trajectory, which is an indication that for healthy patients, this gene has a low distribution but the gene increases and reaches a peak at vertex 6. Subsequently, for pancreatic cancer in Fig. 6b, gene 219787_s_at shows a similar increasing trend though to a lesser degree, whilst 212992_at shows a decreasing trend. For the renal tumour plots in Fig. 6c, the gene distribution for all 3 gene peaks at the same point where the class distribution of the vertex become dominantly class 3 (renal tumour).

Gene 219787_s_at has been identified as the epithelial cell transforming sequence 2 oncogene (ECT2) [25]. ECT2 has an oncogenic role in lung adenocarcinoma cells and it is stated to be commonly upregulated at the early stage lung adenocarcinoma [26]. From Fig. 6 we can see that ETC2 has the largest increase in distribution when the trajectory goes towards a vertex which is predominantly occupied by lung cancer patients. Hence, this is a strong indication that this gene may be a potential target for the treatment of lung cancer and can work as a signal for early stage intervention. Gene 212992_at, also known as AHNAK nucleoprotein 2 (AHNAK2) and gene 222646_s_at, also known as endo-plasmic reticulum oxidoreductase 1 alpha (ERO1A) are proteins within humans. These proteins have been identified by the TDA-PTS approach as possibly being an indication to disease progression. This is further insight on how effectively the gene distribution for the 3 top-ranked genes can help in discovering key stages in disease progression. It helps

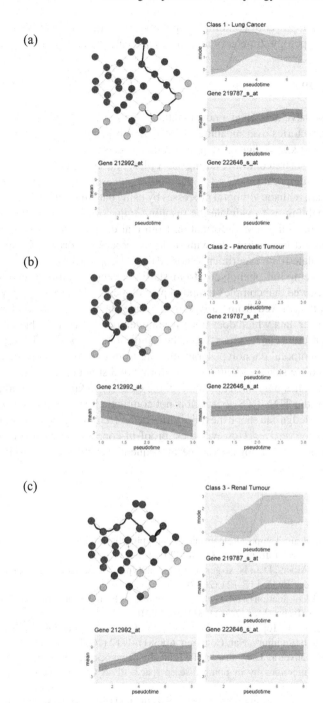

Fig. 6. (Left) TDA plots with sample PTS where colours indicate the majority class at each vertex. (Right) Distribution of the 3 top-ranked genes in each vertex as they travel along their associated PTS. (Color figure online)

to demonstrate the power of combining topology with trajectory analysis in identifying key points in a topology /trajectory that can enable earlier intervention.

4 Conclusions

In this paper we have described a novel method, TDA-PTS with the aim to create realistic disease trajectories over meaningful topologies based upon graph theory, distance metrics and expert knowledge on staging within a disease.

We have demonstrated how resulting TDA plots and the associated PTS trajectories capture realistic temporal processes in three different case-studies. Firstly, we assessed the ability to learn realistic temporal processes by using data that has underlying temporal information enabling us to validate the resulting trajectories: Time-indexed simulated data and time-since-diagnosis information from real diabetes data was used to enrich our topologies and trajectories showing realistic processes form early stages to late stages. The simulated data experiments showed that the approach can successfully extract the underlying temporal phenotypes from starting states to multiple end states. The diabetes data showed that complex temporal phenotypes could be extracted with distinct characteristics that moved from early stages to late stages. We also explored the use of genomic cancer data which does not have any temporal validation but allowed us to explore three different cancer types. From the sample topologies and PTS trajectories we found realistic temporal phenotypes transitioning from uniform healthy states, through diverse intermediate states and ending in uniform but distinct cancer states.

The approach has only been applied to three datasets so far and so validation of the effectiveness of the TDA-PTS approach is not complete. For example, we will explore how expert knowledge can shape the trajectories better (removing any risks of impossible transitions between vertices) However, these proof-of-concept results give an incentive to further explore how combining both shape and sequential analysis can assist in explaining complex disease processes.

References

1. Dagliati, A., et al.: Temporal electronic phenotyping by mining careflows of breast cancer patients. J. Biomed. Inform. **66**, 136–147 (2017)
2. Hripcsak, G., Albers, D.J.: Next-generation phenotyping of electronic health records. J. Am. Med. Inf. Assoc. **20**(1), 117–121 (2013)
3. Li, L., et al.: Identification of type 2 diabetes subgroups through topological analysis of patient similarity. Sci. Transl. Med. **7**(311), 311ra174 (2015)
4. Nielson, J.L., et al.: Topological data analysis for discovery in preclinical spinal cord injury and traumatic brain injury. Nat. Commun. **6**(8581), 1–12 (2015)
5. Torres, B.Y., Oliveira, J.M., Tate, A.T., Rath, P., Cumnock, K., Schneider, D.S.: Tracking resilience to infections by mapping disease space. PLoS Comput. Biol. **14**(4), e1002436 (2016)
6. Singh, G., Memoli, F., Carlsson, G.: Topological methods for the analysis of high dimensional data sets and 3D object recognition. In: SPBG: Eurographics Symposium on Point Based Graphics, Prague, pp. 91–100. The Eurographics Association (2007)

7. Nicolau, M., Levine, A., Carlsson, G.: Topology based data analysis identifies a subgroup of breast cancers with a unique mutational profile and excellent survival. Proc. Natl. Acad. Sci. **108**(17), 7265–7270 (2011)
8. Lum, P.Y., et al.: Extracting insights from the shape of complex data using topology. Sci. Rep. **3**(1), 1236 (2013)
9. Torres-Tramón, P., Hromic, H., Heravi, B.R.: Topic detection in twitter using topology data analysis. In: Daniel, F., Diaz, O. (eds.) ICWE 2015. LNCS, vol. 9396, pp. 186–197. Springer, Cham (2015). https://doi.org/10.1007/978-3-319-24800-4_16
10. Gholizadeh, S., Seyeditabari, A., Zadrozny, W.: Topological signature of 19th century novelists. Big Data Cogn. Comput. **2**(4), 33 (2018)
11. Nilsson, D., Ekgren, A.: Topology and Word Spaces. Stockholm: KTH Computer Science and Communication (2013)
12. Zhu, X.: Persistent homology: an introduction and a new text representation for natural language processing. In: IJCAI International Joint Conference on Artificial Intelligence. International Joint Conferences on Artificial Intelligence Organization, Beijing, pp. 1953–1959 (2013)
13. Sardiu, M., Gilmore, J., Groppe, B., Florens, L., Washburn, M.: Identification of topological network modules in perturbed protein interaction networks. Sci. Rep. **7**(43845), 1–13 (2107)
14. Rizvi, A., et al.: Single-cell topological RNA-seq analysis reveals insights into cellular differentiation and development. Nat. Biotechnol. **35**(6), 551–560 (2017)
15. Romano, D., et al.: Topological methods reveal high and low functioning neuro-phenotypes within fragile X syndrome. Hum. Brain Mapp. **35**, 4904–4915 (2014)
16. Campbell, K.R., Yau, C.: Uncovering pseudotemporal trajectories with covariates from single cell and bulk expression data. Nat. Commun. **9**(1), 2442 (2018)
17. Tucker, A., Garway-Heath, D.: The pseudotemporal bootstrap for predicting glaucoma from cross-sectional visual field data. IEEE Trans. Inf. Technol. Biomed. **14**(1), 79–85 (2010)
18. Dagliati, A., et al.: Inferring temporal phenotypes with topological data analysis and pseudo time-series. In: Riaño, D., Wilk, S., ten Teije, A. (eds.) AIME 2019. LNCS (LNAI), vol. 11526, pp. 399–409. Springer, Cham (2019). https://doi.org/10.1007/978-3-030-21642-9_50
19. Li, Y., Tucker, A.: Uncovering disease regions using pseudo time-series trajectories on clinical trial data. In: 2010 3rd International Conference on Biomedical Engineering and Informatics (BMEI 2010), Yantai, pp. 2356–2362. IEEE (2010)
20. Li, Y., Swift, S., Tucker, A.: Modelling and analysing the dynamics of disease progression from cross-sectional studies. J. Biomed. Inform. **46**(2), 266–274 (2013)
21. Floyd, R.: Algorithm 97: shortest path. Commun. ACM **5**(6), 345 (1962)
22. Sanchez-Palencia, A., et al.: Gene expression profiling reveals novel biomarkers in nonsmall cell lung cancer. Int. J. Cancer **129**(2), 355–364 (2011)
23. Pei, H., et al.: FKBP51 affects cancer cell response to chemotherapy by negatively regulating Akt. Cancer Cell **16**(3), 259–266 (2009)
24. The National Center for Biotechnology Information: Gene Expression Omnibus (GEO) – Accession Display. https://www.ncbi.nlm.nih.gov/geo/query/acc.cgi?acc=GSE 11151. Accessed 04 Mar 2020
25. Rosty, C., et al.: Identification of a proliferation gene cluster associated with HPV E6/E7 expression level and viral DNA load in invasive cervical carcinoma. Oncogene **24**(47), 7094–7104 (2005)
26. Tan, H., Wang, X., Yang, X., Li, H., Liu, B., Pan, P.: Oncogenic role of epithelial cell transforming sequence 2 in lung adenocarcinoma cells. Exp. Ther. Med. **12**(4), 2088–2094 (2016)

Data Decomposition Based Learning for Load Time-Series Forecasting

Jatin Bedi$^{(\boxtimes)}$ and Durga Toshniwal

Department of Computer Science and Engineering, Indian Institute of Technology,
Roorkee 247667, India
jatinbedi278@gmail.com, durgatoshniwal@gmail.com

Abstract. With the deployment of smart grid technologies and management modernization, the large amount of fine-grained electricity consumption data become readily available. So, the process of knowledge extraction from such a vast amount of data should be optimized to efficiently and reliably utilize such information for future strategies making, network optimization and power system planning. In this context, we proposed a hybrid approach that combines decomposition algorithm with deep learning model for improved accuracy and reduced complexity. The approach adds an additional novel perspective to the existing studies by selecting appropriate prediction models on the basis of decomposed components intrinsic features. Experiments are conducted on the Australian National Electricity Market (specifically, Queensland) dataset and prediction results are compared to two different state-of-the-art decomposition based hybrid approaches. The comparison results are evidence that the proposed approach outperforms other decomposition based hybrid approaches by generating 1.63% average prediction error.

Keywords: Time-series forecasting · Load forecasting · Data decomposition based learning

1 Introduction

In recent years, India's electricity sector has witnessed exponential growth in electricity demand [6]. This increased energy demand has been caused by a number of different factors including population growth, urban development, deployment of smart grid technologies and industrial expansion. With respect to increasing energy demand, efficient generation capacity planning and decision-making strategies are needed to satisfy nationwide electricity demand while taking care of natural resources [7]. Since the process of storing excess energy amount is very difficult and expensive, the energy should be generated in a way to satisfy current demand i.e. supply-demand should be coordinated. In this context, energy load forecasting [9,15] has gained significant attention in the power industry for energy grid network optimization, future decision strategies planning and reducing energy wastage. Based on target prediction horizon, load

© Springer Nature Switzerland AG 2020
I. Koprinska et al. (Eds.): ECML PKDD 2020 Workshops, CCIS 1323, pp. 62–74, 2020.
https://doi.org/10.1007/978-3-030-65965-3_5

forecasting can be performed at three different levels [6] [27]: long term demand forecasting (makes prediction for 1 to 50 years ahead, useful for long-term strategies planning), medium-term demand forecasting (makes prediction for months to year ahead, useful for operational planning) and short term demand forecasting (has a prediction span from days to week ahead, useful for distribution network optimization).

In the past years, numerous research efforts have been made for improving prediction performance of the forecasting models. These load forecasting techniques can be broadly divided into three major categories, namely traditional methods, Artificial Intelligence (AI) based methods and hybrid methods. Traditional load demand forecasting has been addressed using various statistical approaches, namely Auto-regressive (AR) models [39], Auto-regressive Moving Average (ARIMA) [43], Auto-regressive Integrated Moving Average (ARIMAX) [17] and so on. These models are simple and easy to implement, but have low generalization capabilities. AI-based models implement variants of Neural Network (NN) or deep learning models (such as feed-forward network [11], Multi-layer Perceptron (MLP) [14], Recurrent Neural Network (RNN) [34], Long Short Term Memory Network (LSTM) [7] and Deep Belief Network (DBN)), genetic algorithms and fuzzy-logic to forecast electricity demand. AI-based models are capable of handling non-linear data complexities and have good approximation capabilities, but their performance gets highly affected by the increasing noise level and sudden fluctuations in the load time series. Hybrid models amalgamate different type of techniques to support improved prediction accuracy. In the last five years, various research studies have investigated the benefits of integrating signal processing techniques (such as wavelet decomposition [38], mode decomposition [6]) with deep learning models. These techniques have been widely implemented to estimate future electricity demand and are found to be more accurate and reliable than the traditional models. However, there are still need for more robust solutions as the existing approaches suffer from some major drawbacks such as high complexity and limited accuracy.

In the current work, we proposed a hybrid approach that combines Empirical Mode Decomposition (EMD) [36] with deep learning model for improved prediction accuracy. The proposed model provides support for improved accuracy and reduced complexity by: (a) performing timestamp data (day-wise) decomposition/segmentation based Learning. (b) performing EMD based decomposition for reduced components intra-correlation. (c) selecting the appropriate prediction model for extracted components on the basis of its intrinsic features such as Hurst, seasonality and non-linearity.

The rest of this paper is organized as follows: the related work done in the field of energy load forecasting is described in Sect. 2. The detailed methodology of the proposed energy demand forecasting approach is explained in Sect. 3. Experimental results of the proposed approach on the real-world dataset are described in Sect. 4. Finally, the conclusion is stated in Sect. 5.

2   Literature Review

Energy load forecasting has widely gained remarkable attention in the last few years [17]. It plays a crucial role in decision making, strategies planning, energy optimization and stable operation of the power grids. With the development of mathematical theory and computational methods, various research studies have significantly contributed to the field. These research studies can be categorized into three major classes, namely statistical approaches, computational intelligence methods and hybrid methods.

Statistical methods implement regression analysis (such as linear regression [29], non-linear regression [9,16,31], step-wise regression [25,42] and least-square regression [15,32]), uni-variate time-series methods (such as moving average [39,43], ARIMA [43], SARIMA [10,21], ARIMAX [3,17]), multi-variate time-series methods (such as Bayesian vector [26], auto-regression [12], multivariate ARIMA [2,35]) and auto-regressive models (such as generalized auto-regressive conditional heteroskedasticity, winters model) for energy load time-series forecasting. Despite of several advantages, these methods have several limitations that limits their usage such as linear dependence and large historic data requirement.

Computational intelligence methods including Artificial neural network (ANN) [5,11], Multi-layer Perceptron network (MLP) [4], Decision-trees, Support Vector Machine (SVM) [22,41] and genetic algorithm were highly utilized in the field of load forecasting. From the experimental results of various research studies, it was found that these methods have better approximation capabilities than the traditional methods. Furthermore, in the recent years, several deep learning techniques such as Convolutional Neural Network (CNN) [23], Recurrent Neural Network (RNN) [7,34], Deep residual network [13] are successfully implemented to effectively forecast the energy demand while taking care of data dependencies. These models are capable of efficiently handling non-linearity and complex features of time-series data.

Hybrid models [8,33,37] implement combination of statistical and computational intelligence techniques to support reliable and efficient load forecasting. Furthermore, in the recent years, various hybrid approaches were introduced that coupled signal processing techniques with learning models. Li. et al. [24] combined wavelet extraction with gray neural network for optimized performance. Changhao et al. [38] proposed a hybrid approach that combined wavelet analysis with machine learning model for electricity power load forecasting. Bedi et al. [6] combined empirical mode decomposition with LSTM model for load forecasting at the state level. He et al. [20] integrated variation model decomposition with LSTM model for load demand forecasting. These hybrid deep neural network based models have gained a lot of attention for energy demand modelling. The experimental results of various research studies have shown that the hybrid approaches provide more accurate and reliable prediction results than that of other existing state-of-the-art data-driven techniques. However, these models suffer from some major shortcomings such as high computational complexity, deciding optimal mode component for noise reduction, handling long-term data dependencies and so on.

To rectify the major drawbacks of these hybrid learning approaches, we propose a hybrid decomposition based learning approach for improved prediction accuracy and reduced complexity. The approach integrates timestamp data decomposition (day-wise segregation) and mode generation algorithm with LSTM [18] and MLP [30] models to provide support for handling long-term data dependencies, abrupt data fluctuations, non-linear complexities and to reduce series intrinsic data correlation.

3   Methodology

In this section, we explicate the methodology of the proposed energy demand forecasting approach. Figure 1 represents the multi-level block diagram of the proposed approach.

3.1   Input Dataset

In the present work, we utilize the historical timestamp electricity load data recorded by the Australian National Electricity Market (NEM) [1]. NEM provides electricity services for six states and territories in Australia, namely, Queensland, Tasmania, Victoria, New South Wales, South Australia and Australian Capital Territory. For the purpose of our current analysis, we utilize the electricity demand data of the second largest (with a land area of 1.853 million km^2) and third most populous state Queensland for the year 2018. The demand data is available at a sample rate of 30 min.

3.2   Data Preprocessing

The accurate execution of the process of knowledge discovery from data is of utmost importance as it forms the basis for various decision-making policies. The efficacy of patterns extraction process is highly dependent on the quality of data available for the current analysis. As, in the case of the real-world scenarios, the data collected from sensors is highly vulnerable to noise and various other errors. So, there is a need for data pre-processing [19] to make it appropriate for the task of analysis. In the current work, we make use of the following data pre-processing steps to improve the generalized performance of the regression models:

- Data segmentation: The energy demand dataset provided by NEM is not appropriate for our current research analysis. So, data segmentation is carried out to generate weekday-wise segmented data.
- Data Transformation: This data pre-processing step includes various techniques [19,30] such as data normalization or standardization, smoothing and data integration.

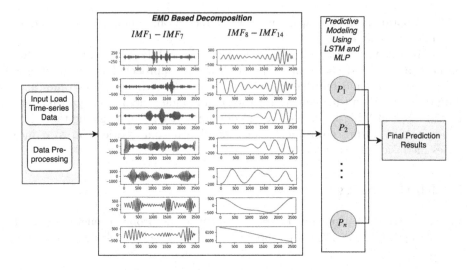

Fig. 1. Architecture of the proposed load forecasting approach

3.3 Load Characterization

Load Characterization aims to generate an in-depth analysis of the historical energy demand patterns. Depending on the current research objectives, it can be performed at different levels of granularity [7] such as periodical analysis, seasonal analysis, yearly analysis and week-day analysis. As in the present research work, our aim is to analyse the impact of timestamp segmentation on the overall model performance. Hence, day-wise trend characterization is performed to improve the performance of the regression models i.e. the overall energy consumption dataset is divided into several subsets namely l_{mon}, l_{tue}, l_{wed}, l_{thr}, l_{fri}, l_{sat} and l_{sun}, where, l_{mon} denotes the historical energy demand dataset for the Mondays in the years 2018, l_{tue} denotes the historical energy demand dataset for the Tuesdays in the years 2018 and so on.

3.4 Decomposition Based Learning

The next step after performing weekday-wise data decomposition is to implement decomposition based learning for improved prediction accuracy. In the current work, we implement Empirical Mode decomposition (EMD) [36] algorithm to decompose non-stationary weekday-wise load time series into various sub-signals or Intrinsic Mode Functions (IMFs). It is very useful data de-noising techniques that works well for non-stationary time series. The step by step working of the EMD algorithm is given as follows:

1. For an input load time-series $x(t)$, calculate mean of the upper and the lower envelope (obtained from the interpolation of local maxima and minima of input signal $x(t)$) and denote it as *mean*.

2. Calculate the first IMF component as $h(t) = x(t)\text{-}mean$.
3. Subtract h(t) from the original signal x(t): $res = x(t) - h(t)$
4. iterate over the steps 2 and 3, until all IMFs are obtained (residual becomes a monotonic function).

The final results of the EMD algorithm are given by [36]:

$$x(t) = \sum_{i=1}^{m} h_i(t) + res \qquad (1)$$

The decomposition steps listed above are repeated for energy load time series of each day of a week (l_{mon}, l_{tue}, l_{wed}, l_{thr}, l_{fri}, l_{sat} and l_{sun}). After successful execution of EMD based decomposition on input load time-series, the next step is to build prediction models to approximate future energy demand on the basis of available historical dependencies. Initially, the transformation steps listed in the Algorithm 1 are applied to include available historical demand observations for predicting future energy demand. Subsequently, the prediction models are trained to delineate the hidden characteristics of the extracted energy load patterns.

Algorithm 1. *Data Transformation* (Input Load Time Series Data)

1: **for each** Input load time series signal **do**
2:     Extract IMFs using EMD algorithm (steps listed in section 3.4)
3:         **for each** IMF of the form $< a_1, a_2, a_3, \ldots, a_n >$, where a_i denotes value at a timestamp i **do**
4:             Substitute each a_i with a vector $< a_{i-95}, a_{i-94}, \ldots, a_{i-1}, a_i >$
5:         **end for**
6: **end for**

The recent studies in the field of energy demand forecasting have implemented deep learning techniques such as LSTM [18], DBN [18], CNN [18] to model each of the extracted sub-signals or modes. However, the extracted IMFs exhibit properties that might vary highly from each other, for example, from the extracted IMF-components shown in Fig. 1, it can be clearly seen that variations in some of the initial components are relatively very higher than the other components. So, the choice of an appropriate prediction model for extracted IMFs on the basis of their properties would intuitively contribute to the improved system performance i.e. the IMFs with high Hurst and non-linear characteristics require more sophisticated models as compared to the other IMFs with small Hurst and stable characteristics. Furthermore, the decomposition process also reduces the degree of intra-correlation of the IMFs, which contributes to the reduced model complexity. Hence, in the present work, we use these data characteristics for improved prediction accuracy and reduced system complexity.

Among the various deep learning based demand prediction models, Long-Short Term Memory Network (LSTM) [7] have been found to be very promising

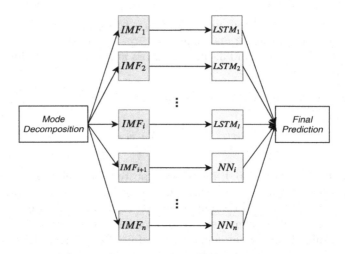

Fig. 2. Core structure of the proposed framework

at capturing trends of high frequency, complex and non-linear demand patterns whereas the conventional neural network models are good for less complex, more stable and seasonal data sequences. Therefore, these models have been chosen in the current work to characterize and predict the extracted IMFs components (based on their characteristics such as Hurst component, non-linearity etc.). The core structure of the proposed hybrid prediction approach is demonstrated in Fig. 2.

In addition to selecting appropriate prediction models, there are various hyper-parameters related to the prediction models that might affect the overall model accuracy. These hyper-parameters are determined by executing iterative runs of training, testing and validation phase to provide an unbiased evaluation of the model fit. The important parameters names and values range used in the current work are: number of input neurons (n_i), number of output neurons (n_o), number of hidden layers LSTM $(n_{h(lstm)} = 2-6)$, $window\_size = 96$, $batch\_size$, number of hidden layers NN $(n_{h(MLP)} = 1-3)$, optimization $=$ "$adam$", loss function $=$ "MSE", number of epochs $= 50 - 300$, regularization parameter (to avoid model overfit) and learning rate parameter (η). Furthermore, the following performance measures are used to evaluate the proposed prediction model.

– *Root Mean Squared Error* [19]: It is given as

$$RMSE = \sqrt{\frac{1}{n}\sum_{i=1}^{n}(P_i - A_i)^2} \tag{2}$$

where n denotes the number of demand observations and P_i, A_i represent the actual and predicted values respectively.
– *Mean Absolute Percentage Error* [19]: It represents the amount by which predicted values differ/deviate from the real time demand observations.

$$MAPE = \frac{1}{n}\sum_{i=1}^{n} |\frac{P_i - A_i}{A_i}|$$ (3)

For the purpose of model building, the entire dataset is divided into three parts: train data (70%), validation data (10%) and test data (20%). After proper validation of model hyper-parameters on train and validation parts, the model performance is evaluated on the test part.

Table 1. Prediction results of proposed approach versus other existing approaches

Day	$Model_1$ [6]		$Model_2$ [40]		$Model_3$ (Proposed)	
	RMSE	MAPE (%)	RMSE	MAPE(%)	RMSE	MAPE(%)
Monday (l_{mon})	126.31	1.99	87.83	1.38	80.34	**1.24**
Tuesday (l_{tue})	182.14	2.85	123.26	1.94	121.06	**1.90**
Wednesday (l_{wed})	145.56	2.29	152.63	2.4	134.69	**2.1**
Thursday (l_{thr})	159.12	2.49	145.09	2.27	138.83	**2.17**
Friday (l_{fri})	169.01	2.67	91.86	1.45	79.51	**1.26**
Saturday (l_{sat})	162.94	2.72	79.14	1.32	77.71	**1.28**
Sunday (l_{sun})	149.47	2.52	89.58	1.51	86.90	**1.46**

4 Results and Discussion

In the recent past, two different decomposition based hybrid strategies were introduced for modelling energy demand at state/household levels. The comparative prediction results of these approaches are evident that the hybrid approaches perform better than traditional data-driven approaches. So, in order to evaluate the performance of the proposed approach, we compare the prediction results of the proposed approach with these two different state-of-the-art demand modelling strategies [6,28,40] in terms of several evaluation measures. The details of existing decomposition based strategies are as follows:

- $Model_1$: a) *Generate IMFs*: Implement EMD for Data Decomposition.
  b) Train Separate LSTM models for each extracted IMFs.
  c) Aggregate and return final prediction results.
  d) Evaluate Prediction model.
- $Model_2$: a) *Generate IMFs*: Implement EMD for Data Decomposition.
  b) Calculate *average_IMF* and subtract it from the original load time series (name it as l_{new}).
  c) Train LSTM model for generated load time series (l_{new}) and return final prediction results.
  d) Evaluate Prediction model.

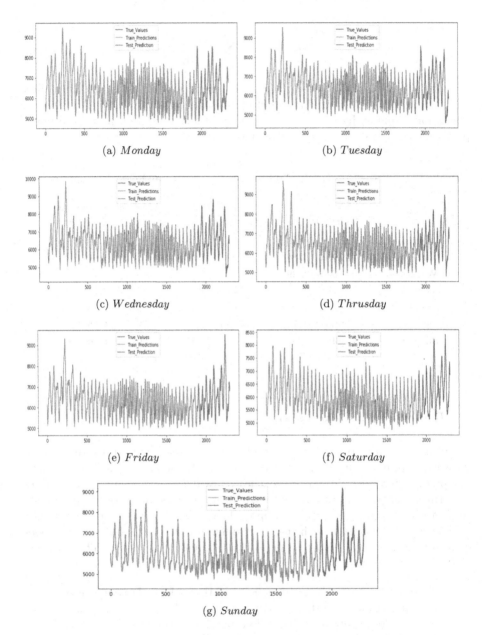

(a) *Monday*   (b) *Tuesday*

(c) *Wednesday*   (d) *Thrusday*

(e) *Friday*   (f) *Saturday*

(g) *Sunday*

Fig. 3. Energy load demand prediction results of the Proposed Approach

- *Model₃* (Proposed Approach): Implements combination of *LSTM* and *MLP* (as depicted in Fig. 2) for improved accuracy and reduced complexity (as explained in Sect. 3.4).

These prediction models utilizes the concept of historical lag values to estimate future energy demand and the corresponding prediction results are shown in Table 1. From the comparison of prediction results listed in Table 1, it is apparent that the proposed approach outperforms other state-of-the-art demand modelling strategies in terms of various evaluation measures described in Sect. 3.4. Furthermore, Fig. 3 provides a visual representation of the prediction results of the proposed approach where blue, orange and green lines represent real-time observations, train prediction and test prediction values respectively. The x-axis represents the number of samples and y-axis denotes the corresponding demand values. From the prediction results demonstrated in Fig. 3, it can be stated that the proposed framework is capable of handling fluctuations and non-linearity of the energy load time series. The working environment of the proposed approach is as follows:

– Software Configuration: Operating System-Ubuntu 14.04, Python, Tensorflow back end.
– Hardware Configuration: 64 GB RAM, Xeon Processor with 48 cores, 2 TB Hard Disk.

5   Conclusion

An efficient load forecasting is paramount for making future decision strategies, stable and reliable operation of power grids and minimizing energy wastage. In this context, the current work has proposed a hybrid data decomposition based learning approach for electricity demand forecasting at the state level. This approach captures the day-wise cyclic patterns of the energy demand by implementing data segregation in conjunction with mode decomposition algorithm. Furthermore, the mode components intrinsic features have been used for selecting the target prediction models. In order to evaluate the performance of the proposed model, experiments are conducted on the timestamp electricity demand dataset of the state Queensland, Australia and the prediction results are evaluated using the two different performance measures i.e. root mean squared error and mean absolute percentage error. Two recent demand prediction models have been compared to signify the effectiveness of the proposed approach. From the comparative experimental results, the following inferences are drawn:

– The data decomposition based learning in conjunction with prediction models provides support for improved accuracy.
– The proposed approach shows better performance in handling compound relationship across time intervals.
– The selection of appropriate prediction models on the basis of component intrinsic features contributes to the improved system accuracy and reduced model complexity.
– The proposed model outperforms other two state-of-the-art hybrid demand prediction model by providing 1.63% average prediction error.

References

1. Australian energy market operator. https://www.aemo.com.au/Electricity/National-Electricity-Market-NEM/Data/. Accessed 30 Feb 2019
2. Adom, P.K., Bekoe, W.: Conditional dynamic forecast of electrical energy consumption requirements in Ghana by 2020: a comparison of ARDL and PAM. Energy **44**(1), 367–380 (2012)
3. Bakhat, M., Rosselló, J.: Estimation of tourism-induced electricity consumption: the case study of Balearics Islands, Spain. Energy Econ. **33**(3), 437–444 (2011)
4. Baliyan, A., Gaurav, K., Mishra, S.K.: A review of short term load forecasting using artificial neural network models. Procedia Comput. Sci. **48**, 121–125 (2015)
5. Barbulescu, C., Kilyeni, S., Deacu, A., Turi, G.M., Moga, M.: Artificial neural network based monthly load curves forecasting. In: 2016 IEEE 11th International Symposium on Applied Computational Intelligence and Informatics (SACI), pp. 237–242. IEEE (2016)
6. Bedi, J., Toshniwal, D.: Empirical mode decomposition based deep learning for electricity demand forecasting. IEEE Access **6**, 49144–49156 (2018)
7. Bedi, J., Toshniwal, D.: Deep learning framework to forecast electricity demand. Appl. Energy **238**, 1312–1326 (2019)
8. Bhanot, S., Jalandhar, P., Mehta, S.: Long term load forecasting using k-mean clustering and ANN approach (2018)
9. Bilgili, M., Sahin, B., Yasar, A., Simsek, E.: Electric energy demands of turkey in residential and industrial sectors. Renew. Sustain. Energy Rev. **16**(1), 404–414 (2012)
10. Cadenas, E., Rivera, W.: Wind speed forecasting in the south coast of Oaxaca, Mexico. Renewable Energy **32**(12), 2116–2128 (2007)
11. Chakravorty, J., Shah, S., Nagraja, H.: ANN and ANFIS for short term load forecasting. Eng. Technol. Appl. Sci. Res. **8**(2), 2818–2820 (2018)
12. Chandramowli, S., Lahr, M.L.: Forecasting new jersey's electricity demand using auto-regressive models. Available at SSRN 2258552 (2012)
13. Chen, K., Chen, K., Wang, Q., He, Z., Hu, J., He, J.: Short-term load forecasting with deep residual networks. IEEE Trans. Smart Grid **10**(4), 3943–3952 (2018)
14. Dudek, G.: Multilayer perceptron for GEFCom2014 probabilistic electricity price forecasting. Int. J. Forecast. **32**(3), 1057–1060 (2016)
15. Ekonomou, L.: Greek long-term energy consumption prediction using artificial neural networks. Energy **35**(2), 512–517 (2010)
16. Ghiassi, M., Nangoy, S.: A dynamic artificial neural network model for forecasting nonlinear processes. Comput. Ind. Eng. **57**(1), 287–297 (2009)
17. González, V., Contreras, J., Bunn, D.W.: Forecasting power prices using a hybrid fundamental-econometric model. IEEE Trans. Power Syst. **27**(1), 363–372 (2011)
18. Goodfellow, I., Bengio, Y., Courville, A.: Deep Learning. MIT Press, Cambridge (2016)
19. Han, J., Pei, J., Kamber, M.: Data Mining: Concepts and Techniques. Elsevier, Amsterdam (2011)
20. He, F., Zhou, J., Feng, Z.K., Liu, G., Yang, Y.: A hybrid short-term load forecasting model based on variational mode decomposition and long short-term memory networks considering relevant factors with Bayesian optimization algorithm. Appl. Energy **237**, 103–116 (2019)

21. Jeong, K., Koo, C., Hong, T.: An estimation model for determining the annual energy cost budget in educational facilities using SARIMA (seasonal autoregressive integrated moving average) and ANN (artificial neural network). Energy **71**, 71–79 (2014)
22. Ju, F.Y., Hong, W.C.: Application of seasonal SVR with chaotic gravitational search algorithm in electricity forecasting. Appl. Math. Model. **37**(23), 9643–9651 (2013)
23. Kim, J., Moon, J., Hwang, E., Kang, P.: Recurrent inception convolution neural network for multi short-term load forecasting. Energy Build. **194**, 328–341 (2019)
24. Li, B., Zhang, J., He, Y., Wang, Y.: Short-term load-forecasting method based on wavelet decomposition with second-order gray neural network model combined with ADF test. IEEE Access **5**, 16324–16331 (2017)
25. Meng, M., Niu, D.: Annual electricity consumption analysis and forecasting of china based on few observations methods. Energy Convers. Manag. **52**(2), 953–957 (2011)
26. Miranda, M.S., Dunn, R.W.: One-hour-ahead wind speed prediction using a Bayesian methodology. In: 2006 IEEE Power Engineering Society General Meeting, pp. 6-pp. IEEE (2006)
27. Mohan, N., Soman, K., Kumar, S.S.: A data-driven strategy for short-term electric load forecasting using dynamic mode decomposition model. Appl. Energy **232**, 229–244 (2018)
28. Premanode, B., Vonprasert, J., Toumazou, C.: Prediction of exchange rates using averaging intrinsic mode function and multiclass support vector regression. Artif. Intell. Res. **2**(2), 47 (2013)
29. Song, K.B., Baek, Y.S., Hong, D.H., Jang, G.: Short-term load forecasting for the holidays using fuzzy linear regression method. IEEE Trans. Power Syst. **20**(1), 96–101 (2005)
30. Tan, P.N.: Introduction to Data Mining. Pearson Education India (2018)
31. Tsekouras, G., Dialynas, E., Hatziargyriou, N., Kavatza, S.: A non-linear multi-variable regression model for midterm energy forecasting of power systems. Electr. Power Syst. Res. **77**(12), 1560–1568 (2007)
32. Tso, G.K., Yau, K.K.: Predicting electricity energy consumption: a comparison of regression analysis, decision tree and neural networks. Energy **32**(9), 1761–1768 (2007)
33. Wang, Y., Chen, Q., Sun, M., Kang, C., Xia, Q.: An ensemble forecasting method for the aggregated load with subprofiles. IEEE Trans. Smart Grid **9**(4), 3906–3908 (2018)
34. Wang, Y., Gan, D., Sun, M., Zhang, N., Lu, Z., Kang, C.: Probabilistic individual load forecasting using pinball loss guided LSTM. Appl. Energy **235**, 10–20 (2019)
35. Wang, Y., Wu, C.: Forecasting energy market volatility using GARCH models: can multivariate models beat univariate models? Energy Econ. **34**(6), 2167–2181 (2012)
36. Wu, Z., Huang, N.E.: Ensemble empirical mode decomposition: a noise-assisted data analysis method. Adv. Adapt. Data Anal. **1**(01), 1–41 (2009)
37. Wu, Z., Zhao, X., Ma, Y., Zhao, X.: A hybrid model based on modified multi-objective cuckoo search algorithm for short-term load forecasting. Appl. Energy **237**, 896–909 (2019)
38. Xia, C., Zhang, M., Cao, J.: A hybrid application of soft computing methods with wavelet SVM and neural network to electric power load forecasting. J. Electr. Syst. Inf. Technol. **5**(3), 681–696 (2018)

39. Xu, G., Wang, W.: Forecasting China's natural gas consumption based on a combination model. J. Nat. Gas Chem. **19**(5), 493–496 (2010)
40. Yaslan, Y., Bican, B.: Empirical mode decomposition based denoising method with support vector regression for time series prediction: a case study for electricity load forecasting. Measurement **103**, 52–61 (2017)
41. Yuan, X., Chen, C., Yuan, Y., Huang, Y., Tan, Q.: Short-term wind power prediction based on LSSVM-GSA model. Energy Convers. Manag. **101**, 393–401 (2015)
42. Zhang, M., Mu, H., Li, G., Ning, Y.: Forecasting the transport energy demand based on PLSR method in china. Energy **34**(9), 1396–1400 (2009)
43. Zhu, S., Wang, J., Zhao, W., Wang, J.: A seasonal hybrid procedure for electricity demand forecasting in China. Appl. Energy **88**(11), 3807–3815 (2011)

Mitigating Bias in Online Microfinance Platforms: A Case Study on Kiva.org

Soumajyoti Sarkar[(✉)] and Hamidreza Alvari

Arizona State University, Tempe, USA
{ssarka18,halvari}@asu.edu

Abstract. Over the last couple of decades in the lending industry, financial disintermediation has occurred on a global scale. Traditionally, even for small supply of funds, banks would act as the conduit between the funds and the borrowers. It has now been possible to overcome some of the obstacles associated with such supply of funds with the advent of online platforms like Kiva, Prosper, LendingClub. Kiva, in particular, allows lenders to fund projects in different sectors through group or individual funding. Traditional research studies have investigated various factors behind lender preferences purely from the perspective of loan attributes and only until recently have some cross-country cultural preferences been investigated. In this paper, we investigate lender perceptions of economic factors of the borrower countries in relation to their preferences towards loans associated with different sectors. We find that the influence from economic factors and loan attributes can have substantially different roles to play for different sectors in achieving faster funding. We formally investigate and quantify the hidden biases prevalent in different loan sectors using recent tools from causal inference and regression models that rely on Bayesian variable selection methods. We then extend these models to incorporate fairness constraints based on our empirical analysis.

Keywords: Linear regression · Causal inference · Machine learning · Online lending

1 Introduction

Online lending in recent years has been considered to be an important contributor to financial restructuring in developing and underdeveloped nations by way of opening access to alternate sources of funding for them [4]. Online platforms that enable such peer-to-peer transactions whereby certain groups of people invest in projects from poor entrepreneurs, have become very popular. There exist different types of microlending services including for-profit lending services like LendingClub, Prosper and the pro-social platforms like Kiva[1] where the lenders offer interest-free money to the borrowers. Platforms like Kiva are beneficial to

---

[1] http://www.kiva.org.

© Springer Nature Switzerland AG 2020
I. Koprinska et al. (Eds.): ECML PKDD 2020 Workshops, CCIS 1323, pp. 75–91, 2020.
https://doi.org/10.1007/978-3-030-65965-3_6

borrowers, since lenders typically are risk-free indicating they do not expect any interest returns for the loan and hence can select their portfolio being less biased. Additionally, such pro-social platforms overcome the biases in loan disbursement through auctions in online platforms which is unfavorably inclined towards the credit-trustworthy users and undermines new users.

Broadly, there have been a few groups of research studies conducted on understanding and promoting microfinance lending on such platforms. (1) Investigating biases: previous studies have focused on understanding and predicting bilateral trade transactions based on migration and GDP differences between country pairs [23]. (2) Borrower and lender features: past studies include understanding various platform-external lender and borrower personal and regional characteristics that facilitate the transactions between countries [8] and the role of matching characteristics. However, the loan attribute concerning the loan sector is often overlooked especially to its connections to philanthropic and pro-social motivations of investors [16], (3) Fairness aware lending: recent studies have acknowledged the existence of bias in lending models and the need to diversify the distribution of donations to reduce the inequality of loans [12], and (4) Social networks: the role of networks have been studied from the perspective of facilitating bidding behavior in platforms [14].

What is often overlooked is the impact of external factors pertaining to the borrower countries that influence lender preferences and which cannot be directly observed from the platform data. Furthermore, there has been substantial evidence in the recent past that supports Lucas paradox, which indicates that, counter-intuitively the liberalization of international capital regimes using the internet platforms has not produced an open club, rather a rich club, a group of countries that exhibit the country-pair bias [1]. Since recommendation models typically do not consider such external data while building their models [21], such latent biases arising from external factors including lender perceptions of countries[2] can be quite detrimental for certain projects especially ones from specific countries.

To this end, we investigate the factors behind the funding speed of loans using the dataset available from Kiva. The goal is to see whether the lenders fall for region specific economic factors that they expect would help them avoid loan defaults from borrowers and whether that affects funding projects in certain sectors. We compare the effect of different sectors on project funding times when the economic external factors form part of the models in consideration. Using data from 143,856 loans over a period of 4 years and economic indicators from World Bank Data, we make the following contributions:

- We gather data from Kiva loans and heterogeneous data sources and build regression models to estimate the impact of such factors on the funding speed. We observe the role of the project or loan sector as a sensitive attribute in the models especially when its correlation with the funding speed differs for different sectors.

---

[2] https://bit.ly/2LF9Mpp.

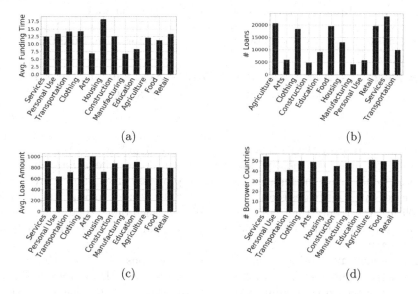

Fig. 1. Distribution of (a) average funding times, (b) number of loans, (c) average loan amount by loan sectors and (d) number of borrower countries by each sector.

- We use recent causal inference and machine learning tools to estimate the effects the sector attribute on funding times. We specifically find that loans catering to Retail are funded 4 days slower relative to the other sectors on aggregate and loans for Arts are funded 6 days faster - all these when considering the economic factors of the location of the borrowers and the loan attributes. This is in contrast to observations from data that do not reveal such hidden discrepancies when excluding external factors.
- Following this, we incorporate fairness driven constraints to mitigate some of the biases arising from these loan specific attributes for particular sectors of loans. Our results suggest that even with such fairness constraints, the model performances are not too far-off from baselines, thus giving hope for future systems that take into account such constraints.

We note that this is the first work in attempting to understand the existing biases from loan attributes when external factors are also considered to be the contributors to such decisive disparities. Throughout our work, we mainly focus on linear regression models, however we adopt the models to use Bayesian variable selection techniques.

2   Data and Modeling Issues

Kiva is a non-profit micro-financial organization and its lending model is based on crowdfunding in which any individual can fund a particular loan by contributing to a loan individually or as a part of a lender team. The choice behind this

Table 1. Basic statistics for loans used in our study

# Loans	# Lender Countries	# Borrower Countries
143856	216	57
# Languages	Avg. Loan Amount (USD)	Avg. Funding Time (std)
7	836.18	12.58 (14.6)

platform is driven by the motivation to test a few hypotheses in this research - we want to be able to understand the presence or absence of behavioral and social bias that could create preferences for certain projects. Since public perceptions of societies can elicit biases towards countries with specific geographical, cultural or political fabric and that can affect funding in such online platforms, we set out to test the interplay of economic externalities and the loan specific attributes in such settings.

The publicly available Kiva dataset[3] contains various entities: (1) the data for the loans that contains various attributes associated with the borrowers, (2) the lenders' information containing various attributes regarding a lender's history of funding projects (3) the borrowers' information containing various attributes regarding a borrower's project and repayment history, (4) field partner which acts as the mediator and allocates loans from the lenders to the borrowers. Since our objective in this study is to understand the role of developmental factors when paired with the sector that receives the most funding, we use the following attributes that are associated with a loan in Kiva's platform from January 2010 to December 2014: (1) sector: categorical attribute denoting the sector of loan activity. The sectors considered in our study after removing sparse data is shown in Fig. 1. Note that the set of sector tags are fixed for all loans and are not randomly generated. (2) currency policy - binary attribute to reduce risk of currency fluctuation[4], (3) language - the language of the loan description - since 70% of the loans we considered were in English, we converted this to a binary attribute by considering all non-English languages as one category, (4) loan amount - numerical attribute denoting the amount of loan requested for the project, (5) borrower gender - binary attribute denoting the gender of the borrower, and (6) funding time - this is a derived numerical attribute calculated as the difference between the time of the loan request and the time when it was fully funded. We use this attribute for measuring the preference of the investors towards particular projects and our models are based on understanding what attributes account for lesser funding times. We plot the distribution of the funding times and the number of loans by sectors in our dataset in Fig. 1. However, unlike similar analyses, we do not found any substantial difference in the average loan amounts by sectors that get funded. Apart from entertainment, most of the sectors have similar funding requests that ultimately get funded.

---

[3] https://www.kiva.org/build/data-snapshots.

[4] https://pages.kiva.org/blog/new-kiva-feature-currency-risk-protection.

As a first task, we try to investigate the causal effects of borrower-lender differences arising from lender perceptions of the borrower countries as well as implicit economic and cultural variations. We try to measure the extent of impact it has on the funding times when considered alongside the sector of the loans. To this end, for each loan, we gather the following data from the world bank metrics dating back to 2010 [5]. We gather the following attributes: (1) ease of business: an ordinal attribute denoting the rank of the borrower country for ease of business, (2) loan access - numerical attribute denoting the ease of access to loan in the borrower country through formal financial institutions, (3) women ratio - numerical attribute measuring the ratio of women in labor force compared to men, (4) affordability - numerical attribute pertaining to the costs associated with using services, including both interest rates and fees, (5) VC financing - ordinal attribute that indicates how easy it is for the borrower to seek capital locally or otherwise in their country, (6) capacity innovation - ordinal attribute denoting the capacity of people in the borrower country to innovate and (7) internet penetration - numerical attribute denoting the percentage of people in the borrower country using the internet. To measure the cross-cultural similarities, we proceed as done in [23] to use the following features: (8) colonization - binary attribute denoting whether the borrower country was colonized by lender country, (9) distance - geographical distance between borrower and lender countries obtained from [17], (10) migrants - numerical attribute that measures the number of people or borrower country origin living in the lender country obtained from world bank data and (11) GDP difference - numerical attribute denoting the GDP Difference between borrower and lender countries obtained from world bank data. For the derived attributes which were calculated based on borrower and lender countries, we used the following method: for numerical attributes, for a specific loan we took the average of all the borrower-lender pairs for that loan. For categorical or binary attributes like colonization, we randomly picked one of the borrower-lender pairs for that loan and used that for the loan feature. This however introduces some approximation into the feature measurements. For all numerical attributes, we performed standardization for the regression models which would be described henceforth.

The dataset is publicly available for download[5]. After merging the data from these heterogeneous sources, we list the basic statistics of the loans used in this study (see Table 1). We find that while the average funding time is 12.5 days, the standard deviation is 14.6 days, which demands further investigation behind the variations.

3 Preliminary Analysis of Potential Disparities

We begin with a simple linear regression model to investigate the importance that these economic indicators capturing the borrower's nations, have on the funding time and how they play a role compared to the loan sector. When we regress the variables of the economic factors and the loan attributes barring the

---

[5] https://bit.ly/2TnqhL7.

Table 2. Table: OLS Regression estimates on funding time for a project loan. For model **M1**, we do not include the Sector attribute and for model **M2**, the attribute Sector (categorical) is used as the dummy variable.

OLS estimates	M1	M2 (Sector)	M3 (Services)	M4 (Agri.)	M5 (Retail)
Intercept	21.0346	20.2312	22.3927	20.4209	19.9626
Sector			−1.5268	−0.5921	2.3072
Currency policy [T.shared]	−1.0349	−1.1697	−3.2858	−0.894	−0.2923
Language	−2.5225	−2.0611	−1.3739	−2.1189	−2.3513
Ease of business	−0.0313	−0.027	−0.0309	−0.0282	−0.0281
Colonization	−1.6048	−2.0484	1.5085	−3.7422	−0.8401
Borrower gender [T.female]	−4.2708	−4.609	−4.4875	−4.1959	−4.7179
Loan amount	3.8751	4.1365	3.6231	5.1564	3.6773
Distance	−0.7032	−0.6359	−0.6739	−0.8225	−0.3331
Migrants	−2.1397	−2.4934	−1.9945	−2.3797	−2.4833
GDP difference	−0.3162	−0.2086	−0.0415	−0.2439	0.0622
Loan access	−1.2037	−0.526	1.619	−1.582	0.2476
Women ratio	−2.9224	−3.2598	−2.1065	−2.0469	−3.3524
Affordability	−2.2799	−2.2284	2.4288	−2.2366	−2.7703
VC finance	2.2952	2.0675	0.4367	2.3493	1.042
Capacity innov.	−0.0378	−0.0177	0.5504	0.5695	−0.0052
Internet pen.	−0.2639	0.4767	0.7634	−1.3048	0.9828

loan sector, on the funding time denoted by model **M1**, we find from Table 2 instantly that there are some borrower-lender attributes that have a larger role to play - the distance, and GDP difference have a negligible impact on the funding time whereas the feature measuring the migrants of borrower country in lender country has a negative correlation with funding times - it suggests that the cultural similarities arising from cross-border migration results towards faster funding for borrowers with such cultural advantages. Similarly, the women ratio factor has a significant negative correlation on the funding time along with the borrower gender in line with previous research [1]. This indicates that the perception about the role of women in such economies is a significant driver towards deciding whether the project would receive faster funding.

Next, we include the project sector attribute in the regression model as a dummy variable with the corresponding one-hot encodings denoted by model **M2**. We observe that while there are minor changes in the magnitude of the coefficients, the correlations of these variables do not change in the presence of the sector variable. This tempts us to conclude that when recommendation systems rely on these attributes to predict the best projects in terms of having better chances of funding, they can make a pretty fair classification for all projects based on these attributes. However, upon closer analyses, we look into the effect that these attributes have when considering each sector at a time. Taking each loan sector category s as the main category in contention, we build sector specific models. For a model on sector s, we consider all loans belonging to s as one category and all other categories as a unified dummy sector category separate from the sector s. We build regression models for all 12 sectors in a similar fashion. We show four of the models corresponding to four different sectors in Table 2 - in model **M3** we convert the multi-category sector attribute into a binary category by considering the services sector and loans belonging to that category as one cluster and all the other loans belonging to other sectors as the other cluster. When we compare M3 with model **M4** catering to the agriculture sector, we can observe that not only do some of the attributes differ in the magnitude significantly, but the influence from the attributes also reverses in some cases. Particularly, we find that the influence from the attribute colonization has opposite effects for the two sectors and similarly for attributes like affordability and loan access.

When comparing the role of sectors, we observe that the coefficient magnitude demonstrates that the relative number of days by which each sector gets funded faster or slower relative to the other sectors. However, the fact that these results are also heavily affected by the varying sparsity of the data. This leads us to turn our attention to recent literature on more robust causal reasoning tools that allow for explaining the effect of sectors on funding speed in the presence of such externalities [2, 20].

4   Causal Inference

Note that the treatment of interest here is the loan sector assignment for the loan requested and we are interested in estimating the effects of loan sector relative to the economic, cultural and other loan characteristics, on the funding time. Following the work done in [20], we would use the Robin Causal Model (RCM) or the Potential Outcome Framework to estimate the treatment effects. We use the RCM model in this study due to the principled framework on which it applies - the treatment of unit i (loan in our case) only affects i and that the treatment is homogeneous across the units.

4.1   Treatment Effects Indicators

We describe in this section how we measure the causal impact metrics for each sector s. We estimate the treatment effects of sector on loan funding time considering separate models for each sector and treating the whole batch of data separately for each sector. Let the features be denoted by X, which in our case are all the attributes except the project sector s. Let Y be the outcome of interest, in our case the funding time of the loans. For each sector s, we consider W to be the binary treatment variable (whether a loan belongs to s or not). Following this, for each sector s, we represent the dataset in the form $(Y_i, X_i, W_i)_{i=1}^n$, where W_i denotes whether the sector for loan i is s or not ($W_1 = 1$ when loan belongs to s), n denoting the number of loans in the data. Note that W_i would be different for loan i when considering different sectors since the observational data gives us the actual loan sector. We will drop the subscripts from W when generalizing the inference settings for all loans. We will also refrain from attaching s as sub/super-scripts to notations since we perform all the following steps and estimate models in the same was irrespective of the sectors. We are interested in estimating the average treatment effects (ATE) of W on Y for each sector s and this is given by:

$$\tau = \mathbb{E}[Y(1) - Y(0)] \tag{1}$$

where $Y(1)$ is the potential outcome of a loan that belongs to s while $Y(0)$ is the one that does not belong to s. However, in the data, only one of them is observed for each loan when considering models for a specific sector. The three assumptions that are made during this estimation procedure are: (1) $(SUTVA)$ - The apriori assumption that the value of Y_i when instance i is exposed to treatment W_i will be the same, no matter what mechanism is used to assign the treatment to i and no matter what treatments others receive, (2) the probability of outcome Y_i is independent of the features X_i given W_i - it means that the features X_i do not simultaneously affect W_i and Y_i. In our case this is more intuitive since firstly the external economic factors in itself have no bearing on the choice of the loan sectors and secondly, the loan sector also has little in relation to other loan features like gender, loan amount, and (3) both treatment and control groups have has at least one instance assigned to them (see [20] for more details on these assumptions).

4.2   Estimating Treatment Effects

With recent advances in machine learning to create estimators for ATE [3,9], we use the Doubly Robust Estimator (DRE) [11,22] to measure τ. We briefly lay out the steps for estimating τ using DRE for our data - note we follow these steps for all sectors individually:

1. **Outcome Model** - For loan sector s, we consider the loans i belonging to s as having $W_i = 1$ and all other loans as $W_i = 0$. Then we use the treated data $\{i : W_i = 1\}$ to estimate $\mu(1, x) = \mathbb{E}[Y(1)|X = x]$ with estimator $\hat{\mu}(1, x)$ and use control data $\{i : W_i = 0\}$ to estimate $\mu(0, x) = \mathbb{E}[Y(0)|X = x]$ with estimator $\hat{\mu}(0, x)$.
2. **Propensity Score Model**: We then estimate the propensity score model - use all loans data to estimate $e(x) = \mathbb{P}(W = 1|X = x)$ with estimator $\hat{e}(x)$.
3. The DRE $\hat{\tau}_{DRE}$ is given by $\hat{\tau}_{DRE} = \frac{1}{n} \sum_{i=1}^{n} \left[W_i \times \frac{Y_i - \hat{\mu}(1,X_i)}{\hat{e}(X_i)} - (1 - W_i) \times \frac{Y_i - \hat{\mu}(0,X_i)}{1 - \hat{e}(X_i)} - \hat{\mu}(1, X_i) - \hat{\mu}(0, X_i) \right]$.
4. The standard error is then estimated following [15] by using an empirical sandwich estimator. For each instance/loan i, we have $IC_i = W_i \times \frac{Y_i - \hat{\mu}(1,X_i)}{\hat{e}(X_i)} - (1 - W_i) \times \frac{Y_i - \hat{\mu}(0,X_i)}{1 - \hat{e}(X_i)} + \hat{\mu}(1, X_i) - \hat{\mu}(0, X_i) - \hat{\tau}_{DRE}$ and $\sigma^2 = \frac{1}{n} \sum_{i=1}^{n} IC_i^2$. The standard error is estimated as $\frac{\sigma}{\sqrt{n}}$.

The DRE has the double robustness property: given that either the outcome model or the propensity score model or both are correctly specified, the estimator is consistent.

4.3   Learning Outcome Models

In order to estimate $\hat{\mu}(1, x)$ and $\hat{\mu}(0, x)$ for each sector s, we use regression models, however we observe from Table 2 that not all variables are equally important when measuring their outcome on funding times and these differ substantially among the sectors. To this end, we adopt some variable selection techniques while building separate regression models for $\hat{\mu}(1, x)$ and $\hat{\mu}(0, x)$ for a sector s. We specifically adopt Bayesian methods where sparsity can be favored by assuming sparsity-enforcing priors on the model coefficients. These types of priors are characterized by density functions that are peaked at zero and also have a large probability mass in a wide range of non-zero values. Ideally, the posterior mean of truly zero coefficients should be shrunk towards zero and the posterior mean of non-zero coefficients should remain unaffected by the assumed prior. We use spike-and-slab priors which have some advantages when compared to other sparsity enforcing priors like Laplace and Student's t priors [19]. We briefly review the spike-and-slab model [10] as the regression model in choice and we learn separate models for $\hat{\mu}(1, x)$ and $\hat{\mu}(0, x)$ for a specific sector.

Let $\mathbf{y} \in \mathbb{R}^{n \times 1}$ be an n-dimensional row vector denoting the target variable and $\mathbf{X} \in \mathbb{R}^{n \times p}$ denote the design matrix, p denoting the number of attributes in our model except the sector attribute. Briefly, the spike-and-slab model specifies the prior hierarchy in the following way:

$$y_i \sim N(\beta x_i, \sigma^2)$$
$$\beta_i \sim (1 - \pi_i)\delta_0 + \pi_i N(0, \sigma^2 \tau^2)$$
$$\tau^2 \sim \text{Inverse-Gamma}(\frac{1}{2}, \frac{s^2}{2})$$
$$\pi_i \sim \text{Bern}(\theta)$$
$$\theta \sim \text{Beta}(a, b)$$
$$\sigma^2 \sim \text{Inverse-Gamma}(\alpha_1, \alpha_2)$$

$$(2)$$

where $i \in [1, p]$ indexes the features in the regression model, β denotes the coefficients in the regression model. The first equation defines a regression model where the response y_i follows a normal distribution conditioned on $\mathbf{x}_i$ and the parameters β. The second equation models the way in which sparsity is enforced on the model coefficients. The sparsity of β can be favored by assuming a spike-and-slab prior for the components of this vector - the slab $N(0, \sigma^2 \tau^2)$ is a zero mean broad Gaussian whose variance τ^2 is large and the scale σ^2 is multiplied so that the prior scales with outcome. The spike δ_0 is a Dirac Delta function (point probability mass) centered at 0 and this component is responsible for deciding whether the posterior for these coefficients would be zeroed out. $\pi \in [0, 1]$ is a mixture weight between the spike-and-slab components in the prior. The rest of the equations denote the hierarchical structure of the parameters σ^2, τ^2 and π. Note that τ^2 and θ are common to all predictors. We briefly describe how we sample the parameters for Gibbs sampling, with details added to Appendix[6].

---

[6] Appendix to the manuscript can be accessed here.

Sampling θ: The parameter is sampled from the conditional posterior using $\theta|\pi$ $\sim Beta\Big(a + \sum_{i=1}^{p}\pi_i, b + \sum_{i=1}^{n}(1-\pi_i)\Big)$.

Sampling τ^2: The conditional posterior of τ^2 can be derived from the probability $p(\tau^2|\mathbf{y},\beta,\pi,\theta,\sigma^2) = p(\tau^2|\pi,\beta)$. Here since π can assume values 0 or 1 we tackle each case independently and derive the following. We sample from the prior if all π_i's are zero. Let $\pi = \{\pi_1,\ldots,\pi_p\}$ be the vector of mixture weights and let $\mathbf{0}$ be a vector of zeros of length p. Following this, we have

$$p(\tau^2|\pi,\beta) = \frac{1}{Z}p(\beta|\tau^2,\pi)p(\pi)p(\tau^2)$$

$$= \frac{1}{Z}\prod_{i=1}^{p}\pi_i(2\pi\sigma^2\tau^2)^{-\frac{1}{2}}exp\Big(-\frac{1}{2\sigma^2\tau^2}\beta^T\beta\Big)\frac{\Big(\frac{s^2}{2}\Big)^{\frac{1}{2}}}{\Gamma\Big(\frac{1}{2}\Big)}(\tau^2)^{-\frac{1}{2}-1}exp\Big(-\frac{\frac{s^2}{2}}{\tau^2}\Big) \tag{3}$$

which is a Gamma distribution and therefore we sample $\tau^2|\beta,\pi \sim$ Inverse-Gamma$(\frac{1}{2} + \frac{\sum_{i=1}^{p}\pi_i}{2}, \frac{s^2}{2} + \frac{\beta^T\beta}{2\sigma^2})$. On the other hand, when $\pi = 0$, the β_i's are 0 and we simply sample from the prior $\tau^2|\beta,\pi \sim$ Inverse-Gamma$(\frac{1}{2}, \frac{s^2}{2})$.

Sampling σ^2: The conditional posterior of τ^2 can be derived in a similar manner as above from the probability $p(\sigma^2|\mathbf{y},\beta,\pi,\theta,\sigma^2) = p(\sigma^2|\mathbf{y},\beta)$. Proceeding as before, we can derive the sampling as follows: $\sigma^2|\mathbf{y},\beta \sim$ Gamma$\Big(\alpha_1 + \frac{n}{2}, \alpha_2 + \frac{(\mathbf{y}-\mathbf{X}\beta)^T(\mathbf{y}-\mathbf{X}\beta)}{2}\Big)$.

Sampling β: Proceeding as before, when all π_i's are zero, the corresponding β_i's are all sampled from the Dirac Delta function δ_o resulting in all zeros. We can now sample all β_i's as follows

$$\beta_i|\mathbf{y},\pi_i,\sigma^2,\tau^2 \sim \begin{cases} \delta_0, & \pi_i = 0 \\ N\Big(\Big(\mathbf{X}^T\mathbf{X}\frac{1}{\sigma^2}+\mathbf{I}\frac{1}{\sigma^2\tau^2}\Big)^{-1}\mathbf{X}^T\mathbf{y}\frac{1}{\sigma^2}, \\ \Big(\mathbf{X}^T\mathbf{X}\frac{1}{\sigma^2}+\mathbf{I}\frac{1}{\sigma^2\tau^2}\Big)^{-1}\Big), & \pi_i = 1 \end{cases} \tag{4}$$

Sampling π

The individual π_j's are conditionally independent given θ. We compare two cases: one when the jth element of β is zero or π_j is zero and the other when $\pi_j = 1$. We denote by π_{-j} the state of the variables barring j. Let $\pi_j = 1|\mathbf{y},\beta_{-j},\pi_{-j},\sigma^2,\tau^2,\theta \sim$ Bern(ζ_j). Let $a = p(\pi_j = 1|\mathbf{y},\beta_{-j},\pi_{-j},\sigma^2,\tau^2,\theta)$ and $b = \pi_j = 1|\mathbf{y},\beta_{-j},\pi_{-j},\sigma^2,\tau^2,\theta$. Then $\zeta_j = \frac{a}{a+b}$. We then draw π_j from a Bernoulli with a chance parameter ζ_j and we repeat this for all predictors β_j. For the case when $\pi_j = 0$,

$$p(\pi_j = 0|\mathbf{y},\beta_{-j},\pi_{-j},\sigma^2,\tau^2,\theta)$$

$$= \frac{1}{Z}exp\Big(-\frac{1}{2\sigma^2}(\mathbf{y}-\mathbf{X}_{-j}\beta_{-j})^T(\mathbf{y}-\mathbf{X}_{-j}\beta_{-j})\Big)(1-\theta) \tag{5}$$

Table 3. Result comparison on the test set. For p-score estimation, we use F1 score and accuracy (the higher, the better); for outcome estimations, we use RMSE (the lower the better).

Sector name	Treatment (RMSE)		Control (RMSE)		p - score	
	SSR	LR	SSR	LR	F1	Acc. %
Manufacturing	12.34	12.39	5.44	5.38	0.68	64.84
Transportation	12.68	12.83	13.98	14.17	0.69	61.76
Clothing	10.01	10.01	4.89	5.02	0.64	62.52
Personal use	9.84	10	10.71	10.84	0.65	64.32
Housing	12.1	12.23	11.79	11.93	0.68	60
Food	11.42	11.61	10.17	10.36	0.69	66.96
Arts	11.11	11.21	12.03	12.11	0.7	59.69
Retail	11.35	11.69	11.32	11.45	0.74	71.82
Construction	10.15	10.21	10.15	10.21	0.7	69.33
Agriculture	10.66	10.75	11.39	11.55	0.71	62.89
Services	12.72	12.94	12.83	13	0.74	68.35
Education	12.57	12.67	6.18	6.36	0.66	61.05

where we have absorbed all the irrelevant terms into Z, the normalizing constant. The expression for $\pi_j = 1$ can be written similarly except that it would require integration over β_j. Defining $\mathbf{z} = \mathbf{y} - \mathbf{X}_{-j}\beta_{-j}$, we have

$$p(\pi_j = 1|\mathbf{y}, \beta_{-j}, \pi_{-j}, \sigma^2, \tau^2, \theta)$$
$$= \frac{1}{Z}\theta(2\pi\sigma^2\tau^2)^{-\frac{1}{2}}exp\left(-\frac{1}{2\sigma^2}(\mathbf{y} - \mathbf{X}_{-j}\beta_{-j})^T(\mathbf{y} - \mathbf{X}_{-j}\beta_{-j})\right)exp\left(\frac{(\sum_{i=1}^n x_i z_i)^2}{2\sigma^2(\sum_{i=1}^n x_i^2 + \frac{1}{\tau^2})}\right)$$
(6)

The conditional posterior of $\pi = 0$ is therefore a Bernoulli distribution with chance parameter $1 - \zeta_j = \dfrac{1-\theta}{(\sigma^2\tau^2)^{-\frac{1}{2}}exp(K)\left(\frac{\sigma^2}{(\sum_{i=1}^n x_i^2+\frac{1}{\tau^2})}\right)^{\frac{1}{2}}\theta + (1-\theta)}$, where $K = $

$\frac{(\sum_{i=1}^n x_i z_i)^2}{2\sigma^2(\sum_{i=1}^n x_i^2 + \frac{1}{tau^2})}$ and where z_j changes depending on which β_j we sample.

5   Experiments and Results

In this section, we first start by evaluating the effectiveness of the learning methods in modeling individual estimators that form the components of $\hat{\tau}_{DRE}$. The outcome models through spike-and-slab Bayesian variable selection models have been described in the previous sections. For estimating the propensity score $e(x)$ $= \mathbb{P}(W = 1|X = x)$ with estimator $\hat{e}(x)$ in step 2 outlined in Sect. 4.2, we use a logistic regression model with the same attributes as the outcome model. We further experimented with Random Forests, but did not observe any substantial

Table 4. Summary of ATE Estimation for different sectors comparing models. Numbers marked in asterisk indicate substantial differences in the estimates from the regression coefficients estimated in Table 2.

Sector name	Naive		Baseline		DRE (SSR)	
	ATE	std	ATE	std	ATE	std
Construction	1.04	0.28	−0.09	0.27	0.51	0.29
Clothing	1.85	0.16	3.12	0.15	2.63	0.29
Retail	0.59	0.15	3.25	0.15	4.81*	0.18
Education	−4.86	0.2	−5.48	0.19	−5.37	0.19
Services	−0.52	0.15	−0.92	0.14	−0.85	0.15
Manufacturing	−5.16	0.25	−5.53	0.23	−5.38	0.24
Transportation	1.34	0.22	1.6	0.2	1.05	0.22
Agriculture	−0.61	0.16	−0.28	0.15	−0.6	0.15
Housing	6.34	0.19	6.77	0.18	7.9*	0.22
Arts	−5.46	0.23	−5.4	0.22	−5.61	0.26
Personal use	1.61	0.27	1.35	0.25	−2.26*	0.71
Food	−1.43	0.15	0.34	0.14	−0.4	0.17

difference in the results. For the Gibbs sampling procedure, we set the following hyper-parameter values: $a = b = 1$, $a_1 = a_2 = 0.01$, $\theta = 0.5$ and $s = 1/2$ for all the models. We use a burn-in of 1000 samples for the procedure and use 4000 samples for the sampling procedure. We use these posterior estimates as the coefficient estimates in the spike-and-slab regression model for predictive purposes.

As mentioned before, for each sector, we consider treated and control groups considering that sector and evaluate the outcome models for treatment and control and the propensity score (p-score) models. We use Root Mean Squared Error (RMSE) for the outcome regression models and F1 sore and Accuracy for the p-score model using logistic regression. For each model we split the data into 70%–30% train-test and evaluate the models using these metrics on the held-out test set. The results shown for all sectors in Table 3 compares Linear Regression (LR) without any regularization with the Spike and Slab (SSR) model. We find that while for most sectors the models fare comparably for both treated and control groups, for 3 sectors namely Manufacturing, Clothing and Education where the regression models for Treatment are an order of magnitude worse than control groups evidenced by their RMSE scores. This can be attributed to the relatively low number of projects in these areas shown in Fig. 1. We also find that the SSR model outperforms the LR model in most cases in terms of lower RMSE scores for the SSR model. For the p-score model, we find that the logistic regression model performs similar for most sectors showing lesser disparity among the several models used for the purpose.

Next, we compare the ATE for different sectors against a model where the ATE is estimated with just the target variable - the funding time. We compare 3 models for measuring the Average Treatment Effect (ATE):

1. **Naive** - ATE is calculated using the differences in means of Y for treatment and control groups, and the standard deviation is calculated using the group standard deviations.
2. **Baseline** - Here we use the Linear Regression (LR) model as discussed above to estimate 2 relations: (1) $Y(1) = \mathbf{X}\beta_1$ with estimate $\hat{\beta}_1$ using the treated data and $Y(0) = \mathbf{X}\beta_0$ with estimate $\hat{\beta}_0$ using the control data. The estimator $\hat{\tau} = \frac{1}{n}\sum_{i=1}^{n}(\hat{Y}_{1,i} - \hat{Y}_{0,i})$. The standard error is then calculated as $\sqrt{\frac{var(Y_i - \hat{Y}_{1,i}|i:W_i=1)}{n_t-1} + \frac{var(Y_i - \hat{Y}_{0,i}|i:W_i=0)}{n_t-1}}$.
3. **DRE (SSR)** - Here we use the SSR models for the estimators $\hat{Y}_1$ and $\hat{Y}_0$ from the treated and control data and $\hat{\tau}_{DRE}$ and teh standard errro is calculated as described in Sect. 4.2.

The results for the model is shown in Table 4. From the table, we find that the four sectors where the ATE from the DRE estimator is substantially different from the naive estimator are Retail, Housing, Arts and Personal Use (we keep the 3 sectors, Manufacturing, clothing and education out of our discussion since the SSR models for the treated data in these 3 sectors were substantially worse than control data). In fact, we find that the funding time for Arts loans have almost 6 days (ATE $= -5.61$) faster funding when compared to all other sectors using our DRE (SSR) model, whereas the naive estimator suggests a slower funding. This suggests that when we combine these economic factors along with the loan attributes for these specific sectors, the effect of this loan sector actually helps in faster funding which in other situations would have been difficult to be funded. Similarly, for the Retail loans, we find that funding is generally disfavored compared to other factors by being funded slower by 5 (ATE $= 4.81$) days. The standard errors for all the 3 models are comparable and so as such the ATE estimates can be compared reliably across the models. These observations suggest that when such economic disparities or similarities exist which can affect lender trust and perceptions of funding a project in a particular sector, biases are bound to arise. Therefore, predictive models which try to model the risk of loan defaults must also incorporate fairness constraints to not allow favoritism towards certain sectors. To this end, we conclude this study by modifying our SSR model to incorporate fairness constraints.

6   Controlling the Disparities from Sectors

To control the disparities arising from the different attributes for different sectors in our regression setting, we adopt the procedure described in [7] and incorporate the constraint in the sampling procedure for the parameter estimates. For each sector s, we divide the dataset as done before into two groups: $D_s^\uparrow$ and $D_s^\downarrow$ based on s. The specific goal here is to build one regression model for each sector and learn the parameters of that model while minimizing bias associated with predicting the target variables when conditioned over the loan sector attribute. To this end, we use the constraint that ensures that the mean predictions for the two groups $D_s^\uparrow$ and $D_s^\downarrow$ are equal irrespective of what the target or outcome exhibits.

Adding Regularization: We use the same model based on Bayesian variable selection introduced in Sect. 4.3 with the addition of new regularization terms. We add the sector attribute to the features $\mathbf{X}$, however we now build one single model for each sector with the entire batch of data. We use the balanced means constraint based on the following criteria: $\frac{\sum_{(\mathbf{x}_i, t_i) \in D_s^\uparrow} \beta.\mathbf{x}_i}{|D_s^\uparrow|} = \frac{\sum_{(\mathbf{x}_i, t_i) \in D_s^\downarrow} \beta.\mathbf{x}_i}{|D_s^\downarrow|}$, where $D_S^\uparrow$ and $D_S^\downarrow$ denote control and treatment data. It denotes the constraint that the predictions from our model should be the same for both the treated and the control groups for the loan sector in consideration irrespective of what the target variable differences in the model exhibit. Using the same notations used in Eqs. 2, we make the following adjustment to sample the target variable. Denoting $\frac{\sum_{(\mathbf{x}_i, t_i) \in D_s^\uparrow} \beta.\mathbf{x}_i}{|D_s^\uparrow|} = \frac{\sum_{(\mathbf{x}_i, t_i) \in D_s^\downarrow} \beta.\mathbf{x}_i}{|D_s^\downarrow|}$ as $\mathbf{d}$, we add the regularization term as: $y_i \sim N(\beta x_i, \sigma^2) + \lambda\beta\mathbf{d}$, where λ is the hyper-parameter controlling the effect of the regularization term. With this modification, the sampling equations are modified following from Sect. 4.3 and have been added to the Appendix.

Results: Finally, we compare the results of the models with the regularization constraint for the sectors with models discussed prior to this. Additionally, we also compare the results from the model in the absence of external factors and only considering loan attributes available from Kiva data. We adopt a similar validation approach as previous where we perform a 70%–30% train-test split and test on the held-out 30% data. For training the SSR models, we use the same settings as explained in Sect. 5 for the Gibbs sampling procedure. For evaluating the regression models, we use the metric RMSE on the test data as done in the previous section. The regularization hyper-parameter λ, we set it to 0.6 after cross-validating it with several values. The results have been shown in Table 5 - the column LR-LA shows the results for the model with only loan attributes from Kiva. The last column shows results incorporating the regularization term. Additionally, we only test the models with the 4 sectors that showed the highest ATE explained in Sect. 5. We observe that in all these sectors, addition of external factors like the economic attributes and borrower-lender country pair attributes improve the model over the model LR-LA. The model with SSR performs the best in the absence of any regularization for all the sectors having the least RMSE, indicating that variable selection helps improve the predictions. However, when we compare these results with the model SSR (with regularization), we find that the performance drops at the cost of the equality constraints, however what we observe is that the results are still comparable to the simple LR model. We find that for Housing loans, the model with regularization performs comparably worse and this can be attributed to the pre-existing disparities shown by high ATE for these loans as shown in Table 4. Therefore, the equal

Table 5. RMSE results of regression models. Models with LA denote only loan attributes from Kiva are used in the model. The lower values indicate better results.

Sector	LR	LR - LA	SSR	SSR (regularization)
Housing	10.76	11.34	10.61	13.82
Personal use	9.6	10.02	9.46	10.24
Retail	12.06	13.18	11.91	12.73
Arts	9.31	10.25	9.19	9.52

means constraint does result in performance degradation. However, these results suggest that we can still build models by reducing disparities in the resulting predictions while limiting the drop in performance.

7 Related Work and Conclusions

Understanding the effect of loan attributes towards funding speeds have been studied extensively in [16] albeit only with factors from the loans data. The effects of cultural differences have also been studied in [6] where the authors present evidence that lenders prefer culturally similar borrowers in Kiva. However, the extent to which that affects the actual interests towards particular sectors was not presented. Our work here opens an entire body of research into fairness aware recommendation systems [13] that might be necessary when promoting projects so as to lessen the inherent biases arising from existing lenders. Especially when designing portfolio recommendations as a tool for decision support for lenders as done in [24], it is important to adjust the multi-objective optimization problems incorporating constraints as described in this paper. Such conclusions can also be extended to platforms which are designed for lenders to profit from investments such as Lendingclub [18]. In this paper, we first demonstrated how simple economic factors can play a role in deciding the speed of funding for particular loans and how they can be intertwined with the loan sector. We then measured the existing disparities arising from such factors using causal reasoning estimators and proposed a method to control the differences in outcome. One area where our work can be extended is to develop a single model taking all models into account - this is where the Bayesian variable selection method can be extended to incorporate priors that take into account fairness constraints for all sectors and using empirical bayes to drive the priors.

References

1. Alfaro, L., Kalemli-Ozcan, S., Volosovych, V.: Why doesn't capital flow from rich to poor countries? An empirical investigation. Rev. Econ. Stat. **90**(2), 347–368 (2008)
2. Athey, S., Imbens, G., Pham, T., Wager, S.: Estimating average treatment effects: supplementary analyses and remaining challenges. Am. Econ. Rev. **107**(5), 278–81 (2017)

3. Athey, S., Imbens, G.W., Wager, S., et al.: Efficient inference of average treatment effects in high dimensions via approximate residual balancing. Technical report (2016)
4. Banerjee, A., Duflo, E., Glennerster, R., Kinnan, C.: The miracle of microfinance? Evidence from a randomized evaluation. Am. Econ. J.: Appl. Econ. **7**(1), 22–53 (2015)
5. World bank data. World Bank (2013)
6. Burtch, G., Ghose, A., Wattal, S.: Cultural differences and geography as determinants of online prosocial lending. MIS Q. **38**(3), 773–794 (2014)
7. Calders, T., Karim, A., Kamiran, F., Ali, W., Zhang, X.: Controlling attribute effect in linear regression. In: 2013 IEEE 13th International Conference on Data Mining, pp. 71–80. IEEE (2013)
8. Choo, J., Lee, C., Lee, D., Zha, H., Park, H.: Understanding and promoting microfinance activities in kiva.org. In: Proceedings of the 7th ACM International Conference on Web Search and Data Mining, pp. 583–592 (2014)
9. Hill, J.L.: Bayesian nonparametric modeling for causal inference. J. Comput. Graph. Stat. **20**(1), 217–240 (2011)
10. Ishwaran, H., Rao, J.S., et al.: Spike and slab variable selection: frequentist and Bayesian strategies. Ann. Stat. **33**(2), 730–773 (2005)
11. Kang, J.D., Schafer, J.L., et al.: Demystifying double robustness: a comparison of alternative strategies for estimating a population mean from incomplete data. Stat. Sci. **22**(4), 523–539 (2007)
12. Lee, E.L., et al.: Fairness-aware loan recommendation for microfinance services. In: Proceedings of the 2014 International Conference on Social Computing, pp. 1–4 (2014)
13. Li, Y., Ning, Y., Liu, R., Wu, Y., Hui Wang, W.: Fairness of classification using users' social relationships in online peer-to-peer lending. In: Companion Proceedings of the Web Conference 2020, pp. 733–742 (2020)
14. Lin, M., Prabhala, N.R., Viswanathan, S.: Judging borrowers by the company they keep: friendship networks and information asymmetry in online peer-to-peer lending. Manag. Sci. **59**(1), 17–35 (2013)
15. Lunceford, J.K., Davidian, M.: Stratification and weighting via the propensity score in estimation of causal treatment effects: a comparative study. Stat. Med. **23**(19), 2937–2960 (2004)
16. Ly, P., Mason, G.: Individual preferences over NGO projects: evidence from microlending on kiva. Available at SSRN 1652269 (2010)
17. Mayer, T., Zignago, S.: Notes on CEPII's distances measures: the GeoDist database (2011)
18. Nowak, A., Ross, A., Yencha, C.: Small business borrowing and peer-to-peer lending: evidence from lending club. Contemp. Econ. Policy **36**(2), 318–336 (2018)
19. O'Hara, R.B., Sillanpää, M.J., et al.: A review of Bayesian variable selection methods: what, how and which. Bayesian Anal. **4**(1), 85–117 (2009)
20. Pham, T.T., Shen, Y.: A deep causal inference approach to measuring the effects of forming group loans in online non-profit microfinance platform. arXiv preprint arXiv:1706.02795 (2017)
21. Rakesh, V., Lee, W.C., Reddy, C.K.: Probabilistic group recommendation model for crowdfunding domains. In: Proceedings of the Ninth ACM International Conference on Web Search and Data Mining, pp. 257–266 (2016)
22. Robins, J.M.: Robust estimation in sequentially ignorable missing data and causal inference models. In: Proceedings of the American Statistical Association, Indianapolis, IN, vol. 1999, pp. 6–10 (2000)

23. Singh, P., et al.: Peer-to-peer lending and bias in crowd decision-making. PLoS ONE **13**(3), e0193007 (2018)
24. Zhao, H., Liu, Q., Wang, G., Ge, Y., Chen, E.: Portfolio selections in P2P lending: a multi-objective perspective. In: Proceedings of the 22nd ACM SIGKDD International Conference on Knowledge Discovery and Data Mining, pp. 2075–2084 (2016)

A Left Realist Critique of the Political Value of Adopting Machine Learning Systems in Criminal Justice

Fabio Massimo Zennaro$^{(\boxtimes)}$ (ID)

Department of Informatics, University of Oslo, 0316 Oslo, Norway
fabiomz@ifi.uio.no

Abstract. In this paper we discuss the political value of the decision to adopt machine learning in the field of criminal justice. While a lively discussion in the community focuses on the issue of the social fairness of machine learning systems, we suggest that another relevant aspect of this debate concerns the political implications of the decision of using machine learning systems. Relying on the theory of Left realism, we argue that, from several points of view, modern supervised learning systems, broadly defined as functional learned systems for decision making, fit into an approach to crime that is close to the law and order stance. Far from offering a political judgment of value, the aim of the paper is to raise awareness about the potential implicit, and often overlooked, political assumptions and political values that may be undergirding a decision that is apparently purely technical.

Keywords: Machine learning · Supervised learning · Fairness · Left realism · Law and order

1 Introduction

The success of machine learning systems in recent years (see, for instance, the breakthroughs in image recognition [23] or audio classification [20]) has led to a wide adoption of automated systems in several fields and applications, ranging from biomedical research to computer security [16].

The prototypical application of machine learning consists of *supervised learning*, that is learning a functional relationship between inputs and outputs by relying on samples demonstrating this relationship. Normally, such a relationship is inferred by tuning the learned model to be as close to data as possible, that is, practically, by optimizing the accuracy of its predictions. This simple learning process, designed to reflect a human inductive learning process, can be easily applied to a surprisingly large number of problems. For instance, any sort of decision-making may be reduced to the problem of taking a decision (output) as a function of a set of signals (input). In several instances, when deployed, this form of machine learning can achieve a level of accuracy that can equal or surpass human experts.

© Springer Nature Switzerland AG 2020
I. Koprinska et al. (Eds.): ECML PKDD 2020 Workshops, CCIS 1323, pp. 92–107, 2020.
https://doi.org/10.1007/978-3-030-65965-3_7

The enthusiasm generated by the success of these systems combined with their flexibility and applicability has led, most recently, to their deployment in socially-critical applications, including criminal justice [9]. From a formal point of view, criminal justice problems, such as sentencing or parole decisions, can be easily modeled in functional terms: for instance, deciding on a sentence or a parole may be seen as the result of a complex evaluation performed by a judge on a set of information. At first sight, it seems that machine learning systems could efficiently support or automate decision-making in criminal justice, maybe even improving its accuracy and removing human biases.

However, it has been noted that algorithms designed to optimize the accuracy of their model may lead to decisions that would not be considered fair from a social or legal point of view [6]. Decisions in modeling, choices in optimization, and biases implicit in the data inevitably cause learned models to be socially unfair. As a result, fair machine learning quickly developed as an active area of research that aims to tackle the problem of designing algorithms able to learn models that are not only accurate but also fair. Debate in fair machine learning has been actively concerned with the definition of fairness and its implications. For instance, [12] studied the cost of adopting fairness criteria in learning; [36] reviewed several measures of fairness; [10] and [22] derived trade-offs and impossibility results in satisfying multiple definitions of fairness; [34] reviewed the trade-off between accuracy and fairness; [27] evaluated how the enforcement of fairness may impact individuals in the long term; [35] explored the use of causal models in defining fairness.

Even if challenges in fair machine learning constitute an interesting and important strand of research, these topics are not the main focus of this work. In this paper, we would like to shift the level of discussion from *the fairness of adopted machine learning algorithms* to *the fairness of adopting machine learning algorithms*. In other words, instead of focusing on the fairness of the outcome suggested by an algorithm, we want to question the more fundamental decision of relying on machine learning systems in the specific setting of criminal justice.

Holding that any technological application has a political value, we try to investigate what political outlook may drive the adoption of machine learning in the field of criminal justice. While it may be suggested that such an adoption is just the necessary and unavoidable consequence of technological progress (i.e., machine learning systems may improve our decision making, therefore it is right and natural to adopt them), we want to argue, instead, that such a choice has a political valence, and, therefore, it should be discussed (also) in a political arena. Thus, *while elsewhere the adoption of machine learning in socially-sensitive fields may be taken for granted, in this paper we question this assumption and analyze the potential political significance that machine learning systems, as tools available to society, may carry.*

In particular, we will focus on the field of criminal justice because of its relevance to political decision-making and its active involvement with statistical models. Indeed, the use of statistical tools in this field has a long history [3], and debates about fairness are very active [6]. Here, disregarding specific definitions of fairness, we will instead consider: *what is the political significance of using modern supervised learning systems in criminal justice? What are the hidden assumptions and potential implications of adopting such systems?*

Relying on the analysis and critique of the problem of crime proposed by *Left realism* [25], we consider the use of standard modern machine learning systems in the light of relevant criminological theories. We restrict our attention to supervised learning systems because of their success and wide adoption. We suggest that features of these systems such as causal-agnosticism, opacity, and reactive stance are particularly suited for a *law-and-order* approach to the problem of crime. Moreover, we draw an instructive analogy between the issue of deploying close-camera television (CCTV) recording systems in the 1980s and the contemporary adoption of machine learning systems. In conclusion, we discuss the limitations of our analysis and point out current developments in machine learning research that may be consistent with different political values.

This paper itself has no intention of expressing a political judgment of value with respect to the problem of adopting machine learning in the sphere of criminal justice (and in other fields). Its main aim is instead to raise awareness concerning the potential political weight of the adoption of machine learning systems in order to instigate an informed debate.

The paper is organized as follows. Section 2 introduces the main concepts in machine learning that are relevant to our discussion. Section 3 offers a presentation of the main criminological theory of interest, that is Left realism. Section 4 provides an analysis of machine learning systems through the conceptual categories of Left realism. Section 5 discusses our observations and their implications. Finally, Sect. 6 summarizes our contributions.

2   Machine Learning Systems

In this section, we provide a concise conceptual definition of the type of machine learning systems which are being discussed. Machine learning provides many models which can be used for learning in different contexts and which may significantly vary in their expressive and representational power (for an overview of different machine learning models, refer to standard machine learning textbooks, such as [28] or [7]). Given this variety, making sweeping general statements about machine learning systems would be impossible. We therefore focus on supervised learning systems as defined below.

Supervised Learning Systems. In this paper, we will focus primarily on supervised learning systems because of their easy deployability and their broad success and adoption. Supervised learning systems are statistical models that learn from data a complex functional relationship between an input, encoded as a set of quantitative features, and an output, representing a result dependent on the input. As *statistical* models, supervised learning systems are defined through a set of assumptions and modeling choices that determine their domain of applicability and their level of abstraction [18]. By *complex* functional relationship we mean that these models learn a non-trivial function which, while commonly used, cannot be easily defined by a human designer (think, for instance, of facial recognition which can be easily performed by humans, thus implying the existence of a functional relationship between facial features and identity, but which can hardly be expressed in an algorithm by a programmer). Formally, a supervised learning system learns a model

$$y = f(\mathbf{x}),$$

where $\mathbf{x}$ is a vector of input features, y is the output, and f is the learned function. The function f is inferred from a data set containing a large number of samples of inputs and outputs. A machine learning algorithm processes each pair of inputs and outputs, $(\mathbf{x}_i, y_i)$, and tunes the learned function f accordingly. By default, most machine learning algorithms tune f by optimizing their accuracy, that is, by minimizing the discrepancy between the results produced by the learned model and results observed in the real-world:

$$\min \mathcal{L}\left(f(\mathbf{x}_i) - y_i\right),$$

over all samples i, and where $\mathcal{L}(\cdot)$ is a chosen loss function evaluating the difference between the predictions of the model and reality.

We take this essential and paradigmatic presentation of a learning system that infers a functional relationship from data via a loss optimization technique as our working definition of a supervised machine learning system. We thus ignore practical details about learning (e.g., how the parametric family over which we optimize is defined or how the evaluation of the degree of generalization is computed), implementation differences between the algorithms (e.g., whether we instantiate a simple linear regression or a neural network) and assumptions underlying concrete instantiations (e.g., independence of the samples, linear separability of the data). Elsewhere, this broad category of machine learning algorithms has been referred to with other terms, such as *regression systems* [3] or *function-based systems* [14].

Supervised Learning Systems in Criminal Justice. The adoption of statistical tools in criminal justice has a history that dates back to the 1920s (see [3] for a review of different generations of statistical models used by the criminal justice community).

The use of modern machine learning techniques is a current topic of debate in criminal justice [1,5], especially in relation to fairness concerns [6]. Indeed, the deployment of supervised learning systems for tasks such as risk assessment and decisional support to judges has been accompanied by discussions on how to evaluate their social fairness. A representative case, that brought the topic to the attention of a wider public, was the Northpointe-ProPublica case. Northpointe was the developer of COMPAS, a predictive tool based on linear regression that can be used to attribute a numerical risk of recidivism to a defendant [8]. COMPAS was deployed in Broward County, Florida, and the results it produced were analyzed by the nonprofit organization ProPublica, which showed the presence of a racial bias in terms of unequal false negative rates [2] (see [13] for a brief synthesis of the argument). The case of COMPAS is representative both of the types of machine learning systems we are considering, and of the kind of discussion we want to extend, shifting the attention from the question of the fairness of systems like COMPAS to the question of the political value of adopting such systems.

The actual effects and efficacy of machine learning in criminal justice has also been a topic of research [33]. Recently, a careful statistical study of the effect of using machine learning systems for supporting the decision making of judges has been carried out in [21]. These results are extremely valuable in the discussion about the adoption of supervised learning systems from a practical point of view, once politically-agreed quantitative measures of efficacy have been established; in contrast, our work will focus on the question of adopting machine learning systems from a theoretical perspective, that is, considering, before its concrete effects, what political value may be attached to the choice of relying on machine learning systems in criminal justice.

3 Approaches to Crime

In this section, we offer a brief review of the main criminological theory relevant to our work. The theory of Left realism was developed in the 1980s as a consistent alternative to the contemporary approaches to crime.

Theory of Left Realism. The foundations of Left realism were laid down by Lea and Young in their study and critique of the *law and order* approach to crime adopted in the UK in the 1980s [25]. Left realism was proposed as a new criminological stance in between *left idealism* (a stance biased towards seeing the criminal as the structural product of oppression in an unfair society) and *law and order* (a stance biased towards seeing the criminal as a deviant individual that must be confronted) [25]. Differently form left idealism, Left realism was founded on the central tenet that crime is a serious and real issue affecting everyday life. However, in distinction to law and order approaches, it strongly emphasized the complexity of crime, both in its causes and its prevention. It promoted a cautious and careful approach to crime data, aimed at avoiding simplistic and ungrounded readings and preventing mass-media distortion and moral panic. It suggested that crime and its causes should be examined in terms of discontent, marginalization, and sub-cultural group dynamics. More importantly, it advocated that crime should be fought in terms of deterrence and consensus policing, as a joint effort between communities and law enforcement, not as a battle carried on by the state through military policing [25]. Over time, attention to Left realism theories has lost traction, partly because of changes in the forms of crime with which society is concerned, and partly because of an inappropriate application of its theories [24]. Despite this decline, however, discussion is still alive around Left realism and the contributions that it may offer to contemporary debates [15].

In the following, we will not present an organic revision or modern declination of Left realism for machine learning. This task, while interesting, is beyond the scope of this work. Rather, we appeal to some core ideas of Left realism and investigate how they can help us to better understand the political relevance of the adoption of machine learning systems in criminal justice.

4   Left Realist Critique of Machine Learning Systems for Criminal Justice

In this section we examine the central question of this paper, that is, what is the political relevance of adopting a machine learning system, paying special attention to the field of criminal justice. More precisely, we rely on the theory of Left realism to investigate where the adoption of machine learning systems in criminal justice would fall in the spectrum of criminological approaches ranging from law and order to Left realism. We examine this question by analyzing a set of issues raised and discussed in [25] that are particularly relevant to the adoption of machine learning systems.

4.1   Focus on Effects and Correlations

Left Realism. Understanding the causes of crime is a central endeavor of Left realism. According to this system, a serious and successful approach to crime must move beyond the simple apprehension of crime to the uncovering of the causes underlying these behaviors[1]. The aim should be to determine which social factors (e.g.: marginalization, lack of political voice) are causally related to anti-social behaviors, so that effective crime policies may be defined in relation to these aspects[2]. This stance contrasts with more conventional approaches to crime, such as law and order, which prioritize fighting crime in itself and which are often uninterested in determining its actual causes[3]. Law and order approaches often explain away anti-social behaviors through the misuse of sociological categories[4] (such as condemning behaviors as psycho-pathological or under-socialized) or relying on simplistic explanations[5] (such as blaming the criminal as evil or lacking human values). From the perspective of Left realism, law and order tends to vainly struggle with the effects of social factors; that is, it focuses on the crime itself disregarding its origin; Left realism, instead, favors an approach that concentrates on the social factors that are seen as the underlying causes of crime.

---

[1] [25], p. 265.
[2] [25], p. 74.
[3] [25], p. 265.
[4] [25], p. 77.
[5] [25], p. 95.

Machine Learning. Supervised machine learning systems such as those defined above are designed to model a direct relationship between a set of inputs and outputs. It is well known that, in statistical terms, standard supervised models learn correlations between inputs and outputs, and not causal relationships. A model $f(\mathbf{x}) = y$ may learn to predict the output y based on features that do not determine it. As long as what matters is a prediction, this may work fine; however, if we were interested in prevention through intervention, then acting on the correlated, but not-necessarily causative, features may not produce the desired result. Standard machine learning models are agnostic of causes; they process static sets of features with no explicit information about causal links. Understanding and analyzing causes is just beyond the concern of standard supervised learning systems.

Also, the common use of binary or discrete labels as outputs seems to comply with a methodology in which understanding subtle causal dynamics is disregarded; discrete categories may be seen as a way to bin cases or individuals into coarse classes; at the extreme, the use of binary output classes may be interpreted as a way to partition cases or behaviors into normal and deviant (or psycho-pathological or under-socialized or evil), with no interest for uncovering deeper dynamics.

Overall, then, supervised learning systems seem to fit better an approach to crime which is more concerned with tackling well-categorized effects by predicting them, instead of engaging and working on the causes of the crimes.

4.2   Focus on Specific Crimes

Left Realism. A starting point of Left realist thought is the awareness of the political value undergirding the definition of crimes; deciding which crimes to focus on, and how to delimit them, are choices that are inevitably bound to shape, and to be shaped by, political programs and public opinion[6]. The very decision to focus on violent crimes or crimes against property, instead of highlighting, say, "white-collar" crimes or financial crimes, is a choice that Left realism tries to bring to the forefront[7]. While not arguing against the importance of dealing with violent crimes, Left realism points out that the definition of what constitutes violent crimes has profound effects on public perception and policies. Official definitions and public opinion may not match and, at times, diverge, as shown, for instance, in the gap between official statistics (based on given definitions of crimes) and self-victimization reports (based on the understanding of crime by a victim)[8].

Machine Learning. By definition, supervised machine learning is very dependent on data. Limitations on the available data sets may severely restrict the

---

[6] [25], pp. 11, 68.

[7] [25], p. 65.

[8] [25], p. 17.

sub-domains of criminal justice to which machine learning may be applied. Following the actual concerns of criminal policies and the definitions of crime previously approved, more data may be available about certain crimes than others (e.g., more data is generally available about violent crimes than financial crimes), and this may improperly justify the adoption of machine learning in those particular sub-domains. What should be a political decision may be implicitly (and fallaciously) justified by the actual availability of data, which may have been determined by entrenched definitions of crime. This, in turn, leads to generation of more data in those specific fields that are the concern of the policymaker.

It is important to remember that algorithms cannot learn but what is provided to them through the data; a given definition of crime, encoded in the pairing of inputs and outputs, will necessarily inform all the results produced by a machine learning system. In their working, supervised learning systems conform and reiterate given definitions. While their accuracy may be quantitatively measured and celebrated, it is always an accuracy with respect to definitions that are often implicitly hidden in the preparation of the data or in the setup of the algorithm. Disagreement or misunderstanding of these definitions may once again give rise to a gap between machine learning results and other reports such as self-victimization reports.

In conclusion, supervised learning systems may feed a self-reinforcing loop in which pre-existing ideas and definitions of crimes are constantly re-affirmed by algorithms trained on the same concepts, making it progressively harder to discuss and challenge the existing and efficient "working" definitions.

4.3 Sensitivity to Data Interpretation

Left Realism. Related to the issue of the dependence of statistics on the definition of crimes, Left realism also argues against simplistic readings of statistics. While statistics are precious resources for studying crime, they should never be taken as hard facts; instead, they should be interpreted with special care for understanding the assumptions and the conditions under which such statistics were generated[9]. Data and results are often characterized by complex behaviors; for instance, special attention should be devoted to aggregated statistics, as they may hide highly biased or skewed distributions with respect to sensitive parameters, such as gender or race[10]. Superficial readings may be responsible for inadequate decisions or may be used opportunistically to justify political choices.

Machine Learning. Results produced by supervised machine learning systems are also non-trivial to analyze. The outcome of the learning process critically depends on the data provided and on the statistical assumptions defining the behavior of the system. All machine learning algorithms have limitations in their modeling power. Their capacity to deal with complex data, such as highly-skewed data or multi-modal data, strictly depends on the specific implementation adopted.

---

[9] [25], p. 12.
[10] [25], p. 28.

A proper model choice would require a careful study of the data at hand, as well as a deep understanding of the assumptions and the limits of the selected supervised algorithm. Unfortunately, supervised learning algorithms are often applied as black-boxes to data that do not conform to their assumptions (as may be in the case of highly biased criminal justice data sets), and this may lead to grossly approximated conclusions that hide, instead of uncover, the subtlety of the data.

To make things worse, supervised learning systems tend to return non-transparent shallow results in the form of a numeric value that can be readily used for decision-making. Such a simple output, however, combined with the opaqueness of many modern supervised learning systems, tends to hinder the possibility of properly understanding and interpreting the result. After carrying out the hard and menial work of crunching data for us, a supervised learning system often does not provide a transparent or justified output. Despite the job performed by the machine, the crucial and sensitive part of interpreting the data and taking a responsible decision cannot be delegated to a machine. Unfortunately, though, full understanding of the results of a supervised system is often not possible.

A supervised learning system may then be easily exploited and presented as an oracle able to perform a complete and reliable statistical analysis, inviting a superficial acceptance of its output instead of stimulating an engaged interpretation.

4.4   Tool for Military Policing

Left Realism. A central concern for criminology and criminal justice relates to policing. In its critique, Left realism identifies two abstract and opposite types of policing. The form of *consensus policing* it advocates is based on a strict and beneficial cooperation between police forces and the community; in this setting, information is voluntarily provided by the community, and police may act with the support and in the interest of the locals[11]. On the opposite end, the form of *military policing* enacted by law and order approaches is based on a unilateral enforcement of law by the police in a context where the cooperation with the community is reduced or has been severed. Deprived of information sources within the community, police have to carry out complex and costly investigations and then act on the uncertain conclusions achieved without local support[12]. According to this perspective, mistakes and prejudices lead to a self-reinforcing loop of antagonizing the masses at large, mobilization of neutral bystanders, and alienation within the community, all of which, in turn, progressively isolate police forces[13].

Machine Learning. Machine learning systems can be powerful tools for the definition of security policies and for policing. Referring to the policing spectrum

---

[11] [25], p. 169.
[12] [25], p. 172.
[13] [25], p. 182.

identified by Left realism, supervised learning systems seem to lean towards one of the two extremes. Modern learning systems seem weakly related to the paradigm of consensual information gathering from the community: learning systems are not designed to ease the relationship between locals and police, nor they are apt to integrate varied data acquired from heterogeneous data sources; instead, they are meant to process uniform data that are acquired in a standardized fashion with or without explicit consent. As tools developed to process data and improve decision-making, supervised learning systems seem more suited at enhancing the investigative expertise of a police force that has been reduced to work on data it gathered by itself. Supervised learning systems can indeed become efficient tools to improve the accuracy and the precision of military policing; at the same time, though, because of the mistakes they are bound to commit, they may cause an increase in the distance between police forces and local communities.

Between the two alternative approaches to policing presented above, current supervised learning systems seem more fit to a military policing approach than a consensus one.

4.5   Issues of Accountability

Left Realism. Connected to the issue of policing is the problem of trust and accountability of law enforcement. Left realism asserts that transparent policies are a necessary requirement to guarantee a democratic overview and control of the activities of police forces[14]. Through accountability, a sense of mutual trust and confidence can be built between communities and state representatives. In contrast to Left realism, other approaches often present several arguments, including the technical nature of decisions related to policing or the necessary secrecy of some operations, in order to justify the opaqueness and the autonomy of police forces[15]. The reduction of policing to a technical question of efficiency tends in turn to overshadow the question of accountability and the role that politics should have in defining policing[16].

Machine Learning. Machine learning raises new and challenging questions about accountability and trust. Most of the current successful supervised learning systems are opaque, behaving like *black boxes* that, provided with an input, return an output without any explanation or justification for it. The result is often the product of an optimization process with respect to a simple and quantifiable definition of accuracy or efficiency. The problem of interpreting the dynamics and the outputs of supervised learning is a problem relevant to many fields beyond criminal justice and is now a very active area of research in machine learning (see, for instance, [26] for a discussion of the definition of interpretability of machine learning models). Without a way to explain results, supervised

---

[14] [25], p. 269.
[15] [25], p. 233.
[16] [25], p. 257.

learning systems may end up diluting accountability, making it hard to trace responsibility through its opaque internals. Currently, trust is not built upon an understanding of the systems, but over a technical confidence in their efficiency. Such trust is, however, bound to fall if the decisions of the system were to be questioned or put into discussion.

The adoption of current black-box supervised learning systems poses a strong challenge to any form of democratic oversight: unless such systems are carefully validated in their assumptions and their definitions, their results may be hard to assess. This may turn machine learning into another technical tool that can be used to justify policing decisions not being disclosed and discussed within the community.

4.6   Analogy with CCTV

Left Realism. Expanding on the topic of policing within criminal justice, a telling parallel may be drawn between the adoption of close-camera television (CCTV) for surveillance in the 1980s and supervised learning systems in the current time. Interestingly, in its analysis of the causes of a rise in military policing in the UK in the 1980s, Left realism identified, beyond an increase in street lifestyle and a rise in prejudices, the widespread adoption of new technologies[17]. New technological resources, such as CCTV, promoted among police forces a "fire-brigade" mentality: instead of being present among the community, an officer could monitor its neighborhood from afar and intervene only when and where necessary[18]. Thanks to the simplicity of interacting with these surveillance devices, CCTV often became the source information of choice, thus favoring the development of a distant and reactive model to policing instead of an integrated and proactive model based on a constant presence among the community. Ahead of times, it was foreseen that this attitude would lead to the development of technologies, such as computerized preventive tools, that would rely on collecting and storing vast amount of data about citizens[19] and which would naturally raise ethical, legal, and political questions.

Machine Learning. Supervised machine learning algorithms are one of the most prominent modern technologies currently deployed in criminal justice. Like CCTVs, these systems generally foster a "fire-brigade" mentality: they offer the possibility of understanding and controlling the community remotely; and, like any technological innovation, they promise unprecedented accuracy and success whenever intervention is necessary. However, the side effect of this development, as it was in the case of CCTVs in the 1980s, is that criminal policies may end up relying more and more on machine-processed data instead of information volunteered by locals, thus further deepening the rift with the community.

It is also clear that modern supervised learning systems meet the prediction about the craving for data. They frequently need to acquire large amounts of

---

[17] [25], p. 179.
[18] [25], p. 181.
[19] [25], p. 243.

data to be trained, to the point that often the term *big data* systems is just used as a synonym for many contemporary machine learning systems. As foreseen, this hunger for data is the source of ethical and political debates, concerning, for instance, the scope, the transparency and the accountability of scoring systems [11]. Debate about the privacy of users and the extent of legal use of their data constitute the topic of relevant and current discussion in the political and economical arena.

In conclusion, there are significant similarities between the adoption of CCTV in the past and the current trend of the adoption of supervised learning systems in the present days. The doubts and the questions about trust, accountability, and control raised by the deployment of CCTV should be asked for supervised learning systems as well. The reflections and the answers about the political values (such as, privacy and security) raised in the debate about CCTV may enlighten similar evaluations on the political implications of adopting supervised learning systems today.

5   Discussion

In the previous sections we saw how a Left realist critique may be used to analyze the decision of adopting machine learning from a political standpoint. Several features of supervised learning algorithms (focus on effect, restriction to certain crimes, favoring investigation over cooperation with the community) seem to align their adoption in the field of criminal justice to a law and order political view. Table 1 offers a simplified and essential overview of the connections we drew between assumptions and features of supervised learning systems in machine learning and their potential political value or meaning interpreted using the theory of Left realism. This analysis of the political significance of supervised learning systems in criminal justice is, of course, far from being exhaustive. We focused our analysis on those aspects that have an overt parallel with observations and critiques offered by Left realism in [25]. However, other more technical aspects of supervised learning systems, such as the assumption of stationarity of data, the definition of a loss function with its terms and constraints, or the assumption of independence of the data samples, could also be investigated for their political implications.

In general, a supervised learning system constitutes an abstract representation of a phenomenon, in this case a criminal justice process. The reduction of a complex reality to a mathematical model often requires strong assumptions and coarse simplifications. Modeling in a socially sensitive context opens the space for political debate. Even if the primary motivation in modeling is practicality and efficiency, the decision of considering or omitting certain aspects of the problem has a political relevance. In contexts such as criminal justice, any choice, from the decision to collect data in a certain environments to the definition of output classes, may be interpreted in a political light.

Despite its limits, this study reveals a potential implicit political bias in the decision of adopting supervised learning systems in criminal justice. Paraphrasing the infraethics position [19], this bias may follow from the fact that machine

Table 1. Summary of the political value or meaning of some of the features of supervised learning systems, as they were analyzed in this paper.

ML assumption or feature	Political value or meaning	Section
Working on correlations	Disregard of actual cause-effect links	4.1
Coarse categorical outputs	Oversimplification of actual sociological/criminological explanations	4.1
Availability of data for limited problems	Restricted political concern with only certain types of crime	4.2
Dependence on given labelling	Implicit enforcement of certain definitions of crime	4.2
Sensitivity to data interpretation	Possible instrumental misinterpretation of the data	4.3
Automatic support for decision making	Possible complete delegation of decision to a legalistic algorithm	4.3
Functional relationship input-output	Better support for military policing rather than consensus policing	4.4
Lack of interpretability	Possible promotion of certain policies solely on the ground of efficiency	4.5
Opaque internals	Dilution of responsibility for the choices of the algorithm	4.5
Remote fast processing of data	Better support for enforcement of "fire-brigade" mentality	4.6
Reliance on big data	Justification for collection of large amounts of data	4.6

learning and the decision of adopting supervised learning systems cannot be a purely politically-neutral choice; instead, as with every technical decision, it inevitably embeds, even in a minimal way, certain values, and thus favors certain choices, becoming a tool to promote political agendas.

An awareness of this reality is important in order to make critical decisions about the adoption of machine learning in sensitive fields like criminal justice. This understanding would allow us to reflect more clearly on the issue of using supervised learning systems by helping us to avoid at least two mistakes.

(i) By uncovering the political value of adopting machine learning systems, it would prevent us from making the *naive* mistake of adopting these systems simply on the ground of efficiency and enthusiasm.

(ii) It would prevent the mistake of accepting the *instrumental* use of technical arguments as justifications to make certain political decisions in the arena of criminal justice more acceptable. Indeed, a stance like law and order may be dangerously and fallaciously defended by appealing to the technicalities we have discussed: focus on crimes instead of their causes may be justified by the nature of most supervised systems ("efficient machine learning systems can only deal with correlations, not causes"), restriction to certain crimes may be defended in terms of data availability ("we can tackle only those crimes for which we have data"), the use of simplified definitions and statistics may be explained in terms of historical data ("we can tackle only crimes as we have observed them until now"), a reactive stance may be motivated over consensus policing by the features of predictive systems ("machine learning systems are designed to improve police investigation"), and opaque decisions may attributed to the intrinsic non-transparency of supervised systems ("results are effective but we cannot explain them").

It is important, though, to underline the limits of the applicability of these considerations. The observations of political value made here apply particularly well to supervised machine learning as we have defined it. However, although supervised learning systems are by far the most widely adopted, these statements can be hardly extended to machine learning in general. Different approaches may be susceptible only to some of the critiques presented in this paper.

For instance, the use of machine learning systems based on the theory of *causality* [31,32] may be immune to the criticism of focusing only on correlations and effects (see Sect. 4.1). While agreement on the definition and the identification of causes may be debatable as there may be disagreement over the causal models to consider or the causal assumptions to accept, a causality-based system would allow not only to work with effects and predictions, but also with causes and policies. Arguments in favor of adopting a causal inference framework, such as the one proposed in the insightful analysis of [3], may be indeed read as addressing some of the political concerns of Left realism.

Other forms of machine learning may be seen as addressing other concerns expressed in this paper. *Bayesian machine learning* [4] models outputs and their uncertainty in the form of probability distributions, thus tackling, in part, the problem of working with discrete outputs (see Sect. 4.1); *transfer learning* [30] studies how to exploit data in a source domain in order to learn in a target domain, thus opening the possibility of deploying learning systems in domain where data are scarce (see Sect. 4.2); similarly, improvements in *statistical modeling* may, for instance, be used to avoid the narrow focus on few specific crimes following from positive feedback effects [17] (see Sect. 4.2); *interpretable machine learning* [26,29], comprising simple understandable algorithms or methods aimed at opening black-boxes, may potentially offer a future solution to the problem of opaqueness and lack of trust (see Sect. 4.5).

All these technical efforts need to be analyzed more closely and deeply in order to assess their contributions and their value from a political viewpoint.

6   Conclusions

In this paper we offered an analysis of the choice of adopting supervised learning systems in criminal justice as a political decision, reviewed through the lens and the categories of Left realism. Our aim was not to promote a particular political stance, but, rather, to raise awareness about the political value of a choice that, at first sight, may look purely technical and apolitical. An informed debate about the opportunity to adopt supervised learning systems in criminal justice should then revolve not only around the question of their efficiency and fairness in a specific setting, but also on the question of which sort of political project they endorse more generally. Adopting machine learning systems in sensitive fields should be not just a question of social fairness, but also of political values.

Already in the 1980s, [25] observed that technological developments did not solve the problems posed by crime; instead they made decisions about the adoption and the use of technology *more political*[20]. The adoption of machine learning, in the present days, in the field of criminal justice and beyond, deserves to be also considered and analyzed in a political light. In any social field, the choice of using a supervised learning system is, in itself, already a political decision.

References

1. Andrews, D.A., Bonta, J., Wormith, J.S.: The recent past and near future of risk and/or need assessment. Crime Delinq. **52**(1), 7–27 (2006)
2. Angwin, J., Larson, J., Mattu, S., Kirchner, L.: Machine bias. ProPublica, 23 May 2016
3. Barabas, C., Dinakar, K., Virza, J.I., Zittrain, J., et al.: Interventions over predictions: reframing the ethical debate for actuarial risk assessment. arXiv preprint arXiv:1712.08238 (2017)
4. Barber, D.: Bayesian Reasoning and Machine Learning. Cambridge University Press, Cambridge (2012)
5. Berk, R.: Criminal Justice Forecasts of Risk: A Machine Learning Approach. Springer, New York (2012). https://doi.org/10.1007/978-1-4614-3085-8
6. Berk, R., Heidari, H., Jabbari, S., Kearns, M., Roth, A.: Fairness in criminal justice risk assessments: the state of the art. arXiv preprint arXiv:1703.09207 (2017)
7. Bishop, C.M.: Pattern Recognition and Machine Learning. Springer, New York (2006)
8. Brennan, T., Dieterich, W., Ehret, B.: Evaluating the predictive validity of the COMPAS risk and needs assessment system. Crim. Justice Behav. **36**(1), 21–40 (2009)
9. Brennan, T., Oliver, W.L.: The emergence of machine learning techniques in criminology: implications of complexity in our data and in research questions. Criminol. Public Policy **12**(3), 551–562 (2013)
10. Chouldechova, A.: Fair prediction with disparate impact: a study of bias in recidivism prediction instruments. Big Data **5**(2), 153–163 (2017)
11. Citron, D.K., Pasquale, F.: The scored society: due process for automated predictions. Wash. L. Rev. **89**, 1 (2014)
12. Corbett-Davies, S., Pierson, E., Feller, A., Goel, S., Huq, A.: Algorithmic decision making and the cost of fairness. In: Proceedings of the 23rd ACM SIGKDD International Conference on Knowledge Discovery and Data Mining, pp. 797–806. ACM (2017)
13. Courtland, R.: Bias detectives: the researchers striving to make algorithms fair. Nature **558**(7710), 357–357 (2018)
14. Darwiche, A.: Human-level intelligence or animal-like abilities? arXiv preprint arXiv:1707.04327 (2017)

---

[20] [25], p. 242.

15. DeKeseredy, W.S., Donnermeyer, J.F.: Contemporary issues in left realism. Int. J. Crime Justice Soc. Democracy **5**(3), 12–26 (2016)
16. Deng, L.: A tutorial survey of architectures, algorithms, and applications for deep learning. APSIPA Trans. Signal Inf. Process. **3** (2014)
17. Ensign, D., Friedler, S.A., Neville, S., Scheidegger, C., Venkatasubramanian, S.: Runaway feedback loops in predictive policing. arXiv preprint arXiv:1706.09847 (2017)
18. Floridi, L.: The Philosophy of Information. OUP Oxford (2013). https://books. google.it/books?id=l8RoAgAAQBAJ
19. Floridi, L.: Infraethics-on the conditions of possibility of morality. Philos. Technol. **30**(4), 391–394 (2017)
20. Hinton, G., et al.: Deep neural networks for acoustic modeling in speech recognition. IEEE Signal Process. Mag. **29**, 82–97 (2012)
21. Kleinberg, J., Lakkaraju, H., Leskovec, J., Ludwig, J., Mullainathan, S.: Human decisions and machine predictions. Q. J. Econ. **133**(1), 237–293 (2017)
22. Kleinberg, J., Mullainathan, S., Raghavan, M.: Inherent trade-offs in the fair determination of risk scores. arXiv preprint arXiv:1609.05807 (2016)
23. Krizhevsky, A., Sutskever, I., Hinton, G.E.: Imagenet classification with deep convolutional neural networks. In: Advances in Neural Information Processing Systems, pp. 1097–1105 (2012)
24. Lea, J.: Left realism: a radical criminology for the current crisis. Int. J. Crime Justice Soc. Democracy **5**(3), 53–65 (2016)
25. Lea, J., Young, J., et al.: What is to be done about law and order? (1984)
26. Lipton, Z.C.: The mythos of model interpretability. arXiv preprint arXiv:1606.03490 (2016)
27. Liu, L.T., Dean, S., Rolf, E., Simchowitz, M., Hardt, M.: Delayed impact of fair machine learning. arXiv preprint arXiv:1803.04383 (2018)
28. MacKay, D.J.: Information Theory, Inference, and Learning Algorithms. Cambridge University Press, Cambridge (2003)
29. Murdoch, W.J., Singh, C., Kumbier, K., Abbasi-Asl, R., Yu, B.: Interpretable machine learning: definitions, methods, and applications. arXiv preprint arXiv:1901.04592 (2019)
30. Pan, S.J., Yang, Q.: A survey on transfer learning. IEEE Trans. Knowl. Data Eng. **22**(10), 1345–1359 (2009)
31. Pearl, J.: Causality. Cambridge University Press, Cambridge (2009)
32. Peters, J., Janzing, D., Schölkopf, B.: Elements of Causal Inference: Foundations and Learning Algorithms. MIT Press, Cambridge (2017)
33. Richardson, R., Schultz, J., Crawford, K.: Dirty data, bad predictions: how civil rights violations impact police data, predictive policing systems, and justice. New York University Law Review Online (2019, forthcoming)
34. Wick, M., Tristan, J.B., et al.: Unlocking fairness: a trade-off revisited. In: Advances in Neural Information Processing Systems, pp. 8780–8789 (2019)
35. Wu, Y., Zhang, L., Wu, X., Tong, H.: PC-fairness: a unified framework for measuring causality-based fairness. In: Advances in Neural Information Processing Systems, pp. 3399–3409 (2019)
36. Zliobaite, I.: A survey on measuring indirect discrimination in machine learning. arXiv preprint arXiv:1511.00148 (2015)

Workshop on Parallel, Distributed and Federated Learning (PDFL 2020)

Preface

Parallel, Distributed, and Federated Learning

Many of today's parallel machine learning algorithms were developed for tightly coupled systems like computing clusters or clouds. However, data volumes generated from machine-to-machine or human-to-machine interaction, such as mobile phones or autonomous vehicles, surpass the amount that can conveniently be centralized. Thus, traditional cloud computing approaches are rendered infeasible. In order to scale machine learning to these amounts of data, computation needs to be pushed towards the edge, that is, towards the data generating devices. By learning models directly on the data sources - which often have computation power of their own, for example, mobile phones, smart sensors and tablets - network communication is reduced by orders of magnitude. Moreover, it facilitates obtaining a global model without centralizing privacy-sensitive data. This novel form of parallel, distributed, and federated machine learning has gained substantial interest in recent years, both from researchers and practitioners, and may allow for disruptive changes in areas such as smart assistants, machine learning on medical or industrial data, and autonomous driving.

The workshop on Parallel, Distributed, and Federated Learning (PDFL'20) was held online in conjunction with ECML PKDD. It is the third edition of the successful DMLE workshop series, but was renamed to broaden the scope and integrate novel directions in the field.

The accepted papers presented interesting novel aspects of distributed and federated machine learning, in particular on event detection via blockchains and resource-constrained and energy-efficient distributed learning. We want to thank the authors for their valuable contributions, great presentations, and lively and fruitful discussions. We would also like to thank the PDFL'20 program committee, whose members made the workshop possible with their rigorous and timely reviews. Finally, we would like to thank ECML PKDD for hosting the workshop and the workshop chairs, Myra Spiliopoulou and Willem Waegeman for their valuable support.

Organization

PDFL'20 Chairs

Linara Adilova   Fraunhofer IAIS
Michael Kamp   Monash University
Yamuna Krishnamurthy   Royal Holloway University of London

Program Committee

Stefan Wrobel   Fraunhofer IAIS
Katharina Morik   TU Dortmund
Tamas Horvath   University of Bonn
Jochen Garke   Fraunhofer SCAI
Mario Boley   Monash University
Christian Bauckhage   Fraunhofer IAIS
Janis Keuper   HS Offenburg
Mark Jelasity   University of Szeged
Dino Oglic   King's College London
Henning Petzka   Lund University
Michael Mock   Fraunhofer IAIS
Daniel Paurat   Deutsche Telekom Technik
Xiaoxiao Li   Yale University
Sven Giesselbach   Fraunhofer IAIS
Tim Wirtz   Fraunhofer IAIS
Pascal Welke   University of Bonn
Nico Piatkowski   Fraunhofer IAIS
Rafet Sifa   Fraunhofer IAIS
Dorina Weichert   Fraunhofer IAIS

Knowledge Discovery on Blockchains: Challenges and Opportunities for Distributed Event Detection Under Constraints

Cedric Sanders[1] and Thomas Liebig[1,2,3(✉)]

[1] Artificial Intelligence Unit, TU Dortmund, 44269 Dortmund, Germany
{cedric.sanders,thomas.liebig}@tu-dortmund.de
[2] Artificial Intelligence Unit, Universtiy of Nicosia, PO 24005, 1700 Nicosia, Cyprus
[3] Artificial Intelligence Unit, Materna Information and Communications SE,
44141 Dortmund, Germany
http://www-ai.cs.uni-dortmund.de/index.html

Abstract. We study the applicability of blockchain technology for distributed event detection under resource constraints. Therefore we provide a test-suite with several promising consensus methods (Proof-of-Work, Proof-of-Stake, Distributed Proof-of-Work, and Practical Proof-of-Kernel-Work).

This is the first work analyzing the communication costs of blockchain consensus methods for knowledge discovery tasks in resource constraint devices. The experiments reveal that our proposed implementations of Distributed Proof-of-Work and Practical Proof-of-Kernel-Work provide a benefit over Proof-of-Work in CPU usage and communication costs. The tests show further that in cases of low data rates, where latencies by mining do not cause harm proposed blockchain implementations could be integrated. However, usage of blockchain requires data broadcasts, which leads to communication overhead as well as memory requirements based on the address list.

Keywords: Blockchain · Consensus method · Ubiquitous knowledge discovery

1 Introduction

The current shift towards edge analysis and distributed knowledge discovery [8,11] is mostly driven by making use of large computation clusters and the internet of things. Indeed, applications that benefit from decentralized data management and analysis are, amongst others, sensor networks and mobility

Supported by German Research Foundation DFG under grant SFB 876 "Providing Information by Resource-Constrained Data Analysis" project B4 "Analysis and Communication for Dynamic Traffic Prognosis".

I. Koprinska et al. (Eds.): ECML PKDD 2020 Workshops, CCIS 1323, pp. 113–128, 2020.
https://doi.org/10.1007/978-3-030-65965-3_8

based services. In both scenarios, a potentially large number of heterogeneous devices is connected and forms a system. The differences amongst the devices could be vast: computation power, memory limitations, energy consumption, etc. Besides, possible applications pose varying requirements for data management. While security is more critical in case of processing vulnerable private information (e.g., medical data), memory consumption or power consumption could be more essential for other application domains.

Once the sensor data in the mesh should be analyzed, one faces the challenge of how to store the data distributedly and how to perform the analysis on this data. This also incorporates the problem of keeping the information amongst the devices consistent. A possible technology that might provide a solution to these issues is the blockchain. These are sequences of unbreakably linked tuples, so-called blocks, of data, transactions, timestamp and the hash value of the ancestral block. A consensus method is required to extend such a blockchain; this is a procedure how multiple network participants find a new block which is added to the blockchain. Existing consensus methods have requirements in computation costs that ubiquitous devices hardly meet.

Thus, the paper-at-hand fits under the topic of ubiquitous knowledge discovery [13]. Which connects current advances of data mining and machine learning with the latest developments in internet-of-things and mobile, distributed systems of heterogeneous devices. This work, therefore, aims at answering the question, whether blockchains are a technical-ready method to process data in distributed heterogeneous networks. We will examine various consensus methods. With well-suited experiments, figures are provided which assist in assessing the general utility of the different blockchain technologies. This raises the following questions:

– How should a consensus method operate that meets requirements of cpu usage, memory usage and power consumption originating from a decentralized usage?
– Which drawbacks make current consensus method implacable? and How could they be tackled?
– Which challenges and requirements remain after analysis of the consensus methods?

Many domains for decentralized knowledge discovery could be imagined. Especially citizen science projects, where citizens build sensors and voluntary collect data poses opportunities to distributed immutable knowledge extraction without any centralized coordinator. As a blockchain does not alter the data nor restrict access, the analysis results will not differ from a knowledge discovery in databases [5] or streaming method [4]. However, different consensus methods are more suitable than others. To assess the methods and evaluate communication load, memory consumption, and CPU load, we carry out experiments using publicly available distributed sensor data from opensensemap[1]. It is a citizen science project (maintained by the University of Münster) and guides the direction

---

[1] https://opensensemap.org/.

for future applications. We use a state-of-the-art event monitoring method, geometric monitoring [19], which uses very few communication to monitor a global function. Thus, we propose a fully decentralized application of the previously coordinated geometric monitoring process. As another contribution, we are first to implement and evaluate the initially vague proposal of Distributed Proof-of-Work [2]. Thus, we borrow some concepts from the Practical Proof-of-Kernel Work. The latter is included in our software library and (in contrast to previously proprietary implementation) for the first time made available for open public development[2].

The following second section of the paper presents different works that are related to the presented topic. It is followed by a general introduction of the functionality of a blockchain. The fourth section describes different approaches for achieving consensus in a blockchain and analyzes them by evaluating their advantages and disadvantages. After understanding the different methods it is time to put them to the test in the form of an experiment, which will be evaluated in the fifth section. This evaluation is followed by the last section containing the conclusion of the paper.

2   Related Work

While the field of ubiquitous knowledge discovery is established [13,20] and nowadays receives much attention [8,11] not only at major data mining and machine learning symposiums but with the spread of Industry 4.0 and internet-of-things also in application domains, just a few works focus on the chances a decentralized immutable storage of data could have for knowledge discovery and information retrieval. One famous exception is the application with health care data [7], which focuses on automated distributed monitoring of patients.

Another highlight was the recent initial coin offering of a machine learning blockchain [3]. The authors offered a market space for algorithms and data, based on smart contracts, but it lacked balancing the workload with a smart consensus method. In the following we briefly describe how a blockchain operates.

3   Blockchain Fundamentals

In the following, we give a brief introduction to the blockchain technology. Hash functions will play an important role in the next sections. Thus it is important to recall that those are one-way functions which are easy to compute but hard to reverse. A common choice for such a hash function is SHA256 [18]. This hash function is a combination of bitwise logical functions (AND, OR, XOR) and shifts (LSHIFTS, RSHIFTS), for the details, we refer the interested reader to the secure hash standard definition in [18]. The bitwise manipulation is part of the basic instruction set of most computer chips nowadays, this speeds computation

---

[2] Our sources and link to the data are available at https://bitbucket.org/cedric_sanders/abschlussarbeit/src/master/.

up. Another important property of these hash functions is to map different input most likely to different output[3].

Blockchains first gained attention with the publication of the white paper "Bitcoin: A Peer-to-Peer Electronic Cash System" of Satoshi Nakamoto [16]. The blockchain is described as a data structure which consists of smaller elements, the so-called blocks. A block comprises of

1. data[4]: contains the actual observations (e.g., transactions or sensor readings),
2. timestamp: is used to define a temporal order on blocks,
3. hash: hash value of the previous block.

Every block contains the hash of the previous block, which in turn holds the hash of its predecessor. In case one of the old blocks is modified it is simple to recognize in future blocks as the hash value will not fit the one stored previously. To use this data structure in a decentralized network, a consensus method has to be added.

4   Consensus Methods

The consensus is an essential part of distributed systems. With blockchains, consensus methods are the class of algorithms that describe how multiple parties find consent on blocks and which novel blocks are added to the chain. Nakamoto describes in his work [16] Proof-of-Work, which is still in use nowadays in Bitcoin, as one of these methods. In the meantime a bunch of new methods was introduced, for example, Proof-of-Burn [17], Proof-of-Luck [15], Proof-of-Stake [10], and Proof-of-Authority. Ethereum (a distributed platform empowering developers to develop blockchains on existing infrastructure) uses a slightly modified version of Proof-of-Work that may cope with large memory requirements of the participating devices [1,21].

A recent development with the potential to solve the current problem is the Distributed Proof-of-Work (vaguely proposed in [2]) and Practical Proof-of-Kernel-Work of Xain [12].

Cicada [2] is a group of programmers that suggest a decentralized democratic system based on unique human identifiers. Their vaguely proposed consensus method, however, has some strong points. In the paper at hand, we are the first implementing and analyzing this consensus method.

The origin of Xain [12] is a group of British scientist with a background in machine learning. The primary focus is the improvement of blockchains by online adjusting block mining difficulties using reinforcement learning. Their distributed method to grant temporary access to physical doors was successfully implemented in vehicular prototypes.

---

[3] We are aware that by reduction of dimensionality collisions must occur, but as the hash function is hard to reverse also the collisions are hard to find.
[4] Due to the strong connection to cryptocurrencies often named transactions.

4.1   Proof-of-Work

As described beforehand, Proof-of-Work (compare Algorithm 1.1) is the original concept for consensus on a blockchain, introduced in [16]. The basic idea is that a party has to gain the right to publish a novel block. This is done by proving that he spent work in terms of computational power for the generation of the block. The proof is enabled by requiring the answer to a complex problem for publishing a block. Usually, a so-called nonce has to be found, which in combination with the new block has a hash value ending on a specific sequence. By changing the length of this predefined sequence, the hardness of the proof could be adjusted.

As no party knows in advance which party will add a new block, data needs to be broadcasted to all parties. Parties that aim for publication of a block have to collect the data and combine them in a novel block. Afterward, they could start to find a nonce such that the necessary hash condition is met. Whoever performs these steps fastest may publish the new block.

It might happen that multiple parties mine the block at the same time, this causes the creation of branches (alternative versions of the blockchain). Proof-of-Work tolerates them for a couple of iterations until one of the branches is longer than its alternatives. As a longer branch represents more computational power, it will be considered correct and alternatives will be deleted.

Blockchain participants do not need to participate in the mining process. As some incentive, there is a reward in crypto-currencies per block and processing fees for transactions.

Input : Last Block
Output : New Block
1: $nonce \leftarrow 0$
2: **while** *proof* is not valid **do**
3:      $proof \leftarrow ProofofWork(Last Block, nonce)$
4:      $nonce \leftarrow nonce + 1$
5: **end while**
6: $RewardMiner()$
7: $CreateBlock(Last Block, proof)$

Algorithm 1.1: Mining with Proof-of-Work

Proof-of-Work is the oldest consensus method incorporated in this study. And since it is the most popular, it is used most often in literature. Thus, the following techniques were introduced to cope with its challenges. Proof-of-Work has been introduced to implement a decentralized cryptocurrency. Therefore, safety, decentralism, and resilience were the most critical aspects of the design.

In his paper, Nakamoto describes attack scenarios and clarifies that one party needs to be faster in adding blocks to the chain than all others to cause damage. At the same time, he estimates the probability an attacker could do this [16, 11. Calculations]. However, this safety has its cost. The blockchain is safe as long as a majority of the computation power is used for mining novel blocks.

This has several properties: The energy consumption of parties that aim for maintaining consistency is exceptionally high. From the very beginning till a possible shut down. This is a problem especially for potentially small or mobile devices which have limited energy budget. Another drawback is the distribution of computational power which is directly coupled with the integrity of the chain. The problem is often also called 51% problem, as any cooperative group of parties holding 51% of the computational power gains a higher impact on the system and attacks on the integrity get easier. In the blockchain, parties may join or leave the network at any time, without any inconsistencies (e.g., duplicate or missing data). Therefore data storage has some redundancy. So blockchains are excellent for applications where memory consumption does not matter, and a high resilience needs to be guaranteed.

The last point is the high communication cost with blockchains in general. The distributed storage blockchain requires lots of communication as broadcasts are necessary for transmission of transactions or data, for distribution of novel blocks, for finding the longest blockchain and resolving branches.

4.2 Proof-of-Stake

Proof-of-Stake (compare Algorithm 1.2) is a concept introduced by Sunny King and Scott Nadal, for the PPCoin [10]. It follows an entirely different approach which is stronger coupled with the application as currency. A party does not need to prove an amount of workload but has to prove it owns a certain amount of the currency. For this reason, Proof-of-Stake uses coinage. Coinage describes the ownership of coins over a certain period. If a party owns 100 coins over 10 time slices, he holds coinage 1.000. The coinage sinks if coins are spent. If a party wants to add a block, it transfers itself coins to reduce its coinage. By this transaction, it gains as a reward a simplification of the mining problem.

Input : Last Block
Output : New Block
1: *coinage* ← *CalculateCoinAge()*
2: *investment* ← *Random(coinage)*
3: *MakeInvestment()*
4: *nonce* ← 0
5: **while** *proof* is not valid **do**
6:    *proof* ← *ProofofWork(Last Block, nonce, investment)*
7:    *nonce* ← *nonce* + 1
8: **end while**
9: *RewardMiner()*
10: *CreateBlock(Last Block, proof)*

Algorithm 1.2: Mining with Proof-of-Stake

Proof-of-Stake requires any form of ownership to invest it for gaining impact on the blockchain. This reduces its applicability in practice. For sure application domains could be extended with such a concept (as done with Ether tokens in Ethereum). But if the consensus method does not provide a considerable benefit over the other methods this workaround should be scrutinized.

Implementing this method raises new questions. For example, an investment strategy of tokens for miners to spend their tokens. This provides a vast potential for ubiquitous devices with limited computational power. They could take high investments at a low frequency to optimally use their limited computation capabilities.

4.3 Distributed Proof-of-Work

The novel consensus method of cicada is called distributed-Proof-of-Work and bases on Proof-of-Work [2]. It structures the mining process into small contests called mining races. In contrast to Proof-of-Work, access to mining is limited. For each mining race, a set of participants is randomly selected. Using, Distributed Proof-of-Work any party needs to take part in mining, making them eligible for mining races.

Distributed Proof-of-Work restricts access to the original Proof-of-Work to overcome some of its problems. However, the description of the authors is somewhat vague; for example the selection of the miners which causes difficulties for implementation. In the following section on Practical Proof-of-Kernel Work verifiable random functions (VRF) are applied for that purpose. Thus we borrow the concept also for Distributed Proof-of-Work. VRF is a concept to execute a random function, i.e., a function with an unknown result while the processor is capable of proving to other parties that the obtained value is correct. Variable random functions could be constructed with different cryptographic methods. One example is the approach by Goldberg [6] using elliptic curve cryptography. The basic procedure follows these steps [14]:

- A so-called generator provides public pk and private keys sk to each party.
- Given its private key sk and a publicly known seed x a party is capable of computing a random function f which calculates a proof p.
- Every other party could now verify that the proof is the result of the random function given p, pk and x.

```
Input : Last Block
Output : New Block
1:  selected ← False
2:  if enough nodes selected then
3:    if selected then
4:      nonce ← 0
5:      while proof is not valid do
6:        proof ← ProofofWork(Last Block, nonce)
7:        nonce ← nonce + 1
8:      end while
9:      RewardMiner()
10:     CreateBlock(Last Block, proof)
11:   else
12:     Wait for next mining race
13:   end if
14: else
15:   selected ← VerifiableRandomFunction(seed, difficulty)
16:   if selected then
17:     Let the other nodes verify the Verifiable Random Function
18:   else
19:     Wait for other nodes to do the lottery
20:     if not enough nodes selected then
21:       Reduce the difficulty of being selected
22:     end if
23:   end if
24: end if
```

Algorithm 1.3: Mining with Distributed Proof-of-Work

4.4   Practical Proof-of-Kernel-Work

Practical Proof-of-Kernel-Work (compare Algorithm 1.4) also bases on Proof-of-Work but includes access control. The used methods are more complex than those of Distributed Proof-of-Work. Three mechanisms control participation in Proof-of-Work:

- A whitelist that lists trustable parties.
- A set of dynamic rules. For example the creator of the last block could be banned for the next three iterations.
- A random selection of parties from the whitelist.

This latter selection routine uses a continuous seed that is embedded in the blockchain. This seed may be used by the parties to perform a lottery based on variable random functions. The selection process not only guarantees a random selection but also prevents others from obtaining any knowledge on the selected parties. This prevents an attacker from performing targetted attacks on parties. The chosen parties, in turn, can prove that they have been selected.

The access control reduces energy consumption and weakens the 51% problem described above (compare Sect. 4.1) as neither computation nor ownership has an impact on future selection. Practical Proof-of-Kernel-Work reduces the likelihood of branches as fewer parties participates in mining. Storing a whitelist on the blockchain holds potential problems for its scalability. In large networks, this would cause huge memory consumption which restricted memory devices may have issues with. Also, the computation of a verifiable random function possesses challenges to computationally weak devices.

5   Experiments

Especially for the two novel and promising consensus methods Distributed Proof-of-Work and Practical Proof-of-Kernel-Work (compare Sects. 4.3 and 4.4) no implementation was available and description was rather vague. Thus, we contribute implementations of these consensus methods. With the focus on potentially heterogeneous devices and latest developments of micropython and circuitpython as rapid prototyping 'operating systems' for ultra-low power devices, we picked python as a programming language[5]. To obtain comparable results also the two established consensus methods Proof-of-Work and Proof-of-Stake are part of our library. The use of a blockchain could expect no improvement or drawback, thus we will not report on the performance of geometric monitoring, but on our measures of interest CPU load, memory usage, through-put and communication costs.

In the following, we briefly describe the problems we faced. The analysis presumes random access to the data. Thus the choice of the algorithm is not crucial for a comparison. We implemented nodes that are processed on a system and hold essential functions:

- running transactions,
- mining blocks,
- syncing the blockchain,
- reading a stream of observations from a file and inserting observations to the blockchain,
- logging of metrics for the analysis we present next,
- running a local model for data analysis.

The overall goal is to keep different methods comparable. Thus we did not focus on implementing individual cases but a plain structure of the methods, as described in Sect. 4.

All our implementations consist of three building blocks 1) a RESTful server that provides an API to other parties, 2) a part for mining and maintenance of the blockchain and 3) a part that performs the actual calculations. For the basic Proof-of-Work, the difficulty was set to 6 leading zeros, which corresponds to 40 seconds block time and fits quite well to the sampling interval of the

---

[5] The resulting sources are made publicly available at https://bitbucket.org/ cedric_sanders/blockchain-experiments/src/master/.

Input : Last Block
Output : New Block
1: *selected* ← *False*
2: **if** enough nodes selected **then**
3:     **if** selected **then**
4:         *nonce* ← 0
5:         **while** *proof* is not valid **do**
6:             *proof* ← *ProofofWork(Last Block, nonce)*
7:             *nonce* ← *nonce* + 1
8:         **end while**
9:         *RewardMiner()*
10:         *CreateBlock(Last Block, proof)*
11:     **else**
12:         Wait for next mining race
13:     **end if**
14: **else**
15:     **if** Node on Whitelist **then**
16:         **if** *CheckRuleset()* **then**
17:             **if** *VerifiableRandomFunction(seed, difficulty)* **then**
18:                 *selected* ← *True*
19:             **end if**
20:         **end if**
21:     **end if**
22:     **if** selected **then**
23:         Let the other nodes verify the Selection
24:     **else**
25:         Wait for other nodes to do the lottery
26:         **if** not enough nodes selected **then**
27:             Reduce the difficulty of being selected
28:         **end if**
29:     **end if**
30: **end if**

Algorithm 1.4: Mining with Practical Proof-of-Kernel-Work

opensensemap data[6] we use. The practical Proof-of-Kernel-Work requires the inclusion of the verifiable random functions. We applied the approach of [6, Definition 4.1] for the lottery. Syncing the needed seed amongst the parties, however, caused some unexpected problems as the operations are not atomic and there might already be consensus for a new seed once a node finished mining, we overcame this chance of asynchronicity by relaxing the verification. Thus, we allow also ancestor and of current seed as valid. Another important decision is when the results of the lottery are broadcasted. If the set of miners is published directly (before the actual creation of the block) the other parties could send their data or transactions directly to the selected ones. An alternative method would be to reveal the decision of the lottery after mining of the new block,

---

[6] https://opensensemap.org/.

this requires a broadcast of all observations. The latter techniques would be more secure. It prevents targetted attacks on single nodes. But, as we want to see the potential benefit of the consensus method, We decided for the first option which reduces energy consumption and communication cost. Besides, we added a white list that keeps a record of the trustable devices. As soon as a malicious party sends fraudulent blocks to the network, it will be removed from the whitelist. Distributed Proof-of-Work operates similar as Practical Proof-of-Kernel-Work, but the time and memory consuming additions are removed. This includes dynamic rules and whitelist.

To compare the consensus methods on their feasibility. We need to test it with a distributed data analysis task. Usage of the blockchain does not alter the data, neither do the considered consensus methods. A distributed analysis, therefore, produces the same result as without using a blockchain. The application we are aiming for is a distributed monitoring task with multiple sensors. We perform analysis with the well suited geometric monitoring approach [19] that reduces communication costs and bases on a simple concept. Recent improvements were published in [9,11]. The primary task is that a global threshold function should be monitored without communicating every single data item. The communication is reduced by introducing local threshold conditions which need to be raised to start communication with the coordinator. The coordinator checks the global function and updates the threshold parameters of the parties. Challenge for the application of geometric monitoring is the design of the local conditions. The requirements to local conditions are:

– Correctness: As long as all local conditions are below the threshold, also the global threshold is not reached.
– Communication efficiency: The number of necessary communications is minimal.
– Efficient computation: the calculation required to test local conditions is low.

As recently shown in [11], finding these local threshold functions is more straightforward when the global function is convex. Then it is sufficient to find a close upper bound for the global function.

In combination with blockchain, the geometric monitoring approach could be applied coordinator free, fully decentralized. Every node has the required information to test global functions.

As described above (compare Sect. 1), we perform the tests using data from opensensemap[7]. This is a network of citizen sensor data consisting of 3909 so-called senseboxes. In general, they are situated around the globe, but mostly they are in Germany. The attributes of each sensor records differ much. While just a few sensors record special features as gamma radiation, temperature and wind speeds are prevalent attributes. To perform tests with geometric monitoring, in

---

[7] https://opensensemap.org/.

this study, we decided for the temperature feature[8]. Setting a global threshold on the average temperature is easy.

The experiments were conducted on a cluster of multi-core computers each running a process of a node. We tested for 5, 10, 20 and 40 participants. To validate even larger networks future implementation could make use of MPI or other interprocess communication protocols. Direct test in a distributed sensor mesh is another option but in a fully distributed coordinator free setup analysis of the experiment also requires centralization and eventually clock synchronization.

We analyze four aspects: communication, mining, memory and CPU usage.

The communication analysis is split into the types, data request, transaction received, coordinating blocks and transactions.

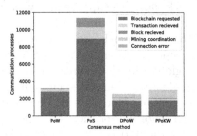

Fig. 1. Average communicationcost for 5 nodes over 1 h

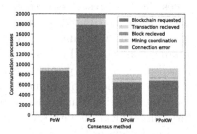

Fig. 2. Average communicationcost for 10 nodes over 1 h

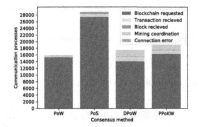

Fig. 3. Average communicationcost for 20 nodes over 1 h

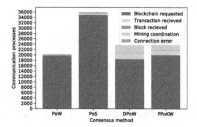

Fig. 4. Average communicationcost for 40 nodes over 1 h

The Figs. 1, 2, 3 and 4 reveal that Proof-of-Stake requires more communication than the other methods. One reason is additional transactions to communicate the coinage. The additional checks of the coinage cause more communication rounds on the blockchain. Most communication originates from the access on the blockchain data. The transmission of transactions and blocks are neglectable.

---

[8] The data we apply the method to is obtained in the interval from March, 23rd 2019 till March, 24th 2019, in the WGS 84 box [5.98865807458, 47.3024876979, 15.0169958839, 54.983104153].

Next, we test the temporal performance of the blockchain. How much time is required for block generation and whats the block through-put? In Figs. 5, 6, 7 and 8 Proof-of-Stake stands out again. The time between consecutive mining Figs. 9, 10, 11 and 12 processes of one party could become quite high. Therefore broadcast of the transactions is important; otherwise, they would be available with a huge delay.

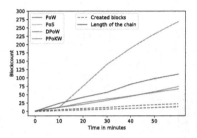

Fig. 5. Average created/total blocks for 5 nodes over 1 h

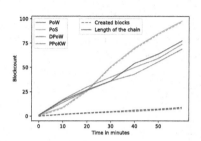

Fig. 6. Average created/total blocks for 10 nodes over 1 h

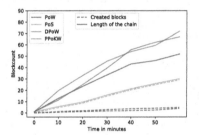

Fig. 7. Average created/total blocks for 20 nodes over 1 h

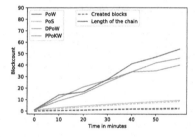

Fig. 8. Average created/total blocks for 40 nodes over 1 h

Next Figs. 13, 14, 15 and 16 depict the memory consumption of the methods. All four methods require a similar amount of memory. Proof-of-Work a little bit less, whereas the two methods with access control need a bit more memory.

The CPU usage is depicted in Figs. 17, 18, 19 and 20. Proof-of-Work requires a high percentage of the calculation power continuously. The two methods Practical Proof-of-Kernel-Work and Distributed Kernel-Work distribute the computation load more amongst the partners, and thus each CPU is used less.

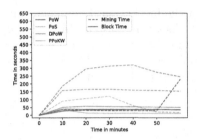

Fig. 9. Average mining time/block time for 5 nodes over 1 h

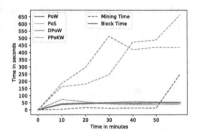

Fig. 10. Average mining time/block time for 10 nodes over 1 h

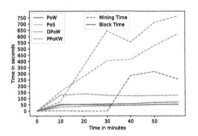

Fig. 11. Average mining time/block time for 20 nodes over 1 h

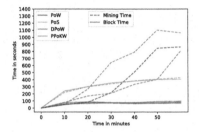

Fig. 12. Average mining time/block time for 40 nodes over 1 h

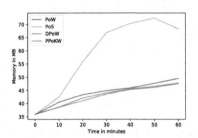

Fig. 13. Average memory usage for 5 nodes over 1 h

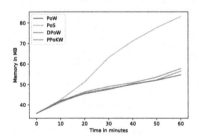

Fig. 14. Average memory usage for 10 nodes over 1 h

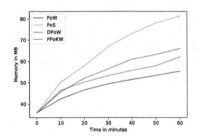

Fig. 15. Average memory usage for 20 nodes over 1 h

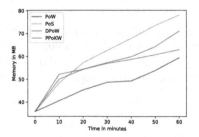

Fig. 16. Average memory usage for 40 nodes over 1 h

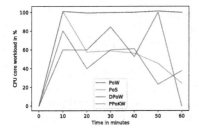

Fig. 17. Average CPU-workload for 5 nodes over 1 h

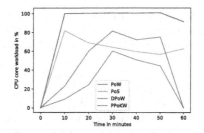

Fig. 18. Average CPU-workload for 10 nodes over 1 h

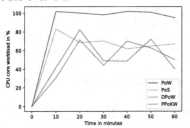

Fig. 19. Average CPU-workload for 20 nodes over 1 h

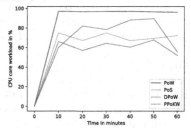

Fig. 20. Average CPU-workload for 40 nodes over 1 h

6   Conclusion and Future Works

The paper-at-hand assessed the suitability of blockchains to decentralized data processing scenarios. After we discussed promising consensus methods, we performed an event monitoring task. Thus we used a fully decentralized geometric monitoring. The analysis reveals that in cases of low data rates, where latencies by mining do not cause harm the methods could be integrated. A major drawback of blockchain is the requirement for broadcasts in the network. Besides communication costs, it also causes a blockchain on restricted memory parties to have a limit of participants given by the address list of the parties. CPU usage does not cause a problem anymore as Distributed Proof-of-Work and Practical Proof-of-Kernel-Work overcome shortcomings of Proof-of-Work.

The current analysis reveals that Proof-of-Work and Proof-of-Stake are not well suited for resource-constrained devices. In future work, the hardness and the verifiable random functions can be studied more. Also, investment strategies of coinage in combination with the restrictive consensus methods are promising.

References

1. Buterin, V., et al.: A next-generation smart contract and decentralized application platform. White paper (2014)
2. CICADA: Cicada: a distributed direct democracy and decentralized appilcation platform. iamcicada.com/whitepaper/. Accessed 30 Mar 2019

3. DML: Decentralized machine learning. https://decentralizedml.com/DML_whitepaper_31Dec_17.pdf. Accessed 02 Apr 2019
4. Domingos, P., Hulten, G.: Mining high-speed data streams. In: KDD, vol. 2, p. 4 (2000)
5. Fayyad, U., Piatetsky-Shapiro, G., Smyth, P.: From data mining to knowledge discovery in databases. AI Mag. **17**(3), 37 (1996)
6. Goldberg, S., Naor, M., Papadopoulos, D., Reyzin, L.: Nsec5 from elliptic curves: Provably preventing dnssec zone enumeration with shorter responses. IACR Cryptology ePrint Archive **2016**, 83 (2016)
7. Griggs, K.N., Ossipova, O., Kohlios, C.P., Baccarini, A.N., Howson, E.A., Hayajneh, T.: Healthcare blockchain system using smart contracts for secure automated remote patient monitoring. J. Med. Syst. **42**(7), 130 (2018)
8. Kamp, M., et al.: Efficient decentralized deep learning by dynamic model averaging. In: Berlingerio, M., Bonchi, F., Gärtner, T., Hurley, N., Ifrim, G. (eds.) ECML PKDD 2018. LNCS (LNAI), vol. 11051, pp. 393–409. Springer, Cham (2019). https://doi.org/10.1007/978-3-030-10925-7_24
9. Keren, D., et al.: Geometric monitoring of heterogeneous streams. IEEE Trans. Knowl. Data Eng. **26**(8), 1890–1903 (2014)
10. King, S., Nadal, S.: Ppcoin: peer-to-peer crypto-currency with proof-of-stake. Self-published paper, 19 August 2012
11. Lazerson, A., Keren, D., Schuster, A.: Lightweight monitoring of distributed streams. ACM Trans. Database Syst. (TODS) **43**(2), 9 (2018)
12. Lundbæk, L.N., Beutel, D.J., Huth, M., Kirk, L.: Practical proof of kernel work & distributed adaptiveness, manuscript Version 1.2 (2018)
13. May, M., Berendt, B., Cornue, A., et al.: Research challenges in ubiquitous knowledge discovery. In: Next Generation of Data Mining, pp. 154–173. Chapman and Hall/CRC (2008)
14. Micali, S., Rabin, M., Vadhan, S.: Verifiable random functions. In: 1999 40th Annual Symposium on Foundations of Computer Science, pp. 120–130. IEEE (1999)
15. Milutinovic, M., He, W., Wu, H., Kanwal, M.: Proof of luck: an efficient blockchain consensus protocol. In: Proceedings of the 1st Workshop on System Software for Trusted Execution, p. 2. ACM (2016)
16. Nakamoto, S.: Bitcoin: a peer-to-peer electronic cash system (2008)
17. P4Titan: Slimcoin: a peer-to-peer crypto-currency with proof-of-burn (2014)
18. PUB, F.: Secure hash standard (SHS). FIPS PUB **180**(4) (2012)
19. Sharfman, I., Schuster, A., Keren, D.: A geometric approach to monitoring threshold functions over distributed data streams. ACM Trans. Database Syst. (TODS) **32**(4), 23 (2007)
20. Wolff, R., Bhaduri, K., Kargupta, H.: A generic local algorithm for mining data streams in large distributed systems. IEEE Trans. Knowl. Data Eng. **21**(4), 465–478 (2009)
21. Wood, G.: Ethereum: a secure decentralised generalised transaction ledger. Ethereum Proj. Yellow Paper **151**, 1–32 (2014)

Resource-Constrained On-Device Learning by Dynamic Averaging

Lukas Heppe[1(✉)], Michael Kamp[2], Linara Adilova[3,4], Danny Heinrich[1],
Nico Piatkowski[3], and Katharina Morik[1]

[1] TU Dortmund, Dortmund, Germany
{lukas.heppe,danny.heinrich,katharina.morik}@tu-dortmund.de
[2] Monash University, Melbourne, Australia
michael.kamp@monash.edu
[3] Fraunhofer IAIS, Sankt Augustin, Germany
{linara.adilova,nico.piatkowski}@iais.fraunhofer.de
[4] Fraunhofer Center for Machine Learning, Sankt Augustin, Germany

Abstract. The communication between data-generating devices is partially responsible for a growing portion of the world's power consumption. Thus reducing communication is vital, both, from an economical and an ecological perspective. For machine learning, on-device learning avoids sending raw data, which can reduce communication substantially. Furthermore, not centralizing the data protects privacy-sensitive data. However, most learning algorithms require hardware with high computation power and thus high energy consumption. In contrast, ultra-low-power processors, like FPGAs or micro-controllers, allow for energy-efficient learning of local models. Combined with communication-efficient distributed learning strategies, this reduces the overall energy consumption and enables applications that were yet impossible due to limited energy on local devices. The major challenge is then, that the low-power processors typically only have integer processing capabilities. This paper investigates an approach to communication-efficient on-device learning of integer exponential families that can be executed on low-power processors, is privacy-preserving, and effectively minimizes communication. The empirical evaluation shows that the approach can reach a model quality comparable to a centrally learned regular model with an order of magnitude less communication. Comparing the overall energy consumption, this reduces the required energy for solving the machine learning task by a significant amount.

1 Introduction

Today more and more data is generated by physically distributed sources, e.g., smartphones, sensors, and IoT devices. Performing machine learning on this data not only poses severe challenges on the bandwidth, on storing and processing it, but also requires enormous amounts of energy: currently, the world communicates around $20 \cdot 10^{10}$ GB per month [11] with a power consumption of around $0.3 \, \text{kWh/GB}$ [18], resulting in a total energy consumption of 6TWh per month. In comparison, the largest nuclear plant in the US, the R.E. Gina reactor in Arizona, generates around 0.39TWh per month [1], so more than 15 such reactors are

© Springer Nature Switzerland AG 2020
I. Koprinska et al. (Eds.): ECML PKDD 2020 Workshops, CCIS 1323, pp. 129–144, 2020.
https://doi.org/10.1007/978-3-030-65965-3_9

needed just to power the communication. With an estimated number of $5 \cdot 10^{10}$ connected devices by the end of 2020 [14], the amount of communication will grow substantially, with some of them (e.g., autonomous vehicles or airplanes) communicating up to 5GB per second [19]. Thus, machine learning on this data could become responsible for a large portion of the world's power consumption.

In order to reduce the communication load, models can be trained locally and only model parameters are centralized periodically [13] or dynamically [7,10]. However, this approach requires sufficient computation power at the local data sources - this is usually available on smartphones, but not necessarily on sensors or IoT devices. Most sensors or IoT devices could be fit with efficient, low-power processors which typically only have integer processing capabilities - no floating point unit. Recently, it was shown that learning exponential families can be performed on such devices using only integer and bit operations [17]. Scaling this learning to the internet of things requires to implement communication-efficient distributed learning on these devices, too.

This work proposes a resource- and communication-efficient distributed learning approach for exponential families that uses only integer and bit operations. The key idea is to only communicate between local devices if their model is sufficiently different from the global mean, implying that it has learned truly novel information. Hence, we adapt dynamic averaging [8] to require only integer operations. In this approach, each device checks a sufficient local condition and only communicates if it is violated. In case of a violation, model parameters are centralized and averaged into a joint model, which is redistributed to the devices. Setting the maximum allowed divergence between a model and the global mean allows users to the trade-off between communication-efficiency and joint model quality.

We theoretically analyze this approach and provide guarantees on the loss and bounds on the amount of communication. We show empirically that using resource-constrained dynamic averaging on integer exponential families allows to reach a model performance close to full floating point models and reduces the required communication substantially.

Related Work. Several works have been published, minimizing the resource-consumptions in federated learning environments. However, most publications already consider smartphones as resource-constrained environments, while we go one step further and focus on ultra-low-power hardware without access to floating-point-units. A similar work has been done by Piatkowski [15], who also considered resource-constrained family models for a distributed learning task. Albeit, the reduced resource-consumption is based on parameter-sparsification and one-shot averaging. Besides, the model aggregates reside in regular model space and thus cannot be applied on ultra-low-power hardware. Alternative methods, proposed by Wang et. al., focus on selecting a trade-off between global aggregation and local updates, while we follow a distinct approach based on dynamic conditions. A survey on federated learning concepts and the challenges can be found in [12].

2   Resource-Constrained Exponential Family Models

Probabilistic graphical models form a subset of machine learning and combine graph with probability theory [20]. They are used to model complex probability distributions, which can be utilized to solve a variety of tasks. The following subsections will introduce the notation and background of graphical models in general as well as highlight the specifics for resource-constrained models.

2.1   Undirected Graphical Models

Let $G = (V, E)$ be an undirected graph with $|V| = n$ vertices which are connected by the edges $(s, t) \in E \subseteq V \times V$. A clique $C \subseteq V$ is formed by some fully connected subset of the vertices: $\forall\, u, v \in C, u \neq v : (u, v) \in E$. The maximal cliques of the graph are those, who are not contained in any larger clique. We denote the set of all maximal cliques by $\mathcal{C}$. In addition, let $\boldsymbol{X} = (\boldsymbol{X}_1, \ldots, \boldsymbol{X}_p)^\top$ denote some random vector where each variable $\boldsymbol{X}_i$ can take values of a discrete set $\mathcal{X}_i$. In turn the vector can take values of the cross product from each variable $\mathcal{X} = \mathcal{X}_1 \times \ldots \times \mathcal{X}_p$. Besides, we allow the indexing of $\boldsymbol{X}$ and $\mathcal{X}$ by subsets like cliques, e.g., $\boldsymbol{X}_C$ and $\mathcal{X}_C$. Specific assignments $\boldsymbol{x}_C$ to those random variables are denoted by bold lowercase letters.

An undirected graphical model represents the joint distribution of $\boldsymbol{X}$ by exploiting conditional independencies between the variables. We model those using a graph, if $(s, t) \notin E \implies \boldsymbol{X}_s \perp\!\!\!\perp \boldsymbol{X}_t \mid \boldsymbol{X} \setminus \{\boldsymbol{X}_s, \boldsymbol{X}_t\}$. Thus, the graph encodes the conditional independence structure of the distribution. If we introduce potential functions $\psi_C : \mathcal{X}_C \mapsto \mathbb{R}_+$ for each maximal clique of the graph, then according to the Hammersley-Clifford-theorem [5] the density factorizes as follows

$$\mathbb{P}(\boldsymbol{X} = \boldsymbol{x}) = \frac{1}{Z} \prod_{C \in \mathcal{C}} \psi_C(\boldsymbol{x}_C), \tag{1}$$

where $Z = \sum_{\boldsymbol{x} \in \mathcal{X}} \prod_{C \in \mathcal{C}} \psi_C(\boldsymbol{x}_C)$ acts as normalizer in order to ensure that $\mathbb{P}$ is a valid probability distribution. By utilizing probabilistic inference algorithms like belief propagation, this distribution can be used for a variety of tasks like querying marginal- or conditional probabilities as well as computing (conditional) maximum-a-posteriori estimates, which, in turn, can be used for predictive tasks.

2.2   From Regular to Resource-Constrained Models

Let $C \in \mathcal{C}$ be a maximal clique of G, $\boldsymbol{\theta}_C \in \mathbb{R}^{|\mathcal{X}_C|}$ a parameter vector and $\phi : \mathcal{X}_C \mapsto \{0, 1\}^{|\mathcal{X}_C|}$ some feature function or sufficient statistic, which maps assignments of the variables to one-hot-encoded vectors. By defining $\psi_C(\boldsymbol{x}_C) = \exp \langle \boldsymbol{\theta}_C, \phi_C(\boldsymbol{x}_C) \rangle$, concatenating all $\boldsymbol{\theta}_C$ in $\boldsymbol{\theta}$ as well as all ϕ_C in ϕ, the joint distribution can be represented as the canonical exponential family [20]

$$\mathbb{P}_{\boldsymbol{\theta}}(\boldsymbol{X} = \boldsymbol{x}) = \exp(\langle \boldsymbol{\theta}, \phi(\boldsymbol{x}) \rangle - A(\boldsymbol{\theta})), \tag{2}$$

with $A(\boldsymbol{\theta}) = \log Z(\boldsymbol{\theta})$, which contains many well known distributions like the gamma, normal, and exponential distribution. Despite its compactness, in contrast to other models like neural networks with millions of parameters, the model cannot be evaluated on ultra low power devices since it requires the presence of floating point units.

Driven by the cheap availability of ultra low power hardware, the increased power consumption of machine learning models and the trend to push those towards the edge, Piatkowski [16] developed a variation of the regular exponential family, which is capable of running on devices, that only have access to integer arithmetic units. By replacing the base in Eq. 2 from e to 2 and restricting the parameters to be a subset of $\mathbb{N}_{<k}$ with fixed word size k, the resource constrained exponential family is defined as follows

$$P_{\boldsymbol{\theta}}(\mathbf{X} = \boldsymbol{x}) = 2^{\langle \boldsymbol{\theta}, \phi(\boldsymbol{x}) \rangle - A(\boldsymbol{\theta})}$$

with

$$A(\boldsymbol{\theta}) = \log_2 \sum_{\boldsymbol{x} \in \mathcal{X}} 2^{\langle \boldsymbol{\theta}, \phi(\boldsymbol{x}) \rangle - A(\boldsymbol{\theta})}.$$

The availability of specialized integer versions of the inference- and optimization-algorithms does allow not only the application, but also the learning of these models directly on local devices. Moreover, Piatkowski has proven [17], that despite the limitations the models still provide theoretical guarantees on the quality.

Learning. The parameters $\boldsymbol{\theta}$ of the distribution $\mathbb{P}_{\boldsymbol{\theta}}$ are estimated using a (regularized) maximum likelihood estimation. Suppose we are given a dataset $\mathcal{D} = \{\boldsymbol{x}_1, \ldots, \boldsymbol{x}_n\}$ with n samples, the negative average log-likelihood is defined as follows

$$\ell(\boldsymbol{\theta}; \mathcal{D}) = \log_2 A(\boldsymbol{\theta}) - \left\langle \boldsymbol{\theta}, \frac{1}{|\mathcal{D}|} \sum_{\boldsymbol{x} \in \mathcal{D}} \phi(\boldsymbol{x}) \right\rangle$$

Setting $\hat{\boldsymbol{\mu}} = \frac{1}{|\mathcal{D}|} \sum_{\boldsymbol{x} \in \mathcal{D}} \phi(\boldsymbol{x})$ the partial derivative of ℓ is as follows

$$\frac{\partial \ell(\boldsymbol{\theta}; \mathcal{D})}{\partial \boldsymbol{\theta}_i} = \mathbb{E}_P[\phi(\boldsymbol{x})_i] - \hat{\boldsymbol{\mu}}_i,$$

which is just the difference between the empirical and the model's distribution. The model's distribution is computed using the BitLength-Propagation-algorithm [17], which returns the probabilities as quotients a/b to avoid floating point numbers. Likewise for $\hat{\boldsymbol{\mu}}$, we store the raw counts as well as the cardinality of the dataset as integers. Using a proximal block coordinate descent method, the parameters for each clique are updated by either increasing or decreasing the current value by one. In-depth details on those specialized integer algorithms can be found in [17]. If the samples $\boldsymbol{x}$ arrive as stream, e.g., sensor readings, the ϕ's and example's counters will be accumulated iteratively and used for a gradient step. This is showcased in Algorithm 1.

Algorithm 1. Integer Learning Algorithm

Input: Graph $G = (V, E)$, bytes $k \in \mathbb{N}$
Initialization:
   local sufficient statistics $\hat{\boldsymbol{\mu}}_1^1, \ldots, \hat{\boldsymbol{\mu}}_1^m \leftarrow \mathbf{0}$
   local example counter $c_1^1, \ldots, c_1^m \leftarrow 0$
Round t at learner i:
   observe $S_t^i \subset \mathcal{X}$
   for $x \in S_t^i$ **do**
     $\hat{\boldsymbol{\mu}}_t^i \leftarrow \hat{\boldsymbol{\mu}}_t^i + \phi(\boldsymbol{x})$
   $c_t^i \leftarrow c_t^i + |S_t^i|$
   $\boldsymbol{\mu}_t^i \leftarrow \texttt{BitLengthBP()}$;   // Compute models distribution
   $\nabla \leftarrow \texttt{Grad}(\boldsymbol{\mu}_t^i, \boldsymbol{\mu}_t^i, c_t^i)$;   // Compute grad using Int-Prox
   $\boldsymbol{\theta}_t^i \leftarrow \texttt{ApplyGrad}(\boldsymbol{\theta}_{t-1}^i, \nabla)$
   return $\boldsymbol{\theta}_t^i$

3 Distributed Learning of Integer Exponential Families

The integer exponential families described above can be trained on a data-generating device using only integer computations. The goal of distributed learning is to jointly train a model across multiple devices. That is, we assume a set of $m \in \mathbb{N}$ local devices, denoted **learners**, learning a joint task defined by a target distribution $\mathcal{D} : \mathcal{X} \times \mathcal{Y} \mapsto \mathbb{R}_+$. The learners obtain local samples over time. For simplicity, we assume rounds $t = 1, 2, \ldots$ where in each round, each learner $l \in [m]$ obtains a local dataset $S_t^l \subset \mathcal{X} \times \mathcal{Y}$ drawn iid. from $\mathcal{D}$.

The most straight-forward approach to solve this task is to compute local data summaries $\hat{\boldsymbol{\mu}}_t^l$ on all observed data $\bigcup_{i=1}^t S_i^l$ as

$$\hat{\boldsymbol{\mu}}_t^l = \frac{1}{t} \sum_{i=1}^t \frac{1}{|S_i^l|} \sum_{\boldsymbol{x} \in S_i^l} \phi(\boldsymbol{x}).$$

These data summaries can then be centralized and the global data summary $\hat{\boldsymbol{\mu}}$ is computed as the weighted average, where n_l is the number of samples the learner l received and $n = \sum_{i=1}^l n_l$ is total amount of samples accros all learners

$$\hat{\boldsymbol{\mu}}_t = \sum_{l=1}^m \frac{n_l}{n} \hat{\boldsymbol{\mu}}_t^l. \tag{3}$$

With this data summary, the respective $\boldsymbol{\theta}_t$ can be computed centrally and thus we call this the **centralized** approach. Since $\hat{\boldsymbol{\mu}}_t$ is the exact data summary of the union of local dataset, this approach results in the same model as learning on the union of all local datasets, directly. However, it has two major disadvantages: it does not make use of the local computing power at the data-generating devices and it requires centralizing potentially sensitive data.

To overcome these disadvantages, we propose to train models locally to obtain both $\boldsymbol{\theta}^l$ and $\boldsymbol{\mu}^l$ for each learner $l \in [m]$. We synchronize these local models by

Table 1. Summary of transmitted data

Protocol	Centralized	Naïve	Privacy
Send	$\boldsymbol{\mu}_i^t$	$\boldsymbol{\mu}_i^t + \boldsymbol{\theta}_i^t$	$\boldsymbol{\theta}_i^t$
Receive	$\boldsymbol{\theta}_{Global}^t$	$\widehat{\boldsymbol{\mu}_i^t + \boldsymbol{\theta}_i^t}$	$\widehat{\boldsymbol{\theta}_i^t}$

averaging the parameters. The average of a set of integer vectors, however, is not necessarily an integer. Instead, the floored average can be computed using only integer operations[1]. Of course, averaging both, $\boldsymbol{\theta}$ and $\boldsymbol{\mu}$, does not solve the privacy issue, since $\boldsymbol{\mu}$ is shared just like in the centralized approach. Thus, we refer to this as **naïve averaging** and use it only as a baseline. Instead, we propose to only average the model parameters $\boldsymbol{\theta}$ and maintain local data summaries $\boldsymbol{\mu}$. We call this approach **privacy-preserving resource constrained averaging** (Table 1).

This averaging can be performed periodically, i.e., after observing $b \in \mathbb{N}$ batches, hence we call this **periodic averaging**. The frequency of averaging allows to balance communication and model quality: communication effort can be saved by averaging less frequently at the expense of model quality.

Communication can be further reduced by deciding in a data-driven way when averaging has the largest impact. **Dynamic averaging** [7,8] checks local conditions to determine when to communicate. The algorithm is presented in Algo. 2. It shows the local computation at each round using the (integer) or real-value learning and the local test of the conditions. That is, with a common reference point $\boldsymbol{r} \in \mathbb{Z}^d$, each local learner checks its local condition

$$\|\boldsymbol{\theta}^i - \boldsymbol{r}\|_2^2 = \sum_{j=1}^{d} \left(\boldsymbol{\theta}_j^i - \boldsymbol{r}\right)^2 \le \Delta,$$

where $\Delta \in \mathbb{Z}$ is a predefined threshold. If all model parameters $\boldsymbol{\theta}^1, \ldots, \boldsymbol{\theta}^m \in \mathbb{Z}^d$ and the reference point $\boldsymbol{r} \in \mathbb{Z}^d$ are d-dimensional integer vectors, and the divergence threshold $\Delta \in \mathbb{Z}$ is also an integer, then the local conditions can be checked using only integer operations.

The algorithm also shows the coordinator processing the submitted models. The augmentation requests additional parameter vectors in case of the dynamic averaging. The number of models received is doubled until the conditions are fulfilled. Hence, it may happen, that finally all learners are used for the central processing which gives a new global model to all local learners.

As mentioned before, using integer exponential families introduces an error into the models. Similarly, using rounded averaging introduces an error. This error can be bounded. Training regular exponential families is a convex learning problem. Indeed, it is trivial to show that the error of using $\widehat{\boldsymbol{\theta}}$ instead of

---

[1] Indeed, the average of two integers in binary representation can be computed using only the logical "and" & and "or" + operations, as well as the bit-shift operator ">>" as $\lfloor \frac{a+b}{2} \rfloor = (a \mathbin{\&} b) + ((a \; XOR \; b) >> 1)$.

the standard average $\overline{\boldsymbol{\theta}}$, i.e., $\|\widehat{\boldsymbol{\theta}} - \overline{\boldsymbol{\theta}}\|_2$ is bounded by $\sqrt{d}$, where d denotes the number of parameters. Let $\epsilon \in \mathbb{R}_+$ denote a bound on the error of using an integer exponential family instead of a real-valued one. Furthermore, define the cumulative loss on $m \in \mathbb{N}$ learners until time $t \in \mathbb{N}$ as

$$L(t,m) = \sum_{i=1}^{t}\sum_{l=1}^{m}\sum_{(\boldsymbol{x},y)\in S_t^l} \ell(\boldsymbol{x},y),$$

where $\ell : \mathcal{Y} \times \mathcal{Y} \to \mathbb{R}_+$ is a loss function. Then, it follows directly from Cor. 3.33 in [6] that when using stochastic gradient descent to train the local models, the cumulative loss of using resource-constrained dynamic averaging over normal periodic averaging is bounded.

Corollary 1. *Assume $m \in \mathbb{N}$ learners jointly training an integer exponential family with stochastic gradient descent with learning rate $\eta \in \mathbb{R}_+$. Furthermore, assume there exists $\rho \in \mathbb{R}_+$ such that $\|x\|_2 \leq \rho$ for all $x \in \mathcal{X}$. Let L_{Per}, L_{Dyn} denote the cumulative loss when local models are maintained by resource-constrained periodic, resp. dynamic averaging. Then it holds that*

$$L_{Dyn}(t,m) - L_{Per}(t,m) \leq \frac{t}{b\eta^2\frac{\rho}{\rho^2+1}}(\Delta + 2d + \epsilon).$$

Using the observation that for stochastic gradient descent, periodic averaging on $m \in \mathbb{N}$ learners with batch size $b = 1$ is equal to centralized mini-batch SGD with mini-batch size m and learning rate η/m [cf. 7, Prop. 3], as well as using the standard learning rate of $\eta = \sqrt{t}$ and $\Delta = \sqrt{t}$, it follows that the regret of using resource-constrained dynamic averaging over centralized training is a constant in d and ϵ. In the following section, we empirically compare dynamic averaging to periodic averaging, as well as the centralized approach, both in terms of model quality and communication demand.

4   Experiments

In our experiments, we want to empirically investigate the centralized, the public, and the private scheme of communication and distributed learning. We compare the periodic and the dynamic update in the distributed learning setting for both, the regular and the resource-constrained averaging operator. Before we introduce the specific research questions and results, we describe the experimental setup. To emphasize reproducible research, we selected two open-source-frameworks for our implementation and experiments. To simulate a distributed learning environment, we utilized the `Distributed-Learning-Platform`[2]. The model implementation was based on the `Randomfields`-library[3]. Also, the source code for the new aggregation-operator and experiments can be found online[4].

---

[2] https://github.com/fraunhofer-iais/dlplatform.
[3] https://randomfields.org/.
[4] https://bitbucket.org/zagazao/dynamic-rc-averaging/src/master/.

Algorithm 2. Resource-Constrained Dynamic Averaging Protocol

Input: learning algorithm $\mathcal{A}$, divergence threshold $\Delta \in \mathbb{N}$, parameter $b \in \mathbb{N}$, m learners

Initialization:

    local models $\theta_1^1, \ldots, \theta_1^m \leftarrow$ one random θ

    reference vector $r \leftarrow \theta$

    violation counter $v \leftarrow 0$

Round t at learner i:

    observe $S_t^i \subset \mathcal{X} \times \mathcal{Y}$

    update θ_{t-1}^i using the learning algorithm $\mathcal{A}$

    if $t \mod b = 0$ **and** $\|\theta_t^i - r\|_2^2 > \Delta$ **then**

        send θ_t^i to coordinator (violation)

At coordinator on violation:

    let $\mathcal{B}$ be the set of learners with violation

    $v \leftarrow v + |\mathcal{B}|$

    if $v = m$ **then** $\mathcal{B} \leftarrow [m]$, $v \leftarrow 0$

    while $\mathcal{B} \neq [m]$ **and** $\left\| \lfloor \frac{1}{\mathcal{B}} \sum_{i \in \mathcal{B}} \theta_t^i \rfloor - r \right\|^2 > \Delta$ **do**

        augment $\mathcal{B}$ by augmentation strategy

        receive models from learners added to $\mathcal{B}$

    send model $\widehat{\theta} = \lfloor \frac{1}{\mathcal{B}} \sum_{i \in \mathcal{B}} \theta_t^i \rfloor$ to learners in $\mathcal{B}$

    if $\mathcal{B} = [m]$ also set new reference vector $r \leftarrow \widehat{\theta}$

4.1 Model Quality and Communication

During the simulation of the distributed learning environment, we limited ourselves to $m = 16$ learners, however, in future work we want to investigate, how this approach scales with an increasing number of learners. For each integer learner, we limited the number of bits for each parameter to $k = 3$, which results in 2^3 possible choices. Lower choices of k resulted in significantly worse performance in comparison to regular exponential family models. Increasing the number of bits did not result in a sufficient increase in performance and had the disadvantage of higher memory- and thus communication complexity. For the evaluation, we chose three different datasets – DOTA2, COVERTYPE and SUSY – of the UCI-Repository [4]. The datasets possess different properties. While the DOTA2-dataset features mostly discrete columns, has many features but a low amount of samples, the SUSY dataset consists of only a few real-valued columns, while consisting of many samples. The COVERTYPE-dataset sits in between those two with a mix of discrete and numerical features and is a medium dataset size. Details on those datasets can be found in Table 2.

All datasets have undergone the same preprocessing: numerical columns have been discretized into ten bins based on their quantiles. Furthermore, a random subset of 10.000 examples was selected as a holdout set, which in turn was used to estimate the model's structure via the Chow-Liu-algorithm [3]. This step has to be done in order to ensure that all models share the same structure. Otherwise, the aggregation would not be possible. Note that this a serious limitation and future work could also investigate if aggregation can be applied to nodes

Table 2. Dataset and model properties

Dataset	Samples	Features	Classes	Discrete	Numerical	Model dimension
SUSY	5.000.000	19	2	1	18	1620
COVERTYPE	581.012	55	7	45	10	1596
DOTA2	102.944	117	2	117	0	2790

with distinct graph structures. The remaining data was partitioned horizontally alongside the nodes.

During the running-phase, at each time step t all learners received a batch of $bs = 10$ new samples. As soon as the batch arrived, learners are asked to predict the labels for each of the samples. Afterwards, the learner uses the new samples in order to update its local data summary $\hat{\mu}$. Thereafter, except for the centralized approach, where a global model is fitted on the accumulated data summaries, learners run an optimization-algorithm with the current data summaries and weights for a specified optimization-budget o in terms of iterations. The budget allows for a further trade-off between model-quality and battery life of some device. Finally, each learner checks if synchronization should be performed. In case of the periodic protocol, the model parameters and/or data summaries are transmitted to the central coordinator after b batches have been processed. In contrast, the dynamic protocol checks if its local conditions hold and only communicates if some condition is violated.

Specifically we want to answer the following **questions**:

- How does the periodic protocol compare against the dynamic one?
- How do resource-constrained models compare to regular ones in terms of predictive quality?

We compare the methods against **two baselines**:

- **Global Learning** We want to compare ourselves against the traditional machine learning setting, where all the data is centralized first. The performance of the global model, a regular exponential family, is evaluated using a 5-fold cross-validation procedure. In the plots this is denoted by Global.
- **Local learning** In this setting each device fits a model based on its local data. No communication takes place, thus this setting acts as a guard, showing that communication helps to improve model quality. In the plots this is denoted by NoSync.

We have plotted the resource constrained performance of dynamic versus periodic updates for the three datasets and aggregation-mechanisms in Fig. 1, 2 and 3. The y-axis shows the error and the x-axis shows the communication consumption in bytes. The baseline of no synchronization is shown by a dashed-dotted line. We further include the performance of the global baseline as dotted line. The periodic and dynamic approaches are displayed with different markers, while different periods and deltas are displayed with varying color choices. Some

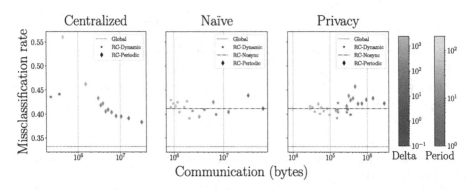

Fig. 1. Missclassification rate vs Communication (`Covertype`)

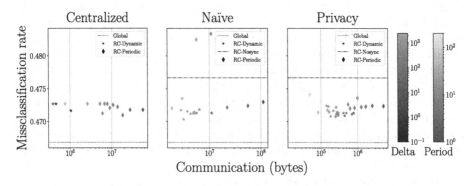

Fig. 2. Missclassification rate vs Communication (`DOTA2`)

periodically updated models are worse, but most models are superior to the base line. As expected, for `DOTA2` and `COVERTYPE`, we see that the dynamic update requires less communication in both, the private and the public setting (little stars in the lower left corner). In the numerical dataset `SUSY`, the dynamic update uses less communication resources, but has less accuracy than the periodic one in the public setting. We also see that the quality of the periodically updated models varies much more than the one of the dynamically updated ones. Although for the dataset with only numerical attributes, `SUSY`, the results are not clearly favoring the dynamic update, overall, the answer to the first question leans towards the dynamic protocol. Furthermore, we notice the privacy-preserving aggregation retains the same predictive quality as the naïve approach while reducing the required communication substantially. Thus we focus on the privacy-preserving protocol for the next question.

Figure 4 shows the privacy-preserving scheme for the three datasets comparing the resource-constrained and the normal graphical models. Again, the y-axis shows the error and the x-axis shows the communication consumption. The dotted baseline shows the performance of the global model, while the dotted baseline stands for not synchronizing normal models and the dashed-dotted line

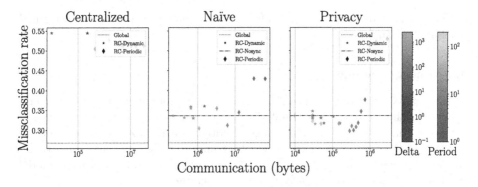

Fig. 3. Missclassification rate vs Communication (SUSY)

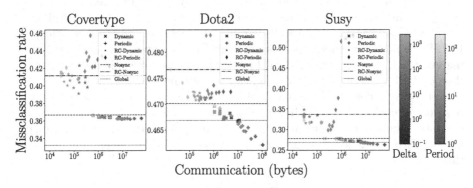

Fig. 4. Privacy-preserving-resource-constrained-averaging

for not synchronizing resource-constrained models. We have varied the frequency of updates for the normal models as well as for the resource constrained ones using the periodic or the dynamic scheme. The parameters for the frequency of update show not surprisingly that more frequent synchronization leads to better model quality which introduces more communication costs as can be seen below the benchmark spreading towards the right. Many of the resource constrained private models outperform the RC baseline. The variance is due to the frequency of updates. The most accurate model is the not resource constrained one in the lower right corner. It uses by far the most communication. We have varied the parameters and see that actually most models of the resource-constrained dynamic updates (stars) outperform the resource-constrained baseline and approach the regular one. However, we must admit that there are models of the resource-constrained periodically and dynamically updated schemes that are worse than the baseline. These have a low frequency of update in common. In the plots, we easily recognize the parameter choice, which balances quality (low) and communication (left). Though, in all settings, we can save communication cost of 1–3 magnitudes while dropping a few percents of classification performance. This is a natural trade-off we encounter in resource-constrained machine learning methods.

4.2   Energy Savings

In this section we provide a rough estimate on the amount of energy that could be saved using resource-constraint distributed learning instead of centralizing data. For that, we compare the energy required to centralize all data and train a model to the energy required for locally training models and averaging them. In this simplified scenario, we do not assume that the centrally computed model needs to be transferred regularly to the local learners.

   To compute the energy required for communication, we assume the data is transmitted over 3G, requiring around 2.9 kWh/GB [18], i.e., $\sigma = 0.0029$ Wh/GB. Furthermore, we assume the central computation is performed on a $p_c = 100$ W processor and one of the parallel low-energy processors consume $p_p = 1$ W. Since these low-energy processors (e.g., FPGAs) are specialized hardware, the execution time for aggregating data or training a models is usually shorter than on CPUs [2]. However, for simplicity we assume similar runtimes.

   Let $c_c \in \mathbb{R}$ denote the amount of communication in GB required by the central approach and $c_p \in \mathbb{R}$ the amount for the parallel one. Let $a, t \in \mathbb{R}$ denote the time required for aggregating $N \in \mathbb{N}$ data points, respectively training a model. With $m \in \mathbb{N}$ local learners, the energy consumed by the central approach then is

$$e_c = \underbrace{(mNa + t)p_c}_{\text{central training}} + c_c\sigma$$

and the energy for the parallel approach is

$$e_p = m\underbrace{(Na + t)p_p}_{\text{local training}} + \underbrace{map_p}_{\text{model aggr.}} + c_p\sigma$$

As reference, we use the empirical results on the SUSY dataset, where the centralized approach achieves an accuracy of 0.73 using $6200640B$ of communication and dynamic averaging achieves a comparable accuracy of 0.69 with $34020B$ of communication. With $a = 10^{-12}$ (roughly the cost of an integer operation on a 1 GHz processor) and $t = 10^{-10}$ (roughly 100 integer operations on a 1 GHz processor), $m = 16$ and $N = 100$ the rough estimates are $e_c = 0.22\mu$Wh and $e_p = 0.0033\mu$Wh, i.e., the centralized approach requires more than 67 times more energy than the parallel one. Note that this estimate is conservative since it does not take into account the energy required in the centralized approach for running an operating system or powering additional components of a computer.

   To analyze the potential scaling behavior we make one more simplifying assumptions: We assume that the ratio of central to parallel communication remains constant with the number of learners. This assumption is not very realistic, but the actual scaling behavior depends on the underlying learning problem. Increasing the number of learners typically leads to an even more favorable ratio

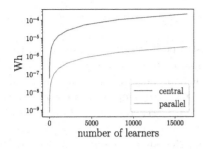
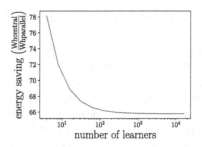

Fig. 5. Scaling behavior of the esti-mated energy consumption with the number of learners.

Fig. 6. Scaling behavior of the energy sav-ing's ratio with the number of learners.

for simple learning problems, whereas for hard learning problems it can be less favorable [6]. Under this assumption, we show the estimated energy consump-tion in Fig. 5. It shows that the energy consumption of the parallel approach remains substantially lower for larger amounts of learners. We show the relative reduction in energy consumption (i.e., e_c/e_p) in Fig. 6. It shows that the relative reduction decreases with the number of learners, but remains above 65 even for large numbers of learners.

5   Discussion

As the empirical evaluation has shown, using only integer operations allows to successfully train models distributedly. However, when using the integer average the relationship between communication and model quality is not as clear as for normal averaging, where more communication reliably leads to higher model quality. The results for resource-constrained averaging indicate that the errors through rounding the average lead to less predictable behavior. The results on SUSY furthermore indicate that too much communication can even be harmful. A possible explanation is that when averaging very often, small changes of local models will get leveled out by the rounding. Thus, the effect of local training is nullified, delaying the overall training process.

This rounding effect might vanish when using larger numbers of learners (in the experiments, we only used $m = 16$ learners). At the same time, this can influence the communication reduction. When computing the energy savings, we assumed the reduction remains constant with larger numbers of learners. It is conceivable for dynamic averaging that larger numbers of learners lead to an even greater reduction in communication when compared to the centralized approach. However, the effects of rounding might similarly lead to more local violations and ultimately a higher amount of communication. To answer this question and determine whether the approach is useful in practice, it is necessary to further study the effects of rounding the average, both empirically and theoretically.

6 Conclusion and Future Work

In this paper, we proposed a new resource-constrained averaging operator, which can be evaluated on ultra-low-power hardware using only integer operations. Besides, we have shown, that the same applies to the evaluation of the local conditions, which consecutively allows performing every step in this distributed learning setting in a resource-constrained fashion. Furthermore, we have shown that the excess loss of using the dynamic averaging protocol over the periodic protocol is bounded. In our experiments we verified that using resource-constrained averaging of integer exponential family models, we reach a similar performance in terms of prediction quality compared to regular exponential family models with access to the non-restricted parameter space, while reducing network requirements substantially. Besides, we do not only save energy by reducing network communication, but also by employing these models on specific, cheap available hardware. However, there is still a decrease in predictive quality from using resource-constrained models, so this trade-off has to be taken into account: Are we willing to drop $x\%$ accuracy for the sake of energy or bandwidth savings?

Future Work. This work opens many new exciting research questions, e.g., how does the averaging perform if we vary the number of nodes in our learning environment. Does it increase the error or do more nodes provide more information for faster convergence? Furthermore, it would be interesting to investigate the effects of resource-constrained-averaging on the parameter vectors in a controlled environment using artificial datasets with known parameters. Besides, the dynamic averaging protocol might yield better results in terms of communication cost in the presence of more nodes, since the partial synchronization mechanism will be triggered more often. Another way to reduce communication could be the clique-wise transmission of data summaries and/or parameters. This technique could possibly help to overcome the limitations of the fixed graph structure by matching the cliques of the different learners and only averaging their parameters. Also, we saw that using incorrect choices for the synchronization period and/or delta, we receive sub-optimal solutions with low predictive quality. This raises the need for informed methods to choose those hyperparameters, incorporating the parameter space, the number of processed samples as well as the optimization budget. Furthermore, since we only considered plain averaging in this work, we could also try to adopt different aggregation mechanisms, e.g., performance-weighted averages or the Radon machine [9], to the resource-constrained setting. Further work could also examine the adaptivity to time-variant distributions as well as the performance/convergence on non i.i.d datasets.

Acknowledgement. This research has been funded by the Federal Ministry of Education and Research of Germany as part of the competence center for machine learning ML2R (01|S18038A/B/C).

References

1. U.S. Energy Information Administration: How much electricity does a typical nuclear power plant generate? (2018). https://www.americangeosciences.org/critical-issues/faq/how-much-electricity-does-typical-nuclear-power-plant-generate. Accessed 02 Dec 2019
2. Asano, S., Maruyama, T., Yamaguchi, Y.: Performance comparison of FPGA, GPU and CPU in image processing. In: 2009 FPL, pp. 126–131. IEEE (2009)
3. Chow, C., Liu, C.: Approximating discrete probability distributions with dependence trees. IEEE Trans. Inf. Theor. **14**(3), 462–467 (2006)
4. Dua, D., Graff, C.: UCI machine learning repository (2017). http://archive.ics.uci.edu/ml
5. Hammersley, J.M., Clifford, P.E.: Markov random fields on finite graphs and lattices. Unpublished manuscript (1971)
6. Kamp, M.: Black-box parallelization for machine learning. Ph.D. thesis, Rheinische Friedrich-Wilhelms-Universität Bonn (2019)
7. Kamp, M., et al.: Efficient decentralized deep learning by dynamic model averaging. In: Berlingerio, M., Bonchi, F., Gärtner, T., Hurley, N., Ifrim, G. (eds.) ECML PKDD 2018. LNCS (LNAI), vol. 11051, pp. 393–409. Springer, Cham (2019). https://doi.org/10.1007/978-3-030-10925-7_24
8. Kamp, M., Boley, M., Keren, D., Schuster, A., Sharfman, I.: Communication-efficient distributed online prediction by dynamic model synchronization. In: Calders, T., Esposito, F., Hüllermeier, E., Meo, R. (eds.) ECML PKDD 2014. LNCS (LNAI), vol. 8724, pp. 623–639. Springer, Heidelberg (2014). https://doi.org/10.1007/978-3-662-44848-9_40
9. Kamp, M., Boley, M., Missura, O., Gärtner, T.: Effective parallelisation for machine learning. In: Advances in Neural Information Processing Systems, vol. 30, pp. 6477–6488. Curran Associates, Inc. (2017)
10. Kamp, M., Bothe, S., Boley, M., Mock, M.: Communication-efficient distributed online learning with kernels. In: Frasconi, P., Landwehr, N., Manco, G., Vreeken, J. (eds.) ECML PKDD 2016. LNCS (LNAI), vol. 9852, pp. 805–819. Springer, Cham (2016). https://doi.org/10.1007/978-3-319-46227-1_50
11. Kemp, S.: Digital 2019 global digital overview (2019). https://datareportal.com/reports/digital-2019-global-digital-overview. Accessed 02 Dec 2019
12. Lim, W.Y.B., et al.: Federated learning in mobile edge networks: a comprehensive survey. CoRR abs/1909.11875 (2019). http://arxiv.org/abs/1909.11875
13. McMahan, B., Moore, E., Ramage, D., Hampson, S., y Arcas, B.A.: Communication-efficient learning of deep networks from decentralized data. In: Artificial Intelligence and Statistics, pp. 1273–1282 (2017)
14. Mohan, N., Kangasharju, J.: Edge-fog cloud: a distributed cloud for internet of things computations. In: 2016 Cloudification of the Internet of Things (CIoT), pp. 1–6. IEEE (2016)
15. Piatkowski, N.: Distributed generative modelling with sub-linear communication overhead. In: Cellier, P., Driessens, K. (eds.) ECML PKDD 2019. CCIS, vol. 1167, pp. 281–292. Springer, Cham (2020). https://doi.org/10.1007/978-3-030-43823-4_24
16. Piatkowski, N., Lee, S., Morik, K.: Integer undirected graphical models for resource-constrained systems. Neurocomputing **173**, 9–23 (2016)
17. Piatkowski, N.P.: Exponential families on resource-constrained systems. Ph.D. thesis, TU Dortmund (2018)

18. Pihkola, H., Hongisto, M., Apilo, O., Lasanen, M.: Evaluating the energy consumption of mobile data transfer-from technology development to consumer behaviour and life cycle thinking. Sustainability **10**(7), 2494 (2018)
19. Shi, W., Cao, J., Zhang, Q., Li, Y., Xu, L.: Edge computing: vision and challenges. IEEE Internet Things J. **3**(5), 637–646 (2016)
20. Wainwright, M.J., Jordan, M.I.: Graphical models, exponential families, and variational inference. Found. Trends Mach. Learn. **1**(1–2) (2008)

Second Workshop on Machine Learning for Cybersecurity (MLCS 2020)

Preface

Machine Learning for Cybersecurity

The last decade has been a critical one regarding cybersecurity, with studies estimating the cost of cybercrime to be up to 0.8 percent of the global GDP. Cyberthreats have increased dramatically, exposing sensitive personal and business information, disrupting critical operations and imposing high costs on the economy. The number and sophistication of threats will only increase and become more targeted in nature. Furthermore, today's computing systems operate under increasing scales and dynamic environments, ingesting and generating more and more functional and non-functional data. The capability to detect, analyse, and defend against threats in (near) real-time conditions is not possible without employing machine learning techniques and big data infrastructure. This gives rise to cyber threat intelligence and analytic solutions, such as (informed) machine learning on big data and open-source intelligence, to perceive, reason, learn, and act against cyber adversary techniques and actions. Moreover, organisations'security analysts have to manage and protect these systems and deal with the privacy and security of all personal and institutional data under their control. This calls for tools and solutions combining the latest advances in areas such as data science, visualization, and machine learning. We strongly believe that the significant advance of the state-of-the-art in machine learning over the last years has not been fully exploited to harness the potential of available data, for the benefit of systems-and-data security and privacy. In fact, while machine learning algorithms have been already proven beneficial for the cybersecurity industry, they have also highlighted a number of shortcomings. Traditional machine algorithms are often vulnerable to attacks, known as adversarial learning attacks, which can cause the algorithms to misbehave or reveal information about their inner workings. As machine learning-based capabilities become incorporated into cyber assets, the need to understand adversarial learning and address it becomes clear. On the other hand, when a significant amount of data is collected from or generated by different security monitoring solutions, big-data analytical techniques are necessary to mine, interpret and extract knowledge of these big data.

The second international workshop on Machine Learning for Cybersecurity (MLCS'20) was held online in conjunction with ECML PKDD. The accepted papers presented interesting novel aspects of machine learning applied to cybersecurity, in particular attack, malware, and community detection, as well as adversarial examples. We want to thank the authors for their valuable contributions, great presentations, and lively and fruitful discussions. We would also like to thank the MLCS'20 program committee, whose members made the workshop possible with their rigorous and timely reviews. Finally, we would like to thank ECML PKDD for hosting the workshop and the workshop chairs, Myra Spiliopoulou and Willem Waegeman for their valuable support.

Organization

MLCS'20 Chairs

Annalisa Appice	Università degli Studi di Bari
Pedro M. Ferreira	Universidade de Lisboa
Michael Kamp	Monash University
Donato Malerba	Università degli Studi di Bari
Ibéria Medeiros	Universidade de Lisboa

Program Committee

Alysson Bessani	University of Lisbon - LASIGE
Cagatay Turkay	University of Warwick
Fabio, Pierazzi	King's College London
Giorgio Giacinto	University of Cagliary
Leonardo Aniello	University of Southampton
Lorenzo, Cavallaro	King's College London
Luis Muñoz-González	Imperial College London
Marc Dacier	Eurecom
Marco Vieira	University of Coimbra
Miguel Correia	University of Lisbon
Rogério de Lemos	University of Kent
Sara Madeira	University of Lisbon
Shihao Ji	Georgia State University
Tommaso Zoppi	University of Florence
Vasileios Mavroeidis	University of Oslo

MitM Attack Detection in BLE Networks Using Reconstruction and Classification Machine Learning Techniques

Abdelkader Lahmadi[1]([✉]), Alexis Duque[2], Nathan Heraief[3], and Julien Francq[3]

[1] Université de Lorraine, CNRS, Inria, Loria, 54000 Nancy, France
`lahmadi@loria.fr`
[2] Rtone, 120 rue de Saint-Cyr, 69009 Lyon, France
`alexis.duque@rtone.fr`
[3] Airbus CyberSecurity SAS, 78996 Elancourt Cedex, France

Abstract. Internet of Things (IoT) devices, including smartphones and tablets, are widely deployed in various application domains ranging from smart homes to industrial environments. Many of these devices rely on Bluetooth Low Energy (BLE) as a communication protocol for their control or the transfer of data. Trivial attacks can easily target these devices to compromise them due to their low security features and inherent vulnerabilities in their software and communication components. In this paper, we firstly demonstrate a Man-in-the-Middle (MitM) attack against BLE devices while collecting datasets of network traffic data exchange with and without the attack. Secondly, we study the use of machine learning to detect this attack by combining unsupervised and supervised techniques. We applied and compared two unsupervised techniques to reconstruct the model of BLE communications and detect suspicious data batches. We then applied a classification method based on Text-CNN technique to classify packets as normal or attack inside each suspicious batch. Our model reconstruction results show that we are able to discriminate normal and attack models with high precision and our classification method achieves high accuracy (≈ 0.99) and low false positive rate (≈ 0.03).

Keywords: IoT security · Bluetooth Low Energy · Neural networks · Machine learning · Attack detection

1 Introduction

BLE (Bluetooth Low Energy) is a widely used radio technology by connected devices including smartwatches, smartphones, smart plugs and smart locks, that are referred as Internet-of-Things (IoT). The number of these devices and their

This work is funded by the French Government under grant FUI 23 PACLIDO (Protocoles et Algorithmes Cryptographiques Légers pour l'Internet Des Objets).

I. Koprinska et al. (Eds.): ECML PKDD 2020 Workshops, CCIS 1323, pp. 149–164, 2020.
https://doi.org/10.1007/978-3-030-65965-3_10

deployment in particular for smart homes and industrial environment is growing, and they are also becoming a subject of potential security issues. They are vulnerable even to trivial attacks and can be easily compromised due their limited security features and lacking of secure development practices. Multiple existing research works have shown real world discovered vulnerabilities [11] in BLE devices and demonstrated attacks against them [20]. An easy to deploy and perform attack on BLE devices is the Man-in-the-Middle (MitM) attack by using several available tools (BTLeJuice, GATTack, Mirage) and with low cost hardware (few BLE adapters) [7]. This attack could be performed even if the device is not too close to the attacker by abusing BLE-enabled smartphones or by remotely controlling a mobile malware. In addition, with special radio adapters and amplifiers, an attacker can intercept BLE signals up to 1,000 m while initially the BLE radio range is up to 100 m [20].

Plenty of work has been done to improve the security of IoT devices by providing detection and protection methods [18]. In particular, several work rely on machine learning techniques to identify anomalies in network traffic through offline or online analysis [8]. Nguyen *et al.* [13] proposed a machine learning based system for detecting compromised IoT devices. Their system uses devices specific communication patterns to detect anomalous behaviours deviation caused by attacks. They applied a federated learning approach using Deep Neural Networks (DNN) to train models locally and then update a centralised model. However, most of existing work focused on volumetric attacks, such as Mirai [2] and few and rare work interested in attacks with sporadic network activity such as MitM, in particular for BLE based systems [1]. Oliff *et al.* [14] proposed a detection method based on machine learning for spoofing attacks in BLE enabled occupancy system. Their method uses three classifiers with location labeled BLE advertising packets and under identity spoofing attacks. The proposed method is able to detect attack with an accuracy ranging from 80% to 91%. Zuo *et al.* [20] have shown that a large number of deployed BLE devices and their companion mobile app are easy to fingerprint and rely on "Just Works" pairing mode which allows attackers to hijack their connections using MitM attack. Yaseen *et al.* [19] addressed the issue of detecting MitM in BLE based eHealth care systems by using anomaly detection metrics.

In this paper, we propose a machine learning based method for detecting MitM attacks by using datasets of a concrete attack scenario on BLE devices. Our method relies on reconstruction and classification techniques to detect suspicious network data batches that have large deviations from benign patterns of behaviour and then detect inside each of them attack packets. For the reconstruction technique, we compared the performance of Long Short-Term Memory (LSTM) and Temporal Convolutional Network (TCN) based auto-encoders to learn normal models of BLE packets. Our results show that a TCN approach is more accurate and provides higher temporal memory effect since our datasets are of small size. The classification technique combines payload bytes embedding and statistical features to learn, by using a Convolutional Neural Network (CNN) architecture, latent features of packets and in a second stage we use a

Random Forest algorithm to classify packets. By combining the two techniques, we were able to detect and classify the BLE packets with high accuracy ($\approx$0.99) and low false positive rate ($\approx$0.03).

The rest of the paper is organised as follows. In Sect. 2, we provide an overview of the BLE protocol and its main features, packets and operations. In Sect. 3, we detail our experimental set-up of the MitM attack and the process of collecting the datasets. In Sect. 4, we describe our ML-based detection method by jointly applying reconstruction and classification techniques. Section 5 concludes the paper and provides perspectives of this work.

2 BLE Overview

Bluetooth Low Energy (BLE) was introduced by the Bluetooth Special Interest Group (SIG) in [15] as a variant targeted towards battery-powered Internet of Things (IoT) applications such as fitness trackers, headphones and smartwatches. BLE is becoming one of the most common wireless standards used today in IoT devices. According to the Bluetooth SIG, more than two billion devices supporting BLE have been shipped in 2018 [16]. Likewise, it is also becoming more commonly used in applications where sensitive information is being transferred.

2.1 BLE Advertising and Connection

BLE uses the same 2.4 GHz ISM band as Bluetooth Classic and Wi-Fi. The BLE specification divides the band into 40 channels of 1 MHz spaced 2 MHz apart. Three of these channels are called advertising and are used by devices exclusively to send beaconing packets called advertising packets.

BLE specification defines two roles: Peripheral and Central. Central devices are the ones that initiate connection, while Peripherals accept. In this way a Central devices acts as a master, on which many Peripheral slaves can be attached. Figure 1 provides an overview of BLE workflow between a peripheral and a central (smartphone). The Central device will listen for advertisements from Peripheral devices but once the advertisement from the desired Peripheral device is received, the Central may connect by entering the initiating state. For the Peripheral device, the advertising state is also the initial state before the connection state. The connection state is the final state in which the Peripheral and Central devices can exchange data.

The BLE Link Layer offers two mechanisms for exchanging data in BLE: advertising and connections. Advertising allows sending unidirectional but broadcast data. The Peripheral device sends data using Advertising and Scan Response packets. Because it is broadcast in nature, multiple devices can listen to the advertising data. Each advertising packet is configurable by the product developer and can contain a wealth of information. It is not necessary to connect to a device to get these packets, but the Central cannot send any data back. Connections allow the Central and Peripheral to exchange data bidirectionally,

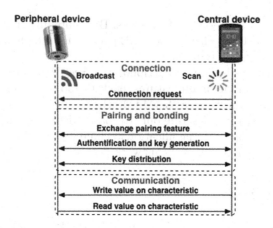

Fig. 1. BLE workflow between peripheral and central devices.

controlling the device and sending it information, as opposed to the unidirectional nature of advertising. So advertising packets serve dual roles: they enable Central devices to find devices and connect, and also able to convey information.

2.2 Data Exchange

Data is transmitted on 37 data channels which are not used for advertising. When devices are in a connection, they periodically exchange packets during connection events. The rate of these events is defined by parameters such as *Connection Interval*. The BLE specification allows the peripheral device to skip connection events if there are no data to exchange.

The logical link control and adaptation protocol (L2CAP) within the BLE stack fragments and re-assembles packets from other layers. It takes packets received by the Link Layer and forwards them the Generic Attribute (GATT) protocol for accessing data or the Security Manager. Data exposed by a Peripheral are presented in a GATT profile which is a hierarchical structure of attributes allowing the transfer of information between a Central device and a Peripheral device. Within a GATT profile, attributes can be either services or characteristics and are identified by a universally unique identifier (UUID). In addition to their UUID, characteristics are made up of an attribute handle, a set of properties and a value. The handle specifies the position of the characteristic in the profile and the value holds the actual data of the characteristic. Properties specify which operations (read, write, etc.) can be executed on each particular attribute and with which specific security requirements (encryption, authentication).

2.3 BLE Security

A BLE connection is said to operate at a specific security mode for which there are several security levels. The required security mode and level of a connection may change from time to time, leading to procedures to increase that level. When two devices which initially do not have security, wish to do something which requires security, the devices must pair first. This process is triggered (for example) by a Central device (e.g. a smartphone) that is attempting to access a data value of a characteristic on a Peripheral device that requires authenticated access. Pairing involves authenticating the identity of two devices, encrypting the link using a Short-Term Key (STK), and then distributing Long-Term Keys (LTK) used for encryption. The LTK is saved for faster reconnection in the future, that is termed Bonding.

The security level of the connection is based on the method of pairing performed and this is selected based on the I/O capabilities of each device. The security level of any subsequent reconnection is based on the level achieved during the initial pairing. When pairing, the method chosen determines if the pairing performs a strong authentication or not. Unauthenticated pairing occurs in situations where the device could not authenticate itself, for example if it has no Input/Output (I/O) capabilities. Pairing involves authenticating the identity of the two devices to be paired, usually through a secret-sharing process. Once authenticated, the link is encrypted and keys distributed to allow security to be restarted on a reconnection much more quickly. If these keys are saved for a future time, the devices are said to be *Bonded*. A pairing procedure involves an exchange of Security Manager protocol packets to generate a temporary encryption key called the Short Term Key (STK). During the packet exchange, the two peers negotiate one of the following STK generation methods: 'Just Works' where the STK is generated on both sides, based on the packets exchanged in plain-text, 'Passkey Display' where one of the peers displays a randomly generated 6-digit passkey and the other side is asked to enter it, 'Out of Band (OOB)' where additional data is transferred by means other than the BLE radio, such as another wireless technology like Near Field Communication (NFC), 'Numeric Comparison' (Low Energy Secure Connections Pairing) which is only available with BLE 4.2 and it uses an algorithm called Elliptic Curve Diffie-Hellman (ECDH) for key generation, and a new pairing procedure for the key exchange. However, many BLE devices rely on the Just Works pairing method which is insecure and the devices become vulnerable to MitM attacks.

3 Experimental Set-Up

In this work, we consider the scenario of a BLE-enabled torque wrench device controlled remotely by a user through an App running on a smartphone to adjust and calibrate with high precision the torque settings (angle and force) as depicted in Fig. 1 of Sect. 2. In this case study, the attacker could be located nearby the device or it could act remotely by compromising the smartphone with a malware. In the second situation, attacks made by a malware could be broad, and they require the exploitation of specific vulnerabilities to the smartphone, its OS or the running App that controls the torque wrench. In this work, we focus more on nearby attackers that perform Man-in-the-Middle (MitM) attacks to connect, pair, read, and even write to the device. This attack does not require specific vulnerabilities. The only constraint is that the attacker has to be within the communication range of BLE which is at most 100 m which could be extended to 1,000 m by using long range BLE sniffers [20].

We performed the MitM attack with a cloned BLE device identical to the torque wrench. The clone is realised by using 2 USB dongles Bluetooth 4.0 Cambridge Silicon Radio (CSR) and the Mirage tool [5]. The attacker uses this clone to read, modify and write the settings of the torque wrench which may alter its accuracy and the quality of operations. In particular, when the operator is adjusting the settings of the torque wrench with the desired values, the attacker will modify them and the applied torque will be different from the expected. In our experimental environment, we used the following devices and tools:

- Two devKits nRF52840. One is used by the torque wrench device, and the second is used as a sniffing interface for BLE packets.
- A smartphone with the nRFConnect installed and running to control remotely the torque wrench device.
- Two USB dongles to perform the MitM attack.
- Two hosts: one is used to perform the MitM attack by using the Mirage tool, and the second is running Wireshark tool for packets capture using the BLE sniffer.

3.1 Experimental Methodology

In our case study, we define two main scenarios. The first is a nominal scenario without any attack, and in a second scenario we introduced the MitM attack. For each scenario, using the experimental environment described above, we collect the BLE packets exchanged between the device and the smartphone while varying the distance between them. The distance as explained in Sect. 4 will be used as a feature for detecting the attack and allows us to measure the detection accuracy according to the closeness of the attacker to the device.

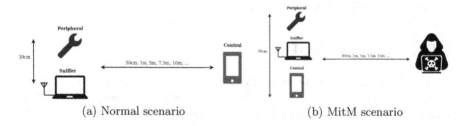

(a) Normal scenario   (b) MitM scenario

Fig. 2. Experimental Set-up for normal and MitM scenarios.

Normal Scenario. In this scenario, as depicted in Fig. 2a, we collect the BLE packets exchanged between the BLE device and the App while performing these operations over time: from 0 to 1 min the App reads 4 values, from 1 to 5 min the App activates and receives notifications, at 5 min the App deactivates the notifications, from 5 to 6 min the App writes 4 values, from 6 to 10 min the App activates and receives the notifications, at 10 min the App deactivates the notifications and reads the Device Name characteristic. These operations allows us to simulate a behaviour of the App running on the smartphone and generate different BLE packets including reading, writing and notifications.

MitM Scenario. In this attack scenario, as depicted in Fig. 2b, the attacker will modify values written by the smartphone App on the BLE device. From 5 to 6 min, the values written by the App are inverted by the attacker before being sent to the BLE device. From 6 to 10 min, the notifications sent by the BLE device to smartphone are modified. The timing of the modifications and the different operations are used for labelling the captured packets with "normal" and "attack" labels.

3.2 Datasets Building

Using the two experiments described above, we collect different datasets of BLE packets exchanged between the device and the smartphone. We build multiple datasets by varying the distance between the smartphone and the BLE device for the normal scenario, and between the attacker and the smartphone for the attack scenario. As depicted in Fig. 3, at time $t = 0$, the first seen packets are advertising messages. Then a connection is established between the smartphone and the device at $t = 2.792896$ with packet number 200.

No.	Time	Source	PHY	Protoco	Length	Delta time (μ	SN	NESN	More Di	Event cc	Info
1 0.000000		d2:57:fb:23:43:43	LE 1M	LE LL	21	46886				0	ADV_IND
2 0.000539		d2:57:fb:23:43:43	LE 1M	LE LL	21	497				0	ADV_IND
				••••							
200 2.792896		77:87:db:4e:87:75	LE 1M	LE LL	34	159				0	CONNECT_REQ
201 2.893677		Master_0xb5b3ad99	LE 1M	LE LL	9	28851	0	0	False	0	Control Opcode: LL_FEATURE_REQ
202 2.894161		Slave_0xb5b3ad99	LE 1M	LE LL	0	159	0	1	False	0	Empty PDU
203 2.894514		Master_0xb5b3ad99	LE 1M	LE LL	0	44618	1	1	False	1	Empty PDU
204 2.894904		Slave_0xb5b3ad99	LE 1M	LE LL	9	151	1	0	False	1	Control Opcode: LL_FEATURE_RSP
205 2.995608		Master_0xb5b3ad99	LE 1M	LE LL	9	44617	0	0	False	2	Control Opcode: LL_LENGTH_REQ

Fig. 3. BLE advertising and connection packets exchanged between the device and the smartphone in a normal scenario with a distance of 1 m between them.

We vary the distance between the devices in the set of values {30 cm, 1 m, 5 m, 7.5 m, 10 m}. In total we obtain 10 datasets that we merge in a single dataset with the distance value as a feature and each sample is labeled as attack or normal. The obtained dataset has a size of 19 MB and 77680 samples. We use 80% of this dataset for the training phase of ML algorithms and 20% for testing.

4   Detection Approach

Our detection approach of the attack described in Sect. 3 relies on two machine learning techniques: reconstruction and classification. This first technique aims at building a baseline model of normal patterns by using a machine learning algorithm and then we measure deviations and errors from that model [6]. Reconstruction is applied on batches of data and when one of them has a significative reconstruction error, it is considered as abnormal. The second technique applies a classification method to classify packets marked with attack features. The two techniques are applied jointly to detect respectively suspicious data and identify attacks in these suspicious packets. Figure 4 depicts the processing steps of our detection approach where reconstruction and classification techniques are applied jointly.

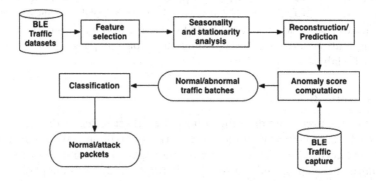

Fig. 4. Our MitM attack detection approach by using jointly reconstruction and classification techniques.

4.1 Features Extraction and Analysis

In this section, we describe our analysis of features extracted from BLE packets to select among them the most important for the reconstruction and classification techniques. We used the following 4 feature selection methods to identify an optimal set of features:

- Variance: this method applies a variance threshold to remove all low-variance features.
- Chi2: this method selects the features with the highest values of the chi-squared test.
- Recursive Feature Elimination (RFE): this method selects the features by recursively considering smaller and smaller sets of features while computing their importance.
- Extra trees: this method applies ensemble learning technique using decision tree provided with a random sample of k features and then select from them the most important features by using the Gini index.

Let $\mathbb{F} = (f_1, f_2, ..., f_n)$ the set of features extracted from a BLE packet, with $n = 250$. Each method i provides a subset of features $F_{k,i}$ composed of k features.

We apply then the intersection operator on the subsets F_k to obtain $\mathbb{F}_{final}$ with $\mathbb{F}_{final} = \bigcap_{i=1}^{4} F_{k,i}$. We applied the 4 methods while computing the performance of the machine learning algorithms until we obtain the optimal set of features. Our analysis shows that the following 4 features in a BLE packets dataset are the most important:

- Channel numbers: the channels used during the exchange of the BLE packets.
- Delta_time: the difference of time between two successive packets.
- Received Signal Strength Indication (RSSI): the signal-to-noise ratio value available in BLE packets.
- Distance: it denotes the distance between the mobile and the BLE device.

After selecting this set of optimal features, we analysed the stationarity and the seasonality of datasets. The stationarity denotes that the statistical properties of a feature are all constant over time. The seasonality denotes periodic patterns in the datasets that should be eliminated prior to building reconstruction models. To guarantee that our selected features represented as time series are stationary, we applied the following tests: Augmented Dickey-Fuller test, and Kwiatkowsk-Phillips-Schimdt-Shin test [4]. Our tests show that the 4 selected features are stationary and we eliminated from them the seasonality patterns.

4.2 LSTM Based Model Reconstruction

The reconstruction method consists in learning the normal behaviour of the BLE packets exchange. In the training phase we are looking to minimise the error between the learned data and the original dataset. In the testing phase, if the data contains an abnormal behaviour, the reconstruction will decrease which allows us to detect such behaviour in the observed packets. A technique to realise a model construction is to rely on a neural network of type Long Short-Term Memory (LSTM) [9]. In this way, we are able to approximate the BLE applications behaviour while considering their temporal patterns. By using this technique, we applied the following steps:

- Train the neural network on the dataset X_{train};
- Evaluate the obtained model on the $X_{validation}$ part while computing the reconstruction error;
- Set a detection threshold to determine the presence of anomalies. We can set, for instance, this threshold to 3 standard deviations of the mean value of the error, which is an empirical choice and a widely used threshold value for anomaly and outliers detection.

We realised this technique by using an LSTM auto-encoder which is a neural network with an Encode-Decoder LSTM architecture [17]. The hyperparameters of the used LSTM neural network are presented in Table 1. To set the detection threshold, we compute the residual defined as $R(X, \widehat{X}) = |X - \widehat{X}|$ with $\widehat{X} = f(X)$ and f represents the transformation of our auto-encoder. At the end of the

Table 1. The hyperparameters of the LSTM neural network.

Hyperparameter	Value
Optimizer	Adam
Learning rate	0.001
Batch size	40
Epoch number	150
Loss function	MSE
Validation metric	Accuracy
Validation split	0.2
DL framework	Tensorflow 1.13.1, Keras 2.2.4, Keras-tcn 2.6.7

training phase, we compute the mean and the standard-deviation of the residual $R(X_{train}, \widehat{X_{train}})$.

In the testing phase, we evaluate the residual $R(X_{test}, \widehat{X_{test}})$ to determine for each data batch its anomaly score α defined as following:

$$\alpha = \begin{cases} 0 & \text{if } |R(X_{test}, \widehat{X_{test}}) - \mu(R(X_{train}, \widehat{X_{train}}))| \leq 3 * \sigma(R(X_{train}, \widehat{X_{train}})) \\ 1 & \text{otherwise.} \end{cases}$$

We used the score α to detect the presence of an anomaly in a data batch if the residual is greater than 3 standard-deviations of the average. We obtain thus $X_{train} \in \mathcal{M}_{T,F}(\mathbb{R})$ which is the dataset of the nominal communication patterns of BLE with $T = 28918$ the number of samples, and $F = 4$ the number of features. We obtain in total: $T * F = 115672$ values. Then, as shown in Fig. 5, we convert our training dataset to a tensor $T^{s,t,F}$ with $s = 4819$ the number of samples, $t = 6$ the time-step (*empirical choice*) and $F = 4$ the number of features. Indeed, we obtain in total $s * t * F = T * F$.

In a first step, during the training phase we build a normal model of BLE communications from a subset of the training dataset. If the model is close to the normal behaviour of these communications, the reconstruction error should be low. Figure 6a shows the details of this phase. We observe that the real values fit well the predicted values with a very low reconstruction error (close to 0).

In a second step, we tested the reconstruction model obtained from X_{train} on X_{test} which contains the MitM attack packets. Figure 6b shows the details of the reconstruction of the attack model. We clearly observe large reconstruction errors and the testing data does not fit with the training model which indicates the presence of anomalies.

To measure the reconstruction error between the normal and attack models, we compared several error metrics which are BIAS (Bias of an estimator), MSE (Mean Squared Error), RMSE (Root Mean Squared Error) and MAE (Mean Absolute Error) [3]. The construction errors using these metrics are shown in Fig. 7. We observe that the metric MSE measures with high precision the reconstruction error of the MitM attack traffic from the normal traffic. We observe

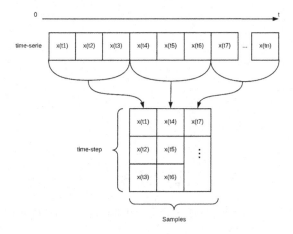

Fig. 5. Transformation of time series into training samples with a time-step = 3.

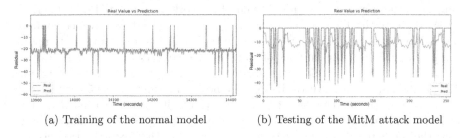

(a) Training of the normal model   (b) Testing of the MitM attack model

Fig. 6. Training and testing of models reconstruction using LSTM.

also that all the metrics provide a low reconstruction error when predicting the same normal traffic as input.

A major drawback when applying the LSTM based auto-encoder technique in our case is the low value of the time-step, which is equal to 6 used for building the input sequences. We have thus a low memory effect in the training neural network. We can hardly increase this value, since our dataset is small and the training phase will face the gradient vanishing or exploding problem where the gradient becomes vanishingly small which prevents the neural network weights from changing their values during the training phase with.

4.3 TCN Based Model Reconstruction

Another technique for model reconstruction is using a Temporal Convolutional Network (TCN) [10] instead of a LSTM based auto-encoder. A TCN is a class of time-series model that employs a hierarchy of temporal convolutional with an encoder-decoder architecture. It has the advantage of obtaining better results with less samples which allows us to increase the time-step when building the

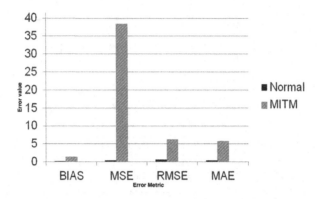

Fig. 7. Reconstruction error between normal and attack patterns using LSTM.

input sequences. The hyperparameter values of the TCN neural network are similar to those used for the LSTM neural network, as presented in Table 1.

As input to the TCN, we used the $X_{train} \in \mathcal{M}_{T,F}(\mathbb{R})$ dataset which contains normal communication patterns of BLE, with $T = 28918$ the number of temporal samples and $F = 4$ the number of features. We convert these time series to a tensor $T^{s,t,F}$ with $s = 963$ the number of samples, $t = 30$ the time-step and $F = 4$ the number of features. Using this model the time-step is 5 times higher than the LSTM based model. The prediction results of the normal behaviour of BLE communications using TCN are depicted in Fig. 8a. We mainly observe that the predicted values fit well the real values and the reconstruction error is close to 0.

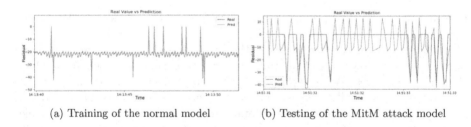

(a) Training of the normal model   (b) Testing of the MitM attack model

Fig. 8. Training and testing of models reconstruction using TCN.

The results of the testing phase by comparing the real and predicted values are shown in Fig. 8b. Similar to the LSTM based models, we observe that the predicted values do not fit the real values and we obtain large reconstruction errors. The reconstruction errors using different metrics when comparing normal and attack enabled BLE traffic are depicted in Fig. 9. The TCN model has more accurate and lower reconstruction error with high memory effect compared to LSTM architecture (Fig. 7) when predicting attack traffic behaviour from normal traffic behaviour. Using the same anomaly score α, we are able to discriminate data batches containing suspicious packets. However, both LSTM and TCN models are only able to detect suspicious batches, without detecting packets involved in the attack.

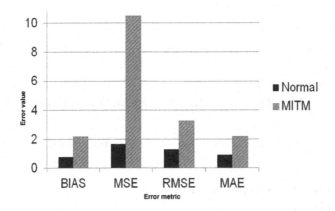

Fig. 9. Reconstruction error between normal and attack patterns using TCN.

4.4   Classification of BLE Packets

After detecting suspicious batches of traffic with attack packets, the next step of our detection process is to classify these packets according to their class: "normal" or "attack". In our work, we applied the technique developed in [12] by jointly using Text-Convolutional Neural Network (Text-CNN) for feature extraction and a Random Forest algorithm for classification. In [12], the authors show that combining Text-CNN for payload feature extraction and a Random Forest algorithm for final packets classification outperforms a CNN model with a *softmax* classifier. For BLE packets available in the dataset, we extract from them their traffic statistics and we convert their payload into word embedding to extract salient features with Text-CNN. The hyperparameters of the Text-CNN neural network are presented in Table 2.

The statistical features that we extracted from the BLE traffic data are presented in Table 3.

The payload based features are extracted by converting packet payload bytes to low dimensional vectors using Word2Vec technique and then provide these vectors as an input to a Text-CNN neural network. The extracted features are then concatenated with the statistical features and provided as input to a Random Forest algorithm using a number of estimators equal to 200 to classify the packets. Our classification results are shown in the confusion matrix of Table 4. We observe that mostly all the packets are classified correctly with only 2 normal packets misclassified as attack and 12 attack packets misclassified as normal.

Table 2. The hyperparameters of the Text-CNN neural network.

Hyperparameter	Value
Optimizer	Adam
Learning rate	0.0001
Batch size	50
Epoch number	50
Loss function	Binary cross-entropy
Validation metric	Accuracy
Validation split	0.2
DL framework	Tensorflow 1.13.1, Keras 2.2.4, Gensim (Word2Vec) 3.7.1

Table 3. Statistical features of BLE traffic data.

Features
Number of packets per second
Number of bytes per second
Max, min and average packets length
Max, min and average time interval between 2 packets
Number of packets for each BLE packets type (ADV, DATA, etc.)

Table 4. Confusion matrix of the classification of BLE packets.

		Predicted labels	
		Normal	Attack
Actual label	Normal	100% (9541/9543)	0% (2)
	Attack	0.3% (12)	99.7% (4207/4219)

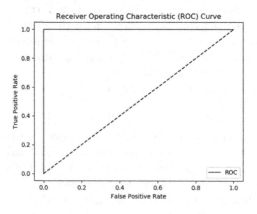

Fig. 10. ROC curve of the BLE packets classifier.

The ROC curve of our classifier is depicted in Fig. 10 with an Area Under the Curve (AUC) close to 1 which confirms that our classification model has a good measurement of separability between "normal" and "attack" packets. However, we have to note that our obtained results with high classification performance, are limited to the collected datasets within our experimental setup environment, and it is still difficult to generalise the learned models on new datasets with different settings.

5   Conclusion and Future Work

In this paper, we presented a study on the use of machine learning techniques to detect MitM attack targeting BLE enabled IoT devices. This attack is trivial to deploy and may be used easily by attackers to stole users private information or alter control data exchanged between a companion mobile app and the device. We demonstrated the feasibility of the attack in a real-world deployment while varying the distance between the BLE mobile and devices and collecting datasets of exchanged BLE packets. We applied jointly reconstruction and classification models based on neural networks to detect suspicious network data traffic batches and then identify from them attack packets. Our evaluation results show high detection accuracy ($\approx$0.99) and low false positive rate ($\approx$0.03). In future work, we will extend the proposed method for detecting more classes of BLE attacks including DoS and connection hijacking within various BLE environments. We will also study efficient protection mechanisms for BLE networks.

References

1. Albahar, M., Haataja, K., Toivanen, P.: Bluetooth MITM vulnerabilities: a literature review, novel attack scenarios, novel countermeasures, and lessons learned. Int. J. Inf. Technol. Secur. **8**, 25–49 (2016)
2. Antonakakis, M., et al.: Understanding the Mirai Botnet. In: 26th USENIX Security Symposium (USENIX Security 17), pp. 1093–1110, August 2017
3. Botchkarev, A.: Performance metrics (error measures) in machine learning regression, forecasting and prognostics: properties and typology (2018)
4. Box, G.E.P., Jenkins, G.M.: Time Series Analysis: Forecasting and Control, 3rd edn. Prentice Hall PTR, USA (1994)
5. Cayre, R., Roux, J., Alata, E., Nicomette, V., Auriol, G.: Mirage: un framework offensif pour l'audit du bluetooth low energy. In: Symposium sur la Sécurité des Technologies de l'Information et des Communications (SSTIC 2019) (2019)
6. Friedman, E., Dunning, T.: Practical Machine Learning: A New Look at Anomaly Detection (2014)
7. Goyal, R., Dragoni, N., Spognardi, A.: Mind the tracker you wear: a security analysis of wearable health trackers. In: Proceedings of the 31st Annual ACM Symposium on Applied Computing, SAC 2016, pp. 131–136 (2016)
8. Hafeez, I., Antikainen, M., Ding, A.Y., Tarkoma, S.: IoT-KEEPER: detecting malicious IoT network activity using online traffic analysis at the edge. IEEE Trans. Netw. Serv. Manage. **17**(1), 45–59 (2020)

9. Hochreiter, S., Schmidhuber, J.: Long short-term memory. Neural Comput. **9**(8), 1735–1780 (1997)

10. Lea, C., Flynn, M.D., Vidal, R., Reiter, A., Hager, G.D.: Temporal convolutional networks for action segmentation and detection. abs/1611.05267 (2016). http://arxiv.org/abs/1611.05267

11. Matheus E. Garbelini, Sudipta Chattopadhyay, C.W.: SweynTooth: unleashing Mayhem over bluetooth low energy. Technical report, Singapore University of Technology and Design (2020)

12. Min, E., Long, J., Liu, Q., Cui, J., Chen, W.: TR-IDS: anomaly-based intrusion detection through text-convolutional neural network and random forest. Secur. Commun. Netw. **2018**, 1–9 (2018)

13. Nguyen, T., Marchal, S., Miettinen, M., Fereidooni, H., Asokan, N., Sadeghi, A.: DIoT: a federated self-learning anomaly detection system for IoT. In: 2019 IEEE 39th International Conference on Distributed Computing Systems (ICDCS)

14. Oliff, W., Filippoupolitis, A., Loukas, G.: Impact evaluation and detection of malicious spoofing attacks on BLE based occupancy detection systems. In: Proceedings of the 1st International Conference on Internet of Things and Machine Learning, IML 2017. ACM (2017)

15. Bluetooth SIG: Bluetooth Core Specification 4.0, December 2010. https://www.bluetooth.com/specifications/bluetooth-core-specification/

16. Bluetooth SIG: Bluetooth Market Update 2019 (2019). https://www.bluetooth.com/wp-content/uploads/2018/04/2019-Bluetooth-Market-Update.pdf

17. Srivastava, N., Mansimov, E., Salakhutdinov, R.: Unsupervised learning of video representations using LSTMs. In: Proceedings of the 32nd International Conference on International Conference on Machine Learning, ICML2015, vol. 37, pp. 843–852. JMLR.org (2015)

18. Vasilomanolakis, E., Daubert, J., Luthra, M., Gazis, V., Wiesmaier, A., Kikiras, P.: On the security and privacy of internet of things architectures and systems. In: 2015 International Workshop on Secure Internet of Things (SIoT)

19. Yaseen, M., et al.: MARC: a novel framework for detecting MITM attacks in ehealthcare BLE systems. J. Med. Syst. **43**(11), 324:1–324:18 (2019)

20. Zuo, C., Wen, H., Lin, Z., Zhang, Y.: Automatic fingerprinting of vulnerable BLE IoT devices with static UUIDs from mobile apps. In: Proceedings of the 2019 ACM SIGSAC Conference on Computer and Communications Security (2019)

Advocating for Multiple Defense Strategies Against Adversarial Examples

Alexandre Araujo[1,2](✉), Laurent Meunier[1,3], Rafael Pinot[1,4],
and Benjamin Negrevergne[1]

[1] Miles Team, PSL, Université Paris-Dauphine, Paris, France
{alexandre.araujo,laurent.meunier,rafael.pinot,
benjamin.negrevergne}@dauphine.psl.eu
[2] Wavestone, Paris, France
[3] Facebook AI Research, Paris, France
[4] CEA, Université Paris-Saclay, Paris, France

Abstract. It has been empirically observed that defense mechanisms designed to protect neural networks against ℓ_∞ adversarial examples offer poor performance against ℓ_2 adversarial examples and vice versa. In this paper we conduct a geometrical analysis that validates this observation. Then, we provide a number of empirical insights to illustrate the effect of this phenomenon in practice. Then, we review some of the existing defense mechanisms that attempt to defend against multiple attacks by mixing defense strategies. Thanks to our numerical experiments, we discuss the relevance of this method and state open questions for the adversarial examples community.

1 Introduction

Deep neural networks achieve state-of-the-art performances in a variety of domains such as natural language processing [19], image recognition [9] and speech recognition [10]. However, it has been shown that such neural networks are vulnerable to *adversarial examples*, *i.e.*, imperceptible variations of the natural examples, crafted to deliberately mislead the models [3,7,22]. Since their discovery, a variety of algorithms have been developed to generate adversarial examples (a.k.a. attacks), for example FGSM [8], PGD [15] and C&W [5], to mention the most popular ones.

Because it is difficult to characterize the space of visually imperceptible variations of a natural image, existing adversarial attacks use surrogates that can differ from one attack to another. For example, [8] use the ℓ_∞ norm to measure the distance between the original image and the adversarial image whereas [5] use the ℓ_2 norm. When the input dimension is low, the choice of the norm is of little importance because the ℓ_∞ and ℓ_2 balls overlap by a large margin, and the adversarial examples lie in the same space. An important insight in this paper is to observe that the overlap between the two balls diminishes exponentially quickly as the dimensionality of the input space increases. For typical image

© Springer Nature Switzerland AG 2020
I. Koprinska et al. (Eds.): ECML PKDD 2020 Workshops, CCIS 1323, pp. 165–177, 2020.
https://doi.org/10.1007/978-3-030-65965-3_11

datasets with large dimensionality, the two balls are mostly disjoint. As a consequence, the ℓ_∞ and the ℓ_2 adversarial examples lie in different areas of the space, and it explains why ℓ_∞ defense mechanisms perform poorly against ℓ_2 attacks and vice versa.

Building on this insight, we advocate for designing models that incorporate defense mechanisms against both ℓ_∞ and ℓ_2 attacks and review several ways of mixing existing defense mechanisms. In particular, we evaluate the performance of *Mixed Adversarial Training* (MAT) [8] which consists of augmenting training batches using *both* ℓ_∞ and ℓ_2 adversarial examples, and *Randomized Adversarial Training* (RAT) [20], a solution to benefit from the advantages of both ℓ_∞ adversarial training, and ℓ_2 randomized defense.

Outline of the Paper. The rest of this paper is organized as follows. In Sect. 2, we recall the principle of existing attacks and defense mechanisms. In Sect. 3, we conduct a theoretical analysis to show why the ℓ_∞ defense mechanisms cannot be robust against ℓ_2 attacks and vice versa. We then corroborate this analysis with empirical results using real adversarial attacks and defense mechanisms. In Sect. 4, we discuss various strategies to mix defense mechanisms, conduct comparative experiments, and discuss the performance of each strategy.

2   Preliminaries on Adversarial Attacks and Defenses

Let us first consider a standard classification task with an input space $\mathcal{X} = [0,1]^d$ of dimension d, an output space $\mathcal{Y} = [K]$ and a data distribution $\mathcal{D}$ over $\mathcal{X} \times \mathcal{Y}$. We assume the model f_θ has been trained to minimize the expectation over $\mathcal{D}$ of a loss function $\mathcal{L}$ as follows:

$$\min_\theta \mathbb{E}_{(x,y)\sim\mathcal{D}} \left[\mathcal{L}(f_\theta(x), y) \right]. \tag{1}$$

2.1   Adversarial Attacks

Given an input-output pair $(x, y) \sim \mathcal{D}$, an *adversarial attack* is a procedure that produces a small perturbation $\tau \in \mathcal{X}$ such that $f_\theta(x + \tau) \neq y$. To find the best perturbation τ, existing attacks can adopt one of the two following strategies: (i) maximizing the loss $\mathcal{L}(f_\theta(x + \tau), y)$ under some constraint on $\|\tau\|_p{}^1$ (a.k.a. loss maximization); or (ii) minimizing $\|\tau\|_p$ under some constraint on the loss $\mathcal{L}(f_\theta(x + \tau), y)$ (a.k.a. perturbation minimization).

(i) Loss maximization. In this scenario, the procedure maximizes the loss objective function, under the constraint that the ℓ_p norm of the perturbation remains bounded by some value ϵ, as follows:

$$\underset{\|\tau\|_p \leq \epsilon}{\operatorname{argmax}} \mathcal{L}(f_\theta(x + \tau), y). \tag{2}$$

---

[1] With $p \in \{0, \cdots, \infty\}$.

The typical value of ϵ depends on the norm $\|\cdot\|_p$ considered in the problem setting. In order to compare ℓ_∞ and ℓ_2 attacks of similar strength, we choose values of ϵ_∞ and ϵ_2 (for ℓ_∞ and ℓ_2 norms respectively) which result in ℓ_∞ and ℓ_2 balls of equivalent volumes. For the particular case of CIFAR-10, this would lead us to choose $\epsilon_\infty = 0.03$ and $\epsilon_2 = 0.8$ which correspond to the maximum values chosen empirically to avoid the generation of visually detectable perturbations. The current state-of-the-art method to solve Problem (2) is based on a projected gradient descent (PGD) [15] of radius ϵ. Given a budget ϵ, it recursively computes

$$x^{t+1} = \prod_{B_p(x,\epsilon)} \left(x^t + \alpha \underset{\delta \text{ s.t. } \|\delta\|_p \leq 1}{\operatorname{argmax}} \left(\Delta^t | \delta \right) \right) \tag{3}$$

where $B_p(x,\epsilon) = \{x + \tau \text{ s.t. } \|\tau\|_p \leq \epsilon\}$, $\Delta^t = \nabla_x \mathcal{L}(f_\theta(x^t), y)$, α is a gradient step size, and $\prod_S$ is the projection operator on S. Both PGD attacks with $p = 2$, and $p = \infty$ are currently used in the literature as state-of-the-art attacks for the loss maximization problem.

(ii) Perturbation minimization. This type of procedure search for the perturbation that has the minimal ℓ_p norm, under the constraint that $\mathcal{L}(f_\theta(x + \tau), y)$ is bigger than a given bound c:

$$\underset{\mathcal{L}(f_\theta(x+\tau),y) \geq c}{\operatorname{argmin}} \|\tau\|_p. \tag{4}$$

The value of c is typically chosen depending on the loss function $\mathcal{L}^2$. Problem (4) has been tackled in [5], leading to the following method, denoted C&W attack in the rest of the paper. It aims at solving the following Lagrangian relaxation of Problem (4):

$$\underset{\tau}{\operatorname{argmin}} \|\tau\|_p + \lambda \times g(x + \tau) \tag{5}$$

where $g(x + \tau) < 0$ if and only if $\mathcal{L}(f_\theta(x + \tau), y) \geq c$. The authors use a change of variable $\tau = \tanh(w) - x$ to ensure that $-1 \leq x + \tau \leq 1$, a binary search to optimize the constant c, and Adam or SGD to compute an approximated solution. The C&W attack is well defined both for $p = 2$, and $p = \infty$, but there is a clear empirical gap of efficiency in favor of the ℓ_2 attack.

In this paper, we focus on the *Loss Maximization* setting using the PGD attack. However we conduct some of our experiments using *Perturbation Minimization* algorithms such as C&W to capture more detailed information about the location of adversarial examples in the vector space[3].

2.2 Defense Mechanisms

Adversarial Training (AT). Adversarial Training was introduced in [8] and later improved in [15] as a first defense mechanism to train robust neural networks.

---

[2] For example, if $\mathcal{L}$ is the 0/1 loss, any $c > 0$ is acceptable.

[3] As it has a more flexible geometry than the *Loss Maximization* attacks.

It consists in augmenting training batches with adversarial examples generated during the training procedure. The standard training procedure from Eq. (1) is thus replaced by the following min max problem, where the classifier tries to minimize the expected loss under maximum perturbation of its input:

$$\min_{\theta} \; \mathbb{E}_{(x,y)\sim\mathcal{D}} \left[\max_{\|\tau\|_p \leq \epsilon} \mathcal{L}\left(f_\theta(x+\tau), y\right) \right] . \tag{6}$$

In the case where $p = \infty$, this technique offers good robustness against ℓ_∞ attacks [1]. AT can also be used with ℓ_2 attacks but as we will discuss in Sect. 3, AT with one norm offers poor protection against the other. The main weakness of Adversarial Training is its lack of formal guarantees. Despite some recent work providing great insights [21,25], there is no worst case lower bound yet on the accuracy under attack of this method.

Noise Injection Mechanisms (NI). Another important technique to defend against adversarial examples is to use Noise Injection. In contrast with Adversarial Training, Noise Injection mechanisms are usually deployed after training. In a nutshell, it works as follows. At inference time, given a unlabeled sample x, the network outputs

$$\tilde{f}_\theta(x) := f_\theta(x+\eta) \quad (\text{instead of } f_\theta(x)) \tag{7}$$

where η is a random variable on $\mathbb{R}^d$. Even though, Noise Injection is often less efficient than Adversarial Training in practice (see *e.g.*, Table 3), it benefits from strong theoretical background. In particular, recent works [13,14], followed by [6,18] demonstrated that noise injection from a Gaussian distribution can give provable defense against ℓ_2 adversarial attacks. In this work, besides the classical Gaussian noises already investigated in previous works, we evaluate the efficiency of Uniform distributions to defend against ℓ_2 adversarial examples.

3   No Free Lunch for Adversarial Defenses

In this Section, we show both theoretically and empirically that defenses mechanisms intending to defend against ℓ_∞ attacks cannot provide suitable defense against ℓ_2 attacks. Our reasoning is perfectly general; hence we can similarly demonstrate the reciprocal statement, but we focus on this side for simplicity.

3.1   Theoretical Analysis

Let us consider a classifier f_∞ that is provably robust against adversarial examples with maximum ℓ_∞ norm of value ϵ_∞. It guarantees that for any input-output pair $(x, y) \sim \mathcal{D}$ and for any perturbation τ such that $\|\tau\|_\infty \leq \epsilon_\infty$, f_∞ is not misled by the perturbation, *i.e.*, $f_\infty(x+\tau) = f_\infty(x)$. We now focus our study on the performance of this classifier against adversarial examples bounded with a

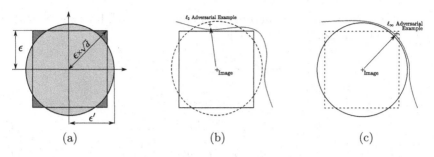

Fig. 1. Left: 2D representation of the ℓ_∞ and ℓ_2 balls of respective radius ϵ and ϵ'. Middle: a classifier trained with ℓ_∞ adversarial perturbations (materialized by the red line) remains vulnerable to ℓ_2 attacks. Right: a classifier trained with ℓ_2 adversarial perturbations (materialized by the blue line) remains vulnerable to ℓ_∞ attacks. (Color figure online)

ℓ_2 norm of value ϵ_2. Using Fig. 1(a), we observe that any ℓ_2 adversarial example that is also in the ℓ_∞ ball, will not fool f_∞. Conversely, if it is outside the ball, we have no guarantee.

To characterize the probability that such an ℓ_2 perturbation fools an ℓ_∞ defense mechanism in the general case (*i.e.*, any dimension d), we measure the ratio between the volume of the intersection of the ℓ_∞ ball of radius ϵ_∞ and the ℓ_2 ball of radius ϵ_2. As Theorem 1 shows, this ratio depends on the dimensionality d of the input vector x, and rapidly converges to zero when d increases. Therefore a defense mechanism that protects against all ℓ_∞ bounded adversarial examples is unlikely to be efficient against ℓ_2 attacks.

Theorem 1 (Probability of the intersection goes to 0).
Let $B_{2,d}(\epsilon) := \left\{ \tau \in \mathbb{R}^d \ s.t \ \|\tau\|_2 \leq \epsilon \right\}$ and $B_{\infty,d}(\epsilon') := \left\{ \tau \in \mathbb{R}^d \ s.t \ \|\tau\|_\infty \leq \epsilon' \right\}$. If for all d, we select ϵ and ϵ' such that $Vol(B_{2,d}(\epsilon)) = Vol(B_{\infty,d}(\epsilon'))$, then

$$\frac{Vol(B_{2,d}(\epsilon) \bigcap B_{\infty,d}(\epsilon'))}{Vol(B_{\infty,d}(\epsilon'))} \to 0 \ when \ d \to \infty.$$

Proof. Without loss of generality, let us fix $\epsilon = 1$. One can show that for all d,

$$\mathrm{Vol}\left(B_{2,d}\left(\frac{2}{\sqrt{\pi}} \Gamma\left(\frac{d}{2} + 1 \right)^{1/d} \right) \right) = \mathrm{Vol}\left(B_{\infty,d}\left(1 \right) \right) \qquad (8)$$

where Γ is the gamma function. Let us denote

$$r_2(d) = \frac{2}{\sqrt{\pi}} \Gamma\left(\frac{d}{2} + 1 \right)^{1/d}. \qquad (9)$$

Then, thanks to Stirling's formula

$$r_2(d) \sim \sqrt{\frac{2}{\pi e}} d^{1/2}. \qquad (10)$$

Finally, if we denote $\mathcal{U}_S$, the uniform distribution on set S, by using Hoeffding inequality between Eq. 14 and 15, we get:

$$\frac{\text{Vol}(B_{2,d}(r_2(d)) \cap B_{\infty,d}(1))}{\text{Vol}(B_{\infty,d}(1))} \tag{11}$$

$$= \mathbb{P}_{x \sim \mathcal{U}_{B_{\infty,d}(1)}} \left[x \in B_{2,d}(r_2(d)) \right] \tag{12}$$

$$= \mathbb{P}_{x \sim \mathcal{U}_{B_{\infty,d}(1)}} \left[\sum_{i=1}^{d} |x_i|^2 \leq r_2^2(d) \right] \tag{13}$$

$$\leq \exp\left\{ -d^{-1} \left(r_2^2(d) - d\mathbb{E}|x_1|^2 \right)^2 \right\} \tag{14}$$

$$\leq \exp\left\{ -\left(\frac{2}{\pi e} - \frac{1}{3} \right)^2 d + o(d) \right\}. \tag{15}$$

Then the ratio between the volume of the intersection of the ball and the volume of the ball converges towards 0 when d goes to ∞.   □

Theorem 1 states that, when d is large enough, ℓ_2 bounded perturbations have a null probability of being also in the ℓ_∞ ball of the same volume. As a consequence, for any value of d that is large enough, a defense mechanism that offers full protection against ℓ_∞ adversarial examples is not guaranteed to offer any protection against ℓ_2 attacks[4].

Table 1. Bounds of Theorem 1 on the volume of the intersection of ℓ_2 and ℓ_∞ balls at equal volume for typical image classification datasets. When $d = 2$, the bound is $10^{-0.009} \approx 0.98$.

Dataset	Dim. (d)	Vol. of the intersection
–	2	$10^{-0.009}$ (≈ 0.98)
MNIST	784	10^{-144}
CIFAR	3072	10^{-578}
ImageNet	150528	10^{-28946}

Note that this result defeats the 2-dimensional intuition: if we consider a 2 dimensional problem setting, the ℓ_∞ and the ℓ_2 balls have an important overlap (as illustrated in Fig. 1(a)) and the probability of sampling at the intersection of the two balls is bounded by approximately 98%. However, as we increase the dimensionality d, this probability quickly becomes negligible, even for very simple image datasets such as MNIST. An instantiation of the bound for classical image datasets is presented in Table 1. The probability of sampling at the intersection of the ℓ_∞ and ℓ_2 balls is close to zero for any realistic image setting. In large dimensions, the volume of the corner of the ℓ_∞ ball is much bigger than it appears in Fig. 1(a).

---

[4] Theorem 1 can easily be extended to any two balls with different norms. For clarity, we restrict to the case of ℓ_∞ and ℓ_2 norms.

3.2 No Free Lunch in Practice

Our theoretical analysis shows that if adversarial examples were uniformly distributed in a high-dimensional space, then any mechanism that perfectly defends against ℓ_∞ adversarial examples has a null probability of protecting against ℓ_2-bounded adversarial attacks. Although existing defense mechanisms do not necessarily assume such a distribution of adversarial examples, we demonstrate that whatever distribution they use, it offers no favorable bias with respect to the result of Theorem 1. As we discussed in Sect. 2, there are two distinct attack settings: loss maximization (PGD) and perturbation minimization (C&W). Our analysis is mainly focusing on loss maximization attacks. However, these attacks have a very strict geometry[5]. This is why, to present a deeper analysis of the behavior of adversarial attacks and defenses, we also present a set of experiments that use perturbation minimization attacks.

Table 2. Average norms of PGD-ℓ_2 and PGD-ℓ_∞ adversarial examples with and without ℓ_∞ adversarial training on CIFAR-10 ($d = 3072$).

	Attack PGD-ℓ_2		Attack PGD-ℓ_∞	
	Unprotected	AT-ℓ_∞	Unprotected	AT-ℓ_2
Average ℓ_2 norm	0.830	0.830	1.400	1.640
Average ℓ_∞ norm	0.075	0.200	0.031	0.031

Adversarial Training vs. Loss Maximization Attacks. To demonstrate that ℓ_∞ adversarial training is not robust against PGD-ℓ_2 attacks we measure the evolution of ℓ_2 norm of adversarial examples generated with PGD-ℓ_∞ between an unprotected model and a model trained with AT-ℓ_∞, *i.e.*, AT where adversarial examples are generated with PGD-ℓ_∞[6]. Results are presented in Table 2.[7]

The analysis is unambiguous: the average ℓ_∞ norm of a bounded ℓ_2 perturbation more than double between an unprotected model and a model trained with AT PGD-ℓ_∞. This phenomenon perfectly reflects the illustration of Fig. 1(c). The attack will generate an adversarial example on the corner of the ℓ_∞ ball thus increasing the ℓ_∞ norm while maintaining the same ℓ_2 norm. We can observe the same phenomenon with AT-ℓ_2 against PGD-ℓ_∞ attack (see Fig. 1(b) and Table 2). PGD-ℓ_∞ attack increases the ℓ_2 norm while maintaining the same ℓ_∞ perturbation thus generating the perturbation in the upper area.

As a consequence, we cannot expect adversarial training ℓ_∞ to offer any guaranteed protection against ℓ_2 adversarial examples .

---

[5] Due to the projection operator, all PGD attacks saturate the constraint, which makes them all lies in a very small part of the ball.

[6] To do so, we use the same experimental setting as in Sect. 4 with ϵ_∞ and ϵ_2 such that the volumes of the two balls are equal.

[7] All experiments in this section are conducted on CIFAR-10, and the experimental setting is fully detailed in Sect. 4.1.

Adversarial Training vs. Perturbation Minimization Attacks. To better capture the behavior of ℓ_2 adversarial examples, we now study the performances of an ℓ_2 perturbation minimization attack (C&W) with and without AT-ℓ_∞. It allows us to understand in which area C&W discovers adversarial examples and the impact of AT-ℓ_∞. In high dimensions, the red corners (see Fig. 1(a)) are very far away from the ℓ_2 ball. Therefore, we hypothesize that a large proportion of the ℓ_2 adversarial examples will remain unprotected. To validate this assumption, we measure the proportion of adversarial examples inside of the ℓ_2 ball before and after ℓ_∞ adversarial training. The results are presented in Fig. 2 (left: without adversarial training, right: with adversarial training).

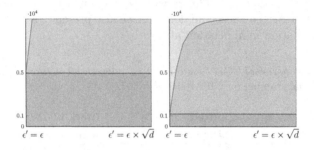

Fig. 2. Comparison of the number of adversarial examples found by C&W, inside the ℓ_∞ ball (lower, blue area), outside the ℓ_∞ ball but inside the ℓ_2 ball (middle, red area) and outside the ℓ_2 ball (upper gray area). ϵ is set to 0.3 and ϵ' varies along the x-axis. Left: without adversarial training, right: with adversarial training. Most adversarial examples have shifted from the ℓ_∞ ball to the cap of the ℓ_2 ball, but remain at the same ℓ_2 distance from the original example. (Color figure online)

On both charts, the blue area represents the proportion of adversarial examples that are inside the ℓ_∞ ball. The red area represents the adversarial examples that are outside the ℓ_∞ ball but still inside the ℓ_2 ball (valid ℓ_2 adversarial examples). Finally, the brown-beige area represents the adversarial examples that are beyond the ℓ_2 bound. The radius ϵ' of the ℓ_2 ball varies along the x-axis from ϵ' to $\epsilon'\sqrt{d}$. On the left chart (without adversarial training) most ℓ_2 adversarial examples generated by C&W are inside both balls. On the right chart most of the adversarial examples have been shifted out the ℓ_∞ ball. This is the expected consequence of ℓ_∞ adversarial training. However, these adversarial examples remain in the ℓ_2 ball, *i.e.*, they are in the cap of the ℓ_2 ball. These examples are equally good from the ℓ_2 perspective. This means that even after adversarial training, it is still easy to find good ℓ_2 adversarial examples, making the ℓ_2 robustness of AT-ℓ_∞ almost null.

4   Reviewing Defenses Against Multiple Attacks

Adversarial attacks have been an active topic in the machine learning community since their discovery [3,7,22]. Many attacks have been developed. Most of them

Table 3. This table shows a comprehensive list of results consisting of the accuracy of several defense mechanisms against ℓ_2 and ℓ_∞ attacks. This table main objective is to compare the overall performance of 'single' norm defense mechanisms (AT and NI presented in the Sect. 2.2) against mixed norms defense mechanisms (MAT & RAT mixed defenses presented in Sect. 4).

	Baseline	AT		MAT		NI		RAT-ℓ_∞		RAT-ℓ_2	
	–	ℓ_∞	ℓ_2	Max	Rand	$\mathcal{N}$	$\mathcal{U}$	$\mathcal{N}$	$\mathcal{U}$	$\mathcal{N}$	$\mathcal{U}$
Natural	0.94	0.85	0.85	0.80	0.80	0.79	0.87	0.74	0.80	0.79	0.87
PGD-ℓ_∞	0.00	0.43	0.37	0.37	0.40	0.23	0.22	0.35	0.40	0.23	0.22
PGD-ℓ_2	0.00	0.37	0.52	0.50	0.55	0.34	0.36	0.43	0.39	0.34	0.37

solve a loss maximization problem with either ℓ_∞ [8,12,15], ℓ_2 [5,12,15], ℓ_1 [23] or ℓ_0 [16] surrogate norms. As we showed, these norms are really different in high dimension. Hence, defending against one norm-based attack is not sufficient to protect against another one. In order to solve this problem, we review several strategies to build defenses against multiple adversarial attacks. These strategies are based on the idea that both types of defense must be used simultaneously in order for the classifier to be protected against multiple attacks. The detailed description of the experimental setting is described in Sect. 4.1.

4.1 Experimental Setting

To compare the robustness provided by the different defense mechanisms, we use strong adversarial attacks and a conservative setting: the attacker has a total knowledge of the parameters of the model (white-box setting) and we only consider untargeted attacks (a misclassification from one target to any other will be considered as adversarial). To evaluate defenses based on Noise Injection, we use *Expectation Over Transformation* (EOT), the rigorous experimental protocol proposed by [2] and later used by [1,4] to identify flawed defense mechanisms.

To attack the models, we use state-of-the-art algorithms PGD. We run PGD with 20 iterations to generate adversarial examples and with 10 iterations when it is used for adversarial training. The maximum ℓ_∞ bound is fixed to 0.031 and the maximum ℓ_2 bound is fixed to 0.83. As discussed in Sect. 2, we chose these values so that the ℓ_∞ and the ℓ_2 balls have similar volumes. Note that 0.83 is slightly above the values typically used in previous publications in the area, meaning the attacks are stronger, and thus more difficult to defend against.

All experiments are conducted on CIFAR-10 with the Wide-Resnet 28-10 architecture. We use the training procedure and the hyper-parameters described in the original paper by [24]. Training time varies from 1 day (AT) to 2 days (MAT) on 4 GPUs-V100 servers.

4.2 MAT – Mixed Adversarial Training

Earlier results have shown that AT-ℓ_p improves the robustness against corresponding ℓ_p-bounded adversarial examples, and the experiments we present in this section corroborate this observation (See Table 3, column: AT). Building on this, it is natural to examine the efficiency of *Mixed Adversarial Training* (MAT) against mixed ℓ_∞ and ℓ_2 attacks. MAT is a variation of AT that uses both ℓ_∞-bounded adversarial examples and ℓ_2-bounded adversarial examples as training examples. As discussed in [23], there are several possible strategies to mix the adversarial training examples. The first strategy (MAT-Rand) consists in randomly selecting one adversarial example among the two most damaging ℓ_∞ and ℓ_2, and to use it as a training example, as described in Eq. (16):

MAT-Rand:

$$\min_{\theta} \mathbb{E}_{(x,y)\sim\mathcal{D}} \left[\mathbb{E}_{p\sim\mathcal{U}(\{2,\infty\})} \max_{\|\tau\|_p \leq \epsilon} \mathcal{L}\left(f_\theta(x+\tau), y\right) \right]. \tag{16}$$

An alternative strategy is to systematically train the model with the most damaging adversarial example (ℓ_∞ or ℓ_2). As described in Eq. (17):

MAT-Max:

$$\min_{\theta} \mathbb{E}_{(x,y)\sim\mathcal{D}} \left[\max_{p\in\{2,\infty\}} \max_{\|\tau\|_p \leq \epsilon} \mathcal{L}\left(f_\theta(x+\tau), y\right) \right]. \tag{17}$$

The accuracy of MAT-Rand and MAT-Max are reported in Table 3 (Column: MAT). As expected, we observe that MAT-Rand and MAT-Max offer better robustness both against PGD-ℓ_2 and PGD-ℓ_∞ adversarial examples than the original AT does. More generally, we can see that AT is a good strategy against loss maximization attacks, and thus it is not surprising that MAT is a good strategy against mixed loss maximization attacks. However efficient in practice, MAT (for the same reasons as AT) lacks theoretical arguments. In order to get the best of both worlds, [20] proposed to mix adversarial training with randomization.

4.3   RAT – Randomized Adversarial Training

We now examine the performance of Randomized Adversarial Training (RAT) first introduced in [20]. This technique mixes Adversarial Training with Noise Injection. The corresponding loss function is defined as follows:

$$\min_{\theta} \mathbb{E}_{(x,y)\sim\mathcal{D}} \left[\max_{\|\tau\|_p \leq \epsilon} \mathcal{L}\left(\tilde{f}_\theta(x+\tau), y)\right) \right]. \tag{18}$$

where $\tilde{f}_\theta$ is a randomized neural network with noise injection as described in Sect. 2.2, and $\|\cdot\|_p$ define which kind of AT is used. For each setting, we consider two noise distributions, Gaussian and Uniform as we did with NI. We also consider two different Adversarial training AT-ℓ_∞ as well as AT-ℓ_2.

The results of RAT are reported in Table 3 (Columns: RAT-ℓ_∞ and RAT-ℓ_2). We can observe that RAT-ℓ_∞ offers the best extra robustness with both noises, which is consistent with previous experiments, since AT is generally more effective against ℓ_∞ attacks whereas NI is more effective against ℓ_2-attacks. Overall, RAT-ℓ_∞ and a noise from uniform distribution offers the best performances but is still weaker than MAT-Rand. These results are also consistent with the literature, since adversarial training (and its variants) is the best defense against adversarial examples so far.

5 Conclusion and Perspective

In this paper, we tackled the problem of protecting neural networks against multiple attacks crafted from different norms. We demonstrated and gave a geometrical interpretation to explain why most defense mechanisms can only protect against one type of attack. Then we reviewed existing strategies that mix defense mechanisms in order to build models that are robust against multiple adversarial attacks. We conduct a rigorous and full comparison of *Randomized Adversarial Training* and *Mixed Adversarial Training* as defenses against multiple attacks.

We could argue that both techniques offer benefits and limitations. We have observed that MAT offers best empirical robustness against multiple adversarial attacks but this technique is computationally expensive which hinders its use in large-scale applications. Randomized techniques have the important advantage of providing theoretical guarantees of robustness and being computationally cheaper. However, the certificate provided by such defenses is still too small for strong attacks. Furthermore, certain Randomized defenses also suffer from the curse of dimensionality as recently shown by [11].

Although, randomized defenses based on noise injection seem limited in terms of accuracy under attack and scalability, they could be improved either by Learning the best distribution to use or by leveraging different types of randomization such as discrete randomization first proposed in [17]. We believe that these certified defenses are the best solution to ensure the robustness of classifiers deployed into real-world applications.

Acknowledgement. This work was granted access to the HPC resources of IDRIS under the allocation 2020-101141 made by GENCI. We would like to thank Jamal Atif, Florian Yger and Yann Chevaleyre for their valuable insights.

References

1. Athalye, A., Carlini, N., Wagner, D.: Obfuscated gradients give a false sense of security: circumventing defenses to adversarial examples. In: Dy, J., Krause, A. (eds.) Proceedings of the 35th International Conference on Machine Learning. Proceedings of Machine Learning Research, vol. 80, pp. 274–283, Stockholmsmässan, Stockholm Sweden, 10–15 July 2018. PMLR (2018)
2. Athalye, A. Engstrom, L., Ilyas, A., Kwok, K.: Synthesizing robust adversarial examples. arXiv preprint arXiv:1707.07397 (2017)

3. Biggio, B., et al.: Evasion attacks against machine learning at test time. In: Blockeel, H., Kersting, K., Nijssen, S., Železný, F. (eds.) ECML PKDD 2013. LNCS (LNAI), vol. 8190, pp. 387–402. Springer, Heidelberg (2013). https://doi.org/10.1007/978-3-642-40994-3_25

4. Carlini, N., et al.: On evaluating adversarial robustness. arXiv preprint arXiv:1902.06705 (2019)

5. Carlini, N., Wagner, D.: Towards evaluating the robustness of neural networks. In: 2017 IEEE Symposium on Security and Privacy (SP), pp. 39–57. IEEE (2017)

6. Cohen, J.M., Rosenfeld, E., Kolter, J.Z.: Certified adversarial robustness via randomized smoothing. CoRR, abs/1902.02918 (2019)

7. Globerson, A., Roweis, S.: Nightmare at test time: robust learning by feature deletion. In: Proceedings of the 23rd International Conference on Machine Learning, pp. 353–360 (2006)

8. Goodfellow, I., Shlens, J., Szegedy, C.: Explaining and harnessing adversarial examples. In: International Conference on Learning Representations (2015)

9. He, K., Zhang, X., Ren, S., Sun, J.: Deep residual learning for image recognition. In: The IEEE Conference on Computer Vision and Pattern Recognition (CVPR), June 2016

10. Hinton, G., et al.: Deep neural networks for acoustic modeling in speech recognition. IEEE Signal Process. Mag. **29** (2012)

11. Kumar, A., Levine, A., Goldstein, T., Feizi, S.: Curse of dimensionality on randomized smoothing for certifiable robustness. arXiv preprint arXiv:2002.03239 (2020)

12. Kurakin, A., Goodfellow, I., Bengio, S.: Adversarial examples in the physical world. arXiv preprint arXiv:1607.02533 (2016)

13. Lecuyer, M., Atlidakais, V., Geambasu, R., Hsu, D., Jana, S.: Certified robustness to adversarial examples with differential privacy. In: 2019 IEEE Symposium on Security and Privacy (SP), pp. 727–743 (2018)

14. Li, B., Chen, C., Wang, W., Carin, L.: Certified adversarial robustness with additive noise. In: Advances in Neural Information Processing Systems, vol. 32, pp. 9459–9469. Curran Associates Inc. (2019)

15. Madry, A., Makelov, A., Schmidt, L., Tsipras, D., Vladu, A.: Towards deep learning models resistant to adversarial attacks. In: International Conference on Learning Representations (2018)

16. Papernot, N., McDaniel, P., Jha, S., Fredrikson, M., Celik, Z.B., Swami, A.: The limitations of deep learning in adversarial settings. In: 2016 IEEE European Symposium on Security and Privacy (EuroS&P), pp. 372–387. IEEE (2016)

17. Pinot, R., Ettedgui, R., Rizk, G., Chevaleyre, Y., Atif, J.: Randomization matters. How to defend against strong adversarial attacks. arXiv preprint arXiv:2002.11565 (2020)

18. Pinot, R., et al.: Theoretical evidence for adversarial robustness through randomization. In: Advances in Neural Information Processing Systems, vol. 32, pp. 11838–11848 (2019)

19. Radford, A., Wu, J., Child, R., Luan, D., Amodei, D., Sutskever, I.: Language models are unsupervised multitask learners. Technical report, OpenAi (2018)

20. Salman, H., et al.: Provably robust deep learning via adversarially trained smoothed classifiers. In: Advances in Neural Information Processing Systems, pp. 11289–11300 (2019)

21. Sinha, A., Namkoong, H., Volpi, R. Duchi, J.: Certifying some distributional robustness with principled adversarial training (2017)

22. Szegedy, C., et al.: Intriguing properties of neural networks. In: International Conference on Learning Representations (2014)

23. Tramèr, F., Boneh, D.: Adversarial training and robustness for multiple perturbations. arXiv preprint arXiv:1904.13000 (2019)
24. Zagoruyko, S., Komodakis, N.: Wide residual networks. arXiv preprint arXiv:1605.07146 (2016)
25. Zhang, H., Yu, Y., Jiao, J., Xing, E.P., Ghaoui, L.E., Jordan, M.I.: Theoretically principled trade-off between robustness and accuracy. arXiv preprint arXiv:1901.08573 (2019)

Hybrid Connection and Host Clustering for Community Detection in Spatial-Temporal Network Data

Mark Patrick Roeling[1,2]([✉]), Azqa Nadeem[1], and Sicco Verwer[1]

[1] Department Intelligent Systems, Cyber-Security, Technical University of Delft,
Delft, The Netherlands
m.p.roeling@tudelft.nl
[2] Department of Statistics, University of Oxford, Oxford, UK

Abstract. Network data clustering and sequential data mining are large fields of research, but how to combine them to analyze spatial-temporal network data remains a technical challenge. This study investigates a novel combination of two sequential similarity methods (Dynamic Time Warping and N-grams with Cosine distances), with two state-of-the-art unsupervised network clustering algorithms (Hierarchical Density-based Clustering and Stochastic Block Models). A popular way to combine such methods is to first cluster the sequential network data, resulting in connection types. The hosts in the network can then be clustered conditioned on these types. In contrast, our approach clusters nodes and edges in one go, i.e., without giving the output of a first clustering step as input for a second step. We achieve this by implementing sequential distances as covariates for host clustering. While being fully unsupervised, our method outperforms many existing approaches. To the best of our knowledge, the only approaches with comparable performance require manual filtering of connections and feature engineering steps. In contrast, our method is applied to raw network traffic. We apply our pipeline to the problem of detecting infected hosts (network nodes) from logs of unlabelled network traffic (sequential data). On data from the Stratosphere IPS project (CTU-Malware-Capture-Botnet-91), which includes malicious (Conficker botnet) as well as benign hosts, we show that our method perfectly detects peripheral, benign, and malicious hosts in different clusters. We replicate our results in the well-known ISOT dataset (Storm, Waledac, Zeus botnets) with comparable performance: conjointly, 99.97% of nodes were categorized correctly.

Keywords: Network data · Unsupervised learning · Clustering · Spatio-temporal

1 Introduction

Spatial-temporal network data have a spatial structure, where observations are linked via single or multiple features, and a temporal structure, meaning multiple time-points are (partly) available. The analyses of the spatial element is

© Springer Nature Switzerland AG 2020
I. Koprinska et al. (Eds.): ECML PKDD 2020 Workshops, CCIS 1323, pp. 178–204, 2020.
https://doi.org/10.1007/978-3-030-65965-3_12

usually performed via network clustering, which is a large field of research where a graph ($\mathcal{G}$), consisting of nodes ($\mathcal{V}$) and edges ($\mathcal{E}$), is represented by one or more pairwise distance matrices subject to an algorithm to group observations with, relatively speaking, small distances [21,25,40,44,48]. There are roughly two kinds of clustering methods: those that cluster edges (e.g. spectral-, density-, or centroid based clustering methods [10,30]) and those that cluster nodes (e.g. community detection algorithms like Louvain clustering [4] or mixture clustering like the Stochastic Block Model [1]).

The analyses of the temporal aspect is equally complex. Apart from collapsing time-points by analyzing the mean of multiple events [11], some methods allow to analyse time-series as discrete windows. Examples of these methods are 1) creating windows and train models for each window so that state-changes over time can be identified [31]; 2) treating time as a latent variable in latent variable growth models [22]; 3) creating temporal graphs so that every pairwise interaction over time becomes a link [24]; 4) the analyses of network evolution with Stochastic Actor Based Models [41]; 5) Temporal Exponential Random Graph Models [18]; and 6) Time-contrastive learning [19]. Even more complex is the analyses of streaming data, where time cannot be treated as a strictly discrete variable either due to an arbitrary sequence in time where cutting windows is difficult, or a negative balance between the volume of time windows and the specificity (larger time windows equals lower specificity).

This paper focuses on unsupervised clustering of streaming spatial-temporal network data by combining node and edge clustering. We aim to present a reliable procedure to communities of nodes with converging behavior, without the need for a labelled dataset and not requiring manual feature engineering or filtering steps. Our method computes pairwise edge distances based on the sequential behavior of network connections using Dynamic Time Warping (distance measure for continuous sequences) and N-grams with Cosine distances (for nominal sequences), as implemented in the MalPaCA tool [33]. In order to include these distances in node clustering, the pairwise distances are aggregated via Principal Component Analysis into a small set of features. These features are added as co-variates to a node clustering algorithm based on Stochastic Block Models (SBMs), which is a well-known generative model for random graphs that produces graphs containing communities. Here, those subgroups represent hosts characterized by being connected with one another with particular edge densities [32]. Our SBM-definition is based on a recent review [27].

SBMs are attractive because they seek highly connected blocks in network connections while allowing the inclusion of features, in a statistically tractable way. This removes the need to first cluster the sequential data before analyzing the network structure or attributes as both are considered in one single node clustering algorithm. Our approach is complementary to earlier work [36] where hosts and connections were classified sequentially by first filtering P2P hosts and then categorizing P2P traffic. Using sequential features is beneficial since it reduces the required number of features as all variation is (assumed to be) captured by the pairwise sequential distance [26,33]. Our approach (shown graphically in Fig. 1) does not require a priori (manual) host or sequence filtering and uses as input raw packet capture (.pcap) files.

We test our method in the setting of botnet-infected computers. Botnets are networks of computers that are infected with malware and are under the control of a botnet controller, able to use the computers for nefarious activities. Infection status is usually unknown to users or controllers and incomplete, meaning that in a large network not all computers are infected but only a relatively small number of machines can be part of a botnet. This motivates an unsupervised approach to cluster the hosts in a computer network, thereby uncovering yet unknown (latent) groups of similarly behaving hosts. The idea is that all infected hosts show different behavior from the normal hosts in a network and can thus be singled out, preferably in one or more dedicated clusters. We experiment with different packet thresholds to show which data-specific cutoffs are optimal (i.e. short but still informative). The reliability of our method is investigated by replicating the main result with another dataset containing different botnet captures.

This paper presents the following contributions:

- We present a clustering method of network data that does not require manual filtering of observations.
- Clustering of nodes as well as edges in spatial-temporal network data is conducted in one procedure.
- We present a competitive performance in the setting of detecting malware infected computers (bots) and replicate our main result in different types of botnets.

2   Related Work

To date, a common strategy is to collapse temporal data into aggregate values and neglect spatial structure [2,7,11,13,15,17,29,34,36,38,39,42,50,51]. This causes a loss of information as researchers remove streams of data that only occur once (e.g. because these connections are uninformative when calculating the variance of inter arrival time between packets in a sequence of connections). Apart from some studies using time-windows [16], removing temporal information by collapsing streaming data complicates botnet classification [37]. Neglecting spatial structure in botnet detection is equally problematic because this structure is informative for infection status [9]: the members of a botnet are more likely to have mutual contacts with each other than with benign hosts.

Another issue is that many studies apply some kind of manual filtering prior to analysis (e.g. removing approved DNS addresses via white-listing based on Alexa [17,39] or other rule based exclusion criteria (e.g. [5,36,46]). It is unclear whether the obtained results are due to the analysis or filtering steps. Manual feature engineering may also bias the results of these experiments [20], especially when combined with sparsely reported procedures and outcomes (e.g. [45,49]). Finally, only a few studies apply methods that do not require a labelled dataset (unsupervised learning: [15,50]). Especially in the botnet setting where computers are *zombies* per definition, the dependence on a labelled dataset is an important shortcoming for operational usefulness.

3 Methods

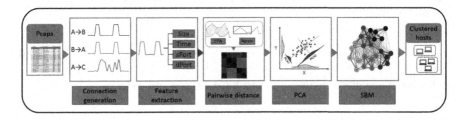

Fig. 1. Schematic illustration of the proposed pipeline

3.1 Connection Features

We build on a sequential feature paradigm presented recently in MalPaCA [33]: a behavior discovery framework for network traffic which uses Hierarchical Density-Based Spatial Clustering of Applications with Noise (HDBScan) [6], providing clusters of connection sequences.

From the original packet capture (.pcap file), we define dataframe C which is a matrix with $t \times p$ dimensions, with t rows (one row for every packet) and p features on the columns. C was made to include unidirectional connections, defined as an uninterrupted list of all packets sent from a source IP to destination IP. MalPaCA proposed to include four sequential features: packet size (bytes), time interval (gaps), source port (sport), and destination port (dport).

From every column of C we created the symmetric distance matrices D_{bytes}, D_{gaps}, D_{sport}, and D_{dport}. All distance matrices had $n_c \times n_c$ dimensions, with n_c unique unidirectional connections, and zero diagonals. For D_{bytes} and D_{gaps} the pairwise distance over time (t) was calculated via Dynamic Time Warping (DTW). For each pair of hosts we had time series $X \in \{1, ..., N\}$ and $Y \in \{1, ..., M\}$ and the average accumulated difference between X and Y is

$$d_\phi(X,Y) = \sum_{k=1}^{T} \frac{d(\phi_x(k), \phi_y(k)) m_\phi(k)}{M_\phi} \tag{1}$$

with warping functions: $\phi(k) = (\phi_x(k), \phi_y(k))$, $\phi_x(k) \in \{1...N\}$, $\phi_y(k) \in \{1...M\}$, which shape the warping curve $\phi(k); k \in \{1, ..., T\}$. $m_\phi(k)$ is a weighting coefficient and M_ϕ is the corresponding normalization constant, which ensures that the accumulated differences in time series are comparable along different paths [14]. DTW optimises by finding the minimum the difference: $dtw(X,Y) = \arg\min_\phi d_\phi(X,Y)$ and we normalized the DTW estimates to range [0–1] with

$$\hat{x}_i = \frac{x_i - min(x)}{max(x) - min(x)} \tag{2}$$

where $\mathrm{x} = [dtw(X_1,Y_1), dtw(X_1,Y_2), ..., dtw(X_{n_c},Y_{n_c})]$.

For source and destination port, the pairwise distances were calculated with the cosine similarity

$$cos(X,Y) = \frac{\sum_{k=1}^{T}(X_k * Y_k)}{\sqrt{(\sum_{k=1}^{T}(X_k^2))}\sqrt{(\sum_{k=1}^{T}(Y_k^2))}} \tag{3}$$

which were normalized as described to form D_{sport} and D_{dport}.

3.2 Host Features

The Stochastic Block Model (SBM) required to transform the connection distance matrices (D_{bytes}, D_{gaps}, D_{sport} and D_{dport}) to host distance matrices, which was achieved via Principal Component Analyses (PCA). The PCA works by calculating the singular value decomposition of the distance matrices so that by maximizing the variation captured per component a small number of components (ideally) captures a major proportion of the variation. We input the distance matrices so the aim was to acquire a number of dimensions less than the number of unique connections, accomplished by selecting the m components explaining at least 40% cumulative variation. For each of the 4 features, the PCA thus resulted in a matrix W with n_c rows and m columns, so that for each unique $a \rightarrow b$ connection m, component weights were available. We used W to create m host-host SBM covariates. Since every row of W referred to a unique $a \rightarrow b$ connection, the connection source (a) and destination (b) are used to indicate the rows and columns for each SBM covariate matrix Y_m with dimensions $n_h \times n_h$ where n_h is the unique number of hosts. Hence, the values in Y_{bytes,m_1}, the SBM covariate matrix for the first component of $bytes$, were inherited from m_1 of W_{bytes} (see Table 1).

Table 1. A fictional example of a distance matrix D_{bytes}, PCA component weights matrix W_{bytes}, and corresponding SBM covariate matrix Y_{bytes,m_1}.

D	ab	ac	bc	ca	W	m_1
ab	0	689	1262	512	ab	−3.18
ac	689	0	1169	680	ac	−2.96
bc	1262	1169	0	1062	bc	−4.60
ca	512	680	1062	0	ca	−2.92

Y_{m_1}	a	b	c
a	0	−3.18	−2.96
b	0	0	−4.60
c	-2.92	0	0

3.3 Stochastic Block Model

The SBM took as input a graph $G = (\mathcal{V}, \mathcal{E})$, where $\mathcal{V}$ was the node set of size $n_h := |\mathcal{V}|$, and $\mathcal{E}$ was the edge list of size $M := |\mathcal{E}|$. The corresponding $n_h \times n_h$ adjacency matrix was denoted by Y, where $Y_{ab} = 1$ if there was a connection between hosts a and b and 0 otherwise. The main input graph was an undirected binary node matrix Y_{class} which held a 1 if there was any connection between nodes a and b; $Y_{class,ab} = 1$ or zero otherwise. The generated SBM covariate matrices are added to the model as covariates

$$SBM(Y_{class,ab}, List(Y_{packetSize,m}, Y_{gapsDist,m}, Y_{sourcePort,m}, Y_{destPort,m}))$$

Since group (g) membership is unknown, the membership labels for every host are captured by a latent variable Z_a, which elements are all 0, except exactly one that takes the value 1 and represents the group host a belongs to. This Z_a is assumed to be independent of Z_b for $a \neq b$. Finally, SBM outputs a $n \times g$ matrix $Z := (Z_1, ..., Z_n)^T$, such that $Z_{a,i}$ is the ith element of Z_a. Graph generation and likelihood are explained elsewhere [27]. The lower and upper bound of fitted SBM models were 2 and 10. Model fit was evaluated with the Integrated Classification Likelihood (ICL), via a variational expectation maximization approach implemented in R [28].

3.4 Experimental Setup

This study used data from the Malware Capture Facility Project, which is a sister project of the Stratosphere IPS Project: an initiative to obtain malware and normal data. From all the published samples, a dataset was selected which included both normal ($N_b = 12$) and infected ($N_i = 10$) hosts and included the entire network. The malicious hosts were infected with the Conficker botnet. The data were downloaded from https://mcfp.felk.cvut.cz/publicDatasets/CTU-Malware-Capture-Botnet-91/ as a .pcap file consisting of 198818 lines (packets), capturing 1011 unique $(a \rightarrow b)$ connections. There were 3 isolated clusters which were removed, leaving 917 unique connections. The correlation between covariates was low (see Table 7) so instead of combining the distance matrices they were included in the SBM as individual predictors.

Not all observed connections are necessarily informative, so we experimented with a minimum number of packets-threshold (P_t) to ensure that the remaining connections represented sufficient information for effective behavioral modeling. The thresholds tested were $P_t \in \{5, 10, 15, 20\}$, respectively pruning to 631 (62.4%), 565 (55.9%), 523 (51.7%), and 483 (47.8%) connections (see Table 2). From analyses we determined that for this dataset a packet threshold of 10 is desirable, balancing the number of connections, nodes, MalPaCA and SBM clusters (see Supplementary Material). Higher thresholds resulted in too much pruning of the network structure, hindering accurate classification in this dataset.

Table 2. Descriptives of the Stratosphere CTU-91 data with different behavioral thresholds

Covariate	N_{seq}	N_{ip}	$Q_{MalPaCA}$	outliers	Q_{SBM}
5 packets	631	205	10	120	4
10 packets	565	182	9	154	4
15 packets	523	165	7	40	4
20 packets	483	148	6	38	5

This Table presents the number of unique $a \rightarrow b$ sequences (N_{seq}), unique hosts (N_{ip}), the optimal number of clusters ($Q_{MalPaCA}$) and *outliers* determined by MalPaCA, and optimal SBM-cluster solution (Q_{SBM}).

3.5 Replication Sample

For replication of our main finding we used the ISOT dataset from the University of Victoria (https://www.uvic.ca/engineering/ece/isot/datasets) as presented in [38], which included of a collection of neutral/background data and 4 samples (Waledac, Storm, Zeus) of botnet data. Storm, Waledac, and Zeus are Windows targeting botnets predominantly used in spamming campaigns which peaked in 2007–2008. They can all be managed via a Command and Control as well as Peer to Peer communication. From the neutral data we selected the data from the Traffic Lab at Ericsson Research in Hungary [43]. The latter contained a large number of general traffic from a variety of applications, including HTTP web browsing behavior, World of Warcraft gaming packets, and packets from popular bittorrent clients. ISOT documentation states IP addresses of infected machines were mapped to the background traffic and all trace file were replaced to homogenize network behavior. The infected data contained 747264 packets with 25308 unique connections and the Ericsson lab data included 2300385 packets from 12778 unique connections. These two sets were combined so that MalPaCA features could be extracted.

4 Results

4.1 Stratosphere Data

MalPaCA Directly. Applying MalPaCA directly to the data assigned the connections to 9 dense clusters (see Table 3). Visual inspection of the nodes belonging to the connections classified as outliers revealed that these were mostly peripheral, supporting the notion that nodes on the edges of the network, with negligible activity, are more likely to fall outside a MalPaCA cluster.

Different subsets of connections were identified. Cluster 1 captured all traffic from 192.168.0.118 to peripheral hosts. Cluster 3 included bidirectional traffic

Table 3. MalPaCA clusters and infection status in the CTU-91 data. Connections in
-1 are unclustered. $srcip_p, srcip_n, scrip_i$ are connections where the source host was
peripheral, normal, or infected (respectively). The same for destination ports $dstip$.

Cluster	$srcip_p$	$srcip_n$	$srcip_i$	$dstip_p$	$dstip_n$	$dstip_i$
-1	8	6	23	17	10	10
1	0	0	14	14	0	0
2	10	0	0	0	0	10
3	119	0	0	0	0	119
4	62	0	0	0	0	62
5	0	0	125	125	0	0
6	0	12	78	73	10	7
7	0	4	4	0	0	8
8	0	0	8	0	8	0
9	0	10	0	0	0	10

between normal and infected hosts as well as connections from normal to normal, infected, and peripheral hosts. Clusters 4 and 5 included connections from
normal and infected to peripheral hosts (opposite to cluster 2: peripheral to
infected and normal), but apparently specific clusters were required to capture
specific connections from peripheral to infected (clusters 6 and 7) and infected
to peripheral hosts (clusters 8 and 9), illustrating the heterogeneity in connections from and to infected nodes. Relating the connections to their respective
nodes, we identified 11 true negatives (cluster 1), 11 false positives (clusters 2:5),
and 389 true positives, yielding an accuracy of 97.32%, sensitivity of 100% and
specificity of 50%.

SBM Directly. Fitting the SBM directly on the network matrix, ignoring the
MalPaCA features, resulted in a 6-class solution. This solution was incapable of
distinguishing normal and peripheral nodes (as described earlier in [37]). Class
1 and 3 captured 11 peripheral and 2 normal hosts, class 2 and 5 respectively
captured 2 and 3 infected hosts, class 4 included 3 normal and 5 infected hosts,
and class 6 only included 148 peripheral hosts. Hence, there are 10 true positives,
3 false positives (class 4), and 312 true negatives, resulting in a performance of:
accuracy $= 99.08\%$, sensitivity $= 100\%$ and specificity $= 99.05\%$.

Our Approach. Applying MalPaCA to obtain the distance matrices, representing the distances between connections for the four features, resulted in 565
surviving connections. The average connection length was 348.48, with a minimum of 10 packets ($P_t = 10$) and a maximum of 5333. The PCA solution on
the MalPaCA distance matrices commended a 1 (bytesDist), 3 (destPort), 1

(gapsDist), and 3 (sourcePort) component solution that cumulatively explained >40% of the variation. This result was P_t invariant; including more packets per connection does not change the amount of variation explained by the components.

Fitting the SBM on the PCA derived covariates favoured a 4-class solution. The network with original- and cluster labels is visualized in Fig. 2 and the performance matrix for the 10 threshold solution is provided in Table 4. After obtaining the cluster solution we used straightforward descriptive analyses and visualization to interpret the clusters (see Supplementary Material and [33]). We found that all malicious hosts were assigned to one cluster with a posterior probability of >.998. Most of the peripheral hosts were captured by one cluster, indicating behavioral similarity, with a class assignment posterior probability of .9982. The non-infected/normal hosts were divided over two clusters, that also included peripheral hosts. Only one normal host had a posterior probability <.95, which was host 192.168.1.6 with .82, with the remaining probability belonging to the other *normal/mixed* class. If we consider all peripheral hosts $(136 + 9 + 1)$ and normal hosts $(4+3)$ to be true negatives, and the correctly clustered infected hosts as true positives, the classification is perfect. These findings are consistent for all four tested packet thresholds (P_t).

Table 4. Performance matrix from the SBM node-based clustering in the CTU-91 data

Cluster	*Peripheral*	*Normal*	*Infected*
1	–	–	10
2	136	4	–
3	9	–	–
4	1	3	–

Table 5. Performance comparison with other studies using ISOT data

Method	*Accuracy*	*Sensitivity*	*Specificity*	*Study*
BClus	.5	.4	.5	[12]
CAMNEP	.5	0	.9	[12]
BotHunter	.4	.01	.9	[12]
BotGM	.91	.83	n.p	[26]
Decision tree	.99	.98	n.p	[51]
Decision tree	.75	.99	n.p	[3]

n.p. = not provided

(a) Network with original labels   (b) Network with MalPaCA and SBM labels

Fig. 2. Network plots of a subset of the CTU-91 network (including hosts with a packet threshold $P_t = 10$). Left: network with original host labels, used in this analyses as ground truth (blue = peripheral, red = infected, green = normal). Right: network with the MalPaCA connection label colours and SBM host labels (blue = peripheral, red = infected, green & turquoise = normal & peripheral). (Color figure online)

4.2 ISOT Data

Previous studies have used the ISOT data for botnet identification purposes and Table 5 presents a selection of the performance reported in related works. As mentioned before, most of these methods require manual feature engineering and connection filtering to be applied, while others operate in a supervised setting. We compare our unsupervised clustering method to these results.

Creating the distance matrices with MalPaCA pruned the network (see Fig. 3a) to 7683 surviving connections with $P_t = 20$. Average connection length was 365.95, with a minimum of 20 and a maximum of 525256. This amounted to 3847 nodes. There was one isolated sub-network of hosts connected to 172.16.2.3, of which only the connection between 172.16.2.3 and 193.88.8.59 survived the packet threshold of 20. Isolation supported their removal from subsequent clustering analyses, leaving 3845 nodes (running the analyses with these two nodes included yielded similar results in the optimal SBM solution; both were allocated to the cluster with infected nodes).

Identical to the Stratosphere data, a PCA fitting resulted 1, 1, 3, 3 components for respectively bytes, gaps, dport and sport to explain >40% of the variation. The SBM model fitted on the binary adjacency matrix, with the PCA features resulted in an optimal 5 class solution (see Figs. 3b and Table 6). Of these 5 clusters, clusters 1 and 2 captured the peripheral nodes, where the peripheral nodes in cluster 1 were all linked to host 172.16.2.11 (Storm + non-malicious) which was the only host allocated to cluster 3. Cluster 4 consisted of the Waledac and Storm hosts, confirming the comparability of Waledac and Storm activity. Cluster 5 captures eight hosts, of which seven are non-malicious: 172.16.2.2, 172.16.2.13-14, 172.16.2.111-114, and one host in cluster 5 (172.16.2.12) had combined (non-malicious & malicious) traffic. If we consider 1734 and 2100 peripheral

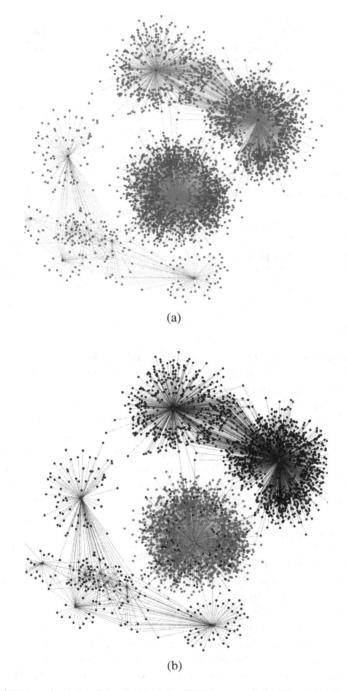

(a)

(b)

Fig. 3. (a) Network plots of a subset of the ISOT network for $P_t = 20$. Network with original host labels, used here as ground truth (blue = peripheral, red = malicious, orange = malicious + non-malicious, green = non-malicious. (b) Network with labels assigned by our method: Turquoise (cluster 1) & blue (cluster 4) = peripheral, red (cluster 2) = malicious + misclasification, orange (cluster 3) and purple (cluster 5) = Waledac, and green (cluster 6) = non-malicious. (Color figure online)

nodes (cluster 1 and 2) and 7 non-malicious nodes (cluster 5) as true negatives, the Waledac and Storm nodes in cluster 3 and 4 as true positives, and the combined traffic node in cluster 5 as a false negative, the accuracy and sensitivity = 99.97 % and the specificity = 100%. This performance is similar to other work on supervised learning using decision trees [26,51] and nearest neighbours [13] on manually curated collapsed data. We outperform the methods listed in [12].

Table 6. Performance matrix from the SBM node-based clustering in the ISOT replication data

Cluster	*Peripheral*	*Normal*	*Normal + infected*	*Infected*
1	1734	–	–	–
2	2100	–	–	–
3	–	–	1	–
4	–	–	–	2
5	–	7	1	–

5 Discussion

Here, we combined two unsupervised methods to solve the problem of analysing spatio-temporal data so that botnet infected computers can be identified via connection- and host clustering. In our discovery sample (CTU-91) we identified all infected machines and classification was perfect. The infected machines were all allocated to one cluster, indicating marked similarities between infected machines infected with the Conficker botnet. In the replication sample (ISOT), one host with malicious and non-malicious traffic was allocated to a cluster of non-malicious nodes, yielding one false negative with an overall accuracy of 99.97%. This procedure outperforms other botnet detection studies using the ISOT dataset [3,8,26,38,47] and has comparable performance to [13,36]. Compared to the studies that report similar classification performance, our method does not require any type of filtering [36] or manual feature selection [13], and is therefore less sensitive to external factors. In the discovery sample, the normal and peripheral hosts were allocated together in a cluster, whereas in the replication data, the peripheral hosts formed a separate cluster. This may be due to the mapping procedure used in the ISOT dataset, where botnet data were collected in a VM and mapped a posteriori, so that the differences in the ISOT data may be captured by our model, underlining the sensitivity of our approach. Furthermore, although not explicitly illustrated, the output of MalPaCA has been found to be informative to identify malware families or other specifically tuned categories of traffic [33], and other similar connection profile based approaches exist [36].

A potential limitation of this study is the relatively short time window in which the data were collected. Ideally one would capture the temporal structure of the network traffic in more specific analyses. A prominent example of such analyses is creating snapshots [23], which facilitates network clustering within snapshots, so that state changes (nodes hopping to another cluster) between snapshots can be analysed [31]. However, given the length of the CTU-91 capture (roughly 20 min, compared to for example one year of data from mobile devices in [31]) we argue there is little sense in making 5-min snapshots, since this would result in many, difficult to compare, local network clusters. Again, these packet thresholds are data specific, and shorter or other snapshots may be applicable in other types of network data (e.g. social network data where snapshots represent school-years). Although our approach does not require manual curation, understanding the effects of sample specific factors is a focus of future research. Another limitation of this approach is the speed of Variational Inference when fitting a SBM with covariates to large datasets (>2500 nodes). The runtime of our discovery (CTU-91) sample was about 2.5 h on a Windows 10 (i7-7700K CPU, 4.2 GHZ, 8-core, 16 GB ram) machine, but new developments in fast optimization [35] will reduce run-time from hours to minutes.

6   Conclusion

The overarching aim of this study is to present a combination of clustering methods to simultaneously cluster nodes and host in spatial-temporal network data, where the features capture a sequential or time series structure. In the setting of botnet detection, our method is able to allocate labels to distinguish different types of nodes, with near-perfect classification, while ingesting raw unfiltered network traffic data. This makes it an easy-to-use and effective tool for network traffic analysis.

Our method and results add to existing studies that botnets are relatively easy to detect. Indeed, our performance is higher compared to most earlier studies and we depend less on manual curating of the data, but methods solely based on community detection, or collapse temporal variation in composite features yield excellent results as well.

In future work, we aim to make our approach less computationally intensive using sketching and related methods from data-stream mining. Moreover, we afterwards intend to apply it to large network captures, and simplify the connection-to-host transformation to a PCA independent yet robust implementation.

7   Supplementary Material

Location of R-scripts and raw input file: https://drive.google.com/drive/folders/ 121pnmgob-f-T0lE60yQmFlnnq6MW2VQy?usp=sharing (Fig. 4).

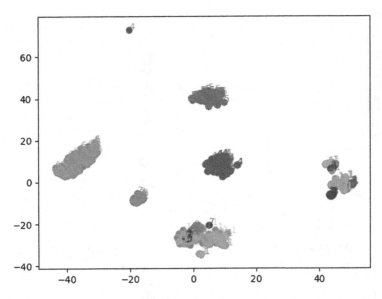

Fig. 4. This Figure shows the connections clustered with MalPaCA on the CTU-91 data. The grey dots indicate connections labeled as outliers by HDBScan. For this plot, the multidimensional sample space was reduced to two axes by TSNE, resulting in the ability to visually identify 7 clusters, of which the top cluster belongs to the middle cluster (letter 4), the right cluster decomposes into 3 sub-clusters (blue, red, brown) and outliers, and the bottom cluster consist of 2 sub-clusters (magenta, darkgreen) and outliers. Hence, 9 clusters are displayed. (Color figure online)

7.1   Host Clustering CTU-91 Dataset

Node assignment to a cluster does not immediately inform which cluster(s) contain the infected nodes. Descriptive analyses are typically used to interpret the cluster output. For example, when comparing cluster 1 (10 hosts) with cluster 2 (140 hosts), we observed an almost 3-fold increase of packets send (93100 versus 33917), a higher occurrence of bigger packets send ($Mean_{c1} = 138.22(SD = 180.51), Mean_{c2} = 118.97(SD = 135.63), t = 1.9547, p = .051$) and received ($Mean_{c1} = 167.26(SD = 226.31), Mean_{c2} = 142.92(SD = 194.23), t = 1.6614, p = .09703$), and higher frequencies of HTTPS, UDP, and SMTP/IMF protocol traffic, whereas SMTP, TCP, NBNS, and BROWSER protocol traffic was significantly higher in cluster 2. This behavior of nodes (more connections via specific protocols) is coherent for botnets. Further visualisation (not provided) resulted in the identification of cluster 1 as likely malicious (and verified with the original labels). All of the malicious hosts (192.168.1.238, 192.168.1.239, 192.168.1.236, 192.168.1.91, 192.168.1.71, 192.168.1.9, 192.168.1.243, 192.168.1.242, 192.168.1.247, 192.168.1.245) were assigned to one cluster with a posterior probability of >.998 (Figs. 5 and 6).

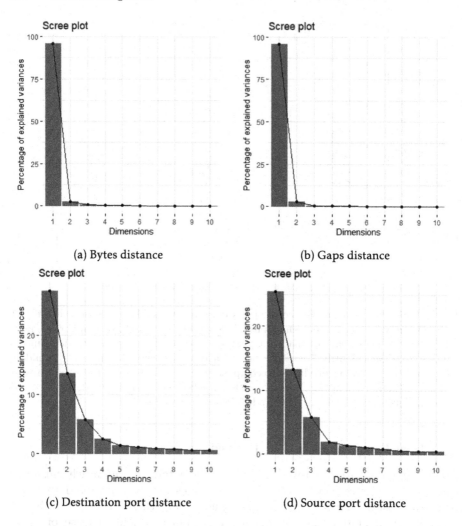

(a) Bytes distance

(b) Gaps distance

(c) Destination port distance

(d) Source port distance

Fig. 5. CTU-91 data: Explained variance of components from the Principal Component Analysis on the four distance matrices, where the packet threshold was 10 packets. The connection distances in the bytes and gaps matrices were captured by one component approximately explaining 90% of the variance, whereas 3 components were required to capture >40% of the variance in the destination and source port distances.

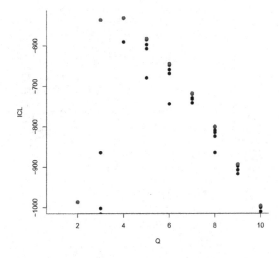

Fig. 6. Plots of the ICL fit evaluation statistic based on the CTU-91 data. The peak at $Q = 4$ illustrates that the optimal SBM clustering solution is reached at 4-classes, and model fit decays when Q increases.

Table 7. Correlation between distance matrices in the CTU-91 data

	bytes	gaps	dport	sport
bytes	–			
gaps	.04	–		
dport	.13	.09	–	
sport	.05	−.03	−.04	–

Our observation that mean differences between clusters (as exampled above) show a trend but are not significant, illustrates that just comparing mean differences to detect groups, with a straightforward anomaly detection approach, would be less successful in this particular setting (Fig. 8).

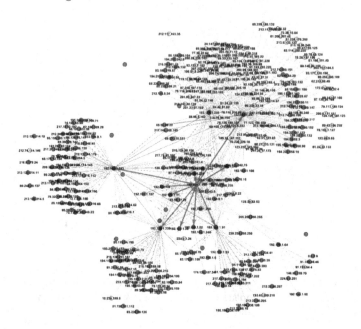

Fig. 7. This Figure shows the full network with the nodes coloured according to the labels from the optimal 4-class SBM solution. This plot is based on the analyses of 483 connections and 148 hosts (nodes) with packet threshold = 20. Nodes are coloured blue (normal), green (normal), turquoise (normal), red (infected), or white (outliers). (Color figure online)

Most of the peripheral hosts were captured by one cluster, indicating behavioral similarity, with a class assignment posterior probability of .9982. The non-infected/normal hosts (192.168.1.155, 192.168.1.52, 192.168.1.157, 192.168.1.36, 192.168.1.6, 192.168.1.53, 192.168.1.64) were divided over two clusters, that also included peripheral hosts. Only one normal host had a posterior probability <.95, which was host 192.168.1.6 with .82, with the remaining probability belonging to the other *normal/mixed* class (Figs. 9, 10, 7, 11, 12 and 13 (Tables 8, 9, 10 and 11).

Fig. 8. This Figure shows the full network with the nodes coloured according to the labels from the optimal 4-class SBM solution. This plot is based on the analyses of 631 connections and 205 hosts (nodes) with packet threshold = 5. Nodes are coloured blue (normal), green (normal), turquoise (normal), red (infected), or white (outliers). (Color figure online)

Table 8. Performance matrix from the SBM node-based clustering when packet threshold = 5

Cluster	Peripheral	Normal	Infected
1	9	0	0
2	0	0	10
3	1	4	0
4	158	3	0

Table 9. Performance matrix from the SBM node-based clustering when packet threshold = 15

Cluster	Peripheral	Normal	Infected
1	133	4	0
2	3	1	10
3	0	1	0

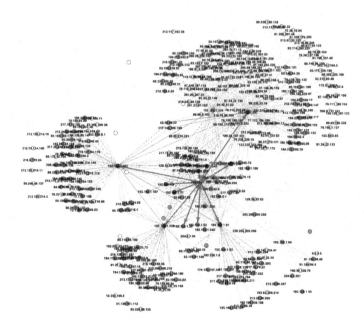

Fig. 9. This Figure shows the full network with the nodes coloured according to the labels from the optimal 4-class SBM solution. This plot is based on the analyses of 565 connections and 182 hosts (nodes) with packet threshold = 10. Nodes are coloured blue (normal), green (normal), turquoise (normal), red (infected), or white (outliers). (Color figure online)

Table 10. Performance matrix from the SBM node-based clustering when packet threshold = 20

Cluster	*Peripheral*	*Normal*	*Infected*
1	123	5	0
2	0	0	6
3	0	0	4
4	2	1	0

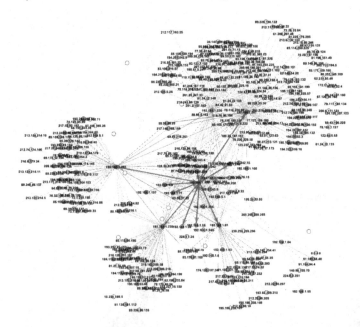

Fig. 10. This Figure shows the full network with the nodes coloured according to the labels from the optimal 4-class SBM solution. This plot is based on the analyses of 523 connections and 165 hosts (nodes) with packet threshold = 15. Nodes are coloured blue (normal), green (normal), turquoise (normal), red (infected), or white (outliers). (Color figure online)

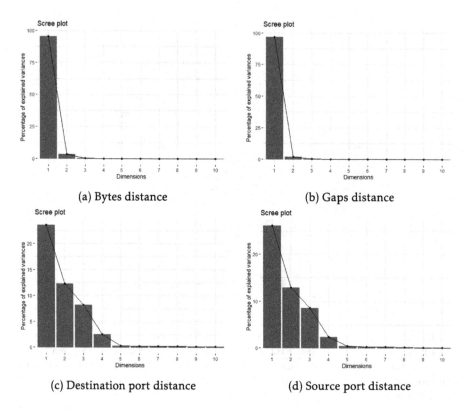

(a) Bytes distance

(b) Gaps distance

(c) Destination port distance

(d) Source port distance

Fig. 11. ISOT data: Explained variance of components from the Principal Component Analysis on the four distance matrices, where the packet threshold was 5 packets. The connection distances in the bytes and gaps matrices were captured by one component approximately explaining 90% of the variance, whereas 3 components were required to capture >40% of the variance in the destination and source port distances.

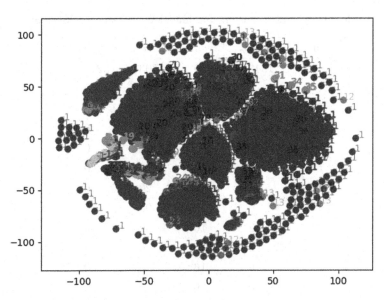

Fig. 12. This Figure shows the connections clustered with MalPaCA on the ISOT data. The green dots indicate connections labeled as outliers by HDBScan. For this plot, the multidimensional sample space was reduced to two axes by TSNE. By colour we different clusters (e.g. orange and purple). Compared to the CTU-91 dataset we see the connections occupy a larger sample space, indicating more variance in the ISOT replication data. (Color figure online)

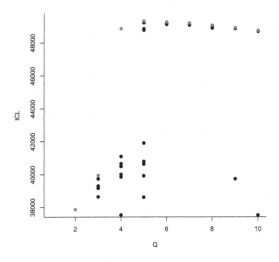

Fig. 13. Plots of the ICL fit evaluation statistic in the ISOT data. The subtle peak at $Q = 5$ indicates that the optimal SBM clustering solution is reached at 5-clusters, and model fit decays when Q increases.

Table 11. MalPaCA clusters and infection status in the ISOT data

Cluster	$srcip_n$	$srcip_i$	$dstip_n$	$dstip_i$
-1	1948	3415	1703	3216
1	0	0	9	10
2	12	12	0	0
3	21	0	0	0
4	0	0	24	0
5	22	0	0	0
6	0	0	20	6
7	0	0	90	17
8	92	10	0	0
9	0	0	0	10
10	0	16	0	0
11	0	9	0	0
12	0	43	0	0
13	0	48	0	0
14	0	38	0	0
15	0	0	0	10
16	0	0	0	11
17	0	0	0	22
18	0	0	0	8
19	0	0	0	8
20	0	0	0	10
21	0	0	0	49
22	0	0	0	10
23	0	0	0	27
24	0	0	0	7
25	0	0	0	40
26	0	7	0	0
27	0	7	0	0
28	0	11	0	0
29	0	7	0	0
30	0	4	0	4
31	0	27	0	0

(*continued*)

Table 11. (*continued*)

Cluster	$srcip_n$	$srcip_i$	$dstip_n$	$dstip_i$
32	11	11	0	0
33	8	8	0	0
34	8	8	0	0
35	11	11	0	0
36	11	11	0	0
37	8	8	0	0
38	15	15	0	0

Interpretation of rows and columns equal to Table 3. Clusters 1, 6, and 7 contain connections from peripheral hosts to normal and infected hosts. Clusters 2, 8, 32–38 contain connections from both infected and normal host to peripheral nodes. Clusters 3 and 5 both include connections from a normal source ip to a peripheral nodes. Cluster 9 includes connections from peripheral nodes to infected destination hosts. Clusters 10–14, 26–29, and 31 comprise of connections from infected source hosts to peripheral hosts. Cluster 30 includes connections from infected source IPs to infected destination IPs.

References

1. Abbe, E.: Community detection and stochastic block models: recent developments. J. Mach. Learn. Res. **18**(1), 6446–6531 (2017)
2. Barthakur, P., Dahal, M., Ghose, M.K.: A framework for P2P botnet detection using SVM. In: 2012 International Conference on Cyber-Enabled Distributed Computing and Knowledge Discovery, pp. 195–200 (2012)
3. Beigi, E.B., Jazi, H.H., Stakhanova, N., Ghorbani, A.A.: Towards effective feature selection in machine learning-based botnet detection approaches. In: 2014 IEEE Conference on Communications and Network Security (CNS), pp. 247–255 (2014)
4. Blondel, V.D., Guillaume, J.-L., Lambiotte, R., Lefebvre, E.: Fast unfolding of communities in large networks. J. Stat. Mech.: Theory Exp. **2008**(10), P10008 (2008)
5. Cai, T., Zou, F.: Detecting HTTP botnet with clustering network traffic. In: 2012 8th International Conference on Wireless Communications, Networking and Mobile Computing, pp. 1–7 (2012)
6. Campello, R.J.G.B., Moulavi, D., Sander, J.: Density-based clustering based on hierarchical density estimates. In: Pei, J., Tseng, V.S., Cao, L., Motoda, H., Xu, G. (eds.) PAKDD 2013. LNCS (LNAI), vol. 7819, pp. 160–172. Springer, Heidelberg (2013). https://doi.org/10.1007/978-3-642-37456-2_14

7. Carl, L., et al.: Using machine learning techniques to identify botnet traffic. In: Proceedings of the 31st IEEE Conference on Local Computer Networks. IEEE (2006)
8. Chowdhury, S., et al.: Botnet detection using graph-based feature clustering. J. Big Data **4**(1), 14 (2017). https://doi.org/10.1186/s40537-017-0074-7
9. Coskun, B., Dietrich, S., Memon, N.: Friends of an enemy: identifying local members of peer-to-peer botnets using mutual contacts. In: Proceedings of the 26th Annual Computer Security Applications Conference, pp. 131–140 (2010)
10. Ester, M., Kriegel, H.-P., Sander, J., Xu, X., et al.: A density-based algorithm for discovering clusters in large spatial databases with noise. In: KDD, pp. 226–231 (1996)
11. Feizollah, A., Anuar, N.B., Salleh, R., Amalina, F., Shamshirband, S., et al.: A study of machine learning classifiers for anomaly-based mobile botnet detection. Malays. J. Comput. Sci. **26**(4), 251–265 (2013)
12. Garcia, S., Grill, M., Stiborek, J., Zunino, A.: An empirical comparison of botnet detection methods. Comput. Secur. **45**, 100–123 (2014)
13. Garg, S., Singh, A.K., Sarje, A.K., Peddoju, S.K.: Behaviour analysis of machine learning algorithms for detecting P2P botnets. In: 2013 15th International Conference on Advanced Computing Technologies (ICACT), pp. 1–4 (2013)
14. Giorgino, T., et al.: Computing and visualizing dynamic time warping alignments in R: the DTW package. J. Stat. Softw. **31**(7), 1–24 (2009)
15. Gu, G., Perdisci, R., Zhang, J., Lee, W.: BotMiner: clustering analysis of network traffic for protocol-and structure-independent botnet detection (2008)
16. Gu, G., Zhang, J., Lee, W.: BotSniffer: detecting botnet command and control channels in network traffic (2008)
17. Haddadi, F., Morgan, J., Gomes Filho, E., Zincir-Heywood, A.N.: Botnet behaviour analysis using IP flows: with HTTP filters using classifiers. In: 2014 28th International Conference on Advanced Information Networking and Applications Workshops (WAINA), pp. 7–12 (2014)
18. Handcock, M.S., et al.: Temporal exponential random graph models (TERGMs) for dynamic network modeling in statnet. In: Sunbelt 2015 (2015)
19. Hyvarinen, A., Morioka, H.: Unsupervised feature extraction by time contrastive learning and nonlinear ICA. In: Advances in Neural Information Processing Systems, pp. 3765–3773 (2016)
20. Ioannidis, J.P.A.: Why most published research findings are false. PLos Med. **2**(8), e124 (2005)
21. Jain, A.K., Murty, M.N., Flynn, P.J.: Data clustering: a review. ACM Comput. Surv. (CSUR) **31**(3), 264–323 (1999)
22. Jung, T., Wickrama, K.A.S.: An introduction to latent class growth analysis and growth mixture modeling. Soc. Pers. Psychol. Compass **2**(1), 302–317 (2008)
23. Kostakis, O., Tatti, N., Gionis, A.: Discovering recurring activity in temporal networks. Data Min. Knowl. Discov. **31**(6), 1840–1871 (2017). https://doi.org/10.1007/s10618-017-0515-0
24. Kostakos, V.: Temporal graphs. Phys. A: Stat. Mech. Appl. **388**(6), 1007–1023 (2009)
25. Kumar, V., Dhok, S.B., Tripathi, R., Tiwari, S.: A review study of hierarchical clustering algorithms for wireless sensor networks. Int. J. Comput. Sci. Issues (IJCSI) **11**(3), 92 (2014)
26. Lagraa, S., François, J., Lahmadi, A., Miner, M., Hammerschmidt, C., State, R.: BotGM: unsupervised graph mining to detect botnets in traffic flows. In: 2017 1st Cyber Security in Networking Conference (CSNet), pp. 1–8 (2017)

27. Lee, C., Wilkinson, D.J.: A review of stochastic block models and extensions for graph clustering. arXiv preprint arXiv:1903.00114 (2019)

28. Leger, J.-B.: Blockmodels: a R-package for estimating in latent block model and stochastic block model, with various probability functions, with or without covariates. arXiv preprint arXiv:1602.07587 (2016)

29. Liu, F., Li, Z., Nie, Q.: A new method of P2P traffic identification based on support vector machine at the host level. In: 2009 International Conference on Information Technology and Computer Science, pp. 579–582 (2009)

30. Lloyd, S.: Least squares quantization in PCM. IEEE Trans. Inf. Theory **28**(2), 129–137 (1982)

31. Masuda, N., Holme, P.: Detecting sequences of system states in temporal networks. Sci. Rep. **9**(1), 1–11 (2019)

32. Mossel, E., Neeman, J., Sly, A.: Stochastic block models and reconstruction. arXiv preprint arXiv:1202.1499 (2012)

33. Nadeem, A., Hammerschmidt, C., Gañán, C.H., Verwer, S.: MalPaCA: malware packet sequence clustering and analysis. arXiv preprint arXiv:1904.01371 (2019)

34. Nagaraja, S., Mittal, P., Hong, C.-Y., Caesar, M., Borisov, N.: BotGrep: finding P2P bots with structured graph analysis. In: USENIX Security Symposium, pp. 95–110 (2010)

35. Park, Y., Bader, J.S.: Fast and reliable inference algorithm for hierarchical stochastic block models. arXiv preprint arXiv:1711.05150 (2017)

36. Rahbarinia, B., Perdisci, R., Lanzi, A., Li, K.: PeerRush: mining for unwanted P2P traffic. In: Rieck, K., Stewin, P., Seifert, J.-P. (eds.) DIMVA 2013. LNCS, vol. 7967, pp. 62–82. Springer, Heidelberg (2013). https://doi.org/10.1007/978-3-642-39235-1_4

37. Roeling, M.P., Nicholls, G.: Stochastic block models as an unsupervised approach to detect botnet-infected clusters in networked data. Data Sci. Cybersecur. **3**, 161 (2018)

38. Saad, S., et al.: Detecting P2P botnets through network behavior analysis and machine learning. In: 2011 Ninth Annual International Conference on Privacy, Security and Trust (PST), pp. 174–180 (2011)

39. Sakib, M.N., Huang, C.-T.: Using anomaly detection based techniques to detect HTTP-based botnet C&C traffic. In: 2016 IEEE International Conference on Communications (ICC), pp. 1–6 (2016)

40. Saxena, A., et al.: A review of clustering techniques and developments. Neurocomputing **267**, 664–681 (2017)

41. Snijders, T.A.B.: Stochastic actor-oriented models for network dynamics. Ann. Rev. Stat. Appl. **4**, 343–363 (2017)

42. Strayer, W.T., Lapsely, D., Walsh, R., Livadas, C.: Botnet detection based on network behavior. In: Lee, W., Wang, C., Dagon, D. (eds.) Botnet Detection. ADIS, vol. 36, pp. 1–24. Springer, Boston (2008). https://doi.org/10.1007/978-0-387-68768-1_1

43. Szabó, G., Orincsay, D., Malomsoky, S., Szabó, I.: On the validation of traffic classification algorithms, In: Claypool, M., Uhlig, S. (eds.) PAM 2008. LNCS, vol. 4979, pp. 72–81. Springer, Heidelberg (2008). https://doi.org/10.1007/978-3-540-79232-1_8

44. Tavse, P., Khandelwal, A.: A critical review on data clustering in wireless network. Int. J. Adv. Comput. Res. **4**(3), 795 (2014)

45. Torres, P., Catania, C., Garcia, S., Garino, C.G.: An analysis of recurrent neural networks for botnet detection behavior. In: 2016 IEEE Biennial Congress of Argentina (ARGENCON), pp. 1–6 (2016)

46. Wang, C.-Y., et al.: BotCluster: a session-based P2P botnet clustering system on NetFlow. Comput. Netw. **145**, 175–189 (2018)

47. Wang, J., Paschalidis, I.C.: Botnet detection based on anomaly and community detection. IEEE Trans. Control Netw. Syst. **4**(2), 392–404 (2016)

48. Xu, R., Wunsch, D.C.: Clustering algorithms in biomedical research: a review. IEEE Rev. Biomed. Eng. **3**, 120–154 (2010)

49. Yamauchi, K., Hori, Y., Sakurai, K.: Detecting HTTP-based botnet based on characteristic of the C & C session using by SVM. In: 2013 Eighth Asia Joint Conference on Information Security, pp. 63–68 (2013)

50. Zhang, J., Perdisci, R., Lee, W., Sarfraz, U., Luo, X.: Detecting stealthy P2P botnets using statistical traffic fingerprints. In: 2011 IEEE/IFIP 41st International Conference on Dependable Systems & Networks (DSN), pp. 121–132 (2011)

51. Zhao, D., Traore, I., Ghorbani, A., Sayed, B., Saad, S., Lu, W.: Peer to peer botnet detection based on flow intervals. In: Gritzalis, D., Furnell, S., Theoharidou, M. (eds.) SEC 2012. IFIPAICT, vol. 376, pp. 87–102. Springer, Heidelberg (2012). https://doi.org/10.1007/978-3-642-30436-1_8

Collaborative Learning Based Effective Malware Detection System

Narendra Singh, Harsh Kasyap$^{(\boxtimes)}$, and Somanath Tripathy

Department of Computer Science and Engineering,
Indian Institute of Technology Patna, Patna, India
{1811cs10,harsh_1921cs01,som}@iitp.ac.in

Abstract. Malware is overgrowing, causing severe loss to different institutions. The existing techniques, like static and dynamic analysis, fail to mitigate newly generated malware. Also, the signature, behavior, and anomaly-based defense mechanisms are susceptible to obfuscation and polymorphism attacks. With machine learning in practice, several authors proposed different classification and visualization techniques for malware detection. Images have proved worth analyzing the behavior of malware. Deep neural networks extract much information from it without having expert domain knowledge. On the other hand, the scarcity of diverse malware data available with clients, and their privacy concerns about sharing data with a centralized curator makes it challenging to build a more reliable model. This paper proposes a lightweight Convolution Neural Network (CNN) based model extracting relevant features using call graph, n-gram, and image transformations. Further, Auxiliary Classifier Generative Adversarial Network (AC-GAN) is used for generating unseen data for training purposes. The model is extended for federated setup to build an effective malware detection system. We have used the Microsoft malware dataset for training and evaluation. The result shows that the federated approach achieves the accuracy closer to centralized training while preserving data privacy at an individual organization.

Keywords: Malware detection · Machine learning · Federated Learning · Feature extraction · Generative Adversarial Network

1 Introduction

Malware or malicious software has been an evolutionary area of research. It was initially intended as a software program to test architectural loopholes. With increasing technologies and money factors involved, programmers started exploiting those to disrupt the service and gain unauthorized access to another system. It led to research in this new field coined as malware detection. A variety of malware exists with different names as worms, viruses, trojans, ransomware, adware, and spyware. Some malware immediately reveals their presence while

© Springer Nature Switzerland AG 2020
I. Koprinska et al. (Eds.): ECML PKDD 2020 Workshops, CCIS 1323, pp. 205–219, 2020.
https://doi.org/10.1007/978-3-030-65965-3_13

others reside inside the machine to steal the identity. In the age of social-computing, targeted attacks can be more frequent than generalized ones, due to the exposed profiles and public news of an organization.

Static analysis techniques [1, 2] have been used since long to detect malware. These techniques rely on the signature-based analysis of malicious programs without running it. They check for the file name, type, and size, checksums or hashes. On the other hand, malware authors have successfully written intelligent programs that trick static analysis techniques, with a small change of malware code and signature. Thus, encrypting and obfuscating the malware code evades detection. Down the lane, several researchers [2–4] used dynamic analysis techniques for classifying malware. It runs the malware and observes the infected files' behavior, including traffic analysis, registry keys, etc. These techniques require a secure and controlled environment like an emulated or virtual sandbox, which might affect the real-time running host.

With the machine and deep learning in practice, many works have been proposed which learn characteristics and relations from the malicious program and classifies them into respective categories. Authors trained different algorithms based on probabilistic and knowledge-based approaches including Hidden Markov Model [5], Naive-Bayes [6], Machine learning-based models, and Multi-layer perceptrons [7]. Unfortunately, these techniques do not suffice against a different dataset or real-time traffic and fail to mitigate targeted malware attacks. Meanwhile, deep learning-based approaches [8–10] do not require in-depth domain knowledge as compared to previous static, dynamic, or machine learning models.

Deep learning-based approaches require more data sets in order to learn inherent characteristics. For dynamic analysis, it becomes challenging to feed large samples, especially from backdoor families. Therefore collaborative approaches would be suitable, which collects data from different sources. Decentralized and collaborative learning is the current alternative and collects the data to make intelligent model. However, the data gets moved from its place, which raises security and privacy concerns. Even with a distributed and decentralized computing paradigm, the data may be kept or processed parallelly or at different locations. Federated Learning [11], a new approach where the model is trained, keeping the data in-place, and a central curator aggregates all the models. It runs the same process for thousands and millions of iterations. It faces trade-offs of energy, not independent and identically distributed data, network, and random participants. However, it preserves the data, which is most crucial for the organizations. We use Federated Learning with multiple participants contributing malware data to train an aggregated malware detection model.

This paper discusses the properties of malware, existing methods to mitigate them, and proposes a novel deep learning approach using a federated setup. The following are the major contributions.

- Features are extracted using call graph from .asm files, image transformations, and n-gram techniques from .bytes file. Preprocessing and combining these features and feeding to convolutional neural networks showed an improved accuracy of 99.72%.

- Auxiliary Classifier GAN (AC-GAN) is used for generating unseen data, preparing the model for targeted attacks.
- We trained the model using a federated setup using the TensorFlow federated API with data distributed across clients and achieved 97.93% accuracy in a few iterations with scope for improvement.

The remainder of this paper is organized as follows. Section 2 discusses the background and related works. Section 3 briefs the concepts of Federated Learning and Auxiliary Classifier GAN (AC-GAN). Section 4 proposes the framework with dataset preprocessing, feature extraction, and the use of underlying concepts to run this experiment. Section 5 describes model configuration, experimental setup, result and comparison. Section 6 concludes and briefs the scope for future work.

2 Related Work

Malware detection is a state of the art to prevent intrusion of malicious software. The long is the history of malware, that long is the history of its detection and prevention. They both started all together, tricking and competing with each other. Every time a more robust defense mechanism comes, malware authors outsmart them by tweaking something new. In this section, We will discuss the existing defense techniques to mitigate malware and their drawbacks.

Lu et al. [10] discussed a malware detection method based on the word embedding technique and LSTM. It automatically learns the correlation between opcodes and feature representation of the opcode sequence. It achieves an accuracy of 95.73% for skip-gram and a continuous bag of words on the Microsoft malware dataset. Le et al. [12] used a CNN architecture with BiLSTM. They used a recurrent layer on top of the CNN architecture. It summarizes the content of the whole file into one feature vector. It achieves an accuracy of 98.8% on the Microsoft malware dataset.

Zhao et al. [9] proposed MalDeep, a novel deep learning-based malware classification technique based on texture visualization. They studied this classification through code mapping, texture partitioning, and texture extracting. The model works on CNN with two convolutional layers and down-sampling layers, and many full connection layers. It achieved higher accuracy of 99% on the Microsoft malware dataset (with nine malware families). The dataset has an uneven distribution of malware families, and this approach reached a better classification accuracy for backdoor families.

Azar et al. [8] used an unsupervised feature learning approach for malware classification and network-based anomaly detection using auto-encoder (AE). It produces a fixed (ten) size vector for both classification and detection of attacks, making it more useful for real-time detection. It achieves a classification accuracy of 96% on the Microsoft malware dataset.

Vasan et al. [13] proposed a deep learning model Image-based Malware Classification using Fine-tuned Convolutional Neural Network (IMCFN), which talks about the image visualization approach and uses CNN architecture. It is computationally cost-effective and provides a scalable solution. It incurs low run-time overhead and proves to be secure against obfuscated malware. It is tested on the Malimg dataset (with twenty-five malware families) and predicts the resilience of the obfuscated malware attack. It achieved an accuracy of 98.82%.

Generative Adversarial Network (GAN) [14], has been used to generate unseen data. It adds noise to the existing data and generates new samples that can not be distinguished from the real samples. These samples often trick the model. Therefore, prior training is done with these samples to boost confidence and be prepared for unknown attacks. Authors in [15,16] have used GAN for handling malware detection. Kim et al. [15] introduced GAN based approaches tGAN and tDCGAN, achieving an accuracy of 96.39% and 95.74% respectively. They compared different deep learning techniques, including multi-layer perceptron, auto-encoder, along with concepts of transfer learning. Authors in [17] ran multiple experiments using Auto-Encoders, and Deep Neural Networks with varying layers over Malicia malware dataset achieving an accuracy of 99.21%. However, they relied on the fact that Deep Learning-based systems are good in automatically extracting higher conceptual features.

3   Preliminaries

This section briefs about Federated Learning, Auxiliary Classifier Generative Adversarial Network (AC-GAN), and illustrates their mathematical description.

3.1   Federated Learning

We are aware of individual organizations' capabilities in terms of generating data and training a smart machine learning model. Previous centralized collaborative approaches were supposed to collect all these data to the central server and train, which induces a high data leak risk and violates various security principles and pacts. It does not guarantee security, privacy, and anonymity. Federated Learning brings the model to the data while keeping the data to the device itself.

Google introduced this concept of Federated Learning back in 2016, a collaborative learning approach that makes learning secure by keeping the data to the device itself. It is an iterative process, and each time the device trains the model with its data and updates the parameters to the central server. The server collects the data, computes federated average, and updates the devices with the latest parameters. This iterative process involves significant communication overhead, and multiple parameter exchanges make the system vulnerable and exposed to attackers. The central curator may allow the use of any optimization and aggregation algorithm depending on the problem. The whole process is illustrated in Fig. 1.

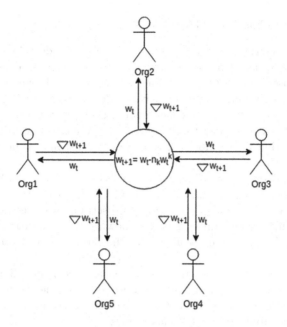

Fig. 1. Federated setup

FedSGD (a variant of stochastic gradient descent (SGD)) is a widely used optimization and aggregation algorithm for federated averaging. SGD samples a subset of summand functions and updates the weight.

$$w := w - \eta \nabla Q_i(w) \tag{1}$$

SGD is effective and scalable for large training sets coupled with complex gradient calculation formulae. In FedSGD, each participant trains the model in-place with some random samples chosen in every iteration and sends the delta change in the gradient to the central aggregator.

$$w_{t+1} = w_t + \eta \frac{\sum_{k \in S_t} n_k \Delta w_t^k}{\sum_{k \in S_t} n_k} \tag{2}$$

The central aggregator sums up the weighted contribution of the delta updates received from all the participants and updates the global weight. Let the system has a total K number of users. In every iteration, a fraction of clients participate, some may drop out. The set comprising of participating clients be S_t and n_k be the number of samples held by client k with the server having a learning rate of η. Let w_t be the global weight of the previous iteration, server updates it, and evaluates w_{t+1} using distributed approximate Newton method [18].

3.2   Auxiliary Classifier GAN (AC-GAN)

Generative Adversarial Network (GAN) is an advanced deep learning approach that generates new data from scratch, which does not exist in real-world training data. It composes of two players, which are also deep learning models called generator and discriminator. A Generative model G takes latent space, and noise from the sample distributes. It concatenates them to convert into a complex distribution, which is similar to the real data. A Discriminator model D is a binary classification neural network that aims to distinguish between real and fake samples generated by Generator model G.

AC-GAN is an extension of the conditional GAN (cGAN). cGAN handles the conditional generation of images, while AC-GAN allows the targeted generation of images of respective types. It makes the discriminator predict the target of input and stabilizes the training process allowing the generation of large-high-quality images. It learns representation in the latent space without knowledge of the target.

In the AC-GAN, every generated sample has a corresponding class label c and the noise z. The generator uses both c and z to generate images $X_{fake} = G(c, z)$. The discriminator gives both a probability distribution over sources and a probability distribution over the class labels.

$$P(S|X), P(C|X) = D(X) \tag{3}$$

The objective function has two parts: the log-likelihood of the correct source, L_S, and the log-likelihood of the correct class, L_C [19]. Discriminator is trained to maximize $L_S + L_C$ while Generator is trained to maximize $L_C - L_S$.

$$L_S = E[\log P(S = \text{real } |X_{\text{real}})] + E\left[\log P\left(S = \text{fake}|X_{\text{fake}}\right)\right] \tag{4}$$

$$L_C = E[\log P(C = c| \ X_{real})] + E\left[\log P\left(C = c|X_{fake}\right)\right] \tag{5}$$

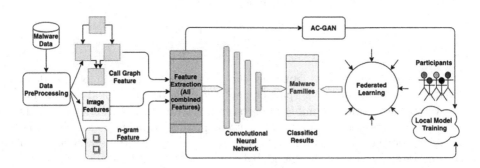

Fig. 2. Proposed framework

4 Proposed Framework

The proposed Malware detection framework facilitates the participants to operate collaboratively and build an effective machine learning model. Each participant and organization hold different data, and the central server acts as an aggregator. They train the model in-place and send the update to the server. The whole process is repeated multiple times. The proposed framework comprising of following major components. The rest of the process is finding relevant features using different transformations and feeding it to a convolutional neural network that classifies malware. It also uses AC-GAN to generate unseen data and defend against targeted attacks (Fig. 2).

4.1 Data Collection

We have used Microsoft Malware data[1] for analysis. The total train dataset size is 200 GB, out of which 50 GB is .bytes file, and the remaining 150 GB is .asm file. It consists of 10,868 .bytes files and 10,868 .asm files with total 21,736 files. In the dataset, .byte files are a combination of 256 hex numbers (a decimal value ranging between 0 to 255) and a special character (??). .asm files are the outputs of the disassembler.

Table 1. Types of Malware in Microsoft Malware dataset

Sr No	Name	Samples	Type
1	Ramnit	1541	Worm
2	Lollipop	2478	Adware
3	kelihosver3	2942	Backdoor
4	Vundo	475	Trojan
5	Simda	42	Backdoor
6	Tracur	751	Trojan downloader
7	Kelihosver1	398	Backdoor
8	Obfuscator.ACY	1228	Obfuscated
9	Gatak	1013	Backdoor

4.2 Data Preprocessing

Data Preprocessing involves Exploratory Data Analysis, Dimensionality Reduction, and Data Normalization. It identifies the meaning and aspects of feature engineering and standardizes data features with feature scaling by analyzing datasets and their examples. After analyzing the data, we observed the uneven

---

[1] https://www.kaggle.com/c/malware-classification/data.

distribution of target classes, as shown in Table 1. Samples with the label- one two and three are more than four, five, and six. It helped in useful dynamic classification to assign the respective families of new malware files encountered or generated, especially the backdoor families.

4.3   Feature Extraction

Many works discussed above have used n-gram and image transformation techniques to achieve higher accuracy. It incurs a higher computing cost in preprocessing and extraction. Authors in [20] discussed the conversion of the function-call graph to a vector in low-dimensional feature space for malware detection. It achieves optimum efficiency with less cost as we aim to propose a lightweight model that can be easily deployed on a federated setup with resource-constrained devices. We use call-graph features with 3-gram analysis and less intensive image operations. Our feature extraction component uses call graphs, n-gram features, and image transformation.

First, .asm files are transformed to extract call graph features by converting it into a control flow graph by tracing the flow sequentially. Control flow graph of an assembly program P is a directed graph $G = (V, E)$, where V is the set of basic blocks, and $E \subseteq V \times V$ is the set of edges representing control flow between basic blocks. A control flow edge from block u to v is $e = (u, v) \in E$. Call Graph represents the relationship between different subroutines in a program. The nodes in the graphs denote the subroutines, and the link to them tells how they call each other. It is of both static and dynamic types. Though, a perfect static graph is an undecidable problem. It can be generated manually or using the software. We wrote a small piece of code to make the control flow graph from the given assembly files. The control flow graph is represented differently for statements, loops, and function calls. It can be used in extracting features for malware detection. It identifies uncalled procedures which can be inside a program for malicious intentions.

We extracted the features like the number of nodes and edges, maximum degree and density of the graph from the call graph. Table 2 lists some rows of features extracted from .asm files of the Microsoft malware dataset.

Table 2. Sample call graph features

File	nodes	edges	maxDeg	density
01lsAbcXXXX	274	333	137	0.0813
01sUzbxXXXX	187	196	82	0.1813
01kzSrtXXXX	158	1533	95	0.1409
01kxPcsXXXX	26	126	35	0.6

We can adequately describe malware through an n-gram analysis as a sequence of hex values. It is a contiguous sequence of n hexadecimal values from a given malware file. Each sequence takes one out of 257 different values, i.e., the 256-byte range plus the special '??' symbol. For each .bytes file, we have made an array and added each element to the array. The length of these arrays is used as a feature. The .asm files consist of various segments, opcodes, and keywords, registers, etc. We have taken the count of segments as a feature and considered the bag-of-words representation of .bytes.

We convert the malware file into binary and take the first eight bits where four most significant bits map to rows and four least significant bits map to columns to make pixels. Images converted were of different sizes. So, we used padding to make them of the same size. The image visualization approach is very efficient but susceptible to noise. It raises data augmentation and motivates us to generate new unseen samples. Thus, We used GAN for generating unseen images and targeted files.

We combined all those different features extracted from .asm and .bytes files for our model. We extracted a total of 1024 features. After Applying dimensionality reduction and normalization techniques, we reduced it to 256 for feeding into a convolutional neural network of (16×16) input vector and 784 for feeding into GAN of (28×28) input vector. As limited data available with individual clients, it is challenging to model a robust defensive mechanism. So we set up a federated environment for collaborative learning.

4.4 Model Configuration

Convolutional Neural Network (CNN): We have used a lightweight model for running our experiment. It runs with fewer layers than the dense networks and requires optimal infrastructure to run, which can be easily deployed in any setting.

The convolutional layer is composed of 32 filters of size 3×3. It takes input as (None, 16, 16, 1). The output of this layer is (None, 14, 14, 32). Next, it is fed to a max-pooling layer, which takes the convolutional layer's output as input. It is of size 2×2, reducing the output to $7 \times 7 \times 32$. Then, the pooling layer is followed by another Flatten layer, which gives (None,1568) output. Another Dense layer follows that takes the output of the previous Flatten layer as input. Then we use the Dropout layer with a rate of 0.5, followed by a densely-connected layer with 256 neurons.

Auxiliary Classifier GAN (AC-GAN): We have used AC-GAN for generating new unseen malware at the client-side. In centralized training, these samples are generated at the server end. In Federated Learning, each participant will train their local data to create new samples that look exactly similar to the original malware and could have tricked the model.

AC-GAN takes a vector input. It concatenates the point in latent space (100 dimensions) and categorically encoded (9 dimensions). A fully connected layer interprets the point in latent space with sufficient activations to generate a grayscale image with the shape 28 * 28 and pixel values in the range $[-1, 1]$ with tanh activation function. The discriminator predicts the probability of the generated image belonging to a real or fake class, taking an input of shape 28 * 28 * 1 given by the generator. It is defined using Gaussian weight initialization, batch normalization, LeakyReLU, Dropout, and a 2 * 2 stride for downsampling instead of pooling layers. This architecture constructs the image with a single input and two outputs. It is trained with two loss functions, binary cross-entropy for the first output layer, and categorical cross-entropy loss for the second output layer using the Adam version of stochastic gradient descent with a small learning rate and modest momentum.

Federated Learning: It is a decentralized collaborative training approach. We have already discussed its benefits of limiting data exposure. In malware context, it can be argued that the malware families are already well known and exposed. So, It may not motivate to go with Federated Learning incurring more cost and similar accuracy. However, with ever-increasing malware families and in-house defense techniques developed for mitigating them, the companies can not afford to make the data public. This study proposes a federated setup for developing special defense techniques and securely improving a global malware detection system.

We have tested the above proposed lightweight convolutional network, with five participants randomly distributing the malware dataset with them. The section below discusses the implementation and API's used in detail.

5   Experimental Setup and Evaluation

This section describes the model configuration and setup carried out for running the proposed framework.

5.1   Setup

This experiment has been run on the federated testbed. The Tensorflow federated installation guide[2] lists different installation methods. Docker setup with ubuntu image has been used to run these experiments. It helps in easy installation and migration. We configured a host machine with processor Intel® Core™ i7-7700 CPU @ 3.60 GHz 8, and Memory 8 GB. Data preprocessing and feature extraction takes significant time due to massive data set.

5.2   Collaborative Training and Evaluation

We evaluated the proposed federated malware detection technique on the Microsoft malware data set, including 10868 files for model training and the same number of files for experimental evaluation. Although the data set is huge and comprises around two hundred fifty gigabytes, the number of samples is

---

[2] https://github.com/tensorflow/federated/blob/master/docs/install.md.

smaller. The data set consists of two types of files .bytes and .asm. The .bytes files contain the address and byte codes in hexadecimal format, while .asm files contain the address, segments, opcodes, registers, function calls, and APIs.

For running this experiment, the dataset is split with an approximate 60:20:20 ratio for training, validation, and test sets. We did data processing on the dataset and extracted features, as mentioned in the above section. We picked a thousand features from the images and twenty features using the n-gram technique. Using the above-discussed call graph technique, four features, i.e., no. of nodes, number of edges, max degree of a graph, and density of graph, were extracted by converting .asm files to control flow graph. Combining all features, we have a total of 1024 features to train our model.

We build our lightweight deep learning model using a convolutional neural network on a federated testbed with the setup mentioned above. The training model's structure derives from CNN with the Input layer followed by Conv layers, Maxpool, Fully Connected, Densely Connected, Dropout, and then Densely Connected layers. We implemented AC-GAN for generating adversarial samples for targeted training and enriching our sample space.

For running on the federated testbed, the data set has been randomly split into six equal-sized subsets. One subset is assigned to the central aggregator to initialize the model and its weights. It is also known as dummy data set and needs to be given iteratively. More help for the same can be found in Tensorflow federated documentation[3]. The rest five subsets are assigned to five participants. While training the model locally, participants use a batch size of twenty and run ten epochs for training a local model in one iteration. We trained the global model by running a different number of iterations to see improvement in model accuracy. We ran from 50 to 100 iterations denoted as F-50, F-60, F-70, F-80, F-90, and F-100 to see an increasing graph of model accuracy. The setup above failed to run more iterations. We expect an improved accuracy on a slightly higher configuration by running more number of iterations.

5.3   Result

Using Auxiliary Classifier GAN (AC-GAN), the central server generated 6200 new malware samples and confidently classified 35.2% of them as malware assigning corresponding class labels. These samples were used along with the (original/collected) training data and prove helpful in improving model accuracy of 99.72%. However, running the experiment with the only participant holding data in silos dips the accuracy to 96.34%. The confusion matrix for the centralized lightweight model is illustrated in Table 3. Precision, Recall, and F1-score are also shown for every malware family. The macro-avg for precision and recall comes 99% and 98%, respectively. It even shows high accuracy for backdoor malware families.

---

[3] Tensorflow federated. https://www.tensorflow.org/federated.

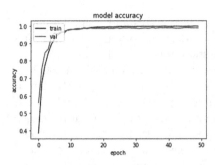

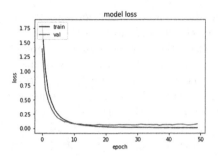

Fig. 3. Model accuracy   **Fig. 4.** Model loss

Table 3. Confusion matrix

Malware Family	Ramnit	Lollipop	kelihosver3	Vundo	Simda	Tracur	Kelihosver1	O.ACY	Gatak
Ramnit	0.9936	0.0004	0	0	0	0	0	0	0
Lollipop	0	1	0	0	0	0	0	0	0
kelihosver3	0	0	1	0	0	0	0	0	0
Vundo	0	0	0	1	0	0	0	0	0
Simda	0	0	0	0	1	0	0	0	0
Tracur	0.0032	0	0.0105	0	0	0.9933	0	0	0
Kelihosver1	0	0	0	0	0	0	1	0	0
O.ACY	0.0032	0	0	0	0	0	0.0067	0.9756	0.0197
Gatak	0	0	0	0	0	0	0	0	1
Precision	0.99	1	1	0.98	1	0.96	0.99	1	1
Recall	0.99	1	1	1	0.88	0.99	0.97	0.99	1
F1-score	0.99	1	1	0.99	0.93	0.98	0.98	0.99	1

In federated setup, with five clients and a central curator, it slightly reduced to 94.66% with 50 iterations. It gained and started showing significant improvement with an increasing number of iterations and reached to 97.93% with 100 iterations. Model accuracy and loss are plotted in Fig. 3 and Fig. 4. It illustrates the gain in accuracy with more local stochastic training at the client-side. It is expected to gain significant improvement with more global and local iterations. Table 4 lists the comparison of proposed architecture with and without federated setup along with previous works. The central setup has slightly higher accuracy compared to the federated setup but is not privacy-preserving in nature.

Table 4. Comparison Report with previous works

Sr No	Authors	Approach	Description	Accuracy
1	Lu et al. [10]	LSTM	Based on natural language processing, the word embedding technique, and LSTM	95.73%
2	Kim et al. [15]	tDCGAN	Deep Autoencoder-based GAN	95.74%
3	Kim et al. [15]	tGAN	Pre-train the generator of GAN using the transfer learning and Detection Using Deep Transferred GAN	96.39%
4	Le et al. [12]	CNN-BiLSTM	Classifies the one dimensional representation of the binary file using local patterns of each malware class	98.8%
5	Azar et al. [8]	AE-SVM	Autoencoder-based feature learning	96.3%
6	Zhao et al. [9]	CNN	Conversion from binary file to gray images including code mapping, texture partitioning, and texture extracting	99%
7	Centralized Model	CNN	Feature Extraction using call graph, Image features and training CNN model, generating unseen data with AC-GAN	99.72%
8	Federated Learning	CNN	Five clients and a central curator running above model in 100 iterations, expecting improved performance with more iterations	97.93%

6 Conclusion

The existing malware detection techniques are sufficient to mitigate against known attacks. However, targeted attacks against companies and individuals pose a severe threat as they model in-house defense techniques and can not publicize them due to privacy threats. In a federated setting, every participant can develop its own model and helps to improve the global model keeping their data private. We presented such a collaborative learning approach to model a malware detection system. The proposed approach transformed, extracted, and merged relevant features from Microsoft malware data and modeled a light convolutional network. Using Auxiliary Classifier GAN (AC-GAN), 6200 generated samples helped to mitigate targeted and adversarial attacks. With the Federated setting, five clients, and a central curator, the accuracy is found to be degraded gracefully, while the privacy of each participant is preserved.

Though, Federated Learning is privacy-preserving in nature, but, it poses issues of significant communication overhead and inference attack with presence of malicious server or adversarial participants. There is a scope to study poisoning attacks in a similar direction and handle the latency trade-offs. Introducing anomalies in networks will result in a dropout of clients. It may introduce error in synchronization of updates, which will affect the results. Any model does not suffice without heterogeneous data and makes a scope for improvement to work with, not IID malware data.

Acknowledgement. We acknowledge the Ministry of Human Resource Development, Government of India, for providing fellowship to complete this work.

References

1. Moser, A., Kruegel, C., Kirda, E.: Limits of static analysis for malware detection. In: Twenty-Third Annual Computer Security Applications Conference, ACSAC 2007, pp. 421–430, December 2007
2. Shijo, P., Salim, A.: Integrated static and dynamic analysis for malware detection. Proc. Comput. Sci. **46**, 804–811 (2015)
3. Carlin, D., Cowan, A., O'Kane, P., Sezer, S.: The effects of traditional anti-virus labels on malware detection using dynamic runtime opcodes. IEEE Access **5**, 17 742–17 752 (2017)
4. Harel, D. (ed.): First-Order Dynamic Logic. LNCS, vol. 68. Springer, Heidelberg (1979). https://doi.org/10.1007/3-540-09237-4
5. Pechaz, B., Jahan, M.V., Jalali, M.: Malware detection using hidden Markov model based on Markov blanket feature selection method. In: 2015 International Congress on Technology, Communication and Knowledge (ICTCK), pp. 558–563, November 2015
6. Liu, C., Zhang, Z., Wang, S.: An android malware detection approach using Bayesian inference. In: 2016 IEEE International Conference on Computer and Information Technology (CIT), pp. 476–483, December 2016
7. Rathore, H., Agarwal, S., Sahay, S.K., Sewak, M.: Malware detection using machine learning and deep learning. CoRR, vol. abs/1904.02441 (2019). http://arxiv.org/abs/1904.02441
8. Yousefi-Azar, M., Varadharajan, V., Hamey, L., Tupakula, U.: Autoencoder-based feature learning for cyber security applications. In: 2017 International Joint Conference on Neural Networks (IJCNN), pp. 3854–3861, May 2017
9. Zhao, Y., Xu, C., Bo, B., Feng, Y.: MalDeep: a deep learning classification framework against malware variants based on texture visualization. Secur. Commun. Netw. **2019**, 1–12 (2019)
10. Lu, R.: Malware detection with LSTM using opcode language. ArXiv, vol. abs/1906.04593 (2019)
11. McMahan, H.B., Moore, E., Ramage, D., y Arcas, B.A.: Federated learning of deep networks using model averaging. CoRR, vol. abs/1602.05629 (2016). http://arxiv.org/abs/1602.05629
12. Le, Q., Boydell, O., Namee, B.M., Scanlon, M.: Deep learning at the shallow end: malware classification for non-domain experts. CoRR, vol. abs/1807.08265 (2018). http://arxiv.org/abs/1807.08265
13. Vasan, D., Alazab, M., Wassan, S., Naeem, H., Safaei, B., Zheng, Q.: IMCFN: image-based malware classification using fine-tuned convolutional neural network architecture. Comput. Netw. 107138 (2020). http://www.sciencedirect.com/science/article/pii/S1389128619304736
14. Goodfellow, I., et al.: Generative adversarial nets. In: Ghahramani, Z., Welling, M., Cortes, C., Lawrence, N.D., Weinberger, K.Q. (eds.) Advances in Neural Information Processing Systems 27, pp. 2672–2680. Curran Associates Inc. (2014). http://papers.nips.cc/paper/5423-generative-adversarial-nets.pdf
15. Kim, J.Y., Bu, S.J., Cho, S.B.: Malware detection using deep transferred generative adversarial networks. In: Liu, D., Xie, S., Li, Y., Zhao, D., El-Alfy, E.S. (eds.) ICONIP 2017. LNCS, vol. 10634, pp. 556–564. Springer, Cham (2017). https://doi.org/10.1007/978-3-319-70087-8_58
16. Hu, W., Tan, Y.: Generating adversarial malware examples for black-box attacks based on GAN. CoRR, vol. abs/1702.05983 (2017). http://arxiv.org/abs/1702.05983

17. Sewak, M., Sahay, S.K., Rathore, H.: An investigation of a deep learning based malware detection system. CoRR, vol. abs/1809.05888 (2018). http://arxiv.org/abs/1809.05888
18. Shamir, O., Srebro, N., Zhang, T.: Communication efficient distributed optimization using an approximate newton-type method. CoRR, vol. abs/1312.7853 (2013). http://arxiv.org/abs/1312.7853
19. Odena, A., Olah, C., Shlens, J.: Conditional image synthesis with auxiliary classifier GANs. In: Precup, D., Teh, Y.W. (eds.) Proceedings of the 34th International Conference on Machine Learning, Series Proceedings of Machine Learning Research, 06–11 Aug 2017, vol. 70, pp. 2642–2651. International Convention Centre. PMLR, Sydney, Australia. http://proceedings.mlr.press/v70/odena17a.html
20. Jiang, H., Turki, T., Wang, J.T.L.: DLGraph: malware detection using deep learning and graph embedding. In: 2018 17th IEEE International Conference on Machine Learning and Applications (ICMLA), pp. 1029–1033 (2018)

Ninth International Workshop on New Frontiers in Mining Complex Patterns (NFMCP 2020)

New Frontiers in Mining Complex Patterns (NFMCP 2020)

The analysis of complex data represents the new frontier in data mining and knowledge discovery. There are several emerging technologies and applications where complex patterns can be extracted: examples are blogs, event or log data, medical data, spatio-temporal data, social networks, mobility data, sensor data and streams. The abundance, variety and velocity of data poses new challenges which can be hardly coped with traditional data mining techniques. This asks for new contributions which allow for efficiently identifying patterns and enable effective decision making.

The Ninth International Workshop on New Frontiers in Mining Complex Patterns (NFMCP 2020) was held virtually in conjunction with the European Conference on Machine Learning and Principles and Practice of Knowledge Discovery in Databases (ECML-PKDD 2020) on September 14, 2020. It was aimed at bringing together researchers and practitioners of data mining and knowledge discovery, interested in the advances and latest developments in mining complex data. The workshop is establishing a premiere event with this goal.

This book includes a collection of four revised and extended versions of papers accepted for presentation at the workshop. These papers went through a rigorous review process and each paper has been reviewed by at least three reviewers.

Three papers pertain to the broad area of process mining and tackle different tasks: the first one concerns detection of deviant process instances, the second concerns activity prediction using multi-target regression, and the third concerns activity prediction using temporal convolution. The fourth paper presents a hybrid recommendation system which is based on bidirectional encoder representations.

We would like to thank all the authors who submitted papers for publication in this book and all the workshop participants and speakers. We are also grateful to the members of the program committee and external referees for their excellent work in reviewing submitted and revised contributions with expertise and patience. We would like to thank Fabrizio Maria Maggi for his invited talk on "Rule Mining: Goals and Challenges - Process mining based on declarative process models". A special thank is due to both the ECML PKDD Workshop Chairs and to the ECML PKDD organizers who made the event possible.

October 2020

Michelangelo Ceci
Corrado Loglisci
Giuseppe Manco
Elio Masciari
Zbigniew Ras

Organization

Program Chairs

Michelangelo Ceci   University of Bari "Aldo Moro", Bari, Italy
Corrado Loglisci   University of Bari "Aldo Moro", Bari, Italy
Giuseppe Manco   ICAR-CNR, Rende, Italy
Elio Masciari   Federico II University Naples, Italy
Zbigniew Ras   University of North Carolina, Charlotte, NC, USA

Program Committee

Petr Berka   University of Economics, Prague, Czech Republic
Roberto Corizzo   American University, Washington DC, USA
Massimo Guarascio   ICAR-CNR, Rende, Italy
Angelo Impedovo   University of Bari Aldo Moro, Italy
Dragi Kocev   Jozef Stefan Institute, Slovenia
Gianvito Pio   University of Bari Aldo Moro, Italy
Domenico Potena   Università Politecnica delle Marche, Italy
Jerzy Stefanowski   Poznań University of Technology, Poland
Herna Viktor   University of Ottawa, Canada
Alicja Wieczorkowska   Polish-Japanese Academy of Information Technology, Poland

Process Mining Based on Declarative Process Models: Goals and Challenges (Invited Talk)

Fabrizio Maria Maggi

Free University of Bozen-Bolzano, Italy

Abstract. Process mining is the part of Business Process Management (BPM) that is focused on the analysis of business processes based on process execution logs (event logs). Another central artifact in process mining are process models that are used as inputs and/or outputs of process mining techniques. Two different approaches can be followed for representing process models: procedural or declarative. Procedural process models aim at describing end-to-end processes and allow only for the process behavior that is explicitly specified in the model. However, procedural process mining techniques applied to processes characterized by a high number of different paths and exceptions produce as output process models that are often unreadable (spaghetti-like models). In these cases, it may be a better choice to use declarative process models that model the process as a (small) set of rules that the process should follow. In this way, everything that is not constrained is allowed and several execution paths can be represented in a compact model. In this keynote, we illustrate goals and challenges of rule mining (i.e., the branch of process mining based on declarative process models) by presenting different rule mining techniques and by showing how these techniques can be applied in practice using RuM, the first comprehensive toolset for rule mining.

A Hybrid Recommendation System Based on Bidirectional Encoder Representations

Irem Islek$^{(\boxtimes)}$ and Sule Gunduz Oguducu

Department of Computer Engineering, ITU AI Research and Application Center,
Istanbul Technical University, Istanbul, Turkey
{isleki,sgunduz}@itu.edu.tr

Abstract. Using auxiliary data about items provides more accurate item recommendations when utilizing deep learning in the recommendation system. Users often read item descriptions during online shopping, which contain key information about the item and its features. However the item descriptions are in unstructured form and using them in the deep learning model is a problem. In this study, we integrate a pioneering Natural Language Processing technique into a recommendation system to create an item embedding vector from unstructured item description text. The experimental results show that the proposed approach is efficient in generating more accurate recommendations by creating item embedding vectors from unstructured item description text.

Keywords: Bidirectional encoder representations · Recommendation models · Hybrid recommendation systems

1 Introduction

Recommendation Systems utilize users' historical behaviors to find items which they will most likely interested in. Although recommendation systems are widely studied and a mature research field, this problem is quite popular because of the fact that successful recommendation systems increase company earning, dramatically. In addition to that, accurate recommendations provide user satisfaction and engagement which are essential for websites. Google states that 40% of app installs on Google Play and 60% of watch time on Youtube come from recommendation systems [1].

If we look from the viewpoint of users, recommendation systems help users to reach related items with little effort. Thanks to recommendation systems, users explore new items without wasting time. For instance, instead of searching for a new song within millions of songs, a recommendation system provides you a new song list considering your musical taste.

In recent years, deep learning models are widely applied in recommendation models due to their capability to handle sparse data and capture latent relationship between items and users especially when items' or users' metadata are available. That's why recent studies try to integrate items' metadata (such as

© Springer Nature Switzerland AG 2020
I. Koprinska et al. (Eds.): ECML PKDD 2020 Workshops, CCIS 1323, pp. 225–236, 2020.
https://doi.org/10.1007/978-3-030-65965-3_14

item description, item category information etc.) to the deep learning based recommendation model when available [3, 4, 7]. One of the problems is that in most cases metadata is not structured and it is another issue to handle it inside the recommendation model.

Since the item description contains the most beneficial details about the item, it is expected that using item description vector will provide an increase in the recommendation model performance. This approach can be thought as an efficient item embedding step for deep learning based recommendation models. Differently from other approaches, proposed item embedding approach utilizes the item description text to create more informative item embedding vector.

To achieve this goal, we proposed in this study a novel approach that utilizes item descriptions with different lengths by transforming them into a fixed length item description vector using a state of the art NLP technique. First step of this approach is preprocessing item description texts. After that, Bidirectional Encoder Representations from Transformers (BERT) [8] model is fine-tuned with item descriptions to obtain more accurate vector representations which yields better recommendations. The item description embedding vector is created using specific layers' outputs from fine-tuned model. Lastly, a selected recommendation model is modified to integrate it with the item description embedding vectors.

One contribution of this paper is that fine-tuning BERT model using a large number of item descriptions from different domains. Also, thanks to proposed approach, it is possible to create a fixed size item embedding vector for each item, regardless of the length of the item description. The proposed approach has been integrated into state-of-the art deep learning based recommendation models SASRec [20] and GRU4Rec [15] and these models are tested with 4 real dataset from Amazon. It has been shown that the recommendation performance for these models has increased.

The paper is organized as follows. Section 2 presents the literature review. In Sect. 3, the details of the proposed method are given. Section 4 gives the test results of the experiments and a discussion of these results. Finally, in Sect. 5 we conclude the paper and discuss future work.

2   Literature Review

The recommender system studies can be categorized under three headings: Collaborative Filtering, Content Based Recommendation and Hybrid Models [2]. As can be seen in [5], Collaborative Filtering based models use only users' interaction history whereas Content Based models use item's content. Hybrid models aim to utilize strengths of both Collaborative Filtering and Content Based models. These models have some limitations such as cold start, lack of modeling the non-linearity, auxiliary data usage (image, review, etc.), sequence modeling. In recent years, deep learning is used in recommendation models to overcome these limitations. Since the method proposed in this study utilizes deep learning approaches, we summarize recommendation models based on these approaches.

There are a quite number of deep learning based recommender studies which use Multi Layer Perceptron (MLP) for recommendation [10, 12, 13, 24]. Because of the fact that, MLP has the ability to model non-linear relationships, these studies outperform most of the previous studies. In addition to given studies, there are some other studies which combine non-linear and linear relationships to have more accurate recommendations such as DeepFM [11] and Wide & Deep Learning [6]. However, although these models provide better results than previous ones, they are unable to model sequential user behavior.

To circumvent the limitations of previous studies, Recurrent Neural Network (RNN) based recommendation studies which use Gated Recurrent Unit (GRU) [9,16,18,22,27,28,30] or Long-Short Term Memories (LSTM) [19,23,29,35,36] are proposed. These models are quite suitable for sequential data modeling. Sequential modeling is advantageous for considering user interactions as a evolving process and and provides a recommendation model that can keep pace with changing user interests. GRU4Rec [15] is one of the session-based recommendation studies in which user's previous interactions are represented as a vector and are processed in a sequential way thanks to GRU (Gated Recurrent Unit). There is an improved version of GRU4Rec which uses another loss function and has a new sampling technique [14]. Convolutional Sequence Embedding Recommendation Model (Caser) [31] which is proposed by Tang et al. is a study which uses both horizontal and vertical convolutionals to modeling sequential behavior.

After it has been shown that attention mechanism is quite successful for modeling sequential data in natural language processing domain, it has been started to use also in recommendation problems [17,32,33,37]. In general, attention mechanism can be described as a mapping relationship between the input sequence and predicted output sequence. For example, Vaswani et al. describe an attention function as mapping a query and a set of key-value pairs to an output. The query, keys, values, and output are all vectors. In this function, the weight assigned to each value is computed by a compatibility function of the query with the corresponding key and output is calculated as a weighted sum of the values [34].

In addition to its success in sequential modelling, attention mechanism is more interpretable than other networks. That's why, it is quite popular among recent studies on recommendation systems. There is a study [21] which uses attention mechanism with GRU for session-based recommendation. On the other hand, SASRec [20] uses only attention-based neural network to have more successful sequential behavior modeling. Even though given studies are successful for sequential modeling, the content of the items are not considered in these studies.

To make progress in recommendation domain, some recent studies utilize the content information of the items. There is a study which uses convolutional neural network (CNN) on the top of Word2Vec [25] representation to create item vectors from item descriptions [4]. There is another study [3] which proposes an item embedding algorithm Item2Vec and uses item embeddings in item-based collaborative filtering.

Even though, using the detailed item description to improve recommendation system performance comes to mind easily, several problems make it difficult to implement. The most important problem about item descriptions is that each description has different lengths and converting them to meaningful vectors with a fixed size is an issue. The most basic approach for this problem can be using bag of words approach. The disadvantage of bag of words approach is that, the total word count is going to be quite high and we obtain a sparse matrix for item description dataset. Using such sparse matrix in complex recommendation models is not an efficient approach in terms of performance. For sparsity issue, creating a fixed size embedding vector will be a solution. Using a word embedding approach will be a solution for this problem but embedding vectors of each word should be combined to create a fixed length final embedding vector. Another problem is selecting appropriate word embedding approach to create meaningful embedding vector for a description text. Using a context independent word embedding approach such as Word2Vec [25] or Glove [26] creates word embedding without considering the context of the word. For example, a context-independent word embedding approach will give same embedding vector for the word "right" to indicate direction and "right" to say correct. In this study, we propose an approach based on a state of the art NLP model to solve these problems.

3   Bidirectional Encoder Representations of Item Descriptions

In this study, we propose an approach to utilize free text type item description in a recommendation model. In this approach, we use bidirectional encoder representations with recommendation models in a hybrid way. The basic steps of the proposed approach are preprocessing step, bidirectional encoder representation model fine-tuning step, item embedding vector creation step, recommender step and evaluation step.

In the first step of the proposed approach, we preprocess item description data. Item description texts have numerous html tags coming from different style features of the Amazon website's item description area. We clean the item description texts from these html tags in the beginning of the preprocessing step. After that, we remove any punctuation, numerical and special character from item description text. Then, we split item description text into words. By this way, we obtain a word array for each item description text.

In the second step of the proposed approach, we fine-tune the BERT model to get a bidirectional encoder representation model for our down-stream task. BERT's model architecture is a multi-layer bidirectional Transformer encoder as can be seen in Fig. 1. The input of the BERT model is a sequence of words, which one of the words is replaced with a [MASK] token, randomly. In BERT model structure, there is a transformer encoder which contains 12 transformer layers. A transformer layer is an attention mechanism that learns contextual relations between words in a text. In each transformer layer of the BERT, 12 separate attention mechanisms are used. Therefore, each word can focus on 12 different aspects of other words, at each layer. Because of that transformer layers use 144 distinct attention heads, each head can focus on different type of combinations. The output of the transformer encoder is a sequence of vectors, in which each vector corresponds to an input word with the same index. On the top of the transformer encoder, there is a classification layer. In this classification layer, the probability of the each word in the vocabulary is calculated with softmax to predict the original value of the masked word, based on the context provided by the other words in the sequence [8].

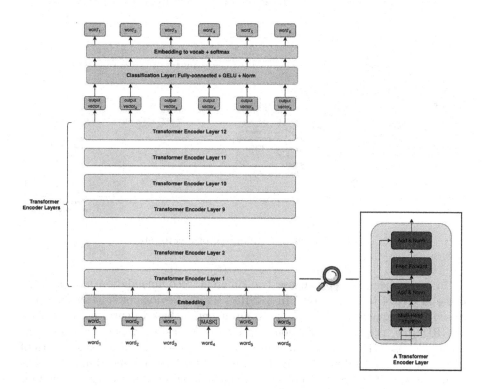

Fig. 1. BERT model.

The BERT model contains multiple bidirectional transformer encoder layers which gives quite accurate results for predicting the randomly masked word. Because of the fact that, BERT uses encoders and provides satisfying results, we decided to use BERT to create an embedding for each word in the item description. Our item description dataset is quite small compared to the large corpus which is used for training general purpose BERT and thus we decided to fine-tuning the BERT model instead of training it from scratch. During this step, the same pre-trained model parameters are used for initialization the model and all parameters are fine-tuned using the dataset of our down-stream task.

In the next step of the proposed approach, we use some selected transformer encoder layers of the fine-tuned BERT model. We will only use the outputs of the last 4 transformer encoder layers to get a fixed length embedding vector for each word in the description text. In this step, we concatenate last 4 transformer encoder layers because of that it is recommended in BERT paper [8].

In this step, we separate the input item description to a words array and for each word we get a fixed size embedding vector by concatenating the last 4 transformer encoder layers' outputs as can be seen in Fig. 2. After that we get embedding vectors for each word in the description, we average these vectors and obtain a 3072 length embedding vector for each item description text.

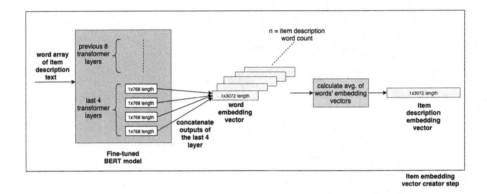

Fig. 2. Item embedding vector creator step.

In recommender step, we use two different recommendation models SAS-Rec and GRU4Rec, seperately. In SASRec, user's previous interactions are processed in a sequential way, thanks to an attention based neural network. Also in GRU4Rec, the user interactions are considered as a sequential process, but this model uses Gated Recurrent Units to modeling sequential behavior. Both of these models are modified to handle array of 3072 length embedding vectors as input, instead of an array of integers. By this way, we obtain two different hybrid recommender systems based on bidirectional encoder representations which we called "SASRec with BERT" and "GRU4Rec with BERT", to compare with original SASRec and GRU4Rec.

In the evaluation step which is the last step of the proposed approach, we compare the results of the modified models and the original models using evaluation metrics. The details of implementation and tests can be seen in Results section.

4   Results

4.1   Dataset

Amazon dataset is one of the datasets which contain auxiliary information such as user reviews and item descriptions. In this study, we use datasets from four different categories provided by Amazon[1]: Beauty, Electronics, Video Games and Movies & TV. The detailed information about these datasets can be seen in Table 1. In this table, the action means that the user has written a review about the item.

Table 1. Dataset details table.

Dataset name	# users	# items	# actions	Avg. actions/user	Avg. actions/item
Amazon Beauty	0.052 m	57,289	0.3 m	7.6	6.9
Amazon Electronics	9.8 m	756,489	20.9 m	2.1	27.7
Amazon Video Games	1.5 m	71,982	2.6 m	1.6	35.6
Amazon Movies & TV	3.8 m	182,032	8.7 m	2.3	48.1

For Amazon datasets, we have user-item review data and item metadata. We use review data to get user-item interactions (actions), in this problem. Amazon datasets, we do not have data of items bought by the user. Therefore, if a user had written a review about an item, this means user is interested in this item. In addition to that, item metadata contains item description text which the seller of the item had written to describe features of the item. In this problem, we use these item description texts to create an embedding vector to represent an item.

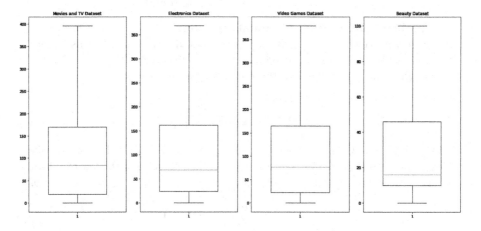

Fig. 3. Description text word count stats

As we mentioned before, there are some item descriptions which are quite long and quite short. For a detailed analysis, we calculated the mean, median, maximum and minimum unique word counts for each dataset and created a box-plot as can be seen in Fig. 3. Because of the fact that the total unique word count

---

[1] http://jmcauley.ucsd.edu/data/amazon/.

of all of these datasets is very high, we can say that the item description data is quite sparse for these datasets and it is a problem to handle it with classical approaches. As can be seen in Fig. 3, Movies and TV, Electronics and Video Games datasets have similar values for item description word count statistics. Differently from these datasets, Beauty dataset contains shorter item descriptions which means that it has lower values for median and maximum word count of item description texts. We can say that, Beauty dataset is more sparse than the other ones, in terms of item description text data.

4.2   Evaluation

For training dataset, we take each user's action sequence and exclude the last action. The last action is used as output while the rest of the user sequence is used as input. For evaluation, we take the ground-truth item and 99 randomly selected items which the user did not interact with. Thanks to given metrics, we can compare the ranking success of baselines and proposed recommendation model. The selected evaluation metrics are Hit Rate@10 and NDCG@10. Details of these metrics can be seen in below:

- **Hit Rate:** This metric calculates the proportion of relevant items found in the top-k recommendations. The formula of Hit Rate@k can be seen in Eq. 1.

$$HitRate@k = \frac{|\{relevant\_items\} \cap \{recommended\_items@k\}|}{|\{relevant\_items\}|} \quad (1)$$

- **Normalized Discounted Cumulative Gain:**
  DCG at a particular rank position p is calculated as in Eq. 2. In this equation p denotes the position up to which the relevance is accumulated. The rel_i shows the graded relevance of the result at position i.

$$DCG_p = \sum_{i=1}^{p} \frac{rel_i}{log_2(i+1)} \quad (2)$$

Ideal DCG (IDCG) is obtained by sorting items of a result list by relevance as can be seen in Eq. 3. In this equation, REL_p represents the list of relevant items which are ordered by their relevance, in the corpus up to position p.

$$IDCG_p = \sum_{i=1}^{|REL_p|} \frac{2^{rel_i} - 1}{log_2(i+1)} \quad (3)$$

As can be seen in Eq. 4, to calculate normalized DCG which is called nDCG, ideal DCG value should be used.

$$nDCG_p = \frac{DCG_p}{IDCG_p} \quad (4)$$

To obtain an average performance measure of the ranking algorithm, the nDCG values for all queries can be averaged.

As we mention before, the selected baseline models are SASRec [20] and GRU4Rec [15] which are recent successful deep learning models for recommendation. These two baselines use only item ids' in their original implementations. During tests, we integrated our item embedding approach to these models to utilize item descriptions.

All hyperparameters and initialization strategies are those suggested by authors of the methods. For SASRec, the Adam optimizer is used. The learning rate is set to 0.001, and the batch size is 128. The dropout rate is 0.5. The maximum sequence length is 50. For GRU4Rec, the learning rate is 0.01, dropout rate is set to 0. The batch size is 32. If validation performance does not improve for 5 epochs, we terminate the training during tests.

4.3   Test Results

Obtained comparative results can be seen in Table 2. The table columns "SASRec with BERT" and "GRU4Rec with BERT" gives results of the modified models which use bidirectional encoder representations. The results show that using BERT as an item embedding creator improves performance in both models, especially for NDCG@10. Detailed discussion about results can be seen in Sect. 5.

Table 2. Test results.

Dataset name	metric	SASRec	SASRec with BERT	GRU4Rec	GRU4Rec with BERT
Beauty	Hit@10	0.4399	0.4522	0.2125	0.2416
	NDCG@10	0.2794	0.3212	0.1203	0.1784
Electronics	Hit@10	0.6820	0.7004	0.2662	0.2998
	NDCG@10	0.4750	0.5412	0.1794	0.2246
Video Games	Hit@10	0.7302	0.7492	0.2938	0.3122
	NDCG@10	0.4796	0.5518	0.1837	0.2470
Movies & TV	Hit@10	0.8251	0.8442	0.3201	0.3656
	NDCG@10	0.5918	0.6308	0.2246	0.2612

If we look in more detail, we can say that using item descriptions provides more improvement for NDCG@10 metric which considers ranks. Item embeddings which are obtained from item descriptions provides some information about the important features of the item. By this way, deep learning model learns to establish a relationship between user and preferred item features.

One of the strengths of the proposed approach is that, using this approach helps us to obtain fixed size item embedding vectors from item description text with different lengths. An item description with 500 words and another description with 10 words are both represented by a vector which has 3072 length. This situation give us the flexibility that using all words of item description text, in an efficient way.

Another strength of the approach is using a context-dependent NLP approach to create an embedding vector from an item description. By this way, we obtain more meaningful item embedding vectors for each item description text.

In addition to that, by fine-tuning the BERT model using item description texts, we obtained a specialized BERT model for our context. As we mention before, the BERT model trained with a corpus for general usage, but more different words are used in writing item descriptions. For this reason, fine-tuning BERT model with item descriptions provides us a more suitable model.

5   Conclusion

In this paper, we proposed a recommendation system in order to combine a deep learning based recommendation model with an approach which creates embedding vector from item description text using bidirectional encoders. Thanks to bidirectional encoder representations, it is possible create an embedding vector to use item description text, in an efficient way. By using these embedding vectors to define an item, it is possible to utilize the features of an item in the recommendation model. We tested our approach with two recent baseline models which are quite successful and obtained results show that performances of these models improved. The experimental results verify that to be able to utilize item descriptions efficiently in deep recommendation models improves recommendation performance, remarkably.

As a future work, we are planning to extend the study by including item review texts in addition to item descriptions as input. Also, the item images can be used with item descriptions to represent an item in a recommendation model.

References

1. Recommendations: What and Why? https://developers.google.com/machine-learning/recommendation/overview
2. Adomavicius, G., Tuzhilin, A.: Toward the next generation of recommender systems: a survey of the state-of-the-art and possible extensions. IEEE Trans. Knowl. Data Eng. **6**, 734–749 (2005)
3. Barkan, O., Koenigstein, N.: Item2Vec: neural item embedding for collaborative filtering. In: 2016 IEEE 26th International Workshop on Machine Learning for Signal Processing (MLSP), pp. 1–6. IEEE (2016)
4. Barkan, O., Koenigstein, N., Yogev, E., Katz, O.: CB2CF: a neural multiview content-to-collaborative filtering model for completely cold item recommendations. In: Proceedings of the 13th ACM Conference on Recommender Systems, pp. 228–236 (2019)
5. Bobadilla, J., Ortega, F., Hernando, A., Gutiérrez, A.: Recommender systems survey. Knowl.-Based Syst. **46**, 109–132 (2013)
6. Cheng, H.T., et al.: Wide & deep learning for recommender systems. In: Proceedings of the 1st Workshop on Deep Learning for Recommender Systems, pp. 7–10. ACM (2016)

7. Cheng, Z., Chang, X., Zhu, L., Kanjirathinkal, R.C., Kankanhalli, M.: MMALFM: explainable recommendation by leveraging reviews and images. ACM Trans. Inf. Syst. (TOIS) **37**(2), 1–28 (2019)
8. Devlin, J., Chang, M.W., Lee, K., Toutanova, K.: BERT: pre-training of deep bidirectional transformers for language understanding. arXiv preprint arXiv:1810.04805 (2018)
9. Donkers, T., Loepp, B., Ziegler, J.: Sequential user-based recurrent neural network recommendations. In: Proceedings of the Eleventh ACM Conference on Recommender Systems, pp. 152–160. ACM (2017)
10. Dziugaite, G.K., Roy, D.M.: Neural network matrix factorization. arXiv preprint arXiv:1511.06443 (2015)
11. Guo, H., Tang, R., Ye, Y., Li, Z., He, X.: DeepFM: a factorization-machine based neural network for CTR prediction. arXiv preprint arXiv:1703.04247 (2017)
12. He, X., Chua, T.S.: Neural factorization machines for sparse predictive analytics. In: Proceedings of the 40th International ACM SIGIR Conference on Research and Development in Information Retrieval, pp. 355–364. ACM (2017)
13. He, X., Liao, L., Zhang, H., Nie, L., Hu, X., Chua, T.S.: Neural collaborative filtering. In: Proceedings of the 26th International Conference on World Wide Web, pp. 173–182. International World Wide Web Conferences Steering Committee (2017)
14. Hidasi, B., Karatzoglou, A.: Recurrent neural networks with top-k gains for session-based recommendations. In: Proceedings of the 27th ACM International Conference on Information and Knowledge Management, pp. 843–852. ACM (2018)
15. Hidasi, B., Karatzoglou, A., Baltrunas, L., Tikk, D.: Session-based recommendations with recurrent neural networks. arXiv preprint arXiv:1511.06939 (2015)
16. Hidasi, B., Quadrana, M., Karatzoglou, A., Tikk, D.: Parallel recurrent neural network architectures for feature-rich session-based recommendations. In: Proceedings of the 10th ACM Conference on Recommender Systems, pp. 241–248. ACM (2016)
17. Hu, B., Shi, C., Zhao, W.X., Yu, P.S.: Leveraging meta-path based context for top-n recommendation with a neural co-attention model. In: Proceedings of the 24th ACM SIGKDD International Conference on Knowledge Discovery & Data Mining, pp. 1531–1540. ACM (2018)
18. Jannach, D., Ludewig, M.: When recurrent neural networks meet the neighborhood for session-based recommendation. In: Proceedings of the Eleventh ACM Conference on Recommender Systems, pp. 306–310. ACM (2017)
19. Jing, H., Smola, A.J.: Neural survival recommender. In: Proceedings of the Tenth ACM International Conference on Web Search and Data Mining, pp. 515–524. ACM (2017)
20. Kang, W.C., McAuley, J.: Self-attentive sequential recommendation. In: 2018 IEEE International Conference on Data Mining (ICDM), pp. 197–206. IEEE (2018)
21. Li, J., Ren, P., Chen, Z., Ren, Z., Lian, T., Ma, J.: Neural attentive session-based recommendation. In: Proceedings of the 2017 ACM on Conference on Information and Knowledge Management, pp. 1419–1428. ACM (2017)
22. Li, P., Wang, Z., Ren, Z., Bing, L., Lam, W.: Neural rating regression with abstractive tips generation for recommendation. In: Proceedings of the 40th International ACM SIGIR conference on Research and Development in Information Retrieval, pp. 345–354. ACM (2017)
23. Li, Z., Zhao, H., Liu, Q., Huang, Z., Mei, T., Chen, E.: Learning from history and present: next-item recommendation via discriminatively exploiting user behaviors. In: Proceedings of the 24th ACM SIGKDD International Conference on Knowledge Discovery & Data Mining, pp. 1734–1743. ACM (2018)

24. Lian, J., Zhou, X., Zhang, F., Chen, Z., Xie, X., Sun, G.: xDeepFM: combining explicit and implicit feature interactions for recommender systems. In: Proceedings of the 24th ACM SIGKDD International Conference on Knowledge Discovery & Data Mining, pp. 1754–1763. ACM (2018)
25. Mikolov, T., Sutskever, I., Chen, K., Corrado, G.S., Dean, J.: Distributed representations of words and phrases and their compositionality. In: Advances in Neural Information Processing Systems, pp. 3111–3119 (2013)
26. Pennington, J., Socher, R., Manning, C.D.: Glove: global vectors for word representation. In: Proceedings of the 2014 Conference on Empirical Methods in Natural Language Processing (EMNLP), pp. 1532–1543 (2014)
27. Quadrana, M., Karatzoglou, A., Hidasi, B., Cremonesi, P.: Personalizing session-based recommendations with hierarchical recurrent neural networks. In: Proceedings of the Eleventh ACM Conference on Recommender Systems, pp. 130–137. ACM (2017)
28. Smirnova, E., Vasile, F.: Contextual sequence modeling for recommendation with recurrent neural networks. In: Proceedings of the 2nd Workshop on Deep Learning for Recommender Systems, pp. 2–9. ACM (2017)
29. Suglia, A., Greco, C., Musto, C., de Gemmis, M., Lops, P., Semeraro, G.: A deep architecture for content-based recommendations exploiting recurrent neural networks. In: Proceedings of the 25th conference on user modeling, adaptation and personalization, pp. 202–211. ACM (2017)
30. Tan, Y.K., Xu, X., Liu, Y.: Improved recurrent neural networks for session-based recommendations. In: Proceedings of the 1st Workshop on Deep Learning for Recommender Systems, pp. 17–22. ACM (2016)
31. Tang, J., Wang, K.: Personalized top-n sequential recommendation via convolutional sequence embedding. In: Proceedings of the Eleventh ACM International Conference on Web Search and Data Mining, pp. 565–573. ACM (2018)
32. Tay, Y., Anh Tuan, L., Hui, S.C.: Latent relational metric learning via memory-based attention for collaborative ranking. In: Proceedings of the 2018 World Wide Web Conference, pp. 729–739. International World Wide Web Conferences Steering Committee (2018)
33. Tay, Y., Luu, A.T., Hui, S.C.: Multi-pointer co-attention networks for recommendation. In: Proceedings of the 24th ACM SIGKDD International Conference on Knowledge Discovery & Data Mining, pp. 2309–2318. ACM (2018)
34. Vaswani, A., et al.: Attention is all you need. In: Advances in Neural Information Processing Systems, pp. 5998–6008 (2017)
35. Wu, C.Y., Ahmed, A., Beutel, A., Smola, A.J.: Joint training of ratings and reviews with recurrent recommender networks (2016)
36. Wu, C.Y., Ahmed, A., Beutel, A., Smola, A.J., Jing, H.: Recurrent recommender networks. In: Proceedings of the Tenth ACM International Conference on Web Search and Data Mining, pp. 495–503. ACM (2017)
37. Zhou, C., Bai, J., Song, J., Liu, X., Zhao, Z., Chen, X., Gao, J.: ATRank: an attention-based user behavior modeling framework for recommendation. In: Thirty-Second AAAI Conference on Artificial Intelligence (2018)

Leveraging Multi-target Regression for Predicting the Next Parallel Activities in Event Logs

Michelangelo Ceci, Angelo Impedovo$^{(\boxtimes)}$, and Antonio Pellicani

Department of Computer Science, Knowledge Discovery
and Data Engineering Laboratory, University of Bari "Aldo Moro",
70125 Bari, Italy
{michelangelo.ceci,angelo.impedovo}@uniba.it,
a.pellicani8@studenti.uniba.it

Abstract. Next activity prediction is one of the most important problems concerning the operational monitoring of processes, that is, supporting the user in predicting the activity that will be executed as the next step during process execution. However, traditional algorithms do not cope with the presence of parallel activities, thus failing to devise accurate prediction of multiple parallel activities that will be simultaneously executed. Moreover, they often require a trace alignment pre-processing step, which can be infeasible during process executions. In this paper, we propose the ParallAct methodology, in which multi-target regression is used to predict the next parallel activities in event logs without the need of aligning traces during process executions. Experimental results show that the proposed solution achieve more accurate predictions compared to the single-target setting.

Keywords: Process mining · Multi-target regression · Next activity prediction

1 Introduction

In recent years, process mining emerged as a research area between business process management and data mining, which aims to model and study real-world processes with data mining techniques. Process mining techniques have been adopted for studying real processes' executions from different perspectives. Firstly, for *process discovery*, that is, to learn accurate and actionable process models (such as Petri nets or heuristic maps) from event logs of process executions. Secondly, for *conformance checking* purposes, that is to check whether a given process execution is compliant with a given process model. Thirdly, for *process enhancement*, that is to improve a given process model based on events recorded in event logs.

Typically, process discovery, conformance checking, and process enhancement are investigated in an offline scenario, under the main assumption that every

© Springer Nature Switzerland AG 2020
I. Koprinska et al. (Eds.): ECML PKDD 2020 Workshops, CCIS 1323, pp. 237–248, 2020.
https://doi.org/10.1007/978-3-030-65965-3_15

process execution should be only considered after his termination. Over time, this assumption has become quite unrealistic, since management and operational environments require process executions to be monitored while still running, in an *online* fashion. This is the case of the next activity prediction problem, in which a given process model is used to predict the activity which is more likely to be executed as the next step in a given partial trace of a running process.

However, next activity prediction becomes a challenging problem when dealing with multiple events which are executed in parallel. Indeed, predicting only a single activity as the next one in a trace could give the users a significantly distorted expectation of the execution outcomes. While this sort of parallelism has been taken into account when devising advanced process discovery and conformance checking algorithms, to the best of our knowledge, no previous attempt has been done for operational support tasks, such as next activity prediction.

Our main claim is that prediction of the next parallel events in a given partial trace can be accomplished with multi-target regression. To this end, in this paper we propose a novel operational support tool, called ParallAct, which learns a multi-target regression model starting from a numerical encoding of structured data, such as the observed traces. Thus, the proposed approach does not require a previously learned process model to be used as a reference for predicting the next activities. Furthermore, ParallAct requires partial traces to be aligned before making predictions. Experiments on real-world processes show that the multi-target learning setting leads to more accurate predictions than in the single-target one.

The rest of this paper is organized as follows: Sect. 2 discusses some related works concerning the next activity prediction problem, Sect. 3 introduces some preliminary notions before discussing, in Sect. 4, the proposed solution. The results of a comparative evaluation are presented in Sect. 5, then we draw the conclusions in Sect. 6.

2   Related Works

Recently, many process mining algorithms working under the parallelism assumption have been proposed. Our contribution strives to study the problem of next activity prediction under the same assumption, which is hereafter referred to as the parallelism assumption. Therefore, what we propose concerns two research perspectives: firstly, existing process mining techniques which take into account the parallelism, and secondly, existing next activity prediction algorithms.

Indeed, parallelism is an important facet of real processes involving the execution of multiple activities, by human or artificial actors, at the same time. As a consequence, traditional process mining techniques, which were not originally designed for processes with parallel activities, had to be extended in order to cope with such a concurrent scenario. For instance, discovering process models is difficult since parallel or concurrent activities may appear as different permutations of activities in traces from an event log. Traditional process discovery algorithms, such as the α-algorithm [1], fails in their purpose. As a solution, [2] proposed a trace alignment pre-processing step, in which traces are aligned in order to let subsequent discovery algorithms to inspect a polished event logs. Process conformance checking under the parallelism assumption is also difficult for two main reasons: on the one hand, conformance checking assumes the presence of a previously learned process model, which for the reason stated above is not easily learned for processes with parallelism. on the other hand, the trace to be validated could contain a random permutation of concurrent activities which should be accounted for in the process model. Also for this reason, [6] proposed a conformance checking which balances the *fitness* and the *appropriateness* scores of event logs against process models.

As for the operational support perspective, to the best of our understanding, no prior attempt has been done before concerning the prediction of multiple parallel activities to be executed. In fact, traditional operational support tools of next activity prediction algorithms first discover a process model of the given process, then they enrich it using temporal and statistical data. Finally, a predictive model, typically a classification one, is learned and used to predict the single next activity of a given partial trace whose execution is running. As an example, the NextAct algorithm [3] is a two-stepped solution in which descriptive data mining and predictive data mining algorithms are used to learn the process model and the next activity prediction model, respectively. More specifically, NextAct learns the process model via the approximate learning of frequent sequential patterns, stored in a SE-Tree data structure, which are later used to train classification models. In particular, NextAct is based upon two main assumptions: firstly, frequent sequences denote the sequences of subsequent activities that are frequently occurring in traces from the training set. Secondly, the traces in which a frequent sequence occur collectively form a training set on which to learn a predictive model, a classification model, of the most promising next activity to be executed in the sequence. However, since NextAct is inherently based on the concept of sequences, which by definition are strongly determined by the ordering of activities in traces, it is affected by the same ambiguity in representing parallel activities in traces of the afore-mentioned algorithms, thus requiring a trace alignment step. Moreover, discovering the set of frequent sequences in an event log is a time-consuming task, due to their combinatory explosion, which closely depends on the frequency threshold considered. As a consequence, learning a process model via frequent sequence mining can rapidly become both memory and time inefficient. Lastly, the situation worsen considering that a given partial trace could match different frequent sequences and, consequently, should be tested against different classification models.

To solve the drawbacks mentioned above, we propose the ParallAct framework, a next activity prediction framework where multi-target regression is preferred to classification for predicting the next parallel activities. The first and foremost difference between ParallAct and NextAct is that the former is a numerical approach based on the regression framework, while the second is a symbolic one based on the sequence mining framework. As a consequence, ParallAct requires traces and activities to be represented in a numerical format, compatible with the regression framework, so that the follow-up relationships between activities is kept. This way, ParallAct implicitly learns a process model by fitting the dependency between a given activity and the next ones via multi-target regression, thus without requiring an expensive sequence mining step and the learning of multiple classification models based on sequences.

3   Preliminaries

Before introducing the computational solution, we give some preliminaries. In particular, we discuss how traces are represented before introducing the multi-target regression problem. Then, we state the problem to be solved by the proposed approach.

Let A be the set of activities, for our convenience we consider each activity $a \in A$ uniquely identified by $id(a)$. An event log over A is defined as the time series of n traces $E = \{T_t\}_{t=1}^n$. Each trace $T_i = \langle a_1, \ldots, a_k \rangle \in \mathcal{L}_A$ is a *word*, drawn from the language $\mathcal{L}_A$ defined on the alphabet of activities A, which captures the sequence of $|T_i| = k$ activities.

Given the trace $T = \langle a_1, \ldots, a_k \rangle$, every $T' = \langle a_1, \ldots, a_j \rangle$ having $0 \le j \le k$ activities is a partial trace of T. Consequently, the mapping $next(T') = \{a_{j+1}, \ldots, a_{j+m}\}$, defined as $next : \mathcal{L}_A \to \mathcal{P}(A)$, maps a partial trace T' with the set $\{a_{j+1}, \ldots, a_{j+k}\}$ of m activities that will be executed in parallel. Intuitively, traces collect activities sorted in their execution order, without specifying the parallelism between some of them. As a consequence i) an activity may be followed by 0 or more activities $next(T')$ executed in parallel and ii) the activities in $next(T')$ may appear in different permutations for different traces.

Clearly, the mapping $next$ is unknown and, when performing next activity prediction, the objective is to accurately estimate it from observed traces in the event log E. Then, such an estimated map, conveniently called $next_P$, is used for predicting the next activities of unseen partial traces T', that is traces for which the next activities are unknown. In the remaining parts of the paper we will resort to the multi-target regression framework to learn a map $next_P$ such that $next_P(T') = next(T')$ for an unseen partial trace T'. Typically, multi-target regression models predict the value of multiple target variables which, in our case, correspond to the next parallel activities.

3.1   Data Representation

Multi-target regression models maps a set of *descriptive features* to a set of *target variables*. Adopting regression algorithms for next activity prediction of multiple parallel events is not immediate, mainly because they i) are often designed for numeric and categorical descriptive and target features and not for process data, and ii) do not learn process models or the dependency between subsequent activities and parallel ones, consequently partial traces cannot be matched against a reference process model, when predicting the next activities based on regularities observed in a set of observed variables.

To solve the afore-mentioned problems, we adopt a matrix encoding of traces. In particular, let $E = \{T_t\}_{t=1}^n$ be the event log of n traces over $|A| = m$ distinct activities. Then, starting from E, we compute two real-valued blockwise defined matrix, that is the *data matrix* D and the *target matrix* B, on which to learn the regression model.

Let $T_i = \langle a_1, \ldots, a_k \rangle$ be a trace. Then, the data matrix is defined as $D = [D_1^T \ldots D_n^T]^T$, each block $D_i = g(T_i) \in \mathbb{R}^{k \times 3}$ denotes the descriptive features of activities involved in T_i. More specifically, the k-th row vector of D_i, denoted as $[D_i]_k = \langle i, k, id(a_k) \rangle$, records the descriptive features associated to the activity a_k in T_i. We only consider the trace id, the index of the activity in the trace, and the unique activity id. Similarly, the target matrix is defined as $B = [B_1^T \ldots B_n^T]^T$. Each block $B_i = f(T_i) \in \mathbb{R}^{k \times m}$ denotes the values of the m target variables associated to activities involved in trace T_i. In particular, the k-th row vector of B_i, denoted as $[B_i]_k$, is an m-dimensional vector in which the j-th element equals to 1 if the corresponding activity in A succeeds a_k in trace T_i, 0 otherwise.

The rationale of this data representation is to train multi-target regression model by observing descriptive features of activities, collected in the *data matrix* D, for predicting the value of the m target variables, in the *target matrix* T.

3.2   Problem Statement

Let A be a set of activities, $E = \{T_t\}_{t=1}^n$ be an event log over A. Then:

- the *data matrix* $D = [g(T_1)^T \ldots g(T_n)^T]^T$ is built as a pre-processing step.
- the *target matrix* $T = [f(T_1)^T \ldots f(T_n)^T]^T$ is built as a pre-processing step.
- the *predictive model* $next_P$ is estimated from D to fit target variables in T.
- *next parallel activities* for every partial trace T' is predicted by:
    - testing T' against the predictive model by computing $N = next_P(T')$ and returning the predicted activities N.

4   Proposed Method

The aforementioned problem can be solved by various computational strategies in which a learner is used to estimate a predictive model from data collected in the event log, then the learner is used for predicting the next parallel activities of an unseen partial trace.

To this purpose we propose the ParallAct framework seen in Fig. 1, in which a multi-target regression algorithm learns a regression model for predicting the next activities of unseen partial traces. Being based on a learner specifically designed for numeric data, ParallAct carefully handles the data representation so that both traces in the event log and unseen partial ones are represented in numerical format, and are also consistent between each other, that is represented by considering the same features. In particular, at training time, ParallAct computes the data matrix D and the target matrix B from traces in E. Specifically, descriptive features and target variables of each trace T_i are extracted by computing the blocks $D_i = g(T_i)$ and $B_i = f(T_i)$, in the data matrix and target matrix, respectively (Steps 1–2), as discussed in Sect. 3.1. The same happens at prediction time, since ParallAct extracts the same descriptive features of a partial trace T' by computing the matrix $D' = g(T')$. Once data is transformed in such a numerical representation, ParallAct learn a multi-target regression model by estimating $next_P$ using the DENCAST multi-target regression algorithm [4] (Step 3). Such a model, is then used at test time for predicting the next parallel activities L based on the numerical representation of the partial trace T' stored in B' (Step 6).

In the following sections we detail how model training and model testing is performed in the ParallAct framework using DENCAST algorithm. Firstly, we focus our attention on how DENCAST estimates $next_P$ from both the data and the target matrix. Secondly, we clarify how the model solves the predictive problem by focusing on the operational details of how $next_P$ is computed, this is particular important since regression models usually predicts numerical targets and not symbolic labels as done by classification model.

4.1   Model Learning

In ParallAct the prediction model is learned by using the DENCAST algorithm, a density-based clustering algorithm which is able to handle large-scale, high-dimensional data.

The rationale behind DENCAST is to exploit the identified clusters, built on labeled data, to predict the value assumed by one or more target variables of unlabeled objects in an inductive, supervised learning setting. This characteristic allows the algorithm to solve any single or multi-target predictive task. As a consequence, we deem DENCAST particularly suitable for fitting predictive models solving next activity prediction problems, because i) the numeric representation of traces is inherently multidimensional, ii) the number of activities that can be executed in parallel is unknown to the users and, potentially, ranges between 1 and $|A|$. As a consequence, the prediction task can easily degenerate into a single-target regression problem.

Given a training set of k activities, described by 3 descriptive features in the data matrix D, and the associated m target variables, described by the target matrix B, DENCAST first apply a Locality-Sensitive Hashing (LSH) [5] algorithm to identify a neighborhood graph, in which two nodes are connected by an edge if the LSH algorithm finds two similar labeled objects. Such a neighborhood graph is an approximate representation of the activities and their distances instead of activity vectors represented in their original feature space. Then, nodes from the neighborhood graph are assigned to clusters with a density-based clustering approach, this is done by propagating cluster IDs from core objects through their neighbors. By doing so, the model learned from DENCAST consists in a set of clusters of similar activities which are used during model testing for solving a multi-target predictive task.

4.2 Model Testing

Once learned, the set of clusters are used for making predictions on unseen traces. From a clustering point of view, the model learnt by DENCAST gathers similar vectors, that is activity vectors from traces, under same cluster. The rationale of this approach is that activities with similar vectors should proceed the same set of parallel activities. Clearly, the same applies for the unseen trace $T' = \langle a_1, \ldots, a_i \rangle$, for which the parallel activities L are to be predicted by testing them against the clusters learned by DENCAST. This is computationally done by quantitatively evaluating computing $L = next_P(T')$, in this section we give the reader some additional details of how $next_P$ is actually computed starting from T' and clusters previously learned.

Since the clustering model has been fitted on activity vectors from the training data, thus being an activity-centric model, the first step for making predictions on T' is to compute its activity vectors $D' = g(T')$ (as seen in Fig. 1, Step 5). Recall that D' is a matrix of i activity vectors, one row per each activity in T'. Of all those vectors we deem as interesting only the activity vector $[D']_i$ associated to the last executed activity in T', that is a_i. This is due to different reasons: firstly, this allows us to make activity-centric predictions based only on the activity which has been currently executed, and secondly, allows us to forget the sequence of previously executed events which could carry little information in the process. This choice is in line with what process models naturally describe, that is workflows in which the dependency between an activity and the next is not determined by those previously executed but, on the contrary, is based only on the activity which is being currently executed.

Since we make predictions based solely on the i-th activity vector of D', that is $[D']_i$, the function we compute becomes $L = next_P(T') = next_P([D']_i)$. This way, given $[D']_i$, our approach exploits the clusters learned by DENCAST for multi-target regression in a two-stepped process in which i) a forecasting step predicts the numerical values for the target variables given the activity vector $[D']_i$, and ii) a decision criteria is used to generate activity labels from the predicted target values.

Specifically, in the forecasting step, DENCAST first assigns $[D']_i$ to the cluster c to which $[D']_i$ ideally belongs: that is, the cluster to which it would have been assigned, if it had been known during the clustering process. This is done by assigning $[D']_i$ to the same cluster C of his most similar labeled activity vector, computed by maximizing the cosine similarity between the two ones. Then, the k dimensional target vector $\vec{b}'$ associated to $[D']_i$ is predicted by averaging the target vectors of all the objects v falling in the cluster C, weighted according to their similarity with $[D']_i$. For our convenience, given the object v in a cluster C, we term the corresponding data vector in D and target vector in B as $D(v)$ and $B(v)$, respectively.

$$\vec{b}' = \frac{\sum_{v \in C} B(v) \cdot cosSim(D(v), [D']_i)}{\sum_{v \in C} cosSim(D(v), [D']_i)}$$

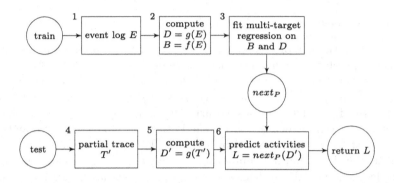

Fig. 1. The ParallAct flowchart

Once the k-dimensional target vector $\vec{b}'$ has been predicted, we apply a decision criteria to each j-th target variable: a threshold is used to establish whether $\vec{b}'_j$ denotes sufficient evidence for predicting the activity $a_j \in A$ as one of the next parallel activities, this is done as in the following:

$$L = next_P([D']_i) = \{a_j \in A \mid \vec{b}'_j \geq \alpha\}$$

Where $\alpha \in \mathbb{R}$ is a user-defined minimum threshold. This way, ParallAct leverages multi-target regression, based on a density-based clustering approach as the one adopted by DENCAST, for predicting the next parallel activities of an unseen trace T', based solely on the last executed activity.

5 Experiments

In this section we present the results of a comparative evaluation between two variants of the ParallAct framework, one operating in the single-target setting, the other in the multi-target setting. In particular, the experiments were designed to answer the following research question: **RQ1)** is the proposed solution more accurate in the multi-target setting rather than in the single-target one on real dataset? **RQ2)** is the proposed solution more efficient in the multi-target setting rather than in the single-target one on real dataset? All the experiments have been executed on a PC equipped with a Xeon E5-1620 quadcore CPU and 32 GB of RAM. We compared the running time and the precision of ParallAct in the multi-target and single-target setting respectively, on four publicly available real world event logs[1] reported in Table 1.

In particular, BPI13 collects traces recorded by Volvo IT Belgium. The log contains events from an incident and problem management system called VINST. The primary goal of the Handle Incidents Process was to restore regular service operation as quickly as possible and by that ensuring that the best possible levels of service quality and availability are maintained. Most IT departments and

---

[1] https://data.4tu.nl/repository/.

Table 1. Statistics describing the event logs considered in the experiments. We report i) the number $|E|$ of traces, ii) the overall count of activities, iii) the number $|A|$ of distinct activities, and iv) the maximum length of traces, resp.

Dataset	$|E|$	$\sum |T_i|$	$|A|$	$\max |T_i|$
BPI13	7554	65533	5	122
BPI15	1119	52217	398	98
WABO	398	1157601	380	3000
NASA	2566	73638	47	48

specialist teams contribute to handling Incidents at some time. Incidents that cannot be resolved by the service desk or expert helpdesk should be escalated to the second line and/or third-line teams. The process is mostly reactive. To react efficiently and effectively, therefore, demands a formal method of working that can be supported by software tools. A workaround or solution should be established as quickly as possible to restore the service to normal with minimum disruption to the business. After implementing a workaround or a solution and verifying that the service is restored the Incident is closed. If the action owner suspects that the incident might reoccur a problem record shall be registered.

BPI15 contains information by five dutch municipalities. The data contains all building permit applications over approximately four years. There are many different activities present, denoted by both codes and labels, both in Dutch and English. The cases in the log contain information on the main application as well as objection procedures in various stages. Furthermore, information is available about the resource that carried out the task and on the cost of the application. The processes in the five municipalities should be identical but may differ slightly. Especially when changes are made to procedures, rules, or regulations, the time at which these changes are pushed into the five municipalities may differ. Of course, over the four years, the underlying processes have changed.

The Wabo dataset collects data originating from the CoSeLoG project. Within the CoSeLoG project, the (dis)similarities between several processes of different municipalities in the Netherlands has been investigated. The dataset, similarly to BPI15, consists of 5 event logs that record the execution of a building permit application process in five different anonymous municipalities. The recording of these processes is comparable, which means that activity labels in the different event logs refer to the same activities performed in the five municipalities.

The NASA dataset contains data describing a single run of an exhaustive unit test suite for the NASA Crew Exploration Vehicle (CEV). CEV was the conceptual component of the NASA Vision for Space Exploration which later became known as the Orion spacecraft. The Orion CEV was part of the program to send human explorers to the moon, and then to Mars and other destinations in the solar system. Each trace represents the execution of a different unit test method, logging both input and output data.

5.1 The Most Accurate Next Activity Prediction Approach

In this set of experiments we have executed ParallAct both in the multi-target and in the single-target setting, on the four considered datasets, then we measured the accuracy of the two approach in predicting the next activities when tuning the threshold $\alpha = \{0, 0.25, 0.5, 0.75\}$. In particularly, every dataset has been randomly split into training and test set using the holdout method. 70% of each dataset has been assigned to the training set and the remaining 30% for the test set. After the training phase, each model has been tested using the respective test set. Since regression models have been trained, it is logical to expect error metrics like Mean Absolute Error (MAE) or Root Mean Square Error (RMSE). However, during these experiments, precision has been preferred since the results of the regression task have been used to decide whether or not a specific activity had to be predicted. The results are depicted in Table 2.

Table 2. Balanced accuracy of ParallAct running in single-target and multi-target setting on real world datasets.

Dataset	Balanced accuracy @ α							
	ParallAct (single-target)				ParallAct (multi-target)			
	0	0.25	0.5	0.75	0	0.25	0.5	0.75
bpi13	0.503	0.51	0.506	0.504	0.751	0.754	0.69	0.556
bpi15	0.528	0.501	0.500	0.5	0.691	0.563	0.561	0.551
wabo	0.53	0.5	0.501	0.5	0.685	0.532	0.532	0.521
nasa	0.737	0.51	0.502	0.501	0.76	0.515	0.504	0.5

Indeed, ParallAct running in the multi-target setting is more accurate than in the single-target setting for every considered dataset and every value of α. Clearly, this is an expected results since the single-target setting usually is not the optimal learning setting for predicting multiple parallel events, which on the contrary suits well the multi-target settings. In fact, predicting the next activities in the single-target setting forces ParallAct to accurately model at most one parallel execution branch, therefore a correct prediction is always made, although not considering the remaining parallel activities. Moreover, we see a decreasing tendency of the accuracy for increasing values of α, in both the single and multi-target settings. This is also an expected results, in fact very high values of k leads to filter out the activities associated to high scores of b_i', thus missing the prediction of really executed parallel events. Therefore, we conclude that predicting the next activities under the multi-target setting leads to more accurate predictions.

5.2 The Most Efficient Next Activity Prediction Approach

In this set of experiments we have executed ParallAct both in the multi-target and in the single-target setting, on the four considered datasets, then we measured the running times of the two approaches when fixing the threshold $\alpha = 0.5$. Models were trained and tested using the same splits considered in Sect. 5.1, results are depicted in Fig. 2.

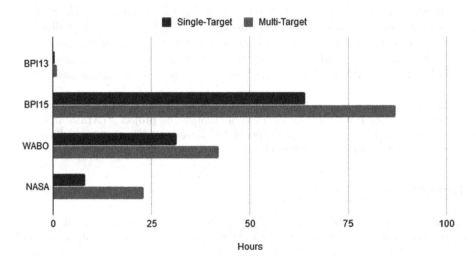

Fig. 2. Running times in hours of ParallAct running in the single-target and multi-target setting on four real-world datasets.

Independently from the dataset considered, ParallAct running in the single-target setting is more efficient than in the multi-target setting. This is an expected results since, when running in the single-target setting, DENCAST solves a more simple multiple regression problem, in terms of target variables involved, than in the multi-target regression problem. In this sets of experiments we have not tuned the threshold α because such parameter does not affect the running times of the overall process. In fact, filtering each element of the predicted vectors $\vec{b}'$ against α requires a time proportional to k, that is the number of target variables.

6   Conclusions

In this paper we have proposed ParallAct, a process mining framework for next activity prediction of parallel events in a supervised fashion. ParallAct is a business operational support tool which leverages multi-target regression, as performed by the DENCAST algorithm, for predicting the next possible parallel activities of a partial trace.

The solution we propose extends the problem to the multi-target setting, while previous solutions are only able of predicting only single activities, ParallAct is able of predicting a set of multiple activities which will be concurrently executed by the actors of the process. The comparative evaluation we performed has shown that the multi-target learning setting achieves an increased prediction accuracy while retaining comparable efficiency.

The framework paves the way to multiple future research directions. For instance, while our prediction is based only on the workflow perspective recorded by features in activity vectors, different features, perhaps concerning the state of actors and resources involved in the process, could lead to significantly different results. Moreover, being a modular framework, ParallAct can be executed with different learner also leading in different conclusions, for instance a multi-label classification algorithm or alternative multi-target regression algorithms.

Acknowledgments. We acknowledge the support of the MIUR - Ministero dell'Istruzione dell'Università e della Ricerca through the project "TALIsMan - Tecnologie di Assistenza personALizzata per il Miglioramento della quAlità della vitA" (Grant ID: ARS01_01116), funding scheme PON RI 2014–2020.

References

1. van der Aalst, W.M.P., Weijters, T., Maruster, L.: Workflow mining: discovering process models from event logs. IEEE Trans. Knowl. Data Eng. **16**(9), 1128–1142 (2004). https://doi.org/10.1109/TKDE.2004.47
2. Jagadeesh Chandra Bose, R.P., van der Aalst, W.: Trace alignment in process mining: opportunities for process diagnostics. In: Hull, R., Mendling, J., Tai, S. (eds.) BPM 2010. LNCS, vol. 6336, pp. 227–242. Springer, Heidelberg (2010). https://doi.org/10.1007/978-3-642-15618-2_17
3. Ceci, M., Spagnoletta, M., Lanotte, P.F., Malerba, D.: Distributed learning of process models for next activity prediction. In: Desai, B.C., Flesca, S., Zumpano, E., Masciari, E., Caroprese, L. (eds.) Proceedings of the 22nd International Database Engineering & Applications Symposium, IDEAS 2018, Villa San Giovanni, Italy, 18–20 June 2018, pp. 278–282. ACM (2018). https://doi.org/10.1145/3216122.3216125
4. Corizzo, R., Pio, G., Ceci, M., Malerba, D.: DENCAST: distributed density-based clustering for multi-target regression. J. Big Data **6**, 43 (2019). https://doi.org/10.1186/s40537-019-0207-2
5. Ravichandran, D., Pantel, P., Hovy, E.H.: Randomized algorithms and NLP: using locality sensitive hash functions for high speed noun clustering. In: Knight, K., Ng, H.T., Oflazer, K. (eds.) ACL 2005, 43rd Annual Meeting of the Association for Computational Linguistics, Proceedings of the Conference, 25–30 June 2005, University of Michigan, USA, pp. 622–629. The Association for Computer Linguistics (2005). https://doi.org/10.3115/1219840.1219917. https://www.aclweb.org/anthology/P05-1077/
6. Rozinat, A., van der Aalst, W.M.P.: Conformance checking of processes based on monitoring real behavior. Inf. Syst. **33**(1), 64–95 (2008). https://doi.org/10.1016/j.is.2007.07.001

A Multi-view Ensemble of Deep Models for the Detection of Deviant Process Instances

Francesco Folino, Gianluigi Folino, Massimo Guarascio[(⊠)], and Luigi Pontieri

ICAR Institute, National Research Council, Rende, CS, Italy
{francesco.folino,gianluigi.folino,
massimo.guarascio,luigi.pontieri}@icar.cnr.it

Abstract. Mining deviances from expected behaviors in process logs is a relevant problem in modern organizations, owing to their negative impact in terms of monetary/reputation losses. Most proposals to deviance mining combine the extraction of behavioral features from log traces with the induction of standard classifiers. Difficulties in capturing the multi-faceted nature of deviances with a single pattern family led to explore the possibility to mix up heterogeneous data views, obtained each with a different pattern family. Unfortunately, combining many pattern families tends to produce sparse and redundant representations that likely lead to the discovery of poor deviance-oriented classifiers. Using a multi-view ensemble learning approach to combine alternative trace representations was recently proven effective for this induction task. On the other hand, Deep Learning methods have been gaining momentum in prediction/classification tasks on process log data, owing to their flexibility and expressiveness. We here propose a novel multi-view ensemble-based framework for the discovery of deviance-oriented classifiers that profitably combines different single-view deep classifiers, sharing an ad hoc residual-like architecture (simulating fine-grain ensemble-like capabilities over each single data view). The approach, tested over real-life process log data, significantly improves previous solutions.

Keywords: Business process intelligence · Ensemble learning · Deviance detection · Deep neural networks

1 Introduction

Deviance mining [11] is a branch of Process Mining (PM) [24] that focuses on the problem of detecting and analyzing "deviant" process instances (i.e. instances featuring abnormal/undesired behavior, such as security breaches, faults, KPI violations) in a collection of log *traces* (representing each the sequence of events occurred when executing a process instance). This problem gained momentum in recent years, owing to the fact that such deviances may endanger severely a business process, and may lead to monetary costs and reputation loss. Notably,

© Springer Nature Switzerland AG 2020
I. Koprinska et al. (Eds.): ECML PKDD 2020 Workshops, CCIS 1323, pp. 249–262, 2020.
https://doi.org/10.1007/978-3-030-65965-3_16

this problem is tightly related to the outcome-prediction one, which amounts to forecasting the final outcome (e.g., in terms of compliance to non-functional requirements or performance constraints) of an ongoing process instance, based on its partial trace [9].

Most deviance-mining solutions (e.g., [2,18,19]) rely on extracting sequential patterns from the traces and then reusing standard Machine Learning (ML) methods to discover a deviance-oriented classifier from a pattern-based representation of the traces. Notably, the usage of concurrency-aware patterns was recently studied in [12].[1]

Since selecting an optimal pattern family for making such vector-space encodings of the traces is not easy, some works [2,19] proposed to mix up heterogeneous representations obtained by using different pattern families. However, using a high number of pattern families is likely to yield redundant and sparse representations, which may eventually lead to poor and/or overfitting deviance detection models.

To overcome such problems, in [5] the authors introduced a multi-view learning scheme to combine different classifiers trained against multiple heterogenous pattern-based view. This approach was extended in [6] to exploit the multi-dimensional nature of log events, with the help of a clustering-based trace abstraction method. However, a more systematic and effective solution to the problem of detecting deviances, also exploiting active learning and self-training mechanisms, was proposed in in [7] where a stacking procedure is used to combine the discovered base models into an overall probabilistic model.

In fact, the usage of multiple data views in the detection of deviant behaviors has also been employed outside the field of PM, e.g. in the area malware discovery [1].

Even though most current solutions for both deviance mining and outcome prediction hinge on traditional ML classifiers (in particular, XGBoost and Random Forest (RF) [22]), there was recently a surge of interest towards using Deep Learning (DL) methods in predictive Process Mining tasks [4,10,17,20,23]. Notably, according to the extensive empirical study on outcome prediction methods conducted in [15], DL methods (based on either feed-forward or recurrent architectures) outperform some very popular ML models (namely, RF and SVM), especially when (a) the process under analysis is complex and exhibits a high number of variants, and (b) the outcome classes are imbalanced, which are both very common situations in real-life deviance-detection scenarios (e.g., especially those concerning the detection of frauds or security attacks).

By contrast, to the best of our knowledge, no attempt has been made in the above-mentioned fields (i.e., deviance mining and outcome prediction) in order to combine ensemble/multi-view learning methods with deep neural architectures.

---

[1] Despite such patters can explain more effectively deviances of processes with a high degree of parallelism, it was shown in [12] that they do not improve significantly the accuracy of deviance predictions, which is the main objective of our work. Thus, we here only focus on classical sequential patterns, for the sake of comparison with previous deviance-mining work.

Contribution and Organization. A novel multi-view deep learning framework for the discovery of deviance-oriented trace classifiers is proposed here (in Sect. 3), after introducing the problem and background concepts (in Sect. 2).

Differently from [7], we here propose to train a single base classifier, taking the form of a Deep Neural Network (DNN), on each feature-based view of the given traces. However, each of these DNN-based classifiers is somehow equipped with ensemble-like capabilities, which descend from the usage of both dropout layers and residual-like connections. Moreover, all the base classifiers are trained with an ad-hoc cost-sensitive loss function to better deal with the imbalanced nature of the training data.

As the class of deviant instances usually features a wide range of heterogeneous behaviors, one single DNN-based classifier hardly covers this class as a whole, and it is likely to play as a specialized detector for some sub-types of deviant instances (i.e. those that can be captured by only looking at the specific pattern-based view employed to train the classifier). Incidentally, this peculiarity makes simple combination schemes, such as weighted voting/averaging, unsuitable for our setting. Thus, we here propose to put the base classifiers into an overall deep neural network, equipped with a combiner sub-net (playing similarly to meta-classifiers in classic stacked generalization approaches), which combines the predictions and some high-level features returned by the base-classifier sub-nets into a final classification.

The approach was implemented into a prototype system, and tested on two real-life datasets (both extracted from the BPIC 2011, one of the logs recently used in [15]). The analysis of the experimental results (discussed in Sect. 4) confirmed the validity of the proposed approach, which obtained compelling achievements compared to state-of-the-art methods. Some final remarks and future work directions are drawn in Sect. 5.

2   Background, Problem and Solution Strategy

Problem and Background. The ultimate task that our framework is meant to support is deciding if a process instance (a.k.a. *case*) is deviant or not, based its (execution) *trace*—i.e. the list of (temporally ordered) events representing the history of the process instance, where each event is assumed to be associated with a process activity (and possibly with other properties, concerning, e.g., who executed the activity, activity's parameters, and performance measures).

This task is a binary (normal vs. deviant) trace classification task. Assuming that example traces are given, with their associated ground-truth class labels, the problem amounts to discover a model that can assign any new trace to one of the two classes. As done in [7], let us name such a classification model a *Deviance Detection Model* (*DDM*) and the associated discovery problem as *DDM mining*—indeed this problem was referred to as "deviance mining" in Process Mining literature [2,7,18,19].

Most of the solutions in this field rely on applying standard classifier induction methods to a vector-space encoding of the given traces. The prevalent encoding strategy relies on first abstracting each trace into a sequence of symbols (usually, the activities appearing in the trace, but possibly also other event data, such as resources/executors), and then using patterns extracted from these sequences as (behavioral) features for mapping each trace onto a vector.

The main *pattern families* that have been employed to this end in previous Process Mining work are: *individual activities* (IA) [21], *tandem repeats* (TR), *maximal repeats* (MR), *alphabet tandem repeats* (ATR), *alphabet maximal repeats* (ATR) [3], and *discriminative patterns* (DP) [18]. In the simple case of IA patterns, each activity a play as a pattern. A *maximal repeat* in a given sequence s is a maximal sequence α occurring in at least two non-overlapping segments of s. A *tandem repeat* in a sequence s is a sequence α such that: *(i)* α^k is a segment of s for some integer $k \geq 2$, and *(ii)* there is no β such that $\alpha = \beta^q$ with $q \in \mathbb{N}$ and $q \geq 2$. The "alphabet" version of a maximal/tandem repeat is the set of symbols in the latter.

Usually, a fixed number of patterns (e.g., the k most frequent ones) is computed for any of the families above, in order to obtain a flat representation of the traces. Each pattern p is turned into a non-negative integer attribute in any trace, storing the number of times p occurs in the trace.

Basic Solution Strategy: Multi-view Ensemble Learning. As noticed in [7], there is no consensus on which pattern family is the best choice for encoding log traces, and always using one of them only may lead to loss in information (and then in classification accuracy). By contrast, mixing up very many pattern families into a single data view would produce a sparse, heterogeneous and redundant representation of the traces, which may yield an overfitting DDM.

A multi-view ensemble learning approach to the DDM mining problem, named *HO-DDM-mine* was defined in [7] to deal with these issues. Essentially, the approach relies on inducing an ensemble of DDMs from different feature-based views of a given set L (usually named a *log*) of labelled traces, according to the following learning scheme:
1) A number of relevant patterns are extracted from L for different families, say $F_1, \ldots, F_n$ of sequential patterns (of the kinds described before). **2)** A distinguished data view L_i is derived for each family F_i, by projecting each trace t in L onto the space of the patterns discovered for F_i and extending this representation with global case-oriented properties of t (if any) and context-related data; **3)** A number of DDMs is then discovered from each view L_i by using different classifier-induction algorithms (after possibly applying a resampling method to L_i in the case of imbalanced classes). **4)** Finally, a combiner model is built for the ensemble (for fusing the heterogeneous base DDMs discovered) through a stacked-generalization scheme, which consists on training a probabilistic (meta) classification model (namely, AODE [25]) on a view of L containing, for each trace t in L, the predictions returned for t by all the base DDMs.

3   The Proposed Deep Ensemble Model: Architecture and Training

As above mentioned, we propose an integrated Deep Learning (DL) framework that simplifies and enhances the basic multi-view learning strategy described in Sect. 2. In particular, our proposal hinges on a novel multi-view ensemble model, named *MVDE* (*Multi-View Deep Ensemble*), following the three-layer high-level structure in Fig. 1.

The first layer in the architecture (shown in the top of the figure) consists of a number n of *Feature Extractor* modules, each of which allows for projecting any given log trace onto a vector space, based on extracting a distinguished kind of features. Such modules can be implemented by training sequence-oriented feature-learning neural networks, and/or pattern-based schemes like those summarized in Sect. 2. In the experimentation presented in Sect. 4, we have focused on using the latter kind of feature-extraction modules, which was shown effective in capturing process-deviance patterns [2,7,19]. This choice mainly serves our desire to evaluate the benefit of using ad hoc neural-network architectures for implementing the other two levels (i.e., those of the base DDMs and of the combiner) in the ensemble. However, we pinpoint that the ensemble model proposed here is parametric to this choice, and that we plan to test other kinds of feature extractors in the future.

The data representation returned by each of the Feature Extractor modules is given as input to a single base DDM (rather than to a heterogeneous collection of ML classifiers) that takes the form of a Deep Neural Network (*DNN*) returns, for each process instance, a fuzzy "deviance score" in [0, 1] that represents an estimate for the probability that the instance is deviant. All of these base DDMs (denoted in the figure as $DNN_1, \ldots, DNN_n$) share the same DNN architecture, including both dropout layers and residual-like connections that allow each base DDM to "mimic" an ensemble of sub-models (reasoning on the same representation of the process instances)—details on the architecture of the base models are given later on.

The last layer of the ensemble model module, named here *NN combiner*, is devoted to encode the function for combining the outputs of the base DNN classifiers into an overall deviance score – see Subsect. 3.2 for more details.

We pinpoint that the proposed ensemble model, if excluding the Feature Extractor modules (in the current implementation of our approach) consists of an integrated neural network composed of all the base DDMs and the combiner sub-net.

Definition 1 (Training scheme). *The induction of a model from a given set L of training traces is performed according to the following steps:*

1. *A number, say n, of Feature Extractor modules are constructed and used to derive a list $L_1, \ldots, L_n$ of different views of L, which are possibly made undergo a resampling procedure when dealing with imbalanced data.*

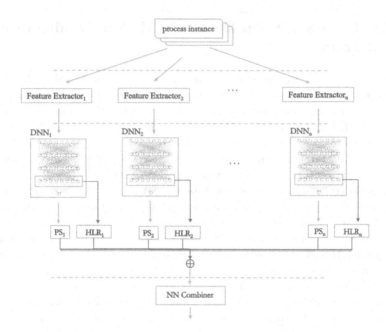

Fig. 1. Proposed multi-view ensemble model *MVDE*: high-level architecture.

2. *Each view L_i, for $i \in \{1, ..n\}$ is used to train a distinguished instance DNN_i of the proposed base-DDM architecture (see Sect. 3.1), by possibly using an ad hoc cost-sensitive loss function (described later on) in the case of imbalanced data.*
3. *An instance of* MVDE *is built that incorporates the DDMs (DNN_1, ..., DNN_n) found in Step 2 as its base classifiers, and it is possibly trained over (the feature-based representations of) the traces in L, when using a trainable NN combiner, in order to fine-tune the base classifiers and learn the combiner function (while leaving the Feature Extractor modules unchanged).* □

The rest of this section is meant to give a detailed description the DNN architectures adopted for the base learners (Sect. 3.1) and for the combiner subnet (Sect. 3.2).

3.1 Base DDMs' Architecture

As stated above, the base DDM classifiers in the proposed ensemble model *MVDE* share the same DNN architecture, summarized in the left side of Fig. 2. The architecture consists of the following stack of components:

- an *input* layer devoted to encode the vectorial representation (yielded by one of the Feature Extractor modules in the *MVDE*) of any input process instance;

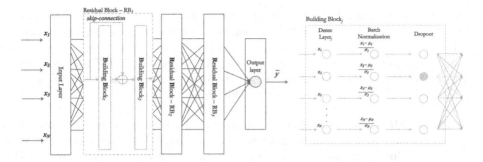

Fig. 2. DNN Architecture adopted for all the base DDMs in a *MVDE* (left), and details on the Building Block sub-net (right).

- three instances of a *Residual Block* sub-net (denoted in the figure as RB_1, ..., RB_3), consisting each of two instances of a *Building-block* sub-net linked one another by a skip connection as shown in the right side of Fig. 2;
- an output layer consisting of a single neuron equipped with a *sigmoid* activation function (returning a deviance score in $[0, 1]$).

In more detail, the building block of our solution is composed of three main components: *(i)* a fully-connected dense layer equipped with a *tanh* activation function for each neuron of the layer, *(ii)* a batch-normalization layer [14] (helping improve stability and performances of the current dense layer) and *(iii)* a dropout [13] layer (helping reduce the risk of overfitting).

A weighted variant of the *Mean Absolute Error* (MAE) is employed as the loss function for training the above described base DDM's architecture, which is defined as follows: $\frac{1}{n} \sum_{i=1}^{n} |y^{(i)} - \tilde{y}^{(i)}| \cdot weight(y^{(i)})$, where n is the number of process instances in the training set, while $y^{(i)}$ and $\tilde{y}^{(i)}$ are the real[2] and predicted deviance score of the i-th process instance, respectively, and $weight(y^{(i)})$ is a function that associates each class with a real number representing its associated misclassification cost. In the current implementation of the proposed approach, these weights have been set to 1 and 2 for the normal and deviant classes, respectively.

3.2   Combiner Sub-net: Two Alternative Instantiations

Defining the strategy to combine the base models into a collective decision is a critical issue in each ensemble classification model. In our framework, two alternatives types of neural-network models can be used to instantiate the NN combiner sub-net of a *MVDE*: *(a)* a simple non-trainable architecture that just selects the deviance score yielded by the "most self-confident" base model, and

---

[2] Notice that $y^{(i)} = 1$ iff the i-th instance in the training set is deviant, and $y^{(i)} = 0$ otherwise.

(b) a trainable architecture that implements a variant of classical stacked generalization allowing for possibly learning a "context-aware" meta-classification scheme.

Two alternative variants of the proposed DDM model *MVDE* are obtained when using the options *a* or *b* mentioned above, denoted hereinafter as *MVDE-Max* and *MVDE-Stack*, respectively. More precisely:

- In *MVDE-Max*, the combiner is a non-trainable sub-net encoding a fixed function that returns, for any process instance x, the highest class-membership probability among those estimated for x by the base DNN models—i.e. (i) $p_{max}^{dev}(x)$ if $p_{max}^{dev}(x) > p_{max}^{norm}(x)$, or (ii) $1 - p_{max}^{norm}(x)$ otherwise, with $p_{max}^{norm}(x) = \max_{i \in \{i,\dots,n\}}(1 - \tilde{y}^{(i)})$ and $p_{max}^{dev}(x) = \max_{i \in \{i,\dots,n\}} \tilde{y}^{(i)}$.
- In *MVDE-Stack*, the combiner is a trainable feed-forward sub-net, consisting of just one Dense layer, that takes as input both the predictions (i.e. deviance scores) $PS_1, \dots, PS_n$ made on any process instance x by the base DNN classifiers and the high-level representations $HLR_1, \dots, HLR_n$ produced for x by the last hidden layers of these classifiers. This allows the combiner to reason on n different high-level representations of x that are more informative than the base predictions $PS_1, \dots, PS_n$ and/or the low-level features of x, and to possibly apprehend expressive context-aware scheme for fusing these predictions.

4   Experimental Evaluation

To assess the capability our approach to recognize deviant behaviors, we compared it with some single-view learning schemes and some competitors over datasets derived from the real-life log associated with the *2011 BPI Challenge* [8]—used in most previous work in the field.

4.1   Datasets, Parameters and Measures

The datasets used in this section were derived from a log concerning the activities performed (in a Dutch hospital) on patients suffering from some kinds of cancers. The raw event log contains 150,291 events, referring to 624 distinct activities, and 1,142 cases, corresponding each to a distinguished patient. Each case was enriched with two contextual (derived) attributes, i.e. the *duration* of the case (in years) and the *number of events* appearing in the respective trace.

In order to use these data for a DDM learning task, we labeled each trace as either "normal" (label = 0) or "deviant" (label=1) by using the same criteria as in [7,19]. In practice, we generated two datasets, namely BPI_{dM13} and BPI_{dM16}, where a trace is labelled as deviant iff the value of attribute *Diagnosis* is "M13"and "M16", respectively. Table 1 reports some statistics related to these two datasets.

For the sake of significance and to avoid any favorable bias, each dataset was pre-processed by removing all the attributes (including those of categories

Table 1. Summary statistics of datasets BPI_{dM13} and BPI_{dM16}. Clearly, the percentage of deviant traces can be regarded as a measure of the degree of class imbalance.

Dataset	#traces	%deviant traces	Avg. length (dev.)	Avg. length (norm.)
BPI_{dM13}	1,142	27.1%	74	144
BPI_{dM16}	1,142	18.9%	113	127

"diagnosis code", "diagnosis", and "treatment code") that are directly linked to the class label.

As done in [7,19], we considered the following pattern families (cf. Sect. 2) for obtaining different feature-based representations of the traces: *(i)* {IA}, i.e. individual activities used alone (producing a bag-of-activity representation of traces' structure); *(ii)* {IA, TR}, i.e. a heterogeneous family containing individual activities and tandem repeats; *(iii)* {IA, ATR}, i.e. heterogeneous family containing individual activities and alphabet tandem repeats; *(iv)* {IA, MR}, i.e. heterogeneous family containing individual activities and maximal repeats; *(v)* {IA, AMR}, i.e. a heterogeneous family containing individual activities and alphabet maximal repeats; *(vi)* {IA, DP}, i.e. heterogeneous family containing individual activities and discriminative patterns; *(vii)* {DP}, i.e. discriminative patterns alone.

As for the base DNN classifiers, we configured each of the dense layers in all building blocks with 128 neurons, and used a dropout rate of 0.5. The whole architecture of a single base model is composed of three residual blocks stacked on an initial building block, then a number of seven fully-connected dense layers, equipped with *tanh* activation functions, are included in the model. On the top of the architecture, an output layer equipped with a *sigmoid* activation function, is further stacked to provide the final prediction. The one-layer combiner sub-net in the variant *MVDE-Stack* was equipped instead with 1024 neurons. RMSProp was used as the optimizer for all training steps.

Since both datasets are imbalanced, we adopted a resampling procedure similar to that of [7], and duplicated each deviant trace a number of times such that the ratio between the sizes of the minority (deviant) and majority (normal) classes became 0.4.

To evaluate the quality of discovered deviance-oriented classifiers, we resorted to three metrics that suit better the case of imbalanced classes than classic accuracy scores: (i) the *area under the ROC curve*, denoted as *AUC*; (ii) the *G-mean* measure defined in [16] (computed as the geometric mean between the True-Positive and True-Negative rates); and (iii) the *F1-score* for the class of deviant instances (computed as their harmonic mean between the *Precision* and *Recall* scores of this class).

All the aggregated results shown in the rest of this section were computed by averaging the measures obtained in 5 trials, according to a 5-fold cross-validation scheme.

Table 2. Comparing the two variants of the proposed approach with all single-view learning schemes on dataset BPI_{dM13}. The best outcomes on each metrics are in bold.

View type	Abstraction type	AUC	G-Mean	F1-Score
Single-View	{IA}	0.832 ± 0.038	0.735 ± 0.046	0.606 ± 0.048
	{IA, AMR}	0.798 ± 0.047	0.720 ± 0.046	0.587 ± 0.048
	{IA, ATR}	0.783 ± 0.057	0.694 ± 0.045	0.561 ± 0.050
	{IA, DP}	0.817 ± 0.048	0.731 ± 0.075	0.615 ± 0.062
	{IA, MR}	0.765 ± 0.075	0.680 ± 0.071	0.548 ± 0.068
	{IA, TR}	0.807 ± 0.039	0.717 ± 0.032	0.579 ± 0.036
	{DP}	0.787 ± 0.037	0.725 ± 0.024	0.588 ± 0.028
Multi-View	MVDE-Max	0.849 ± 0.019	0.774 ± 0.019	0.657 ± 0.026
	MVDE-Stack	$\mathbf{0.871 \pm 0.018}$	$\mathbf{0.794 \pm 0.020}$	$\mathbf{0.677 \pm 0.023}$

Table 3. Comparing the two variants of the proposed approach with all single-view learning schemes on dataset BPI_{dM16}. The best outcomes on each metrics are in bold.

View type	Abstraction type	AUC	G-Mean	F1-Score
Single-View	{IA}	0.806 ± 0.052	0.693 ± 0.037	0.461 ± 0.040
	{IA, AMR}	0.715 ± 0.039	0.633 ± 0.044	0.403 ± 0.044
	{IA, ATR}	0.813 ± 0.019	0.703 ± 0.034	0.476 ± 0.039
	{IA, DP}	0.849 ± 0.032	0.727 ± 0.049	0.505 ± 0.078
	{IA, MR}	0.745 ± 0.070	0.624 ± 0.073	0.394 ± 0.072
	{IA, TR}	0.811 ± 0.052	0.724 ± 0.038	0.493 ± 0.040
	{DP}	0.803 ± 0.045	0.719 ± 0.031	0.488 ± 0.031
Multi-View	MVDE-Max	0.874 ± 0.028	0.776 ± 0.032	0.570 ± 0.044
	MVDE-Stack	$\mathbf{0.884 \pm 0.025}$	$\mathbf{0.805 \pm 0.021}$	$\mathbf{0.617 \pm 0.031}$

4.2 Comparison with a Single-View Deep-Learning Baseline

A first suite of experiments was conducted to compare the proposed deep ensemble learning framework, compared to a scenario where a single-view deep classifier is discovered by training the base DDM architecture described in Sect. 3.1 on one of the considered pattern-based views of the dataset at hand. These experiments were aimed at assessing whether combining (and possibly fine-tuning) these deep single-view classifiers according to our approach improves the performance of each classifier alone.

Tables 2 and 3 report the performances (in terms of AUC, G-Mean and F1-Score) achieved on the two datasets by the two variants (MVDE-Max and MDVE-Stack) of our approach, compared with those of the single-view base DNNs (as they were discovered at the end of Step 2 of the training procedure in Definition 1).

Table 4. Comparing the two variants of the proposed approach with the approach defined in [7] (HO-DDM-mine) and an extended version (SV^+) of that defined in [19] on dataset BPI_{dM13}. For each metrics, the best outcomes are shown in bold.

Method	AUC	G-Mean	F1-Score
AUC winner SV⁺ (AODE on {IA})	0.817 ± 0.020	0.747 ± 0.014	0.622 ± 0.019
G-Mean winner SV⁺ (AODE on {IA})	0.817 ± 0.020	0.747 ± 0.014	0.622 ± 0.019
F1-measure winner SV⁺ (MRNB on {IA,AMR})	0.792 ± 0.052	0.746 ± 0.052	0.631 ± 0.070
HD-DDM-mine	0.841 ± 0.017	0.741 ± 0.021	0.633 ± 0.033
MVDE-Max	0.849 ± 0.019	0.774 ± 0.019	0.657 ± 0.026
MVDE-Stack	$\mathbf{0.871 \pm 0.018}$	$\mathbf{0.794 \pm 0.020}$	$\mathbf{0.677 \pm 0.023}$

As expected (see Tables 2 and 3), both proposed multi-view combiners outperform considerably all the single-view DDMs in all measures and for both datasets. In particular, the MDVE-Stack combiner performs neatly better than the MDVE-Max one in the BPI_{dM16} dataset—less evident are the differences between the two proposed combiners, especially in terms of AUC metric, in the BPI_{dM13} dataset.

4.3 Comparison with State-of-the-art Competitors

In order to assess the validity of our approach, we compared both its variants MVDE-Max and MVDE-Stack with two state-of-the-art deviance-mining approaches (both relying on standard machine-learning methods): (i) the *HD-DDM-mine* method defined in [7] and (ii) an empowered version, denoted hereinafter as SV^+, of the non ensemble-based approach proposed in [19].

Notice that the original approach in [19] consisted in applying three classifier-induction algorithms separately to each of the pattern-based views described in Sect. 4.1, and then selecting (based on some chosen metrics) the best of the models discovered. In our extended version SV^+ of this competitor approach, we used the same resampling method as in *HO-DDM-mine* and a wider range of alternative induction methods (see [7] for related references): *AODE*, *HNB*, *MetaCost* with AODE as base learner (a costs of 40 and 25 for false negatives and false positives, respectively), a multi-layer perceptron, the *SVM* method *SMO* with an RDF kernel ($c = 1$, and $\gamma = 0.01$), *J48*, a 10 nearest-neighbor classifier and the rule-based methods *MRNB* and *JRipper*.

Clearly, the single-view approach SV^+ generates many independent DDMs, one for each of the pattern families considered in our tests (see in Sect. 4.1). In order to present the results of this competitor more compactly, we only report here the best of the evaluation scores obtained by the resulting models. Specifically, for each evaluation metrics, we have selected the "winner" combination of pattern family (i.e. one among {IA}, {IA, TR}, {IA, ATR}, {IA, MR}, {IA, AMR}, {IA, DP}) and learning algorithm (i.e. one among AODE, HNB, MetaCost, SMO, MRNB, JRipper, J48 and 10-NN) that got the highest score on that metrics. These three "optimal" instantiations of SV^+ are denoted hereinafter as: *AUC winner SV^+*, *G-mean winner SV^+* and *F1 winner SV^+*.

Table 5. Comparing the two variants of the proposed approach with the approach defined in [7] (HO-DDM-mine) and an extended version (SV^+) of that defined in [19] on dataset BPI_{dM16}. For each metrics, the best outcomes are shown in bold.

Method	AUC	G-Mean	F1-Score
AUC winner SV⁺ (HNB on {IA,AMR})	0.866 ± 0.016	0.781 ± 0.021	0.589 ± 0.035
G-Mean winner SV⁺ (HNB on {IA,AMR})	0.866 ± 0.016	0.781 ± 0.021	0.589 ± 0.035
F1-measure winner SV⁺ (JRip on {IA,AMR})	0.778 ± 0.033	0.756 ± 0.038	0.610 ± 0.050
HD-DDM-mine	0.878 ± 0.011	0.778 ± 0.021	$\mathbf{0.643 \pm 0.036}$
MVDE-Max	0.874 ± 0.028	0.776 ± 0.032	0.570 ± 0.044
MVDE-Stack	$\mathbf{0.884 \pm 0.025}$	$\mathbf{0.805 \pm 0.021}$	0.617 ± 0.031

Tables 4 and 5 show the results achieved (in terms of AUC, G-Mean and F1-Score) by both the two variants of our MVDE approach and the two competitors over the datasets BPI_{dM13} and BPI_{dM16}, respectively.

From Tables 4 and 5, it is evident that the variant MVDE-Stack of our approach (using a trainable combiner) outperforms all the other competitors for all the metrics, with the exception of the F1-Score for the BPI_{dM16} dataset, in which the best performance is reached by the *HO-DDM-mine* method. However, MVDE-Max, employing a fast non-trainable combiner, reaches the second highest score for the BPI_{dM13} dataset.

5 Conclusion and Future Work

A novel multi-view deep learning framework for the discovery of deviance-oriented trace classifiers is proposed in this work. The framework, first build a number of deviance detection models, each one trained by using a DNN on each feature-based view of these traces and then, combine them in an ensemble model by adopting two different combination functions, i.e. a stacked-generalization scheme and a maximum-confidence classification one. In addition, a training data resampling method and a cost-sensitive training loss are exploited to cope with the case of imbalanced classes.

The experiments, conducted on two real-life datasets, demonstrated the capability of ensemble-based approach to provide more accurate predictions than selected competitors in terms of the different metrics. In particular, the stacked-based combiner obtains the best performance in comparison with the other combiner (MVDE-Max).

Our approach can be extended to the classification of unfinished ("pre-mortem") traces work, in order to support online deviance detection tasks. This only requires all DDMs (both the base models and the combiner one) to be trained on labeled partial traces. Implementing and testing such an extension and a wider variety of feature extraction/learning methods are two interesting directions of future research.

References

1. Appice, A., Andresini, G., Malerba, D.: Clustering-aided multi-view classification: a case study on Android malware detection. J. Intell. Inf. Syst. **55**(1), 1–26 (2020). https://doi.org/10.1007/s10844-020-00598-6
2. Bose, R.P.J.C., van der Aalst, W.M.P.: Discovering signature patterns from event logs. In: IEEE Symposium on Computational Intelligence and Data Mining (CIDM 2013), pp. 111–118 (2013)
3. Bose, R.P.J.C., van der Aalst, W.M.P.: Trace clustering based on conserved patterns: towards achieving better process models. In: Rinderle-Ma, S., Sadiq, S., Leymann, F. (eds.) BPM 2009. LNBIP, vol. 43, pp. 170–181. Springer, Heidelberg (2010). https://doi.org/10.1007/978-3-642-12186-9_16
4. Camargo, M., Dumas, M., González-Rojas, O.: Learning accurate LSTM models of business processes. In: Hildebrandt, T., van Dongen, B.F., Röglinger, M., Mendling, J. (eds.) BPM 2019. LNCS, vol. 11675, pp. 286–302. Springer, Cham (2019). https://doi.org/10.1007/978-3-030-26619-6_19
5. Cuzzocrea, A., Folino, F., Guarascio, M., Pontieri, L.: A multi-view learning approach to the discovery of deviant process instances. In: Debruyne, C., et al. (eds.) OTM 2015. LNCS, vol. 9415, pp. 146–165. Springer, Cham (2015). https://doi.org/10.1007/978-3-319-26148-5_9
6. Cuzzocrea, A., Folino, F., Guarascio, M., Pontieri, L.: A multi-view multidimensional ensemble learning approach to mining business process deviances. In: 2016 International Joint Conference on Neural Networks (IJCNN), pp. 3809–3816 (2016)
7. Cuzzocrea, A., Folino, F., Guarascio, M., Pontieri, L.: A robust and versatile multi-view learning framework for the detection of deviant business process instances. Int. J. Cooper. Inf. Syst. **25**(04), 1740003 (2016)
8. van Dongen, B.: Real-life event logs - hospital log (2011). https://doi.org/10.4121/uuid:d9769f3d-0ab0-4fb8-803b-0d1120ffcf54
9. Dumas, M., La Rosa, M., Mendling, J., Reijers, H.A.: Fundamentals of Business Process Management. Springer, Heidelberg (2018). https://doi.org/10.1007/978-3-662-56509-4
10. Evermann, J., Rehse, J., Fettke, P.: Predicting process behaviour using deep learning. Decis. Support Syst. **100**, 129–140 (2017)
11. Folino, F., Pontieri, L.: Business process deviance mining. In: Sakr, S., Zomaya, A. (eds.) Encyclopedia of Big Data Technologies. Springer, Cham (2018). https://doi.org/10.1007/978-3-319-63962-8_100-1
12. Genga, L., Potena, D., Chiorrini, A., Diamantini, C., Zannone, N.: A latitudinal study on the use of sequential and concurrency patterns in deviance mining. In: Appice, A., Ceci, M., Loglisci, C., Manco, G., Masciari, E., Ras, Z.W. (eds.) Complex Pattern Mining. SCI, vol. 880, pp. 103–119. Springer, Cham (2020). https://doi.org/10.1007/978-3-030-36617-9_7
13. Hinton, G.E., Srivastava, N., Krizhevsky, A., Sutskever, I., Salakhutdinov, R.: Dropout: a simple way to prevent neural networks from overfitting. J. Mach. Learn. Res. **15**, 1929–1958 (2014)
14. Ioffe, S., Szegedy, C.: Batch normalization: accelerating deep network training by reducing internal covariate shift. In: Proceedings of the 32nd International Conference on Machine Learning, ICML 2015, vol. 37, pp. 448–456 (2015)
15. Kratsch, W., Manderscheid, J., Röglinger, M., Seyfried, J.: Machine learning in business process monitoring: a comparison of deep learning and classical approaches used for outcome prediction. Bus. Inf. Syst. Eng. 1–16 (2020)

16. Kubat, M., Holte, R., Matwin, S.: Learning when negative examples abound. In: van Someren, M., Widmer, G. (eds.) ECML 1997. LNCS, vol. 1224, pp. 146–153. Springer, Heidelberg (1997). https://doi.org/10.1007/3-540-62858-4_79
17. Lin, L., Wen, L., Wang, J.: MM-PRED: a deep predictive model for multi-attribute event sequence. In: SIAM International Conference on Data Mining, pp. 118–126 (2019)
18. Lo, D., Cheng, H., Han, J., Khoo, S.C., Sun, C.: Classification of software behaviors for failure detection: a discriminative pattern mining approach. In: Proceedings of 15th International Conference on Knowledge Discovery and Data Mining (KDD 2009), pp. 557–566 (2009)
19. Nguyen, H., Dumas, M., La Rosa, M., Maggi, F.M., Suriadi, S.: Mining business process deviance: a quest for accuracy. In: Meersman, R., et al. (eds.) OTM 2014. LNCS, vol. 8841, pp. 436–445. Springer, Heidelberg (2014). https://doi.org/10.1007/978-3-662-45563-0_25
20. Pasquadibisceglie, V., Appice, A., Castellano, G., Malerba, D.: Using convolutional neural networks for predictive process analytics. In: International Conference on Process Mining, pp. 129–136 (2019)
21. Suriadi, S., Wynn, M.T., Ouyang, C., ter Hofstede, A.H.M., van Dijk, N.J.: Understanding process behaviours in a large insurance company in Australia: a case study. In: Salinesi, C., Norrie, M.C., Pastor, Ó. (eds.) CAiSE 2013. LNCS, vol. 7908, pp. 449–464. Springer, Heidelberg (2013). https://doi.org/10.1007/978-3-642-38709-8_29
22. Teinemaa, I., Dumas, M., La Rosa, M., Maggi, F.M.: Outcome-oriented predictive process monitoring: review and benchmark. ACM Trans. Knowl. Discov. Data (TKDD) 13(2), 1–57 (2019)
23. Teinemaa, I., Dumas, M., Leontjeva, A., Maggi, F.M.: Temporal stability in predictive process monitoring. Data Min. Knowl. Disc. 32(5), 1306–1338 (2018). https://doi.org/10.1007/s10618-018-0575-9
24. Van Der Aalst, W.: Process Mining: Discovery, Conformance and Enhancement of Business Processes, vol. 2 (2011)
25. Webb, G.I., Boughton, J.R., Wang, Z.: Not so Naive Bayes: aggregating one-dependence estimators. Mach. Learn. 58(1), 5–24 (2005)

Exploiting Temporal Convolution for Activity Prediction in Process Analytics

Francesco Folino$^{(\boxtimes)}$, Massimo Guarascio, Angelica Liguori, Giuseppe Manco,
Luigi Pontieri, and Ettore Ritacco

ICAR Institute, National Research Council, I87036 Rende, CS, Italy
{francesco.folino,massimo.guarascio,angelica.liguori,
giuseppe.manco,luigi.pontieri,ettore.ritacco}@icar.cnr.it

Abstract. Process Mining (PM) is meant to extract knowledge on the behavior of business processes from historical log data. Lately, an increasing attention has been gained by the *Predictive Process Monitoring*, a field of PM that tries to extend process monitoring systems with prediction capabilities and, in particular. Several current proposals in literature to this problem rely on Deep Neural Networks, mostly on recurrent architectures (in particular LSTM) owing to their capability to capture the inherent sequential nature of process data. Very recently, however, an alternative solution based on a convolutional architecture (CNN) has been proposed in the literature, which was shown to achieve compelling results. Inspired by this line of research, we here propose a novel convolution-based deep learning approach to the prediction of the next activity which relies on: *(i)* extracting high-level features (at different levels of abstraction) through the computation of time-oriented dilated convolutions over traces, and *(ii)* exploiting residual-like connections to make the training of the predictive model more robust and faster. Preliminary results on real-life datasets confirm the validity of our proposal, compared with an LSTM-based and a CNN-based approach in the literature.

Keywords: Predictive process monitoring · Convolutional neural networks · Next activity prediction

1 Introduction

Process Mining techniques [19] aim at extracting knowledge on the behavior of business processes from historical log data, and constitute a valuable means for improving the quality and performances of such processes. Increasing attention in this research field has been gained by *Predictive Process Monitoring* approaches [11,13], which try to extend process monitoring systems with prediction capabilities, in order to support anticipated decisions and pro-active optimisation mechanisms.

© Springer Nature Switzerland AG 2020
I. Koprinska et al. (Eds.): ECML PKDD 2020 Workshops, CCIS 1323, pp. 263–275, 2020.
https://doi.org/10.1007/978-3-030-65965-3_17

These approaches rely on discovering a model capable to make forecasts for an ongoing process instance based on its partial trace, i.e. the sequence of events stored for the process instance up to the time of prediction. The main task considered in this context consists in predicting the next activity that will be executed in a process instance [2,4,9,12,15,16,18].

Several approaches to this problem have been proposed in recent years that take advantage of Deep Neural Network (DNN) models [2,4,9,12,16,18], most of which rely on the usage of architectures [2,4,9,12,18]. Although LSTMs, and RNNs in general, are a natural choice for making predictions on process traces, owing to their capability to learn effective fixed-length representations from such sequential data, they are known to suffer from slow convergence, as well as from vanishing gradients and lack of memory in the case of long event sequences [5].

An alternative solution was recently proposed in [16], which consists in applying a stack of convolutional layers to an image-like representation of the process traces, and was shown to improve the LSTM-based approach in [18]. However, as discussed in [16], the specific feature-engineering scheme employed to transform the traces (relying on a bag-of-activity representation of the trace prefixes) suffers from some limitations, such as the difficulty to predict non-frequent activities and the risk of producing sparse representations when dealing with traces of very different lengths.

Following the interesting direction of research started in [16], we here propose a novel convolution-based deep learning framework for next-activity predictions, which consists in making the traces undergo a sophisticated sequence-oriented CNN architecture without feature-engineering steps. In a nutshell, the architecture can compute hierarchies of time oriented (dilated) convolutions over the traces, while taking advantage of residual-like connections that make the training more robust and faster. The main benefits to adopt residual nets are: (*i*) their capability to make the convergence faster mitigating the *degradation problem* [6], (*ii*) their improved performances in terms of generalization. Preliminary results on real-life datasets confirmed the validity of our proposal, compared to both the popular LSTM-based approach of [18] and the CNN-based approach defined in [16].

Organization. The rest of the paper is organized as follows. After discussing some major related work in Sect. 2, we introduce background notions and an informal statement of the problem addressed in Sect. 3. Section 4 then provides the reader with a detailed description of the CNN-based neural architecture adopted in our framework for training a next-activity predictor. The results of experiments performed on real-life datasets are discussed in Sect. 5. In Sect. 6, we draw some concluding remarks and directions for future work.

2 Related Work

Several *Machine Learning* approaches to the prediction of the next activity in an ongoing process instance have been developed in recent years. For example, in [3] it was proposed to extract frequent activity patterns from a given log, through a pattern mining method, which are represented in form of sequence trees. Each node of the tree is thus associated with a specific prediction model.

More recently, Deep Neural Networks (DNNs) have become a reference tool for this prediction task [2,4,9,12,16,18], owing to their advantages in terms of both accuracy and usability. Most of these approaches rely on adopting Recurrent Neural Network (RNN) layers, typically LSTM ones [2,4,9,12,18], provided with some suitable encoding of the given events, considering control-flow information (i.e. the activities performed), possibly combined with temporal event features (e.g. [16,18]) and other non-functional event properties such as the executor or activities' parameters (e.g. [2,4,9,12]). Specifically, Tax et a. [18] used an LSTM-based network architecture to predict the next activity and the time until the next event, while encoding each event into a feature vector that combines a one-hot encoding of the associated activity and a number of temporal features derived from the the event's timestamp.

Evermann et al. [4] also applied LSTM networks to predict the activity associated with the next event, but differently from [18], they only adopted an embedding layer for two categorical attributes of the events (namely, the activity and the executor/resource). Lin et al. [9] proposed an LSTM-based model for predicting the next activity (together with all of the other categorical attributes of the next event) that takes as input information on all the attributes of the past events. A peculiar feature of this architecture lies in the usage of an "attention-like" mechanism for weighting the event attributes on the basis of their relevance in the prediction of future events. Camargo et al. [2] proposed different LSTM-based architectures for the prediction of next event, in terms of the associated activity, timestamp and resource (abstracted at the level of groups, in a preprocessing phase). Combining features of [18] and of [4], this approach can deal with both categorical and numerical attributes in the traces.

A notable attempt to evaluate alternative solutions for predictive process monitoring was recently made in [16], which proposed the application of a Convolutional Neural Network (CNN) architecture to image-like representations of each process trace τ. Essentially, the control-flow information stored in τ is encoded into a bi-dimensional matrix, where the rows and columns correspond to the trace's prefixes and the process activities, respectively, while each cell (i, j) stores the number of times the j-th activity occurs in the i-th prefix of the trace. A similar matrix is constructed to capture the performance perspective of the traces, with each cell (i, j) storing the time elapsed from the starting of τ until the latest occurrence of the j-th activity in the i-th prefix. Such an encoding scheme allows for reusing standard spatial convolution layers to predict the next activity of any ongoing trace —precisely, a three-layer CNN architecture with max-pooling was adopted in [16] (featuring 32, 64, and 128 filters, respectively), by using the control-flow and performance matrices as distinguished image channels. Notably, this CNN-based approach was shown to mark an improvement over a popular LSTM-based approach (namely, the one proposed in [18]) using the same kind of information on the trace events (i.e. only the associated activities and timestamps). However, as discussed in [16], the specific feature-engineering scheme employed to transform a trace (relying on a bag-of-activity view of the trace's prefixes) suffers form some limitations, such as the difficulty to predict non-frequent activities and the risk of producing sparse representations when dealing with traces of very different lengths.

A major difference between our proposal and the approach defined in [16] lies in the fact that the former does not requires any substantial preliminary data-engineering step, but directly extracts a hierarchy of representations for the process traces by computing dilated convolutions [8] directly on event sequences. Moreover, the DNN model proposed here is equipped with residual-like connections that make the training of the model both more robust to vanishing gradients and faster than existing RNN-based solutions in the field.

3 Background and Problem Statement

Background and Notation. The data considered in this work are execution traces of a business process, i.e. sequences of events, recorded each along a single execution of the process (a.k.a. *process instance* or *case*).

Every event in a trace is marked temporally and it refers to a process activity (i.e. the activity that was executed correspondingly to the event).

More precisely, let $\mathcal{E}$ denote the reference universe of events that may appear in any trace. Each event $e \in \mathcal{E}$ is associated with two data attributes:

- $act : \mathcal{E} \to A$, which associates each event e with an activity label taken from a given vocabulary A, and represents the type/class of e, and
- $time : \mathcal{E} \to \mathbb{R}$, which associates each event e with a real-valued timestamp $time(e)$; as commonly done in the literature, let us assume that the events in any trace τ are ordered temporally based on their timestamps, i.e. $time(\tau[i]) \leq time(\tau[j])$ for any $i, j \in [1, len(\tau)]$ such that $i \leq j$, where $len(\tau)$ stands for the number of events in trace τ.

It is worth noting that in some application settings, log events can be associated with further information (concerning, e.g., activities' executors and parameters), and that the framework proposed here could be extended to also exploit such data –by possibly treating each of these event dimensions as a distinguished "channel" of the input data. However, for the sake of fair comparison with previous works relying on the usage of convolution-based DNNs, we have decided to abstract from these additional event features in this work, and to simply regard each trace as a sequence of activity labels.

Let $\mathcal{T}$ be the reference universe of all possible traces (i.e. sequences of events from $\mathcal{E}$) that could be generated by the process under analysis. For any trace $\tau \in \mathcal{T}$, let $len(\tau)$ be the total number of events in τ, and $\tau[i]$ be the i-th event of τ, for $i \in [1 \ldots len(\tau)]$. Moreover, $\tau[: i]$ and $\tau[i:]$ are *prefix* and *suffix* (sub-)trace of τ, respectively —containing the first and last i events of τ, respectively.

For any trace or trace prefix/suffix τ, let $act(\tau)$ be the sequence of activities resulting from projecting each event of τ onto its associated activity attribute, i.e. $act(\tau) = \langle act(\tau[1]), \ldots, act(\tau[len(\tau)]) \rangle$.

Finally, a *log* L is a collection of "post-mortem" traces, encoding each the history of a fully unfolded process instance, from its start to its end.

Problem Statement. The prediction problem addressed here (as a form of predictive process monitoring task) amounts to forecasting the next activity that will be executed for an ongoing (i.e. unfinished) process instance p, based on the partial trace that is currently available for p (i.e. the prefix gathered for p up to the moment of prediction). Let $\mathbf{x} = \langle \mathbf{x}_1, \ldots, \mathbf{x}_n \rangle$ and $\mathbf{y} = \langle \mathbf{y}_1, \ldots, \mathbf{y}_m \rangle$ be the sequences of activities appearing in the partial (prefix) trace and the unknown suffix traces of p, then this problem can be stated as that of predicting $\mathbf{y}_1$ based on the information contained in the given sequence $\mathbf{x}$. As usually done in the literature, we assume that the given prefix $\mathbf{x}$ is not empty, i.e. it contains at least one event.

This prediction problem gives rise to an auxiliary inductive-learning one, which amounts to train a model, capable to support this prediction task, against a historical log L, i.e. a sample of complete traces. Usually, after abstracting each trace $\tau^{(i)}$ in L into a sequence $\mathbf{x}^{(i)} \equiv act(\tau^{(i)})$ of activity labels, a number of labeled prefixes are derived from the trace. Each of these prefixes of size k takes the form $\mathbf{x}^{(i,k)} = act(\tau[: k])$ (for $k \in [1 \ldots len(\tau) - 1]$) and is labeled with the activity label $act(\tau^{(i)}[k + 1])$ occurring in the subsequent step of the trace.

As a result, the given log L is turned into a collection D of activity sequences, encoding each an abstracted representation of a process instance's partial unfolding, and labelled with the respective ground-truth next activity: $D = \{(\mathbf{x}^{(i,k)}, a^{(i,k)}) \mid \tau^{(i)} \in L, k \in [1 \ldots len(\tau^{(i)}) - 1], \mathbf{x}^{(i,k)} = act(\tau[: k]), \text{ and } a^{(i,k)} = act(\tau^{(i)}[k + 1])\}$.

Clearly, a predictive model discovered from such a dataset D can be applied to any novel partial trace τ' to predict the activity that will be executed in the next step of the process instance associated with τ', once having abstracted τ' into the activity sequence $act(\tau')$.

4   DNN Model

This section is devoted to offer an overview of the model adopted in our framework to cope with the problem, presented in Sect. 3, of predicting the next activity that will appear in a given sequence $\mathbf{x}$.

The model founds on the architectural scheme of *Temporal Convolutional Networks* (TCNs) [8] (cf. Fig. 1), which were shown able to provide more accurate predictions on sequence data than their RNN-based counterparts, without experiencing certain well-known drawbacks of the latter [1,20].

Technically, TCNs are a family of sequence-oriented DNN models that were conceived to enjoy two nice properties: *(i)* similarly to RNNs, they return as many output elements as those in the input sequence; *(ii)* no "leakage" of information from future steps is allowed. As a matter of fact, these properties make a TCN model a suitable solution for our prediction task.

In more detail, a TCN ensures the first property by simply exploiting a *1D fully-convolutional network* [10], where each hidden layer has the same length

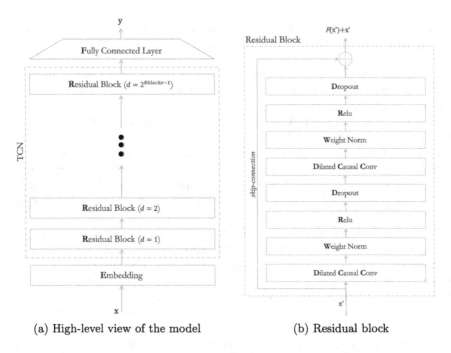

(a) High-level view of the model   (b) Residual block

Fig. 1. Model architecture: high-level view (left) and details on the internal structure of each residual block (right).

as the input sequence, combined with a zero-padding (of length kernel size-1) mechanism for keeping the layers' length constant across the network. The second property is attained instead by resorting to *causal convolutions*, i.e. a restricted variant of standard convolutions that, when computing a value for a sequence element, can only used the element itself and those appeared earlier than it.

In order to possibly capture long-term correlations, such a basic architecture should be implemented by stacking many convolution layers, equipped each with large enough filter sizes. However, this leads to models with a lot of parameters, which are hard to train and exposed to overfitting risks. To cope with this issue, two strategies are typically integrated in the TCNs: (1) using *dilated convolutions* (in place of causal convolutions) to expand the amount of past input elements considered in the computation of each output element, and (2) exploiting *residual blocks* [6] to make faster and more stable the training procedure when the problem calls for (particularly) deep architectures.

As to point (1), it is worth observing that a network N using standard causal convolutions is only able to look back at sub-sequences of input elements having a size (a.k.a. *receptive field*) that is linear in the depth of the network. To be more precise, letting l be the number of N's layers and k be the size of filters used in each layer, then N can account for $(k-1) \times l$ input elements per time —for example, if $l = 10$ and $k = 2$, then N only achieves a modest receptive field h of 10 input elements. Clearly, this is a severe limitation when long-range temporal dependencies among process activities need to be captured.

Compared to standard causal convolutions, dilated convolutions allow for considering an exponentially (rather than linearly) large receptive field. Formally, given an 1-D input sequence $\mathbf{x} \in \mathbb{R}^n$ and a filter $f : \{0, \ldots, k-1\} \to \mathbb{R}$, the dilated convolution operator $\mathcal{F}$ applied to a generic element s of the input sequence is defined as follows:

$$\mathcal{F}(s) = (\mathbf{x} *_d f)(s) = \sum_{i=0}^{k-1} f(i) \cdot \mathbf{x}_{s-d \cdot i}$$

where d is the *dilation factor*, k is the size the filter, and $s - d \cdot i$ is the "gap" separating s from the next element back in the history to convolve —clearly, when $d = 1$, dilated convolutions coincide with regular convolutions.

Interestingly, the receptive field of a TCN using dilated convolutions can be widened by increasing both k and d, since each layer is able to go $(k-1) \times d$ steps back in its own input's history (see Fig. 2). In particular, using an exponentially increasing dilated factor $d = 2^i$ for the i-th hidden layer in the TCN, we allow the latter to consider an exponentially large history windows of the input data. For instance, a TCN featuring 4 layers (i.e. $i = 0, 1, 2, 3$) using dilation factors $d = 2^i = \{1, 2, 4, 8\}$ and filter size $k = 2$, achieves a receptive field of 16 at its last layer.

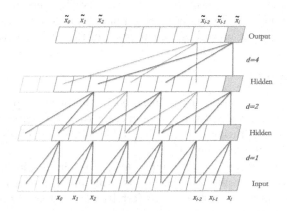

Fig. 2. An example of dilated causal convolution with $d = \{1, 2, 4\}$ and $k = 3$.

The second distinctive feature of a TCN is the presence of *residual blocks*. Basically, residual blocks [6] differ from regular ones by the mere addition (trough a *skip connection*) of an identity function to the block's output. More formally, the output of a residual block is defined as $activation(\mathbf{x}' + F(\mathbf{x}'))$, where F denotes the function that the residual block is learning to transform the input $\mathbf{x}'$ of the block itself.

Residual architectures are recognized to converge in fewer epochs than non-residual ones due to the mitigation of the so-called *degradation problem* [6] (i.e. the risk of learning with a lower rate when a new layer is stacked up) as well as to provide improved performances in terms of generalization.

All the residual blocks used in the TCNs takes a specific structure, sketched in Fig. 1b. Specifically, each block features two stacked dilated causal convolution nets, where some degree of non-linearity is provided through REctified Linear Units (ReLU) [14]. Weights are normalized and a spatial dropout [7] is added after each dilated convolution layer to help preventing overfitting.

The overall TCN architecture (shown in Fig. 1a) is a stack of such residual blocks (associated with increasing values of the dilation factor), which allows for transforming an activity sequence $\mathbf{x}$ (suitably mapped to an encoded form $\mathbf{x}'$, through an automatically-learnt Embedding layer) into a hierarchy of abstract features. This stack is topped by a prediction module consisting of a linear fully-connected layer with Softmax normalization, which eventually returns a distribution of probabilities over the activity labels for each output element.

5   Experiments

Our approach has been implemented in Python 3.8 with PyTorch 1.5 as deep learning framework. The experiments were executed on a GPU V100 32 GB running into a NVidia DGX Station. The code has been used to test our approach in the specific task of predicting the next activity for every possible prefix of all traces in the logs. In particular, we compared our results, obtained on two benchmark datasets, against those of two state-of-the-art competitors.

5.1   Competitors

Among the plethora of approaches proposed in the business process literature using deep learning architectures for predicting the next activity (cf. Sect. 2), we selected two competitors: the LSTM-based architecture proposed in [18], and the CNN architecture described in [16].

Our selection was not, despite appearances, a "cherry-picking" procedure, but founded on two specific criteria: (1) selecting archetypes for recurrent and non-recurrent architectures in order to test to what extent the specific model influences the quality of prediction; and (2) choosing approaches that, similarly to ours, focus on control-flow only, with at most time-related information (actually not used by our model) –i.e. approaches disregarding events' payload.

We then chose the only two approaches that met these two criteria. Indeed, the competitor [18] was the only LSTM-based proposal, among all those cited in Sect. 2, where all events' attributes but the activity and timestamp were disregarded. On the other hand, the competitor [16] was the sole technique using a (non-recurrent) CNN-based architecture (which makes it as our main term of comparison), in addition to using no event information beyond the activity performed and its associated timestamp.

Table 1. Some statistics on datasets.

Log	Traces	Events	Activities	Min len.	Max len.	Avg len.
Helpdesk	3,804	13,710	9	1	14	3.60
BPI12_W_Complete	9,658	72,413	6	1	74	7.49

It is also worth noticing that the current version of our framework mainly focuses on the control-flow perspective of the traces, without exploiting performance values derived from the events' timestamps (as done in both [18] and [16]). In fact, we believe that extending our approach with such a capability is likely to further improve its achievements.

5.2 Datasets

Our approach has been validated against two publicly-available real-life event logs. In particular, for the sake of comparison, we used the same datasets adopted by our competitors [16,18]. These datasets store information on traces of two real-life business processes, concerning different domains and exhibiting diverse characteristics. Descriptive statistics on datasets are reported in Table 1.

Helpdesk Dataset. This dataset[1] contains events from a ticketing management process of the helpdesk of an Italian software company. The business process consists of 9 activities. All cases in the log start with the insertion of a new ticket into the management system and terminate with the closing of the ticket when the issue is solved. The log contains 3,804 traces and 13,710 events. The length of the traces ranges between a minimum of 1 and a maximum of 14, with an average length of 3.60.

BPI12_W_Complete Dataset. This dataset, extracted from the *BPI 2012* log[2], contains traces coming from a loan application process from a German financial institution. The overall process is composed by three sub-processes, where the first tracks the state of the application (A), the second the states of work items (W), and the third the state of the offer (O). In particular, we decided to test our approach against the 'W' sub-process in order to enable a comparison against our direct competitors [16,18]. The dataset has been filtered in order to retain only the completion events. In more detail, this version of the log contains 9,658 traces with 72,413 events and 6 activities. The length of traces varies in a range between 1 and 74 with an average length of 7.49.

5.3 Evaluation Procedure and Parameters' Setting

For the sake of comparison, we decided to adopt the same evaluation protocol as in [16,18]. In particular, for each dataset, we used a hold-out strategy, where the

---

[1] https://doi.org/10.17632/39bp3vv62t.1.

[2] https://doi.org/10.4121/uuid:3926db30-f712-4394-aebc-75976070e91f.

Table 2. Accuracy (%) obtained by Ours and its two competitors [16,18] for the next activity prediction on *Helpdesk* and *BPI12_W_Complete* datasets.

Approach	Accuracy	
	Helpdesk	*BPI12_W_Complete*
Ours	**80.79%**	**81.77%**
Pasquadibisceglie et al. [16]	73.93%	78.17%
Tax et al. [18]	71.23%	76.00%

first (chronologically ordered) 2/3 of traces are used to train our model, while the last 1/3 to test it. The next activity is predicted for all possible prefixes extracted from the traces in the test set.

As an effectiveness metric, we adopted the same *Accuracy* score as in [16, 18] to compute the fraction of correct predictions returned by the model when applied to the traces in the test set.

Specifically, let us assume that each trace $\tau^{(i)}$ in the test set is broken down into all its corresponding (*activity-prefix, next-activity*) pairs $(\mathbf{x}^{(i,k)}, a^{(i,k)})$ s.t. $1 < k < len(\tau^{(i)}) - 1)$. Let D_{test} be the resulting set of such pairs. Then, the accuracy of a model M over the test set D_{test} can be computed as follows:

$$Accuracy = \frac{|\{(\mathbf{x}, a) \in D_{test} \mid nextAct(M(\mathbf{x})) = a\}|}{|D_{test}|}$$

where $nextAct(M(\mathbf{x}))$ is the hard prediction obtained by applying an `argmax` operator to the output returned by M correspondingly to the last step of $\mathbf{x}$.

In our solution, we adopt a TCN including five residual blocks composed by convolutional layers with filter size set to 2 and stride set to 1, while the numbers of filters for each block are $2048, 1024, 512, 256$, and 128, respectively. A batch size of 16 and 200 epochs are used to learn the model. Finally, Adam [17], with a learning rate of $1e - 4$, is used as optimization algorithm.

5.4   Test Results

Table 2 reports the overall accuracy obtained by our approach *Ours* and its two competitors Tax et al. [18] and Pasquadibisceglie et al. [16] in the task of predicting the next activity for each prefix extracted from the traces in the *Helpdesk* and *BPI12_W_Complete* logs.

Results show that *Ours* manages to achieve a compelling overall accuracy of 80.79% on *Helpdesk* and 81.77% on *BPI12_W_Complete*, respectively. Notably, *Ours* easily outperforms the LSTM-based approach in [18] that reaches an accuracy of only 71.23% on *Helpdesk* and of 76.00% on *BPI12_W_Complete*.

Even though our results are preliminary, by matching them with the observation that also the other CNN-based approach in [16] performs better than the one in [18], they clearly show that a convolution-based architecture is able to provide, at least in the considered setting, more accurate predictions for the next activity than a LSTM-based one.

More interesting, however, is the fact that the specific convolutional architecture we use (see the scores of *Ours* in Table 2) performs even better than that proposed in [16] (reaching accuracy scores of 73.93% and 78.17% on *Helpdesk* and *BPI12_W_Complete* logs, respectively), despite we do not exploit any precise information on trace performances. Such a result reveals that the CNN-based architecture we propose, hinging on its primary capability to directly convolve over time on traces' prefixes and to build high-level features at different levels of abstraction for them, better captures the inherent sequential nature of process data. We hence believe that our work can be used as a basis for the development of even more accurate CNN-based solutions for predictive process monitoring.

6 Conclusion and Future Work

Following the promising line of research (started in [16]) on the exploitation of CNN models for predictive process monitoring (in the place of traditional RNN ones), we have propose a novel framework that mainly relies on extracting a hierarchy of trace representations through the computation of time-oriented dilated convolutions. Differently from [16], the framework does not require the preliminary application of ad-hoc data engineering/transformation mechanisms to the log data, which might lead to data losses/distortions.

Preliminary results on real-life datasets confirm the validity of our proposal, compared with the popular LSTM-based method in [18] and the CNN-based one of [16] –which, as ours, only require the log events to contain an activity label and a timestamp. This result is particularly interesting if considering the fact that, differently from [18] and [16], our framework does not exploit in full the information conveyed by the event timestamps –which are currently used only to turn each trace into a temporally-ordered sequence of activity labels.

As to future work, we plan to extend the framework with the capability to use both time-oriented performance measurements, defined in terms of the events' timestamps (similarly to [16,18]), and other kinds of event data (concerning, e.g., activity executors, or activity parameters) that may be available in the log. We believe, indeed that all these kinds of information can turn useful in the prediction task, and can improve substantially our framework's performances.

Moreover, we will investigate on the problems of predicting other properties (e.g., the timestamp, the executor) of the next event, or a trace suffix (i.e. the entire sequence of events that will be registered in the future for an ongoing process instance).

References

1. Bai, S., Kolter, J.Z., Koltun, V.: An empirical evaluation of generic convolutional and recurrent networks for sequence modeling. CoRR abs/1803.01271 (2018)
2. Camargo, M., Dumas, M., González-Rojas, O.: Learning accurate LSTM models of business processes. In: Hildebrandt, T., van Dongen, B.F., Röglinger, M., Mendling, J. (eds.) BPM 2019. LNCS, vol. 11675, pp. 286–302. Springer, Cham (2019). https://doi.org/10.1007/978-3-030-26619-6_19
3. Ceci, M., Lanotte, P.F., Fumarola, F., Cavallo, D.P., Malerba, D.: Completion time and next activity prediction of processes using sequential pattern mining. In: Džeroski, S., Panov, P., Kocev, D., Todorovski, L. (eds.) DS 2014. LNCS (LNAI), vol. 8777, pp. 49–61. Springer, Cham (2014). https://doi.org/10.1007/978-3-319-11812-3_5
4. Evermann, J., Rehse, J.R., Fettke, P.: Predicting process behaviour using deep learning. Decis. Support Syst. **100**, 129–140 (2017)
5. Goodfellow, I., Bengio, Y., Courville, A.: Deep Learning. MIT (2016)
6. He, K., Zhang, X., Ren, S., Sun, J.: Deep residual learning for image recognition. In: Proceedings of the IEEE Conference on Computer Vision and Pattern Recognition, pp. 770–778 (2016)
7. Hinton, G.E., Srivastava, N., Krizhevsky, A., Sutskever, I., Salakhutdinov, R.: Dropout: a simple way to prevent neural networks from overfitting. J. Mach. Learn. Res. **15**, 1929–1958 (2014)
8. Lea, C., Vidal, R., Reiter, A., Hager, G.D.: Temporal convolutional networks: a unified approach to action segmentation. In: Hua, G., Jégou, H. (eds.) ECCV 2016. LNCS, vol. 9915, pp. 47–54. Springer, Cham (2016). https://doi.org/10.1007/978-3-319-49409-8_7
9. Lin, L., Wen, L., Wang, J.: MM-PRED: a deep predictive model for multi-attribute event sequence. In: Proceedings of the 2019 SIAM International Conference on Data Mining, pp. 118–126. SIAM (2019)
10. Long, J., Shelhamer, E., Darrell, T.: Fully convolutional networks for semantic segmentation. In: Proceedings of the IEEE Conference on Computer Vision and Pattern Recognition, pp. 3431–3440 (2015)
11. Maggi, F.M., Di Francescomarino, C., Dumas, M., Ghidini, C.: Predictive monitoring of business processes. In: Jarke, M., et al. (eds.) CAiSE 2014. LNCS, vol. 8484, pp. 457–472. Springer, Cham (2014). https://doi.org/10.1007/978-3-319-07881-6_31
12. Mehdiyev, N., Evermann, J., Fettke, P.: A novel business process prediction model using a deep learning method. Bus. Inf. Syst. Eng. **62**(2), 143–157 (2018). https://doi.org/10.1007/s12599-018-0551-3
13. Metzger, A., et al.: Comparing and combining predictive business process monitoring techniques. IEEE Trans. Syst. Man Cybern. Syst. **45**(2), 276–290 (2015)
14. Nair, V., Hinton, G.E.: Rectified linear units improve restricted Boltzmann machines. In: Proceedings of the 27th International Conference on International Conference on Machine Learning, ICML 2010, pp. 807–814 (2010)
15. Navarin, N., Vincenzi, B., Polato, M., Sperduti, A.: LSTM networks for data-aware remaining time prediction of business process instances. In: IEEE Symposium Series on Computational Intelligence (SSCI), pp. 1–7 (2017)
16. Pasquadibisceglie, V., Appice, A., Castellano, G., Malerba, D.: Using convolutional neural networks for predictive process analytics. In: International Conference on Process Mining (ICPM), pp. 129–136 (2019)

17. Ruder, S.: An overview of gradient descent optimization algorithms. CoRR abs/1609.04747 (2016). http://arxiv.org/abs/1609.04747
18. Tax, N., Verenich, I., La Rosa, M., Dumas, M.: Predictive business process monitoring with LSTM neural networks. In: Dubois, E., Pohl, K. (eds.) CAiSE 2017. LNCS, vol. 10253, pp. 477–492. Springer, Cham (2017). https://doi.org/10.1007/978-3-319-59536-8_30
19. Van Der Aalst, W.: Process Mining: Discovery, Conformance and Enhancement of Business Processes. Springer, Heidelberg (2011). https://doi.org/10.1007/978-3-642-19345-3
20. Zhao, W., Gao, Y., Ji, T., Wan, X., Ye, F., Bai, G.: Deep temporal convolutional networks for short-term traffic flow forecasting. IEEE Access (2019). https://doi.org/10.1109/ACCESS.2019.2935504

Workshop on Data Integration and Applications (DINA 2020)

Data Integration and Applications Workshop (DINA 2020)

Luiza Antonie[1] and Peter Christen[2]

[1] University of Guelph, Canada
lantonie@uoguelph.ca
[2] The Australian National University, Australia
peter.christen@anu.edu.au
https://sites.google.com/view/dinaworkshop2020/home

The sixth Data Integration and Applications Workshop (DINA 2020) was held in conjunction with the European Conference on Machine Learning and Principles and Practice of Knowledge Discovery in Databases (ECML/PKDD 2020) as a virtual online workshop.

Data are at the core of research in many domains outside of computer science, such as healthcare, social sciences, and business. Combining diverse sources of data provides potentially very useful and powerful data, but it is also a challenging research problem. There are a multitude of challenges in data integration: the data collections to be integrated may come from different sources; the collections may have been created by different groups; their characteristics can be different (different schema, different data types); and the data may contain duplicates. Solving these challenges requires substantial effort and domain experts need to be involved. In the era of Big Data, with organizations scaling up the volume of their data, it is critical to develop new and scalable approaches to deal with all these challenges. In addition, it is important to properly assess the quality of the source data as well as the integrated data. As a consequence, the quality of the source data will drive the methods needed for its integration. Data integration is an important phase in the data mining process, by creating new and enriched records from a multitude of sources. These new records can be queried, searched, mined and analyzed for discovering new, interesting and useful patterns.

The goal of this workshop was to bring together computer scientists with researchers from other domains and practitioners from businesses and governments to present and discuss current research directions on multi source data integration and its application. The workshop provided a forum for original high-quality research papers on record linkage, data integration, population informatics, mining techniques of integrated data, and applications, as well as multidisciplinary research opportunities.

The call for papers included the following (non-exhaustive) list of topics of interest:

- Data Integration Methodologies
  - Automating data cleaning and pre-processing
  - Algorithms and techniques for data integration
  - Entity resolution, record linkage, data matching, and duplicate detection

- Big Data integration
- Integrating complex data
– Population Informatics
  - Algorithms and techniques for managing, processing, analyzing, and mining large population databases
  - Requirements analysis for population informatics
  - Models and algorithms for population informatics
  - Architectures and frameworks for population informatics
  - Research case studies of population informatics in health, demographics, ecology, economics, the social sciences, and other research domains
– Evaluation, Quality and Privacy
  - Evaluation of linkage/matching/data integration methods
  - Data quality evaluation for source data and/or integrated data
  - Bias and quality of longitudinal data
  - Preserving privacy in data integration
– Integrated Data and Longitudinal Data Applications
  - Mining and analysis of longitudinal data
  - Data integration applications for healthcare, social sciences, digital humanities, bioinformatics, genomics, etc.
  - Applications of population informatics in governments and businesses

The ten submitted workshop papers were assessed through a double blind peer-reviewed process in which each submitted paper was assigned to at least three members of the program committee. The main selection criteria were the novelty of the application and its social impact. Seven papers (4 long and 3 short) were accepted for presentation.

The program included a keynote presentation, "Splink: An open source package for record linkage at scale using Apache Spark" by Robin Linacre, Ministry of Justice, UK

More information about the workshop can be found on the workshop website at: https://sites.google.com/view/dinaworkshop2020/home.

We like to thank all authors who submitted their work to DINA 2020, all presenters of accepted papers for their video presentations; and the members of the DINA 2020 program committee for their timely submissions of valuable review reports.

Workshop Organization

Workshop Co-chairs

Luiza Antonie	University of Guelph, Canada
Peter Christen	The Australian National University, Australia
Erhard Rahm	University of Leipzig, Germany
Osmar Zaïane	University of Alberta, Canada

Program Committee

Jose-Luis Ambite	University of Southern California, USA
Kerina Jones	Swansea University, Wales, UK
Dimitrios Karapiperis	Hellenic Open University, Greece
Abel Kho	Institute for Public Health and Medicine (IPHAM), USA
Graham Kirby	University of St Andrews, Scotland
Brad Malin	Vanderbilt University, USA
Brendan Murphy	University College Dublin, Ireland
Rebecca Nugent	Carnegie Mellon University, USA
Thilina Ranbaduge	The Australian National University, Australia
Sean Randall	Curtin University, Australia
Reza Sherkat	SAP, Canada
Rainer Schnell	University of Duisburg-Essen, Germany
Jeffrey Sukharev	Apple Inc, USA
Dinusha Vatsalan	CSIRO, Australian National University, Australia
Vassilios Verykios	Hellenic Open University, Greece
William Winkler	US Census Bureau, USA

Hyper-Parameter Optimization for Privacy-Preserving Record Linkage

Joyce Yu[1]($\boxtimes$), Jakub Nabaglo[2], Dinusha Vatsalan[1], Wilko Henecka[1], and Brian Thorne[3]

[1] CSIRO's DATA61, Eveleigh, NSW 2015, Australia
{joyce.yu,dinusha.vatsalan,wilko.henecka}@data61.csiro.au
[2] Ntropy Network, San Francisco, USA
j@nab.gl
[3] Hardbyte, Christchurch, New Zealand
brian@hardbyte.nz

Abstract. Linkage of records that refer to the same entity across different databases finds applications in several areas, including healthcare, business, national security, and government services. In the absence of unique identifiers, quasi-identifiers (e.g. name, age, address) must be used to identify records of the same entity in different databases. These quasi-identifiers (QIDs) contain personal identifiable information (PII). Therefore, record linkage must be conducted in a way that preserves privacy. Using Cryptographic Long-term Key (CLK)-based encoding is one popular privacy-preserving record linkage (PPRL) technique where different QIDs are encoded independently into a representation that preserves records' similarity but obscures PII. To achieve accurate results, the parameters of a CLK encoding must be tuned to suit the data. To this end, we study a Bayesian optimization method for effectively tuning hyper-parameters for CLK-based PPRL. Moreover, ground-truth labels (match or non-match) would be useful for evaluating linkage quality in the optimization, but they are often difficult to access. We address this by proposing an unsupervised method that uses heuristics to estimate linkage quality. Finally, we investigate the information leakage risk with the iterative approach of optimization methods and discuss recommendations to mitigate the risk. Experimental results show that our method requires fewer iterations to achieve good linkage results compared to two baseline optimization methods. It not only improves linkage quality and computational efficiency of hyper-parameter optimization, but also reduces the privacy risk.

Keywords: Hyper-parameters · Bloom filters · Bayesian optimization · Unsupervised · Heuristic measures · Information leakage risk

1 Introduction

Privacy-preserving record linkage (PPRL) is the process of identifying matching records across different databases that correspond to the same real-world

© Springer Nature Switzerland AG 2020
I. Koprinska et al. (Eds.): ECML PKDD 2020 Workshops, CCIS 1323, pp. 281–296, 2020.
https://doi.org/10.1007/978-3-030-65965-3_18

entities without revealing private or sensitive information about the entities. Since unique entity identifiers across different databases are not often available, the linkage needs to be conducted using the personal identifiable information (PII) that is commonly available in quasi-identifier (QID) attributes, such as name, address, and date of birth [14]. PPRL is generally a classification problem where a pair of records from different databases is classified as a match or a non-match depending on the similarity between QIDs of those records.

However, QIDs often contain personal and sensitive information about the entities and therefore PPRL aims to preserve the privacy by using encoding and/or encrypted functions [14]. Bloom filter encoding is one such encoding function that has widely been used in the PPRL literature due to the efficiency of encoding in terms of operational time and space, and has been employed in several real-world linkage applications [3,7,14]. Cryptographic Long-term Key (CLK) encoding is a popular method of Bloom filter encoding that hash-maps several QIDs of a record into one single Bloom filter [9]. With appropriate parameter settings, CLKs have shown to be successful in providing high quality linkage [7,8].

Nevertheless, the success of linkage based on Bloom filter encoding highly depends on the parameters used [7–9], which are saturation of the filter (depending on the length of the Bloom filter and the number of hash functions used to hash-map a record into the Bloom filter), weights used for each of the QIDs when hash-mapping, and the type of tokenisation used to hash-map QIDs to allow approximate/fuzzy matching. These parameters need to be tuned appropriately in order to optimize the linkage results.

Different parameter tuning techniques have been used in the literature, which are (1) Grid Search, (2) Random Search, and (3) Bayesian optimization. The former two search the full space of different parameter values in an isolated way without paying attention to previous results. Tuning parameters using these techniques is a time-consuming process, especially with Bloom filter-based PPRL due to the large parameter space. The search space grows exponentially with the number of parameters to be tuned, whilst for each parameter combination the PPRL algorithm has to be trained, linkage results have to be generated on the validation data, and the validation results have to be evaluated.

Bayesian Optimization, on the other hand, is an efficient parameter tuning method, which can bring down the time spent to get the optimal set of parameters as well as result in better generalisation performance on the test set [10]. It does this by taking into account information on the parameter combinations it has previously seen thus far when choosing the parameter set to evaluate next. We therefore study hyper-parameter optimization using Bayesian optimization method for CLK-based PPRL. Another challenge with PPRL is that accessing to ground-truth labels (of 'matches' and 'non-matches') is not trivial in a privacy-preserving context [14]. We therefore propose to use heuristic measures based on a greedy matching approach to evaluate/validate PPRL in an unsupervised way (in the absence of true match/non-match labels).

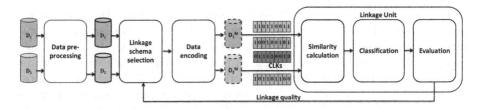

Fig. 1. Linkage model for PPRL of two databases

Further, hyper-parameter optimization using iterative encoding and evaluation can be susceptible to inference attacks. We study the information leakage risk in hyper-parameter optimization and discuss recommendations to overcome the associated risk. Specifically, we propose an attack method and a set of disclosure risk measures to quantify and evaluate the information leakage risk.

We conduct experimental evaluation and show that the disclosure risk increases with the number of iterations of encoding and validating, and that the number of iterations required to achieve improved linkage results is less with our unsupervised Bayesian method compared to the grid search and random search methods [2]. Further, we also show that the heuristic measures used by our method have a strong correlation with the standard $F1$-measure, validating the effectiveness of our unsupervised hyper-parameter optimization method.

Outline: We describe the linkage model in Sect. 2 and the hyper-parameter optimization method in Sect. 3. We propose heuristic measures for unsupervised method in Sect. 3.1, and discuss the information leakage risk in Sect. 3.2. We present experimental evaluation results in Sect. 4, and discuss the outcomes and provide recommendations to reduce the information leakage risk in hyper-parameter optimization in Sect. 5. Finally, we conclude the paper in Sect. 6 with an outlook to future research directions.

2   Linkage Model

The linkage model for linking two databases in a privacy-preserving context is outlined in Fig. 1. As a first step, the databases to be linked need to be pre-processed by the database owners. Real-world data often contain errors, variations and missing values leading to low quality linkage results. This requires data to be pre-processed before conducting the linkage. Next, the linkage hyper-parameters need to be selected and agreed upon by the database owners. Linkage hyper-parameters refer to both the selection of QIDs (feature selection) and their weights as well as the parameter setting for the encoding function.

Records in the databases are masked or encoded before sharing or exchanging them among the parties involved in the PPRL protocol. The remaining steps of linkage are conducted on the encoded records. Two major categories of techniques developed for privacy-preserving algorithms are: (1) cryptographic-based secure multi-party computation (SMC) techniques and (2) perturbation-based efficient masking techniques [12]. Techniques developed under the former category are generally more expensive with regard to the computation and communication complexities while providing strong privacy guarantees and high linkage quality [14]. Perturbation techniques, on the other hand, efficiently perturb or modify the original values (to preserve privacy) while still allowing to perform approximate matching between the masked values using the functional relationship between original and masked data [12,14].

Bloom filter encoding falls under the second category of techniques, which has widely been used in both research and practical applications of PPRL [6,7,11]. A Bloom filter b_i is a bit vector of length l bits where all bits are initially set to 0. k independent hash functions, $h_1, \ldots, h_k$, each with range $1, \ldots l$, are used to map each of the tokens s in a set S into the Bloom filter by setting the bit positions $h_j(s)$ with $1 \leq j \leq k$ to 1. The set S can contain, for example, n-grams (substrings of length n) extracted from string QID values (e.g. name), neighbouring values for numerical QIDs (e.g. age), or exact values of categorical QIDs (e.g. gender) [8,11]. Cryptographic Long-term Key (CLK) encoding is a Bloom filter encoding method that hash-maps different QIDs independently with different weights into one single Bloom filter which improves privacy against attacks on Bloom filters while preserving utility of encoding [8,9].

The encoded records (CLKs) output by the encoding step are next compared at the linkage unit by calculating the similarity between pairs of CLKs using a comparison/similarity function. The similarity function returns a similarity value between 0 and 1, where 1 means the QID values encoded into the CLKs are highly similar (exactly matching) and 0 means totally dissimilar QID values. Any token-based similarity function (such as overlap, Jaccard, and Dice coefficient) can be used to calculate the similarity between CLKs. In PPRL, the Dice coefficient has been used for matching of CLKs, since it is insensitive to many matching zeros (bit positions to which no elements are hash-mapped) in long CLKs [8]. The Dice coefficient similarity of two CLKs (b_1 and b_2) is: $sim(b_1, b_2) = \frac{2 \times \sum b_1 \cap b_2}{\sum b_1 + \sum b_2}$.

The calculated similarities are then used in the classification step to classify record pairs (CLK pairs) into either 'matches' or 'non-matches'. For example, a similarity threshold-based classifier classifies a pair as a 'match' if the similarity of corresponding CLKs is equal to at least the minimum similarity threshold, and as a 'non-match' if not. Machine learning classifiers can be used to improve the linkage quality of classification, however, they require training data with ground-truth labels of 'matches' and 'non-matches'.

Finally, the linkage quality needs to be evaluated in the evaluation step and the results are used to tune/select the hyper-parameters in the next iteration. Hyper-parameter optimization is an iterative process that continues until a specified criteria is met or for a certain number of iterations. However, in the PPRL context, the ground-truth labels are often not available to evaluate the linkage quality, making hyper-parameter optimization for PPRL a challenging task.

3   Hyper-Parameter Optimization

Grid search is the naïve method for tuning parameters [2]. For every set of parameters a classifier is trained and evaluated after which the combination with the best results is put forward. In small parameter spaces grid search can turn out to be quite effective, but in case of a large number of parameters (as with the case of CLK-based PPRL), the number of parameter combinations exponentially grows with the number of parameters. A popular alternative to grid search is **random search**. Random search samples combinations of random parameters from a statistical distribution provided by the user. This approach is based on the assumption that in most cases, parameters are not uniformly important. In practice random search is often more efficient than grid search due to reduced number of randomly chosen parameters, but it might fail to select important points in the search space. Both approaches tune in an isolated way disregarding past evaluations of parameter combinations. They further consider the full domain of parameters available, which might lead them to evaluate unpromising areas of the search space.

Bayesian optimization in turn takes into account past evaluations when choosing the parameter set to evaluate next. By choosing its parameter combinations in an informed way, it enables to focus on those areas of the parameter space that it believes will bring the most promising validation scores. This approach typically requires less number of iterations to get to the optimal set of parameter values, as it disregards those areas of the parameter space that it believes not be important for improving the validations scores. This in turn limits the number of times a classifier needs to be trained for validation as only those parameter combinations that are expected to generate a higher validation score are passed through for evaluation. There are four main components for the Bayesian optimization: 1) the search space to sample parameter values from, 2) an objective function, 3) a surrogate function, and 4) a selection function.

The objective function evaluates the parameter combinations. It takes in a set of parameters and outputs a score that indicates how well a set of parameters performs on the validation set. If ground-truth data is available, then 'accuracy score' can be used as the evaluation metric of choice. In this case, clearly the aim is to maximise the objective function. However, evaluating each set of parameters by means of maximizing the accuracy score can become a costly operation when dealing with large parameter space as each time the PPRL classifier needs to be trained in order to evaluate the linkage quality on the validation set. Hence, calling this evaluation function should ideally be restricted to a minimum. Maximising accuracy scores is equal to minimising negative validation scores (such as Root Mean Square Error or Error Rate). Therefore, the objective function is:

$$accuracy\_loss = f(x), \tag{1}$$

where f is the classifier used in PPRL to classify record pairs into matches or non-matches based on the similarity scores, x is the parameter set, and accuracy_loss is the metric (Root Mean Square Error or Error Rate) used to evaluate the correctness of f. The optimal set of parameters $x*$ that minimises the accuracy_loss (in other words maximises the accuracy score) is:

$$x* = argmin_{x \in X} \ f(x) \tag{2}$$

The evaluation function takes in a set of parameters X, trains a PPRL classifier and returns $x*$ that yields the lowest accuracy_loss score. Since accuracy_loss cannot be computed directly for PPRL as the class labels are generally not known, we propose to use heuristic loss metrics in an unsupervised greedy matching method (as will be detailed in Sect. 3.1), which shows high correlation with accuracy of linkage measured using the standard $F1$-measure.

Bayesian optimization tracks parameter sets evaluated thus far to select the parameters to be used next in the objective function. This is achieved through the (3) surrogate and (4) selection functions, as will be described below. Both work together to propose the parameters of which it potentially will bring the lowest accuracy_loss (highest accuracy) on the objective function.

The surrogate function can be interpreted as an approximation of the objective function. It is the probability representation of the objective function built using previous evaluations. It is used to propose parameter values to the objective function that likely yield an improvement in terms of accuracy score. There are several different forms of the surrogate function including Gaussian Processes, Random Forest regression, and Tree-structured Parzen Estimator (TPE). We use TPE as the surrogate function as it outperforms the other methods in terms of accuracy (error rate), as validated in [1].

The TPE builds a model by applying Bayes rule. Given y is the value of the objective function and x is the set of parameters, instead of directly representing $p(y|x)$, it uses:

$$p(y|x) = \frac{p(x|y)p(y)}{p(x)} \tag{3}$$

Th probability of parameters x given the validation score of the objective function y (i.e. $p(x|y)$) is broken into two different distributions for the parameters, $l(x)$ and $g(x)$. The former defines the distribution of parameters when the (negative) validation score is lower than a score threshold, $y*$ (e.g. the top accuracy score achieved thus far), while the latter represents the distribution for scores above $y*$.

$$p(x|y) = \begin{cases} l(x) \ if \ y < y* \\ g(x) \ if \ y \geq y* \end{cases} \tag{4}$$

Ideally, we want to draw values of x from $l(x)$ and not from $g(x)$ because this distribution is based only on values of x that yielded lower scores than the threshold. The TPEs works by drawing samples x from $l(x)$, evaluating them in terms of $l(x)/g(x)$, and returning the set that yields the highest value under $l(x)/g(x)$ corresponding to the selection function (as will be described next). These parameters are then evaluated on the objective function, which would yield a better validation score.

As discussed above, the parameters that are to be used for evaluation by the objective function are selected by applying a criterion to the surrogate function.

This criterion is defined by a selection function. A common approach is using the Expected Improvement metric [1].

$$EI_{y*}(x) = \int_{-\infty}^{y*} (y * -y)p(y|x)dy, \tag{5}$$

where $y*$ is a threshold value of the objective function, x is a set of parameters, y is the actual value of the objective function using x, and $p(y|x)$ is the surrogate probability model expressing the probability of y given x. The aim is to maximize the Expected Improvement with respect to x, i.e. finding the best parameters under the surrogate function $p(y|x)$. If $p(y|x) == 0$, then x are not expected to yield any improvement. If the integral is positive, then it means that x are expected to yield a better result than the threshold value.

3.1 Heuristic Loss as Alternative Metrics

Unlike the general classification problem where we have access to ground-truth data to train the model, there is no ground-truth data available for PPRL problems because generating or manually assigning ground-truth labels is either a time-consuming and erroneous process or it is not allowed in the privacy-preserving context due to privacy concerns. Therefore, we propose several heuristics to approximate the ground-truth data. Instead of using accuracy_loss metrics (such as Root Mean Square Error or Error rate) that require ground-truth data to be measured, we propose to use heuristic_loss metrics for minimizing the objective function (Eqs. 1 and 2).

We calculate heuristic_loss in terms of different functions. The input to these functions is a sequence of 0s and 1s, where 1 represents a match of a candidate pair by the greedy matching algorithm and 0 represents a non-match pair by the greedy matching algorithm. Assuming two sets of records X and Y from two parties, for example, the greedy matching algorithm matches a record $x_i \in X$ with the record $y_j \in Y$ that has the highest similarity (i.e. the pair consisting of x_i and y_j is a match represented as 1), while all other record pairs consisting of x_i and y_k with $y_k \neq y_j$ are considered as non-matches (represented as 0). Given the output by the greedy matching algorithm for all candidate record pairs as 0s and 1s, we define several heuristic functions to evaluate the linkage quality:

1. **Index of first low:** It returns the index of the first low value/non-match (0) in the sequence multiplied by (-1). For example, a sequence $[1, 1, 0, 1, 0, 0]$ returns -2 for this function as the first value of 0 appears in the index of 2 in the sequence (zero-based numbering, i.e., the initial element of the sequence is assigned with the index 0).
2. **Number of swaps:** It is calculated as the difference between number of matches (1s), which we denote as m, and the number of matches in the first m values in the sequence. With the previous example sequence of $[1, 1, 0, 1, 0, 0]$, this function returns 1 as $m = 3$ and the sum of the first 3 values is 2.
3. **Number of swaps by 1:** This heuristic calculates the sum of steps required to bring matches forward in the sequence multiplied by (-1). For the running example sequence of $[1, 1, 0, 1, 0, 0]$, it returns $-(0 - 0 + 1 - 1 + 2 - 3) = 1$

4. **Sum of low indices:** It returns the sum of all indices that have the low value/non-match (0) in the sequence multiplied by (-1). In the example sequence of $[1, 1, 0, 1, 0, 0]$, it returns $-(2 + 4 + 5) = -11$.
5. **Harmonic weights of sum of low indices:** It calculates the sum of weighted low indices (0s) where each of the low index is divided by the count (starting from 1) and the resulting sum of weighted indices is multiplied by (-1). With the running example of $[1, 1, 0, 1, 0, 0]$, this function returns $-(2/1 + 4/2 + 5/3) = -5.667$.
6. **Exponential weights of sum of low indices:** It calculates the sum of weighted low indices (0s) where each of the low index is divided by the exponential value of the count and the resulting sum of weighted indices is multiplied by (-1). For the running example of $[1, 1, 0, 1, 0, 0]$, this function returns $-(2/e^1 + 4/e^2 + 5/e^3) = -1.526$.

The accuracy of linkage quality evaluation using one of these heuristic measures relies on the output provided by the greedy matching algorithm. More advanced mapping functions, such as Hungarian matching algorithm, can be used to improve the accuracy (which is left as a future work). In Sect. 4, we experimentally evaluate the accuracy of these heuristic measures by comparing them with the $F1$-measure, which is the standard linkage quality measure calculated based on the ground-truth labels.

3.2 Information Leakage with the Iterative Approach

To evaluate the information leakage in hyper-parameter optimization methods we conduct a frequency inference-based attack on the CLKs and measure the disclosure risk at every iteration. There have been several cryptanalysis attacks developed in the literature to evaluate Bloom filters' susceptibility to such privacy attacks by the linkage unit [4]. All of these attack methods are based on frequency information of bit patterns in the Bloom filters.

Since hyper-parameter optimization involves an iterative approach where multiple iterations of encoding and sharing of CLKs are required, calculating the privacy risk with multiple iterations of encoding and sharing is required. We propose an attack method to calculate the privacy risk with multiple iterations and numerical metrics to quantify the information leakage risk. As with most of the existing attack methods, we assume that the adversary (i.e. the linkage unit) knows or guesses the hyper-parameters used and has access to the frequency distribution of unencoded data of similar distribution. Our attack method is based on a frequency attack where we align the frequency of bits in the CLKs to frequency of elements/tokens in the records (e.g. n-grams of string QIDs, neighbouring values of numeric QIDs or exact values of categorical QIDs [8,11]) and then eventually to the records that contain those tokens.

At every iteration the tokens (in features) hash-mapped into the CLKs are extracted from the unencoded data first to study the frequency distribution of tokens in the unencoded data. Then the frequency distribution of bits in CLKs is identified and matched or aligned to the tokens in the unencoded data based on the frequency distributions. Next, we identify the set of possible records that could have been hash-mapped into for each bit in the CLKs. This is done by extracting all the records that contain the possible tokens which are aligned to the corresponding bits.

However, the frequency alignment can lead to wrong mapping of bits to records due to collisions that occur during the hash-mapping process (this is the case when the frequencies of different bits/tokens are not considerably different from each other). In order to overcome this issue with one-to-one mapping, we group the bits and tokens according to their frequencies, such that bits or tokens with similar frequencies are considered the same and grouped into the same clusters. We then map the clusters of bits to clusters of tokens (many-to-many mapping) using frequency alignment and get the set of possible records for each cluster of bits. More advanced cryptanalysis attacks are required to study further the correct one-to-one mapping between bits and tokens instead of many-to-many mapping.

In the next iterations, we repeat the frequency alignment and identify the possible records for bits based on the frequency distribution. However, a group of frequent bits often would have encoded the same (group of) records at different iterations regardless of the hyper-parameters used, and therefore we calculate the intersection of records that are possibly aligned to each of the bits in the CLKs at different iterations. With multiple iterations, the size of the intersection set would become smaller which increases the probability of suspicion.

The probability of suspicion of a bit β in CLKs is based on the number of potential matching records n_g (that contain the tokens that are aligned to this bit) and is defined as $P_s(\beta) = 1/n_g$. We normalise this value into the 0.0 to 1.0 interval using $P_s(\beta) = \frac{1/n_g - 1/n}{1 - 1/n}$,

where n is the total number of records in the encoded database. Based on the P_s values calculated for each bit, we calculate the disclosure risk metrics. Specifically, we calculate the maximum and mean disclosure risk:

1. mean disclosure risk (DR_{Mean}): the average risk ($\sum_{\beta=1}^{l} P_s(\beta)/l$) of any sensitive bit in CLKs being re-identified [12]
2. maximum disclosure risk (DR_{max}): the maximum risk ($max_\beta P_s(\beta)$) of a sensitive bit in CLKs being re-identified [12]

4   Experimental Evaluation

We conducted our experiments on three datasets with the following parameter settings as illustrated in Fig. 2:

1. **ABS:** This is a synthetic dataset used internally for linkage experiments at the Australian Bureau of Statistics (ABS). It simulates an employment census and two supplementary surveys. We sampled 5000 records for two parties with all seven attributes (integer).

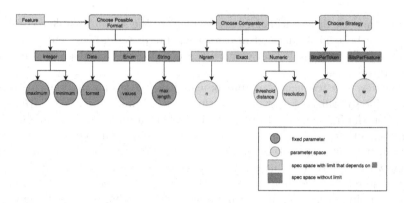

Fig. 2. Parameter Setup for Linkage

Both n-gram (where n is set to either 1 or 2) and exact comparators are used for five of these attributes, while only exact comparator is used for the other two attributes. Only one strategy of choosing bits from features to construct the CLKs is used, and the number of bits per feature is set to $w = 100$ for five of the attributes (including the ones that use only the exact comparator), $w = [10, 100]$ and $w = [20, 100]$ for the other two attributes. Therefore, the search space used for this dataset is 128 ($4 \times 4 \times 2 \times 1 \times 2 \times 2 \times 1 = 128$).

2. **NCVR:** We extracted a pair of datasets with 5000 records each (for a **small-scale study**) and a pair of datasets with 10000 records each (for a **large-scale study**) for two parties from the North Carolina Voter Registration (NCVR) database[1] with 50% of matching records between the two parties. Ground-truth is available based on the voter registration identifiers. We used given name (string), surname (string), suburb (string), and postcode (string) attributes as QIDs for the linkage.

The parameter settings for the **small-scale study** are the max length for the former three attributes is 30 and for the latter is 5, CLK strategies of 1) choosing 150 bits from each of the attributes into a CLK and 2) choosing 5 bits from different tokens (n-grams) of these attributes into a CLK are used for all 4 attributes, and the token sizes are $n = [2, 3]$ for given name and surname, $n = 2$ for suburb, and $n = [1, 2]$ for postcode. This setting provides a total number of parameter combinations (search space) of 128 for a small-scale study of linking two databases of 5000 records each.

In the **large-scale study** of linking databases of 10000 records each, we used the same setting for the fixed parameters, however for the other parameters we used $n = [2, 3]$ for all attributes except postcode which was set to $n = [1, 2]$, and both CLK hash-mapping strategies for all attributes with the number of bits per token set to $w = [5, 10]$ for all except postcode that is set to only $w = 5$ and the number of bits per feature set to $w = [100, 200, 300]$ for given

[1] Available from *ftp://dl.ncsbe.gov/data/*.

name, $w = [100, 150, 300]$ for surname, $w = [150, 300]$ for suburb, and $w = 150$
for postcode, which gives a total search space of 128000 for large-scale study.

3. **DSS:** This is a real dataset from the Department of Social Science (DSS).
Again we sampled 5000 records (for a **small-scale study**) and 10000 records
(for a **large-scale study**) for both parties in a two-party linkage setting
with the attributes of first name (string), last name (string), gender (enum
or categorical), date of birth (string), start date (date) and end date (date).
The search space for the small-scale linkage of 5000 records is 144 and the
large-scale linkage of 10000 records is 30720.

For the **small-scale study**, the parameter settings are n-gram comparator
for the string attributes with either $n = [2, 3]$ or $n = [1, 2]$, exact comparator
for the gender, and both exact and n-gram comparators for the date attributes
with $n = [1, 2]$ for start date and $n = 2$ for the end date. The strategy
of choosing $w = 5$ bits from tokens is used for the gender attribute, both
strategies of choosing $w = 150$ bits from attributes and $w = [5, 10]$ bits from
tokens are used for the first name attribute, and the strategy of choosing
$w = 150$ bits from attributes is used for the remaining attributes. For **large-
scale study**, the comparators and strategies used for different attributes are
the same as for the small-scale study, except that the gender attribute also
uses the strategy of choosing bits from attributes in addition to choosing
bits from tokens. We used $n = [2, 3]$ or $n = [1, 2]$ for the string attributes,
$n = [1, 2]$ for the start date, and $n = 2$ for the end date. The number of bits
chosen from tokens is set to $w = [5, 10]$ for first name and $w = 5$ for gender,
while the number of bits chosen from attributes is set to $w = [100, 150]$ for
first name, start date, and end date, $w = 150$ for last name and gender, and
$w = [100, 200]$ for date of birth.

We implemented our method and the baseline methods (grid search and
random search) in Python 3.7.4[2], and ran all experiments on a server with 4-
core 64-bit Intel 2.8 GHz CPU, 16 GBytes of memory and running OS X 10.15.1.
We used the clkhash library available in the Anonlink, which is an open source
tool for PPRL, for encoding records into CLKs [5]. Computational efficiency
is evaluated using the number of iterations required for optimization, linkage
quality is evaluated in terms of accuracy of linkage results using the $F1$-measure,
and privacy is measured using the disclosure risk metrics (defined in Sect. 3.2).
The stopping criterion for the optimization methods in the experiments is the
maximum number of iterations, which is set to $[100, 125]$.

We first evaluated the correlation between our proposed heuristic measures
(Sect. 3.1) and the standard $F1$-measure. We present the Pearson's correlation
coefficient values between all the proposed heuristic measures and $F1$-measure on
all datasets in Table 1. The sum of low indices measure has a strong correlation
with the $F1$-measure on all datasets followed by the number of swaps by 1
and harmonic weights of sum of low indices measures. Figure 3 shows perfect
correlation between the sum of low indices and $F1$-measure and the number of
swaps by 1 and $F1$-measure on the ABS dataset (please note that due to space

---

[2] The source code is available in http://doi.org/10.5281/zenodo.3971263.

Table 1. Correlation coefficient between heuristic loss measures and $F1$-measure

Heuristics	Datasets		
	DSS	ABS	NCVR
Index of first low	0.37	0.06	0.13
Number of swaps	0.27	0.48	0.39
Number of swaps by 1	0.79	**1.0**	0.77
Sum of low indices	**0.88**	**1.0**	0.71
Harmonic weights of sum of low indices	0.33	0.87	0.94
Exponential weights of sum of low indices	0.54	0.1	**0.98**

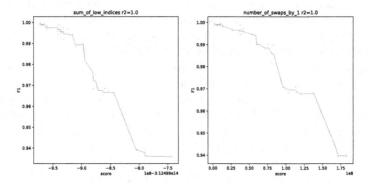

Fig. 3. Heuristic loss calculated using the sum of low indices vs. $F1$-measure (left) and number of swaps by 1 vs. $F1$-measure (right) on ABS dataset

limitation we do not include the plots for all the heuristic measures). These results indicate that the heuristic loss metrics using the number of swaps by 1 and sum of low indices can be effectively used as an alternative metric for evaluating linkage quality in PPRL. However, the performances of other heuristic metrics are not consistent across different datasets (especially with the exponential and harmonic weights of sum of low indices), which needs further investigation of underlying reasons behind the large variance between different datasets.

We then compared the performance of hyper-parameter optimization using the Bayesian optimization with the grid search and random search methods. This set of experiments are two-fold. First, we compare all three methods on small datasets (NCVR and ABS datasets each containing 5000 records for each of the two parties) with relatively small search space for CLK-based PPRL (128). The search space size is quantified using the number of parameter combinations used. The results are shown in Fig. 4. From these results, we found that the grid search method does not perform well compared to other two optimization methods. However, it is difficult to compare the performance of Bayesian and random search methods with these experimental results. Therefore, we next compared the random search and Bayesian methods on large datasets of 10000

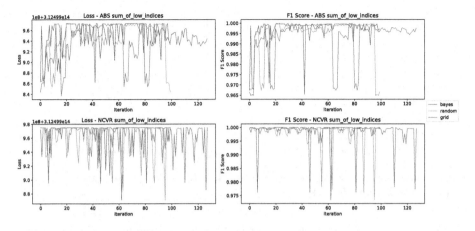

Fig. 4. Comparison of methods on small search space

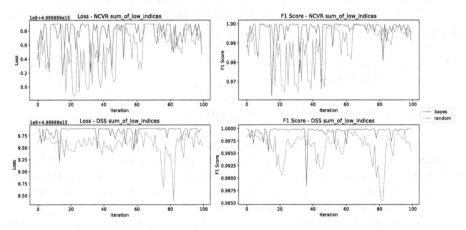

Fig. 5. Comparison of methods on large search space

records from the NCVR and DSS datasets (with larger search spaces of 12800 and 30720, respectively). As can be seen in Fig. 5, these results clearly reveal that the Bayesian method outperforms the random search method on large datasets with large search space.

Finally, we present the disclosure risk results of the iterative hyper-parameter optimization method against a frequency inference attack (as described in Sect. 3.2). We quantified the information leakage from the CLKs to the linkage unit in terms of maximum and mean disclosure risk metrics that are calculated based on the probability of suspicion values (as defined in Sect. 3.2). We used the NCVR-10000 datasets for this experiment. As shown in Fig. 6, the disclosure risk increases with multiple iterations and the maximum disclosure risk reaches to 1.0 after a certain number of iterations (which means that there exists a one-to-one mapping between a bit in the CLKs and a record). However, as can

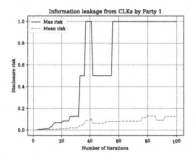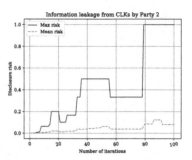

Fig. 6. Information leakage risk with multiple iterations of hyper-parameter optimization on NCVR-10000 datasets

be seen in Fig. 5, we are able to achieve high linkage quality within a smaller number of iterations (within the first 10–20 iterations) that have lower disclosure risk. Therefore, Bayesian hyper-parameter optimization not only improves linkage quality and efficiency (runtime) with a smaller number of iterations, but also improves privacy guarantees against frequency attacks by requiring a smaller number of iterations of encoding and revealing CLKs to the linkage unit for hyper-parameter optimization.

5 Discussion and Recommendation

Our experimental results show that our unsupervised Bayesian hyper-parameter optimization method improves the linkage quality within a smaller number of iterations than the baseline methods. However, the information leakage risk increases with multiple iterations of any hyper-parameter optimization methods. In this section, we discuss some recommendations and directions to reduce the risk and thereby improve the privacy guarantees with the iterative approach of our PPRL hyper-parameter optimization model.

1. Non-uniform record identifiers: The attack model (proposed in Sect. 3.2) assumes that the records have the same (uniform) record identifiers across different iterations. However, the linkage unit does not require consistent or uniform record identifiers (but does require unique identifiers) at different iterations to evaluate/validate the linkage using the unsupervised greedy matching method (described in Sect. 3.1). Using different record identifiers at different iterations could reduce the disclosure risk against such inference attacks.
2. Bloom filter hardening methods: Different hardening methods for enhancing the privacy aspect of Bloom filter encoding have been proposed in the literature [8]. For example, BLIP is a method that flips bits in the Bloom filters using the randomised response method to guarantee differential privacy. The impact of such hardening methods on the information leakage risk as well as on the linkage quality needs to be investigated for hyper-parameter optimization.

3. Counting Bloom filter (CBF): A CBF c is an integer vector that contains the counts of values in each position. Multiple CLKs of length l bits can be summarized into a single CBF c of length l bits, such that $c[\beta] = \sum_{i=1}^{p} b_i[\beta]$, where $1 \le \beta \le l$ and p is the number of CLKs (parties). $c[\beta]$ is the count value in the β bit position of the CBF c. Given p CLKs from p corresponding parties b_i with $1 \le i \le p$, the CBF c can be generated by applying a secure summation operation between the p bit vectors such that $c = \sum_i b_i$, and the similarity between CLKs can be calculated using the CBF [13]. Since the CBF contains only the summary information (count values), it provides more privacy guarantees than CLKs against an inference attack by the linkage unit [13].
4. Local evaluation of disclosure risk: The evaluation of information leakage risk from CLKs in multiple iterations against an attack model can be performed by the database owners/parties individually. The parties can therefore locally evaluate the risk against a frequency attack on the CLKs before sending the CLKs to the linkage unit. If the calculated risk is high, then the parties need to change the CLK parameters and/or the QIDS and their weights.

6 Conclusion

In this paper, we have proposed unsupervised Bayesian hyper-parameter optimization for PPRL and studied two different aspects of hyper-parameter optimization for PPRL: (1) using heuristic measures to evaluate/validate the linkage quality for hyper-parameter optimization in the absence of ground-truth labels which is often the case in PPRL, and (2) evaluating the information leakage risk associated with the iterative approach of hyper-parameter optimization methods. We conducted experiments on three real and synthetic datasets and evaluated these two aspects of our proposed hyper-parameter optimization method and compared with two baseline methods.

While our hyper-parameter optimization method improves the linkage quality with a smaller number of iterations than the baseline methods, our experimental results also show the vulnerability of iterative hyper-parameter optimization approach to frequency inference attacks. We have discussed several recommendations to reduce the privacy risk of hyper-parameter optimization which require more research and study in those directions. Further, developing more comprehensive and advanced attack methods is an important future research to evaluate and compare the privacy risk with PPRL hyper-parameter optimization methods. Similarly, the applicability of heuristic measures to evaluate the linkage quality needs to be studied and evaluated in an extensive empirical study.

In the future, we also aim to address the computation and communication efficiency aspects of iterative hyper-parameter optimization method, and conduct a large-scale experimental study on hyper-parameter optimization for PPRL using large datasets. Moreover, since hyper-parameter optimization for PPRL implies a change in the traditional PPRL protocols, as most real-world Bloom filter-based PPRL applications are a one-shot game, it opens options for developing other iterative PPRL schemes.

Acknowledgements. This work was funded by the Australian Department of Social Sciences (DSS) as part of the Platforms for Open Data (PfOD) project. We would like to thank Waylon Nielsen, Alex Ware, and Maruti Vadrevu from DSS for their support and feedback on this work.

References

1. Bergstra, J.S., Bardenet, R., Bengio, Y., Kégl, B.: Algorithms for hyper-parameter optimization. In: Advances in Neural Information Processing Systems, pp. 2546–2554 (2011)
2. Borgs, C.: Optimal parameter choice for bloom filter-based privacy-preserving record linkage. Ph.D. thesis (2019). https://doi.org/10.17185/duepublico/70274
3. Brown, A.P., Randall, S.M., Boyd, J.H., Ferrante, A.M.: Evaluation of approximate comparison methods on bloom filters for probabilistic linkage. Int. J. Popul. Data Sci. 4(1) (2019)
4. Christen, P., Ranbaduge, T., Vatsalan, D., Schnell, R.: Precise and fast cryptanalysis for Bloom filter based privacy-preserving record linkage. IEEE Trans. Knowl. Data Eng. **31**, 2164–2177 (2018)
5. CSIRO's Data61: Anonlink private record linkage system (2017). https://github.com/data61/clkhash
6. Kuehni, C.E., et al.: Cohort profile: the Swiss childhood cancer survivor study. Int. J. Epidemiol. **41**(6), 1553–1564 (2011)
7. Randall, S.M., Ferrante, A.M., Boyd, J.H., Semmens, J.B.: Privacy-preserving record linkage on large real world datasets. J. Biomed. Inform. **50**(1), 1 (2014)
8. Schnell, R.: Privacy preserving record linkage. In: Harron, K., Goldstein, H., Dibben, C. (eds.) Methodological Developments in Data Linkage, pp. 201–225. Wiley, Chichester (2016)
9. Schnell, R., Bachteler, T., Reiher, J.: A novel error-tolerant anonymous linking code. German Record Linkage Center, Working Paper Series No. WP-GRLC-2011-02 (2011)
10. Snoek, J., Larochelle, H., Adams, R.P.: Practical Bayesian optimization of machine learning algorithms. In: Advances in Neural Information Processing Systems, pp. 2951–2959 (2012)
11. Vatsalan, D., Christen, P.: Privacy-preserving matching of similar patients. J. Biomed. Inform. **59**, 285–298 (2016)
12. Vatsalan, D., Christen, P., O'Keefe, C.M., Verykios, V.S.: An evaluation framework for privacy-preserving record linkage. J. Priv. Confid. **6**(1), 1 (2014)
13. Vatsalan, D., Christen, P., Rahm, E.: Scalable privacy-preserving linking of multiple databases using counting Bloom filters. In: Workshop on Privacy and Discrimination in Data Mining held at IEEE ICDM, Barcelona (2016)
14. Vatsalan, D., Christen, P., Verykios, V.S.: A taxonomy of privacy-preserving record linkage techniques. Inf. Syst. **38**(6), 946–969 (2013)

Group-Specific Training Data

Ben Busath, Jalen Morgan, and Joseph Price[(✉)]

Brigham Young University, Provo, UT 84604, USA
joe_price@byu.edu

Abstract. We examine the degree to which training models for specific sub-groups within a population can help improve precision and recall in linking historical records. We focus on an application of linking individuals between the 1900–1920 US censuses. Our results are an inverse of the transfer learning question and also relate to the ways in which training data built for the full population can result in biased predictions for minority groups in the population. We find that training a model specifically for German-born Americans improves our precision rate for these links from 79.1% to 92.7% while decreasing our recall from 94.5% down to 91.4%, thus dramatically increasing our true match rate for this subgroup. Similar analysis can be done based on gender, birthplace, race, and uniqueness of one's surname.

Keywords: Record linking · Training data · XGBoost

1 Introduction

Data from historical documents can assist in performing significant economic, epidemiological and demographic studies. The value of this data is greatly enhanced through linking individuals across multiple historical documents spanning long periods of time. Census records gathered at regular intervals can provide an important source to create these large population-based linked datasets. Currently there are a number of methods being used to link together the entire US population across the 10 full-count censuses that span from 1850 to 1940 [1–4]. Ultimately, this will result in a longitudinal panel that includes about 217 million people, becoming even larger when the 1950 census becomes publicly available in 2022.

Machine learning approaches will play an important role in making this large-scale linking process possible. Record linking models can determine the likelihood that a person in one record is the same individual as a person in another record, based on a set of features from the two datasets [5]. This process of entity resolution requires a training set that can allow the machine learning algorithm to place the appropriate weights on each of the features when determining if two people are a match or not.

There have been some concerns about how the source of training data in other areas of machine learning that can create biased predictions for particular subgroups of the population. For example, if training data is created using only data for white non-immigrant males, then the predictions from these models may do poorly when applied to

© Springer Nature Switzerland AG 2020
I. Koprinska et al. (Eds.): ECML PKDD 2020 Workshops, CCIS 1323, pp. 297–302, 2020.
https://doi.org/10.1007/978-3-030-65965-3_19

women, immigrants, or non-white individuals. These biases can often only be detected when the training data and validation sets include enough individuals from these other groups. This concern about predictions that are biased for particular subgroups is the inverse of the transfer learning issue which examines whether a machine learning model trained in one context can make accurate predictions in another context [6].

In this paper, we examine these issues using a massive training set that we have created using data from a free online genealogical website, FamilySearch.org. This website includes a public wiki-style family tree that allows anyone to add information about their ancestors and extended relatives. An important type of information that people add are links to historical records for that person. We use pairs of different census records attached to the same person on the Family Tree to create a training set that includes over 9 million true matches between the 1900, 1910, and 1920 US census. In previous work, we have used this training data to develop a machine learning approach to identify 55 million links between these datasets with a precision of 89% [7].

The contribution of this paper is to show that we can dramatically improve the precision we achieve for particular subgroups by using subgroup-specific training data. This type of focused approach is only possible with large training sets. However, the increasing availability of linked administrative datasets is likely to improve access to these larger training sets.

In the following sections, we describe the process that we use to test the value of group-specific training data. In Sect. 2, we describe the records we would like to link and the way in which we created our training data using the data from FamilySearch. In Sect. 3, we provide additional detail about the machine learning model that we employ to do the record linking. In Sect. 4, we provide results about the improvement in performance that we observe when using group-specific training data instead of training data based on the full population.

2 Data

2.1 US Decennial Census

The goal of our record linking application is to link individuals across the 1900, 1910, and 1920 US decennial censuses. The US census is taken every 10 years and the full data becomes publicly available 72 years later. The 1850 census was the first year that the names of all household members were included on the census and 1870 is the first year that many African Americans can be observed because the names of slaves were not included in censuses prior to the Emancipation Proclamation in 1863. The 1890 census was lost, leaving nine individual-level censuses that can be used between 1850 and 1940, with the 1950 census becoming publicly available in 2022.

Figure 1 provides an example image of the upper left section of a 1920 census sheet that depicts the raw data on which our record linking is based. Data from these images were transcribed by FamilySearch using human volunteers. There are at least three possible sources of error in the data: incorrect reporting by the census participant, incorrect notation by the census enumerator, and incorrect transcription by the FamilySearch volunteer. Machine learning becomes important to be able to link individuals across records when much of the information is likely to be incorrect (including misspelled names, incorrect ages, and occasionally an incorrect gender or birth place).

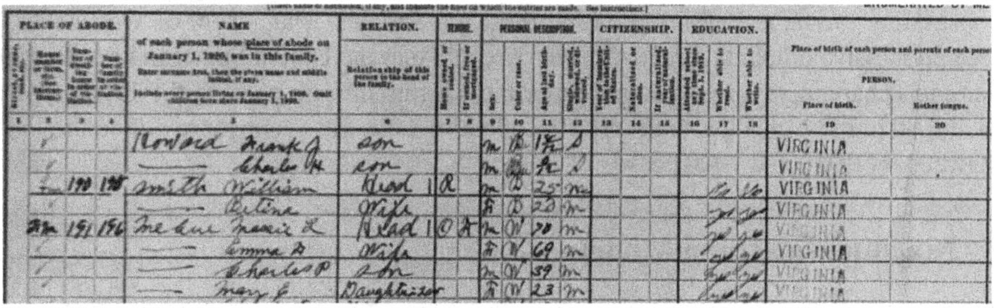

Fig. 1. This is an image of the upper left corner of a sheet of the 1920 census.

Our full sample includes 76.2 million individuals in the 1900 census, 92.2 million in the 1910 census, and 106.6 million in the 1920 census. Based on birth and immigration years and accounting for under-enumeration estimates, we estimate that 63.0 million individuals are linkable between 1900 and 1910 and 76.7 million individuals are linkable between 1910 and 1920 [7].

2.2 Training Data

To create our training data, we utilize record links compiled from individual profiles on a public, wiki-style family tree provided by FamilySearch. When multiple census are attached to the same individual on the family tree, we can treat each pair of records as a true match. Compiling links using this method allows us to have access to millions of 'true' links that cover a diverse set of demographics. These links are likely to be of higher quality, on average, than other methods of labeling links since the people creating the links often have personal information about the individual, access to multiple records, sufficient time to reconcile conflicting information, and a strong interest in finding the correct link.

Upon selecting a subset of true links from this master set, false links can then be created by "blocking" the people associated to the true links from one census to the other census corresponding to these true links. Blocking is a way of specifying a set of criteria that has to be met exactly for a possible match to even be considered. Among this set of possible matches, we then identify the correct match based on the true links from FamilySearch and label the other possible links within the block as false links.

For both the German and full sample models, we block on race, gender, birth year within 3 years, and NYSIIS values for the first and last name. We then create two training sets: one is created from a random sample of the entire set of true matches, while the second is created from a random sample of the true matches where the person is listed as being born in Germany in the 1910 census. We refer to the former training set as the 'Full' sample set and the latter training set as the 'German' sample for the rest of this paper. The full sample includes 19,526 true matches and 71,189 false matches and the German sample includes 5,750 true matches and 54,105 false matches.

2.3 German Americans

The main subgroup that we focus on in this paper are German-born Americans. There were about 2.5 million German-born Americans living in the US during the 1910 census, constituting the largest ethnic group in the United States. The advent of World War I created massive amounts of anti-German prejudice in the United States and resulted in Germans changing their names and reporting a different birth place in the 1920 census [8, 9]. All of these changes in the reported identity make this group more difficult to link between the 1910 and 1920 census.

3   Machine Learning Model

For our record linking algorithm, we use an XGBoost Classifier [10]. XGBoost is well suited for the record linkage task because of its computational speed as well as its high accuracy and efficiency [7, 11]. Another benefit of using decision tree-based models like XGBoost is that they can provide estimates of feature importance to determine which features most inform the scoring of the model.

4   Performance

To compare the performance of the full-sample model to the German model, we observe precision and recall. Precision is the rate of identified matches that are true matches, while recall is the rate of true matches that are identified among those that are possible.

We compare the performance of each model on a holdout set of 64,934 German true and false matches, as well as a holdout set of 90,715 links from the entire collection of true and false matches. We find that training a model specifically for German-born Americans improves our precision rate for these links from 79.1% to 92.7% while decreasing our recall from 94.5% down to 91.4%, thus dramatically increasing our true match rate for this subgroup (Table 1).

Table 1. Comparison of performance based on the training set used.

	Full sample training set		German sample training set	
	Full sample	German sample	Full sample	German sample
Precision	0.922	0.791	0.922	0.927
Recall	0.898	0.945	0.814	0.914
N	90,716		64,934	

Observing the feature importance of each model gives additional insight into how the German model was able to accomplish such a large increase in precision. Feature importance weights the amount that each feature split point improves performance with the number of observations the node is responsible for in order to provide the relative amount of important decisions the given feature makes within the model.

The full model had an immigration year feature importance of only 0.006, while the German model used immigration much more with a feature importance of 0.096. This makes sense as the majority of people in the full sample were born in the US and thus did not have an immigration year on each census, while people born in Germany are much more likely to have a documented immigration year on each census (Table 2).

Table 2. Comparison of feature importance based on the training set used.

Feature	Full model	German model
Residence distance	0.305	0.427
Birth year distance	0.222	0.168
Surname JW	0.114	0.140
Father birthplace	0.112	0.000
Relationship	0.064	0.035
Mother birthplace	0.049	0.000
Surname commonality	0.044	0.046
Given name commonality	0.043	0.020
Given name JW	0.033	0.012
Immigration year	0.006	0.096
Marital status	0.006	0.059

5   Conclusion

The purpose of this paper is to examine if we can improve precision and recall for specific subgroups by using training data just for that subgroup. We use the application of linking German-born Americans between the 1910 and 1920 census since this was a subgroup of the US population that changed aspects of their identity in the face of prejudice during World War I. As such, a model trained on the full population may provide biased predictions for this particular group. We find that this is the case and we can improve the precision of our predictions from 78% up to 93% by creating a training set specific to this subgroup.

Acknowledgements. This work was funded by a grant from the Russell Sage Foundation and from generous research support provided by Brigham Young University.

References

1. Abramitzky, R., Boustan, L.P., Eriksson, K., et al.: Automated linking of historical data. J. Econ. Lit. (forthcoming)

2. Bailey, M., Cole, C., Henderson, M., Massey, C.: How well do automated methods perform in historical samples? Evidence from new ground truth. J. Econ. Lit. (2019, forthcoming)
3. Abramitzky, R., Mill, R., Perez, S.: Linking individuals across historical sources: a fully automated approach. Hist. Methods 53, 94–111 (2020)
4. Feigenbaum, J.J.: Automated Census Record Linking: A Machine Learning Approach. Working Paper (2016)
5. Christen, P.: Data matching: concepts and techniques for record linkage, entity resolution, and duplicate detection. Data-Centric Systems and Applications (2012)
6. Weiss, K., Khoshgoftaar, T., Wang, D.: A survey of transfer learning. J. Big Data 3(9) (2016)
7. Price, J., Buckle, K., Van Leeuwen, J., Riley, I.: Combining Family History and Machine Learning to Link Historical Records. Working Paper (2020)
8. Moser, P.: Taste-based discrimination evidence from a shift in ethnic preferences after WWI. Explor. Econ. Hist. 49, 167–188 (2012)
9. Fouka, V.: Backlash: the unintended effects of language prohibition in us schools after World War I. Rev. Econ. Stud. (forthcoming)
10. Chen, T., Guestrin, C.: Xgboost: a scalable tree boosting system. In: Proceedings of the 22nd ACM SIGKDD International Conference on Knowledge Discovery and Data Mining, KDD 2016, pp. 785–794 (2016)
11. Folkman, T., Furner, R., Pearson, D.: GenERes: a genealogical entity resolution system. In: IEEE International Conference on Data Mining Workshops, pp. 495–501 (2018)

Scalable Blocking for Very Large Databases

Andrew Borthwick, Stephen Ash$^{(\boxtimes)}$, Bin Pang, Shehzad Qureshi,
and Timothy Jones

AWS AI Labs, Seattle, WA, USA
{andborth,ashstep,pangbin,shezq,timjons}@amazon.com

Abstract. In the field of database deduplication, the goal is to find
approximately matching records within a database. *Blocking* is a typical stage in this process that involves cheaply finding candidate pairs
of records that are potential matches for further processing. We present
here *Hashed Dynamic Blocking*, a new approach to blocking designed to
address datasets larger than those studied in most prior work. Hashed
Dynamic Blocking (HDB) extends Dynamic Blocking, which leverages
the insight that rare matching values and rare intersections of values
are predictive of a matching relationship. We also present a novel use
of Locality Sensitive Hashing (LSH) to build blocking key values for
huge databases with a convenient configuration to control the trade-off
between precision and recall. HDB achieves massive scale by minimizing
data movement, using compact block representation, and greedily pruning ineffective candidate blocks using a Count-min Sketch approximate
counting data structure. We benchmark the algorithm by focusing on
real-world datasets in excess of one million rows, demonstrating that the
algorithm displays linear time complexity scaling in this range. Furthermore, we execute HDB on a 530 million row industrial dataset, detecting
68 billion candidate pairs in less than three hours at a cost of $307 on a
major cloud service.

Keywords: Duplicate detection · Blocking · Entity matching · Record
linkage

1 Introduction

Finding approximately matching records is an important and well-studied problem [12]. The challenge is to identify records which represent the same real-world
entity (e.g. the same person, product, business, movie, etc.) despite the fact that
the corresponding data records may differ due to various errors, omissions, or
different ways of representing the same information. For many database dedupli-
cation/record linkage applications a common approach is to divide the problem

---

A. Borthwick and S. Ash—Equal Contribution.

I. Koprinska et al. (Eds.): ECML PKDD 2020 Workshops, CCIS 1323, pp. 303–319, 2020.
https://doi.org/10.1007/978-3-030-65965-3_20

into four stages [17]: Normalization [2], Blocking [7,19,24], Pairwise Matching [6,20], and Graph Partitioning [14,25].

This work focuses on the problem of blocking very large databases with record counts between 1M and 530M records. We focus on databases in this range due to their importance in industrial settings. We make a case that different blocking algorithms will be successful in this range than are effective on databases with fewer than 1 million records. The experimental results that we show on real-world datasets with 50M or more records, in particular, are unusual in the literature.

In contrast to prior work such as [3] which seeks to build an optimal set of fields on which to block records, the philosophy of the dynamic blocking family of algorithms [19] is to avoid selecting a rigid set of fields and instead dynamically pick particular *values* or combinations of values on which to block. As an example of blocking on a fixed, static set of blocking key fields, consider a system to deduplicate U.S. person records by simply proposing all pairs of persons who match on the field *last_name*. This would be prohibitively expensive due to the necessity of executing a pairwise matching algorithm on each of the $\binom{1,400,000}{2}$ pairs of people who share the surname "Jones". A pairwise scoring model averaging 50 μs would take ≈ 567 days to compare all "Jones" pairs.

On the other hand, suppose that we statically select the pair of fields *(first_name, last_name)* as a single blocking key. This solves the problem of too many "Jones" records to compare, but is an unfortunate choice for someone with the name "Laurence Fishburne" or "Shehzad Qureshi". Both of these surnames are rare in the U.S. A static blocking strategy which required both given name and surname to match would risk missing the pair ("laurence fishburne", "larry fishburne") or ("shehzad qureshi", "shezad qureshi"). Differentiating between common and less common field/value pairs in the blocking stage fits with the intuition that it is more likely that two records with the surname "Fishburne" or "Qureshi" represent the same real-world individual than is the case for two records with the surname "Jones", which is an intuition backed up by algorithms that weight matches on rare values more strongly than matches on common values [6,17,28].

This work makes the following contributions: (1) We describe a new algorithm called Hashed Dynamic Blocking (HDB) based on the same underlying principle as dynamic blocking [19], but achieves massive scale by minimizing data movement, using compact block representation, and greedily pruning ineffective candidate blocks. We provide benchmarks that show the advantages of this approach to blocking over competing approaches on huge real-world databases. (2) Our experimental evidence emphasizes very large real-world datasets in the range of 1M to 530M records. We highlight the computational complexity challenges that come with working at this scale and we demonstrate that some widely cited algorithms break down completely at the high end. (3) We describe a version of Locality Sensitive Hashing applied to *blocking* that is easily tunable for increased precision or increased recall. Our application of LSH can generate (possibly overlapping) blocking keys for multiple columns simultaneously, and

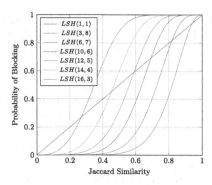

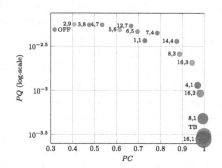

(a) Probability of blocking vs Jaccard of the record pair's attribute under various $LSH(b, w)$ settings

(b) PQ vs PC on SCHOLAR under various LSH(b, w) settings. The diameter of the point relates to the number of pairs produced.

Fig. 1. PQ and PC of various LSH settings on the SCHOLAR dataset

we provide empirical evaluation of LSH versus Token Blocking to highlight the trade-offs and scaling properties of both approaches.

2   LSH and Block Building

Like most other blocking approaches such as Meta-blocking [21], dynamic blocking begins with a set of records and a *block building* step that computes a set of *top-level* blocks, which is a set of records that share a value computed by a block blocking process, t, where t is a function that returns a set of one or more *blocking keys* when applied to an attribute a_k of a single record, r. The core HDB algorithm described in Sect. 3 is agnostic to the approach to block building.

With structured records, one can use domain knowledge or algorithms to pick which block building process to apply to each attribute. We term *Identity Block Building* as the process of simply hashing the normalized (*e.g.* lower-casing, etc.) attribute value concatenated to the attribute id to produce a blocking key. Thus the string "foo" in two different attributes returns two different top-level blocking keys (*i.e.* hash values). For attributes where we wish to allow fuzzier matches to still block together, we propose *LSH Block Building* as described in the next section. Alternatively, *Token Blocking* [21] is a schema-agnostic block building process where every token for every attribute becomes a top-level blocking key. Note that, unlike Identity Blocking Building, the token "foo" in two different attributes will return just a single blocking key.

2.1   LSH Block Building

In this work we propose a new block building approach which incorporates Locality Sensitive Hashing (LSH) [13,15] with configurable parameters to control the precision, recall trade-off per column. LSH block building creates multiple sets of keys that are designed to group similar attribute values into the same block. We leverage a version of the algorithm which looks for documents with high degrees of Jaccard similarity [18,27] of tokens. Here a *token* could be defined as a *word*, a word n-gram, or as a character q-gram.

[18] describes a method in which, for each document d, we first apply a min-hash algorithm [5] to yield m minhashes and we then group these minhashes into b *bands* where each band consists of $w = m/b$ minhashes. In our approach each of these bands constitutes a blocking key. Now consider a function $LSH(b, w, j)$, in which b and w are the LSH parameters mentioned above and j is the Jaccard similarity of a pair of records, then $LSH(b, w, j)$ is the probability that the attributes of two records with Jaccard similarity of j will share at least one key and can be computed as: $LSH(b, w, j) = 1 - (1 - j^w)^b$ $LSH(b, w, \cdot)$ has an attractive property in that the probability of sharing a key is very low for low Jaccard similarity and very high for high Jaccard similarity. Figure 1 graphs $LSH(b, w, \cdot)$ for various values of (b, w), which gives us a range of attractive trade-offs on the Pair-Quality (*i.e.* precision) versus Pair-Completeness (*i.e.* recall) curve by varying the two parameters for LSH, b and w.

2.2 Prior Work on Block Building

Our block building techniques are strongly distinguished from prior work in the field. For example, [9] makes an assumption that the block-building phase yields a strict partitioning of the database, although multiple distinct passes can be used to reduce false negatives [9,12]. Our approach, by contrast leverages the fact that the block building strategies discussed in Sect. 2 yield blocks that are, by design, highly overlapping and all the blocks are processed in a single pass. Another distinction is that [9] generates a single minHash on a single attribute from which it builds blocks, which in terms of our approach would correspond to using a degenerate LSH with the parameters of $b = 1, w = 1$ on only a single column. Figure 1 includes this $LSH(1, 1)$ configuration, which highlights its particular point in the precision, recall curve for the SCHOLAR dataset. In this case, our $LSH(14, 4)$ improves recall by $\approx 20\%$ with only $\approx 1\%$ change in precision.

Use of LSH is fairly common in the literature. [23] has an extensive recent survey. [18] has a useful tutorial on LSH that uses deduplication as an example. However, our approach is new in that we do not apply LSH to the record as a whole, but rather LSH is applied selectively to columns where it makes sense (*e.g.* columns consisting of multi-token text), while columns consisting of scalar values generate top-level blocks through trivial identity block building.

Using the nomenclature of a recent survey on blocking [23], our block building strategy yields top-level blocks which are neither *redundancy-free*, where every entity is assigned to exactly one block, nor is it *redundancy-positive*, in which every entity is assigned to multiple blocks, such that the "more blocks two entities share, the more similar their profiles are likely to be". The latter is due to the fact that by construction LSH bands act as redundant blocking keys that do connote some similarity (*e.g.* higher jaccard) but less similarity than co-occurring non-LSH keys.

Algorithm 1. Hashed Dynamic Blocking

Input: R, a dataset of records, r, to be blocked, with each record having a long identifier, rid

Output: a *blocked* dataset of deduplicated record pairs

1: **function** HASHEDDYNAMICBLOCKING(R)
2:     $K \leftarrow$ BLOCKONKEYS(R)
3:     $(K_R, \tilde{K}_O) \leftarrow$ ROUGHOVERSIZEDETECTION(K)
4:     $(\hat{K}_R, K_O) \leftarrow$ EXACTLYCOUNTANDDEDUPE($\tilde{K}_O$)
5:     $K_R \leftarrow K_R \cup \hat{K}_R$
6:     **while** $K_O \neq \emptyset$ **do**
7:         $K' \leftarrow$ INTERSECTKEYS(K_O)
8:         $(K'_R, \tilde{K}'_O) \leftarrow$ ROUGHOVERSIZEDETECTION(K')
9:         $(\hat{K}'_R, K'_O) \leftarrow$ EXACTLYCOUNTANDDEDUPE($\tilde{K}'_O$)
10:        $K_R \leftarrow K_R \cup \hat{K}'_R$
11:        $K_O \leftarrow K'_O$
12:     **end while**
13:     **return** REMOVEDUPEPAIRS(K_R)
14: **end function**

---

3 Hashed Dynamic Blocking

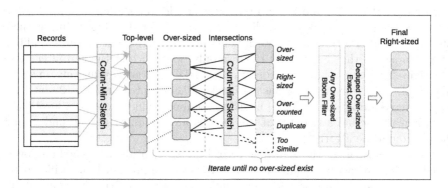

Fig. 2. Diagram illustrating how candidate blocks are processed in Hashed Dynamic Blocking

Dynamic blocking [19] takes the approach of *finding* overlapping subsets of records that share enough blocking key values in common to make the size of each subset small. We impose this subset size threshold as a way to balance the precision and recall of each emitted subset of records. At each iteration of the algorithm, we partition the blocking keys between those which are above and below this threshold: MAX_BLOCK_SIZE. Those below the max block size are deemed to be *accepted* or right-sized. For all accepted blocks b_i, the blocking phase is over. That is, later in the pairwise matching phase, we will compare all $\binom{|b_i|}{2}$ pairs of records from all right-sized blocks. However, for over-size blocks, we need to find additional co-occurring blocking key values. To do this we compute the logical intersections of all pairs of over-size blocks. For example, if the "Jones" block described in Sect. 1 had more than MAX_BLOCK_SIZE records, it could be intersected with other blocks generated by values that also had more than MAX_BLOCK_SIZE records such as the block for the first_name "Tim". The logical intersection of these two blocks may be under the threshold. We progressively intersect blocking key *values* in this way until we have no over-size blocks left. As described below, we use a few heuristics to guide this search for right-sized intersections to make this converge efficiently.

3.1   Algorithm Detailed Description

Algorithm 1 describes the high level algorithm of Hashed Dynamic Blocking (HDB). HDB is implemented in Apache Spark[1]. For clarity we show the pseudocode in an imperative style, but in the implementation everything is implemented as a sequence of lazy map and reduce operations. In particular, we use the keyword **parallel for** to indicate which loops are actually map operations (as in the MapReduce paradigm).

In HASHEDDYNAMICBLOCKING, first, the function BLOCKONKEYS applies the configured block building functions to the input dataset, R, as described in Sect. 2. The resulting dataset, K, is an inverted index of blocking keys for each record ID. It is important to note that we do *not* maintain or materialize the *flipped* view of block key to list of record IDs in that block during these iterations. Materializing this view is relatively expensive as it requires shuffling the data across the cluster, and thus we only do it once at the end after all of the right-sized blocks have been determined. HDB operates exclusively on 64-bit record IDs and a sequence of hashed blocking keys represented by 128-bit hash values derived from the top-level blocking attribute values. After top-level block building, the actual attributes of the records are no longer needed and do not flow through the algorithm.

Figure 2 visualizes the logical steps of how we identify right-sized and oversized blocks. In each iteration, we lazily intersect the previously identified oversize blocking keys. We use fast approximate counting in ROUGHOVERSIZEDETECTION (Algorithm 3) to quickly identify which of these are right-sized blocks, K_R, and possibly over-sized blocks, $\tilde{K}_O$.

---

[1] https://spark.apache.org/.

Algorithm 2. Intersecting Blocking Keys

Input: K, a dataset of rid to blocks, $b_{0..n}$, where b_i is a 2-tuple of the block key hash, $b.key_i$, and the count of records in this block $b.size_i$

Output: R, a dataset of rid to intersected blocks, $b_{0..n}$, where b_i is a 2-tuple of the block key hash, $b.key_i$, and the count of records in the *parent* block $b.psize_i$

1: **function** INTERSECTKEYS(K)
2:    $K \leftarrow \{(rid, b_{0..n}) \mid (rid, b_{0..n}) \in K \wedge n \leq \texttt{MAX\_KEYS}\}$
3:    $R \leftarrow \emptyset$
4:    **parallel for** $(rid, b_{0..n}) \in K$ **do**
    ▷ intersect all block keys, producing $\binom{n}{2}$ new block keys
5:       $P \leftarrow \{b_i, b_j \mid b_i \in b, b_j \in b \wedge b_i < b_j\}$
6:       **parallel for** $(b_i, b_j) \in P$ **do**
7:          $x.key \leftarrow$ MURMUR3($b.key_i, b.key_j$)
    ▷ the new block's size is unknown at this point, but we carry the smallest parent's size
8:          $x.psize \leftarrow min(b.size_i, b.size_j)$
9:          $R[rid] += x$
10:       **end for**
11:    **end for**
12:    **return** R
13: **end function**

Our probabilistic counting data structure *might* over-count, and therefore some of the identified blocks in $\tilde{K}_O$ may in fact be right-sized. The function EXACTLYCOUNTANDDEDUPE (Algorithm 4) post-processes $\tilde{K}_O$ to accurately identify any over-counted right-sized blocks, $\hat{K}_R$. This function also de-duplicates the over-sized blocks efficiently, resulting in the final true, unique set of over-sized blocks left over, K_O, for the next iteration. After all iterations, the set of resultant right-sized blocks may have some duplicate pairs. Thus in function REMOVEDUPEPAIRS, we remove duplicate pairs as described in Sect. 3.1.

Intersecting Keys Algorithm 2 shows how we compute what is semantically a pair-wise intersection of every over-sized block by local operations. The inverted index of blocking keys, K, accepted by INTERSECTKEYS, is logically a map of record ID rid to the set of over-sized blocking keys $b_{0..n}$ for that record. The blocking keys here are represented as a 2-tuple of $(b.key_i, b.size_i)$, where $b.key_i$ is the blocking key hash value and $b.size_i$ is the number of records that share the blocking key $b.key_i$ (as computed by EXACTLYCOUNTANDDEDUPE).

We discard from further processing all records which have more than MAX_KEYS blocking keys (line 2.2) as a guard against a quadratic explosion of keys. The governing hypothesis of dynamic blocking is that, since all blocking keys cover a distinct set of record IDs, this quadratic increase in the number of keys will be counterbalanced by the fact that $|A \cap B| < |A| + |B|$ and thus the intersected blocks will tend to become right-sized. Furthermore, records which have a large number of keys on iteration i are likely to have participated in many right-sized blocks on iterations prior to i.

Algorithm 3. Rough Over-sized Block Detection

Input: K, a dataset of rid to over-sized blocks, $b_{0..n}$ where b_i is a 2-tuple of the block
    key hash, $b.key_i$, and the count of records in the parent block, $b.psize_i$
Output: K_R, a dataset of record to right-sized blocks
Output: $\tilde{K}_O$, a map of record to *possibly* over-sized blocks
 1: **function** ROUGHOVERSIZEDETECTION(K)
 2:    $cms \leftarrow$ APPROXCOUNTBLOCKINGKEYS(K)
 3:    $K_R \leftarrow \emptyset$
 4:    $\tilde{K}_O \leftarrow \emptyset$
 5:    **parallel for** $(rid, b_{0..n}) \in K$ **do**
 6:        **for all** $b_i \in b$ **do**
 7:            $s \leftarrow cms[b.key_i]$
 8:            $p \leftarrow b.psize_i$
 9:            **if** $s \leq$ MAX_BLOCK_SIZE **then**
10:                $K_R[rid] += b_i$ ▷ right-sized
11:            **else if** $(s/p) \leq$ MAX_SIMILARITY **then**
12:                $\tilde{K}_O[rid] += b_i$ ▷ over-sized
13:            **end if**
        ▷ We discard over-sized blocks that are too similar in size to parent
14:        **end for**
15:    **end for**
16:    **return** $K_R, \tilde{K}_O$
17: **end function**

On lines 2.5 to 2.9, we replace the existing, over-sized block keys with $\binom{n}{2}$ new hashes computed by combining every pair of existing over-sized hashes for that record. There are some blocking key intersections which we do *not* want to produce. For example, if a dataset had 4 nearly identical over-sized blocks, then after the first intersection these 4 columns would intersect with each other to produce $\binom{4}{2} = 6$ columns, but since these were already over-sized and nearly identical, the intersected columns would be over-sized as well. This quadratic growth of over-sized blocking keys per record would not converge. To avoid this hazard, we apply a *progress heuristic* and only keep blocking key intersections that reduce the size of the resulting blocks by some fraction, MAX_SIMILARITY. This heuristic filter is applied in Algorithm 3, using the minimum *parent* block size which we propagate on line 2.8.

Rough Over-Sized Block Detection. It is critical that we can accurately count the size of each block. A naïve approach would be to pivot from our inverted index to a view of records per blocking key, at which point counting block sizes is trivial. This requires expensive global *shuffling* of all of the data across the cluster in each iteration of the blocking algorithm. Our approach makes novel use of a Count-Min Sketch (CMS) [10] data structure to compute an approximate count of the cardinality of every candidate blocking key (line 3.2). We compute one CMS per data partition and then efficiently merge them together. Due to the semantics of a CMS, the approximate count

---

Algorithm 4. Correct over-counting and deduplicate blocks

Input: $\tilde{K}_O$, a dataset of rid to $b_{0..n}$ where b_i are block key hashes for r

Output: $\hat{K}_R$, a dataset of record to right-sized blocks that were erroneously over-counted by the Count-min Sketch

Output: K_O, a dataset of truly over-sized blocks, rid to $b_{0..n}$ where b_i is a 2-tuple of the block key hash, $b.key_i$, and the count of records in this block, $b.size_i$

```
 1: function EXACTLYCOUNTANDDEDUPE(K̃_O)
 2:     K̂_R ← ∅
 3:     K_O ← ∅
 4:     H ← COUNTKEYSANDXORIDS(K̃_O)
        ▷ H is dataset of block key hash to tuple of (XOR, size)
 5:     H_O ← {h | h ∈ H ∧ h.size > MAX_BLOCK_SIZE}
 6:     H_U ← DROPDUPLICATES(H_O)                              ▷ based on XOR
        ▷ counts is a broadcasted map of deduped, true over-sized counts
 7:     counts ← BROADCASTCOUNTS(H_U)
 8:     bloom ← BUILDBLOOMFILTER(H_O)
 9:     parallel for (rid, b_{0..n}) ∈ K̃_O do
10:         for all b_i ∈ b do
11:             if b.key_i ∉ bloom then
12:                 K̂_R[rid] += b_i                           ▷ over-counted
13:             else if b.key_i ∈ counts then
14:                 x.key ← b.key_i
15:                 x.size ← counts[b.key_i]
16:                 K_O[rid] += x                             ▷ over-sized
17:             end if
            ▷ keys in bloom but not in counts were duplicate over-sized blocks, which we discard
18:         end for
19:     end for
20:     return K̂_R, K_O
21: end function
```

---

will never be *less* than the true count, and thus no truly over-sized blocks can be erroneously reported as right-sized. In this way, the CMS acts as a filter, dramatically reducing the number of candidate blocks that we need to focus on in each iteration.

Exactly Count and Deduplicate. Algorithm 4 focuses on correcting the possibly over-sized blocks. The goal of this method is to partition the $\tilde{K}_O$ blocking keys in the inverted index into three sets, illustrated in Fig. 2: (1) **right-sized blocks** that were erroneously over-counted by the Count-Min Sketch, $\hat{K}_R$, which we subsequently union into this iteration's right-sized blocks (line 1.10); (2) **duplicate** over-sized blocks, which we discard; (3) **surviving, deduplicated** over-sized blocks, K_O, with precise counts of how many records are in each, which are then further intersected in the next iteration.

Block A duplicates block B if block A's record IDs are equal to block B's. We arbitrarily discard duplicate blocks, leaving only a single surviving block from the group of duplicates, in order to avoid wasting resources on identical blocks that would only continue to intersect with each other, but produce no new pair-wise comparisons. We do this exact count and dedup in parallel in one map-reduce style operation. To *deduplicate* the blocks we build a *block membership* hash key by hashing each record ID in the candidate block and bit-wise XORing them together. Since XOR is commutative, the final block membership hash key is then formed (reduced) by XORing the partial membership hash keys.

On line 4.6, we discard duplicate copies of blocking keys that have the same block membership hash key. From these deduplicated blocking keys, H_U, we create a string multiset, *counts*, to precisely count the over-sized blocking keys. Even in our largest dataset of over 1 billion records, the largest count of oversized blocks in a particular iteration after deduplication is $\approx$2.6M which easily fits into memory, but if this memory pressure became a scaling concern in the future, we could use another Count-Min Sketch here.

Lastly, we need to distinguish the erroneously over-counted blocks which are actually right-sized, $\hat{K}_R$, from the surviving, deduplicated blocks, H_U. On line 4.8 we build a Bloom filter [4] over *all* of the over-sized blocking keys, H_O, which contains both duplicate and surviving over-sized blocks as determined by precise counting. Therefore, the Bloom filter answers the set membership question: is this blocking key possibly over-sized? In this way, we use this filter as a mechanism to detect right-sized blocks that were erroneously over counted. We build the Bloom filter using a large enough bit array to ensure a low expected false positive rate of 1e−8. Even in our largest dataset, the biggest Bloom filter that we have needed is less than $\approx$100 MB.

Pair Deduplication. The final set of right-sized blocks determined after k iterations of Hashed Dynamic Blocking will likely contain blocks that overlap or are entirely subsumed by other blocks. We use a map-reduce sequence to compute all distinct pairs similar to the pair deduplication algorithm presented in [19], retaining only the pair from the *largest* block in the case of duplicates. This results in tuples $(rid_1, rid_2, b.key_i)$ where $b.key_i$ is the identifier for the *largest* block that produced the pair (rid_1, rid_2). We then group the tuples by $b.key_i$ to reconstruct the blocks. For each block, we now have an edgelist of $[1, \binom{n}{2}]$ pairs and have the complete set of n resulting record IDs. We build a bitmap of $\binom{n}{2}$ bits with each representing one pair for pairwise matching. The bit index $b_{i,j}$ for a pair of record IDs rec_a, rec_b is computed by: $b_{i,j} = i * (n-1) - (i-1) * i/2 + j - i - 1$, where i, j are the zero-based *indexes* of rec_a, rec_b in the block of n records, ordered by the record IDs natural order and $i < j$. This is simply a sequential encoding of the strictly upper triangular matrix describing all $\binom{n}{2}$ pairs in the block. In the common case where none of the $\binom{n}{2}$ pairs are filtered out, we omit the bitmap and just score all pairs from the block during pairwise matching.

4   Prior Work

4.1   Prior Work on Dynamic Blocking

The need for Hashed Dynamic Blocking may be unclear since its semantics (the pairs produced after pair deduplication) are essentially the same as that of [19] for scalar-valued attributes. Relative to [19], this work offers the following advantages: (1) [19] had a substantial memory and I/O footprint since the content of the records being blocked had to be carried through each iteration of the algorithm. (2) LSH would have been challenging to implement in the Dynamic Blocking algorithm of [19] as it did not contemplate blocking on array-valued columns.

4.2   Meta-Blocking Based Approaches

Meta-Blocking [21], like dynamic blocking, starts from an input collection of blocks and is independent of the scheme for generating these blocks. It encompasses a broad variety of techniques, but at its most basic, it builds a graph in which a node corresponds to a record and an edge (e_1, e_2) indicates that at least one block contains both e_1 and e_2.

A shortcoming of the Meta-Blocking family of algorithms is that it is linear in the number of comparisons in the input block collection [11], which would be equivalent to the total number of comparisons implied by all blocks (both *oversized* and *right-sized*) in the input block collection. Meta-Blocking approaches generally mitigate this linearity by purging the very largest blocks [11] and by Block Filtering [22] which, for each entity, trims the entity from the largest blocks in which it participates. However, [11] reports only an "at least 50%" reduction in the number of pairwise comparisons using Block Filtering, leaving the algorithm still linear in the comparisons of the input block collection.

Our approach, by contrast, aims to leverage rather than trim large blocks by intersecting them with other large blocks. This is better than either discarding or trimming the large blocks, which may sacrifice recall, or attempting to do even a minimal amount of pairwise processing on the large blocks, which would impact performance.

BLAST [26] is a schema-aware meta-blocking approach. One innovation of BLAST is making records that share high entropy attributes like *name* more likely to be pairwise-compared than low entropy attributes like *year of birth*. HDB, as noted above, takes this approach one step further by making rare values (*e.g.* surname *Fishburne*) more likely to create pairs than common values (*e.g.* surname *Jones*).

Table 1. Datasets used for experiments where BB indicates (L)SH or (T)oken block building strategy and positive labels marked with † are complete ground truth. Datasets marked C are Commercial datasets.

Moniker	Records	+Labels	Cols	BB	Src
VAR1M	1.03M	818	60	L	C
VAR10M	10.36M	8,890	60	L	C
VAR25M	25.09M	20,797	60	L	C
VAR50M	50.02M	40,448	60	L	C
VAR107M	107.58M	80,068	60	L	C
VAR530M	530.73M	76,316	60	L	C

Moniker	Records	+Labels	Cols	BB	Src
VOTER	4.50M	53,653†	108	L	[1]
SCHOLAR	64,263	7,852†	5	L	[16]
CITESR	4.33M	558k†	7	L	[26]
DBPEDIA	3.33M	891k†	—	T	[11]
FREEB	7.11M	1.31M†	—	T	[11]

5 Experimental Results

We present experimental results to explore a few different aspects of Hashed Dynamic Blocking: (1) we present metrics illustrating the overall performance of HDB on a diverse collection of datasets compared to two different baselines: (a) Threshold Blocking (THR) and (b) Parallel Meta-blocking[2] (PMB) [11]. Threshold Blocking refers to blocking based on field values (as in HDB and PMB), but if a block is too large (records >500) then the block is discarded entirely. This simple baseline is useful in illustrating the value of *dynamic* blocking as a means to discover co-occurring values that are discriminating enough to warrant all pairs comparison. (2) we demonstrate the impact of using LSH-based block building with varying parameter values of b bands and w minhashes per band. Unless mentioned otherwise, we use hyper-parameters `MAX_BLOCK_SIZE = 500`, `MAX_KEYS = 80`, and `MAX_SIMILARITY = 0.9`.

We run all of our experiments using AWS ElasticMapReduce (EMR) using Spark 2.4.3 and 100 m4.4xlarge core nodes with 20 GB of executor memory and 16 cores per executor. At the time of writing m4.4xlarge instances on AWS cost $1.04/h (on EMR). Our largest dataset of 530M records 169 min to complete blocking costing ≈$307.

5.1 Datasets

In order to evaluate the effectiveness of Hashed Dynamic Blocking, we evaluate against a diverse collection of datasets. Table 1 lists summary information for each dataset used for evaluation. The **VARxx** datasets are product variations datasets that come from a subset of a large product catalog from a large E-commerce retailer. Each **VARxx** record contains sparsely populated fields such as product name, description, manufacturer, and keywords. We include the bibliographic citation dataset *DBLP-Scholar*, called **SCHOLAR**, from [16] as it is small enough to practically illustrate the differences between LSH-based block building with many different configurations. We include the DBLP-Citeseer bibliographic citation dataset, **CITESR**, from [26]. We also include two token blocking-based datasets, **DBPEDIA** and **FREEB** (Freebase), published in [11].

---

[2] https://github.com/vefthym/ParallelMetablocking.

For these two datasets, instead of using our LSH-based block building method, we use the exact token-blocking input published by the authors in [11].

Finally, we introduce a large, labeled, public-domain dataset: the Ohio Voter dataset, called **VOTER**. We built this by downloading two snapshots of Ohio registrations [1] from different points in time and treating as duplicates records with the same voter ID but different demographic information. Similar work was done previously on North Carolina voter registration data [8], but the Ohio dataset is richer in that it contains 108 columns, including birthday and voter registration.

5.2 Metrics

We present a few different metrics in order to evaluate performance. We use the established PQ, Pair Quality, (analogous to precision) and PC, Pair Completeness, (analogous to recall) metrics [7]. Every dataset described in Table 1 has labeled pair-wise training data. We report the number of positively labeled pairs as $+Labels$. However, as is a common problem in record linkage evaluation, the number of labeled training pairs is usually incomplete and significantly smaller than the possible pairs in the input record set. For these incompletely labeled datasets, we present PC with respect to the labeled pairs, defined as: $|P \cap L^+|/|L^+|$, where P is the set of pairs produced by the blocker and L^+ is the set of positively labeled pairs in the training data.

To measure PQ for datasets without complete ground truth, we follow a similar practice as described in [19] where we employ an *Oracle* pair-wise model previously trained on the complete labeled dataset. We use the same oracle per dataset for all experiments and thus the numbers are relatively comparable, despite containing some error introduced by the imperfect Oracle.

5.3 Comparing Hashed Dynamic Blocking to Other Methods

Table 2 shows the performance of Hashed Dynamic Blocking (HDB). Threshold Blocking is a simple strategy, but comparing the results to HDB shows that

Table 2. Comparing Hash Dynamic Blocking (HDB) to other methods based on Pair Quality (PQ), Pair Completeness (PC), and Elapsed Time (T) in minutes

Dataset	Threshold (THR)			Parallel Meta (PMB)			Hash Dynamic (HDB)		
	PQ	PC	T	PQ	PC	T	PQ	PC	T
VAR1	**0.3003**	**0.9450**	2.6	0.1825	0.5428	13.9	0.2612	**0.9450**	4.9
VAR10	**0.3336**	0.9444	4.8	0.1174	0.7773	16.3	0.3083	**0.9445**	10.6
VAR25	**0.3445**	0.9251	7.8	0.1213	0.7620	23.8	0.2739	**0.9315**	20.7
VAR50	**0.3355**	0.9240	13.9				0.2394	**0.9343**	30.5
VAR107	**0.3227**	0.9102	23.8				0.2168	**0.9277**	54.6
VAR530	0.4787	0.8341	110.3				**0.4834**	0.8588	169.2
VOTER	**6.96e-4**	1.0000	2.6	2.74e-4	0.9986	24.2	5.19e-4	1.0000	5.4
SCHOLAR	**5.52e-3**	0.4749	0.8	1.71e-3	0.3583	10.5	5.52e-3	0.4749	1.2
CITESR	**1.32e-2**	0.9544	2.2	5.02e-4	0.4808	15.5	5.58e-3	**0.9545**	3.6
DBPEDIA	**7.99e-4**	0.9376	3.6	2.60e-4	0.9742	14.5	2.38e-4	**0.9921**	22.1
FREEB	**2.37e-4**	0.7340	6.8	1.50e-4	0.8303	23.8	1.47e-4	**0.8497**	25.9

in all large datasets, recall is hurt when we simply discard over-sized blocks. Table 3 shows the number of pairs produced in each of our experiment setups. Since PMB and HDB have different hyper-parameters that affect the operating point, we configured both through trial and error to produce a similar number of pairs to relatively evaluate PC and PQ at the same operating point. *Naive* here represents the number of pairs produced by simple blocking on the blocking key values; that is comparing all pairs of records that share any blocking key value and not discarding any blocks due to size (as we do in THR). The VAR530 dataset with Naive blocking produces 120 quadrillion pairs, which on our cluster would take over 7,200 years to score, highlighting the need for more sophisticated blocking approaches at massive scale.

We have not been able to successfully execute PMB on some of the larger sets (VAR50, VAR107, VAR530); it fails with out-of-memory errors and we have been unable to get it to complete. We ran into similar issues when running BLAST [26] on our huge datasets, which we expected given that they broadcast hash maps of record ID $\rightarrow$ blocking keys to every node. For our large datasets, this single broadcast map would be multiple TBs of memory.

We note that HDB demonstrates improved recall over PMB despite PMB producing more pairs to evaluate. We believe this may be a consequence of the heuristic of meta-blocking weighting pairs that occur in multiple blocks. In the case of LSH-based blocking keys where there are many highly overlapping blocks, this may result in PMB picking many redundant pairs that don't improve compression. HDB by contrast, prefers to focus on the blocks that are small enough to thoroughly evaluate and find intersections of over-sized blocks. This may produce more diversity in the pairs emitted by HDB compared to PMB.

Table 3. Comparing the number of pairs produced by different blocking algorithms

Dataset	Naive $\|B\|$	THR $\|B\|$	PMB $\|B\|$	HDB $\|B\|$
VAR1	4.5e11	1.1e8	1.8e8	1.6e8
VAR10	4.4e13	1.1e9	1.7e9	1.4e9
VAR25	2.6e14	3.2e9	5.4e9	5.3e9
VAR50	1.1e15	6.4e9		1.3e10
VAR107	5.2e15	1.4e10		3.0e10
VAR530	1.2e17	4.5e10		6.8e10

Dataset	Naive $\|B\|$	THR $\|B\|$	PMB $\|B\|$	HDB $\|B\|$
VOTER	3.5e11	9.3e8	2.3e9	1.3e9
SCHOLAR	2.4e7	2.0e6	4.7e6	2.0e6
CITESR	2.3e11	4.5e7	6.2e8	1.1e8
DBPEDIA	8.0e10	1.0e9	3.2e9	3.7e9
FREEB	2.2e11	4.1e9	7.0e9	7.6e9

5.4   Comparing LSH Configurations

To illustrate the impact of including Locality Sensitive Hashing (LSH) with HDB we present numbers showing how PQ and PC are affected by various LSH configurations. Figure 3 shows the results with varying the number of *bands* b between 3 and 16 and varying the number of minhashes per band w from 8 to 3. As expected, LSH improves recall for datasets that have multi-token text fields, which is most of the datasets evaluated. In some instances, adding LSH dramatically improves recall. As expected, for most datasets the precision decreases as LSH becomes more liberal. Figure 1 shows a scatter plot of many different LSH configurations on the SCHOLAR dataset and includes the Token Blocking ($HDBTB = 0.5$) result for comparison to highlight the differences in PQ and PC. The diameter of each data point in the scatter plot is a linear scaling of the number of pairs produced.

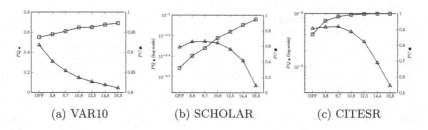

(a) VAR10   (b) SCHOLAR   (c) CITESR

Fig. 3. PQ and PC of various LSH(b, w) settings on three datasets with text fields

6   Conclusions

We have shown Hashed Dynamic Blocking being applied to different large datasets up to 530M records. We also introduced the LSH-based block building technique, and illustrated its usefulness in blocking huge datasets. The Hashed Dynamic Blocking algorithm leverages a fortunate convergence in the requirements for efficiency and accuracy. HDB accomplishes this through a new algorithm which iteratively intersects and counts sets of record IDs using an inverted index and approximate counting and membership data structures. This efficient implementation is fast, robust, cross-domain, and schema-independent, thus making it an attractive option for blocking large complex databases.

References

1. Ohio voter registration and election history statewide data. https://www6.ohiosos. gov/ords/f?p=VOTERFTP:STWD:::#stwdVtrFiles. Accessed 21 Dec 2019 and 08 Feb 2020. These two snapshots are available for research purposes from the authors
2. Ash, S.M., Ip-Lin, K.: Embracing the sparse, noisy, and interrelated aspects of patient demographics for use in clinical medical record linkage. In: AMIA Summits on Translational Science Proceedings, p. 425. AMIA (2015)
3. Bilenko, M., Kamath, B., Mooney, R.J.: Adaptive blocking: learning to scale up record linkage. In: IEEE International Conference on Data Mining, ICDM, pp. 87–96 (2006)
4. Bloom, B.H.: Space/time trade-offs in hash coding with allowable errors. Commun. ACM **13**(7), 422–426 (1970)

318   A. Borthwick et al.

333
33
5. Broder, A.Z., Charikar, M., Frieze, A.M., Mitzenmacher, M.: Min-wise independent permutations. J. Comput. Syst. Sci. **60**(3), 630–659 (2000)
6. Chen, S., Borthwick, A., Carvalho, V.R.: The case for cost-sensitive and easy-to-interpret models in industrial record linkage. In: 9th International Workshop on Quality in Databases (2011)
7. Christen, P.: A survey of indexing techniques for scalable record linkage and deduplication. IEEE Trans. Knowl. Data Eng. **24**(9), 1–20 (2011)
8. Christen, P.: Preparation of a real temporal voter data set for record linkage and duplicate detection research (2013). http://cs.anu.edu.au/~./Peter.Christen/publications/ncvoter-report-29june2014.pdf
9. Chu, X., Ilyas, I.F., Koutris, P.: Distributed data deduplication. Proc. VLDB Endow. **9**(11), 864–875 (2016)
10. Cormode, G., Muthukrishnan, S.: An improved data stream summary: the count-min sketch and its applications. J. Algorithms **55**(1), 58–75 (2005)
11. Efthymiou, V., Papadakis, G., Papastefanatos, G., Stefanidis, K., Palpanas, T.: Parallel meta-blocking for scaling entity resolution over big heterogeneous data. Inf. Syst. **65**, 137–157 (2017)
12. Elmagarmid, A., Ipeirotis, P., Verykios, V.: Duplicate record detection: a survey. IEEE Trans. Knowl. Data Eng. **19**(1), 1–16 (2007)
13. Gionis, A., Indyk, P., Motwani, R.: Similarity search in high dimensions via hashing. In: Proceedings of the 25th International Conference on Very Large Data Bases, pp. 518–529 (1999)
14. Hassanzadeh, O., Chiang, F., Lee, H.C., Miller, R.J.: Framework for evaluating clustering algorithms in duplicate detection. Proc. VLDB Endow. **2**, 1282–1293 (2009)
15. Indyk, P., Motwani, R.: Approximate nearest neighbors: towards removing the curse of dimensionality. In: 30th Annual ACM Symposium on Theory of Computing, pp. 604–613. ACM (1998)
16. Köpcke, H., Thor, A., Rahm, E.: Evaluation of entity resolution approaches on real-world match problems. Proc. VLDB Endow. **3**(1–2), 484–493 (2010)
17. Koudas, N., Sarawagi, S., Srivastava, D.: Record linkage: similarity measures and algorithms. In: ACM SIGMOD International Conference on Management of Data, pp. 802–803. ACM (2006)
18. Leskovec, J., Rajaraman, A., Ullman, J.D.: Finding Similar Items. In: Mining of Masive Datasets, 2nd edn., pp. 72–130 (2014)
19. McNeill, W.P., Kardes, H., Borthwick, A.: Dynamic record blocking: efficient linking of massive databases in mapreduce. In: Quality in Databases (2012)
20. Mudgal, S., et al.: Deep learning for entity matching: a design space exploration. In: 2018 International Conference on Management of Data, pp. 19–34 (2018)
21. Papadakis, G., Koutrika, G., Palpanas, T., Nejdl, W.: Meta-blocking: taking entity resolution to the next level. IEEE Trans. Knowl. Data Eng. **26**(8), 1946–1960 (2014)
22. Papadakis, G., Papastefanatos, G., Palpanas, T., Koubarakis, M.: Scaling Entity Resolution to Large. Heterogeneous Data with Enhanced Meta-blocking, EBDT (February) (2016)
23. Papadakis, G., Skoutas, D., Thanos, E., Palpanas, T.: A Survey of Blocking and Filtering Techniques for Entity Resolution. arXiv e-prints arXiv:1905.06167, May 2019
24. Papadakis, G., Svirsky, J., Gal, A., Palpanas, T.: Comparative analysis of approximate blocking techniques for entity resolution. Proc. VLDB Endow. **9**(9), 684–695 (2016)

25. Reas, R., Ash, S., Barton, R., Borthwick, A.: SuperPart: supervised graph partitioning for record linkage. In: IEEE International Conference on Data Mining (2018)
26. Simonini, G., Gagliardelli, L., Bergamaschi, S., Jagadish, H.: Scaling entity resolution: a loosely schema-aware approach. Inf. Syst. **83**, 145–165 (2019)
27. Van Dam, I., van Ginkel, G., Kuipers, W., Nijenhuis, N., Vandic, D., Frasincar, F.: Duplicate detection in web shops using LSH to reduce the number of computations. In: 31st Annual ACM Symposium on Applied Computing, pp. 772–779 (2016)
28. Wang, X., Sun, A., Kardes, H., Agrawal, S., Chen, L., Borthwick, A.: Probabilistic estimates of attribute statistics and match likelihood for people entity resolution. In: 2014 IEEE International Conference on Big Data, pp. 92–99. IEEE (2014)

Address Validation in Transportation and Logistics: A Machine Learning Based Entity Matching Approach

Yassine Guermazi[(✉)], Sana Sellami, and Omar Boucelma

Aix-Marseille University, University of Toulon, CNRS, LIS, Marseille, France
{yassine.guermazi,sana.sellami,omar.boucelma}@lis-lab.fr

Abstract. In the Transportation and Logistics (TL) industry, address validation is crucial. Indeed, due to the huge number of parcel shipments that are moving worldwide everyday, incorrect addresses generates several shipment returns, leading to useless financial and ecological costs. In this paper, we propose an entity-matching approach and system for validating TL entities. The approach is based on Word Embedding and Supervised Learning techniques. Experiments carried out on a real dataset demonstrate the effectiveness of the approach.

Keywords: Entity matching · Supervised learning · Word embedding · Transport and logistics

1 Introduction

The Transportation and Logistics (TL) industry includes different stakeholders (companies) associated with shipping, trucking and logistics, railways, etc. For the business to run correctly, the identification of these companies is essential for any activity such as, for example, the transport and/or shipment of a parcel. A company can be represented as an entity described by a data structure composed of its (legal) name and address. This identification may seem sufficient to verify the existence of customers as it can be done by the well-known KYC process (Know Your Customer), or even simpler, to ensure that a shipment arrives at (the right) destination. However, in practice, this verification can be tedious and costly, mainly because of (poor) data quality: use of acronyms or abbreviations in company names, typographical errors, or incomplete data.

In this work, we are interested in verifying the existence of TL entities through their addresses in France. In a real setting, and for a vertical domain, this verification often relies on a (possibly unique) data repository that acts as the "ground truth database". However, in France, there is no such repository for the TL domain. As a result, each TL organisation maintains its own repository. Due to a lack of resources and harmonization rules, these repositories are by nature heterogeneous and often prone to error due to data quality issues.

© Springer Nature Switzerland AG 2020
I. Koprinska et al. (Eds.): ECML PKDD 2020 Workshops, CCIS 1323, pp. 320–334, 2020.
https://doi.org/10.1007/978-3-030-65965-3_21

In order to assist the data verification process, some commercial software systems have been proposed in recent years. Examples of such systems are: *altares-IndueD*[1] or *LEI lookup*[2]. However, these systems do not necessarily validate TL entities. For example, *LEI lookup* checks the entities against the LEI database, which contains mainly financial institutions. In addition, these systems store the main (Corporate) addresses while the secondary addresses are often unknown.

The goal of the work described in this paper is to propose an entity-matching approach and system for validating TL entities. This involves, on the one hand, correcting data anomalies and, on the other hand, validating the entities by matching company names and addresses in using several data repositories such as Kompass[3], Societe[4] and Infogreffe[5]. The approach is based on Word Embedding and Supervised Learning techniques and has the following properties: (1) it exhibits a semantic similarity between two entities by means of their (heterogeneous) addresses which share the same geographical context, (2) it determines the syntactic similarity between poor quality data, and (3) it does not require a large dataset for learning.

This paper is organized as follows. In Sect. 2, we present and formalize the entity matching problem. Section 3 is devoted to the state of the art on entity matching. In Sect. 4, we describe our approach to entity matching in Transport and Logistics. Experiments carried out are described in Sect. 5. Section 6 concludes the work and presents some perspectives.

2   Entity Matching Problem

In this section, we define the problem of entity matching.

2.1   TL Entity Definition

A TL entity is described by a structure that includes the company name and address. An address is the street number, the street or road name, the city and the country, and must include rural areas like industrial area and logistics park. In order to take into account rural areas as well as points of interest (POI) of TL such as: airports, terminals and cargo-ports, we extend the model defined by UPU (Universal Postal Union)[6] representing French postal addresses. Figure 1 displays the proposed model.

---

[1] https://www.altares.com/en/your-issues/compliance/speed-up-verifications/.
[2] www.lei-lookup.com/#!aboutNewFeatures.
[3] https://fr.kompass.com/.
[4] https://www.societe.com/.
[5] https://www.infogreffe.fr/.
[6] http://www.upu.int/fileadmin/documentsFiles/activities/addressingUnit/fraFr.pdf.

InBuilding (IB)	ExtBuilding (EB)	PoiLogistic (PL)	Zone (Z)	HouseNum (HN)	RoadName (RN)	PoBox (PB)	ZipCode (ZC)	City (C)	Additional (A)

Fig. 1. Proposed address model

Table 1. Address Matching levels

Matched attributes	Levels
-	NoMatch
City	CityLevel
City + Zone	ZoneLevel
City + (Zone) + PoiLogistic	PoiLevel
City + (Zone) + (PoiLogistic) + RoadName	RoadNameLevel
City + (Zone) + (PoiLogistic) + RoadName + HouseNum	HouseNumLevel
City + (Zone) + (PoiLogistic) + (RoadName) + ExtBuilding	ExtBuildingLevel
City + (Zone) + (PoiLogistic) + (RoadName) + ExtBuilding + InBuilding	InBuildingLevel
City + Additional	AdditionalLevel

2.2 Entity Matching Definition

Entity matching aims to find all tuple pairs (t, t') that are similar, i.e. refer to the same real world entity, between two tables T and T' such as $(t \in T, t' \in T')$.

Both tables follow the same data schema $\{N, A0..A9\}$, where N represents the name of the entity and $\{A0..A9\}$ represent the different attributes of an address.

Let L = (ln, ladd) be the pair of labels of the pair of tuples (t, t') such that:

- $ln \in [$ *"Match"*, *"NoMatch"*$]$ is the label representing the matching result of the two company names of the two tuples.
- $ladd \in [$ *"NoMatch"*, *"CityLevel"*, *"ZoneLevel"*, *"PoiLevel"*, *"RoadNameLevel"*, *"HouseNumLevel"*, *"ExtBuildingLevel"*, *"InBuildingLevel"*, *"AdditionalLevel"*$]$ is the label representing the matching result of two addresses of the two tuples (Table 1).

Two entities are similar if L= (*"Match"*, *"laddM"*) such as: *"laddM"* $\in$ [*"CityLevel"*, *"ZoneLevel"*, *"PoiLevel"*, *"RoadNameLevel"*, *"HouseNumLevel"*, *"ExtBuildingLevel"*, *"InBuildingLevel"*, *"AdditionalLevel"*]. Figure 2 shows an example of entity matching.

2.3 French TL Entity Matching Issues

There are several issues to consider when it comes to TL entity matching: (1) data heterogeneity (structured vs. textual), (2) quality dimensions (incompleteness, duplication), (3) typos. Table 2 illustrates examples of data quality issues.

In our work, matching is performed against company addresses and company names. Table 3 illustrates two examples of name matching. The first example illustrates the match between a person's name and a company name. The second example illustrates a match between the company name and its corresponding

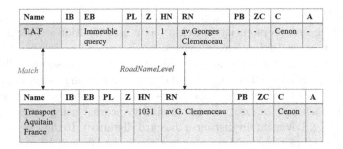

Name	IB	EB	PL	Z	HN	RN	PB	ZC	C	A
T.A.F	-	Immeuble quercy	-	-	1	av Georges Clemenceau	-	-	Cenon	-

Match   RoadNameLevel

Name	IB	EB	PL	Z	HN	RN	PB	ZC	C	A
Transport Aquitain France	-	-	-	-	1031	av G. Clemenceau	-	-	Cenon	-

Fig. 2. Example of entity matching

Table 2. TL Data Quality Examples

Entities	Data quality problems
FC LOGISTIQUE,	**Missing elements:** 93420 (zipcode)
22 Ave des nationsParis nord II,	**Non-standard abbreviations:** Ave (Avenue) and Bt (bâtiment)
parc silic Bt rotand	**Typographical errors:** nationsParis nord II (nations Paris nord II)
villepint france	**Spelling errors:** Villepint (Villepinte) and rotand (rostand)
GLM TRANSIT,	**Address update problem:**
25 rue Jules Lequier 22190 Plerin	Correct address: 31 rue Lequier 22190 Plerin

Table 3. Company Names matching

Name A	Name B	Matching result
Transport Express Caretto	Monsieur Stephane Caretto	"Match"
A.T.B sarl	Affretements et transports becker	"Match"

Table 4. Semantic address matching

Zone	RoadName	City
zac satolas green	-	Pusignan

Zone	RoadName	City
-	chemin du bois des aies	Pusignan

acronym. Table 4 shows an example of semantic matching between two addresses: *"zac satolas green Pusignan"* and *"chemin du bois des aies Pusignan"* which refer the same geographical area.

3   Related Work

We describe in this section related works on Entity Matching as well as existing works in the field of address and company names matching.

3.1   Entity Matching

We distinguish between two categories of entity matching approaches: 1) Rule-based [4,24,25] and 2) Learning-based [2,8,18,19]. The first category of approaches is based on rules fixed by experts who set the conditions for matching pairs of entities. Similarity measures (e.g. Levenshtein distance [11], Jaro-Winkler distance [27], Jaccard distance [7]) are generally used for comparing attributes. We focus on the second category of approaches based on machine learning which considers entity matching as a classification problem. Learning can be either supervised or unsupervised.

Konda et al. [8] have proposed an entity matching system, called Magellan, which covers the entire pipeline including debugging, sampling, blocking and matching. In the matching step, the system generates a vector, containing features for each pair of entities (e.g. similarity scores) using several similarity techniques (e.g. Levenshtein distance, Jaccard distance). It then performs cross-validation on all of these vectors to select the most efficient learning algorithm from those provided by Magellan (e.g. decision trees, Support vector machine). From 2016 to date, Magellan has been successfully applied to various real-world applications [5].

Unlike Magellan, Papadaki et al. [20], propose an entity matching system called Jedai, based on unsupervised learning techniques on structured and semi-structured data. The data matching phase has two sub-steps: 1) *Entity Matching* in which Jedai compares the pairs of entities, associates every pair with a similarity in [0,1] using several techniques (e.g. cosine similarity, Jaccard distance) and generates as output a similarity graph, i.e., an undirected, weighted graph where the nodes correspond to the entities and the edges connect pairs of compared entities and 2) *Entity Clustering* which takes as input the similarity graph produced by the previous step and partitions it into a set of equivalence clusters, with every cluster corresponding to a distinct real-world object using several clustering techniques (e.g Merge-Center Clustering, Correlation Clustering, Best Assignment Clustering).

The evaluation of Jedai, on four real datasets, shows that it outperforms Magellan on three datasets. In addition, Jedai is more efficient and less dependent on experts than Magellan since it does not require data labelling.

Magellan and Jedai are two examples of entity matching systems which mainly use similarity techniques between strings in combination with supervised or unsupervised learning algorithms. However, these systems are not suitable for matching unstructured datasets and do not consider the semantic matching between entities. Indeed, they fail to match entities sharing the same meaning or the same context.

Other works have proposed the use of deep learning. In [2], an Entity Resolution system, called DeepER is proposed. For each value of entity attribute, authors first break it into individual words using a standard tokenizer. Then, a Word Embedding technique Glove [21] is used to assign vectors to each token. The vector representation for an attribute value is obtained by averaging the vectors of its tokens. The similarity vectors between attributes are computed using cosine similarity. Finally, a densely connected neural network maps the vector of similarities to a binary output, 1 if there is a matching between the pair of entities, and 0 otherwise. The evaluation of the approach is carried out on 7 real datasets[7,8,9] covering different areas such as citations, e-commerce, and proteomics. These datasets are partitioned into "Easy" and "Challenging" depending on the data types and noise levels. The approach was compared with Magellan and the results have shown that it performs well on dirty datasets containing unstructured attributes.

In [18], authors apply Word Embedding technique with using fastText [28]. Several methods have been proposed for attribute embedding (e.g *Recurrent Neural Network (RNN), Attention Mechanism*).

Similarity between attributes is computed using either *Fixed distance* (e.g cosine, Euclidean) or *Learnable distance*. Finally, the classification is carried out by a deep learning algorithm: *"ReLU HighwayNet"* [26]. The approach was evaluated against Magellan on different structured, textual and dirty real datasets. Evaluations have shown that the proposed approach performs better on textual and dirty data.

There are different business tools for entity matching such as Informatica Data Quality[10], DataMatch[11] or Tamr[12]. A comparative study was carried out by [3] on 15 commercial solutions of Entity Matching. Most of these tools perform entity matching using rule-based methods.

3.2   Address and Name Matching

Most of the address and name matching works in the literature [6,10,14] rely on syntactic matching using a combination of string similarities with rules or traditional learning algorithms. In [6], authors propose a Record Linkage system for matching companies. They use a combination of Levenshtein distances [11] and Jaccard distance [7] to compute a similarity score between company names. Different weights are assigned to tokens (significant weight for the alias of the company name and a low weight for city and legal entity types). This approach has been evaluated against a distributed indexing system *ApacheSolr*[13]. The evaluation results showed that the proposed approach outperforms Apache Solr in terms of precision and recall. Some recent works [1,12,23] considered semantic matching with using Word Embedding techniques. In [1], authors generate word vectors for each address attribute using Word2vec [17], a Word Embedding method based on two-layer neural networks and seeks to learn vectorial representations of the words composing a corpus. So, words that share similar contexts are represented by similar numeric vectors[14]. Next, a comparison vector

---

[7] https://dbs.uni-leipzig.de/en/research/projects/object_matching/fever/ benchmark_datasets_for_entity_resolution.

[8] http://www.cs.utexas.edu/users/ml/riddle/data.html.

[9] https://sites.google.com/site/anhaidgroup/projects/data.

[10] https://kb.informatica.com/h2l/HowTo%20Library/1/0816-IdentifyingDuplicateRecordsinIDQ9.pdf.

[11] https://dataladder.com/products/datamatch-enterprise/.

[12] https://docs.tamr.com/new/docs/overall-workflow-mastering.

[13] https://lucene.apache.org/solr/.

[14] www.dataanalyticspost.com/Lexique/word2vec/.

for each pair of addresses is created containing similarity values between word vectors using cosine similarity. Finally, three classification methods are applied to classify the pairs in Match/NoMatch: random forest, XGBoost and logistic regression model. The matching is carried out between 2 databases: "Local Data Company (LDC)" and "Valuation Office Agency (VOA)" comprising addresses belonging to the United Kingdom. The precision and recall values obtained are 0.95 and 0.87 respectively (with the XGboost method). However, since the comparison vector of addresses is only composed of similarity values between the same type of attributes, this approach does not take into account matching data injected under the wrong attributes. In [12], an address matching approach combining Word Embedding and deep learning was proposed. The addresses are first converted into vectors using Word2vec. Then, the enhanced sequential inference model (ESIM), a deep text-matching model, is applied to these vectors to make local and global inferences in order to determine if two addresses match. The approach is tested on real addresses in the city of Shenzhen in China. The results obtained show that the proposed approach outperforms non-Deep Learning based approaches. However, this approach requires a large training dataset. In addition, no details are provided about multiclass classification of addresses.

In the industry, tools such as AddressDoctor[15], smartystreets[16] or egon[17] are proposed for the validation of urban addresses. Most of these tools do not cope with rural areas or domain specific addresses such as logistics POIs. In addition, matching techniques used in these tools are considered as a black box.

3.3   Synthesis

Our study of related work shows that: 1) Methods based on similarity techniques combined with rules or Learning techniques perform syntactic matching efficiently on a small dirty dataset, 2) Entity matching techniques based on the use of Word Embedding and deep learning techniques solve the problem of semantic matching of entities and are efficient on dirty unstructured data. However, these techniques require a large learning dataset as demonstrated in [18] and consequently a great human effort in terms of data labeling. In addition, they allow only binary classification of entities.

4   Methodology

In this section, we describe our entity-matching approach for TL entities which consists of two main processes (Fig. 3): 1) Entity standardization and 2) Matching by supervised learning on vector representations of the entities.

---

[15] https://www.informatica.com/fr/demos/data-as-a-service.html.
[16] https://smartystreets.com/products/single-address.
[17] https://www.egon.com/solutions/address-validation.

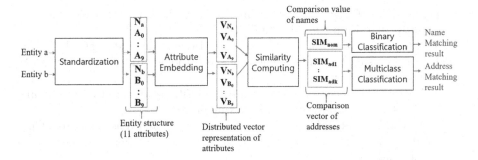

Fig. 3. Entity Matching approach

4.1 Standardization

This 2-steps process consists in transforming data into a standard format: 1) Pre-Processing and 2) Parsing.

Pre-processing. The purpose of this step is to normalize entities and to correct different spelling errors. Normalization consists in abbreviation expansion, acronyms identification (e.g. A.T.B. vs AFFRETEMENTS ET TRANSPORTS BECKER), word capitalization and deletion of punctuation marks.

Abbreviation expansion consists in recognizing shortened form of words and expanding them to their corresponding words in a Keyword-Abbreviation list that contains a set of keywords that are likely to be used to define components of address model (e.g. InBuilding, ExtBuilding, RoadName, City) and their abbreviations. To do this, we extract data from official sources like the French Post, INSEE service[18] and unofficial sources that generally have common abbreviations, like the list of abbreviations recognized by OpenStreetMap[19] query tools.

In addition, we are interested in correcting spelling errors mainly in address keywords. These words have a major role in parsing addresses. To this end, we used a spell checker *pyspellchecker*[20,21]. When it detects a misspelling in a word, pyspellchecker proposes a list of potential candidates to replace this word. Then, we performed an exact matching between each word from this list and address elements keywords.

Parsing. Parsing is performed on addresses and aims at identifying the different elements defined in the model (Fig. 1). It consists of the following steps:

- Identification of the address elements like RoadName, InBuilding, ExtBuilding, PoiLogistic, Zone and PoBox based on the Keyword-Abbreviation list. For example, an address line in the form "Rue de Quebec Zone industrielle

---

[18] https://www.sirene.fr/sirene/public/variable/typvoie.

[19] https://wiki.openstreetmap.org/wiki/Name_finder:Abbreviations.

[20] https://readthedocs.org/projects/pyspellchecker/downloads/pdf/latest/.

[21] https://norvig.com/spell-correct.html.

Chef de Baie BP 2088" is divided into address elements "**Rue** de Quebec", "**Zone industrielle** Chef de Baie","**BP** 2088".
- Identification of the address's digits like HouseNum and ZipCode in the address, by using the rules defined by the National Address Service (SNA) described as follows:
  - A street number (HouseNum) must be positioned before the street name (RoadName) and must have a maximum of 4 digits.
  - A postal code (ZipCode) must contain 5 digits and must precede a City.
- Identification of the City represented by a token or a token sequence in two different cases:
  - It is a known city name from the UN-LOCODE gazetteer[22], which contains French cities and communes with information about their subdivisions and geographical coordinates, and it can be found in the address shortly after a postal code.
  - It is an unknown city but preceded directly by a postal code candidate or followed by a country name. In this case, the validation of city name will be achieved in the address matching step.

4.2   Matching

In this step, we try to find correspondences between TL entities (company names and addresses). First, we manually assign labels to (address, company name) pairs. Second, we apply Attribute Embedding techniques to transform words into vectors. Third, we compute similarities between vectors. Finally, we apply a Supervised Learning algorithm on vectors and labels in order to classify the pairs of entities. Algorithm 1 describes the address matching process.

Attribute Embedding: The creation of vectors for company names and address attributes is performed with fastText [28], a Word Embedding method, that is a variant of Word2vec that includes sequences of characters in the embedding learning. Unlike Word2vec, fastText represents words by all of their n-grams. The representation vector of a word is the sum of the representation vectors of all its n-grams.

Computing Similarity Between Entity Representation Vectors: At the end of the attribute embedding step, each entity will be represented by several vectors (one vector per company name and per address attribute). The comparison of vectors between entities is calculated by cosine similarity, which unlike several similarity techniques, considers vectors' similarity instead of text fields and determines the semantic closeness of word vectors [1,15].

The values of the address comparison vectors have three origins:

- Values representing similarities between vectors of the same attribute type.

---

[22] https://service.unece.org/trade/locode/fr.htm.

- Values representing similarities between the "Additional" attribute and the ExtBuilding, PoiLogistic, Zone and RoadName attributes. We computed these similarity values in order to take into account address elements which are defined as wrong attributes at the end of the address parsing step.
- Values representing the similarities between all possible combinations of pairs including the attributes ExtBuilding, PoiLogistic, Zone, RoadName (except the combination of pairs of vectors that belong to the same attribute which have already been taken into account). We compute these values to exhibit semantic similarities which can occur between attributes that may have "some hidden relationship" (e.g., similarity between "RoadName" and "Zone" since the zone may include the street).

Algorithm 1. Address Matching

1: Input: two Tables T, T' (each tuple is composed of an address with K+1 attributes; $K \in \{0..9\}$), Address Database DB
2: Output: all tuple pairs with their corresponding matching class
3: // For each tuple, compute the distributed representation of all its attributes
4: Train a Word Embedding model WE using the address Database DB.
5: **for** each pair of tuple (t,t') in T x T' **do**
6:     Compute the distributed representation V_k of each attribute's value of t ($t[A_k]$) using WE model.
7:     Compute the distributed representation V'_k of each attribute's value of t' ($t'[A_k]$) using WE model.
8: **end for**
9: // Create similarity vector W for each pair of tuple using cosine similarity (cos)
10: $W := \emptyset$; $W1 := \emptyset$; $W2 := \emptyset$; $W3 := \emptyset$
11: **for** each pair of tuple (t,t') in T x T' **do**
12:     $W1 := cos(V_k, V'_k)$
13:     $W2 := cos(V_9, V'_i) \cup cos(V_i, V'_9)$; $i \in \{1,2,3,5\}$
14:     $W3 := cos(V_x, V'_y)$; $x \in \{1,2,3,5\}$ and $y \in \{1,2,3,5\}$ and $x \neq y$
15:     $W := W1 \cup W2 \cup W3$
16: **end for**
17: // Classification
18: Split T x T' into Training set S and Test set TS
19: Train a classifier C using the similarity vectors for S and true labels
20: **for** each pair of tuple (t,t') in TS **do**
21:     Predict Matching class for (t, t') using C
22: **end for**

Supervised Learning for Classifying of Entity Pairs: Once we get the comparison vector for each pair of entities, we split the dataset into a training set and a test set. Then, we carry out training phase, using the training set, on the comparison vectors as well as the labels of the address pairs and those of company names pairs based on several supervised learning methods (Sect. 5.2). Finally, the test set is used to evaluate the classification of the different learning models used.

5   Experiments and Results

5.1   Dataset

We conducted our experiments with a real dataset composed of 3712 TL entities.

In order to verify these entities, we compared our dataset with entities contained in directories such as Kompass[23]. First, we extracted data in using BeautifulSoup[24], then we assigned labels: at the end, we obtained a dataset composed of 3123 pairs.

5.2   Experimental Study and Evaluation

Metrics. We use F1-score metric to evaluate the effectiveness of the methods where: $F1 - score = 2 \times \frac{Precision \times Recall}{Precision + Recall}$.

Precision is the percentage of correctly matched pairs among all address pairs and *Recall* is the percentage of correctly matched pairs among all address pairs that should be matched.

Experimental Setup. Our approach is based on the combination of Word Embedding techniques with supervised classification algorithms. We implement two Word Embedding methods: Word2vec and fastText using Gensim [22] python library. The training set of Word2vec and fastText is the dataset composed of the pairs of initial entities augmented by a real and public French address database[25] which includes 1 million addresses. It represents the addresses of French establishments sent to the National Industrial Property Institute (INPI) as part of its missions. In the case of company names matching, the training set of fastText is the dataset composed of pairs of company names.

The classification algorithms used in our approach are: Support Vector Machine (SVM), Decision Tree (DT), Random Forest (RF), XGBoost and Multilayer Perceptron with a single hidden layer (MLP). In addition, we used Stratified k-fold Cross-Validation, where k = 10, as evaluation method of all classifiers. This method split data into 10 set of equal size. Each set contains approximately the same percentage of samples of each target class as the complete set. In total, 10 iterations are carried out: in each iteration, the classifier is trained on 9 subsamples and tested on a sub-sample. We report the average of the F-measure values obtained across all the folds.

5.3   Experimental Results

We performed several experiments in order to evaluate our approach.

---

[23] https://fr.kompass.com/.

[24] https://www.crummy.com/software/BeautifulSoup/bs4/doc/.

[25] https://public.opendatasoft.com/explore/dataset/inpi-liste-des-etablissements/table/?disjunctive.nom_greffe.

Entity Matching Results. Table 5 shows Entity Matching results. Pairs of entities labelled as "NoMatch", either in name or address matching, are entities (from our dataset) that proved invalid when compared against Kompass: the total number of such entities is 1431. As expected, verifying entities against a single directory may prove "incomplete" (54% of entities were considered as invalid). In absence of a complete TL repository, we need to query different directories.

Table 5. Entity matching results

Company Name Matching	Address Matching	Frequency
NoMatch	-	1111
Match	NoMatch	320
Match	CityLevel	527
Match	ZoneLevel	177
Match	PoiLevel	12
Match	RoadNameLevel	302
Match	HouseNumLevel	587
Match	ExtBuildingLevel	14
Match	InBuildingLevel	0
Match	AdditionalLevel	73

Comparison with Existing Methods. We compared our address matching approach with Magellan. Table 6 shows that our approach outperforms Magellan in terms of F1-score. Indeed, our approach takes into account semantic similarities between addresses while Magellan is mainly based on lexical similarity.

We also compared company names matching with Magellan. As shown in Table 7, our approach is competitive with Magellan, because existing problems (e.g., spelling errors, abbreviations and acronyms, permutation of words) in company names can be solved with syntactic matching approaches.

Table 6. Evaluation of address matching solutions

Method	F1-score
Magellan	0.907
fastText + SVM	0.942
fastText + DT	0.938
fastText + RF	0.932
fastText + XGBoost	0.938
fastText + MLP	0.94

Table 7. Evaluation of company name matching solutions

Method	F1-score
Magellan	0.917
fastText + SVM	0.925
fastText + DT	0.917
fastText + RF	0.894
fastText + XGBoost	0.915
fastText + MLP	0.917

Table 8. Comparison of different Word Embedding methods

	Word2vec	fastText
SVM	0.914	0.942
DT	0.906	0.938
RF	0.891	0.932
XGBoost	0.895	0.938
MLP	0.912	0.940

Table 9. Impact of Varying fastText's Training Data

	fastText + small training set	fastText + large training set
SVM	0.916	0.942
DT	0.920	0.938
RF	0.912	0.932
XGBoost	0.914	0.938
MLP	0.920	0.940

Comparison of Word Embedding Methods. We compared Word2vec and fastText. Table 8 shows that fastText is more efficient. This is mainly due to the fact that fastText takes into account spelling errors in the vector representation of words: forexample, fastText assigns similar vectors to the two words MARCHAL and MARECHAL when matching AVENUE MARCHAL FOCH with AVENUE MARECHAL FOCH.

Impact of the Word Embedding Training Set. We studied the impact the training set size when using fastText. Given two training sets of different sizes, a *small Training set* which contains both addresses to be checked and those retrieved from Kompass, and a *large Training set* which includes 1 million of French addresses collected by INPI. Table 9 illustrates the results of our approach in using fastText: one can see a drop in F1-score when trained on a smaller dataset. Indeed, Word Embedding methods require a large amount of data to better detect semantic relationships between words.

Varying the Size of the Supervised Training Set. Figure 4 shows the impact of varying the size of supervised training set on the effectiveness of our approach. We compared the effectiveness of our approach with 4 different sizes of the training set: 10%, 30%, 50% and 70% of the initial dataset (3123 pairs of entities). The results obtained show that even with a small training set, i.e. 10% (313 entity pairs) of the initial dataset, our approach remains effective. For all the learning algorithms used, the maximum difference in F1-score between a training set of size 70 % with that of 10 % is equal to 0.02. The robustness of our approach is mainly due to the unsupervised learning phase performed on a large volume of data (1 million addresses) to obtain vector representations of addresses.

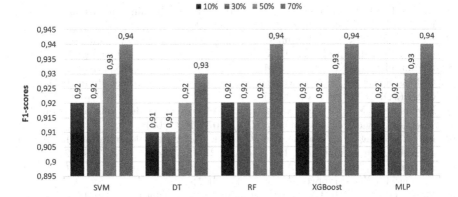

Fig. 4. Impact of varying supervised training data

6   Conclusion and Future Work

In this article, we described our approach and solution for the problem of TL entity matching. The approach is based on Word Embedding and Supervised Learning techniques. An implementation with experiments on real "French" data was carried out. The first results obtained, with F1 score greater than 0.9, are encouraging, but we have to put them into perspective given the size of the samples, and the number of data sources (TL information repositories) that are needed to reach some "completeness". In the future, we intend to extend this work in at least two directions: the management of a larger set of entities (companies), in a wider (international) setting: ultimately this may lead to a unique virtual data repository.

References

1. Comber, S., Arribas-Bel, D.: Machine learning innovations in address matching: a practical comparison of word2vec and CRFs. Trans. GIS **23**(2), 334–348 (2019)
2. Ebraheem, M., Thirumuruganathan, S., Joty, S., Ouzzani, M., Tang, N.: DeepER-Deep Entity Resolution. arXiv preprint arXiv:1710.00597 (2017)
3. Konda, P., et al. Magellan.: toward building entity matching management systems [Technical report]. http://www.cs.wisc.edu/anhai/papers/magellan-tr.pdf (2016)
4. Fan, W., Jia, X., Li, J., Ma, S.: Reasoning about record matching rules. Proc. VLDB Endowment **2**(1), 407–418 (2009)
5. Govind, Y., et al.: Entity matching meets data science: a progress report from the magellan project. In: Proceedings of the 2019 International Conference on Management of Data, pp. 389–403. June 2019
6. Gschwind, T., Miksovic, C., Minder, J., Mirylenka, K., Scotton, P.: Fast record linkage for company entities. In: 2019 IEEE International Conference on Big Data, pp. 623–630. IEEE, December 2019
7. Jaccard, P.: Nouvelles recherches sur la distribution florale. Bull. Soc. Vaud. Sci. Nat. **44**, 223–270 (1908)

8. Konda, P., et al.: Magellan: toward building entity matching management systems. Proc. VLDB Endowment **9**(12), 1197–1208 (2016)
9. Köpcke, H., Thor, A., Rahm, E.: Evaluation of entity resolution approaches on real-world match problems. Proc. VLDB Endow. **3**(1–2), 484–493 (2010)
10. Koumarelas, I., Kroschk, A., Mosley, C., Naumann, F.: Experience: enhancing address matching with geocoding and similarity measure selection. J. Data Inf. Qual. (JDIQ) **10**(2), 1–16 (2018)
11. Levenshtein, V.I.: Binary codes capable of correcting deletions, insertions, and reversals. Soviet physics doklady **10**(8), 707–710 (1966)
12. Lin, Y., Kang, M., Wu, Y., Du, Q., Liu, T.: A deep learning architecture for semantic address matching. Int. J. Geogr. Inf. Sci. **34**(3), 559–576 (2020)
13. Magnani, M., Montesi, D.: A study on company name matching for database integration. Technical report UBLCS-07-15 (2007)
14. Matci, D.K., Avdan, U.: Address standardization using the natural language process for improving geocoding results. Comput. Environ. Urban Syst. **70**, 1–8 (2018)
15. McInnes, B.T., Pedersen, T.: Evaluating measures of semantic similarity and relatedness to disambiguate terms in biomedical text. J. Biomed. Inform. **46**(6), 1116–1124 (2013)
16. Medvedev, T., Ulanov, A.: Company Names Matching in the Large Patents Dataset. Hewlett-Packard Development Company, LP (2011)
17. Mikolov, T., Chen, K., Corrado, G., Dean, J.: Efficient estimation of word representations in vector space. arXiv preprint arXiv:1301.3781 (2013)
18. Mudgal, S., et al.: Deep learning for entity matching: a design space exploration. In: Proceedings of the 2018 International Conference on Management of Data, pp. 19–34, May 2018
19. Papadakis, G., Tsekouras, L., Thanos, E., Giannakopoulos, G., Palpanas, T., Koubarakis, M.: The return of JedAI: end-to-end entity resolution for structured and semi-structured data. Proc. VLDB Endow. **11**(12), 1950–1953 (2018)
20. Papadakis, G., Tsekouras, L., Thanos, E., Giannakopoulos, G., Palpanas, T., Koubarakis, M.: Domain-and structure-agnostic end-to-end entity resolution with JedAI. ACM SIGMOD Rec. **48**(4), 30–36 (2020)
21. Pennington, J., Socher, R., Manning, C. D. Glove: global vectors for word representation. In: Proceedings of the 2014 Conference on Empirical Methods in Natural Language Processing (EMNLP), pp. 1532–1543, October 2014
22. Rehurek, R., Sojka, P.: Software framework for topic modelling with large corpora. In: Proceedings of the LREC 2010 Workshop on New Challenges for NLP Frameworks (2010)
23. Shan, S., et al.: Geographical address representation learning for address matching. World Wide Web **23**(3), 2005–2022 (2020). https://doi.org/10.1007/s11280-020-00782-2
24. Singh, R., et al.: Generating concise entity matching rules. In: Proceedings of the 2017 ACM International Conference on Management of Data, pp. 1635–1638, May 2017
25. Singh, R., et al.: Synthesizing entity matching rules by examples. Proc. VLDB Endow. **11**(2), 189–202 (2017)
26. Srivastava, R.K., Greff, K., Schmidhuber, J.: Highway networks. arXiv preprint arXiv:1505.00387 (2015)
27. Winkler, W.E.: String Comparator Metrics and Enhanced Decision Rules in the Fellegi-Sunter Model of Record Linkage (1990)
28. Bojanowski, P., Grave, E., Joulin, A., Mikolov, T.: Enriching word vectors with subword information. Trans. Assoc. Comput. Linguist. **5**, 135–146 (2017)

Linking Heterogeneous Data for Food Security Prediction

Hugo Deléglise[1,3,4]($\boxtimes$), Agnès Bégué[1,3,4], Roberto Interdonato[1,3,4],
Elodie Maître d'Hôtel[2,3,4], Mathieu Roche[1,3,4], and Maguelonne Teisseire[1,4,5]

[1] TETIS, Univ Montpellier, AgroParisTech, CIRAD, CNRS, INRAE,
Montpellier, France
hugo.deleglise@cirad.fr
[2] MOISA, Univ Montpellier, CIHEAM-IAMM, CIRAD, INRAE, Institut Agro,
Montpellier, France
[3] CIRAD, UMR TETIS, 34398 Montpellier, France
[4] CIRAD, UMR MOISA, 34398 Montpellier, France
[5] INRAE, Montpellier, France

Abstract. Identifying food insecurity situations timely and accurately
is a complex challenge. To prevent food crisis and design appropriate
interventions, several food security warning and monitoring systems are
very active in food-insecure countries. However, the limited types of data
selected and the limitations of data processing methods used make it difficult to apprehend food security in all its complexity.

In this work, we propose models that aim to predict two key indicators of food security: the food consumption score and the household
dietary diversity score. These indicators are time consuming and costly
to obtain. We propose using heterogeneous data as explanatory variables
that are more convenient to collect. These indicators are calculated using
data from the permanent agricultural survey conducted by the Burkinabe government and available since 2009. The proposed models use deep
and machine learning methods to obtain an approximation of food security indicators from heterogeneous explanatory data. The explanatory
data are rasters (population densities, rainfall estimates, land use, etc.),
GPS points (of hospitals, schools, violent events), quantitative economic
variables (maize prices, World Bank variables), meteorological and demographic variables. A basic research issue is to perform pre-processing
adapted to each type of data and then to find the right methods and
spatio-temporal scale to combine them. This work may also be useful in
an operational approach, as the methods discussed could be used by food
security warning and monitoring systems to complement their methods
to obtain estimates of key indicators a few weeks in advance and to react
more quickly in case of famine.

Keywords: Machine learning · Neural network · Heterogeneous data ·
Food security

© Springer Nature Switzerland AG 2020
I. Koprinska et al. (Eds.): ECML PKDD 2020 Workshops, CCIS 1323, pp. 335–344, 2020.
https://doi.org/10.1007/978-3-030-65965-3_22

1   Introduction

Hunger in Africa is growing again after several years of decline. In West Africa, progress in the fight against hunger was stable between 2000 and 2014. During this period, the prevalence of undernutrition gradually decreased from 12.3% to 10.7% before rising again to nearly 15% in 2017 [4]. The prevalence of severe food insecurity characterized by feeling hungry but not eating increased from 20.7% in 2014 to 29.5% in 2017 [3]. Burkina Faso is one of the most food-insecure countries in West Africa, with a prevalence of undernutrition of 21.3% between 2015 and 2017 [3]. The country is heavily affected by the "triple burden of malnutrition", a concept that highlights the complexity of malnutrition and its different expressions: undernutrition, micronutrient deficiency and excess weight/obesity. In 2017, the prevalence of wasting in children, stunting in children and obesity in adults was 7.6%, 27.3% and 4.5% respectively, the first two being among the highest in West Africa [4]. The reasons for the deterioration of the food situation in Burkina Faso in recent years are multiple and interrelated. A first reason is that climate change has led to an increase of extreme weather events such as droughts and floods that affect food availability [17]. A second reason is that conflicts in the Sahel displace populations and cause the fall of food production and distribution channels [9]. Both phenomenons hinder an economic downturn aggravated by an already fragile global economic context.

To prevent food crisis and design appropriate interventions, several food security warning and monitoring systems like the GIEWS (Global Information and Early Warning System) system created by the Food & Agriculture Organisation (FAO), and the FEWSNET one (Famine Early Warning Systems Network) founded by the United States Agency for International Development were set up in the second half of the last century by NGOs and state organizations, and are now very active in food-insecure countries. They do publish regular bulletins on the food situation at regional and national scale. These systems aim at preventing and treating food crisis through the establishment of targeted and appropriate food aid programs.

Given the difficulty of predicting food crisis, some aspects of these systems hinder more accurate and early predictions. First of all, to classify the level of food security (FS) of a territory, the different sources of information are exclusively combined and synthesized manually according to pre-established rules. This exclusively human intervention is time-consuming and limits the complexity and the updating of the decision rules. Moreover, these systems integrate mainly meteorological and remote sensing data, the integration of data from other fields related to FS (commodity prices, violent events, etc.) and other types (time series, high-resolution images) should make it possible to describe it more completely.

The objective of this paper is twofold: (i) To define original and efficient machine learning techniques for the processing of heterogeneous data in the context of FS. (ii) To enrich remote sensing data by linking them to data from different domains in order to make them more suitable for the analysis of complex FS phenomena.

Machine Learning methods are increasingly used to extract relevant information from complex and heterogeneous FS-related data, and several studies have attempted to detect food insecurity and crisis using machine learning techniques [1,10,14] with encouraging but improving results. A group of machine learning methods called deep learning is increasingly being used and is very effective in analysing complex and heterogeneous data [7]. Deep learning has been used with conclusive results for the analysis of FS-related topics such as poverty [15], drought [13] or market prices [12] but has not yet been used with convincing results in the field of FS.

In this work, we propose models that aim to predict two key indicators of FS: the food consumption score and the food diversity score. These indicators are calculated using data from the permanent agricultural survey conducted by the Burkinabe government and available since 2009. The proposed models use deep and machine learning methods to obtain an approximation of FS indicators from heterogeneous explanatory data. The explanatory data are rasters (Population densities, rainfall estimates, land use, etc.), GPS points (of hospitals, schools, violent events), quantitative economic variables (maize prices, World Bank variables), and also meteorological and demographic variables. An important issue was to perform pre-processing adapted to each type of data and then to find the right methods and the right spatio-temporal scale to combine them.

This work can be useful on 2 levels: on the one hand in a basic research approach. Indeed, the problem related to the combination of heterogeneous data is a current question of research, particularly in the field of FS; on the other hand, in an approach operational, the methods applied could be used by FS warning and monitoring systems in complement their methods to obtain estimates of key indicators a few weeks in advance and to be able to react more quickly in the event of famine.

2   Material and Method

2.1   Measuring Food Security

Food security is a complex and multifactorial concept, resulting from multiple and interrelated factors (e.g., climate, economy, wars). Food security holds "when all people have, at all times, physical and economic access to sufficient, safe and nutritious food" [16]. From this definition, four components emerge: (i) the availability in sufficient quantities of food of an appropriate nature and quality; (ii) the access of all persons to the resources necessary to acquire the food necessary for a nutritious diet; (iii) the stability of access to food over time despite natural or economic shocks; (iv) the appropriate use of food (storage, cooking, hygiene, etc.). These components can be appreciated at different levels, through data sources at the national, regional, household or individual level. There are a large number of food security indicators, and the use of several indicators is recommended because of the complexity of food security [2]. Hoddinott [5] estimated the number of food security indicators at about 450.

There are also a large number of proxies indicators related to one or more components of food security, such as vegetation indices, rainfall, food prices, local population densities, number of violent events, road conditions, number of schools and hospitals, etc.

The aim of this work is to propose machine learning models able to use FS proxies as input to predict FS indicators that are time-consuming and costly to obtain with classical methodologies, i.e., with data collected at the household level.

2.2   Study Data

Response Data. The response variables are derived from the Permanent Agricultural Survey, which has been conducted annually in routine by the Burkinabe Ministry of Agriculture since 1982 in Burkina Faso. For this study, we take into account the data that are available from 2009 to 2018 (personal communication, 2018). The resulting dataset contains information from 46400 farm households, i.e. an average of 4640 farm households per year distributed in 351 communes. A farm household is defined as a household practising one of the following activities: temporary crops (rainfed and off-season crops), fruit growing, animal husbandry. In this paper, we focus on two indicators based on answers to household surveys: the Food Consumption Score (FCS) and the Household Dietary Diversity Score ($HDDS$). They provide information on the frequency, quantity and quality of food, and are among the most popular indicators for researchers and organizations [6,11,18]. These indicators are averaged by commune and considered from 2009 to 2018, representing 3066 observations.

Food Consumption Score (FCS): This indicator is a proxy of the quantity of nutrient and energy intake. It is an estimate of the cumulative frequency of the different food groups consumed over 7 days within each household surveyed. The frequency of consumption of each food group is weighted by its nutritional value (Eq. 1; Table 1). Several thresholds to differentiate between households are commonly used. We choose thresholds set by the World Food Program (WFP): acceptable (>42), limit (28–42), and low (<28) [19]

$$FCS = \sum_{i=1}^{9} x_i.p_i \tag{1}$$

$x_i \in$ {Frequency of consumption for each food group i}, $p_i \in$ {Weighting of food groups}

Household Dietary Diversity Score ($HDDS$): It is an indicator of food consumption frequency and diversity more focused on the nutritional quality of the diet. It is an estimate of the number of food groups consumed in the last 24 h. There is no consensus on the choice of the number of groups to use and their boundaries. For example, WFP uses the same groups as the ones used for the FCS, while FAO uses a classification of 12 food groups [8]. The choice of food classification depends on the context (putting more emphasis on products rich in

Table 1. Food groups and their weights for the calculation of the Food Consumption Score (*FCS*). *Source:* [19]

Food group	Weighting
Cereals and tubers	2
Pulses	3
Vegetables and leaves	1
Fruits	1
Animal proteins	4
Dairy products	4
Sugars	0.5
Oils	0.5
Condiments	0

vitamins A, calories, etc.) and the available data. We use the FAO methodology to calculate the HDDS (Eq. 2; Table 2).

$$HDDS = \sum_{i=1}^{12} x_i \tag{2}$$

$x_i \in \{0$: food i not consumed, 1: food i consumed$\}$.

Table 2. Food groups for the calculation of the Household Dietary Diversity Score (*HDDS*). *Source:* [8]

Food group
Cereals
Roots and tubers
Vegetables
Fruits
Meat products
Eggs
Fish and seafood
Legumes, nuts and seeds
Milk and dairy products
Oils and fat
Sweets
Condiments, épices et boissons

Explanatory Data. First, FS proxies are pre-processed to extract relevant explanatory variables by commune, which is the smallest administrative boundary for which the response variables are spatialized. Some proxies have a finer granularity and must be aggregated by commune; other proxies are available at a coarser granularity and must be interpolated on every commune. Then, for each commune and year, the explanatory variables obtained are selected by retaining only the explanatory variables significantly correlated with the response variable under consideration (p-value < 0.05). The selected explanatory variables are classified into 4 groups according to their spatio-temporal granularity to be independently processed by a deep learning method for the prediction of the response variable:

Time Series [Multiple Values Per Year; One Value Per Commune]

- Smoothed Brightness Temperature (SMT); Source: National Oceanic and Atmospheric Administration (Noaa); Frequency: 7 days; Spatial resolution: 4km
- Rainfall estimate; Source: Tropical Rainfall Measuring Mission (Trmm); Frequency: 10 days; Spatial resolution: 6 km
- Maize price; Source: Société Nationale de Gestion du Stock de Sécurité alimentaire (SONAGESS); Frequency: 1 month; Spatial resolution: 64 markets. These data are interpolated on the centroids of each commune using the nearest k neighbour method.
=> These three time series are aggregated into monthly time series (May to November of the year in which the FS indicator is collected and of the previous year)

Conjunctural Data [One Value Per Year; One Value Per Commune]

- Meteorological data (daylight, temperature, humidity, evapotranspiration, wind); Source: Knoema platform; Frequency: 1 year; Spatial resolution: 10 stations. These data are interpolated on the centroids of each commune using the nearest k neighbour method.
- Population density raster; Source: Afripop, Frequency: 1 year; Spatial resolution: 100 m. Extraction by commune of quartiles, spatial autocorrelation, differential entropy and Gini coefficient.
- World Bank data (GDP growth, Consumer Price Index, military spending, etc.); Source: World Bank; Frequency: 1 year; Spatial resolution: Burkina Faso
- Mean SMT, rainfall estimates and maize price by commune

Structural Data [One Value Per Commune]

- Land cover map; Source: European Space Agency (ESA); 2016; Spatial resolution: 20 m. Calculation of the proportions of each type of soil per commune
- Hospitals, schools; Source: Open Street Map; 2018; Spatial resolution: Dot vectors. Calculation of numbers of hospitals and schools per 1000 habitants.
- Violent events; Source: Armed Conflict Location & Event Data Project (ACLED); 2018; Spatial resolution: Dot vectors. Calculation of the number of protests, riots, civil violence and total violence per 1000 habitants.

High Spatial Resolution Data [Multiple Values Per Commune]

– Population density raster; Source: Afripop, Frequency: 1 year; Spatial resolution: 100 m. The raster is split into 10×10 pixel patches.

Finally, each variable is centred reduced in relation to communes and years (consists of subtracting the mean and dividing it by the standard deviation).

2.3   Proposed Frameworks

We perform three types of regression analyses to predict FCS and $HDDS$. To assess performance, we randomly select 85% of the dataset for model learning and 15% for testing.

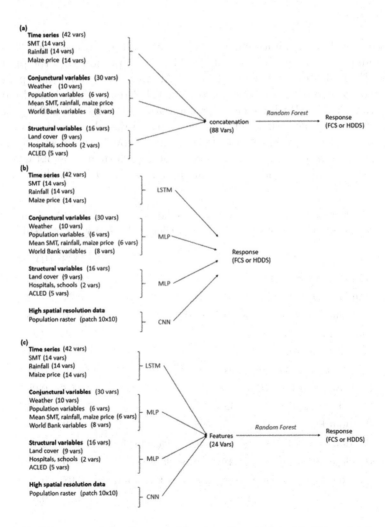

Fig. 1. Architecture of the three machine learning models (a), (b) and (c) used.

- (a) We apply a Random Forest directly on initial variables (for time series, conjunctural variables, structural variables and all variables).
- (b) We use four deep learning models separately on each group of variables. We apply a Long Short Term Memory (LSTM) on time series, a Multilayer Perceptron (MLP) on conjunctural and structural data and a Convolutional Neural Network (CNN) on high spatial resolution data.
- (c) We apply a random forest on features extracted by the deep learning models (for deep learning models associated with time series, conjunctural variables, structural variables, high spatial resolution variables, all variables) (Fig. 1).

3 Results

First, we find that the performance (R^2) is not high, not exceeding 0.38 for the $HDDS$ and 0.35 for the FCS (Table 3). These results show that the prediction of these FS indicators is a complex issue. At present, no published paper has attempted to predict these FS indicators, a WFP team worked on the prediction of the FCS in Burkina Faso for comparable results (R^2=0.34)[1]. Second, we note that it is the structural variables (spatial distribution of schools, hospitals, violent events and land use) that seem to provide the most information: for the prediction of the FCS, the second best performance is obtained using only the structural variables; for the prediction of the $HDDS$, the addition of

Table 3. Performance (R^2) of the 3 types of models - (a): yellow; (b): green; (c): blue - for Food Consumption Score and Household Dietary Diversity Score prediction.

Model	FCS	HDDS
Random forest(Time series)	0.20	0.25
Random forest(Conjunctural variables)	0.27	0.32
Random forest(Structural variables)	0.30	0.38
Random forest(All variables)	0.35	0.37
LSTM(Time series)	0.20	0.21
MLP(Conjunctural variables)	0.10	0.11
MLP(Structural variables)	0.03	0.08
CNN(High spatial resolution data)	0.05	0.06
Random forest(Features(Time series))	0.19	0.20
Random forest(Features(Conjunctural variables)	0.08	0.13
Random forest(Features(Structural variables)	0.30	0.37
Random forest(Features(High spatial resolution data)	0.08	0.10
Random forest(All variables)	0.29	0.36

[1] https://wfp-vam.github.io/HRM/.

non-structural variables do not increase performance. Finally, the use of neural networks is complex for this type of multifactorial indicators and do not allow better performance than using classical machine learning methods for the current time.

4 Conclusion

This study proposes methods to obtain an approximation of FS indicators by integrating heterogeneous data. We faced two scientific obstacles: 1) the choice of input data and the preprocessing to be applied to them. In order to take into account all the facets of FS, we integrated several types of variables (vegetation index, meteorological, economic, demographic variables, etc.) with different spatio-temporal granularities, and we had to perform suitable treatments to extract relevant information; 2) The choice of methods to combine the different variables. We used machine learning and deep learning methods adapted to each group of data (LSTM adapted to time series and CNN adapted to images) and also used deep learning methods to extract features of the same dimension and therefore combinable. The best performances of this study outperform the only comparable (unpublished) work, this is mainly due to the diversity of the data collected and the pre-processing performed. The structural data (spatial distribution of schools, hospitals, violent events and land use) are the most informative in relation to FS. The future work will consist in improving the architecture and settings of the hyper-parameters of the deep learning models in order to take more into account the other types of data and better predict FS.

Acknowledgement. This study was conducted with the help of the Ministry of Agriculture, Water Resources, Sanitation and Food Security of Burkina Faso, the World Food Program (WFP) and the Société Nationale de Gestion du Stock de Sécurité Alimentaire (SONAGESS) which provided data. This work was supported by the French National Research Agency under the Investments for the Future Program #DigitAg, referred as ANR-16-CONV-0004.

References

1. Barbosa, R.M., Nelson, D.R.: The use of support vector machine to analyze food security in a region of Brazil. Appl. Artif. Intell. (2016). ISSN 10876545
2. Coates., J.: Build it back better: Deconstructing food security for improved measurement and action. Global Food Secur. 2(3), 188-194 (2013). ISSN 22119124
3. FAO and ECA: Addressing the threat from climate variability and extremes for food security and nutrition. FAO (2018). ISBN 9789251311578
4. FAO, FIDA, OMS, WFP, and UNICEF. L'état de la sécurité alimentaire et de la nutrition dans le monde en 2018 : renforcer la Résilience face aux changements climatiques pour La sécurité alimentaire et la nutrition. FAO (2018). ISBN 978-92-5-130840-0
5. Hoddinott, J.: Choosing Outcome Indicators Of Household Food Security. International Food Policy Research Institute (1999)

6. Jones, A.D., Nguren, F.M., Pelto, G., Young, S.L.: What are we assessing when we measure food security? A compendium and review of current metrics. Adv. Nutr. (2013). ISSN 0022–3166
7. Julio, J.V.: Extreme learning machines with heterogeneous data types. Neurocomputing (2018). ISSN 18728286
8. Kennedy, G., Ballard, T., Dop, M.-C.: Guide pour mesurer la diversité alimentaire au niveau du ménage et de l'individu. FAO (2013)
9. Lacher, W.: Organized crime and conflict in the Sahel-Sahara region. Carnegie Endowment for International Peace (2012)
10. Lukyamuzi, A., Ngubiri, J., Okori, W.: Tracking food insecurity from tweets using data mining techniques. In: Proceedings of the 2018 International Conference on Software Engineering in Africa - SEiA 2018 (2018)
11. D. Maxwell, B. Vaitla, and J. Coates. How do indicators of household food insecurity measure up? An empirical comparison from Ethiopia. Food Policy **47**, 107-116 (2014). ISSN 03069192
12. Min, W., Ping, L., Lingfei, Z., Yan, C.: Stock market trend prediction using high-order information of time series. IEEE Access **7**, 28299-28308 (2019)
13. Mumtaz, A., Ravinesh, C.D., Nathan, J.D., Tek, M.: Multi-stage committee based extreme learning machine model incorporating the influence of climate parameters and seasonality on drought forecasting. Comput. Electron. Agricult. **152**, 149–165 (2018)
14. W. Okori and J. Obua. Supervised Learning Algorithms For Famine Prediction. Appl. Artif. Intell. **25**(9), 822-835 (2011). ISSN 2078–0958
15. Shailesh, M.P., Tushar, A., Narayanan, C.K.: Multi-task deep learning for predicting poverty from satellite images. In: The Thirtieth AAAI Conference on Innovative Applications of Artificial Intelligence (2018)
16. Shaw, D.J.: World Food Security: A History Since: Palgrave MacMillan (2007). ISBN 10: 0230553559 (1945)
17. Tapsoba, A., Combes Motel, P., Combes, J.-L.: Remittances, food security and climate variability : the case of Burkina Faso. HAL (2019). ISSN 2114–7957
18. Vhurumuku, E.: Food security indicators - WFP. In: Integrating Nutrition and Food Security Programming for Emergency Response Workshop (2014)
19. Wiesmann, D., Bassett, L., Benson, T., Hoddinott., J.: Validation of the world food programme's food consumption score and alternative indicators of household food security. Int. Food Policy Res. Inst. (IFPRI) (2009)

Second Workshop on Evaluation and Experimental Design in Data Mining and Machine Learning (EDML 2020)

2nd Workshop on Evaluation and Experimental Design in Data Mining and Machine Learning (EDML 2020)

The 2nd edition of the *Workshop on Evaluation and Experimental Design in Data Mining and Machine Learning* was held in conjunction with the conference ECML PKDD 2020 on September 14, 2020.

A vital part of proposing new machine learning and data mining approaches is evaluating them empirically to allow an assessment of their capabilities. Numerous choices go into setting up such experiments: how to choose the data, how to preprocess them (or not), potential problems associated with the selection of datasets, what other techniques to compare to (if any), what metrics to evaluate, etc. and last but not least how to present and interpret the results. Learning how to make those choices on-the-job, often by copying the evaluation protocols used in the existing literature, can easily lead to the development of problematic habits. Numerous, albeit scattered, publications have called attention to those questions and have occasionally called into question published results, or the usability of published methods.

Those studies consider different evaluation aspects in isolation, and the issue becomes even more complex because setting up an experiment introduces additional dependencies and biases: having chosen an evaluation metric with in an unbiased manner can be easily undermined by choosing data that cannot appropriately treated by one of the comparison techniques, for instance, and having carefully addressed both aspects is of little worth if the statistical test chosen does not allow to assess significance.

At a time of intense discussions about a reproducibility crisis in natural, social, and life sciences, and conferences such as SIGMOD, KDD, and ECML PKDD encouraging researchers to make their work as reproducible as possible, we therefore feel that it is important to bring researchers together, and discuss those issues on a fundamental level. In non-computational sciences, experimental design has been studied in depth, which has given rise to such principles as randomization, blocking, or factorial experiments. While these principles are usually not applied in machine learning and data mining, one desirable goal that arose during workshop discussions is that of the formulation of a checklist that quickly allows to evaluate the experiment one is about to perform, and to identify and correct weaknesses. An important starting point of any such list has to be: "What question do we want to answer?"

An issue directly related to the dataset choice mentioned above is the following: even the best-designed experiment carries only limited information if the underlying data are lacking. We therefore also want to discuss questions related to the availability of data, whether they are reliable, diverse, and whether they correspond to realistic and/or challenging problem settings. This is of particular importance because our field is at a disadvantage compared to other experimental science: whereas there, data are collected (e.g., in social sciences), or generated (e.g., in physics), we often "only" use existing data.

Finally, we want to emphasize the responsibility of the researchers to communicate their research as objectively as possible. We also want to highlight the critical role of the reviewers: The typical expectation of many reviewers seems to be that an evaluation should demonstrate that a newly proposed method is better than existing work. This can be shown on a few example datasets at most and is still not necessarily true in general. Rather it should be demonstrated in papers (and appreciated by reviewers) to show on what kind of data a new method works well, and also where it does not, and this way in which respect it is different from existing work and therefore is a useful complement. A related topic is therefore also how to characterize datasets, e.g., in terms of their learning complexity and how to create benchmark datasets, an essential tool for method development and assessment, adopted by other domains like computer vision (CV), information retrieval (IR) etc.

We mainly solicited contributions that discuss those questions on a fundamental level, take stock of the state-of-the-art, offer theoretical arguments, or take well-argued positions, as well as actual evaluation papers that offer new insights, e.g. question published results, or shine the spotlight on the characteristics of existing benchmark data sets.

As such, topics included, but were not limited to

- Benchmark datasets for data mining tasks: are they diverse, realistic, and challenging?
- Impact of data quality (redundancy, errors, noise, bias, imbalance, …) on qualitative evaluation
- Propagation or amplification of data quality issues on the data mining results (also the interplay between data and algorithms)
- Evaluation of unsupervised data mining (the dilemma between novelty and validity)
- Evaluation measures
- (Automatic) data quality evaluation tools: What are the aspects one should check before starting to apply algorithms to given data?
- Issues around runtime evaluation (algorithm vs. implementation, dependency on hardware, algorithm parameters, dataset characteristics)
- Design guidelines for crowd-sourced evaluations
- Principled experimental workflows

We received 8 submissions, of which 6 were selected for the workshop (one of which is not included in the post-proceedings as it has since been accepted at DSAA 2020, *Benchmarking network embedding models for link prediction: are we making progress?*, A.C. Mara, J. Lijffijt, T. De Bie in: DSAA2020, the 7th IEEE International Conference on Data Science and Advanced Analytics, 2020). The workshop also featured invited talks on

- "How to Choose Community Detection Methods in Complex Networks—The Case Study of Ulule Crowdfunding Platform" by Cécile Bothorel, IMT Atlantique, France
- "Machine Learning meets Software Development - A challenge for validation" by Ingo Thon, Digital Factory Division, Siemens AG, Germany

Full information about the workshop can be found at the workshop's website at https://imada.sdu.dk/Research/EDML/2020/.

October 2020

Eirini Ntoutsi
Erich Schubert
Arthur Zimek
Albrecht Zimmermann

Organization

Workshop Co-chairs

Eirini Ntoutsi — Leibniz University Hannover, Germany & L3S Research Center, Germany

Erich Schubert — Technical University Dortmund, Germany

Arthur Zimek — University of Southern Denmark, Denmark

Albrecht Zimmermann — Université de Caen Normandie, France

Program Committee

Roberto Bayardo — Google, USA

Marcus Edel — Freie Universität Berlin, Germany

Ricardo J. G. B. Campello — University of Newcastle, Australia

Fatih Gedikli — Hochschule Ruhr West, Germany

Markus Goldstein — Ulm University of Applied Sciences, Germany

Nathalie Japkowicz — American University, USA

Daniel Lemire — LICEF Research Center, Université du Québec, Canada

Juergen Pfeffer — Technical University of Munich, Germany

Miloš Radovanović — University of Novi Sad, Serbia

Maryam Tavakol — TU Dortmund, Germany

Invited Presentations

How to Choose Community Detection Methods in Complex Networks

The Case Study of Ulule Crowdfunding Platform

Cécile Bothorel

IMT Atlantique, France

Abstract. Discovering community structure in complex networks is a mature field since a tremendous number of community detection methods have been introduced in the literature. Nevertheless, it is still very challenging for practitioners to choose in each particular case the most suitable algorithm which would provide the richest insights into the structure of the social network they study. Through a case study of the French crowdfunding platform, Ulule, this talk demonstrates an original methodology for the selection of a relevant algorithm. For this purpose we, firstly, compare the partitions of 11 well-known algorithms, using conventional clustering validation metrics such as NMI. We obtain four clusters of equivalent methods, and select one method of each cluster. Then, we study their complementary in a more qualitative way to match our case study: which organizational patterns are correlated with crowdfunding success? With a bivariate map based on hub dominance and transitivity, we identify the partitions which unveil communities with the most interesting size and internal topologies. Finally, we add business-oriented indicators meaningful in the framework of the crowdfunding platform, in order to select the most significant algorithm of community detection, and to analyze the cooperation patterns among the platform's users and their impact on success of fundraising campaigns. In this talk, we show how both quantitative and qualitative evaluations, combined with business-oriented variables, are relevant when practitioners need to apply machine learning methods.

Machine Learning Meets Software Development

A Challenge for Validation

Info Thon

Siemens AG, Germany

Abstract. Industrial automation utilizes control systems for handling different processes and machineries in industries. The first industrial automation started with the mechanization the textile industry. The second revolution came in the early 20th century when Henry Ford invented the assembly line and started mass production. In the third industrial revolution production went digital and CPUs took over control. In the current – fourth – industrial revolution, industry is adopting novel technologies like IOT, cloud computing, 3d printing, robotics and most importantly artificial intelligence.

Artificial intelligence and especially its sub-field Machine Learning can and will have a large contribution in this revolution. The long history of industrial automation has led to several paradigms which guarantee the safety, reliability, and efficiency, at a level beyond what is known in software development. The paradigms are crucial in build an automation system, as most of these are large scale and distributed.

To enable the mass adoption of Machine Learning in this field, we need to establish an engineering paradigm for Machine Learning. Proper validation of the learned model will play a central role. In this talk, we will look at real world examples where (a) model validation was overlooked, (b) validation measure was based on best practice, (c) methods to overcome this problems based on XAI lead to the wrong conclusion.

Based on these observations we will look at the open challenge that we need a framework analog to unit-tests which supports us in the validation of the classifiers.

Towards Better Evaluation
of Multi-target Regression Models

Evgeniya Korneva[1]([⊠]) and Hendrik Blockeel[1,2]

[1] Department of Computer Science, KU Leuven, Celesteijnenlaan 200A,
3001 Leuven, Belgium
{evgeniya.korneva,hendrik.blockeel}@kuleuven.be
[2] Leuven AI, Leuven, Belgium

Abstract. Multi-target models are machine learning models that simultaneously predict several target attributes. Due to a high number of real-world applications, the field of multi-target prediction is actively developing. With the growing number of multi-target techniques, there is a need for comparing them among each other. However, while established procedures exist for comparing conventional, single-target models, little research has been done on making such comparisons in the presence of multiple targets. In this paper, we highlight the challenges of evaluating multi-target models, focusing on multi-target regression algorithms. This paper reviews the common practice and discusses its shortcomings, indicating directions for future research.

Keywords: Multi-task learning · Multi-target regression · Evaluation

1 Introduction

Multi-target learning refers to building machine learning models that are capable of simultaneously predicting several target attributes, which allows the model to capture inter-dependencies between the targets and, as a result, make better predictions. If the target attributes are binary, the problem is referred to as multi-label classification. Multi-dimensional classification is a more general setting where each instance is associated with a set of non-binary labels. Multi-target regression problems, in turn, refer to predicting multiple numerical attributes at the same time.

Due to a large number of real-world applications, the field of multi-target prediction is rapidly expanding. Multi-target problems often occur in ecological modelling, bioinformatics, life sciences, e-commerce, finance, etc. Consider, for instance, predicting several water or air quality indicators (multi-target regression) or product or text categorization (multi-label classification).

This research is supported by Research Foundation - Flanders (project G079416N, MERCS).

I. Koprinska et al. (Eds.): ECML PKDD 2020 Workshops, CCIS 1323, pp. 353–362, 2020.
https://doi.org/10.1007/978-3-030-65965-3_23

Many widely-used machine learning algorithms have been extended towards multi-target prediction. In addition, various specialized methods have been designed to tackle multi-target prediction tasks.

The more algorithms are being proposed to solve multi-target problems, the higher the need to compare them among each other is. However, no methodology to properly evaluate multi-target algorithms has been developed so far. There exist established techniques for comparing conventional, single-target models, but they are not directly applicable in the multi-target setting.

In this paper, we consider multi-target regression as an example of a multi-target problem and review the current practice of evaluating multi-target regression algorithms. Our goal is to identify key challenges and open problems in evaluating such models, propose possible solutions and start the discussion around the topic.

The rest of the paper is organized as follows. In Sect. 2, we review recent publications on multi-target regression and provide an overview of the most common approaches towards model evaluation. Their shortcomings are then discussed in Sect. 3, where we also suggest possible improvements. Additionally, Sect. 4 inspects widely used benchmark multi-target regression datasets. Finally, Sect. 5 concludes the paper with a summary of key findings and future research directions.

Table 1. To review the common practice in evaluation of multi-target regression models, we consider ten representative papers from the field.

Approach	Method	References	Year
Problem transformation	Random linear target combinations	Tsoumakas et al. [17]	2012
	Regressor chains	Spyromitros-Xioufis et al. [15]	2016
	SVR	Melki et al. [13]	2017
Algorithm adaptation	Multi-target regression trees	Kocev et al. [11]	2013
		Breskvar et al. [3]	2018
	Rules	Aho et al. [1]	2012
	Low-rannk learning	Zhen et al. [21]	2017
	Neural networks	Hadavandi et al. [8]	2015
	Multi-target SVR	Xu et al. [19]	2013
		Tuia et al. [18]	2017

2   Common Practices

A typical machine learning paper introducing a new machine learning algorithm normally contains an evaluation section, where a number of algorithms are run on a set of suitable datasets. The performance of each algorithm on each of the datasets is evaluated using some metric. The obtained scores are compared, sometimes using statistical analysis, in order to make conclusions about the

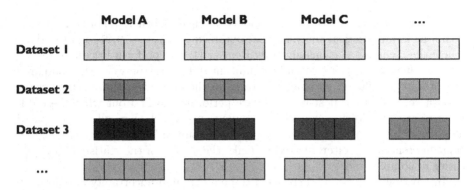

Fig. 1. In the multi-target setting, one obtains several performance scores per dataset (one per each target). It is not trivial to come up with a suitable statistical test to compare such multivariate data. Typical approach is to average scores within a dataset.

predictive performance of the newly proposed approach. This last step, namely comparison of the models based on experimental results, is not trivial in the presence of multiple target attributes.

To review the current practice, we have analyzed a number of papers that introduce a multi-target regression method and evaluate it by comparing it to a number of competitor techniques. We focused on the works published in the past ten years, and selected representative papers from a variety of authors following different approaches towards tackling a multi-target problem, as well as using different machine learning algorithms as a basis for their methods. The summary of the reviewed papers can be found in Table 1.

Most authors chose for Relative Root Mean Squared Error (RRMSE) to measure the accuracy of the target-specific performance. It is a relative measure that is computed as a ratio of the model's Root Mean Squared Error (RMSE) to that of predicting the average value of the target attribute. The lower the RRMSE, the better.

Other common choices are plain RMSE or Mean Squared Error (MSE). In that case, the authors first standardize the targets so that their values are in the same scales and the corresponding errors are comparable. Additionally, correlation coefficient (CC) between the true and predicted values is sometimes computed.

All estimates are typically obtained via cross-validation (an exception is [19], where a holdout set was used to assess the performance).

Whatever metric is chosen, it leaves one with several scores per dataset, namely one per each target attribute, as illustrated in Fig. 1. The common approach is then to average these scores across all targets within each dataset. As a result, a single aggregated performance score per dataset is obtained (e.g., aRRMSE), which makes experimental results look like those in the conventional, single-target case.

The next step is to compare the models among each other. While some papers do not include statistical analysis of the obtained results [18,19,21], most authors follow the recommendations given by Demšar [4] and perform Friedman test to check if there are any statistically significant differences between the compared algorithms (or different parameter settings for the same algorithm). If the answer is positive, additional post-hoc tests are performed to find out what these differences are. In addition, average ranks diagrams, which show all the compared algorithms in the order of their average ranks and indicate statistically significant differences, are often plotted to make the results of the statistical analysis easier to comprehend.

Interestingly, however, there seem to be a common uncertainty about which performance scores to run these statistical tests on. Aho et al. [1] state two options, namely:

1. compare the aggregated scores (e.g., aRRMSE), one per dataset;
2. compare individual, target-specific scores (e.g., RRMSE), one per each target in all the datasets.

The authors explicitly state the drawbacks of both approaches. Aggregation across different targets within a dataset (1) is "summing apples and oranges", while comparing target-specific scores (2) is wrong since targets coming from the same dataset are obviously dependent. Nonetheless, "in the absence of a better solution", the authors present results of the statistical analysis for the both options. Similar remarks can be found in [15]. Also in [3] results are reported for the two scenarios[1], while other works [8,11,13,17] base their statistical evaluation on the within-dataset averages (1) only.

In the next section, we discuss options (1) and (2) in more detail, as well as suggest possible alternative ways of comparing multi-traget models.

3   Can We Do Better?

Both approaches to statistical comparison of multi-target models commonly used in practice have a number of drawbacks. We discuss them below.

3.1   Why Comparing Aggregated Scores is Bad

Apart from not always having a meaningful interpretation, averages are easily affected by the outliers, e.g., when some target is much easier or much more difficult to predict than the others. Excellent performance on an easy target may compensate for the overall bad performance, and vice versa. In addition, when many such targets are strongly correlated, it may appear that the model

---

[1] Per-target analysis (2) always finds more significant differences in performance of the compared techniques than the per-dataset comparison (1) indicates. This is expected, because statistical test is biased and overly confident in the presence of dependent observations.

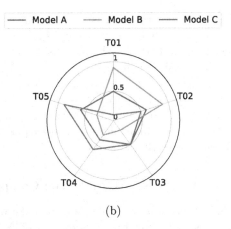

	A	B	C
T1	0.50 (2)	0.90 (3)	0.10 (1)
T2	0.60 (2)	0.90 (3)	0.50 (1)
T3	0.50 (2.5)	0.20 (1)	0.50 (2.5)
T4	0.40 (2)	0.30 (1)	0.60 (3)
T5	0.60 (2)	0.30 (1)	0.90 (3)
	0.52 (2.1)	0.52 (1.8)	0.52 (2.1)

(a)

(b)

Fig. 2. (a) In a fictional example where three multi-target models are compared on a dataset with five targets, aRRMSE is the same. However, the target-specific performances are quiet different. Per-target ranks (in brackets) can help highlight the differences. (b) Visualization is key in understanding such differences. Radar plots can be helpful.

does very well (badly) on the whole dataset, while actually it is just one task that it did (didn't) manage to learn. Besides, and most importantly, averaging always hides a lot of information. Consider a fictional example given in Fig. 2, where three multi-target models are compared on a dataset with five targets. While the average scores across all targets are the same, models A, B and C perform quite differently. It is not true that all three methods are equally good: depending on the application, one of them can be preferred.

Since within-dataset average scores do not fully reflect the performance of multi-target models, comparisons in terms of such aggregates are not informative, and can even be misleading.

3.2 Why Comparing Target-Specific Scores is Bad

As has been mentioned in the previous section, the only alternative strategy sometimes used in practice to avoid averaging is to compare target-specific scores across all datasets. As has already been noticed by some researchers, the scores coming from the same dataset are dependent, which violates the assumptions of the Friedman test, commonly applied to compare these scores across the algorithms. Thus, such an approach is not statistically sound and should not be used in practice because the results of the test are not reliable.

Furthermore, even if a statistical test existed that would take the dependencies between performance scores coming from the same dataset into account, it would allow one to compare multi-target models in terms of their performance on a single randomly selected task. Arguably, this is not what we want: one is rather interested in comparing the models based on their *joint* performance on a *set* of related targets.

But is there a statistically sound way to compare a set of target-specific scores as a whole, i.e., without aggregating them into a single score per dataset, yet keeping track of which dataset the scores are coming from?

The task of comparing multivariate samples often arises in practice and has been extensively studied. Examples include nested ANOVA, global statistical tests [14], and "the method of m rankings" [2]. However, to the best of our knowledge, none of the existing approaches are applicable in the multi-target setting, where multiple observations per dataset are dependent, and their number varies across the datasets.

3.3   How Can We Make the Comparisons Better

Since there is no suitable statistical test one could run on a table of experimental results such as in Fig. 1, some kind of within-dataset aggregation is inevitable. We propose averaging the ranks rather than raw prediction scores. Below, we suggest two ways of introducing ranks.

Target-Specific Ranks. In order to obtain a single aggregated performance score per dataset, one can replace raw target-specific scores by their ranks when averaging across the targets. This will help overcome the issue of non-commensurability of the scores corresponding to different targets, as well as to limit the influence of the outliers.

In the fictional example in Fig. 2a, such ranks for a single dataset are given in brackets. While aRRMSEs are the same, the rank of model B is lower than that of models A and C, indicating that this model "wins" more often.

When such ranks are obtained for multiple datasets, statistical tests can be run to compare the models in terms of their average ranks rather then average performance score.

The disadvantage of this approach is that ranks do not capture the magnitude of the differences in performances. Aligned ranks can be introduced that take it into account, but this will make the hypothesis of the statistical test run on these ranks less interpretable.

Pareto Ranks. Pareto-dominance is an alternative way to compare performances of several algorithms. A model is Pareto-optimal on some dataset if for each target, it yields better prediction accuracy than any other model.

To make Pareto-style comparisons across multiple datasets, Pareto ranks can be introduced as follows. For each dataset, the models that are Pareto-optimal get rank 1. The models that are optimal without considering the models with rank 1, get rank 2, and so on. Once the ranks are computed, statistical tests can be run to check if there is any difference in the Pareto ranks obtained by different models.

The disadvantage of such an approach is that it is quite conservative: improvements across all targets are needed for a model to get a higher rank. It can happen that on some datasets, no model is Pareto-optimal (this is exactly the situation

Table 2. Summary of the 18 benchmark datasets used for evaluating multi-target regression models.

Dataset	# samples	# features	# targets	% missing	Source
atp1d	337	411	6	0	[15]
atp7d	296	411	6	0	[15]
oes97	334	263	16	0	[15]
oes10	403	298	16	0	[15]
rf1	9125	64	8	0.6	[15]
rf2	9125	576	8	6.8	[15]
scm1d	9803	280	16	0	[15]
scm20d	8966	61	16	0	[15]
edm	154	16	2	0	[10]
sf1	323	10	3	0	[5]
sf2	1066	10	3	0	[5]
jura	359	15	3	0	[7,15]
wq	1060	16	14	0	[6]
enb	768	8	2	0	[15,16]
slump	103	7	3	0	[15,20]
andro	49	30	6	0	[9,15]
osales	639	413	12	3.8	[15]
scpf	1137	23	3	35.4	[15]

in the Fig. 2a). In this case, all models get the same rank. If this happens for multiple datasets, no insights can be gained from such a conservative procedure. At the same time, if some algorithm *is* the best in terms of Pareto rank, one can be sure that it outperforms the competitors on all targets, which is not the case when comparison is based on aRRMSE. Every model which is the best in terms of aRRMSE is Pareto-optimal, but the opposite is not true: major improvement on one target can lead to the lowest aRRMSE even if model's performance on the rest of the targets is worse compared to some other methods.

4 Remarks on the Benchmark Datasets

Datasets used to evaluate the models are as important as the procedures used to draw conclusions about models' performances on them. In this section, we take a closer look at the datasets commonly used to evaluate multi-target regression algorithms.

Illustrating some properties of multi-target methods on toy datasets, or evaluating them on synthetic datasets is unfortunately not common. Only in [19], the methods are evaluated on a synthetic dataset generated using a simulated two-output time series process. This synthetic dataset, however, is not constructed

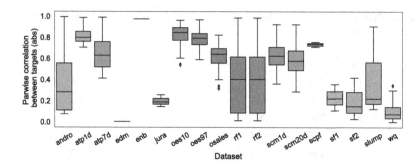

Fig. 3. The distribution of pairwise correlations between targets of benchmark datasets (absolute values are considered to reflect the magnitude of dependencies). Sometimes, all targets are strongly correlated, which can introduce bias in the evaluation process.

to highlight the differences in the behavior of the compared techniques, but is rather used as an addition to the available real-world data.

In 2016, Spyromitros-Xioufis et al. collected a set of 18 real-world datasets [15] that have been commonly used for evaluation of multi-target regression models since then. These datasets are summarized in Table 2. There are datasets of different sizes in terms of the number of examples, features and targets, which is important to guarantee general evaluation. The datasets are also coming from a variety of different domains such as geology (jura), hydrology (rf, wq, andro), astronomy (sf) and engineering (edm, enb, slump), as well as e-commerce (scpf), sales (atp, osales), economics (oes) and management (scm). However, while datasets seem diverse at first glance, there are two aspects that need to be taken into account when using them to evaluate multi-target models.

First, one can notice that some of them come in pairs, e.g., sf1 and sf2, etc. This is because, in some cases, separate datasets were created for the same type of data collected, for instance, in different years. Such datasets are thus very similar, and the algorithms are likely to demonstrate similar performance on them, which can add bias to the evaluation process. Besides, performance scores, both target-specific and aggregated, coming from such similar datasets are also dependent, which is a problem for statistical tests.

The second point worth discussing is the magnitude of dependency between the targets in a single dataset. In Fig. 3, we plot the distribution of the absolute values of the pairwise correlations between the targets per dataset. One can notice that for some datasets such as atp1d, oes10 and oes97, these values are rather high. An extreme case is the enb dataset, where the only two targets are perfectly correlated. An opposite situation can be observed in enb, where there is no correlation between the targets. Of course, this is not 'wrong' per se since the data is coming from the real-world applications and reflects the phenomena that occur in practice. However, these aspects should be taken into account during the evaluation process, since predicting linearly dependent targets is easier than those with more complex inter-dependency. One should therefore not make overly confident statements about the performance of a multi-target model when testing on the datasets with very correlated targets.

5 Conclusions

Multi-target regression, which is a special case of multi-target prediction where several numerical targets are predicted simultaneously, is an actively developing field with diverse real-world applications. A lot of methods to tackle multi-target regression tasks are being proposed by the researchers in the field. In this paper, we have addressed the problem of evaluating multi-target regression models, which is crucial to better understand and modify the existing techniques, as well as to successfully develop new ones. Our analysis of the recent papers publishing the results of several multi-target regression methods over multiple datasets has shown that many authors are unsure about the correct way of making such comparisons.

We argue that comparing multi-target models in terms of averaged scores leaves no possibility to fully understand and meaningfully discuss strengths and weaknesses of different approaches. Besides, it does not help the practitioners to choose an appropriate model to solve a real-world multi-target regression problem. However, we conclude that to run statistical test on experimental results, aggregation is inevitable since no existing test is suitable for comparing multi-target models. We therefore propose two ways on how ranks can be used instead of raw performance scores to overcome such shortcomings of simple averaging as non-commensurability of the target-specific scores and sensitivity to outliers. Note that such ranks, just like any other aggregation, hide a lot of information about models' behavior, and should be reported along with other metrics (e.g., min and max of target-specific errors, median error, etc.).

Simply plotting the per-target results can help highlight the differences between the models. Radar plot, shown for a fictional example in Fig. 2b, is a good example of such visualization. Besides, it is worth to explore why some models perform well on one set of targets and others on another one, as it gives a deeper understanding of the behavior of the model. Such analysis is almost not happening in practice. One example can be found in [17].

In addition, we also inspect benchmark multi-target regression datasets and claim that more diverse datasets are needed to improve the evaluation process. In the absence of more real-world data, one solution is to use artificially generated datasets[2]. Wisely created, such datasets are useful not only to compare the overall predictive performance of multi-target approaches, but also to explore and understand the behavior of individual algorithms in-depth.

References

1. Aho, T., Ženko, B., Džeroski, S., Elomaa, T.: Multi-target regression with rule ensembles. J. Mach. Learn. Res. **13**(Aug), 2367–2407 (2012)

---

[2] An attempt to create such toy benchmarks can be seen in [12].

2. Benard, A.P., vanElteren, P.: A generalization of the method of m rankings. Indagationes Mathematicae **1**(5), 358–369 (1953)
3. Breskvar, M., Kocev, D., Džeroski, S.: Ensembles for multi-target regression with random output selections. Mach. Learn. **107**(11), 1673–1709 (2018). https://doi.org/10.1007/s10994-018-5744-y
4. Demšar, J.: Statistical comparisons of classifiers over multiple data sets. J. Mach. Learn. Res. **7**(Jan), 1–30 (2006)
5. Dua, D., Graff, C.: UCI machine learning repository (2017). http://archive.ics.uci.edu/ml
6. Džeroski, S., Demšar, D., Grbović, J.: Predicting chemical parameters of river water quality from bioindicator data. Appl. Intell. **13**(1), 7–17 (2000)
7. Goovaerts, P.: Geostatistics for natural resources evaluation. Oxford University Press on Demand (1997)
8. Hadavandi, E., Shahrabi, J., Shamshirband, S.: A novel boosted-neural network ensemble for modeling multi-target regression problems. Eng. Appl. Artif. Intell. **45**, 204–219 (2015)
9. Hatzikos, E.V., Tsoumakas, G., Tzanis, G., Bassiliades, N., Vlahavas, I.: An empirical study on sea water quality prediction. Knowl.-Based Syst. **21**(6), 471–478 (2008)
10. Karalič, A., Bratko, I.: First order regression. Mach. Learn. **26**(2–3), 147–176 (1997)
11. Kocev, D., Vens, C., Struyf, J., Džeroski, S.: Tree ensembles for predicting structured outputs. Pattern Recogn. **46**(3), 817–833 (2013)
12. Mastelini, S.M., Santana, E.J., da Costa, V.G.T., Barbon, S.: Benchmarking multi-target regression methods. In: 2018 7th Brazilian Conference on Intelligent Systems (BRACIS), pp. 396–401. IEEE (2018)
13. Melki, G., Cano, A., Kecman, V., Ventura, S.: Multi-target support vector regression via correlation regressor chains. Inf. Sci. **415**, 53–69 (2017)
14. O'Brien, P.C.: Procedures for comparing samples with multiple endpoints. Biometrics 1079–1087 (1984)
15. Spyromitros-Xioufis, E., Tsoumakas, G., Groves, W., Vlahavas, I.: Multi-target regression via input space expansion: treating targets as inputs. Mach. Learn. **104**(1), 55–98 (2016). https://doi.org/10.1007/s10994-016-5546-z
16. Tsanas, A., Xifara, A.: Accurate quantitative estimation of energy performance of residential buildings using statistical machine learning tools. Energy Build. **49**, 560–567 (2012)
17. Tsoumakas, G., Spyromitros-Xioufis, E., Vrekou, A., Vlahavas, I.: Multi-target regression via random linear target combinations. In: Calders, T., Esposito, F., Hüllermeier, E., Meo, R. (eds.) ECML PKDD 2014. LNCS (LNAI), vol. 8726, pp. 225–240. Springer, Heidelberg (2014). https://doi.org/10.1007/978-3-662-44845-8_15
18. Tuia, D., Verrelst, J., Alonso, L., Pérez-Cruz, F., Camps-Valls, G.: Multioutput support vector regression for remote sensing biophysical parameter estimation. IEEE Geosci. Remote Sens. Lett. **8**(4), 804–808 (2011)
19. Xu, S., An, X., Qiao, X., Zhu, L., Li, L.: Multi-output least-squares support vector regression machines. Pattern Recogn. Lett. **34**(9), 1078–1084 (2013)
20. Yeh, I.C.: Modeling slump flow of concrete using second-order regressions and artificial neural networks. Cement Concrete Composites **29**(6), 474–480 (2007)
21. Zhen, X., Yu, M., He, X., Li, S.: Multi-target regression via robust low-rank learning. IEEE Trans. Pattern Anal. Mach. Intell. **40**(2), 497–504 (2017)

Assessing the Difficulty of Labelling an Instance in Crowdworking

Neetha Jambigi$^{(\boxtimes)}$, Tirtha Chanda, Vishnu Unnikrishnan,
and Myra Spiliopoulou

Otto von Guericke University, 39104 Magdeburg, Germany
{neetha.jambigi,tirtha.chanda,vishnu.unnikrishnan,myra}@ovgu.de
https://www.uni-magdeburg.de

Abstract. In supervised machine learning solutions, obtaining labels for data is either expensive or labels are very difficult to come by. This has resulted in reliance on crowdworking for label acquisition. However, these labels come with a penalty of unreliability, which gives rise to the need for assessing the reliability of labels. One such assessment can be performed by determining the difficulty of the labeling task performed by the crowdworker. Assessing annotator stress levels while performing a task can be indicative of its difficulty. We propose a time series classification approach that learns on stress signals of crowdworkers to distinguish between easy and difficult *exemplary* instance-labeling tasks. To transfer this classifier for a labeling task of different nature, we propose two types of time series classification models: a global model trained on the data of all label annotators, and individual-centric models trained on the time series of each annotator. We incorporate this approach into an instance-labeling framework that encompasses one phase for learning on exemplary tasks and one phase for the characterization of unknown tasks. In other words, the model is trained on a data distribution and is then used for classifying data from another distribution. We show that the individual-centric models achieve better performance than their global counterparts on many occasions, and we report notable performance by the classification models overall.

Keywords: Crowdworking · Time series classification · Label reliability

1 Introduction

With the increase in the amount of data available today for machine learning, there is a need for *reliably* labeling them for supervised learning. Crowdworking is a mechanism of choice for the acquisition of labels for large amounts of data, and it is widely used for operational tasks [17], as well as to obtain a ground truth in competitions [2]. It is thereby assumed that agreement among crowdworkers

---

N. Jambigi and T. Chanda—Equal contribution.

ⓒ Springer Nature Switzerland AG 2020
I. Koprinska et al. (Eds.): ECML PKDD 2020 Workshops, CCIS 1323, pp. 363–373, 2020.
https://doi.org/10.1007/978-3-030-65965-3_24

indicates that the assigned label is the correct one [2]. Raebiger et al. have shown though that crowdworker agreement does not necessarily lead to correct labels, because the labeling task may be inherently difficult to accomplish for some data instances [19,20]. In this study, we investigate the interplay between difficulty of the labeling task and the stress level of the annotator, and we present a machine learning approach that can predict task difficulty for a different set of tasks than those used for learning[1].

Quality of the crowdworking outcomes has been extensively studied in literature [3,6,23,24]. One threat to quality is the behaviour of unreliable crowdworkers, so many studies focus on the identification of adversarial and of unreliable crowdworkers, see e.g. [11,14,15]. In [12], Gadiraju et al. have shown that there are further factors affecting outcome quality, including the knowledge of the crowdworker, the environmental factors the crowdworker performed the task in and the inherent difficulty of the task. In this study, we concentrate on the aspect of inherent task difficulty and we propose a mechanism that learns to separate between easy and difficult labeling tasks on the basis of stress in a controlled experimental environment *and then transfers* to an environment where the labeling tasks are of different nature.

Our approach is based on the measurement of stress through Electrodermal Activity (EDA), because EDA is affected by a human's stress levels [8]. For each annotator and instance labeling task we acquire a time series, which we use for task difficulty classification. For this classification, we propose a *global method* that is trained on the data of all annotators and an *individual-centric* method that is trained on each annotator separately. Our contributions are as follows:

- We propose a framework that links difficulty of the annotation task to the stress of the annotator, and thus we address the following question: "Can we identify the inherent difficulty of performing an annotation task through the stress measurements of the annotator?"
- We propose time series classification methods that distinguish between stress signals of easy vs difficult tasks, after being trained on tasks of different duration and different nature.

The rest of the paper is organized as follows: related literature is discussed in Sect. 2. We present our approach in Sect. 3. In Sect. 4, we elaborate on the experimental runs and report on our findings. The last section closes with a summary, limitations and outlook.

2   Related Work

In [12], Gadiraju et al. define task difficulty as a function of objective task difficulty and length of the task. In one of their tasks, a dataset of captcha images which have increasing levels of difficulty in transcribing is used. To figure out whether a task was correctly performed given difficulty, they model crowdworker trustworthiness when performing additional tasks of a different nature

---

[1] In this work, we use the terms *annotation* and *labeling* interchangeably.

interspersed through the transcribing task. In [16], Kurve et al. capture the types of workers using task difficulty as one of the factors along with worker skill and intentions. But how to decide whether a task is *objectively* difficult? In [26], Welinder et al. define discriminatory characteristics of the task eg., image annotation and combine them with the annotator's skill and bias to obtain group of annotator's and groups of images based on difficulty of annotation. In [19], Raebiger et al. have modeled task difficulty based on crowdworker disagreement on a tweet sentiment annotation task. They built a task difficulty predictor by creating a training set from worker-annotated tweets where difficulty was measured by the amount of disagreement on the label. Hence, they use disagreement as indicator of *subjective, perceived* difficulty. In our work, we model *subjective* difficulty through the stress levels experienced by the annotators while performing the task.

The innate difficulty of performing a task affects the stress levels and in turn affects the physiological features due to difficulty induced stress as shown in [4]. In [13], the electrocardiogram, electromyogram, skin conductance, and respiration was recorded to distinguish three levels of drivers' stress and results show skin conductivity and heart rate metrics are most closely correlated with driver stress level. We apply this notion to the crowdworking domain to detect potentially unreliable labels. Among many existing solutions to measure Electrodermal Activity (EDA), we utilize a sensor wristband by Movisens[2]. Thus, annotator stress levels during instance labeling result in time series that correspond to easy vs hard (instance labeling) tasks. The goal of task characterization can be thus (machine) learned with time series classification.

As detailed in [1], there are different ways of handling time series for clustering and classification purposes. In our work we have used HAC clustering using average linkage and cross correlation based distance measure as introduced in [18]. For classification purposes, of the several methods discussed in [5], we have focused on dictionary based methods which essentially employ dimensionality reduction on the time series. Methods like BOSS [21], SAX-VSM [22] can be used for transforming time series into features which can be input to classifiers like SVM, Random Forest, etc. In [25], the authors employ a KNN-inspired approach to exploit the similarity in time series belonging to the same entity. We adopt this approach to create individual-specific models by treating an annotator as an entity.

3   Our Approach

Our approach encompasses an **Experiment-driven Data Collection** and **Time series classification** with model transfer. We collect stress signals emitted by each annotator while performing instance labeling tasks, i.e. we acquire one time series (actually a segment of known length) per task. The data collected in phase 1 constitute the training set for the time series classification, whereupon the classifier is used in phase 2 to characterize instances as easy/hard to

---

[2] https://www.movisens.com/en/products/eda-and-activity-sensor-move-3/.

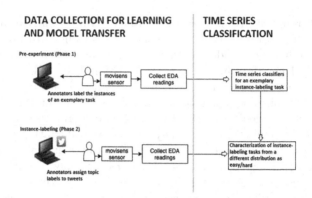

Fig. 1. Workflow

annotate. It is stressed that the tasks of phase 1 (used for training) are different from those of phase 2.

3.1 Experiment Overview

Two phases of user studies were independently conducted: pre-experiment (phase 1) and instance-labeling experiment (phase 2). Both phases consist of annotation tasks interleaved with relaxation breaks, to prevent carry-over stress from one task to another. The job was designed to take approximately 1 hour to complete. An overview of the workflow is given in Fig. 1.

Annotators were students and staff of Otto von Guericke University Magdeburg with English comprehension abilities. The user study took place in a closed room and it was ensured that only 1 annotator took the study at a time to avoid external disruption. In case of any disruption, the signal for the task was discarded. Among all the annotators from phase 1 and phase 2, 9 annotators participated in both phases of the study. Ground truth concerning difficulty was determined by the experimenters, distinguishing between 'Easy' and 'Hard' tasks.

Annotators were instructed not to consume food/beverages that could affect stress levels (e.g. caffeine) and perform no intensive physical activities (e.g. jogging) right before the experiment. Each annotator was presented with the objectives of the study, data collection policies, storage, usage, and anonymity, along with an approved ethics document and were requested to sign the consent form. We measure stress levels with the device Movisens EDAMove3 strapped on to the wrist of the annotator's non-dominant hand. The device captures several parameters like acceleration in three dimensions, temperature, etc. of which we utilize only EDA.

3.2   Design of the Experiment and Data Collection

Tasks and Relaxation Breaks: Each phase consisted of a job containing a total of 42 annotation tasks - 2 learning tasks, 20 easy tasks and 20 relatively difficult tasks. Inspired by [20], the first 2 tasks are considered as a learning phase where the annotator could clarify doubts. All the annotators received the tasks in the same order. Every hard task was followed by a joke/comic strip to help the annotator relax and to divert the annotator's attention before continuing with subsequent tasks. EDA is recorded throughout the experiment and the signals for the learning phase tasks and breaks are excluded from the final dataset.

A simple text joke/comic strip was placed after every hard task. Halfway through the experiment a 2-minute break was provided during which the annotator could choose to see images of landscape/baby animals. After the image display ended, the annotator could prolong the break before resuming the job.

GUI: A GUI was created to present the tasks interleaved with relaxation images to the annotator. The same GUI was used for both phases of the user study with tasks displayed belonging to respective phases. The app collected data - annotator ID, task ID, timestamps which has session start timestamp (when the first task is displayed), session end timestamp (when the last task is submitted), end of in-between tasks (when the task answer is submitted), event type (answer/relaxation), annotator's answer, task label (Easy/Hard/Funny/Relaxation) and stored it in a database. The timestamps were used to segment the time series to obtain the signals for each task and to discard the signals for relaxation, funny, and learning phase tasks. The EDA signals are collected into the Movisens device which is then transferred to a computer for segmentation (1 timeseries per task) using the timestamps from the database.

Design of Phase 1: This job entails identifying if instance B (middle column) is more similar to instance A (left column) or instance C (third column) based on color matching across each row. The instance that got the majority of the votes was defined as the correct answer. Figure 2c is an example. This design was inspired by [10], with an intention of designing a generic job as opposed to a specific job like sentiment labeling.

The easy tasks were created using the Cleveland dataset [9] records by choosing a subset of 9 attributes. Blocks were filled with color, based on attribute values from a range. A KNN algorithm was used to obtain the most near and the most remote neighbours of an instance (instance to be classified) to initialise A and C instances. Hard instances were created by manually initialising instance values such that they required thorough inspection of the colour ranges to arrive at a solution. The actual feature names were masked to avoid ambiguities for annotators. The color palette chosen for the job is color blind friendly.

Design of Phase 2: The job entails classifying the topic in tweet B (middle column) as more similar to the topic of tweet A (left column) or to the topic of tweet C (right column). This job format is designed to be inline with the

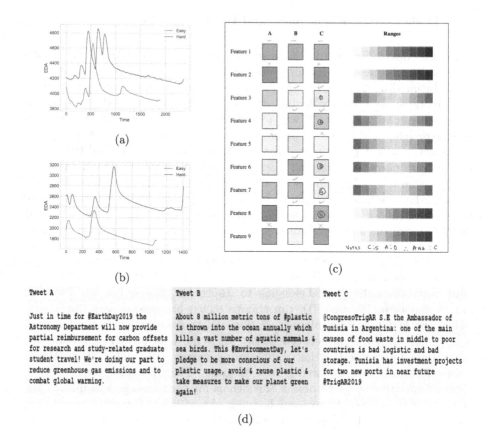

(a)

(b)

(c)

Tweet A

Just in time for #EarthDay2019 the
Astronomy Department will now provide
partial reimbursement for carbon offsets
for research and study-related graduate
student travel! We're doing our part to
reduce greenhouse gas emissions and to
combat global warming.

Tweet B

About 8 million metric tons of #plastic
is thrown into the ocean annually which
kills a vast number of aquatic mammals &
sea birds. This #EnvironmentDay, let's
pledge to be more conscious of our
plastic usage, avoid & reuse plastic &
take measures to make our planet green
again!

Tweet C

@CongresoTrigAR S.E the Ambassador of
Tunisia in Argentina: one of the main
causes of food waste in middle to poor
countries is bad logistic and bad
storage. Tunisia has investment projects
for two new ports in near future
#TrigAR2019

(d)

Fig. 2. (a) Example signal for a phase 1 task (b) Example signal for a phase 1 task (c)
Example Task image phase 1 (d) Example task image phase 2

format of phase 1. Tweets belonging to topics such as global warming, music,
food waste, climate change, travelling were acquired from Twitter. For the easy
tasks, one of the choices were clearly from the same topic as tweet B. In the hard
tasks (e.g., Fig. 2d), we ensured difficulty by choosing all 3 tweets consisting of
very similar topics, making it difficult to come to a decision on similarity.

Example signals from phase 1 and phase 2 are plotted in Fig. 2a, resp. Figure
2b. We see that the signals seem to be of similar nature across both the phases.
The EDA value ranges, however, are quite different across the jobs. Therefore,
the intuition is that the shape of the signals are more informative than the EDA
values when transferring knowledge from the phase 1 job to phase 2.

3.3   Time Series Preprocessing and Classification

Building the Training Set From the Pre-experiment: The signals for each annotator are hierarchically clustered using cross-correlation distance measure with

average linkage for $k = 2$ for the two classes (easy and hard). Each annotator's dendrogram was visually analysed and for *training*, only annotators were chosen for whom there was a clear separation between easy and hard tasks. This would remove noisy data from the training set since some annotators' signals had little distinction between the classes. When the classifier was applied during the experiment, *all* annotators were considered, no matter how clear the distinction between easy and difficult was for them. We observed that the easy task signals were more homogeneously clustered than the hard task signals. We further observed that the segments of different annotators for the same task were distributed to different clusters. This indicates that the perception of hard vs easy tasks may be subjective to each annotator, and led to us to employ individual-centric learning.

Individual-Centric vs Individual-Independent Time Series Classification: Using the EDA data acquired while performing a general job for training enables the learned model to be applied to another job of different nature without being explicitly trained on the other job. For time series classification we used (i) *Individual-centric Models* that are trained on the individual annotator's data of phase 1, and (ii) *Global (Individual-independent) Models* that are trained on the data of all annotators of phase 1.

As base classifiers we chose (from the pyts library[3] and the scikit-learn library[4]) the following methods, setting the hyperparameters on the basis of 3-fold cross validation on the training sets:

- BOSSVS [21]: Converts the time series into Bag-of-Patterns (SFA symbols) with tf-idf weights. For classifying a time series, cosine similarity is calculated between the series tf vector and the tf-idf vectors of each class.
  Hyperparameters: word_size $= 2$, n_bins $= 6$, window_size $= 60$
- WEASEL [22]: Similar to BOSSVS, but uses bi-grams for features and also uses chi-square for feature selection. Then produces a term-document matrix which can be used by any classification algorithm.
  Hyperparameters: word_size $= 2$, n_bins $= 7$, window_sizes $= [36, 100]$
- Feature based [7]: Involves extracting features like number of peaks, count above mean, and so on from the time series, and then these features are fed to a classifier. We chose: SVM with hyperparameters $C = 1.0$, kernel $= $ 'rbf', degree $= 3$, and Random Forest (RF) with hyperparameters n_estimators $= 100$, max_depth $= 5$, random_state $= 0$.

4   Results and Discussion

The models built from the phase 1 data are used to classify data from phase 2. The training set (phase 1) contains 650 (332 easy 318 hard) instances and the test set (phase 2) contains 630 (318 easy 312 hard).

---

[3] https://pyts.readthedocs.io/en/stable/generated/pyts.classification.{BOSSVS.html, WEASEL.html}.

[4] https://scikit-learn.org/stable/modules/generated/sklearn.{svm.SVC.html,ensemble.RandomForestClassifier.html}.

Table 1. Overall performance of the global models - (E-Easy H-Hard)

	Prec E	Rec E	Prec H	Rec H	F1 E	F1 H	Avg Prec	Avg Rec	Avg F1
BOSSVS	0.603	**0.910**	**0.824**	0.412	**0.725**	0.549	**0.713**	0.661	0.637
WEASEL SVM	**0.696**	0.615	0.661	0.736	0.653	**0.696**	0.678	**0.676**	**0.675**
WEASEL RF	0.664	0.628	0.654	0.689	0.646	0.671	0.659	0.658	0.658
Feat.based SVM	0.469	0.439	0.482	0.513	0.454	0.497	0.476	0.476	0.475
Feat.based RF	0.568	0.321	0.533	**0.761**	0.410	0.627	0.551	0.551	0.518

	Feature Based		WEASEL	
Ann.	I	G	I	G
112	**0.68**	0.623	0.774	**0.824**
113	**0.623**	0.540	**0.674**	0.646
116	**0.606**	0.381	0.717	**0.793**
119	**0.742**	0.598	0.554	**0.663**
120	**0.615**	0.404	**0.588**	0.530
122	**0.582**	0.454	0.574	**0.622**
126	**0.481**	0.479	0.563	**0.636**
131	**0.675**	0.427	0.774	**0.799**
133	**0.674**	0.444	0.673	**0.723**

(a)

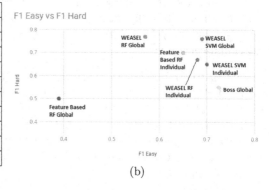

(b)

Fig. 3. (a) Average F1 scores for the individual-centric "I" models and the global models "G", considering feature-based learning and WEASEL RF: the scores refer to predictions for each of the listed 9 annotators separately (b) Juxtaposition of scores for annotator 133: for this annotator, the WEASEL SVM Global model is better than the Individual-centric models, showing that the stress level of some (though not all) annotators can be predicted very well by a global model.

Global Models: The overall performance of the global models is given in Table 1. WEASEL with SVM achieves the best overall performance with an average F1 score of 0.675. When it comes to identifying hard instances, the Feature-based RF performs the best with a recall of 0.76, and BOSS achieves the best performance for identifying the easy instances with a recall score of 0.91.

Individual-Centric Models: The individual-centric models were possible only for annotators who participated in both the phases. The training set contains 37–40 instances and the test set contains 36–40 as well. The evaluation results are presented in Fig. 3. For WEASEL RF, we see that the individual-centric models perform worse than the global models; however, they achieve higher average F1 scores than the global ones when employing the Feature-based RF.

Upon inspecting the trees from the RF Ensemble we found that autocorrelation, counts above mean and number of peaks were class separating: a hard instance was more likely to have an overall 'peaky' signal with repeating patterns of peaks, resulting in higher autocorrelation as well.

In Fig. 3b, we show the performance of all models on the phase 2 data of a randomly selected annotator (#133). WEASEL Global using SVM achieved the best trade-off between the easy and hard class F1 scores. BOSSVS Global performed the best for the easy class, and the Global Feature-based RF method performed the worst overall. Extracting better, more informative features could possibly improve this. The other three individual-centric models are situated around the optimal trade-off, indicating a better balance between the classes than WEASEL Global and BOSS Global. Concluding, the results show that a model trained on the EDA signals of annotators performing a general job, can be used to classify signals for another job.

5 Conclusion

In our work we have presented a method that exploits stress signals to infer whether a crowdsourcing task is relatively difficult to perform, whereupon the time series separation classifier is trained on a handcrafted set of tasks that are independent of the tasks whose difficulty must be assessed.

Our approach entails conducting user studies consisting of a job to be performed, simulating a crowdworker scenario. Two independent user studies were conducted, where the jobs differed in specification from one study to the other. Across both studies the nature of the job was mainly annotation of images/tweets. By training the models using the EDA signals from phase 1 and classifying the EDA signals from phase 2, we have shown that models were able to capture and transfer the learning of stress patterns from one kind of job to another. Our work has two limitations: i) Measuring stress requires sensors. ii) While it is remarkable that the feature-based individual-centric methods perform better than the feature-based global ones, it also means that the extracted features weren't discriminating enough to separate easy and hard tasks. We also plan to investigate whether eye tracking can be associated to stress levels and thus serve as a less obtrusive difficulty separator. Moreover, we intend to study to what extent task annotation duration correlates or at least can be associated with stress levels, i.e. the more objective indicator of difficulty than what we have used in the present work. Task difficulty could be correlated with label confidence, however, we have not attempted this in our work. Concerning applicability, our approach can be used by any institution intending to crowdsource annotation tasks. They can deliver the tasks to a *small* set of annotators and use their behaviour trails to figure out whether the dataset contains many difficult tasks. The institution can subsequently decide against sending the job out to crowd-workers, since the acquired labels would likely be unreliable. They can also perform the difficulty assessment experiment after crowd-sourced labels have been acquired to assess the reliability of the labels. There could also be a benefit in Active Learning where instances are labeled by an oracle and they are incrementally added to the model. Instances that are identified as difficult and potentially unreliable could then be excluded from the set of instances being added to the model.

References

1. Aghabozorgi, S., Shirkhorshidi, A.S., Wah, T.Y.: Time-series clustering-a decade review. Inf. Syst. **53**, 16–38 (2015)
2. Agirre, E., et al.: Semeval-2015 task 2: semantic textual similarity, English, Spanish and pilot on interpretability. In: Proceedings of the 9th International Workshop on Semantic Evaluation, pp. 252–263 (2015)
3. Allahbakhsh, M., Benatallah, B., Ignjatovic, A., Motahari-Nezhad, H.R., Bertino, E., Dustdar, S.: Quality control in crowdsourcing systems: issues and directions. IEEE Internet Comput. **17**(2), 76–81 (2013)
4. Anthony, L., Carrington, P., Chu, P., Kidd, C., Lai, J., Sears, A.: Gesture dynamics: features sensitive to task difficulty and correlated with physiological sensors. Stress **1418**(360), 312–316 (2011)
5. Bagnall, A., Lines, J., Bostrom, A., Large, J., Keogh, E.: The great time series classification bake off: a review and experimental evaluation of recent algorithmic advances. Data Mining Knowl. Disc. **31**(3), 606–660 (2016). https://doi.org/10.1007/s10618-016-0483-9
6. Chandler, J., Paolacci, G., Mueller, P.: Risks and rewards of crowdsourcing marketplaces. In: Michelucci, P. (ed.) Handbook of Human Computation, pp. 377–392. Springer, New York (2013). https://doi.org/10.1007/978-1-4614-8806-4_30
7. Christ, M., Braun, N., Neuffer, J., Kempa-Liehr, A.W.: Time series feature extraction on basis of scalable hypothesis tests (tsfresh-a python package). Neurocomputing **307**, 72–77 (2018)
8. Critchley, H., Nagai, Y.: Electrodermal activity (EDA). Encycl. Behav. Med. **78**, 666–669 (2013)
9. Dua, D., Graff, C.: UCI machine learning repository (2017). http://archive.ics.uci.edu/ml
10. Döbler, A., Moczalla, G.: Design and evaluation of similarity assessment configurations with help of crowdsourcing and active learning. Master Thesis OVGU (2018)
11. Eickhoff, C., de Vries, A.P.: Increasing cheat robustness of crowdsourcing tasks. Inf. Retriev. **16**(2), 121–137 (2013)
12. Gadiraju, U.: Its Getting Crowded!. Improving the Effectiveness of Microtask Crowdsourcing, Gesellschaft für Informatik eV (2018)
13. Healey, J.A., Picard, R.W.: Detecting stress during real-world driving tasks using physiological sensors. IEEE Trans. Intell. Transp. Syst. **6**(2), 156–166 (2005)
14. Ipeirotis, P.G., Provost, F., Wang, J.: Quality management on amazon mechanical turk. In: Proceedings of the ACM SIGKDD Workshop on Human Computation, pp. 64–67 (2010)
15. Jagabathula, S., Subramanian, L., Venkataraman, A.: Identifying unreliable and adversarial workers in crowdsourced labeling tasks. J. Mach. Learn. Res. **18**(1), 3233–3299 (2017)
16. Kurve, A., Miller, D.J., Kesidis, G.: Multicategory crowdsourcing accounting for variable task difficulty, worker skill, and worker intention. IEEE Trans. Knowl. Data Eng. **27**(3), 794–809 (2014)
17. Luz, N., Silva, N., Novais, P.: A survey of task-oriented crowdsourcing. Artif. Intell. Rev. **44**(2), 187–213 (2014). https://doi.org/10.1007/s10462-014-9423-5
18. Paparrizos, J., Gravano, L.: k-shape: efficient and accurate clustering of time series. In: Proceedings of the 2015 ACM SIGMOD International Conference on Management of Data, pp. 1855–1870 (2015)

19. Räbiger, S., Gezici, G., Saygın, Y., Spiliopoulou, M.: Predicting worker disagreement for more effective crowd labeling. In: 2018 IEEE 5th International Conference on Data Science and Advanced Analytics (DSAA), pp. 179–188. IEEE (2018)
20. Räbiger, S., Spiliopoulou, M., Saygın, Y.: How do annotators label short texts? Toward understanding the temporal dynamics of tweet labeling. Inf. Sci. **457**, 29–47 (2018)
21. Schäfer, P.: Bag-of-SFA-symbols in vector space (boss vs) (2015)
22. Schäfer, P., Leser, U.: Fast and accurate time series classification with weasel. In: Proceedings of the 2017 ACM on Conference on Information and Knowledge Management, pp. 637–646. ACM (2017)
23. Sheng, V.S., Provost, F., Ipeirotis, P.G.: Get another label? Improving data quality and data mining using multiple, noisy labelers. In: Proceedings of the 14th ACM SIGKDD International Conference on Knowledge Discovery and Data Mining, pp. 614–622 (2008)
24. Snow, R., O'connor, B., Jurafsky, D., Ng, A.Y.: Cheap and fast-but is it good? Evaluating non-expert annotations for natural language tasks. In: Proceedings of the 2008 Conference on Empirical Methods in Natural Language Processing, pp. 254–263 (2008)
25. Unnikrishnan, V., et al.: Entity-level stream classification: exploiting entity similarity to label the future observations referring to an entity. Int. J. Data Sci. Anal. **9**(1), 1–15 (2019). https://doi.org/10.1007/s41060-019-00177-1
26. Welinder, P., Branson, S., Perona, P., Belongie, S.J.: The multidimensional wisdom of crowds. In: Advances in Neural Information Processing Systems, pp. 2424–2432 (2010)

Experimental Evaluation of Scale, and Patterns of Systematic Inconsistencies in Google Trends Data

Philipp Behnen[1(✉)], Rene Kessler[2], Felix Kruse[2], Jorge Marx Gómez[2], Jan Schoenmakers[1], and Sergej Zerr[3]

[1] HASE & IGEL GmbH, Oldenburg, Germany
{philipp.behnen,jan.schoenmakers}@haseundigel.com
[2] VLBA, Oldenburg University, Oldenburg, Germany
{rene.kessler,felix.kruse,jorge.marx.gomez}@uni-oldenburg.de
[3] L3S Research Center, Leibniz University Hannover, Hannover, Germany
szerr@l3s.de

Abstract. Search analytics and trends data is widely used by media, politicians, economists, and scientists in various decision-making processes. The data providers often use sampling when calculating the request results, due to the huge data volume that would need to be processed otherwise. The representativity of such samples is typically assured by the providers. Often, limited or no information about the reliability and validity of the service or the sampling confidence are provided by the services and, as a consequence, the data quality has to be assured by the users themselves, before using it for further analysis.

In this paper, we develop an experimental setup to estimate and measure possible variation in service results for the example of Google Trends. Our work demonstrates that the inconsistencies in Google Trends Data and the resulting contradictions in analyses and predictions are systematic and particularly large when analyzing timespans of eights months or less. In our experiments, the representativity claimed by the service was disproved in many cases. We found that beyond search volume and timespan, there are additional factors for the deviations that can only be explained by Google itself. When working with Google Trends data, users must be aware of the marked risks associated with the inconsistencies in the samples.

Keywords: Google Trends · Service reliability · Sampling

1 Introduction

Web applications and services are being developed and extensively used around the globe since the start of the Internet revolution at the end of the last century. The user interaction data with those services has been turned into a valuable source of information not only for improving the services themselves but also for

© Springer Nature Switzerland AG 2020
I. Koprinska et al. (Eds.): ECML PKDD 2020 Workshops, CCIS 1323, pp. 374–384, 2020.
https://doi.org/10.1007/978-3-030-65965-3_25

third party market analytics. Media, politicians, economists, and scientists are widely using search analytics in various decision-making processes. Such data is provided by big web companies with a large number of users, with analysts relying on the quality of the services assured by the providers. On the example of Google Trends, our work shows that caution and careful pre-processing are required when using the data in the decision-making processes.

Since its introduction in 2006, Google Trends[1](GT) service has established itself as a tool for investigation, research and forecasting with a broad range of use cases ranging from forecasting epidemics [16], to indicating movements in the stock market [9] or identifying consumer trends and demand [17]. Inconsistencies in GT data may have considerable implications because of the service's regular and widespread use in politics, journalism, economy, and science. Especially during the corona crisis various media are using these resources, basing their research and reports on data from GT[2]. For this service, Google is using ad-hoc samples from the total of searches in its database and assures that the sample sizes are sufficiently large for the data to be representative for all searches on Google.

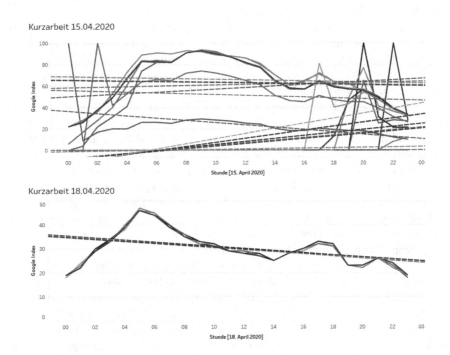

Fig. 1. Google scores and linear regression for "kurzarbeit" for April 15 and 18, 2020. Every request has its own regression.

---

[1] https://trends.google.de.

[2] https://www.finanznachrichten.de/nachrichten-2020-04/49427722-google-trends-as-a-proxy-for-covid-19-incidence-and-deaths-378.htm (accessed 17.07.2020).

376 P. Behnen et al.

During the computation of trends using Google data, however, we observed large deviations between results of identical API requests[3]. While, for example, the values for the (German) term "kurzarbeit" for April 15, 2020, differ so wildly by the time the request was initiated that they sometimes show completely contradictory trends, there is hardly any contradiction in the data for the same search term for April 18 as displayed in Fig. 1. Upon our contacting them, Google posited that such deviations may happen, but should only occur for requests with small search volumes and should be marginal. We tested these hypotheses. This paper aims to provide first insights into our investigation of the observed inconsistencies, with a focus on implications for practitioners using GT data.

2 Related Work

Search analytics and especially GT data have been widely used in research, including computer science, sociology, economics, and medicine. Especially in areas missing official statistics on some subjects, GT is frequently used as a proxy [1]. Whether the conclusions based on GT are sound, stands and falls with the credibility of the data provided.

The research has a high societal impact. Aguilera et al. [1] employed GT to access interest in burnout and models based on GT data outperformed traditional autoregressive approaches in forecasting touristic demand. [7]. GT was reported as a useful tool to acquire evidence for social hierarchy impacting income inequality and racial bias by Connor et al. [5].

In the domain of economics, Xu et al. [18] employed GT as a proxy for event impact to link to US macroeconomic variables. There is a body of work on applicability of GT for monitoring and forecasting of stock markets [2,8,14], new products [4] and cryptocurrencies [15] development.

In the medical domain, search statistics gained especial popularity as official health statistics are often not available for some geographic regions, however, the users tend to develop a certain level of trust for "Dr.Google" [13]. GT was adopted to monitor search interest in epilepsy surgery [11], for monitoring and forecasting deceases outbreaks [3], in particular influenza [12], respiratory syncytial virus [6] and, recently COVID19 [10].

Some criticism concerning GT was reported in research, reflecting anticipated challenges when using it as a data source. This includes the obscure score calculation, irregularly missing data [6], and the fact that user properties behind Google searches can not be identified [5]. Often, Goggle Trends tends to underestimate the real value of observation when the general public has poor knowledge of a given term. For example, the timely popularity of diseases and regional media coverage has more impact on the index as their real spread [3].

---

[3] There is a discussion thread at Google support: https://support.google.com/google-ads/thread/8389370?msgid=26184434 (accessed 17.07.2020).

Recent studies agree that the services should be used only to estimate the public interest for a particular keyword. To the best of our knowledge, none of the works mentioned above report any pre-processing, or data cleaning steps when using GT. In our work, we do the first step towards the systematic evaluation of the data quality provided.

3 Evaluation Setup

In this section, we provide a setup to a) evaluate the overall reliability of GT services, b) access the correlation between the reliability and search volume, and c) evaluate the representativeness of data samples provided by Google.

3.1 GT Service

GT is a service provided by Google free of charge, which can be used to extract time series of index values indicating the search intensity and trends for freely selectable keywords and topics worldwide. The analytics timespan can be chosen at liberty from between a few hours or days up to a time series from the year 2004 until today. It is also possible to filter for specific countries or regions. A single data point is a score that reflects the search popularity of the keyword, compared to the total amount of searches in the same region and timespan. The index score ranges from 0 to 100 with 100 being the data point with the highest search intensity for the selected keyword within the selected timespan. The aggregation granularity level is defined by the service as one of hour/day/week/month, depending on the length of the requested period. The data can be displayed as a graph and exported as a CSV file from a web dashboard.

Table 1. A motivated choice of keywords (German) that were used in our experiments

Keyword	Search Volume⌀ 01.2015–03.2020	Reason
dachdecker	39,800/40,500	Medium sized, relatively constant long-term demand with some seasonal peaks
kurzarbeit	20,900/27,100	Single big peak during corona crisis. Before there was a small search volume, after the peak it was medium sized
sofa	197,000/201,000	Volume increases constantly and on a long-term basis. High volume overall with regular seasonal fluctuations

3.2   Data Acquisition

We systematically retrieved trends data for our experiments, repeating for the same keywords and timespans over and over again for several weeks while limiting the region to Germany. We excluded empty request results (not enough data available) form the analysis.

GT does not provide information about the search volume. To test Google's claim that fluctuations are limited to low-volume keywords, we employed Google Ads data as a proxy. To this end, we used the tool "KWFinder" by Slovakian company Mangools which is well-established on the European market.[4]

We limited our research to German keywords (see Table 1). The keywords used in this report are "dachdecker" ("roofer"), "kurzarbeit" ("short-time work") and "sofa", as they show a range in search volume and volatility. Depending on the length of the timespan, Google automatically aggregates the data on an hourly, daily, weekly, or monthly basis. For the 16 timespans analyzed, the granularity of data is shown in Table 2. We executed requests at different times of day, with varying time intervals between requests and on different days of the week.

3.3   Evaluation Framework

Reliability: To measure the deviation within the GT results, we employ the standard deviation of the scores obtained from different samples of the same query(requested keyword, time period and geographic area), executed ad different times. We additionally employed relative standard deviation (the percentage of deviation from the mean) to make values between different keywords and time spans comparable.

Correlation: According to Google, small deviations may occur for keywords with low search volumes. We use the Spearman correlation coefficient to test this claim, as we are interested in rank correlation. We additionally employ R^2 to measure the amount of explainable variance.

Representativeness: Google emphasizes that the samples used in GT are representative. A representative sample is one that accurately represents and reflects the underlying data distribution. Thus, any two independent representative samples drawn from the same population will not significantly differ. To check the overall representativeness, we employed a Mann-Whitney-U test to measure the proportion of pairs of samples (from all available) that is coming from the same distribution.

---

[4] https://mangools.com/blog/kwfinder-top-questions/ A direct retrieval from Google Ads was not possible for us since Google only provides very rough figures such as "10,000–100,000" by default - only larger advertisers receive more precise data.

Table 2. Used timespans and granularity of data supplied by GT

Timespan	Granularity of GT data
01/2010–04/2020	Monthly
01/2015–04/2020	Monthly
01/2019–04/2020	Weekly
01/2020–04/2020	Daily
Q1, Q2, Q3 und Q4 (2019)	Daily
January, February, and March (2020)	Daily
15.04, 16.04, 17.04, 18.04 and 19.04 (2020)	Hourly

4 Experimental Results

4.1 Descriptive Figures

Figure 2 shows an example of retrieved data. Every column represents the index value as supplied by GT for a single request (keyword "kurzarbeit" – "short-time work" for the timespan of January 2020 and region Germany). Every row is expected to contain only slightly varying or even the same values. In our examples, however, we observe large variations. To further identify patterns in observed inconsistencies, we examined the values for the different keywords (Table 1) and timespans (Table 2). For the shortest timespans - five consecutive days from the April 15 to April 19 with values aggregated on an hourly basis - no clear patterns can be observed (Fig. 4). For the keyword "sofa", which has the highest average search volume, GT returned no values for the vast majority of requests from the 15th to the 18th of April[5]. For April 19, however, a sufficient amount of data points could be retrieved.

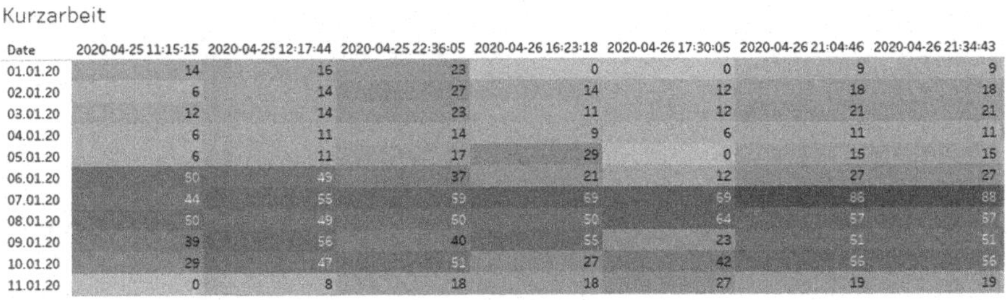
Kurzarbeit

Date	2020-04-25 11:15:15	2020-04-25 12:17:44	2020-04-25 22:36:05	2020-04-26 16:23:18	2020-04-26 17:30:05	2020-04-26 21:04:46	2020-04-26 21:34:43
01.01.20	14	16	23	0	0	9	9
02.01.20	6	14	27	14	12	18	18
03.01.20	12	14	23	11	12	21	21
04.01.20	6	11	14	9	6	11	11
05.01.20	6	11	17	29	0	15	15
06.01.20	50	49	37	21	12	27	27
07.01.20	44	55	69	69	69	88	88
08.01.20	50	49	50	50	64	57	57
09.01.20	39	56	40	55	23	51	51
10.01.20	29	47	51	27	42	56	56
11.01.20	0	8	18	18	27	19	19

Fig. 2. Heatmap for 7 requests for the keyword "kurzarbeit" with the timespan of January 2020, limited to the first 11 days to provide a short overview.

[5] For April 16, 17 and 18, 2020 there are 35 query results each, which have the Google index value 0 for each hour. The corresponding timespans were, therefore, not considered in the analysis.

380   P. Behnen et al.

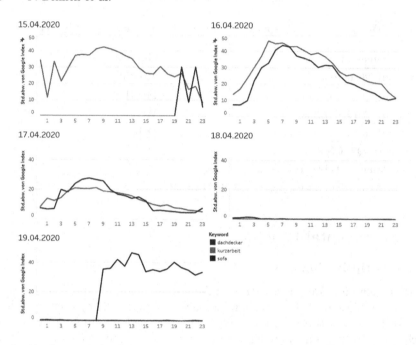

Fig. 3. Absolute standard deviations of hourly aggregated index values for the April 15. to 19., 2020

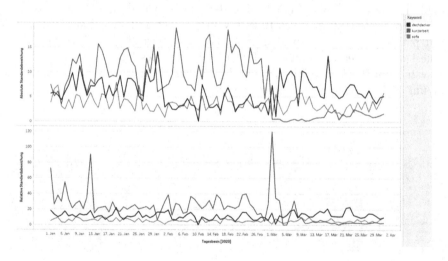

Fig. 4. Absolute standard deviations of daily aggregated index values for the April 15 to 19, 2020

Although both other keywords ("kurzarbeit" and "dachdecker") have much smaller average search volumes, GT returned index scores for all the single days. Between April 15 and 17, those values showed a relative standard deviation of over 100%, which casts serious doubts on the reliability of the retrieved data.

For April 18 and 19, however, the data is very coherent for "kurzarbeit" and "dachdecker" and seems fit for analytic use, while "sofa" displays high deviations despite being the "biggest" keyword.

For the next larger timespan, from January until March 2020, the data is automatically aggregated daily. Here, the values for the keyword "sofa" with the highest search volume is the least deviant, while the index values of the smallest keyword "kurzarbeit" diverge the most (see Fig. 3). While this seems coherent at first glance, it should be noted that the difference in relative standard deviation between "sofa" and "dachdecker" is rather low, although the search volumes differ drastically. Larger search volumes seem to have some impact on the data quality ("sofa" vs. "kurzarbeit"), but do not explain all of the inconsistencies observed ("sofa" vs. "dachdecker"). Table 3 summarizes the results of the descriptive analysis. For the keywords "sofa" and "dachdecker" the hourly aggregated data (for timespans shorter than one week) shows deviations that are too high to be used in practice. Even for daily aggregated index values (timespans shorter than eight months) sometimes deviations of great size persist, depending on when the request is made. For timespans longer than 8 months (and therefore on the aggregation level of weeks or months), index values seem to be robust enough to justify practical use with some level of attention. For the smaller keyword "kurzarbeit" – which has been used by the German expert council for economy to determine the increase of short-time work in the country – the data is so deviant that it is questionable to use it at all. Although the fluctuations are often small in absolute terms, in percentage terms they can be very high, as can be seen in Table 3. Using these data may lead to different conclusions if only individual months are considered. These discrepancies can be explained by the frequent occurrence of null values. If values greater than null occur for the first time after a longer period, the relative standard deviation increases sharply.

4.2   Statistical Evaluation: Correlation with Search Volume

In this section we examine the dependence of the quality of the data on the search volume. To this end, we statistically examined the correlations between the google index (relative values), search volume (absolute values from Google Ads) and the standard deviation (as an indicator for the reliability of the data) by observing the four quarters of 2019. We repeated this calculation with the derivative (change) of the values in order to test whether data quality is affected by the fluctuations of search volume beyond their amount. For these calculations, we used the Spearman correlation measure. The resulting correlations were examined in a significance test and reported along with the proportion of the variance explained using the R^2 value. That way we can observe how strong the effect really is (see Table 4).

On average, the data quality does increase with the search volume. However, this only accounts for approximately a quarter (for the index value), respectively a half (absolute search volume) of the inconsistencies. Additionally, we found that changes in search volume positively correlate with the standard deviation, meaning that the discrepancy is higher when the search volume changes.

382 P. Behnen et al.

Table 3. Relative standard deviation for different index value aggregation levels

Keyword	Index value aggregation level	Relative standard deviation range in %	Average relative standard deviation in %
kurzarbeit	Hourly	0–181	38.4
sofa	Hourly	57–248	87.4
dachdecker	Hourly	0–134	33.3
kurzarbeit	Daily	0–170,8	34.2
sofa	Daily	0–13,4	5.8
dachdecker	Daily	0–36,1	12.8
kurzarbeit	Weekly	0–685,6	75.4
sofa	Weekly	0–3,7	1.7
dachdecker	Weekly	0–9,0	4.6
kurzarbeit	Monthly	0–888,8	100.9
sofa	Monthly	0–4,5	1.8
dachdecker	Monthly	0–5,5	2.4

Table 4. Correlations of the standard deviation, search volume, index volume as well as their derivatives for all keywords and Q1 until Q4 2019

Correlations between the values

	Index	STD
STD	c= -0.49 r^2= 26.33% p<0.05	
Vol	c= 0.79 r^2= 51.39% p<0.05	c= -0.87 r^2= 53.22% p<0.05

Correlations between value changes

	Index	STD
STD	c= 0.44 r^2= 18.16% p<0.05	
Vol	c= -0.06 r^2= 0.49% p= 0.69	c= -0.20 r^2= 4.13% p= 0.23

This effect accounts for approx. $\frac{1}{5}$ of the inconsistencies. This clearly shows that Google's explaining the contradictions in GT data with low search volumes is not wrong in principle, but also far from sufficient: depending on which variable is used as a reference, a half to almost three-quarters of the discrepancies in GT data cannot be explained by the search volume of the respective search terms. Our analyses also reveal that the GT index is a very limited indicator for actual changes in search volume, since it is calculated concerning the total number of Google searches at any given time, and since this number seem to fluctuate massively, changes in actual search volume explain only half of the changes in the Google Index value. In fact, for 2 of the 3 terms examined, there was no significant correlation between the development of the Google index value and the absolute search volume - at least judging from the data available to us.

Lacking further indications from Google on how the total number of searches has developed in the timespan observed, one should have fundamental doubts about the GT index's expressiveness.

4.3   Statistical Evaluation: Pairwise Representativeness

In this section, we analyze the pairwise differences between request results for the same search at different times to check the sample representativity. To this end, we employed the Mann-Whitney-U-Test, as we cannot assume a normal data distribution.

Depending on the timespan and keyword, up to 35% of the compared sample pairs failed the test - and thus the requests cannot be considered representative. On an hourly level (single day timespan), a quarter of all samples fail the test, while on a daily level (timespan of weeks or months), the risk of being shown a non-representative sample remains just as high. From the weekly aggregation of the data (timespan of 8 months and longer), all samples for "sofa" and "kurzarbeit" pass the test and can, therefore, be considered representative. For "dachdecker" however, the proportion of non-representative samples is highest at the weekly level (35%) and falls significantly at the monthly level only (e.g. for periods of at least five years), although even on this scale still more than one in seven samples are not representative.

5   Conclusions and Outlook

In this work, we took a first step towards a comprehensive, systematic analysis of data retrieved from Google Trends. Our experiments show that GT data is risky to use for analysis and forecasts: requests for the same term and period at different times can return very different results. The discrepancies can be unexpectedly large and question the representativity of the samples. The patterns behind these contradictions in GT data are complex and can not be explained with insufficient search volume alone.

Consequently, analyses based on the data provided by the service should not be used in the decision-making process without careful pre-processing. In future work, we plan to analyze the deviation patterns further and include other publicly available web services.

Acknowledgements. This work is partly funded by the European Research Council under grant agreement 833635 (ROXANNE) and 832921(MIRROR) and by the Lower Saxony Ministry of Science and Culture under grant number ZN3492 within the Lower Saxony "Vorab" of the Volkswagen Foundation, supported by the Center for Digital Innovations (ZDIN).

References

1. Aguilera, A.M., Fortuna, F., Escabias, M., Di Battista, T.: Assessing socialinterest in burnout using google trends data. Soc. Indic. Res. (2019). https://doi.org/10.1007/s11205-019-02250-5

2. Alsmadi, I., Al-Abdullah, M., Alsmadi, H.: Popular search terms and stock price prediction. In: Big Data 2019 (2019)
3. Cervellin, G., Comelli, I., Lippi, G.: Is google trends a reliable tool for digital epidemiology? Insights from different clinical settings. J. Epidemiol. Global Health **7**(3), 185–189 (2017)
4. Chumnumpan, P., Shi, X.: Understanding new products' market performance using google trends. Australas. Market. J. **27**(2), 91–103 (2019)
5. Connor, P., Sarafidis, V., Zyphur, M.J., Keltner, D., Chen, S.: Income inequality and white-on-black racial bias in the united states: evidence from project implicit and google trends. Psychol. Sci. **30**(2), 205–222 (2019)
6. Crowson, M.G., Witsell, D., Eskander, A.: Using google trends to predict pediatric respiratory syncytial virus encounters at a major health care system. J. Med. Syst. **44**(3), 1–6 (2020). https://doi.org/10.1007/s10916-020-1526-8
7. Höpken, W., Eberle, T., Fuchs, M., Lexhagen, M.: Google trends data for analysing tourists' online search behaviour and improving demand forecasting: the case of Åre, Sweden. Inf. Technol. Tourism **21**(1), 45–62 (2018). https://doi.org/10.1007/s40558-018-0129-4
8. Hu, H., Tang, L., Zhang, S., Wang, H.: Predicting the direction of stockmarkets using optimized neural networks with google trends. Neurocomputing **285**, 188–195 (2018)
9. Huang, M.Y., Rojas, R.R., Convery, P.D.: Forecasting stock market movements using google trend searches. Empirical Econ. **59**, 1–19 (2019). https://doi.org/10.1007/s00181-019-01725-1
10. Husnayain, A., Fuad, A., Su, E.C.Y.: Applications of google search trends forrisk communication in infectious disease management: a case study of covid-19 outbreak in Taiwan. Int. J. Infect. Dis. **95**, 221–223 (2020)
11. Kinney, M.O., Brigo, F.: What can google trends and wikipedia-pageview analysis tell us about the landscape of epilepsy surgery over time? Epilepsy Behav. **103**, 106533 (2020)
12. Kondo, K., Ishikawa, A., Kimura, M.: Sequence to sequence with attention for influenza prevalence prediction using google trends. In: ICCBB (2019)
13. Lee, K., Hoti, K., Hughes, J.D., Emmerton, L.: Dr google and the consumer: a qualitative study exploring the navigational needs and online health information-seeking behaviors of consumers with chronic health conditions. JMIR **16**(12), e262 (2014)
14. Preis, T., Moat, H.S., Stanley, H.E.: Quantifying trading behavior in financial markets using google trends. Nat. Sci. Rep. **3**, 1684 (2013)
15. Smuts, N.: What drives cryptocurrency prices? An investigation of google trends and telegram sentiment. In: ACM SIGMETRICS (2019)
16. Verma, M., Kishore, K., Kumar, M., Sondh, A.R., Aggarwal, G., Kathirvel, S.: Google search trends predicting disease outbreaks: an analysis from India. Healthc. Inform. Res. **24**(4), 300–308 (2018)
17. Vosen, S., Schmidt, T.: Forecasting private consumption: survey-based indicators vs. google trends. J. Forecast. **30**(6), 565–578 (2011)
18. Xu, Q., Bo, Z., Jiang, C., Liu, Y.: Does google search index really help predicting stock market volatility? Evidence from a modified mixed data sampling model on volatility. Knowl.-Based Syst. **166**, 170-185 (2019)

Assessing the Uncertainty of the Text Generating Process Using Topic Models

Jonas Rieger$^{(\boxtimes)}$ ⓘ, Carsten Jentsch ⓘ, and Jörg Rahnenführer ⓘ

Department of Statistics, TU Dortmund University, 44221 Dortmund, Germany
{rieger,jentsch,rahnenfuehrer}@statistik.tu-dortmund.de

Abstract. Latent Dirichlet Allocation (LDA) is one of the most popular topic models employed for the analysis of large text data. When applied repeatedly to the same text corpus, LDA leads to different results. To address this issue, several methods have been proposed. In this paper, instead of dealing with this methodological source of algorithmic uncertainty, we assess the aleatoric uncertainty of the text generating process itself. For this task, we use a direct LDA-model approach to quantify the uncertainty due to the random process of text generation and propose three different bootstrap approaches to resample texts. These allow to construct uncertainty intervals of topic proportions for single texts as well as for text corpora over time. We discuss the differences of the uncertainty intervals derived from the three bootstrap approaches and the direct approach for single texts and for aggregations of texts. We present the results of an application of the proposed methods to an example corpus consisting of all published articles in a German daily quality newspaper of one full year and investigate the effect of different sample sizes to the uncertainty intervals.

Keywords: Aleatoric uncertainty · Topic model · Machine learning · Stochastic · Text data

1 Introduction

Modeling unstructured data is a big challenge in the field of machine learning. Due to an increase of volume of unstructured data the need for appropriate analytical methods also increases. Text data covers a large share of unstructured data and is often organized in a collection of texts called corpus.

We consider each text to be a sequence of sentences, where each sentence consists of a sequence of tokens of words. The set of all words are denoted as vocabulary, where a token is given by a word at a specific place in a single text. Observed text data is generally subject to a certain degree of aleatoric uncertainty, since an author uses a slightly different choice of words when writing repeatedly the same text. We provide a mechanism to quantify the uncertainty of the text generation directly and by bootstrap simulation based on topic models. For the bootstrap we distinguish between different implementations of the

© Springer Nature Switzerland AG 2020
I. Koprinska et al. (Eds.): ECML PKDD 2020 Workshops, CCIS 1323, pp. 385–396, 2020.
https://doi.org/10.1007/978-3-030-65965-3_26

procedure, that is, we rely on resampling words, sentences or a combination of both. All approaches are compared regarding uncertainty estimation on an example dataset consisting of all 51 026 articles published in the German quality newspaper Süddeutsche Zeitung in 2018.

1.1   Related Work

In the field of text data analysis it is very common to model a corpus of text data using probabilistic topic models [3]. Latent Dirichlet Allocation [5] is clearly one of the most commonly used topic models and numerous extensions of it have been proposed in the literature that are specialized to certain applications including e.g. the Author-Topic Model [22], Correlated Topics Model [4], or the more generalized Structural Topic Model [21]. However, for illustration we will stick to the classical LDA, but our procedure can be easily extended to other topic models as well.

The modeling procedure of LDA using a Gibbs sampler is stochastic in the sense that it depends on initial topic assignments and reassigns tokens based on conditional distributions. This fact is rarely discussed in applications [1], although several approaches have been proposed to overcome this weakness of algorithmic uncertainty: approaches that optimize perplexity [16] or the semantic coherence of topics [6,14,23] and those, that stabilize the results by initializing the topic assignments reasonably [13,15]. In this paper, for the analysis we will use a new method to select a model of a set of LDAs that is named LDAPrototype [19,20], which will be explained in detail in Sect. 2.1.

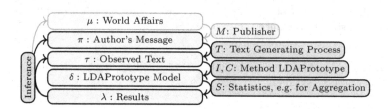

Fig. 1. The stochastic process of text generation: various sources of uncertainty and possible options to do inference on it. Adapted scheme from [2].

When analyzing the evolution of text content over time, it is important to consider various sources of uncertainty in the analysis. Benoit et al. [2] proposed an "Overview of the positions to text to coded data process" visualized in an adapted version in Fig. 1. The diagram relates the following components:

- μ, the true unobservable world affairs researched by journalists and effected by strategic decisions by the publisher M, leading to
- π, the underlying intention of a single text's author,
- τ, the observed text generated by a process T, which is often coded by humans based on a coding scheme that someone devised stochastically, denoted with I. In conjunction with the coding process C itself this leads to

- δ, a table of codings, which are modeled using a preliminarily selected modeling procedure S, resulting in
- λ, values for the coded text, which can be used to do inference on
- the observed text τ, the intended message π and the true preference μ.

The uncertainty of C is well known and can be quantified using intercoder reliability measures like Krippendorff's α [12], which offers the opportunity to do inference on the observed text τ. If we can quantify the uncertainty in T or both, T and M, we can do inference on π or μ, respectively. In fact, there are few works (e.g. [2]) that mention the uncertainty in T or M, respectively.

1.2   Contribution

In the following, we take care especially of the aleatoric uncertainty of the text generating process T. Quality newspapers in general claim to reflect the world affairs, which corresponds to μ in Fig. 1. Besides the fact that the set of world events is not fully observable, we also cannot infer about them objectively from the published newspaper articles. Publishing companies are influenced by a number of (economic and social) factors to select their contents sensibly and to control their quantity. Moreover, the publishers themselves are not even aware of all the world's incidents. This process is condensed in M and it leads to the unobservable messages of the authors π per event or text, respectively. This is the variable about which we want to make a statement. Therefore, we need to know about the text generating process T that maps the author's message to the observed text τ, the articles of the corpus from the Süddeutsche Zeitung.

We show that three natural variants of bootstrap resampling strategies lead to different degrees of captured uncertainty of the text generating process. In addition, we show that these methods lead to uncertainty intervals for aggregations of articles that are considerably different to the model-based one. Our results suggest that this type of aleatoric uncertainty should be considered in particular for small sample sizes, whereas it becomes negligible for larger sample sizes. In our application, it turns out that the simplest approach of resampling words tends to underestimate the uncertainty of T.

2   Methods

For capturing the aleatoric uncertainty in the text generating process, we make use of topic modeling as the measurement instrument I and the coding process C in the inference scheme of Benoit et al. [2] in Fig. 1. That is, in contrast to controlling the stochastic component of the coding process, which is based on manual coding, we need to rule out the algorithmic uncertainty in the modeling process of the topic model.

2.1   Latent Dirichlet Allocation

The topic model we use is a version of the Latent Dirichlet Allocation [5] estimated by a Collapsed Gibbs sampler [10], as a probabilistic topic model that is widely used in text data analysis. The LDA assumes that there is a topic distribution for every text, and it models them by assigning one topic from the set of topics $T = \{T_1, ..., T_K\}$ to every token in a text, where $K \in \mathbb{N}$ is a user-defined parameter, the number of modeled topics. We denote a text (or document) of a corpus consisting of M texts by $D^{(m)}$, where $N^{(m)}$ is the size of text m, while $W = \{W_1, ..., W_V\}$ is the set of words and $V = |W| \in \mathbb{N}$ the vocabulary size. Then, the topic assignments of every text m are given by $T^{(m)}$:

$$D^{(m)} = \left(W_1^{(m)}, ..., W_{N^{(m)}}^{(m)}\right), \quad m = 1, ..., M, \quad W_n^{(m)} \in W, \quad n = 1, ..., N^{(m)},$$

$$T^{(m)} = \left(T_1^{(m)}, ..., T_{N^{(m)}}^{(m)}\right), \quad m = 1, ..., M, \quad T_n^{(m)} \in T, \quad n = 1, ..., N^{(m)}.$$

That is, $T_n^{(m)}$ contains the information of topic assignment of the corresponding token $W_n^{(m)}$ in text m. Let $n_k^{(mv)}, k = 1, ..., K, v = 1, ..., V$ denote the number of assignments of word v in text m to topic k. Then, we define the cumulative count of topic k over all words in document m by $n_k^{(m\bullet)}$ and the vectors of topic counts for the $m = 1, ..., M$ texts by $t^{(m)} = (n_1^{(m\bullet)}, ..., n_K^{(m\bullet)})^T$. Using these definitions, the underlying probability model of LDA [10] can be written as

$$W_n^{(m)} \mid T_n^{(m)}, \phi_k \sim \text{Discrete}(\phi_k), \qquad \phi_k \sim \text{Dirichlet}(\eta),$$

$$T_n^{(m)} \mid \theta_m \sim \text{Discrete}(\theta_m), \qquad \theta_m \sim \text{Dirichlet}(\alpha),$$

where α and η are Dirichlet distribution hyperparameters and must be set by the user. The topic distribution parameters $\theta_m = (\theta_{m,1}, ..., \theta_{m,K})^T \in (0,1)^K$ can be estimated based on the topic counts $t^{(m)}$. Therefore, Griffiths et al. [10] proposed an estimator including a correction for underestimated topics

$$\hat{\theta}_{m,k} = \frac{n_k^{(m\bullet)} + \alpha}{N^{(m)} + K\alpha}.$$

LDAPrototype. Modeling LDAs using a Gibbs sampler is sensitive to the random initialization of topic assignments as mentioned in Sect. 1.1. To control the stochastic nature of LDA we use a recently proposed method to select the "best" model of a set of LDAs. This version of LDA named LDAPrototype [19] leads to an increase of reliability of the conclusions drawn from the prototype model [20]. The increase is obtained by choosing a prototype model as the most central model in the set of all LDA runs, usually from about 100 LDA runs applied to the same dataset. This choice is comparable to the median in the univariate case. The approach is implemented in the R [17] package ldaPrototype [18].

2.2   Text Generating Process

The stochastic component in the process of text generation T in Fig. 1 can be quantified model-based or by bootstrap simulation. For the latter case we will use bootstrap resampling of texts.

Model-Based Uncertainty Estimation. To estimate the aleatoric uncertainty of the random process of text generation we can use our chosen topic model. That is, we assume the underlying text generating process of the LDA model to represent the truth. We estimate topic proportions by $\hat{\theta}_{m,k}$. For the expected value it holds $E(\hat{\theta}_{m,k}) = \theta_{m,k}$, if $\hat{\theta}_{m,k}$ is unbiased, that is on average $\hat{\theta}_{m,k}$ reproduces the true unobservable $\theta_{m,k}$. Then, if $\sum_{k=1}^{K} \theta_{m,k} = 1$ $\forall m = 1, ..., M$ and $(\theta_{m,k})_{k=1,...,K}$ are the true, but unobservable topic proportions of the intended message of text m, we obtain from the multinomial distribution

$$E\left(n_k^{(m\bullet)}\right) = N^{(m)}\hat{\theta}_{m,k} \quad \text{and} \quad \text{Var}\left(n_k^{(m\bullet)}\right) = N^{(m)}\hat{\theta}_{m,k}\left(1 - \hat{\theta}_{m,k}\right),$$

where $n_k^{(m\bullet)} \sim \text{Binomial}\left(N^{(m)}, \theta_{m,k}\right)$ and $t^{(m)} \sim \text{Multinomial}\left(N^{(m)}, \theta_m\right)$.

The binomial distribution offers the possibility to calculate an approximate confidence interval for $\theta_{m,k}$ based on the normal distribution [24] given by

$$\text{Var}\left(\hat{\theta}_{m,k}\right) = \frac{\hat{\theta}_{m,k}\left(1 - \hat{\theta}_{m,k}\right)}{N^{(m)}} \Rightarrow \text{CI}_{\theta_{m,k}} = \left[\hat{\theta}_{m,k} \pm z_{1-\alpha/2}\sqrt{\frac{\hat{\theta}_{m,k}(1 - \hat{\theta}_{m,k})}{N^{(m)}}}\right],$$

where $z_{1-\alpha/2}$ denotes the $(1-\alpha/2)$-quantile of the standard normal distribution. This enables us to quantify the uncertainty of the text generating process of a single text in our corpus based on the chosen topic model LDA. The requirement of a large sample size for an adequate construction of approximate confidence intervals will be not always satisfied for individual texts, but certainly will apply to a (large) number of aggregated texts. Furthermore, it is often of interest to consider those aggregations of texts, especially stratified by time intervals, as for example daily newspaper editions. In Sect. 3, we consider daily newspaper editions of the Süddeutsche Zeitung. However, due to the fact that generally $\text{Cov}(n_k^{(m_1\bullet)}, n_k^{(m_2\bullet)}) \neq 0$ holds for two selected texts $m_1, m_2 \in \{1, ..., M\}$, the analytic derivation of $\text{Var}(n_k^{(m_1\bullet)} + n_k^{(m_2\bullet)})$ is complicated. In this case, the bootstrap approach provides a remedy.

Bootstrap-Based Uncertainty Estimation. The seminal idea of the bootstrap [7,8] is that a random sample x relates to its population in the same manner as a random sample x^* drawn independently with replacement from x relates to the random sample x itself. We will use the bootstrap idea to estimate the uncertainty of the text generating process using resampled texts. There are several natural ways how to bootstrap texts. We will propose and investigate three versions:

1. **BW**ord: The text is understood as one bag of words and these words are bootstrapped. The BWord approach corresponds to the model-based assessment and is equivalent to it for a large number of bootstrap replications.
2. **BS**entence: The text is split into sentences and these sentences are put in a imaginary bag of sentences to create new texts generated by resampled sentences. This approach takes more natural structure of the texts into account.
3. **BS**entence**W**ord: This approach is a kind of intermediate of both. At first the BS approach is executed, that is, sentences are resampled. Afterwards, every resampled sentence is resampled with respect to its words. The second step corresponds to a BW approach for sentences.

In the present case we replicate every text 25 000 times using each of the three introduced methods. For aggregation statistics we resample $R = 100\,000$ combinations based on each set of resampled texts. The words in each bootstrapped text are assigned to the corresponding topics from the LDAPrototype model according to the tokens of the original texts. To save computation time, if a text contains less than ten words, in BW we determine all possible combinations of words. The number of possible combinations is given by $\binom{2n-1}{n-1}$, where n denotes the number of individuals. That is, for $n = 9$ we have 24 310 combinations and for $n = 5$ there are only 126 possibilities to combine these five words with replacement. We proceed analogously for the BS approach; for BSW, only if the according text contains one single sentence consisting of less than ten words. Then, we build bootstrap intervals for θ reaching from the 0.025%- to the 0.975%-quantile of $\hat{\theta}_r, r = 1, ..., R$.

As we investigate a daily newspaper, we also calculate daily aggregation statistics using a rolling window approach for 7, 15 and 29 days. That is, for every single day and topic we calculate the mean of the daily count of topic assignments for ± 3, ± 7 or ± 14 days. The estimator is denoted by $\hat{p}$ and is defined as the simple proportion of topic assignments for each topic at the given day. We determine bootstrap intervals for the real topic proportion p in the style of those for θ. In addition, we measure the relative standard deviation of $\hat{p}$ by the coefficient of variation defined as the ratio of empirical standard deviation and the sample mean $\bar{\hat{p}}$ of the $\hat{p}_r, r = 1, ..., R$, which is given by

$$\text{CV}(\hat{p}) = \frac{1}{\bar{\hat{p}}} \sqrt{\frac{1}{R-1} \sum_{r=1}^{R} \left(\hat{p}_r - \bar{\hat{p}}\right)^2}.$$

This allows us to make uncertainty statements not only in dependence of single topics' proportions but more general depending on the level of $\hat{p}$.

3   Analysis

For the following analysis we refer to a corpus of newspaper articles. We consider the complete set of texts published in the daily German quality newspaper Süddeutsche Zeitung in 2018. It consists of 51 026 articles. We perform classical

Table 1. Statistics of the number of words per text, sentences per text and words per sentence in the preprocessed corpus of Süddeutsche Zeitung in 2018.

	Min	25%	Median	Mean	75%	Max
Words per text	2	59	164	217	321	2 220
Sentences per text	1	7	20	28	37	752
Words per sentence	1	4	7	8	10	171

preprocessing steps for text corpora as removal of numbers, punctuation and distinct German stopwords. In addition, all words that occur ten times or less are deleted from the corpus. The corpus results to consist of $M = 48\,753$ non-empty texts with a vocabulary size of $V = 76\,499$ words. Preprocessing is done with the R packages tosca [11] and tm [9].

Table 1 gives an overview of the resulting number of words or sentences per text and the number of words per sentence. We can conclude that after preprocessing there is a large proportion of rather short texts of less than 300 words, while there is a small number of clearly longer texts with up to 2 220 words. We observe around 28 sentences per text and 8 words per sentence in mean. Mainly due to enumerations of sports results and similar, there is a single text containing 752 sentences and there are 17 sentences with more than 100 words.

3.1   Study Design

We analyze the presented corpus using the proposed methods to quantify the aleatoric uncertainty resulting from the stochastic text generating process T regarding to Fig. 1. For this purpose, we assign each word of a text to a topic using the LDAPrototype approach. This corresponds to the coding scheme I (selection of the model) and coding process C (modeling procedure itself). Based on the resulting model of the prototype method δ, the calculation of estimators for topic proportions per document and aggregation statistics lead to the final results λ. These are used to draw conclusions about the observed text τ as well as about the author's message π. In addition, we once generate stratified subcorpora containing 10, 20, 30 or 50% of the articles per day.

Due to the high combinatorial possibility of parameter selection, some parameters have to be chosen arbitrarily but sensibly. We select $K = 50$ and $\alpha = \eta = 1/K = 1/50$ as parameters for the LDA which implies that we assume 50 topics to be present in the corpus. The mixture parameters α and η are selected rather small to create relatively disjoint topics and to meet the intuitive assumption of few but dominant topics per article. In addition, the Gibbs sampler is supposed to iterate 200 times to the final LDA result. The LDAPrototype parameters are all taken from the default setting [18]. Data and scripts can be retrieved from the GitHub repository https://github.com/JonasRieger/edml2020.

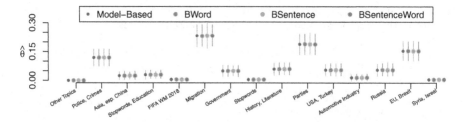

Fig. 2. Estimated topic proportions and corresponding confidence intervals for the article "Wochenchronik vom 30. Juni bis 6. Juli 2018" (weekly chronicle) in Süddeutsche Zeitung published on 7th of July in 2018.

3.2 Results

We analyze the corpus in dependence of the different bootstrap approaches and sample sizes. The topic assignment for a specific token is considered to be constant determined by the LDAPrototype to eliminate the algorithmic uncertainty. Hence, the sample size does not effect the estimation for a single document.

For the analysis of topic proportions on a document level $\hat{\theta}$, we select one article at random. Figure 2 shows the estimation of topic proportions of this random article, which is about a summary of the previous week from the department of politics. The article deals with the topics *Migration, Parties, EU & Brexit* and *Police & Crimes* at most. This is plausible because the text is mainly about the so-called asylum package that the government parties in Germany adopted on 5th of July. Figure 2 shows that all three bootstrap approaches overall match the model-based confidence interval. Only the intervals resulting from the BS approach differ for some topic proportions slightly from the model-based interval. A reason could be that a certain sentence often consists of one dominating topic, which results in wider intervals for those topics and smaller intervals for topics that are spread over many sentences. The latter is true for the topic *Stopwords*

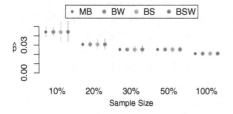

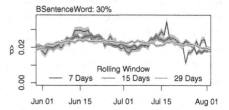

Fig. 3. Estimated topic proportions and corresponding confidence intervals for the topic *Migration* on 7th of July in 2018 for different sample sizes of articles.

Fig. 4. Smoothed estimated topic proportions and corresponding confidence intervals for the topic *Migration* using the BSW approach and a sample size of 30% from 1st of June to 31st of July in 2018.

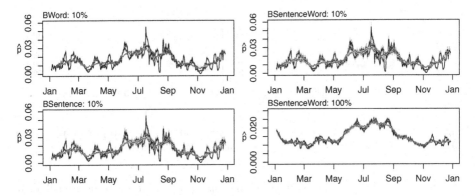

Fig. 5. Smoothed estimated topic proportions and corresponding confidence intervals for the topic *Migration* and for different bootstrap approaches and sample sizes in 2018 using a rolling window over 7 (black), 15 (blue) and 29 days (red). (Color figure online)

& Education, which appears in almost every sentence because of its composition of stopwords, so that the corresponding uncertainty is rather low. Despite the removal of stopwords there are still stopword topics where less distinct stopwords can be found that were not excluded from the outset.

In the following, we focus on the topic *Migration* for an exemplary analysis of the history of media coverage for a single topic. The proportion of the selected topic $\hat{p}$ on 7th of July in 2018, corresponding confidence intervals of the bootstrap approaches and the model-based interval in dependence of the sample size can be seen in Fig. 3. The LDA-based interval differs from its bootstrap counterpart BW because the implicit assumption that the covariance of two texts equals zero is not fulfilled here (see Sect. 2.2). Instead, the uncertainty balances itself out over a large number of articles. The BS intervals are the second widest, while the BSW approach adds some additional uncertainty to it leading to slightly larger intervals. There are 229 articles published at the 7th of July, that is, the sample sizes of 10, 20, 30 and 50% correspond to 22, 45, 68 and 114 articles, respectively. Apparently, a higher number of articles is able to balance itself better, the monotony of the drop in level results from the monotonous selection of articles from the complete data set.

It is common to consider visualizations of topic proportions over time in topic model analysis. Daily topic counts or proportions fluctuate frequently. To overcome this issue, we make use of the rolling window method with window widths of 7, 15 and 29. Figure 5 displays a selection of combinations of those smoothed curves for the topic *Migration*. It is clear that the larger the window size, the smoother the associated curves become and the lower the sample size is, the wider are the intervals that characterize the uncertainty of the text generating process. The topic proportions of the BS and BSW approaches are subject to greater uncertainty than BW. This matches the findings regarding Fig. 3.

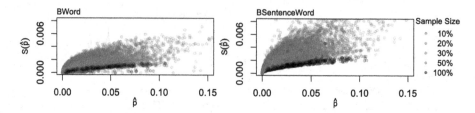

Fig. 6. Coefficient of variation of the daily topic proportion for all topics at all days in 2018, for the BW and BSW approach and for different sample sizes.

Figure 4 makes the uncertainty of the topic proportion even more visible. It zooms into the months June and July in 2018 and considers 30% of the articles for the BSW approach. It shows that larger window widths lead to narrower intervals, which can be explained by the better balance through multiple values.

To generalize the results in a proper way, Fig. 6 visualizes the standard deviations of topic proportions in dependence of the topic proportion itself. It compares the resampling approaches BW and BSW (results for BS and BSW are similar) and the five sample sizes. For BW the uncertainty is easier to estimate, the points are not as scattered as for BSW. The estimated uncertainty in dependence of $\hat{p}$ is for BW less pronounced. For example, for $\hat{p} = 0.1$ one should add about 0.001 in uncertainty, while BSW suggest almost 0.002. For smaller sample sizes the effect increases (10%: BW ≈ 0.004, BS ≈ 0.006, BSW > 0.007).

4   Discussion

We have found that for a single article the aleatoric uncertainty of the text generating process can be well quantified by the presented LDA-based confidence interval. The estimator $\hat{\theta}_{m,k}$ is not unbiased, but it shifts the estimator for each topic towards K^{-1} for small sample sizes to represent the usually symmetric chosen a-priori distribution. This robustness property leads to slightly smaller confidence intervals, that matches the more computational-intensive bootstrap intervals to a sufficient extent for all considered articles.

However this intuitive way of calculating confidence intervals is not suitable for aggregated texts as implicitly the covariances $\mathrm{Cov}(n_k^{(m_1\bullet)}, n_k^{(m_2\bullet)})$ are assumed to be zero for the calculation of the LDA-based confidence intervals. Obviously, this is not true in general, leading to intervals that are too small and do not represent appropriately the aleatoric uncertainty of the text generating process for aggregated texts.

For a large number of texts the uncertainty regarding aggregated values becomes negligibly small. On the other hand, especially for small sample sizes, the aleatoric uncertainty of the text generating process should be considered. The three bootstrap methods presented are suitable for this purpose, whereby BW ignores potential dependencies and thus seems to slightly underestimate the uncertainty and BS and BSW are usually very similar. The more intuitive approach of the two seems to be BSW. One can well imagine that authors make use of certain sentence bodies, but these sentences vary slightly. This corresponds exactly to the BSentenceWord approach, which we therefore recommend for assessing the aleatoric uncertainty of the text generating process for aggregated values in small sample size scenarios.

Acknowledgments. The present study is part of a project of the Dortmund Center for data-based Media Analysis (DoCMA). In addition, the authors gratefully acknowledge the computing time provided on the Linux HPC cluster at TU Dortmund University (LiDO3), partially funded in the course of the Large-Scale Equipment Initiative by the German Research Foundation (DFG) as project 271512359.

References

1. Agrawal, A., Fu, W., Menzies, T.: What is wrong with topic modeling? And how to fix it using search-based software engineering. Inf. Softw. Technol. **98**, 74–88 (2018). https://doi.org/10.1016/j.infsof.2018.02.005
2. Benoit, K., Laver, M., Mikhaylov, S.: Treating words as data with error: uncertainty in text statements of policy positions. Am. J. Polit. Sci. **53**(2), 495–513 (2009). https://doi.org/10.1111/j.1540-5907.2009.00383.x
3. Blei, D.M.: Probabilistic topic models. Commun. ACM **55**(4), 77–84 (2012). https://doi.org/10.1145/2133806.2133826
4. Blei, D.M., Lafferty, J.D.: A correlated topic model of science. Ann. Appl. Stat. **1**(1), 17–35 (2007). https://doi.org/10.1214/07-AOAS114
5. Blei, D.M., Ng, A.Y., Jordan, M.I.: Latent Dirichlet allocation. J. Mach. Learn. Res. **3**, 993–1022 (2003). https://doi.org/10.1162/jmlr.2003.3.4-5.993
6. Chang, J., Boyd-Graber, J., Gerrish, S., Wang, C., Blei, D.M.: Reading tea leaves: how humans interpret topic models. In: Proceedings of the 22nd International NIPS-Conference, pp. 288–296. Curran Associates Inc. (2009). https://dl.acm.org/doi/10.5555/2984093.2984126
7. Efron, B.: Bootstrap methods: another look at the jackknife. Ann. Stat. 7(1), 1–26 (1979), http://www.jstor.org/stable/10.2307/2958830
8. Efron, B., Tibshirani, R.: An Introduction to the Bootstrap. Chapman & Hall/CRC, New York (1994). https://doi.org/10.1201/9780429246593
9. Feinerer, I., Hornik, K., Meyer, D.: Text mining infrastructure in R. J. Stat. Softw. **25**(5), 1–54 (2008). https://doi.org/10.18637/jss.v025.i05
10. Griffiths, T.L., Steyvers, M.: Finding scientific topics. Proc. Natl. Acad. Sci. **101**(suppl 1), 5228–5235 (2004). https://doi.org/10.1073/pnas.0307752101
11. Koppers, L., Rieger, J., Boczek, K., von Nordheim, G.: tosca: Tools for Statistical Content Analysis (2019). https://doi.org/10.5281/zenodo.3591068, R package version 0.1-5
12. Krippendorff, K.: Content Analysis: An Introduction to Its Methodology, 3rd edn. Sage Publications, Thousand Oaks (2013)
13. Maier, D., et al.: Applying LDA topic modeling in communication research: toward a valid and reliable methodology. Commun. Methods Measures **12**(2–3), 93–118 (2018). https://doi.org/10.1080/19312458.2018.1430754
14. Mimno, D., Wallach, H.M., Talley, E., Leenders, M., McCallum, A.: Optimizing semantic coherence in topic models. In: Proceedings of the 2011 EMNLP-Conference, pp. 262–272. ACL (2011). https://dl.acm.org/doi/10.5555/2145432.2145462

15. Newman, D., Bonilla, E.V., Buntine, W.: Improving topic coherence with regularized topic models. In: Proceedings of the 24th International NIPS-Conference, pp. 496–504. Curran Associates Inc. (2011). https://dl.acm.org/doi/10.5555/2986459. 2986515

16. Nguyen, V.A., Boyd-Graber, J., Resnik, P.: Sometimes average is best: the importance of averaging for prediction using MCMC inference in topic modeling. In: Proceedings of the 2014 EMNLP-Conference, pp. 1752–1757. ACL (2014). https://doi.org/10.3115/v1/D14-1182

17. R Core Team: R: A Language and Environment for Statistical Computing. R Foundation for Statistical Computing, Vienna, Austria (2019). http://www.R-project.org/

18. Rieger, J.: ldaPrototype: a method in R to get a prototype of multiple latent Dirichlet allocations. J. Open Source Softw. 5(51), 2181 (2020). https://doi.org/10.21105/joss.02181

19. Rieger, J., Koppers, L., Jentsch, C., Rahnenführer, J.: Improving Reliability of Latent Dirichlet Allocation by Assessing Its Stability Using Clustering Techniques on Replicated Runs (2020). https://arxiv.org/abs/2003.04980

20. Rieger, J., Rahnenführer, J., Jentsch, C.: Improving latent Dirichlet allocation: on reliability of the novel method LDA Prototype. In: Métais, E., Meziane, F., Horacek, H., Cimiano, P. (eds.) NLDB 2020. LNCS, vol. 12089, pp. 118–125. Springer, Cham (2020). https://doi.org/10.1007/978-3-030-51310-8_11

21. Roberts, M.E., Stewart, B.M., Tingley, D., Airoldi, E.M.: The structural topic model and applied social science. In: NIPS-Workshop on Topic Models: Computation, Application, and Evaluation (2013)

22. Rosen-Zvi, M., Griffiths, T., Steyvers, M., Smyth, P.: The author-topic model for authors and documents. In: Proceedings of the 20th UAI-Conference, pp. 487–494. AUAI Press (2004). https://dl.acm.org/doi/10.5555/1036843.1036902

23. Stevens, K., Kegelmeyer, P., Andrzejewski, D., Buttler, D.: Exploring topic coherence over many models and many topics. In: Proceedings of the 2012 Joint EMNLP/CoNLL-Conference, pp. 952–961. ACL (2012). https://dl.acm.org/doi/10.5555/2390948.2391052

24. Wald, A.: Tests of statistical hypotheses concerning several parameters when the number of observations is large. Trans. Am. Math. Soc. 54, 426–482 (1943). https://doi.org/10.1090/S0002-9947-1943-0012401-3

A Ranking Stability Measure for Quantifying the Robustness of Anomaly Detection Methods

Lorenzo Perini$^{(\boxtimes)}$ (iD), Connor Galvin, and Vincent Vercruyssen$^{(\boxtimes)}$ (iD)

DTAI Research Group & Leuven.AI, KU Leuven, Leuven, Belgium
{lorenzo.perini,connor.galvin,vincent.vercruyssen}@kuleuven.be

Abstract. Anomaly detection attempts to learn models from data that can detect anomalous examples in the data. However, naturally occurring variations in the data impact the model that is learned and thus which examples it will predict to be anomalies. Ideally, an anomaly detection method should be robust to such small changes in the data. Hence, this paper introduces a *ranking stability measure* that quantifies the robustness of any anomaly detector's predictions by looking at how consistently it ranks examples in terms of their anomalousness. Our experiments investigate the performance of this stability measure under different data perturbation schemes. In addition, they show how the stability measure can complement traditional anomaly detection performance measures, such as area under the ROC curve or average precision, to quantify the behaviour of different anomaly detection methods.

Keywords: Ranking stability · Anomaly detection · Classifier trust

1 Introduction

Anomaly detection attempts to find examples in a dataset that do not conform normal behaviour. It has many applications in areas such as fraud detection, medical disease detection, and cyber security [5]. Because anomalies are in nature unexpected and happen infrequently, the datasets observed in many anomaly detection tasks are especially prone to variation. Hypothetically, if we could collect a dataset multiple times, it would contain different anomalous and normal examples each time. Consequently, an anomaly detection model learned from the data, will each time be slightly different and make different predictions. It would be valuable to quantify just how consistent a detector's predictions are under variations in the training data. We refer to this as the detector's *stability*.

Anomaly detection is typically tackled from an unsupervised perspective because acquiring labels in real world use cases is expensive [17]. For instance, you will not simulate a medical error simply to have an example of anomalous behaviour. Given some training data, an anomaly detection model assigns an anomaly score to each example in the test set. Because the magnitude of this

© Springer Nature Switzerland AG 2020
I. Koprinska et al. (Eds.): ECML PKDD 2020 Workshops, CCIS 1323, pp. 397–408, 2020.
https://doi.org/10.1007/978-3-030-65965-3_27

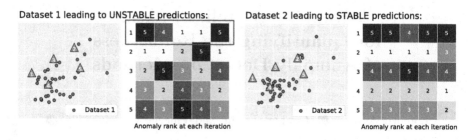

Fig. 1. Illustration of how uncertainty in which training data are observed leads to instability in the rankings. For five iterations (columns), we take a random subset from each dataset (blue dots) to train an LOF model, predict the anomaly scores for the test set examples (orange triangles), and rank them from least anomalous (rank 1) to most anomalous (rank 5). Clearly, small perturbations of dataset 2 have a smaller effect on the consistency of LOF's predictions than small perturbations in dataset 1. (Color figure online)

score conveys the anomalousness of an example, a ranking can be constructed over the test set examples from most to least anomalous. This helps the user to inspect the predictions in a structured way. However, user trust in the anomaly detector's predictions will quickly erode if retraining the model on a slightly different version of the training data yields different predictions (and thus a different ranking). Figure 1 illustrates this process on two toy datasets. Due to different examples being observed in each dataset, the anomaly detection model ranks the test set examples differently each time it is retrained on a subset of the dataset. If the user could quantify the *stability* of a model, it would help her decide which model to use or how to collect her data.

To the best of our knowledge, this paper is the first to contribute a *ranking stability measure* for quantifying the robustness of anomaly detection methods. The stability measure is constructed by retraining an anomaly detector multiple times on different subsets of the training data, each time constructing the ranking over the test set examples, and measuring the consistency between these rankings. The stability measure is computed in a completely unsupervised manner, unlike popular existing performance measures for anomaly detection that require labeled data, such as the area under the ROC curve or average precision [4]. In contrast, our stability measure captures a different aspect of a model's performance, namely its ability to consistently make the same predictions for a set of examples when the training data change.[1] We perform an extensive empirical evaluation of our stability measure and show that it indeed responds meaningfully to changes in the training data. Finally, we conduct a comparison between seven state-of-the-art anomaly detection methods in terms of the stability measure and traditional performance measures.

---

[1] We will experimentally validate this claim in Sect. 4 by measuring correlations between our stability measure and existing performance measures.

2   Related Work

Numerous anomaly detection methods have been developed during the past decades [4, 6]. The focus of this paper, however, is not on any particular method, but on designing a way to measure the stability of a method. The most closely related work in this area is [14]. The authors develop EXCEED, a method to estimate the confidence of any anomaly detector in its example-wise predictions. In contrast, our stability measure does not look at binary predictions but at how different examples are comparatively ranked by an anomaly detector, providing an *aggregate* picture of stability instead.

The idea of stability has sprung up in different areas of machine learning. In particular, [10] proposed a *point stability* measure with respect to clustering. It captures the idea that if two examples belong to the same cluster executed on some subset of the data, they do not necessarily belong to the same cluster if the full dataset is clustered. Similarly, we are interested in the stability of an example's ranking by an anomaly detector. Our measure, however, is not suitable for clustering, while the metrics developed in [10] cannot be applied to anomaly detection or rankings.

Social choice theory studies how individual opinions, preferences, or interests (i.e., rankings of items) can be combined to form a social consensus. Most work is being done on developing algorithms that can derive the consensus ranking from individual's rankings [1]. In addition, rank correlation and rank distance metrics have been developed to measure the agreement between a pair of orderings of items [7]. In contrast, the fundamental insight of our stability measure is that, within the context of anomaly detection, (small) changes in the rank position of an example near the top of the ranking should contribute more to the aggregate stability than (large) changes near the bottom of the ranking.

Ensemble methods for anomaly detection often make use of rank aggregation techniques to aggregate the predictions of the different ensemble members [18, 19]. In contrast, we look at rank aggregation from a post-hoc evaluation perspective. Our stability measure captures consistency in the rankings, but cannot be used to make predictions. This is akin to the intuition behind internal evaluation measures for anomaly detection such as IREOS [12, 13], where the goal is to evaluate the predictive performance of anomaly detectors without access to the ground truth. Our stability measure does not evaluate predictive performance, however, but rather robustness of the predictions.

3   Methodology

This paper tackles the following problem:

Given: a training dataset D_{train} and a test set D_{test}, an anomaly detection model h, and a contamination factor γ;

Design: a stability measure $\mathcal{S}_h$ that quantifies the ability of the model h to rank the examples in D_{test} consistently under variations in D_{train}.

A trained anomaly detection model h computes an anomaly score for each example in D_{test}. These scores can be used to create a *ranking* of the test examples from least to most anomalous. Our key insight is that an unstable model will not produce consistent rankings when retrained on different, uniformly sampled subsets of the training data: the same test set example will sometimes be ranked high and sometimes low. Thus, we can define a model's *stability* in terms of the examples' stabilities:

$$\mathcal{S}_h := \frac{1}{n_t} \sum_{j=1}^{n_t} \mathcal{S}_{x_j}, \tag{1}$$

where, for each example x_j in the test set D_{test} of size n_t, $\mathcal{S}_{x_j}$ captures the consistency in its position in the ranking when retraining h multiple times on variations of D_{train}. We can now estimate the model stability $\mathcal{S}_h$ in three steps. First, we randomly draw subsets from the training set D_{train} to simulate slight changes in the set of available training examples. Each time, we retrain model h and construct a ranking over D_{test}. Second, we assign a stability score to each test set example by taking into account both the variance and the range of its normalized rank positions. Third, we aggregate the stability scores of all test set examples to obtain the model score $\mathcal{S}_h$.

3.1   Generating Anomaly Rankings

Our goal is to design a measure that captures an anomaly detector's consistency in ranking test examples under slight variations of the training data. To simulate these variations, we draw I different subsets D_i from D_{train} without replacement, with $i = 1, \dots, I$ and $|D_i|$ randomly selected as a percentage of $|D_{train}|$. Each time, we retrain h and use it to predict the anomaly score of each test set example. This results in I sets of scores

$$S^{(I)} = \{S^{(i)} \subseteq \mathbb{R}^{n_t} : i = 1, \dots, I\} = \{\{s_1^{(i)}, \dots, s_{n_t}^{(i)} \in \mathbb{R} : n_t \in \mathbb{N}\} : i = 1, \dots, I\},$$

where

$$s_j^{(i)} = h_{D_i}(x_j)$$

is the anomaly score of the example x_j through h when training on subset $D_i \subseteq D_{train}$, and n_t is the number of test set examples. Then, we define the *rank positions* of each example x_j as

$$r_j^{(I)} = \{r_j^{(i)} \in \{1, \dots, n_t\} : i = 1, \dots I\}, \tag{2}$$

where $r_j^{(i)}$ represents the position of the score s_j among the n_t scores when the examples are sorted from lowest anomaly score (position 1) to highest anomaly score (position n_t). We normalize the rank positions by dividing each $r_j^{(i)}$ by n_t. Thus, for any example $x_j \in D_{test}$, its *normalized* list of rank positions will be referred to as $r_j^{(I)}$. For instance, the normalized rank positions of example 1 in dataset 1 of Fig. 1 (red box) are [1.0, 0.8, 0.2, 0.2, 1.0].

3.2   Example-Wise Stability Score

An example's *stability* quantifies the variation in its normalized rank positions. The most obvious way to do this is to measure the standard deviation of an example's rank positions. However, this does not reflect that some changes in ranking are intuitively more important than others. Whether two normal examples change position in the ranking is not so important as whether an anomaly suddenly ranks lower than a normal example. In other words, we care mostly about variations in the top part of the ranking that presumably contains the anomalies (or at least the examples that the model thinks are the anomalies). Knowing the proportion of anomalies in the test set, i.e., the contamination factor γ, we can consider all examples in the top $(1-\gamma)$ % of the ranking to be the anomalies, while the rest are the normals. Thus, for each example $x_j \in D_{test}$, we compute its stability score as:

$$\mathcal{S}_{x_j} = 1 - \frac{1}{Z}\left[\sqrt{\mathrm{Var}\left[r_j^{(I)}\right]} \times \omega\left(r_j^{(I)}; \gamma\right)\right] \tag{3}$$

where the first multiplicative term is the standard deviation of an example's rank positions. This term has values in the range $[0, 0.5]$, as proven in Theorem 1 (see Appendix). The ω-term captures the intuition that an example's ranking should be considered more unstable if its rank positions change near the top as determined by γ. Finally, Z is a normalization constant (see Sect. 3.3).

To model the ω-term, we make use of a $Beta\,(\alpha, \beta)$ distribution defined over the range of all possible normalized rank positions (going from 0 to 1). By carefully setting the α and β parameters, the shape of the distribution can be tailored to our task. First, we set the parameters such that the *mode* of the distribution coincides with the threshold between predicted anomalies and normals:

$$\frac{\alpha - 1}{\alpha + \beta - 2} = 1 - \gamma \implies \gamma\alpha - (1 - \gamma)\beta = 2\gamma - 1. \tag{4}$$

Second, we require that ψ% of the mass of the Beta distribution falls within the interval $[1 - 2\gamma, 1]$. This has the intuitive interpretation that rank changes within this interval have more weight. Hyperparameter ψ is set by the user. To enforce these constraints, we solve the following optimization problem:

$$\min_{\alpha, \beta} \qquad [(1 - \psi) - \mathrm{F}_{\alpha, \beta}(1 - 2\gamma)]^2 \tag{5a}$$

$$\text{subject to} \qquad \alpha \geq 1, \beta \geq 1, \tag{5b}$$

$$\gamma\alpha - (1 - \gamma)\beta = 2\gamma - 1 \tag{5c}$$

where $\mathrm{F}_{\alpha, \beta}(1 - 2\gamma)$ is the cumulative density function of a Beta distribution governed by parameters α and β and evaluated at rank position $1 - 2\gamma$.

The key insight is that the area under the Beta distribution can capture the uncertainty caused by the spread of all possible rankings of an example:

$$\omega\left(r_j^{(I)}; \gamma\right) = \int_{\min_i\left\{r_j^{(i)}\right\}}^{\max_i\left\{r_j^{(i)}\right\}} \frac{x^{\alpha-1}(1 - x)^{\beta-1}}{\mathrm{B}\,(\alpha, \beta)}\, dx, \tag{6}$$

where $B(\alpha, \beta)$ is the beta function. Thus, an example that has a large range of rankings, as indicated by $[\min_i\{r_j^{(i)}\}, \max_i\{r_j^{(i)}\}]$, or whose range is closer to the top of the ranking, is penalized more when computing its stability. If an example is ranked as both the most anomalous (position n_t) and least anomalous (position 1) when training h on different subsets, it gets the maximum penalty possible, which is 1 (the entire area under the Beta distribution).

3.3   The Model Stability Measure

The model stability measure $\mathcal{S}_h$ takes values in the range $[0, 1]$, where a score of 1 means that each of the I rankings is identical. We set the normalization constant Z of Eq. 3 such that a stability score of 0 corresponds to a model that produces completely random rankings each time it is retrained. In fact, we assume that a model performing worse than randomly ranking the examples also gets a stability measure equal to 0, as we are not interested in measuring stability for such unstable scenarios. Thus, in a random scenario (i.e. worst case), the constant Z is equal to the standard deviation of a discrete uniform random variable, as shown in Theorem 2 (see Appendix). The final stability measure for a model h is obtained by taking the average of the stability scores of all test set examples, as defined in Eq. 1. The sample mean allows us to infer a unique stability measure for model h by uniformly weighting all the example-wise stability scores.

4   Experiments

In this section, we try to answer the following questions:[2]

Q1: Does the stability measure behave as we would expect it to?
Q2: How do the hyperparameters of the stability measure influence its value?
Q3: Can we use the stability measure to compare different anomaly detection algorithms, complementing traditional performance measures?

Data. For all experiments in this section, results are presented on 9 datasets that are commonly used in anomaly detection [4]. The datasets vary in number of samples, dimensionality, and γ.[3]

Anomaly Detectors. To test the stability measure, we use 7 well-known anomaly detectors: LOF [3], KNNO [15], IFOREST [11], HBOS [8], INNE [2], OCSVM [16], and CBLOF [9].

---

[2] Code available at: https://github.com/Lorenzo-Perini/StabilityRankings_AD.
[3] Details of data: https://www.dbs.ifi.lmu.de/research/outlier-evaluation/.

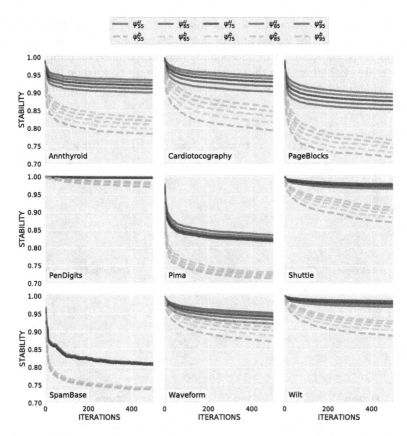

Fig. 2. The figure illustrates how the stability measure behaves under two different strategies to sample the I subsets: uniform sampling (continuous lines) and biased sampling (dashed lines). We vary both the number of iterations I (x-axis) and hyperparameter ψ (lines). Biased sampling of the subsets decreases the stability.

4.1   Results Q1: Behaviour of the Stability Measure

To see whether the stability measure behaves as we would like it to, we test the following hypothesis: "an anomaly detector trained on subsequent *biased* subsets of a dataset, should have a lower stability than the same detector trained on *random* subsets of the same dataset." To simulate this, we compute two versions of our stability measure for a given dataset: (1) a version where the I subsets are drawn uniformly from D_{train}; (2) a version where the subsets are drawn in a biased manner. In practice, we achieve the latter by first clustering D_{train} into 10 clusters and assigning a random weight to all instances in each cluster between every subset iteration. For a given dataset, we repeat this experiment for three anomaly detectors (LOF, KNNO, and IFOREST) using 5-fold cross-validation for each detector, and report the average stability over all folds and detectors. We use different detectors to factor out the dependence on a single model. Figure 2

shows the results for each of the 9 benchmark datasets. The plot also shows how
the stability changes for values of hyperparameters I and ψ. The results confirm
our hypothesis: the stability of an anomaly detector trained on uniformly drawn
subsets is always higher than that of the same detector trained on biased subsets.
This provides evidence that our stability measure conforms our intuitions on how
it should behave.

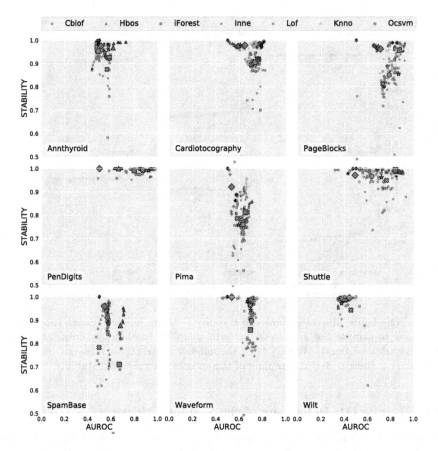

Fig. 3. Each dot of a certain color represents the stability and area under the ROC
curve achieved by one of the 7 anomaly detectors with a given hyperparameter setting
on the dataset. The large dots are the corresponding averages per method. The figure
illustrates that the different detectors have varying stabilities. (Color figure online)

4.2   Results Q2: Hyperparameters

The stability measure has two hyperparameters: the number of iterations I and
the shape of the Beta distribution ψ. Figure 2 shows how the stability measure

changes for different values of these hyperparameters. For each of the 9 datasets, it seems that the stability measure converges after about 250 iterations. For most datasets, the value of ψ does not have a large impact as long as it is around 75%.

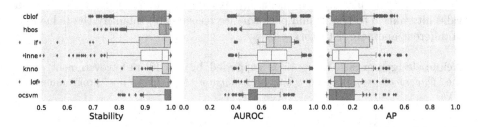

Fig. 4. Comparison of different anomaly detectors in terms of: stability, AUROC, and average precision. For each method and measure, a box plot shows the full range of results obtained over all benchmark datasets and hyperparameter settings.

4.3 Results Q3: Comparing Anomaly Detectors

We apply the 7 anomaly detection methods, each with a variety of hyperparameter settings, to the benchmark datasets and record our stability measure, the area under the ROC curve (AUROC), and the average precision. We compute them using 5-fold cross-validation. Figure 3 plots the results as a scatter plot where each dot represents both the stability and AUROC achieved by applying a method with a certain hyperparameter setting to the corresponding dataset. A large dot corresponds to the performance of a method averaged over all its hyperparameter settings. The figure allows us to compare different methods in terms of their stability. In all datasets, OCSVM has on average the highest stability, meaning that the method is most robust to changes in the training data. The least stable method is CBLOF, which might not be surprising given that it relies on a k-means clustering subroutine and changes in the data easily affect which clusters are found.

Figure 4 aggregates all results for each method and per measure (stability, AUROC, and average precision) over the entire benchmark. Both KNNO and OCSVM seem to be stable methods. Finally, the Pearson correlations between stability and AUROC and average precision are around -0.05 and -0.4 respectively, indicating that our stability measure captures a different aspect of performance than those traditionally used metrics.

5   Conclusion

We proposed a method to quantify the robustness of anomaly detectors by measuring the ranking stability under slight variations of the training data. The method estimates the stability in three steps. First, we simulate perturbations in the training set by drawing i.i.d. subsets. Second, we estimate the example-wise stability score by taking into account both the standard deviation of normalized rankings and the area under a Beta distribution. Third, we derive the stability measure by averaging the normalized stability score. The experiments show that the stability measure can meaningfully capture ranking variations and be a valid alternative to traditional performance measures to quantify the behaviour of different anomaly detectors.

Acknowledgements. This work is supported by the Flemish government under the "*Onderzoeksprogramma Artificiële Intelligentie (AI) Vlaanderen*" programme (LP, VV).

A   Appendix

Theorem 1. *Let $(\Omega, \mathfrak{S}, \mathbb{P})$ be a probability space, where Ω is a set, $\mathfrak{S}$ represents a σ-algebra over Ω and $\mathbb{P}$ is a probability measure. Assume that $X \in L^2$ is a real random variable (continuous or discrete), such that $X \colon \Omega \to \mathcal{V} \subseteq [0,1]$. Then,*

$$0 \leq \mathrm{Var}\,[X] \leq \frac{1}{4}.$$

Proof. Assuming that $0 \leq X \leq 1$,

$$\mathrm{Var}\,[X] = \mathbb{E}\,[X^2] - \mathbb{E}\,[X]^2 \leq \mathbb{E}\,[X] - \mathbb{E}\,[X]^2,$$

where the inequality holds because $0 \leq X \leq 1$. Then,

$$\mathrm{Var}\,[X] \leq \mathbb{E}\,[X] - \mathbb{E}\,[X]^2 = -\left(\mathbb{E}\,[X]^2 - \mathbb{E}\,[X]\right)$$

$$= -\left[\left(\mathbb{E}[X] - \frac{1}{2}\right)^2 - \frac{1}{4}\right] = \frac{1}{4} - \left(\mathbb{E}[X] - \frac{1}{2}\right)^2 \leq \frac{1}{4}.$$

$\square$

Theorem 2. *Let X be a discrete random variable over the probability space $(\Omega, \mathfrak{S}, \mathbb{P})$, where $\Omega = \{1, 2, \dots, n_t\}$, $n_t \in \mathbb{N}$, $\mathfrak{S}$ a σ-algebra over Ω and $\mathbb{P}$ a probability measure. Assume that X follows a discrete uniform distribution. Then, the random variable $\frac{X}{n_t}$ has mean and variance, respectively, equal to*

$$\mathbb{E}\left[\frac{X}{n_t}\right] = \frac{n_t + 1}{2n_t}, \quad \mathrm{Var}\left[\frac{X}{n_t}\right] = \frac{(n_t + 1)(n_t - 1)}{12n_t^2} \tag{7}$$

Proof. We can directly compute the mean and the variance of $\frac{X}{n_t}$ by using the properties of random variables. First, we compute first and second moment of a discrete uniform random variables:

$$\mathbb{E}\,[X] = \sum_{j=1}^{v} x_j \cdot \mathbb{P}(X = x_j) = \frac{1}{n_t} \sum_{j=1}^{n_t} j = \frac{n_t + 1}{2}$$

$$\mathbb{E}\,[X^2] = \sum_{j=1}^{n_t} x_j^2 \cdot \mathbb{P}(X = x_j) = \frac{1}{n_t} \sum_{j=1}^{n_t} i^2 = \frac{(n_t + 1)(2n_t + 1)}{6}. \tag{8}$$

Second, we achieve the goal as follows:

$$\mathbb{E}\left[\frac{X}{n_t}\right] = \frac{1}{n_t}\mathbb{E}[X] = \frac{n_t + 1}{2n_t};$$

$$\text{Var}\left[\frac{X}{n_t}\right] = \frac{1}{n_t^2}\text{Var}[X] = \frac{1}{n_t^2}\left[\mathbb{E}\left[X^2\right] - \mathbb{E}[X]^2\right] = \frac{(n_t + 1)(n_t - 1)}{12n_t^2}. \quad (9)$$

$\square$

References

1. Amodio, S., D'Ambrosio, A., Siciliano, R.: Accurate algorithms for identifying the median ranking when dealing with weak and partial rankings under the kemeny axiomatic approach. Eur. J. Oper. Res. **249**(2), 667–676 (2016)
2. Bandaragoda, T.R., Ting, K.M., Albrecht, D., Liu, F.T., Zhu, Y., Wells, J.R.: Isolation-based anomaly detection using nearest-neighbor ensembles. Comput. Intell. **34**(4), 968–998 (2018)
3. Breunig, M.M., Kriegel, H.P., Ng, R.T., Sander, J.: Lof: identifying density-based local outliers. In: Proceedings of the 2000 ACM SIGMOD International Conference on Management of Data, pp. 93–104 (2000)
4. Campos, G.O., et al.: On the evaluation of unsupervised outlier detection: measures, datasets, and an empirical study. Data Mining Knowl. Disc. **30**(4), 891–927 (2016). https://doi.org/10.1007/s10618-015-0444-8
5. Chandola, V., Banerjee, A., Kumar, V.: Anomaly detection: a survey. ACM Comput. Surv. (CSUR) **41**(3), 1–58 (2009)
6. Domingues, R., Filippone, M., Michiardi, P., Zouaoui, J.: A comparative evaluation of outlier detection algorithms: experiments and analyses. Pattern Recognit. **74**, 406–421 (2018)
7. Emond, E.J., Mason, D.W.: A new rank correlation coefficient with application to the consensus ranking problem. J. Multi-Criteria Decis. Anal. **11**(1), 17–28 (2002)
8. Goldstein, M., Dengel, A.: Histogram-based outlier score (hbos): a fast unsupervised anomaly detection algorithm. KI-2012: Poster and Demo Track, pp. 59–63 (2012)
9. He, Z., Xu, X., Deng, S.: Discovering cluster-based local outliers. Pattern Recognit. Lett. **24**(9–10), 1641–1650 (2003)
10. Höppner, F., Jahnke, M.: Holistic assessment of structure discovery capabilities of clustering algorithms. In: Brefeld, U., Fromont, E., Hotho, A., Knobbe, A., Maathuis, M., Robardet, C. (eds.) ECML PKDD 2019. LNCS (LNAI), vol. 11906, pp. 223–239. Springer, Cham (2020). https://doi.org/10.1007/978-3-030-46150-8_14
11. Liu, F.T., Ting, K.M., Zhou, Z.H.: Isolation-based anomaly detection. ACM Trans. Knowl. Disc. Data (TKDD) **6**(1), 1–39 (2012)
12. Marques, H.O., Campello, R.J.G.B., Zimek, A., Sander, J.: On the internal evaluation of unsupervised outlier detection. In: Proceedings of the 27th International Conference on Scientific and Statistical Database Management (2015)
13. Marques, H.O., Campello, R.J., Sander, J., Zimek, A.: Internal evaluation of unsupervised outlier detection. ACM Trans. Knowl. Disc. Data (TKDD) **14**(4), 1–42 (2020)

14. Perini, L., Vercruyssen, V., Davis, J.: Quantifying the confidence of anomaly detectors in their example-wise predictions. In: The European Conference on Machine Learning and Principles and Practice of Knowledge Discovery in Databases. Springer Verlag (2020)
15. Ramaswamy, S., Rastogi, R., Shim, K.: Efficient algorithms for mining outliers from large data sets. In: Proceedings of the 2000 ACM SIGMOD International Conference on Management of Data, pp. 427–438 (2000)
16. Schölkopf, B., Platt, J.C., Shawe-Taylor, J., Smola, A.J., Williamson, R.C.: Estimating the support of a high-dimensional distribution. Neural Comput. **13**(7), 1443–1471 (2001)
17. Vercruyssen, V., Wannes, M., Gust, V., Koen, M., Ruben, B., Jesse, D.: Semi-supervised anomaly detection with an application to water analytics. In: Proceedings of the IEEE International Conference on Data Mining (2018)
18. Zimek, A., Campello, R.J., Sander, J.: Data perturbation for outlier detection ensembles. In: Proceedings of the 26th International Conference on Scientific and Statistical Database Management, pp. 1–12 (2014)
19. Zimek, A., Gaudet, M., Campello, R.J., Sander, J.: Subsampling for efficient and effective unsupervised outlier detection ensembles. In: Proceedings of the 19th ACM SIGKDD International Conference on Knowledge Discovery and Data Mining, pp. 428–436 (2013)

Second International Workshop on eXplainable Knowledge Discovery in Data Mining (XKDD 2020)

International Workshop on eXplainable Knowledge Discovery in Data Mining (XKDD 2020)

The *2nd International Workshop on eXplainable Knowledge Discovery in Data Mining (XKDD 2020)* was held in conjunction with the *European Conference on Machine Learning and Principles and Practice of Knowledge Discovery in Databases (ECML PKDD 2020)* in Ghent, Belgium, Monday 14th September 2020. The previous edition of the workshop were also held jointly with ECML PKDD in 2019. In line with the organization of ECML-PKDD 2020, the XKDD 2020 workshop has been a fully virtual event with live presentations which were also pre-recorded and are freely available on the workshop website[1].

In the past decade, machine learning based decision systems have been widely used in a plethora of applications ranging from credit score, insurance risk, and health monitoring, in which accuracy is of the utmost importance. Although the application of these systems may bring myriad benefits, their use might involve some ethical and legal risks, such as codifying biases; jeopardizing transparency and privacy, reducing accountability. Unfortunately, these risks increase and are made more serious by the opacity of these systems, which often are complex and their internal logic is usually inaccessible to humans.

Nowadays most of the Artificial Intelligence (AI) systems are based on machine learning algorithms. The relevance and need of ethics in AI is supported and high-lighted by the various initiatives that in the worlds provide recommendations and guidelines in the direction of making AI-based decision systems explainable and compliant with legal and ethical issues. These include the EU's GDPR regulation which introduces, to some extent, a right for all individuals to obtain "meaningful explanations of the logic involved" when automated decision making takes place, the "ACM Statement on Algorithmic Transparency and Accountability", the Informatics Europe's "European Recommendations on Machine-Learned Automated Decision Making" and "The ethics guidelines for trustworthy AI" provided by the EU High-Level Expert Group on AI.

The challenge to design and develop trustworthy AI-based decision systems is still open and requires a joint effort across technical, legal, sociological and ethical domains. For these reasons, the XKDD aimed at encouraging principled research that will lead to the advancement of explainable, transparent, ethical and fair data mining and machine learning. The workshop offered top-quality presentations addressing uncovered important issues related to ethical, explainable and transparent data mining and machine learning.

Topics treated at the XKDD 2020 workshop include:

- Interpretable Machine Learning
- Explainable Artificial Intelligence

---

[1] https://kdd.isti.cnr.it/xkdd2020/.

- Iterative Dialogue Explanations
- Visualization-based Explanations
- Human-in-the-Loop Interactions
- Explanation in Health
- Fair Machine Learning
- Fairness Checking
- Privacy Risk Assessment
- Privacy-Preserving Explanations
- Privacy by Design Approaches for Human Data
- Anonymity and Information Hiding Problems in Comprehensible Models
- Explanation for Privacy Risk
- Ethics Discovery for Explainable AI

The XKDD workshop papers were selected through a single-blind peer-reviewed process in which each submitted paper was assigned to three members of the Program Committee. The main selection criteria were the novelty of the proposal and its impact in explanation/privacy/fairness processes. XKDD received a total of twelve submissions. Seven papers were accepted for presentation. The workshop was organized as a Zoom webinar and we registered an audience of about 270 different users across the whole workshop with a peak of attendees around 130 during the keynote talks.

The program included two excellent and thought-provoking keynotes:

- *Interpretable Machine Learning* by Christopher Molnar, LM University of Munich, Germany
- *Fair Matching and Fair Ranking* by Francesco Bonchi, ISI Foundation, Italy

More information about the workshop, including the videos of the talks, can be found on the workshop website: https://kdd.isti.cnr.it/xkdd2020/. We would like to thank all the participants for making XKDD 2020 a very successful event: Christopher Molnar and Francesco Bonchi for the very fascinating talks, the authors for their interesting works and presentations, and all workshop attendees for their engagement and the questions. A special thank goes to the wonderful Program Committee for their effective and timing reviews.

The organization of XKDD 2020 was supported the European Community H2020 programme under the funding schemes: INFRAIA-1-2014-2015 Res. Infr. G.A. 871042 *SoBigData++* (sobigdata), G.A. 952026 *HumanE AI Net* (humane-ai), G.A. 825619 *AI4EU* (ai4eu), G.A. 834756 *XAI* (xai).

October 2020   Riccardo Guidotti
                                                                   Anna Monreale
                                                                   Salvatore Rinzivillo
                                                                   Przemysław Biecek

XKDD2020 Workshop Organization

XKDD 2020 - Program Chairs

Riccardo Guidotti	University of Pisa, Italy
Anna Monreale	University of Pisa, Italy
Salvatore Rinzivillo	ISTI-CNR, Italy
Przemysław Biecek	Warsaw University of Technology, Poland

XKDD 2020 - Program Committee

Osbert Bastani	University of Pennsylvania, US
Livio Bioglio	University of Turin, Italy
Tobias Blanke	King's College London, UK
Francesco Bonchi	ISI Foundation, Italy
Giuseppe Casalicchio	Ludwig-Maximilians-University of Munich, Germany
Chaofan Chen	Duke University, UK
Luca Costabello	Accenture Labs Dublin, Ireland
Mark Coté	King's College London, UK
Miguel Couceiro	LORIA CNRS, France
Josep Domingo-Ferrer	Universitat Rovira i Virgili, Spain
Boxiang Dong	Montclair State University, US
Alex Freitas	University of Kent, US
Luis Galárraga	Aalborg University, France
Giannotti Fosca	ISTI-CNR Pisa, Italy
Aristides Gionis	KTH Royal Institute of Technology, Sweden
Thibault Laugel	Sorbonne University, France
Paulo Lisboa	Liverpool John Moores University, UK
Pasquale Minervini	University College London, UK
Ioannis Mollas	Aristotle University of Thessaloniki, Greece
Christoph Molnar	Ludwig-Maximilians-University of Munich, Germany
Cecilia Panigutti	Scuola Normale Superiore Pisa, Italy
András Pataricza	Technical University of Budapest, Hungary
Dino Pedreschi	University of Pisa, Italy
Francesca Pratesi	University of Pisa, Italy
Xavier Renard	AXA - LinkedIn, Frances
Fabrizio Sebastiani	ISTI-CNR, Italy
Dylan Slack	University of California Irvine, US
Dominik Slezak	University of Warsaw, Poland
Vicenc Torra	Umeå University, Sweden
Grigorios Tsoumakas	Aristotle University of Thessaloniki, Greece
Franco Turini	University of Pisa, Italy
Cagatay Turkay	University of Warwick, UK

XKDD2020 Keynote Talks

Interpretable Machine Learning

Christopher Molnar

LM University of Munich, Germany

Abstract. We present a brief history of the field of interpretable machine learning (IML), give an overview of state-of-the-art interpretation methods and discuss challenges. Research in IML has boomed in recent years. As young as the field is, it has over 200 years old roots in regression modeling and rule-based machine learning, starting in the 1960s. Recently, many new IML methods have been proposed, many of them model-agnostic, but also interpretation techniques specific to deep learning and tree-based ensembles. IML methods either directly analyze model components, study sensitivity to input perturbations, or analyze local or global surrogate approximations of the ML model. The field approaches a state of readiness and stability, with many methods not only proposed in research, but also implemented in open-source software. But many important challenges remain for IML, such as dealing with dependent features, causal interpretation, and uncertainty estimation, which need to be resolved for its successful application to scientific problems. A further challenge is a missing rigorous definition of interpretability, which is accepted by the community. To address the challenges and advance the field, we urge to recall our roots of interpretable, data-driven modeling in statistics and (rule-based) ML, but also to consider other areas such as sensitivity analysis, causal inference, and the social sciences.

Biography

Christoph Molnar is a PhD candidate at the Statistical Learning and Data Science Chair at the LMU Munich (Germany). He is author of the book Interpretable Machine Learning (https://christophm.github.io/interpretable-ml-book/) and the R package *iml*, which implements interpretation tools for machine learning. His research focuses on model-agnostic interpretation methods for machine learning.

Fair Matching and Fair Ranking

Francesco Bonchi

ISI Foundation, Italy

Abstract. Matching and ranking algorithms are used routinely in many decision making processes in spheres such as health (e.g., recipients list for solid organs transplantation, triage in pandemic), education (e.g., university admission), or employment (e.g., selection for a job), which can have a direct tangible impact on people's life. Although many valid solutions may exist to a given problem instance, when the elements that shall be matched or ranked in a solution correspond to individuals, it becomes of paramount importance that the solution is selected fairly. In this talk I present a new line of research recently started together with David Garcia-Soriano, in which we study individual fairness in combinatorial problems and argue that, given that many different valid solutions may exist, each one satisfying a different set of individuals, the only way to guarantee fairness is through randomization. Our proposal, named distributional max-min fairness, uses randomization to maximize the expected satisfaction of the worst-off individuals.

Biography

Francesco Bonchi is Scientific Director at the ISI Foundation, Turin, Italy, where he's also coordinating the "Learning and Algorithms for Data Analytics" Research Area. Before becoming Scientific Director (April 2020), he was Deputy Director with responsibility over the Industrial Research area and head of the Algorithmic Data Analytics group. Earlier he was Director of Research at Yahoo Labs in Barcelona, Spain, where he was leading the Web Mining Research group. He is also (part-time) Research Director for Big Data & Data Science at Eurecat (Technological Center of Catalunya), Barcelona. His recent research interests include algorithms and learning on graphs and complex networks (e.g., financial networks, social networks, brain networks), fair and explainable AI, and more in general, privacy and all ethical aspects of data analysis and AI. He has more than 200 publications in these areas. He also filed 16 US patents, and got granted 9 US patents. He has been Program Chair and General Chair of several international conferences and workshops in the field of knowledge discovery and machine learning.

Interpretable Machine Learning – A Brief History, State-of-the-Art and Challenges

Christoph Molnar$^{(\boxtimes)}$ ⓘ, Giuseppe Casalicchio ⓘ, and Bernd Bischl ⓘ

Department of Statistics, LMU Munich, Ludwigstr. 33, 80539 Munich, Germany
`christoph.molnar@stat.uni-muenchen.de`

Abstract. We present a brief history of the field of interpretable machine learning (IML), give an overview of state-of-the-art interpretation methods and discuss challenges. Research in IML has boomed in recent years. As young as the field is, it has over 200 years old roots in regression modeling and rule-based machine learning, starting in the 1960s. Recently, many new IML methods have been proposed, many of them model-agnostic, but also interpretation techniques specific to deep learning and tree-based ensembles. IML methods either directly analyze model components, study sensitivity to input perturbations, or analyze local or global surrogate approximations of the ML model. The field approaches a state of readiness and stability, with many methods not only proposed in research, but also implemented in open-source software. But many important challenges remain for IML, such as dealing with dependent features, causal interpretation, and uncertainty estimation, which need to be resolved for its successful application to scientific problems. A further challenge is a missing rigorous definition of interpretability, which is accepted by the community. To address the challenges and advance the field, we urge to recall our roots of interpretable, data-driven modeling in statistics and (rule-based) ML, but also to consider other areas such as sensitivity analysis, causal inference, and the social sciences.

Keywords: Interpretable Machine Learning · Explainable artificial intelligence

1 Introduction

Interpretability is often a deciding factor when a machine learning (ML) model is used in a product, a decision process, or in research[1]. Interpretable machine learning (IML)[2] methods can be used to discover knowledge, to debug or justify

---

[1] This project is funded by the Bavarian State Ministry of Science and the Arts and coordinated by the Bavarian Research Institute for Digital Transformation (bidt) and supported by the German Federal Ministry of Education and Research (BMBF) under Grant No. 01IS18036A. The authors of this work take full responsibilities for its content.

[2] Sometimes the term Explainable AI is used.

© Springer Nature Switzerland AG 2020
I. Koprinska et al. (Eds.): ECML PKDD 2020 Workshops, CCIS 1323, pp. 417–431, 2020.
https://doi.org/10.1007/978-3-030-65965-3_28

the model and its predictions, and to control and improve the model [1]. In this paper, we take a look at the historical building blocks of IML and give an overview of methods to interpret models. We argue that IML has reached a state of readiness, but some challenges remain.

2   A Brief History of IML

A lot of IML research happened in the last couple of years. But learning interpretable models from data has a much longer tradition. Linear regression models were used by Gauss, Legendre, and Quetelet [37, 64, 90, 109] as early as the beginning of the 19th century and have since then grown into a vast array of regression analysis tools [98, 115], for example, generalized additive models [45] and elastic net [132]. The philosophy behind these statistical models is usually to make certain distributional assumptions or to restrict the model complexity beforehand and thereby imposing intrinsic interpretability of the model.

In ML, a slightly different modeling approach is pursued. Instead of restricting the model complexity beforehand, ML algorithms usually follow a non-linear, non-parametric approach, where model complexity is controlled through one or more hyperparameters and selected via cross-validation. This flexibility often results in less interpretable models with good predictive performance. A lot of ML research began in the second half of the 20th century with research on, for example, support vector machines in 1974 [119], early important work on neural networks in the 1960s [100], and boosting in 1990 [99]. Rule-based ML, which covers decision rules and decision trees, has been an active research area since the middle of the 20th century [35].

While ML algorithms usually focus on predictive performance, work on interpretability in ML – although underexplored – has existed for many years. The built-in feature importance measure of random forests [13] was one of the important IML milestones.[3] In the 2010s came the deep learning hype, after a deep neural network won the ImageNet challenge. A few years after that, the IML field really took off (around 2015), judging by the frequency of the search terms "Interpretable Machine Learning" and "Explainable AI" on Google (Fig. 1, right) and papers published with these terms (Fig. 1, left). Since then, many model-agnostic explanation methods have been introduced, which work for different types of ML models. But also model-specific explanation methods have been developed, for example, to interpret deep neural networks or tree ensembles. Regression analysis and rule-based ML remain important and active research areas to this day and are blending together (e.g., model-based trees [128], RuleFit [33]). Many extensions of the linear regression model exist [25, 38, 45] and new extensions are proposed until today [14, 26, 27, 117]. Rule-based ML also remains an active area of research (for example, [52, 66, 123]). Both regression models and rule-based ML serve as standalone ML algorithms, but also as building blocks for many IML approaches.

---

[3] The random forest paper has been cited over 60,000 times (Google Scholar; September 2020) and there are many papers improving the importance measure ([44, 55, 110, 111]) which are also cited frequently.

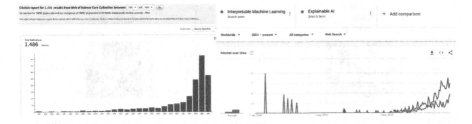

Fig. 1. Left: Citation count for research articles with keywords "Interpretable Machine Learning" or "Explainable AI" on Web of Science (accessed August 10, 2020). Right: Google search trends for "Interpretable Machine Learning" and "Explainable AI" (accessed August 10, 2020).

3 Today

IML has reached a first state of readiness. Research-wise, the field is maturing in terms of methods surveys [1,6,15,23,41,75,96,120], further consolidation of terms and knowledge [17,22,42,82,88,97], and work about defining interpretability or evaluation of IML methods [49,73,74,95]. We have a better understanding of weaknesses of IML methods in general [75,79], but also specifically for methods such as permutation feature importance [7,51,110,111], Shapley values [57,113], counterfactual explanations [63], partial dependence plots [7,50,51] and saliency maps [2]. Open source software with implementations of various IML methods is available, for example, *iml* [76] and *DALEX* [11] for R [91] and *Alibi* [58] and *InterpretML* [83] for Python. Regulation such as GDPR and the need for ML trustability, transparency and fairness have sparked a discussion around further needs of interpretability [122]. IML has also arrived in industry [36], there are startups that focus on ML interpretability and also big tech companies offer software [8,43,126].

4 IML Methods

We distinguish IML methods by whether they analyze model components, model sensitivity[4], or surrogate models, illustrated in Fig. 2.[5]

---

[4] Not to be confused with the research field of sensitivity analysis, which studies the uncertainty of outputs in mathematical models and systems. There are methodological overlaps (e.g., Shapley values), but also differences in methods and how input data distributions are handled.

[5] Some surveys distinguish between *ante-hoc (or transparent design, white-box models, inherently interpretable model)* and *post-hoc* IML method, depending on whether interpretability is considered at model design and training or after training, leaving the (black-box) model unchanged. Another category separates model-agnostic and model-specific methods.

Fig. 2. Some IML approaches work by assigning meaning to individual model components (left), some by analyzing the model predictions for perturbations of the data (right). The surrogate approach, a mixture of the two other approaches, approximates the ML model using (perturbed) data and then analyzes the components of the interpretable surrogate model.

4.1   Analyzing Components of Interpretable Models

In order to analyze components of a model, it needs to be decomposable into parts that we can interpret individually. However, it is not necessarily required that the user understands the model in its entirety (simulatability [82]). Component analysis is always model-specific, because it is tied to the structure of the model.

Inherently interpretable models are models with (learned) structures and (learned) parameters which can be assigned a certain interpretation. In this context, linear regression models, decision trees and decision rules are considered to be interpretable [30,54]. Linear regression models can be interpreted by analyzing components: The model structure, a weighted sum of features, allows to interpret the weights as the effects that the features have on the prediction.

Decision trees and other rule-based ML models have a learned structure (e.g., "IF feature $x_1 > 0$ and feature $x_2 \in \{A, B\}$, THEN predict 0.6"). We can interpret the learned structure to trace how the model makes predictions.

This only works up to a certain point in high-dimensional scenarios. Linear regression models with hundreds of features and complex interaction terms or deep decision trees are not that interpretable anymore. Some approaches aim to reduce the parts to be interpreted. For example, LASSO [98,115] shrinks the coefficients in a linear model so that many of them become zero, and pruning techniques shorten trees.

4.2   Analyzing Components of More Complex Models

With a bit more effort, we can also analyze components of more complex black-box models.[6] For example, the abstract features learned by a deep convolutional neural network (CNN) can be visualized by finding or generating images that activate a feature map of the CNN [84]. For the random forest, the minimal depth distribution [56,85] and the Gini importance [13] analyze the structure of the trees of the forest and can be used to quantify feature importance. Some

---

[6] This blurs the line between an "inherently interpretable" and a "black-box" model.

approaches aim to make the parts of a model more interpretable with, for example, a monotonicity constraint [106] or a modified loss function for disentangling concepts learned by a convolutional neural network [130].

If an ML algorithm is well understood and frequently used in a community, like random forests in ecology research [19], model component analysis can be the correct tool, but it has the obvious disadvantage that it is tied to that specific model. And it does not combine well with the common model selection approach in ML, where one usually searches over a large class of different ML models via cross-validation.

4.3   Explaining Individual Predictions

Methods that study the sensitivity of an ML model are mostly model-agnostic and work by manipulating input data and analyzing the respective model predictions. These IML methods often treat the ML model as a closed system that receives feature values as an input and produces a prediction as output. We distinguish between local and global explanations.

Local methods explain individual predictions of ML models. Local explanation methods have received much attention and there has been a lot of innovation in the last years. Popular local IML methods are Shapley values [69,112] and counterfactual explanations [20,81,116,118,122]. Counterfactual explanations explain predictions in the form of what-if scenarios, which builds on a rich tradition in philosophy [108]. According to findings in the social sciences [71], counterfactual explanations are "good" explanations because they are contrastive and focus on a few reasons. A different approach originates from collaborative game theory: The Shapley values [104] provide an answer on how to fairly share a payout among the players of a collaborative game. The collaborative game idea can be applied to ML where features (i.e., the players) collaborate to make a prediction (i.e., the payout) [68,69,112].

Some IML methods rely on model-specific knowledge to analyze how changes in the input features change the output. Saliency maps, an interpretation method specific for CNNs, make use of the network gradients to explain individual classifications. The explanations are in the form of heatmaps that show how changing a pixel can change the classification. The saliency map methods differ in how they backpropagate [69,80,105,107,114]. Additionally, model-agnostic versions [69,95,129] exist for analyzing image classifiers.

4.4   Explaining Global Model Behavior

Global model-agnostic explanation methods are used to explain the expected model behavior, i.e., how the model behaves on average for a given dataset. A useful distinction of global explanations are feature importance and feature effect. Feature importance ranks features based on how relevant they were for the prediction. Permutation feature importance [16,28] is a popular importance measure, originally suggested for random forests [13]. Some importance measures rely on removing features from the training data and retraining the model [65].

An alternative are variance-based measures [40]. See [125] for an overview of importance measures.

The feature effect expresses how a change in a feature changes the predicted outcome. Popular feature effect plots are partial dependence plots [32], individual conditional expectation curves [39], accumulated local effect plots [7], and the functional ANOVA [50]. Analyzing influential data instances, inspired by statistics, provides a different view into the model and describes how influential a data point was for a prediction [59].

4.5 Surrogate Models

Surrogate models[7] are interpretable models designed to "copy" the behavior of the ML model. The surrogate approach treats the ML model as a black-box and only requires the input and output data of the ML model (similar to sensitivity analysis) to train a surrogate ML model. However, the interpretation is based on analyzing components of the interpretable surrogate model. Many IML methods are surrogate model approaches [10,18,34,61,72,75,89,95] and differ, e.g., in the targeted ML model, the data sampling strategy, or the interpretable model that is used. There are also methods for extracting, e.g., decision rules from specific models based on their internal components such as neural network weights [5,9]. LIME [95] is an example of a local surrogate method that explains individual predictions by learning an interpretable model with data in proximity to the data point to be explained. Numerous extensions of LIME exist, which try to fix issues with the original method, extend it to other tasks and data, or analyze its properties [12,47,53,92–94,103,121].

5 Challenges

This section presents an incomplete overview of challenges for IML, mostly based on [79].

5.1 Statistical Uncertainty and Inference

Many IML methods such as permutation feature importance or Shapley values provide explanations without quantifying the uncertainty of the explanation. The model itself, but also its explanations, are computed from data and hence are subject to uncertainty. First research is working towards quantifying uncertainty of explanations, for example, for feature importance [4,28,124], layer-wise relevance propagation [24], and Shapley values [127].

In order to infer meaningful properties of the underlying data generating process, we have to make structural or distributional assumptions. Whether it is a classical statistical model, an ML algorithm or an IML procedure, these

---

[7] Surrogate models are related to knowledge distillation and the teacher-student model.

assumptions should be clearly stated and we need better diagnostic tools to test them. If we want to prevent statistical testing problems such as p-hacking [48] to reappear in IML, we have to become more rigorous in studying and quantifying the uncertainty of IML methods. For example, most IML methods for feature importance are not adapted for multiple testing, which is a classic mistake in a statistical analysis.

5.2 Causal Interpretation

Ideally, a model should reflect the true causal structure of its underlying phenomena, to enable causal interpretations. Arguably, causal interpretation is usually the goal of modeling if ML is used in science. But most statistical learning procedures reflect mere correlation structures between features and analyze the surface of the data generation process instead of its true inherent structure. Such causal structures would also make models more robust against adversarial attacks [29,101], and more useful when used as a basis for decision making. Unfortunately, predictive performance and causality can be conflicting goals. For example, today's weather directly causes tomorrow's weather, but we might only have access to the feature "wet ground". Using "wet ground" in the prediction model for "tomorrow's weather" is useful as it has information about "today's weather", but we are not allowed to interpret it causally, because the confounder "today's weather" is missing from the ML model. Further research is needed to understand when we are allowed to make causal interpretations of an ML model. First steps have been made for permutation feature importance [60] and Shapley values [70].

5.3 Feature Dependence

Feature dependence introduces problems with attribution and extrapolation. Attribution of importance and effects of features becomes difficult when features are, for example, correlated and therefore share information. Correlated features in random forests are preferred and attributed a higher importance [51,110]. Many sensitivity analysis based methods permute features. When the permuted feature has some dependence with another feature, this association is broken and the resulting data points extrapolate to areas outside the distribution. The ML model was never trained on such combinations and will likely not be confronted with similar data points in an application. Therefore, extrapolation can cause misleading interpretations. There have been attempts to "fix" permutation-based methods, by using a conditional permutation scheme that respects the joint distribution of the data [28,51,78,110]. The change from unconditional to conditional permutation changes the respective interpretation method [7,78], or, in worst case, can break it [57,62,113].

5.4 Definition of Interpretability

A lack of definition for the term "interpretability" is a common critique of the field [22,67]. How can we decide if a new method explains ML models better without a satisfying definition of interpretability? To evaluate the predictive performance of an ML model, we simply compute the prediction error on test data given the groundtruth label. To evaluate the interpretability of that same ML model is more difficult. We do not know what the groundtruth explanation looks like and have no straightforward way to quantify how interpretable a model is or how correct an explanation is. Instead of having one groundtruth explanation, various quantifiable aspects of interpretability are emerging [3,21,31,46,77,86,87,87,102,131].

The two main ways of evaluating interpretability are objective evaluations, which are mathematically quantifiable metrics, and human-centered evaluations, which involve studies with either domain experts or lay persons. Examples of aspects of interpretability are sparsity, interaction strength, fidelity (how well an explanation approximates the ML model), sensitivity to perturbations, and a user's ability to run a model on a given input (simulatability). The challenge ahead remains to establish a best practice on how to evaluate interpretation methods and the explanations they produce. Here, we should also look at the field of human-computer interaction.

5.5   More Challenges Ahead

We focused mainly on the methodological, mathematical challenges in a rather static setting, where a trained ML model and the data are assumed as given and fixed. But ML models are usually not used in a static and isolated way, but are embedded in some process or product, and interact with people. A more dynamic and holistic view of the entire process, from data collection to the final consumption of the explained prediction is needed. This includes thinking how to explain predictions to individuals with diverse knowledge and backgrounds and about the need of interpretability on the level of an institution or society in general. This covers a wide range of fields, such as human-computer interaction, psychology and sociology. To solve the challenges ahead, we believe that the field has to reach out horizontally – to other domains – and vertically – drawing from the rich research in statistics and computer science.

References

1. Adadi, A., Berrada, M.: Peeking inside the black-box: a survey on explainable artificial intelligence (XAI). IEEE Access **6**, 52138–52160 (2018)
2. Adebayo, J., Gilmer, J., Muelly, M., Goodfellow, I., Hardt, M., Kim, B.: Sanity checks for saliency maps. In: Advances in Neural Information Processing Systems, pp. 9505–9515 (2018)
3. Akaike, H.: Information theory and an extension of the maximum likelihood principle. In: Parzen, E., Tanabe, K., Kitagawa, G. (eds.) Selected Papers of Hirotugu Akaike, pp. 199–213. Springer, New york (1998). https://doi.org/10.1007/978-1-4612-1694-0_15
4. Altmann, A., Toloşi, L., Sander, O., Lengauer, T.: Permutation importance: a corrected feature importance measure. Bioinformatics **26**(10), 1340–1347 (2010)

5. Andrews, R., Diederich, J., Tickle, A.B.: Survey and critique of techniques for extracting rules from trained artificial neural networks. Knowl.-Based Syst. **8**(6), 373–389 (1995)
6. Anjomshoae, S., Najjar, A., Calvaresi, D., Främling, K.: Explainable agents and robots: results from a systematic literature review. In: 18th International Conference on Autonomous Agents and Multiagent Systems (AAMAS 2019), Montreal, Canada, 13–17 May 2019, pp. 1078–1088. International Foundation for Autonomous Agents and Multiagent Systems (2019)
7. Apley, D.W., Zhu, J.: Visualizing the effects of predictor variables in black box supervised learning models. arXiv preprint arXiv:1612.08468 (2016)
8. Arya, V., Bellamy, R.K., Chen, P.-Y., Dhurandhar, A., Hind, M., Hoffman, S.C., Houde, S., Liao, Q.V., Luss, R., Mojsilovic, A., et al.: AI explainability 360: an extensible toolkit for understanding data and machine learning models. J. Mach. Learn. Res. **21**(130), 1–6 (2020)
9. Augasta, M.G., Kathirvalavakumar, T.: Rule extraction from neural networks–a comparative study. In: International Conference on Pattern Recognition, Informatics and Medical Engineering (PRIME-2012), pp. 404–408. IEEE (2012)
10. Bastani, O., Kim, C., Bastani, H.: Interpreting blackbox models via model extraction. arXiv preprint arXiv:1705.08504 (2017)
11. Biecek, P.: DALEX: explainers for complex predictive models in R. J. Mach. Learn. Res. **19**(1), 3245–3249 (2018)
12. Botari, T., Hvilshøj, F., Izbicki, R., de Carvalho, A.C.: MeLIME: meaningful local explanation for machine learning models. arXiv preprint arXiv:2009.05818 (2020)
13. Breiman, L.: Random forests. Mach. Learn. **45**(1), 5–32 (2001)
14. Caruana, R., Lou, Y., Gehrke, J., Koch, P., Sturm, M., Elhadad, N.: Intelligible models for healthcare: Predicting pneumonia risk and hospital 30-day readmission. In: Proceedings of the 21th ACM SIGKDD International Conference on Knowledge Discovery and Data Mining, pp. 1721–1730 (2015)
15. Carvalho, D.V., Pereira, E.M., Cardoso, J.S.: Machine learning interpretability: a survey on methods and metrics. Electronics **8**(8), 832 (2019)
16. Casalicchio, G., Molnar, C., Bischl, B.: Visualizing the feature importance for black box models. In: Joint European Conference on Machine Learning and Knowledge Discovery in Databases, pp. 655–670. Springer (2018). https://doi.org/10.1007/978-3-030-10925-7_40
17. Chromik, M., Schuessler, M.: A taxonomy for human subject evaluation of blackbox explanations in XAI. In: ExSS-ATEC@ IUI (2020)
18. Craven, M., Shavlik, J.W.: Extracting tree-structured representations of trained networks. In: Advances in Neural Information Processing Systems, pp. 24–30 (1996)
19. Cutler, D.R., Edwards Jr., T.C., Beard, K.H., Cutler, A., Hess, K.T., Gibson, J., Lawler, J.J.: Random forests for classification in ecology. Ecology **88**(11), 2783–2792 (2007)
20. Dandl, S., Molnar, C., Binder, M., Bischl, B.: Multi-objective counterfactual explanations. arXiv preprint arXiv:2004.11165 (2020)
21. Dhurandhar, A., Iyengar, V., Luss, R., Shanmugam, K.: TIP: typifying the interpretability of procedures. arXiv preprint arXiv:1706.02952 (2017)
22. Doshi-Velez, F., Kim, B.: Towards a rigorous science of interpretable machine learning. arXiv preprint arXiv:1702.08608 (2017)
23. Du, M., Liu, N., Hu, X.: Techniques for interpretable machine learning. Commun. ACM **63**(1), 68–77 (2019)

24. Fabi, K., Schneider, J.: On feature relevance uncertainty: a Monte Carlo dropout sampling approach. arXiv preprint arXiv:2008.01468 (2020)
25. Fahrmeir, L., Tutz, G.: Multivariate Statistical Modelling Based on Generalized Linear Models. Springer, Cham (2013)
26. Fasiolo, M., Nedellec, R., Goude, Y., Wood, S.N.: Scalable visualization methods for modern generalized additive models. J. Comput. Graph. Stat. 29(1), 78–86 (2020)
27. Fasiolo, M., Wood, S.N., Zaffran, M., Nedellec, R., Goude, Y.: Fast calibrated additive quantile regression. J. Am. Stat. Assoc. 1–11 (2020)
28. Fisher, A., Rudin, C., Dominici, F.: All models are wrong, but many are useful: learning a variable's importance by studying an entire class of prediction models simultaneously. J. Mach. Learn. Res. 20(177), 1–81 (2019)
29. Freiesleben, T.: Counterfactual explanations & adversarial examples-common grounds, essential differences, and potential transfers. arXiv preprint arXiv:2009.05487 (2020)
30. Freitas, A.A.: Comprehensible classification models: a position paper. ACM SIGKDD Explor. Newslett. 15(1), 1–10 (2014)
31. Friedler, S.A., Roy, C.D., Scheidegger, C., Slack, D.: Assessing the local interpretability of machine learning models. arXiv preprint arXiv:1902.03501 (2019)
32. Friedman, J.H.: Greedy function approximation: a gradient boosting machine. Ann. Stat. 1189–1232 (2001)
33. Friedman, J.H., Popescu, B.E., et al.: Predictive learning via rule ensembles. Ann. Appl. Stat. 2(3), 916–954 (2008)
34. Frosst, N., Hinton, G.: Distilling a neural network into a soft decision tree. arXiv preprint arXiv:1711.09784 (2017)
35. Fürnkranz, J., Gamberger, D., Lavrač, N.: Foundations of Rule Learning. Springer, Cham (2012)
36. Gade, K., Geyik, S.C., Kenthapadi, K., Mithal, V., Taly, A.: Explainable AI in industry. In: Proceedings of the 25th ACM SIGKDD International Conference on Knowledge Discovery & Data Mining, pp. 3203–3204 (2019)
37. Gauss, C.F.: Theoria motus corporum coelestium in sectionibus conicis solem ambientium, vol. 7. Perthes et Besser (1809)
38. Gelman, A., Hill, J.: Data Analysis Using Regression and Multilevel/hierarchical Models. Cambridge University Press, Cambridge (2006)
39. Goldstein, A., Kapelner, A., Bleich, J., Pitkin, E.: Peeking inside the black box: visualizing statistical learning with plots of individual conditional expectation. J. Comput. Graph. Stat. 24(1), 44–65 (2015)
40. Greenwell, B.M., Boehmke, B.C., McCarthy, A.J.: A simple and effective model-based variable importance measure. arXiv preprint arXiv:1805.04755 (2018)
41. Guidotti, R., Monreale, A., Ruggieri, S., Turini, F., Giannotti, F., Pedreschi, D.: A survey of methods for explaining black box models. ACM Comput. Surv. (CSUR) 51(5), 1–42 (2018)
42. Hall, M., et al.: A systematic method to understand requirements for explainable AI(XAI) systems. In: Proceedings of the IJCAI Workshop on eXplainable Artificial Intelligence (XAI 2019), Macau, China (2019)
43. Hall, P., Gill, N., Kurka, M., Phan, W.: Machine learning interpretability with H2O driverless AI. H2O. AI (2017). http://docs.h2o.ai/driverless-ai/latest-stable/docs/booklets/MLIBooklet.pdf
44. Hapfelmeier, A., Hothorn, T., Ulm, K., Strobl, C.: A new variable importance measure for random forests with missing data. Stat. Comput. 24(1), 21–34 (2014)

45. Hastie, T.J., Tibshirani, R.J.: Generalized Additive Models, vol. 43. CRC Press, Boca Raton (1990)
46. Hauenstein, S., Wood, S.N., Dormann, C.F.: Computing AIC for black-box models using generalized degrees of freedom: a comparison with cross-validation. Commun. Stat.-Simul. Comput. **47**(5), 1382–1396 (2018)
47. Haunschmid, V., Manilow, E., Widmer, G.: audioLIME: listenable explanations using source separation. arXiv preprint arXiv:2008.00582 (2020)
48. Head, M.L., Holman, L., Lanfear, R., Kahn, A.T., Jennions, M.D.: The extent and consequences of p-hacking in science. PLoS Biol. **13**(3), e1002106 (2015)
49. Hoffman, R.R., Mueller, S.T., Klein, G., Litman, J.: Metrics for explainable AI: challenges and prospects. arXiv preprint arXiv:1812.04608 (2018)
50. Hooker, G.: Generalized functional ANOVA diagnostics for high-dimensional functions of dependent variables. J. Comput. Graph. Stat. **16**(3), 709–732 (2007)
51. Hooker, G., Mentch, L.: Please stop permuting features: an explanation and alternatives. arXiv preprint arXiv:1905.03151 (2019)
52. T. Hothorn, K. Hornik, and A. Zeileis. ctree: Conditional inference trees. The Comprehensive R Archive Network, 8, 2015
53. Hu, L., Chen, J., Nair, V.N., Sudjianto, A.: Locally interpretable models and effects based on supervised partitioning (LIME-SUP). arXiv preprint arXiv:1806.00663 (2018)
54. Huysmans, J., Dejaeger, K., Mues, C., Vanthienen, J., Baesens, B.: An empirical evaluation of the comprehensibility of decision table, tree and rule based predictive models. Decis. Support Syst. **51**(1), 141–154 (2011)
55. Ishwaran, H., et al.: Variable importance in binary regression trees and forests. Electron. J. Stat. **1**, 519–537 (2007)
56. Ishwaran, H., Kogalur, U.B., Gorodeski, E.Z., Minn, A.J., Lauer, M.S.: High-dimensional variable selection for survival data. J. Am. Stat. Assoc. **105**(489), 205–217 (2010)
57. Janzing, D., Minorics, L., Blöbaum, P.: Feature relevance quantification in explainable AI: a causality problem. arXiv preprint arXiv:1910.13413 (2019)
58. Klaise, J., Van Looveren, A., Vacanti, G., Coca, A.: Alibi: algorithms for monitoring and explaining machine learning models (2020). https://github.com/SeldonIO/alibi
59. Koh, P.W., Liang, P.: Understanding black-box predictions via influence functions. arXiv preprint arXiv:1703.04730 (2017)
60. König, G., Molnar, C., Bischl, B., Grosse-Wentrup, M.: Relative feature importance. arXiv preprint arXiv:2007.08283 (2020)
61. Krishnan, S., Wu, E.: Palm: machine learning explanations for iterative debugging. In: Proceedings of the 2nd Workshop on Human-In-the-Loop Data Analytics, pp. 1–6 (2017)
62. Kumar, I.E., Venkatasubramanian, S., Scheidegger, C., Friedler, S.: Problems with Shapley-value-based explanations as feature importance measures. arXiv preprint arXiv:2002.11097 (2020)
63. Laugel, T., Lesot, M.-J., Marsala, C., Renard, X., Detyniecki, M.: The dangers of post-hoc interpretability: unjustified counterfactual explanations. arXiv preprint arXiv:1907.09294 (2019)
64. Legendre, A.M.: Nouvelles méthodes pour la détermination des orbites des comètes. F. Didot (1805)
65. Lei, J., G'Sell, M., Rinaldo, A., Tibshirani, R.J., Wasserman, L.: Distribution-free predictive inference for regression. J. Am. Stat. Assoc. **113**(523), 1094–1111 (2018)

66. Letham, B., Rudin, C., McCormick, T.H., Madigan, D., et al.: Interpretable classifiers using rules and Bayesian analysis: Building a better stroke prediction model. Ann. Appl. Stat. **9**(3), 1350–1371 (2015)
67. Lipton, Z.C.: The mythos of model interpretability. Queue **16**(3), 31–57 (2018)
68. Lundberg, S.M., Erion, G.G., Lee, S.-I.: Consistent individualized feature attribution for tree ensembles. arXiv preprint arXiv:1802.03888 (2018)
69. Lundberg,S.M., Lee, S.-I.: A unified approach to interpreting model predictions. In: Advances in Neural Information Processing Systems, pp. 4765–4774 (2017)
70. Ma, S., Tourani, R.: Predictive and causal implications of using Shapley value for model interpretation. In: Proceedings of the 2020 KDD Workshop on Causal Discovery, pp. 23–38. PMLR (2020)
71. Miller, T.: Explanation in artificial intelligence: Insights from the social sciences. Artif. Intell. **267**, 1–38 (2019)
72. Ming, Y., Qu, H., Bertini, E.: Rulematrix: visualizing and understanding classifiers with rules. IEEE Trans. Vis. Comput. Graph. **25**(1), 342–352 (2018)
73. Mohseni, S., Ragan, E.D.: A human-grounded evaluation benchmark for local explanations of machine learning. arXiv preprint arXiv:1801.05075 (2018)
74. Mohseni, S., Zarei, N., Ragan, E.D.: A multidisciplinary survey and framework for design and evaluation of explainable AI systems. arXiv, pages arXiv-1811 (2018)
75. Molnar, C.: Interpretable Machine Learning (2019). https://christophm.github.io/interpretable-ml-book/
76. Molnar, C., Bischl, B., Casalicchio, G.: iml: an R package for interpretable machine learning. JOSS **3**(26), 786 (2018)
77. Molnar, C., Casalicchio, G., Bischl, B.: Quantifying model complexity via functional decomposition for better post-hoc interpretability. In: Cellier, P., Driessens, K. (eds.) ECML PKDD 2019. CCIS, vol. 1167, pp. 193–204. Springer, Cham (2020). https://doi.org/10.1007/978-3-030-43823-4_17
78. Molnar, C., König, G., Bischl, B., Casalicchio, G.: Model-agnostic feature importance and effects with dependent features-a conditional subgroup approach. arXiv preprint arXiv:2006.04628 (2020)
79. Molnar, C., et al.: Pitfalls to avoid when interpreting machine learning models. arXiv preprint arXiv:2007.04131 (2020)
80. Montavon, G., Lapuschkin, S., Binder, A., Samek, W., Müller, K.-R.: Explaining nonlinear classification decisions with deep taylor decomposition. Pattern Recogn. **65**, 211–222 (2017)
81. Mothilal, R.K., Sharma, A., Tan, C.: Explaining machine learning classifiers through diverse counterfactual explanations. In: Proceedings of the 2020 Conference on Fairness, Accountability, and Transparency, pp. 607–617 (2020)
82. Murdoch, W.J., Singh, C., Kumbier, K., Abbasi-Asl, R., Definitions, B.Y.: Methods, and applications in interpretable machine learning. Proc. Nat. Acad. Sci. **116**(44), 22071–22080 (2019)
83. Nori, H., Jenkins, S., Koch, P., Caruana, R.: Interpretml: a unified framework for machine learning interpretability. arXiv preprint arXiv:1909.09223 (2019)
84. Olah, C., Mordvintsev, A., Schubert, L.: Feature visualization. Distill (2017). https://distill.pub/2017/feature-visualization
85. Paluszynska, A., Biecek, P., Jiang, Y.: Random forest explainer: explaining and visualizing random forests in terms of variable importance, R package version 0.10.1 (2020)
86. Philipp, M., Rusch, T., Hornik, K., Strobl, C.: Measuring the stability of results from supervised statistical learning. J. Comput. Graph. Stat. **27**(4), 685–700 (2018)

87. Poursabzi-Sangdeh, F., Goldstein, D.G., Hofman, J.M., Vaughan, J.W., Wallach, H.: Manipulating and measuring model interpretability. arXiv preprint arXiv:1802.07810 (2018)
88. Preece, A., Harborne, D., Braines, D., Tomsett, R., Chakraborty, S.: Stakeholders in explainable AI. arXiv preprint arXiv:1810.00184 (2018)
89. Puri, N., Gupta, P., Agarwal, P., Verma, S., Krishnamurthy, B.: Magix: model agnostic globally interpretable explanations. arXiv preprint arXiv:1706.07160 (2017)
90. Quetelet, L.A.J.: Recherches sur la population, les naissances, les décès, les prisons, les dépôts de mendicité, etc. dans le royaume des Pays-Bas (1827)
91. R Core Team. R: A Language and Environment for Statistical Computing. R Foundation for Statistical Computing, Vienna, Austria (2020)
92. Rabold, J., Deininger, H., Siebers, M., Schmid, U.: Enriching visual with verbal explanations for relational concepts – combining LIME with Aleph. In: Cellier, P., Driessens, K. (eds.) ECML PKDD 2019. CCIS, vol. 1167, pp. 180–192. Springer, Cham (2020). https://doi.org/10.1007/978-3-030-43823-4_16
93. Rabold, J., Siebers, M., Schmid, U.: Explaining black-box classifiers with ILP – empowering LIME with Aleph to approximate non-linear decisions with relational rules. In: Riguzzi, F., Bellodi, E., Zese, R. (eds.) ILP 2018. LNCS (LNAI), vol. 11105, pp. 105–117. Springer, Cham (2018). https://doi.org/10.1007/978-3-319-99960-9_7
94. Rahnama, A.H.A., Boström, H.: A study of data and label shift in the LIME framework. arXiv preprint arXiv:1910.14421 (2019)
95. Ribeiro, M.T., Singh, S., Guestrin, C.: why should i trust you? Explaining the predictions of any classifier. In: Proceedings of the 22nd ACM SIGKDD International Conference on Knowledge Discovery and Data Mining, pp. 1135–1144 (2016)
96. Rosenfeld, A., Richardson, A.: Explainability in human-agent systems. Auton. Agent. Multi-Agent Syst. 33(6), 673–705 (2019)
97. Samek, W., Müller, K.-R.: Towards explainable artificial intelligence. In: Samek, W., Montavon, G., Vedaldi, A., Hansen, L.K., Müller, K.-R. (eds.) Explainable AI: Interpreting, Explaining and Visualizing Deep Learning. LNCS (LNAI), vol. 11700, pp. 5–22. Springer, Cham (2019). https://doi.org/10.1007/978-3-030-28954-6_1
98. Santosa, F., Symes, W.W.: Linear inversion of band-limited reflection seismograms. SIAM J. Sci. Stat. Comput. 7(4), 1307–1330 (1986)
99. Schapire, R.E.: The strength of weak learnability. Mach. Learn. 5(2), 197–227 (1990)
100. Schmidhuber, J.: Deep learning in neural networks: an overview. Neural Netw. 61, 85–117 (2015)
101. Schölkopf, B.: Causality for machine learning. arXiv preprint arXiv:1911.10500 (2019)
102. Schwarz, G., et al.: Estimating the dimension of a model. Ann. Stat. 6(2), 461–464 (1978)
103. Shankaranarayana, S.M., Runje, D.: ALIME: autoencoder based approach for local interpretability. In: Yin, H., Camacho, D., Tino, P., Tallón-Ballesteros, A.J., Menezes, R., Allmendinger, R. (eds.) IDEAL 2019. LNCS, vol. 11871, pp. 454–463. Springer, Cham (2019). https://doi.org/10.1007/978-3-030-33607-3_49
104. Shapley, L.S.: A value for N-person games. Contrib. Theory Games 2(28), 307–317 (1953)

105. Shrikumar, A., Greenside, P., Shcherbina, A., Kundaje, A.: Not just a black box: learning important features through propagating activation differences. arXiv preprint arXiv:1605.01713 (2016)
106. Sill, J.: Monotonic networks. In: Advances in Neural Information Processing Systems, pp. 661–667 (1998)
107. Simonyan, K., Vedaldi, A., Zisserman, A.: Deep inside convolutional networks: visualising image classification models and saliency maps. arXiv preprint arXiv:1312.6034 (2013)
108. Starr, W.: Counterfactuals (2019)
109. Stigler, S.M.: The History of Statistics: The Measurement of Uncertainty Before 1900. Harvard University Press, Cambridge (1986)
110. Strobl, C., Boulesteix, A.-L., Kneib, T., Augustin, T., Zeileis, A.: Conditional variable importance for random forests. BMC Bioinf. 9(1), 307 (2008)
111. Strobl, C., Boulesteix, A.-L., Zeileis, A., Hothorn, T.: Bias in random forest variable importance measures: illustrations, sources and a solution. BMC Bioinf. 8(1), 25 (2007)
112. Štrumbelj, E., Kononenko, I.: Explaining prediction models and individual predictions with feature contributions. Knowl. Inf. Syst. 41(3), 647–665 (2014)
113. Sundararajan, M., Najmi, A.: The many Shapley values for model explanation. arXiv preprint arXiv:1908.08474 (2019)
114. Sundararajan, M., Taly, A., Yan, Q.: Axiomatic attribution for deep networks. arXiv preprint arXiv:1703.01365 (2017)
115. Tibshirani, R.: Regression shrinkage and selection via the lasso. J. Roy. Stat. Soc.: Ser. B (Methodol.) 58(1), 267–288 (1996)
116. Tolomei, G., Silvestri, F., Haines, A., Lalmas, M.: Interpretable predictions of tree-based ensembles via actionable feature tweaking. In: Proceedings of the 23rd ACM SIGKDD International Conference on Knowledge Discovery and Data Mining, pp. 465–474 (2017)
117. Ustun, B., Rudin, C.: Supersparse linear integer models for optimized medical scoring systems. Mach. Learn. 102(3), 349–391 (2016)
118. Ustun, B., Spangher, A., Liu, Y.: Actionable recourse in linear classification. In: Proceedings of the Conference on Fairness, Accountability, and Transparency, pp. 10–19 (2019)
119. Vapnik, V., Chervonenkis, A.: Theory of pattern recognition (1974)
120. Vilone, G., Longo, L.: Explainable artificial intelligence: a systematic review. arXiv preprint arXiv:2006.00093 (2020)
121. Visani, G., Bagli, E., Chesani, F.: Optilime: Optimized LIME explanations for diagnostic computer algorithms. arXiv preprint arXiv:2006.05714 (2020)
122. Wachter, S., Mittelstadt, B., Russell, C.: Counterfactual explanations without opening the black box: automated decisions and the GDPR. Harv. JL Tech. 31, 841 (2017)
123. Wang, F., Rudin, C.: Falling rule lists. In: Artificial Intelligence and Statistics, pp. 1013–1022 (2015)
124. Watson, D.S., Wright, M.N.: Testing conditional independence in supervised learning algorithms. arXiv preprint arXiv:1901.09917 (2019)
125. Wei, P., Lu, Z., Song, J.: Variable importance analysis: a comprehensive review. Reliabil. Eng. Syst. Saf. 142, 399–432 (2015)
126. Wexler, J., Pushkarna, M., Bolukbasi, T., Wattenberg, M., Viégas, F., Wilson, J.: The what-if tool: interactive probing of machine learning models. IEEE Trans. Vis. Comput. Graph. 26(1), 56–65 (2019)

127. Williamson, B.D., Feng, J.: Efficient nonparametric statistical inference on population feature importance using Shapley values. arXiv preprint arXiv:2006.09481 (2020)

128. Zeileis, A., Hothorn, T., Hornik, K.: Model-based recursive partitioning. J. Comput. Graph. Stat. **17**(2), 492–514 (2008)

129. Zeiler, M.D., Fergus, R.: Visualizing and understanding convolutional networks. In: Fleet, D., Pajdla, T., Schiele, B., Tuytelaars, T. (eds.) ECCV 2014. LNCS, vol. 8689, pp. 818–833. Springer, Cham (2014). https://doi.org/10.1007/978-3-319-10590-1_53

130. Zhang, Q., Nian Wu, Y., Zhu, S.-C.: Interpretable convolutional neural networks. In: Proceedings of the IEEE Conference on Computer Vision and Pattern Recognition, pp. 8827–8836 (2018)

131. Zhou, Q., Liao, F., Mou, C., Wang, P.: Measuring interpretability for different types of machine learning models. In: Ganji, M., Rashidi, L., Fung, B.C.M., Wang, C. (eds.) PAKDD 2018. LNCS (LNAI), vol. 11154, pp. 295–308. Springer, Cham (2018). https://doi.org/10.1007/978-3-030-04503-6_29

132. Zou, H., Hastie, T.: Regularization and variable selection via the elastic net. J. Roy. Stat. Soc.: Ser. B (Stat. Methodol.) **67**(2), 301–320 (2005)

Efficient Estimation of General Additive Neural Networks: A Case Study for CTG Data

P. J. G. Lisboa$^{(\boxtimes)}$, S. Ortega-Martorell, M. Jayabalan, and I. Olier

Department of Applied Mathematics, Liverpool John Moores University, Liverpool L3 3AF, UK
p.j.lisboa@ljmu.ac.uk

Abstract. This paper discusses the concepts of interpretability and explainability and outlines desiderata for robust interpretability. It then describes a neural network model that meets all criteria, with the addition of global faithfulness.

This is achieved by efficient estimation of a General Additive Neural Network, seeded by a conventional Multilayer Perceptron (MLP) by distilling the dependence on individual variables and pairwise interactions, so that their effects can be represented within the structure of a General Additive Model. This makes the logic of the model clear and transparent to users, across the complete input space. The model is self-explaining.

The modelling approach used in this paper derives the partial responses from the MLP, resulting in the Partial Response Network (PRN). Its application is illustrated in a medical context using the CTU-UHB Cardiotacography intrapartum database (n = 552) to infer the features associated with caesarean deliveries. This is the first application of the PRN to this data set and it is shown that the self-explaining model achieves comparable discrimination performance to that of Random Forests previously applied to the same data set. The classes are highly imbalanced with a prevalence of caesarean sections of 8.33%. The resulting model uses 4 from 8 possible features and has an AUROC of 0.69 [CI 0.60, 0.77] estimated by 4-fold cross-validation. Its performance and features are compared also with those from a Sparse Additive Models (SAM) which has an AUROC of 0.72 [CI 0.64, 0.80]. This is not significantly different and requires all features.

For clinical utility by risk stratification, the odds-ratio for caesarian section *vs.* not at the prevalence threshold is 3.97 for the PRN, better 3.14 for the SAM. Compared for consistency, parsimony, stability and scalability the models have complementary properties.

Keywords: Explainable machine learning · Interpretable machine learning · Generalised additive model · Self-explaining neural network · Sparse additive model · Knowledge discovery from data · CTG · Physionet · Medical decision support

1 Introduction

Attention has recently focused on a better understanding by end users of inferences made by machine learning models. It is acknowledged that the models can reflect weaknesses

© Springer Nature Switzerland AG 2020
I. Koprinska et al. (Eds.): ECML PKDD 2020 Workshops, CCIS 1323, pp. 432–446, 2020.
https://doi.org/10.1007/978-3-030-65965-3_29

in the data, for instance implicit bias in observational samples. Moreover, the impressive performance figures that can be obtained for generalisation accuracy belie our general ignorance about the failure modes of the models, where application to new data may result in incorrect predictions due to unexpected extrapolation of the non-linear response of the model. Inferences on future data can be controlled only if there is complete transparency about how the model makes at its predictions.

In Europe, this is now regulated by the General Data Protection Regulations (GDPR), which require that in the case of automated decision-making, the data subject has the right to "meaningful information about the logic involved" in arriving at the decision [1]. This is problematic for many current machine learning algorithms, even those used in safety-critical contexts such as medical decision support.

In a thorough review of explainable AI, Adadi and Berrada [2] consider reasons why explanations are needed and categorise them into 4 classes, namely to:

- Justify an inference, which is the nearest category to fulfilling the requirement of the "right to explanation";
- Control the vulnerabilities of the model, in order to mitigate uncontrolled extrapolation to new data;
- Improve the model, for instance when assimilating new data and facilitate transfer learning;
- Discover the main statistical effects that are associated with observations in different classes, so providing specific indications about the features that most inform us on how to separate them.

In contrast, in a review of the human factors involved in explaining complex models, Miller [3] draws a distinction between explainability and interpretability adopting Brian and Cotton's [4] definition that the interpretability of a model is the "the degree to which an observer can understand the cause of a decision". This distinction is subtle but important, as it invokes causality as a condition to test whether the identified elements of decision making are both necessary and sufficient to elicit the inference made by the model. This is not the same as a local statement about the plausibility of a prediction made for a particular instance; rather, it reflects a deeper requirement that more completely defines that output of the model in terms that the user can understand.

In this sense, interpretability is the degree to which a model can be integrated into the logic of human reasoning. A fully interpretable model will explain the model outputs globally, that is to say for all possible inputs. This will automatically fulfil all of the four requirements for explanation that are listed above.

Methods that derive explainable models directly from data are usually constrained in ways that limit their flexibility to fit complex decision boundaries. This is the case typically with decision trees, which apply axis orthogonal separating surfaces. This can lead to a proliferation of rules as is the case for instance with Random Forests (RF), which limits the interpretability of the models.

An alternative is to use rules to explain trained neural networks. There are two approaches, decompositional and pedagogic [5]. The former directly interpret the response of each node in the neural network with the aim of attributing linguistic meaning to each node. While this approach provides an interpretation of a trained Multi-Layer

Perceptron (MLP) in symbolic terms, it has been shown that the hierarchical nature of the decompositional approach does not ensure that the correct logic of the model is identified. Pedagogical approaches to rule extraction from trained neural networks, or indeed from any non-linear response surface (they are model agnostic), treating the model as a black-box and using the response function directly to derive minimal sets of multivariate Boolean rules that are interpretable [5, 6].

Rule tree induction generally effects a compromise between accuracy and interpretability. When the rules are succinct, they are understood by the user and there are numerous examples of applications of flexible models to medical decision making with rule sets [7].

A more common approach to explaining neural network models is to apply *a* posteriori methods akin to sensitivity analysis. This can be effective to find the features that most influence the model output, even in the case of deep convolutional models. These approaches include local interpretable model-agnostic explanations [8], saliency maps and model distillation [2].

Recently, a unified approach was proposed by Lundberg and Lee [9] who prove a theorem that only one possible explanation model complies with the generic framework of additive feature attributions using binary feature selection of variables and satisfying three properties that are required to uniquely determine additive feature attributions, namely local accuracy, lack of impact for features missing in the original input and consistency. The consistency requirement is that "if a model changes so that some simplified input's contribution increases or stays the same regardless of the other inputs, that input's attribution should not decrease". They propose a practical implementation using Shapeley explanation values [9].

It is widely accepted that "the best explanation of a simple model is the model itself; it perfectly represents itself and is easy to understand" [9]. This is the approach followed in this paper.

Our approach is guided by the three desiderata for robust interpretability and explainabilty [10]: explicitness/intelligibility: *"Are the explanations immediate and understandable?"*; faithfulness: *"Are relevance scores indicative of "true" importance?"*; and stability: *"How consistent are the explanations for similar/neighboring examples?"*.

We agree with this set and propose to extend it with two more requirements:

- Parsimony: *"Do the explanatory variables comprise a minimal set?"*
- Consistency: *"How robust are the explanations to perturbations in the data?"*

The principle of parsimony has a long history in statistics and is widely regarded as central to ensure robust generalisation. It relates to the principle of maximising the signal to noise ratio by avoiding redundancy and retaining only the most informative variables.

Consistency is also fundamental if we are to attribute relevance to the input variables and quantify their effect on the model response. It has always been an issue with neural networks to have multiple answers when modelling the same data. Therefore, if a self-explanatory model is parsimonious, this would be expected to leave to greater consistency for multiple implementations of the same network.

A natural extension of the requirement for consistency is to compare different models since, if they provide different interpretations of the same data with similar predictive power, it is likely that the models will be degenerate so the attribution of relevance to individual variables is not safe.

This paper makes the following contributions:

First, it will take a simple but flexible class of General Additive Models, namely General Artificial Neural Networks (GANN) and show that its structure can be efficiently estimated even for a challenging data set. The dataset is challenging by virtue of the low prevalence of events, which makes it difficult to identify the informative variables to explain the model inferences.

Second, it will demonstrate that parsimonious models can beat the performance interpretability trade-off by improving on the performance of the original universal approximator, in this case an MLP.

Third, it will test the principles of parsimony and consistency by comparing with an alternative classifier from the same class but estimated with completely different principles.

The alternative classifier is the Sparse Additive Model (SAM) [11]. This method applies a kernel smoother to a linear combination of functions of a single variable parametrised with splines. It is fitted using the back-fitting algorithm commonly used in GAMs and it decouples smoothing and sparsity through the application of soft-thresholding and smoothing. Like the PRN, it makes use of l_1 regularisation for feature selection. It is formulated as a convex optimisation problem, so it is trained only once for a given data set, in contrast with the PRN which is built on a neural network and therefore is seed dependent.

Both models enforce sparseness with a GAM using flexible functions of fewer variables, to make the model self-explanatory. Both algorithms model the logit of the posterior for class membership, extending the well-known logistic regression model that is still commonly used in high stakes applications such as medical decision support. In this sense, they allow a representation using nomograms, which is important for clinical acceptance and was previously applied to Support Vector Machines (SVM) [12].

2 Data

2.1 Description of the Data

The Czech Technical University, Prague-University Hospital Brno (CTU-UHB) Cardiotacogram (CTG) open-access database shared by Physionet in [13] comprises high level features extracted from 552 records, of which 446 correspond to normal (vaginal) deliveries and 46 to deliveries by caesarean section. The data set is used to illustrate an interpretable application of the MLP to highly imbalanced data (prevalence of 46/552 = 8.33%). – how the data were collected – features present in the data – outcome of interest: caesarean section vs. normal delivery]. The dataset was publicised by Chudáček et al. [14]. It is a measure of how difficult it can be to acquire and curate a quality assured medical data set, that the initial pool of cases consisted of CTG traces from 14,492 deliveries [14]. The inclusion criteria applied include singleton pregnancies, maternal age at least

18, gestational weeks at least 37, no missing values and additional clinico-physiological constraints.

Each CTG trace is represented by a set of 8 non-linear features, some of which were derived by Spilka et al. [15] and others by Fergus et al. [16] who kindly made the data available for this study. The traces measure foetal heartbeat and frequency of uterine contractions. These measurements are routinely made during labour and serve to identify fetal distress which may result birth by caesarean section.

The covariates are listed in Table 1 and their marginal statistics are in Table 2, showing heavy mixing between the two classes.

Table 1. Covariate definitions [14, 15]

Label	Definition
STV	Short-Term Variability: Beat-to-Beat time interval (BB)
FD	Fractal Dimension
DFA	De-trend Fluctuation Analysis
RMS	Root Mean Square
SampEn	Sample Entropy
SD1	Short-term variation in BB
SD2	Long-term variation in BB
SDRatio	SD1/SD2

Table 2. Median and interquartile range

Label	Class 0	Class 1
STV	0.93 (0.63,1.34)	0.82 (0.45,1.19)
FD	0.035 (0.027,0.0420)	0.035 (0.022,0.045)
DFA	1.24 (1.22,1.26)	1.22 (1.19,1.24)
RMS	4.19E-3(3.97E-3,44.6E-3)	4.39E-3(4.06E-3,4.81E-3)
SampEn	136.8 (128.8,144.9)	141.6 (130.9,156.6)
SD1	11.08 (7.85,15.08)	11.11 (7.39,17.13)
SD2	16.725 (11.9,24.6)	14.865 (11.19,22.42)
SDRatio	0.68 (0.54,0.85)	0.81 (0.53,1.04)

The following variable pairs are correlated: RMS & SampEn ($\rho = 0.98$); SD1 & SD2 ($\rho = 0.77$); STV & SD1 ($\rho = 0.52$); STV & SD2 ($\rho = 0.55$). From this, variables RMS, SD1 and SD2 were removed from the study, leaving the following 5 covariates: STV, FD, DFA, SampEn and SDRatio.

2.2 Previous Results

A recent comprehensive review of analysis of fetal heart rate [17] identified 8 studies of which 4 used the CTU-UHB database and only one targeted similar classes to our study, namely [18] which had a class imbalance of 508/44. This refers to a separate sub-classification of cases as normal, suspicious, pathological and uninterpretable. They applied at Least Squares SVM to morphological signals, achieving a sensitivity of 72% and specificity of 65%.

Previous work on classification of pH with a threshold of 7.15, half way in the normal artery range from 7.05 to 7.38, found that non-linear features such as FD and SampEn result in a sensitivity of 78% with specificity of 70% and AUROC of 0.74 for the SVM. However, this was with a smaller subset of 94 records considered normal and 95 abnormal.

The only previous study to use the same data with the same covariates is [16], who note that from the 56 caesarean sections, only 22 (48%) have recorded pathological outcomes which indicate that the baby was certainly in distress, such evidence lacking for the remaining 24 cases (52%). This sets a minimum acceptable value for the sensitivity. The classification performance on the original (imbalanced) data for Fisher Linear Discriminants, Random Forests (RF) and the SVM, had AUROC values of 0.68, 0.70 and 0.63 respectively. This followed the application of Recursive Feature Elimination (RFE) resulted in the eight features forming the original pool of covariates for this study.

3 Description of the Model

The Partial Response Network (PRN) is a representation of the MLP using a GAM [19] with the following properties:

- The model applies the logit link function as this is appropriate for estimating a posterior probability of class membership, when used alongside the log-likelihood cost function for a Bernoulli distribution of the class label. This maintains the statistical rigour of this flexible model for binary classification.
- The additive functions are Partial Responses, that is to say the model outputs for subsets of covariates where most are fixed at their median values and some are varied. In particular, we consider:

  - Univariate terms, where only one input is varied at a time, all of the others remaining fixed;
  - Bivariate interactions, where two inputs are taken from the data, the others remaining fixed.
- The Bivariate terms are made orthogonal to the Univariate terms, in order to capture only additional two-way effects.

These requirements are met by the following GAM that follows the ANOVA decomposition [20]:

$$logit(P(C|x)) = \varphi(0) + \sum_i \varphi_i(x_i) + \sum_{i \neq j} \varphi_{ij}(x_i, x_j) + \ldots + \sum_{i_1 \neq \ldots \neq i_d} \varphi_{i_1 \ldots i_d}(x_{i_1}, \ldots, x_{i_d})$$

(1)

where:

$$\varphi(0) = logit(P(C|0))$$

(2)

$$\varphi_i(x_i) = logit(P(C|(0, .., x_i, .., 0))) - \varphi(0)$$

(3)

$$\varphi_{ij}(x_i, x_j) = logit(P(C|(0, .., x_i, .., x_j, ..0))) - \varphi_i(x_i) - \varphi_j(x_j) - \varphi(0)$$

(4)

The motivation for this approach is to distil from the original MLP the explicit dependence on individual variables and pairs of variables. The above identify makes the component elements clear. The elements are easily calculated by fixing all but one or two variables at their median values, hence they represent partial responses.

In principle the component functions can be represented by any flexible sub-model, whether using splines or a structured neural network such as a GANN. However, it is difficult to derive the structure of a GANN and setting it *a priori* defeats the purpose of data-based modelling. This is achieved by separating smoothing with the MLP from sparsity using the Lasso [21], mirroring the strategy applied by the SAM [10] but within the statistical framework of kernel methods rather than neural networks.

In the PRN algorithm the smoothing function makes use of soft thresholding with the Bayesian framework known as the evidence approximation [22]. This involves considering each weight in the MLP to be described by a distribution:

$$P(w|D, \propto, H) = \frac{P(D|w, \propto, H)P(w|\propto, H)}{Z_W(\alpha)}$$

(5)

The first term in the numerator of Eq. (5) represents the quality of the data fit, which in the case of binary classification is the usual likelihood for a target variable following a Bernoulli distribution. The second term is the prior distribution of weights, which is assumed to take the standard form centered at zero with a set variance, modelled in the MLP as the strength of the gradient descent term, represented by $\propto$.

The denominator $Z_W(\alpha)$ is of course the integral of the numerator over all possible values of the weights and represents $P(D|\propto, H)$ which is the evidence that the model H with hyper parameters $\propto$ fits the data. The model is defined by the configuration of the neural network and choice of transfer functions.

The $P(\alpha|D, H)$ is obtained from the evidence, through application of Bayes theorem, which involves a Taylor expansion of the evidence about the most probable weights, known as the Laplace approximation. The key point is that this provides an analytical expression to automatically set the value of the weight decay.

The availability of closed form estimates for the strength of the weight decay hyper-parameters enables the use of multiple weight decay parameters. There is a separate hyperparameter for each input variable, with additional ones for the bias terms and output node weights. In this way the penalty term will penalize uninformative variables more by raising the value of the hyper parameter, which implements soft pruning.

This is then followed by the use of the Lasso for hard pruning, as noted above, followed by a second iteration of re-training to re-adjust the partial responses without the conditioning on spurious variables that have now been removed from the model.

The PRN algorithm is now outlined:

1. Train an MLP for binary classification;
2. Obtained the univariate and bivariate partial responses in (2)-(4).
3. Apply the Lasso to the Partial Responses. The residual term may be included to represent un-modelled effects.
4. Construct a second MLP as a linear combination of the partial responses so as to replicate the functionality of the Lasso. The modules are assembled into a MLP as shown in Fig. 1.
5. Re-train the resulting multi-layer network using BEP. This further re-calibrates the estimates of the posterior probability of class membership and smooths-out the partial responses.

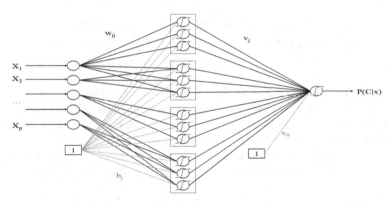

Fig. 1. Structure of the partial response network comprising modular replicates of the relevant weights from the original MLP for each univariate or bivariate response retained by the Lasso.

The method is further detailed and benchmarked in [19], where it is shown that the performance of the PRN is competitive with state-of-the-art classifiers across a range of tabular data sets, that is to say without an inherent signal processing structure. This is typical of clinical decision support applications as distinct from speech, text and image processing.

4   Description of the Model

The PRN was applied to the data in stages. First it was applied to the 5 covariates, to assess the stability of the model given the challenging nature of the data. In 4-fold cross validation this showed that only 4 variables were selected in univariate or bivariate terms, namely {FD, DFA, SampEn and SDRatio}. These occurred as a group in two of four folds and only {DFA, SampEn and SDRatio} in the remaining two folds.

Given that there are only 46 cases of the class of interest in a sample size of 552 cases, the PRN is remarkably consistent.

Table 3. Results obtained by 4-fold cross-validation

Model	MLP-ARD	PRN	SAM
AUROC	0.65	0.69	**0.72**
[CI]	[0.56, 0.74]	[0.60,0.77]	**[0.64,0.80]**
Sensitivity (Recall)	0.587	**0.674**	0.587
Specificity	0.302	**0.312**	0.287
PPV (Precision)	0.150	**0.164**	0.157
Odds Ratio for caesarean sections	2.94	**3.97**	3.15

The model derived by the PRN consists of:

$$logit(P(CSection|FD, DFA, SampEn, SDRatio))$$
$$= \beta_{FD} \cdot \varphi(FD) + \beta_{DFA} \cdot \varphi(DFA) + \beta_{ampEn} \cdot \varphi(SampEn)$$
$$+ \beta_{SDRatio} \cdot \varphi(SDRatio) + \beta_0. \qquad (6)$$

The individual functions $\varphi(.)$ for the first fold are shown in Figs. 2, 3, 4, 5.

There are also two 2-way effects are present for some seeds, which are interactions between FD-SampEn and FD-DFA. These are shown in Figs. 6, 7. All functions are referenced to a logit of zero at the population median.

The AUROC evaluated by 4-fold cross-validation, sensitivity (recall), specificity and precision at the prevalence threshold i.e. for predictions above vs. below 0.0833 are listed in Table 3.

A quantity that has particular clinical utility is the odds ratio for Caesarean Sections either side of the classification threshold. The reason for this is that the PPV (precision) is necessarily limited by the low prevalence of the event of interest, but a more useful purpose for a binary classifier is to stratify the population by risk. The empirical odds ratio for the two classifiers is also listed in Table 3.

The component functions of the SAM model are shown in Figs. 8, 9, 10 and 11. Note that whereas SampEn and RMS are highly correlated, the functions are reversed.

The shape of the univariate functions in both models is generally consistent. For instance FD has a critical point at 0.05 when the risk of a caesarean delivery begins to rise. For DFA it is the opposite, as the risk decreases monotonically with the value of this variable.

Sample entropy is interesting as in both models there is a higher risk outside the mass of the overall population. The PRN has the minimum risk close to the median whereas SAM places it to the right of that point.

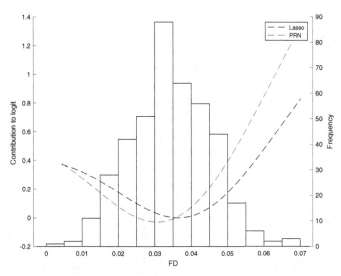

Fig. 2. Contribution to the logit arising from FD. The black line shows the response derived from the original MLP. This changes to the red line after the function is mapped onto the GAMM and is re-trained. The histogram shows the population distribution. (Color figure online)

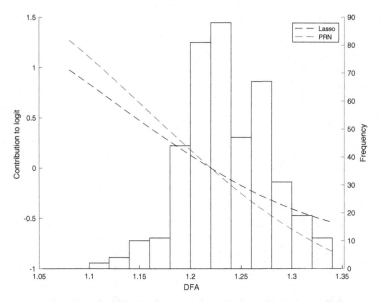

Fig. 3. Contribution to the logit arising from De-trend Fluctuation Analysis (DFA), as in Fig. 2

However, the role of SDRatio has two conflicting interpretations: one model predicts that the risk increases with the value of SDRatio and the other that it decreases. This is an example where a clinician might analyse samples of patients whose measurements of this variable are normal or high, and conclude that one of the models is more clinically

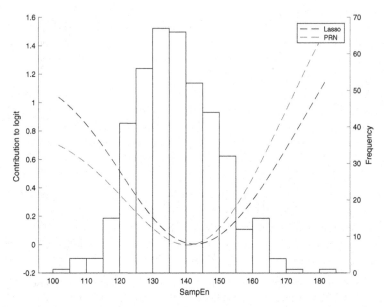

Fig. 4. Contribution to the logit arising from Sample Entropy (SampEn) as in Fig. 2.

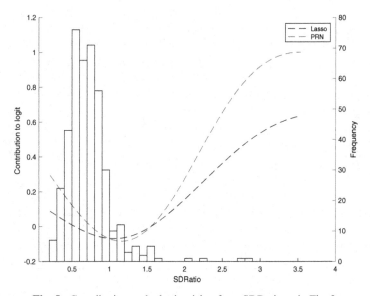

Fig. 5. Contribution to the logit arising from SDRatio as in Fig. 2.

plausible then the other – quantifying the independent effects to make this comparison possible is exactly what we are trying to achieve with sparse GAMs.

These differences are related to the interference that some variables have on how non-linear models use other variables. In effect, the estimation of the weight of each

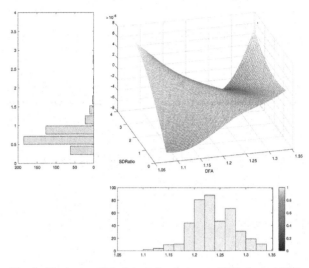

Fig. 6. Heat-map of the interaction between SDRatio and DFA.

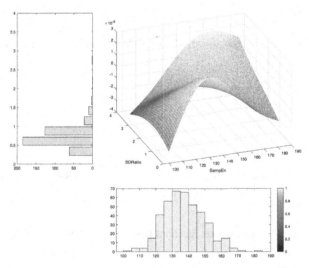

Fig. 7. Heat-map of the interaction between SDRatio and SampEn.

variable is conditional on the presence of all of the others. If this adjustment to the effect sizes is misplaced, artefactual effects will result.

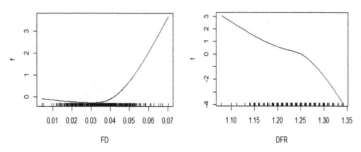

Fig. 8. Component functions from SAM for FD and DFA.

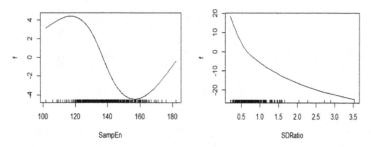

Fig. 9. Component functions from SAM for SampEn and SDRatio.

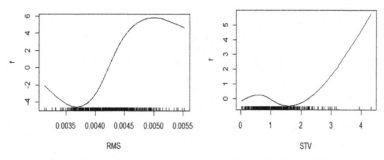

Fig. 10. Component functions from SAM for RMS and STV.

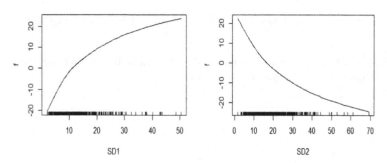

Fig. 11. Component functions from SAM for SD1 and SD2.

5 Conclusion

We demonstrated a neural network model that meets the key requirements for robust interpretability [10] namely isolating and identifying the effects of individual variables, eliminating uninterpretable effects caused by higher order interactions and faithfulness to the model outputs.

These properties are articulated in a desiderata whose principles are met by General Additive Models. We have shown how a General Additive Neural Network can be derived from an MLP, which bucks the performance-interpretability trade-off by virtue of being a self-explanatory neural network that matches or improves on the performance of the original MLP.

The PRN is compared with a statistical sparse model, the SAM. The classification performance and covariate dependence of the two models is comparable but with exceptions. In particular, PRN is more parsimonious. Both models are stable in the sense that similar examples naturally have similar explanations.

Both models are scalable for univariate effects. Clearly including bivariate terms creates a proliferation of component functions that can be unwieldy. Nevertheless, the PRN is well placed to model bivariate effects, since it does not required parameterisation of the component functions.

The AUROC is competitive against that of Random Forests (RF) and Support Vector Machines (SVM).

A strength of the PRN is its ease of implementation. It is built from standard models and exploits the optimal properties of neural networks for non-parametric smoothing and of the Lasso for pruning. Mapping the GAM-Lasso model onto the structure of a GANN initiates a second round of training to refine the component functions, free from the effects of adjusting for the values of variables that do not add to the predictive power of the model.

The main limitation of the model is that the number of events per variable (EPV) needs to be sufficient to allow a clear identification of the most informative models. Without this, it is now possible to derive a parsimonious model using statistical significance. In practice, this makes the model data hungry especially for high dimensional data.

It remains for end users to ascertain the plausibility of the weights attributed to each component of the model and match them with human-interpretable concepts that can be integrated into human reasoning. Both models meet the goals of Quantitative Testing with Concept Activation Vectors [23] since they are accessible to non-ML experts, they explicitly articulate the concepts represented in the model and so make customization possible, and they have plug-in readiness and global quantification since the explanation is the model itself.

References

1. Goodman, B., Flaxman, S.: European union regulations on algorithmic decision making and a 'right to explanation'. AI Mag. **38**, 50–57 (2017)
2. Adadi, A., Berrada, M.: Peeking inside the black-box: a survey on explainable artificial intelligence (XAI). IEEE Access **6** 52138–52160 (2018)

3. Miller, T.: Explanation in artificial intelligence: insights from the social sciences. Artif. Intell. **267**, 1–38 (2019)
4. Biran, O., Cotton, C.: Explanation and justification in machine learning: a survey. In: IJCAI Workshop on Explainable AI (XAI) (2017)
5. Etchells, T.A., Lisboa, P.J.G.: Orthogonal Search-Based Rule Extraction (OSRE) for trained neural networks: a practical and efficient approach. IEEE Trans. Neural Netw. **17**(2), 374–384 (2006)
6. Rögnvaldsson, T., Etchells, T.A., You, L., Garwicz, D., Jarman, I., Lisboa, P.J.G.: How to find simple and accurate rules for viral protease cleavage specificities. BMC Bioinf. **10**(1), 149 (2009)
7. Montani, S., Striani, M.: Artificial intelligence in clinical decision support: a focused literature survey. Yearb. Med. Inform. **28**(1), 120–127 (2019)
8. Ribeiro, M.T., Singh, S., Guestrin, C.: Why should I trust you? In: Proceedings of the 22nd ACM SIGKDD International Conference on Knowledge Discovery and Data Mining - KDD 2016, pp. 1135–1144 (2016)
9. Lundberg, S., Lee, S.-I., A unified approach to interpreting model predictions. In: Advances in Neural Information Processing Systems, vol. 30, pp. 4765–4774 (2017)
10. Alvarez-Melis, D., Jaakkola, T.S.: Towards robust interpretability with self- explaining neural networks. In: NIPS, vol. 31 (2018)
11. Ravikumar, P., Lafferty, J., Liu, H., Wasserman, L.: Sparse additive models. J. Roy. Stat. Soc.: Ser. B (Stat. Methodol.) **71**(5), 1009–1030 (2009)
12. Van Belle, V., Van Calster, B., Van Huffel, S., Suykens, J.A.K., Lisboa, P.: Explaining support vector machines: a color based nomogram. PLoS ONE **11**(10), e0164568 (2016)
13. Goldberger, A.L., et al.: PhysioBank, PhysioToolkit, and PhysioNet. Circulation **101**(23), e215–e220 (2000)
14. Chudáček, V., et al.: Open access intrapartum CTG database. BMC Pregnancy Childbirth **14**(1), 16 (2014)
15. Spilka, J., Chudacek, V., Koucky, M., Lhotska, L.: Assessment of non-linear features for intrapartal fetal heart rate classification. In: 2009 9th International Conference on Information Technology and Applications in Biomedicine, pp. 1–4 (2009)
16. Fergus, P., Selvaraj, M., Chalmers, C.: Machine learning ensemble modelling to classify caesarean section and vaginal delivery types using Cardiotocography traces. Comput. Biol. Med. **93**, 7–16 (2018)
17. Zhao, Z., Zhang, Y., Deng, Y.: A comprehensive feature analysis of the fetal heart rate signal for the intelligent assessment of fetal state. J. Clin. Med. **7**(8), 223 (2018)
18. Georgoulas, G., Karvelis, P., Spilka, J., Chudáček, V., Stylios, C.D., Lhotská, L.: Investigating pH based evaluation of fetal heart rate (FHR) recordings. Health Technol. (Berl). **7**(2–3), 241–254 (2017)
19. Lisboa, P.J.G., Ortega-Martorell, S., Cashman, S., Olier, I.: The partial response network arXiv, pp. 1–10 (2019)
20. Hooker, G.: Generalized functional ANOVA diagnostics for high-dimensional functions of dependent variables. J. Comput. Graph. Stat. **16**(3), 709–732 (2007)
21. Meier, L., Van De Geer, S., Bühlmann, P.: The group lasso for logistic regression. J. R. Stat. Soc. Ser. B Stat. Methodol. (2008)
22. MacKay, D.J.C.: The evidence framework applied to classification networks. Neural Comput. **4**(5), 720–736 (1992)
23. Kim, B., et al.: Interpretability beyond feature attribution: quantitative testing with concept activation vectors (TCAV). In: International Conference on Machine Learning (ICLR) (2018)

What Would You Ask the Machine Learning Model? Identification of User Needs for Model Explanations Based on Human-Model Conversations

Michał Kuźba[1,2]([✉]) [iD] and Przemysław Biecek[1,2] [iD]

[1] Faculty of Mathematics, Informatics and Mechanics, University of Warsaw,
Warsaw, Poland
kuzba.michal@gmail.com
[2] Faculty of Mathematics and Information Science,
Warsaw University of Technology, Warsaw, Poland

Abstract. Recently we see a rising number of methods in the field of eXplainable Artificial Intelligence. To our surprise, their development is driven by model developers rather than a study of needs for human end users. The analysis of needs, if done, takes the form of an A/B test rather than a study of open questions. To answer the question "What would a human operator like to ask the ML model?" we propose a conversational system explaining decisions of the predictive model. In this experiment, we developed a chatbot called dr_ant to talk about machine learning model trained to predict survival odds on Titanic. People can talk with dr_ant about different aspects of the model to understand the rationale behind its predictions. Having collected a corpus of 1000+ dialogues, we analyse the most common types of questions that users would like to ask. To our knowledge, it is the first study which uses a conversational system to collect the needs of human operators from the interactive and iterative dialogue explorations of a predictive model.

Keywords: eXplainable Artificial Intelligence · Iterative dialogue explanations · Human-centred machine learning

1 Introduction

Machine Learning models are widely adopted in all areas of human life. As they often become critical parts of the automated systems, there is an increasing need for understanding their decisions and ability to interact with such systems. Hence, we are currently seeing the growth of the area of eXplainable Artificial Intelligence (XAI). For instance, Scantamburlo et al. [28] raise an issue of understanding machine decisions and their consequences on the example of computer-made decisions in criminal justice. This example touches upon such features as fairness, equality, transparency and accountability. Ribera & Lapedriza [26] identify the following motivations for why to design and use explanations: system

© Springer Nature Switzerland AG 2020
I. Koprinska et al. (Eds.): ECML PKDD 2020 Workshops, CCIS 1323, pp. 447–459, 2020.
https://doi.org/10.1007/978-3-030-65965-3_30

verification, including bias detection; improvement of the system (debugging); learning from the system's distilled knowledge; compliance with legislation, e.g. "Right to explanation" set by EU; inform people affected by AI decisions.

We see the rising number of explanation methods, such as LIME [25] and SHAP [15] and XAI frameworks such as AIX360 [2], InterpretML [22], DALEX [4], modelStudio [3], exBERT [10] and many others. These systems require a systematic quality evaluation [8,13,21]. For instance, Tan et al. [32] describe the uncertainty of explanations and Molnar et al. [20] describe a way to quantify the interpretability of the model.

These methods and toolboxes are focused on the model developer perspective. Most popular methods like Partial Dependence Plots, LIME or SHAP are tools for a post-hoc model diagnostic rather than tools linked with the needs of end users. But it is important to design an explanation system for its addressee (explainee). Both form and content of the system should be adjusted to the end user. And while explainees might not have the AI expertise, explanations are often constructed by engineers and researchers for themselves [19], therefore limiting its usefulness for the other audience [17].

Also, both the form and the content of the explanations should differ depending on the explainee's background and role in the model lifecycle. Ribera & Lapedriza [26] describe three types of explainees: AI researchers and developers, domain experts and the lay audience. Tomsett et al. [33] introduce six groups: creators, operators, executors, decision-subjects, data-subjects and examiners. These roles are positioned differently in the pipeline. Users differ in the background and the goal of using the explanation system. They vary in the technical skills and the language they use. Finally, explanations should have a comprehensible form – textual, visual or multimodal. Explanation is a cognitive process and a social interaction [7]. Moreover, interactive exploration of the model allows to personalize the explanations presented to the explainee [31].

Arya et al. identify a space for interactive explanations in a tree-shaped taxonomy of XAI techniques [2]. However, AIX360 framework presented in this paper implements only static explanations. Similarly, most of the other toolkits and methods focus entirely on the static branch of the explanations taxonomy. Sokol & Flach [29] propose conversation using class-contrastive counterfactual statements. This idea is implemented as a conversational system for the credit score system's lay audience [30]. Pecune et al. describe conversational movie recommendation agent explaining its recommendations [23]. A rule-based, interactive and conversational agent for explainable AI is also proposed by Werner [35]. Madumal et al. propose an interaction protocol and identify components of an explanation dialogue [16]. Finally, Miller [18] claims that truly explainable agents will use interactivity and communication.

To address these problems we create an open-ended dialog based explanation system. We develop a chatbot allowing the explainee to interact with a predictive model and its explanations. We implement this particular system for the random forest model trained on Titanic dataset [1,5]. However, any model trained on this dataset can be plugged into this system. Also, this approach can be applied successfully to other datasets and much of the components can be reused.

Our goal is twofold. Firstly, we create a working prototype of a conversational system for XAI. Secondly, we want to discover what questions people ask to understand the model. This exploration is enabled by the open-ended nature of the chatbot. It means that the user might ask any question even if the system is unable to give a satisfying answer for each of them.

There are engineering challenges of building a dialogue agent and the "Wizard of Oz" proxy approach might be used as an alternative [11,31]. In this work however, we decide to build such a system. With this approach we obtain a working prototype and a scalable dialogue collection process.

As a result, we gain a better understanding of how to answer the explanatory needs of a human operator. With this knowledge, we will be able to create explanation systems tailored to explainee's needs by addressing their questions. It is in contrast to developing new methods blindly or according to the judgement of their developers.

We outline the scope and capabilities of a dialogue agent (Sect. 2). In Sect. 3, we illustrate the architecture of the entire system and describe each of the components. We also demonstrate the agent's work on the examples. Finally, in Sect. 4, we describe the experiment and analyze the collected dialogues.

2 Dialogue System

This dialogue system is a multi-turn chatbot with the user initiative. It offers a conversation about the underlying random forest model trained on the well-known Titanic dataset. We deliberately select a black box model with no direct interpretation together with a dataset and a problem that can be easily imagined for a wider audience. The dialogue system was built to understand and respond to several groups of queries:

- **Supplying data** about the passenger, e.g. specifying age or gender. This step might be omitted by impersonating one of two predefined passengers with different model predictions.
- **Inference** – telling users what are their chances of survival. Model imputes missing variables.
- **Visual explanations** from the Explanatory Model Analysis toolbox [5]: Ceteris Paribus profiles [12] (addressing "what-if" questions) and Break Down plots [9] (presenting feature contributions). Note this is to offer a warm start into the system by answering some of the anticipated queries. However, the principal purpose is to explore what other types of questions might be asked.
- **Dialogue support** queries, such as listing and describing available variables or restarting the conversation.

This system was firstly trained with an initial set of training sentences and intents. After the deployment of the chatbot, it was iteratively retrained based on the collected conversations. Those were used in two ways: 1) to add new intents, 2) to extend the training set with the actual user queries, especially those which were misclassified. The final version of the dialogue agent which is used in the experiment at Sect. 4 consists of 40 intents and 874 training sentences.

3   Implementation

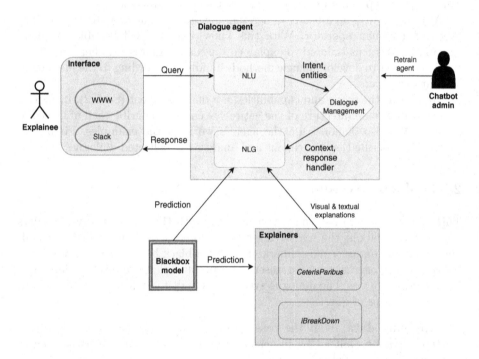

Fig. 1. Overview of the system architecture. **Explainee** uses the system to talk about the **blackbox model**. They interact with the system using one of the **interfaces**. The conversation is managed by the **dialogue agent** which is created and trained by the **chatbot admin**. To create a response system queries the **blackbox model** for its predictions and **explainers** for visual explanations.

A top-level chatbot architecture is depicted in Fig. 1. The system consists of several components:

1. **Explainee**
   Human operator – addressee of the system. They chat about the blackbox model and its predictions.

2. **Interface**
   This dialogue agent might be deployed to various conversational platforms independently of the backend and each other. The only exception to that is rendering some of the graphical, rich messages. We used a custom web integration as a major surface. It communicates with the dialogue agent's engine sending requests with user queries and receiving text and graphical content. The frontend of the chatbot uses `Vue.js` and is based on `dialogflow`[1] repository. It provides a chat interface and renders rich messages, such as plots and suggestion buttons. This integration allows to have a voice conversation using the browser's speech recognition and speech synthesis capabilities.

3. **Dialogue agent**
   Chatbot's engine implemented using `Dialogflow` framework and `Node.js` fulfilment code run on `Google Cloud Functions`.

   – **Natural Language Understanding (NLU)**
   The Natural Language Understanding component classifies query intent and extracts entities. This classifier uses the framework's builtin rule-based and Machine Learning algorithms. NLU module recognizes 40 intents such as posing a what-if question, asking about a variable or specifying its value. It was trained on 874 training sentences. Some of these sentences come from the initial subset of the collected conversations. Additionally, NLU module comes with 4 entities – one for capturing the name of the variable and 3 to extract values of the categorical variables – gender, class and the place of embarkment. For numerical features, a builtin numerical entity is utilized. See examples in Sect. 3.1.

   – **Dialogue management**
   It implements the state and context. Former is used to store the passenger's data and the latter to condition response on more than the last query. For example, when the user sends a query with a number it might be classified as age or fare specification depending on the current context.

   – **Natural-language generation (NLG)**
   Response generation system. To build a chatbot's utterance the dialogue agent might need to use the explanations or the predictions. For this, the NLG component will query explainers or the model correspondingly. Plots, images and suggestion buttons which are part of the chatbot response are rendered as rich messages on the front end.

4. **Blackbox model**
   A random forest model was trained to predict the chance of survival on Titanic[2]. The model was trained in R [24] and converted into REST api with the `plumber` package [34]. The random forest model was trained with default hyperparameters. Data preprocessing includes imputation of missing values. The performance of the model on the test dataset was AUC 0.84 and F1 score 0.73.

---

[1] https://github.com/mishushakov/dialogflow-web-v2.
[2] You can download the model from the `archivist` [6] database with a following hook: archivist::aread("pbiecek/models/42d51").

5. **Explainers**
   REST API exposing visual and textual model explanations from `iBreakDown` [9] and `CeterisParibus` [12] libraries. They explore the blackbox model to create an explanation. See the `xai2cloud` package [27] for more details.
6. **Chatbot admin**
   Human operator – developer of the system. They can manually retrain the system based on misclassified intents and misextracted entities. For instance, this dialogue agent was iteratively retrained based on the initial subset of the collected dialogues.

This architecture works for any predictive model and tabular data. Its components differ in how they can be transferred for other tasks and datasets[3]. The user interface is independent of the rest of the system. When a dataset is fixed, the model is interchangeable. However, the dialogue agent is handcrafted and depends on the dataset as well as explainers. Change in a dataset needs to be at least reflected in an update of the data-specific entities and intents. For instance, a new set of variables needs to be covered. It is also followed by modifying the training sentences for the NLU module and perhaps some changes in the generated utterances. Adding a new explainer might require adding a new intent. Usually, we want to capture the user queries, that can be addressed with a new explanation method.

3.1 NLU Examples

Natural-language understanding module is designed to guess an intent and extract relevant parameters/entities from a user query. Queries can be specified in a open format. Here are examples of NLU for three intents.

Query: What If I had been older?
Intent: ceteris_paribus
Entities: [variable: age]

Query I'm 20 year old woman
Intent: multi_slot_filling
Entities: [age: 20, gender: female]

Query: Which feature is the most important?
Intent: break_down
Entities: []

---

[3] The source code is available at https://github.com/ModelOriented/xaibot.

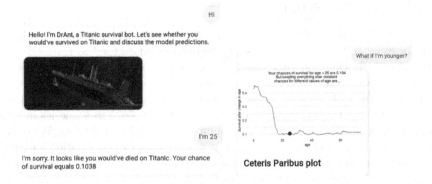

Fig. 2. An example conversation. Explainee's queries in the grey boxes.

3.2 Example Dialogue

An excerpt from an example conversation is presented in Fig. 2. The corresponding intent classification flow is highlighted in Fig. 3.

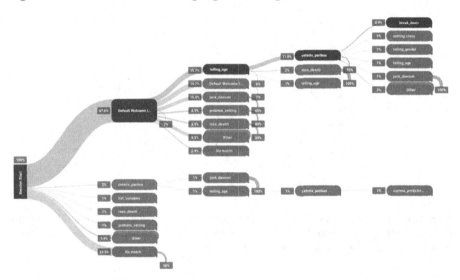

Fig. 3. Screenshot from the `Dialogflow Analytics`. This flow chart demonstrates the results of the NLU module on a sample of collected dialogues. Example conversation from Fig. 2 contributes to the topmost (green) path. Each box corresponds to a classified intention of the query, e.g. *telling_age* or *ceteris_paribus*. (Color figure online)

4   Results

The initial subset of the collected dialogues is used to improve the NLU module of the dialogue agent. As a next step, we conduct an experiment by sharing the chatbot in the Data Science community and analyzing the collected dialogues.

4.1   Experiment Setup

For this experiment, we work on data collected throughout 2 weeks. This is a subset of all collected dialogues, separate from the data used to train the NLU module. Narrowing the time scope of the experiment allows to describe the audience and ensure the coherence of the data. As a next step, we filter out conversations with totally irrelevant content and those with less than 3 user queries. Finally, we obtain 621 dialogues consisting of 5675 user queries in total. The average length equals 9.14, maximum 83 and median 7 queries. We see the histogram of conversations length in Fig. 4. Note that by conversation length we mean the number of user queries which is equal to the number of turns in the dialogue (user query, chatbot response).

The audience acquisition comes mostly from R and Data Science community. Users are instructed to explore the model and its explanations individually. However, they might come across a demonstration of the chatbot's capabilities potentially introducing a source of bias.

We describe the results of the study in the Sect. 4.2 and we share the statistical details about the experiment audience in the Sect. 4.3.

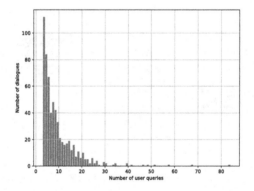

Fig. 4. Histogram of conversations length (number of user queries), after filtering out conversations shorter than 3 queries. As expected, most conversations were short. However, there were also dialogues of over 20 queries.

4.2   Query Types

We analyze the content of the dialogues. Similar user queries, when different only in the formulation, are manually grouped together. For each category, we calculate the number of conversations with at least one query of this type. Numbers of occurrences are presented in Table 1.

Note that users were not prompted or hinted to ask any of these with an exception of the *"what do you know about me"* question. Moreover, the taxonomy defined here is independent of the intents recognized by the NLU module and is defined based on collected dialogues.

Here is the list of the query types ordered decreasingly by the number of conversation they occur in.

1. **why** – general explanation queries, typical examples of such are:
   - "why?"
   - "explain it to me"
   - "how was this calculated?"
   - "why is my chance so low?"
2. **what-if** – alternative scenario queries. Frequent examples: *what if I'm older?*, *what if I travelled in the 1st class?*. Rarely, we see multi-variable questions such as: *What if I'm older and travel in a different class?*.
3. **what do you know about me** – this is the only query hinted to the user using the suggestion button. When the user inputs their data manually it usually serves to understand what is yet missing. However, in the scenario when the explainee impersonates a movie character it also aids understanding which information about the user is possessed by the system.
4. **EDA** – a general category on Exploratory Data Analysis. All questions related to data rather than the model fall into this category. For instance, *feature distribution, maximum values, plot histogram for the variable v, describe/summarize the data, is dataset imbalanced, how many women survived, dataset size* etc.
5. **feature importance** – here we group all questions about the relevance, influence, importance or effect of the feature on the prediction. We see several subtypes of that query:
   - *Which are the most important variable(s)?*
   - *Does gender influence the survival chance?*
   - **local importance** – *How does age influence my survival, What makes me more likely to survive?*
   - **global importance** – *How does age influence survival across all passengers?*
6. **how to improve** – actionable queries for maximizing the prediction, e.g. *what should I do to survive, how can I increase my chances*.
7. **class comparison** – comparison of the predictions across different values of the categorical variable. It might be seen as a variant of the *what-if* question. Examples: *which class has the highest survival chance, are men more likely to die than women*.
8. **who has the best score** – here, we ask about the observations that maximize/minimize the prediction. Examples: *who survived/died, who is most likely to survive*. It is similar to *how to improve* question, but rather on a per example basis.
9. **model-related** – these are the queries related directly to the model, rather than its predictions. We see questions about the algorithm and the code. We also see users asking about metrics (accuracy, AUC), confusion matrix and confidence. However, these are observed just a few times.

10. **contrastive** – question about why predictions for two observations are different. We see it very rarely. However, more often we observe the implicit comparison as a follow-up question – for instance, *what about other passengers, what about Jack*.
11. **plot interaction** – follow-up queries to interact with the displayed visual content. Not observed.
12. **similar observations** – queries regarding "neighbouring" observations. For instance, *what about people similar to me*. Not observed.

Table 1. Results of the analysis for 621 conversations in the experiment. The second column presents the number of conversations with at least one query of a given type. A single dialogue might contain multiple or none of these queries.

Query type	Dialogues count
Why	73
What-if	72
What do you know about me	57
EDA	54
Feature importance	31
How to improve	24
Class comparison	22
Who has the best score	20
Model-related	14
Contrastive	1
Plot interaction	0
Similar observations	0
Number of all analyzed dialogues	**621**

We also see users creating alternative scenarios and comparing predictions for different observations manually, i.e. asking for prediction multiple times with different passenger information. Additionally, we observe explainees asking about other sensitive features, that are not included in the model, e.g. nationality, race or income. However, some of these, e.g. income, are strongly correlated with class and fare.

4.3   Statistics of Surveyed Sample

We use Google Analytics to get insights into the audience of the experiment. Users are distributed across 59 countries with the top five (Poland, United States, United Kingdom, Germany and India, in this order) accounting for 63% of the users. Figure 5 presents demographics data on the subset of the audience (53%) for which this information is available.

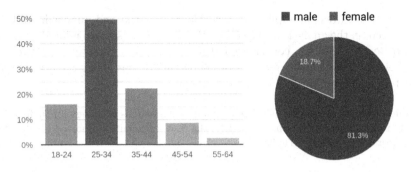

Fig. 5. Demographic statistics for age (left) and gender (right) of the studied group registered by Google Analytics.

5 Conclusions and Future Work

Depending on the area of application, different needs are linked with the concept of interpretability [14,33]. And even for a single area of application, different actors may have different needs related to model interpretability [2].

In this paper, we presented a novel application of the dialogue system for conversational explanations of a predictive model. Detailed contributions are following (1) we presented a process based on a dialogue system allowing for effective collection of user expectations related to model interpretation, (2) we presented a xai-bot implementation for a binary classification model for Titanic data, (3) we conducted an analysis of the collected dialogues.

We conduct this experiment on the survival model for Titanic. However, our prior goal of this work is to understand user needs related to the model explanation, rather than improve this specific implementation. The knowledge we gain from this experiment will aid in designing the explanations for various models trained on tabular data. One example might be survival models for COVID-19 which are currently under large interest.

Conversational agent proved to work as a tool to explore and extract user needs related to the use of the Machine Learning models. This method allowed us to validate hypotheses and gather requirements for the XAI system on the example from the experiment. In this analysis, we identified several frequent patterns among user queries.

Conversational agent is also a promising, novel approach to XAI as a model-human interface. Users were given a tool for the interactive explanation of the model's predictions. In the future, such systems might be useful in bridging the gap between automated systems and their end users. An interesting and natural extension of this work would be to compare user queries for different explainee's groups in the system, e.g. model creators, operators, examiners and decision-subjects. In particular, it would be interesting to collect needs from explainees with no domain knowledge in Machine Learning. Similarly, it is interesting to take advantage of the process introduced in this work to compare user needs across various areas of applications, e.g. legal, medical and financial. Additionally, based on the analysis of the collected dialogues we see two related areas that would benefit from the conversational human-model interaction – *Exploratory Data Analysis* and *model fairness* based on the queries about the sensitive and bias-prone features.

Acknowledgments. We would like to thank 3 anonymous reviewers for their insightful comments and suggestions. Michał Kuźba was financially supported by the 'NCN Opus grant 2016/21/B/ST6/0217'.

References

1. Titanic dataset. https://www.kaggle.com/c/titanic/data
2. Arya, V., et al.: One explanation does not fit all: a toolkit and taxonomy of AI explainability techniques (2019)
3. Baniecki, H., Biecek, P.: modelStudio: interactive studio with explanations for ML predictive models. J. Open Source Softw. (2019). https://doi.org/10.21105/joss.01798
4. Biecek, P.: DALEX: explainers for complex predictive models in R. J. Mach. Learn. Res. **19**, 1–5 (2018)
5. Biecek, P., Burzykowski, T.: Explanatory Model Analysis. Explore, Explain and Examine Predictive Models (2020). https://pbiecek.github.io/ema/
6. Biecek, P., Kosinski, M.: archivist: an R package for managing, recording and restoring data analysis results. J. Stat. Softw. **82**(11), 1–28 (2017)
7. El-Assady, M., et al.: Towards XAI: structuring the processes of explanations (2019)
8. Gilpin, L.H., Bau, D., Yuan, B.Z., Bajwa, A., Specter, M., Kagal, L.: Explaining explanations: an approach to evaluating interpretability of machine learning (2018). http://arxiv.org/abs/1806.00069
9. Gosiewska, A., Biecek, P.: Do Not Trust Additive Explanations. arXiv e-prints (2019)
10. Hoover, B., Strobelt, H., Gehrmann, S.: exBERT: a visual analysis tool to explore learned representations in transformers models (2019)
11. Jentzsch, S., Höhn, S., Hochgeschwender, N.: Conversational interfaces for explainable AI: a human-centred approach (2019)
12. Kuzba, M., Baranowska, E., Biecek, P.: pyCeterisParibus: explaining machine learning models with ceteris paribus profiles in Python. JOSS **4**(37), 1389 (2019). http://joss.theoj.org/papers/10.21105/joss.01389
13. Lage, I., et al.: An evaluation of the human-interpretability of explanation (2019). http://arxiv.org/abs/1902.00006
14. Lipton, Z.C.: The mythos of model interpretability (2016). http://arxiv.org/abs/1606.03490
15. Lundberg, S.M., Lee, S.I.: A unified approach to interpreting model predictions. In: Guyon, I., et al. (eds.) Advances in Neural Information Processing Systems, vol. 30, pp. 4765–4774. Curran Associates, Inc. (2017). http://papers.nips.cc/paper/7062-a-unified-approach-to-interpreting-model-predictions.pdf
16. Madumal, P., Miller, T., Sonenberg, L., Vetere, F.: A grounded interaction protocol for explainable artificial intelligence. In: AAMAS (2019)

17. Madumal, P., Miller, T., Vetere, F., Sonenberg, L.: Towards a grounded dialog model for explainable artificial intelligence (2018). http://arxiv.org/abs/1806.08055
18. Miller, T.: Explanation in artificial intelligence: Insights from the social sciences (2017), http://arxiv.org/abs/1706.07269
19. Miller, T., Howe, P., Sonenberg, L.: Explainable AI: beware of inmates running the asylum or: how I learnt to stop worrying and love the social and behavioural sciences (2017). http://arxiv.org/abs/1712.00547
20. Molnar, C., Casalicchio, G., Bischl, B.: Quantifying interpretability of arbitrary machine learning models through functional decomposition. arXiv e-prints (2019)
21. Mueller, S.T., Hoffman, R.R., Clancey, W.J., Emrey, A., Klein, G.: Explanation in human-AI systems: a literature meta-review, synopsis of key ideas and publications, and bibliography for explainable AI (2019). http://arxiv.org/abs/1902.01876
22. Nori, H., Jenkins, S., Koch, P., Caruana, R.: InterpretML: a unified framework for machine learning interpretability (2019). https://arxiv.org/abs/1909.09223
23. Pecune, F., Murali, S., Tsai, V., Matsuyama, Y., Cassell, J.: A model of social explanations for a conversational movie recommendation system (2019)
24. R Core Team: R: A Language and Environment for Statistical Computing. R Foundation for Statistical Computing, Vienna, Austria (2019). https://www.R-project.org/
25. Ribeiro, M.T., Singh, S., Guestrin, C.: Why Should I Trust You?: Explaining the Predictions of Any Classifier (2016). https://doi.org/10.1145/2939672.2939778
26. Ribera, M., Lapedriza, À.: Can we do better explanations? a proposal of user-centered explainable AI. In: IUI Workshops (2019)
27. Rydelek, A.: xai2cloud: Deploys An Explainer To The Cloud (2020). https://modeloriented.github.io/xai2cloud
28. Scantamburlo, T., Charlesworth, A., Cristianini, N.: Machine decisions and human consequences (2018). http://arxiv.org/abs/1811.06747
29. Sokol, K., Flach, P.: Conversational explanations of machine learning predictions through class-contrastive counterfactual statements. In: Proceedings of the Twenty-Seventh International Joint Conference on Artificial Intelligence Organization, IJCAI-18, pp. 5785–5786, July 2018. https://doi.org/10.24963/ijcai.2018/836
30. Sokol, K., Flach, P.: Glass-box: explaining AI decisions with counterfactual statements through conversation with a voice-enabled virtual assistant. In: Proceedings of the Twenty-Seventh International Joint Conference on Artificial Intelligence Organization, IJCAI-18, pp. 5868–5870 (2018). https://doi.org/10.24963/ijcai.2018/865
31. Sokol, K., Flach, P.: One explanation does not fit all. KI - Künstliche Intelligenz 34(2), 235–250 (2020). https://doi.org/10.1007/s13218-020-00637-y
32. Tan, H.F., Song, K., Udell, M., Sun, Y., Zhang, Y.: Why should you trust my interpretation? Understanding uncertainty in LIME predictions (2019). http://arxiv.org/abs/1904.12991
33. Tomsett, R., Braines, D., Harborne, D., Preece, A., Chakraborty, S.: Interpretable to whom? A role-based model for analyzing interpretable machine learning systems (2018)
34. Trestle Technology, LLC: plumber: an API Generator for R (2018)
35. Werner, C.: Explainable AI through rule-based interactive conversation. In: EDBT/ICDT Workshops (2020)

Analyzing Forward Robustness of Feedforward Deep Neural Networks with LeakyReLU Activation Function Through Symbolic Propagation

Giulio Masetti[(⊠)] and Felicita Di Giandomenico

Institute of Science and Technology "A. Faedo", 56124 Pisa, Italy
giulio.masetti@isti.cnr.it

Abstract. FeedForward Deep Neural Networks (Dnns) robustness is a relevant property to study, since it allows to establish whether the classification performed by Dnns is vulnerable to small perturbations in the provided input, and several verification approaches have been developed to assess such robustness degree. Recently, an approach has been introduced to evaluate forward robustness, based on symbolic computations and designed for the ReLU activation function. In this paper, a generalization of such a symbolic approach for the widely adopted LeakyReLU activation function is developed. A preliminary numerical campaign, briefly discussed in the paper, shows interesting results.

1 Introduction

Deep Neural Networks are increasingly exploited in a number of AI applications, ranging from traditional speech recognition and image recognition to innovative modern sectors such as self-driving cars [8]. However, in addition to great performance capability, employment of Dnns in dependability critical applications, such as autonomous vehicles, requires the satisfaction of high degrees of accuracy/robustness. Therefore, it is paramount to analyze Dnns to verify whether their robustness degree is satisfactory for the application contexts where they are going to be employed. Among the others, abstract interpretation has been proposed in [2] for verifying Dnns. Unfortunately, as recently pointed out in [11], abstract interpretation can result too imprecisely, due to the non-linearity in Dnns.

To mitigate this problem, in [11] a novel symbolic propagation technique has been proposed with the aim of improving the precision of Dnns verification through abstract interpretation. Their idea consists in symbolically representing, for each neuron, how its value can be determined by the values of some neurons at the previous levels. They developed symbolic computations for the ReLU activation function, and proved improvements in the evaluation of Dnns, such as a better lower bound on the robustness property.

© Springer Nature Switzerland AG 2020
I. Koprinska et al. (Eds.): ECML PKDD 2020 Workshops, CCIS 1323, pp. 460–474, 2020.
https://doi.org/10.1007/978-3-030-65965-3_31

As a further contribution in this stream, which showed promising to advance on the robustness evaluation aspects, this paper offers a generalization of the symbolic computation technique to the LeakyReLU activation function case. LeakyReLU was introduced as one of the strategies to mitigate the "dead neuron" problem that affects DNNs with the ReLU activation function: when a neuron outputs zero, it is quite unlikely that a relatively small change of the input can produce an output different from zero. It gained rather high popularity within the community. Actually, ReLU is a special case of LeakyReLU and the common features are exploited to adapt the reasoning of [11] to the one presented in this paper. A preliminary numerical campaign, briefly discussed in the paper, shows interesting results.

Given the narrowed scope of this paper, that focuses on extending the recently proposed approach in [11], we limit the review of the state of the art on DNN robustness verification through symbolic computations to [11], and rely on the positioning of the contribution already addressed there, after verification that there isn't (at the best of our knowledge) other advancements appeared in the literature in the meanwhile.

Enlarging the view on the notion of robustness, it can be observed that, although the formulation as in Definition 3 has been conceived in the context of adversarial training of DNNs, recently it has started to be enlisted under the eXplainable Artificial Intelligence (XAI) umbrella concept. In fact, it can be considered also as a prerequisite for a DNN to be "interpretable", because otherwise the interpretation has to comprise the sensitivity of the DNN to small input changes, resulting in a tedious description of too low level features of the DNN. Even further, the explanation approach itself has to be robust to small changes in the input, and many well-known approaches were proven not robust enough [9]. Robustness is a key feature of linear (regression) models, so one way to impose a certain level of robustness to DNN-based classifiers, designed having in mind interpretability, is to modify the learning process addressing locally difference boundness [7]. Here, instead of imposing "from the outside" some property to the DNN, the focus is on those activation functions for which, given any point other than zero, there exists a neighbourhood where the function is linear, in particular (Leaky)ReLU. This paper has a narrower scope than [7], where higher level features instead of pixels are considered. However, here an explicit dependency of the output from the input is provided.

Another example of training process that can take into consideration the robustness of the DNN is [4], while [5] refers to text classification under adversarial symbol substitutions. Both are originated in the context of robustness to adversarial perturbations of the input, but the reasoning is applicable in the context of XAI. Checking robustness can be formalized as solving a constrained optimization, where the constraints encode the DNN, followed by testing whether the result is less than zero. This computation can be easily integrated within the DNN training process, promoting the definition of robust neural networks. The only requirement on the activation function is that it must be monotonic so that, when propagating a box enclosing the given input through the DNN for solving the optimization, only the intervals' bounds are relevant for the computations. Being designed to work for all the monotonic activation functions, this approach does not exploit a peculiar feature of (Leaky)ReLU: definitely activation/deactivation, as detailed in Sect. 3. In [4,5] all the bounds are propagated through all the layers of the DNN, instead here (following [11]) the bounds are propagated only when strictly necessary, promoting the tightness of the output layer's bounds.

The rest of the paper is structured as follows. Section 2 recalls some preliminaries, in particular Sect. 2.2 justifies the choice of the LeakyReLU activation function. Section 3 extends the work of [11] to the LeakyReLU activation function. Section 4 presents the experimental evaluation. Section 5 draws the conclusions and discusses future work.

2   Preliminaries

We work with deep feedforward neural networks (DNNs), represented as the evaluation of functions $F : \mathbb{R}^m \to \mathbb{R}^n$, where there are m input neurons and n output neurons.

As widely known, a DNN is structured as a sequence of layers: the input layer, comprising all the m input neurons, followed by n_{hl} hidden layers, and an output layer, comprising all the n output neurons, in the end. The output of a layer is the input of the next layer. To ease the notation, in this[1] paper only *fully connected* layers are considered, meaning that the output of each neuron of a layer is connected to the input of each neuron in the next layer. The DNN is then represented as the composition of transformations between layers. In particular, calling m_k the number of neurons within the k-th layer, the transformation between the $(k - 1)$-th and the k-th layer is indicated as $F^{(k)} : \mathbb{R}^{m_{k-1}} \to \mathbb{R}^{m_k}$. Here $m_0 = m$ and $m_{n_{hl}+1} = n$, so that in total there are $m + m_1 + m_2 + \cdots + m_{n_l} + n$ neurons.

Typically, in each layer, a linear transformation is followed by a non-linear activation function, so the application of $F^{(k)}$ requires two intermediate steps:

$$F^{(k-\frac{1}{2})} = W^{(k)} F^{(k-1)} + b^{(k)}, \tag{1}$$

$$F^{(k)} = \text{map } f \text{ over } F^{(k-\frac{1}{2})}, \tag{2}$$

where Eq. (1) is the weighted sum (plus bias) of the neurons of the $(k - 1)$-th layer, Eq. (2) is the application of the non-linear *activation function* $y = f(x)$ over each component of the vector $F^{(k-\frac{1}{2})}$. With a minor notation abuse, we will indicate with $F^{(k)}$ both the function and the vector

$$F^{(k)}(F^{(k-1)}(F^{(k-2)}(\cdots F^{(0)}(\text{in}) \cdots))),$$

where in is the input vector. Here we focus on *classification* DNNs, i.e., the aim of the considered DNNs is to find $c(x)$, the class assigned to $x \in \mathbb{R}^m$, where $c(x) = \arg\max_i F_i(x)$.

---

[1] A discussion about convolutional layers and max pooling layer can be the subject of further studies.

2.1   Formal Verification

A neural network is said to be robust at an input x if it does not change its predicted class on adding some small adversarial noise. Several techniques for verifying DNNs robustness have been proposed; here we focus on *abstract interpretation*. The literature on this subject is vast, but for the aims of this paper it is sufficient to recall that the central idea is: instead of working with a single point x, to work with a set of points $X \ni x$ that have a special "shape" and then to formally verify that a particular property holds.

More formally, we first define the *forward verification problem* for DNN and then *local forward robustness*.

Definition 1 (forward verification problem). *Given F, a domain $X \subseteq \mathbb{R}^m$ of the inputs and a property $C \subseteq \mathbb{R}^n$, we want to establish whether $F(X) \subseteq C$, where $F(X) = \{F(x) s.t.\ x \in X\}$.*

Definition 2 (local forward robustness). *Fixed a norm $||\cdot||_p$, given $in \in \mathbb{R}^m$ and a fixed tolerance $\delta > 0$, we want to investigate the verification problem defined by $X = B(in, \delta) = \{x \in \mathbb{R}^m\ s.t.\ ||x - in||_p \leq \delta\}$ and $C_L = \{y \in \mathbb{R}^n\ s.t.\ \arg\max_i y_i = L\}$, where $L = \arg\max_i F_i(in)$.*

Usually δ is considered constant across all the analysis, so in the literature is often employed the δ-robustness:

Definition 3 (δ-robustness). *A given DNN is said δ-robust if, fixed a norm $||\cdot||_p$ and given $in \in \mathbb{R}^m$, the local forward robustness is verified.*

The most commonly adopted "shapes" include boxes, zonotopes and polyhedra. In this paper we address only boxes, for which it is convenient to consider the infinity norm $||x||_\infty = \max_i |x_i|$. This eases the notation and allows us to focus on the core ideas, observing that our reasoning can be applied almost straightforwardly to polyhedra, whereas polytopes require more care. For a brief, but complete, description of abstract interpretation please refer to [11].

Being X a box, we can represent it as $[l^{(0)}, u^{(0)}]$, i.e., for each i, we keep track of the lower $(l_i^{(0)})$ and upper $(u_i^{(0)})$ bounds of x_i, and propagate these bounds through F, recording in $[l^{(k)}, u^{(k)}]$ the bounds of the box in the k-th layer.

It is well-known that, just considering the propagation of a box through $F^{(k-\frac{1}{2})}$, the first computational step of the k-th neuron as defined in Eq. (1), can lead to precision loss due to the very nature of interval arithmetic (see Example 1). Thus, to mitigate this issue we follow [11] in resorting to a symbolic computation approach. In addition, also the second computational step, defined in Eq. (2), can lead to precision loss (see Example 2) and then the activation function has to be selected with great care.

2.2   Activation Function

In the literature, the activation function at the basis of neurons computation $f : \mathbb{R} \to \mathbb{R}$ is usually chosen among the following: sigmoid(x), tanh(x), ReLU(x),

LeakyReLU(x), eLU(x). Different characteristics of f guide not only the choice of the most appropriate[2] learning algorithm, taking into account the problem at hand and its context of application, but also the kind of robustness analysis we can perform. A summary of the properties for the above mentioned activation functions is reported in Table 1.

Table 1. Classification of activation functions.

	sigmoid	tanh	ReLU	LeakyReLU	eLU
Bounded	✓	✓			
Invertible	✓	✓		✓	✓
Differentiable	✓	✓			
Differentiable for $x \neq 0$	✓	✓	✓	✓	✓
Test + operation			✓	✓	✓
Test + linear			✓	✓	

For the purpose of our study that focuses on symbolic expressions, it is required the property to test "is x greater than zero?", that is a "definitely behavior", as better explained in Sect. 3. This property is shown by ReLU(x), LeakyReLU(x), eLU(x). However, for the last activation function, the transformation following the test is not linear, which is a necessary condition to apply symbolic computation, as we are interested in this work. Therefore, the only two activation functions that are amenable to be treated through symbolic computation are ReLU(x), LeakyReLU(x), whose equations are as follows:

$$\text{ReLU}(x) = \max\{0, x\} \tag{3}$$

$$\text{LeakyReLU}(x) = \max\{0, x\} + \alpha \cdot \min\{0, x\} \tag{4}$$

Since ReLU's robustness through symbolic computation has been already analyzed, in this paper we focus on Eq. (4). Notice that we can also train the parameter α of LeakyReLU, instead of considering it as a constant, obtaining the so called PReLU. However, this has no impact on the reasoning of this paper, so in the following we refer to LeakyReLU only.

3   Symbolic Forward Propagation for DNNs

As already said, we adapt the symbolic computation approach developed in [11] for the ReLU activation function to the case where the activation function is

---

[2] A large body of knowledge is available on this subject, here we just mention [3] as a general overview and [10] for experimental comparisons among ReLU and some of its variants in the context of image recognition (convolutional DNNs are considered, as in [11]).

LeakyReLU. Therefore, as in [11], we consider vectors of expressions $E^{(k-\frac{1}{2})}$ and $E^{(k)}$ together with the functions' min, max : Expr $\rightarrow$ $\mathbb{R}$ for evaluating the minimum and maximum value of an expression, given that the symbols it comprises belong to known intervals.

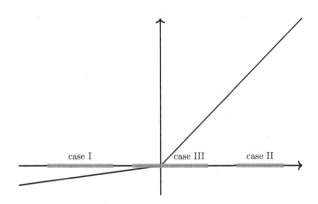

Fig. 1. Relative positions of $[l_i^{(k)}, u_i^{(k)}]$ with respect to 0, considering the LeakyReLU, i.e., Eq. (4). Case I results in a definitely-deactivated neuron, Case II results in a definitely-activated neuron, Case III cannot be resolved in the k-th layer.

Only three cases are possible, according to the relative position of $\min(E_i^{(k-\frac{1}{2})})$ and $\max(E_i^{(k-\frac{1}{2})})$ with respect to 0, as depicted in Fig. 1: case I, where the behavior is "definitely-deactivated", meaning that $E_i^{(k-\frac{1}{2})}$ is always less than 0 because $\max(E_i^{(k-\frac{1}{2})}) < 0$; case II, where the behavior is "definitely-activated", meaning that $E_i^{(k-\frac{1}{2})}$ is always greater than 0 because $\min(E_i^{(k-\frac{1}{2})}) \geq 0$; and case III, where $E_i^{(k)}$ can be either negative or positive, since $\min(E_i^{(k-\frac{1}{2})}) < 0$ and $\max(E_i^{(k-\frac{1}{2})}) > 0$. For $i = 1, \ldots, m_k$, the expression $E_i^{(k-\frac{1}{2})}$ comprises a linear combination of the expressions $E_j^{(k-1)}$, and we can decide how to define $E_i^{(k)}$ taking into account the properties of the activation function.

As shown in Eq. (3) with respect to Eq. (4), ReLU is a special case of LeakyReLU, where $\alpha = 0$. Therefore, the novelty of our approach consists in adapting the previous reasoning, valid for $\alpha = 0$, to the LeakyReLU, where $\alpha > 0$, that is changing the treatment of case I and case III. LeakyReLU is linear when evaluated on $\mathbb{R}^+$ (case II) or $\mathbb{R}^-$ (case I), so we can define $E_i^{(k)}$ always to be linear in the symbol it comprises: if we know for sure that $E_i^{(k-\frac{1}{2})}$ is either in $\mathbb{R}^-$ or $\mathbb{R}^+$ then we can define $E_i^{(k)}$ as $E_i^{(k-\frac{1}{2})}$ times a constant. Otherwise (case III) we can introduce a fresh symbol s_i^k, discard the expression $E_i^{(k-\frac{1}{2})}$ and define $E_i^{(k)} = s_i^k$, so to have again a linear expression in the symbols. More specifically, the action that corresponds to Eq. (1) is $E_i^{(k-\frac{1}{2})} = \sum_j W_{ij}^{(k)} E_j^{(k-1)} - b_i^{(k)}$

followed by a symbolic simplification. Observing that $E_i^{(k)}$ is linear in $E_i^{(k-\frac{1}{2})}$ or s_i^k, $E_i^{(k-\frac{1}{2})}$ is linear in $E_j^{(k-1)}$, and that $E_i^{(0)} = s_i^{(0)}$, we can prove by induction that $E_i^{(k)}$ is linear in the symbols. This fact does not only promote the symbolic computations, but also guarantees that the gradient of $E_i^{(k)}$, with respect to the symbols it comprises, is a constant. Thus, min and max can be easily evaluated.

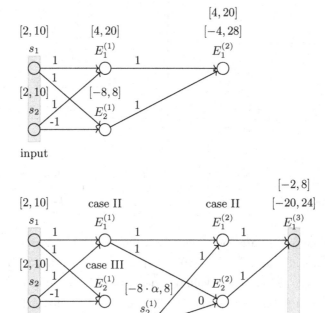

Fig. 2. Representation of Example 1 (top) and Example 2 (bottom). In red are reported the intervals obtained only through interval arithmetic, in blue the intervals obtained exploiting symbolic computations. The second neuron of the first hidden layer in Example 2, being of case III, is replaced by a new neuron with a fresh symbol. Only the relevant neurons and arcs are depicted. (Color figure online)

Evaluating the bounds for each neuron in each layer, just using the interval arithmetic as in [2], can lead to a loss of precision, as illustrated in Example 1, because at increasing of the number of hidden layers the chances of over-approximate the bounds increase due to the very nature of interval arithmetic. Thus, the bounds are actually evaluated only when we are not sure of the sign of $E_i^{(k-\frac{1}{2})}$, i.e., when we introduce a fresh symbol. This gives us also a metric to evaluate how often we compute the bounds because it is sufficient to count the number of new symbols (indicated as Δ_{count}) that are introduced.

The pseudocode of the described procedure is listed in Algorithm 1. The benefits of evaluating the bounds for each neuron in each layer through symbolic computations instead of interval arithmetic are essentially related to the occurrence of *cancellation* [1] and are illustrated through Example 1. Notice that the type of symbolic computation we are interested in is also known as "affine arithmetic".

Example 1. Consider the DNN, depicted on top of Fig. 2, with two-dimensional hidden layers and identity activation function defined by (the second neuron of the second layer is not relevant for the example):

$$E_1^{(1)} = s_1 + s_2, \ E_2^{(1)} = s_1 - s_2,$$
$$\text{input layer: } s_1, s_2 \in [2, 10],$$
$$E_1^{(2)} = E_1^{(1)} + E_2^{(1)} = s_1 + s_2 + s_1 - s_2 = 2s_1,$$

where evaluating the expressions in layer 1 produces $[l_1^{(1)}, u_1^{(1)}] = [4, 20]$ and $[l_2^{(1)}, u_2^{(1)}] = [-8, 8]$, and then in layer 2 we have $[l_1^{(2)}, u_1^{(2)}] = [-4, 28]$, whereas simplifying $E^{(2)}$ and evaluating it only in layer 2 we have $[l_1^{(2)}, u_1^{(2)}] = [4, 20]$, a smaller interval. $\triangle$

Adopting LeakyReLU ensures that $E_i^{(k)}$ is always linear in the symbols it comprises, in particular: $\alpha \cdot E_i^{(k-\frac{1}{2})}$, if in case I; $E_i^{(k-\frac{1}{2})}$, if in case II; introduce a new symbol s_i^k, set $E_i^{(k)} = s_i^k$, $l_i^{(k)} = \alpha \cdot \min(E_i^{(k-\frac{1}{2})})$ and $u_i^{(k)} = \max(E_i^{(k-\frac{1}{2})})$, if in case III.

To appreciate the impact of the activation function, in Example 2 the identity activation function of Example 1 is replaced by the LeakyReLU.

Example 2. Consider the same DNN of Example 1 where we replace the linear activation function with LeakyReLU, setting $\alpha = 0.5$, as depicted at the bottom of Fig. 2. Calling the symbols of input layer $s_1^0, s_2^0 \in [2, 10]$, we have

$$E_1^{(1)} = s_1^0 + s_2^0, \quad E_2^{(1)} = s_1^0 - s_2^0.$$

So $\min(E_1^{(1)}) \geq 0$, and then the first neuron of the first layer is in case II, whereas $\min(E_2^{(1)}) = -8$ and $\max(E_2^{(1)}) = 8$, so the second neuron of the first layer is in case III. Thus, the fresh symbol s_2^1 is introduced, the expression $E_2^{(1)}$ is set equal to s_2^1 and the bounds of s_2^1 are set to $[-8 \cdot \alpha, 8]$. The first neuron of the second layer is

$$E_1^{(2)} = E_1^{(1)} + E_2^{(1)} = s_1^0 + s_2^0 + s_2^1.$$

Thus, $\min(E_1^{(2)}) = 0$, and then the first neuron in the second layer is in case II. Define now the second neuron of the second layer as $E_2^{(2)} = E_1^{(1)}$ and the first neuron of the output layer as $E_1^{(3)} = E_1^{(2)} - E_2^{(2)}$. Taking into account the fact that the first neuron in the second layer is in case II we obtain $[-2, 8]$ as bounds for $E_1^{(3)}$, whereas just propagating the bounds from layer 1 to layer 3 produces $[-20, 24]$ as bounds for $E_1^{(3)}$. $\triangle$

The combined effects illustrated in Examples 1 and 2 show that it is possible to obtain sharper bounds with symbolic computations than just propagating the box through the layers.

4 Experimental Evaluation

The experimental evaluation presented in the following aims at three major objectives: i) demonstrate the feasibility of the symbolic computation approach, described through Algorithm 1, to assess the robustness of the LeakyReLU activation function; ii) analyze the most computationally intensive operations performed by Algorithm 1, as well as evaluate Δ_{count}, that is the number of new symbols s_i^k introduced during its execution. This last corresponds to the number of times case III is encountered, which is the most problematic case inducing precision loss in the computation; and iii) compare the robustness of ReLU and LeakyReLu.

To this purpose, starting from available educational code[3], we have implemented[4] Algorithm 1 in MATLAB. As dataset, we adopted the MNIST[5] dataset of handwritten digits, among the most popular ones used in similar studies (including [11]). Two DNNs have been developed and trained. The first consists of $n_{hl} = 2$ layers, where the first layer is populated by 80 neurons, while the second one has 60 neurons. Since both LeakyReLU and ReLU are considered in the experiments, we denote with $N_{80,60}^R$ the one where the neurons in the hidden layers work with the ReLU activation function, and with $N_{80,60}^L$ the one where neurons work with the LeakyReLU activation function. The LeakyReLU's parameter has been chosen equal to $\alpha = 0.01$. The activation function of the output layer of both $N_{80,60}^R$ and $N_{80,60}^L$ is the identity function $f(x) = x$. The second DNN consists of $n_{hl} = 4$ hidden layers with 128 neurons each. Similarly, two variants $N_{4\times128}^R$ and $N_{4\times128}^L$ are exercised, distinguished by the adoption in the hidden layers of ReLU and LeakyReLU as activation functions, respectively. Again, the output layer's activation function is the identity function.

Considering networks with different numbers of hidden layers allows to investigate how the evaluation of δ-robustness (Definition 3) is impacted by both how deep the DNNs are and by the behavior of the activation function.

4.1 Analysis Results

The accuracy of $N_{80,60}^R$ is 96.65%, whereas the accuracy of $N_{80,60}^L$ is 96.55%. We adopted two DNNs with almost the same accuracy, since we are interested in understanding whether LeakyReLU offers advantages from the robustness evaluation point of view over ReLU.

---

[3] https://it.mathworks.com/matlabcentral/fileexchange/73010-mnist-neural-network-training-and-testing.
[4] https://github.com/106ohm/DeepNeuralNetworkForwardRobustness.
[5] http://yann.lecun.com/exdb/mnist.

Algorithm 1. Forward propagation of boxes for LeakyReLU

Require: a Forward Neural Network
Require: lower and upper bonds $l^{(0)}, u^{(0)} \in \mathbb{R}^m$ of in
Require: $\alpha > 0$
Ensure: lower and upper bonds $l^{(\text{out})}, u^{(\text{out})} \in \mathbb{R}^n$
 for $i = 1, \ldots, m$ **do**
  $E_i^{(0)} \leftarrow s_i^{(0)}$ $\triangleright$ a fresh symbol for each entry of the input vector
 end for
 for $k = 1, \ldots, n_{hl}$ **do**
  $E^{(k-\frac{1}{2})} \leftarrow W^{(k)} \cdot E^{(k-1)} + b^{(k)}$ $\triangleright$ symbolic computations
  $\text{simplify}\left(E^{(k-\frac{1}{2})}\right)$ $\triangleright$ symbolic simplifications
  for $i = 1, \ldots, m_k$ **do**
   if $\max\left(E_i^{(k-\frac{1}{2})}\right) \leq 0$ **then** $\triangleright$ i-th neuron is definitely-deactivated: case I
    $E_i^{(k)} \leftarrow \alpha \cdot E_i^{(k-\frac{1}{2})}$
    continue
   else if $\min\left(E_i^{(k-\frac{1}{2})}\right) \geq 0$ **then** $\triangleright$ i-th neuron is definitely-activated: case II
    $E^{(k)} \leftarrow E^{(k-\frac{1}{2})}$
    continue
   else $\triangleright$ case III
    $l_i^{(k)} \leftarrow \alpha \cdot \min(E_i^{(k-\frac{1}{2})})$
    $u_i^{(k)} \leftarrow \max(E_i^{(k-\frac{1}{2})})$
    $E_i^{(k)} \leftarrow s_i^{(k)}$ $\triangleright$ introduce a fresh symbol
   end if
  end for
 end for
 $E^{(\text{out})} \leftarrow W^{(n_{hl}+1)} \cdot E^{(n_{hl})} + b^{(n_{hl}+1)}$
 for $i = 1, \ldots, m_{n_{hl}+1}$ **do**
  $l_i^{(\text{out})} \leftarrow \min\left(E^{(\text{out})}\right)$
  $u_i^{(\text{out})} \leftarrow \max\left(E^{(\text{out})}\right)$
 end for

Focusing on the 37-th image of the MNIST test suit, both $N_{80,60}^R$ and $N_{80,60}^L$ correctly classify it as a "seven", as can be seen from the *out* columns of Table 2. Setting $\delta = 0.01$, we propagate the box of width δ through both $N_{80,60}^R$ and $N_{80,60}^L$ obtaining the lower and upper bounds reported in Table 2. On one hand, both $N_{80,60}^R$ and $N_{80,60}^L$ are δ-robust, when tested on the 37-th image, and several information can be extracted from Table 2. Examining the upper bounds, particularly relevant for ReLU, of $N_{80,60}^R$ we can notice that digit "two" presents a quite large upper bound (0.846 for $N_{80,60}^R$ and 1.006 for $N_{80,60}^L$), and also other digits have upper bounds close to 0.4. This lead us thinking that we can gain insights about how $N_{80,60}^R$ judges the similarities among digits 7 and 2, and other digits, looking at upper bounds.

Table 2. $N_{80,60}^R$ and $N_{80,60}^L$: lower bound, *out* layer and upper bound taking as *input* the 37-th image of the MNIST test suit.

Digit	$N_{80,60}^R$			$N_{80,60}^L$		
	Lower	Out	Upper	Lower	Out	Upper
0	−0.052	−0.002	0.327	−0.001	$-4.2 \cdot 10^{-5}$	0.048
1	−0.061	−0.004	0.024	−0.001	$-2.9 \cdot 10^{-6}$	0.026
2	−0.083	0.183	**0.846**	−0.005	0.070	**1.006**
3	−0.665	−0.027	0.380	−0.003	0.032	0.453
4	−0.137	−0.001	0.065	−0.002	$-1.6 \cdot 10^{-4}$	0.036
5	−0.275	−0.014	0.093	−0.002	$-2.2 \cdot 10^{-4}$	0.075
6	−0.086	−0.001	0.027	−0.001	$-7.9 \cdot 10^{-5}$	0.158
7	**0.278**	**0.997**	**1.699**	**0.722**	**1.026**	**1.047**
8	−0.351	−0.020	0.425	−0.001	0.004	0.047
9	−0.925	−0.121	0.462	−0.002	$-6.1 \cdot 10^{-5}$	0.046

On the other hand, the bounds of $N_{80,60}^L$ are much tighter than those of $N_{80,60}^R$, demonstrating that, for the 37-th image, $N_{80,60}^L$ is much more robust than $N_{80,60}^R$.

Concerning the evaluation of Δ_{count}, that is the number of fresh symbols added when in case III. For $N_{80,60}^R$ at the end of the output layer there are in total 813 symbols, meaning that the new symbols are 29, since the computation started with $28 \cdot 28 = 784$ symbols. Instead, for $N_{80,60}^L$ we $\Delta_{\text{count}} = 816 - 784 = 31$. The better bounds shown by LeakyReLU are obtained despite the slightly higher value of Δ_{count} with respect to ReLU.

At increasing of n_{hl} the chances of hitting a case III increase, and this is expected to produce a domino effect, leading to a higher number of fresh symbols, and then negatively affecting the tightness of the bounds. In order to study this phenomenon we train and test $N_{4 \times 128}^R$ and $N_{4 \times 128}^L$, the former with an accuracy of 97.78% and the latter of 97.60%, and then we propagate the box of width δ through them to obtain upper and lower bounds, reported in Table 3. $N_{4 \times 128}^R$ results *not* δ-robust because the digit with the greatest upper bound is "three" instead of "seven". Instead, $N_{4 \times 128}^L$ *is* δ-robust. This shows that, even though the bounds of $N_{4 \times 128}^R$ are tighter than those of $N_{4 \times 128}^L$, $N_{4 \times 128}^L$ is more resilient to slightly changes in the input. In addition, the lower bounds of $N_{4 \times 128}^L$ are much smaller than those of $N_{4 \times 128}^R$, so demonstrating that LeakyReLU maintains more information than ReLU. For $N_{4 \times 128}^R$, Δ_{count} results to be equal to $1020 - 784 = 236$, an increment of about 30%, whereas for $N_{4 \times 128}^L$ is $\Delta_{\text{count}} = 1064 - 784 = 280$. So, as before, $N_{4 \times 128}^L$ has slightly more fresh symbols than $N_{4 \times 128}^R$.

Focusing on a single neuron, though, we can observe that the amount of new symbols that affect its behavior are quite limited. For instance, the 67-th neuron of the fourth layer of $N_{4 \times 128}^R$ comprises: the 784 symbols defined within the input

Table 3. $N^R_{4\times128}$ and $N^L_{4\times128}$: lower bound, *out* layer and upper bound taking as *input* the 37-th image of the MNIST test suit.

Digit	$N^R_{4\times128}$			$N^L_{4\times128}$		
	Lower	Out	Upper	Lower	Out	Upper
0	−12.251	0.025	11.638	−0.233	0.003	21.637
1	−12.195	−0.039	13.346	−0.240	−0.001	25.460
2	−15.166	0.014	17.023	−0.294	0.017	24.191
3	−15.546	0.008	**17.404**	−0.159	0.046	17.880
4	−12.302	−0.006	12.466	−0.124	−0.006	24.270
5	−15.717	−0.028	14.635	−0.272	0.041	22.845
6	−13.579	0.007	15.936	−0.224	0.014	28.455
7	−21.041	0.024	13.046	−0.164	0.024	**34.517**
8	−13.160	0.052	15.740	−0.248	−0.034	29.613
9	−11.768	−0.014	15.475	−0.259	−0.003	25.208

layer, 18 symbols defined in layer 1, 28 in layer 2 and 63 in layer 3. In total, this accounts to a 14% increment in the number of symbols.

4.2 Considerations on Computational Performance

Although the current implementation of Algorithm 1 is still preliminary, and does not exploit the inherent parallelism, we can observe a couple of interesting behaviors.

First, even though the overall computation of the bounds can be quite slow (it can take about two hours and a half for $N^R_{80,60}$ and $N^L_{80,60}$, and about five days for $N^R_{4\times128}$ and $N^L_{4\times128}$ on a low-performing laptop[6]) a clear pattern emerges: the computation time is linear in the number of symbols. In fact, in MATLAB the performance of all the expressions' manipulations is highly sensitive to the number of symbols they comprise and then, if Δ_{count} is small compared with the number of symbols within the input layer, then the computation time is linear in n_{hl}. In particular, for neurons in case I and II the expressions are just manipulated through the application of linear functions and the MATLAB function *isAlways*.

Second, when a fresh symbol is needed we also need to compute the bounds of the symbol, and this is the single most expensive atomic computation the algorithm needs to perform. There are several ways to accomplish this task; at the moment we employ the MATLAB *funmincon* function exploiting the fact, pointed out in Sect. 3, that the grading of an expression with respect to the symbols it comprises is a constant. Thus, if the vast majority of the neurons

---

[6] CPU Intel(R) Core(TM) i3-6100U at 2.30 GHz, 4 Gb RAM at 2133 MHz, running Ubuntu 20.04, MATLAB 2019b.

is in case I and II, the longer computations needed for case III are not prevalent. Otherwise, as for $N^R_{4 \times 128}$ and $N^L_{4 \times 128}$, the computations related to case III overwhelm those related to the other cases.

5   From Forward to Backward Propagation: Initial Thoughts

Inspired by [6], we realize that the symbolic computation techniques described in this paper can also impact other areas of Explainable Neural Networks research, in particular those focused on determining which characteristics of a given DNN primarily influence a specific result. The idea is to symbolically propagate back through the DNN a box enclosing a given output, to determine the box enclosing those inputs that are mapped to the selected output. Not being able to classify this kind of reasoning according to already established nomenclature, such as the one discussed in [9], we can refer to it as "backward behavior". So far, this kind of analysis couldn't be considered feasible mainly because of two obstacles related to the activation function: on one side, among the most widely adopted activation functions, those that are invertible (a necessary condition for backward behavior investigations) do not fit well with exact symbolic computations; and, on the other side, the one that is perfect for symbolic computation, i.e. ReLU, is not invertible. Now, the generalization of the work in [11] to the LeakyReLU, that is invertible (Table 1), paves the way to new possibility of explaining the behavior of DNNs.

However, although the premises are encouraging, the research is still at an initial stage. The main challenge about backward behavior of DNNs seems to be related to the inversion of the symbolic expression manipulation that corresponds to Eq. (1). DNNs are often characterized by having hidden layers with different numbers of neurons, so $W^{(k)}$ is rectangular, and it can also happen that $W^{(k)}$ is square but not full rank. Maintaining a symbolic approach, but trading on the abstract interpretation's shape, we could resort to use the Moore-Penrose pseudoinverse, that is the best approximant for $|| \cdot ||_2$, in particular considering that almost always $W^{(k)}$ is full rank. Alternatively, maintaining $||\cdot||_\infty$ but trading on symbolic computations we can define an optimization problem to find one of the $F^{(k-1)}$ such that $W^{(k)}F^{(k-1)} + b^{(k)} = F^{(k+\frac{1}{2})}$ given $F^{(k+\frac{1}{2})}$. Both solutions are not satisfactory: the first, according to our preliminary experiments, produce boxes that are too large to have some meaning; the second because a single point cannot be representative of an interval, so the entire concept of abstract interpretation is not maintained.

It is expected that from these initial thoughts new ideas will be triggered, to possibly find the way to advance in this research direction.

6   Conclusions and Future Work

This paper presented an approach to assess forward robustness of DNNs, where the adopted activation function is LeakyReLU. The approach exploits symbolic computation, as recently proposed in [11] for the case of the ReLU activation function. A preliminary campaign of experiments has demonstrated the feasibility of the approach and the better robustness obtained by DNNs employing LeakyReLU with respect to those employing ReLU. This is mainly due to the dying problem affecting ReLU, that is actually alleviated by LeakyReLu, thus confirming the value of developing our symbolic computation technique for an activation function that has good popularity within the community.

From the initial investigations presented in this paper, several research lines are foreseen as interesting advancements. The most natural ones are to apply the approach to deeper DNNs and to extend the abstract elements to shapes other than boxes. In particular, zonotopes and polyhedra are planned to be investigated. Another direction is testing Algorithm 1 on real-world scenarios to understand whether there are significant limitations to the application of the approach in concrete contexts. Of interest for a niche within the community, we can try to extend the concept of definitely-activated and definitely-deactivated to those complex activation functions defined after ReLU, for which several authors have proposed different ways to trade between holomorphicity and troubles related to the Liouville's theorem.

Of course, extending investigations on the backward behavior as discussed in Sect. 5 is a further study where we see interesting potentialities, although indirectly connected to the forward robustness this paper focuses on.

Acknowledgements. We would like to thank Prof. Laura Semini, University of Pisa, and Prof. Alessandro Fantechi, University of Florence, for the initial fruitful discussion on the subject of the paper, and the reviewers for their constructive suggestions.

References

1. Comba, J.L.D., Stolfi, J.: Affine arithmetic and its applications to computer graphics. In: VI Brazilian Symposium on Computer Graphics and Image Processing
2. Gehr, T., Mirman, M., Drachsler-Cohen, D., Tsankov, P., Chaudhuri, S., Vechev, M.: Ai2: safety and robustness certification of neural networks with abstract interpretation. In: 2018 IEEE Symposium on Security and Privacy (SP), pp. 3–18 (2018)
3. Goodfellow, I., Bengio, Y., Courville, A.: Deep Learning. MIT Press (2016). http://www.deeplearningbook.org
4. Gowal, S., et al.: On the effectiveness of interval bound propagation for training verifiably robust models. arXiv preprint arXiv:1810.12715 (2018)
5. Huang, P.S., et al.: Achieving verified robustness to symbol substitutions via interval bound propagation. arXiv preprint arXiv:1909.01492 (2019)
6. Lapuschkin, S., Wäldchen, S., Binder, A., Montavon, G., Samek, W., Müller, K.: Unmasking clever Hans predictors and assessing what machines really learn. CoRR abs/1902.10178 (2019)
7. Melis, D.A., Jaakkola, T.: Towards robust interpretability with self-explaining neural networks. In: Advances in Neural Information Processing Systems, pp. 7775–7784 (2018)
8. Sze, V., Chen, Y., Yang, T., Emer, J.S.: Efficient processing of deep neural networks: a tutorial and survey. Proc. IEEE **105**(12), 2295–2329 (2017)

9. Vilone, G., Longo, L.: Explainable artificial intelligence: a systematic review (2020)
10. Xu, B., Wang, N., Chen, T., Li, M.: Empirical Evaluation of Rectified Activations in Convolutional Network. arXiv e-prints (2015)
11. Yang, P., Liu, J., Li, J., Chen, L., Huang, X.: Analyzing deep neural networks with symbolic propagation: towards higher precision and faster verification. In: Proceedings of the 26th International Symposium on Static Analysis, pp. 296–319 (2019)

Limeout: An Ensemble Approach to Improve Process Fairness

Vaishnavi Bhargava, Miguel Couceiro$^{(\boxtimes)}$, and Amedeo Napoli

Université de Lorraine, CNRS, Inria N.G.E., LORIA, 54000 Nancy, France
vaishnavi.bhargava2605@gmail.com,
{vaishnavi.bhargava,miguel.couceiro,amedeo.napoli}@loria.fr

Abstract. Artificial Intelligence and Machine Learning are becoming increasingly present in several aspects of human life, especially, those dealing with decision making. Many of these algorithmic decisions are taken without human supervision and through decision making processes that are not transparent. This raises concerns regarding the potential bias of these processes towards certain groups of society, which may entail unfair results and, possibly, violations of human rights. Dealing with such biased models is one of the major concerns to maintain the public trust.

In this paper, we address the question of *process* or *procedural fairness*. More precisely, we consider the problem of making classifiers fairer by reducing their dependence on sensitive features while increasing (or, at least, maintaining) their accuracy. To achieve both, we draw inspiration from "dropout" techniques in neural based approaches, and propose a framework that relies on "feature drop-out" to tackle process fairness. We make use of "LIME Explanations" to assess a classifier's fairness and to determine the sensitive features to remove. This produces a pool of classifiers (through feature dropout) whose ensemble is shown empirically to be less dependent on sensitive features, and with improved or no impact on accuracy.

Keywords: Explainability · Fairness · Feature importance · Feature-dropout · Ensemble classifier · LIME

1 Introduction

Machine Learning (ML) tasks often involve the training of a model based on past experience and data, which are then used for prediction and classification purposes. The practical applications where such models are used include, e.g., loan grants in view of framing laws, detecting terrorism, predicting criminal recidivism, and similar social and economic issues at a global level [11,12,17].

This research was partially supported by TAILOR, a project funded by EU Horizon 2020 research and innovation programme under GA No. 952215, and the Inria Project Lab "Hybrid Approaches for Interpretable AI" (HyAIAI).

© Springer Nature Switzerland AG 2020
I. Koprinska et al. (Eds.): ECML PKDD 2020 Workshops, CCIS 1323, pp. 475–491, 2020.
https://doi.org/10.1007/978-3-030-65965-3_32

These decisions affect human life and may have undesirable impacts on vulnerable groups in society. The widespread use of ML algorithms has raised multiple concerns regarding user privacy, transparency, fairness, and trustfulness of these models. In order to make Europe "fit for the digital age"[1], in 2016 the European Union has enforced the GDPR Law[2] across all organizations and firms. The law entitles European citizens the right to have a basic knowledge regarding the inner workings of automated decision models and to question their results. The unfair automated decisions not only violate anti-discrimination laws, but they also undermine public trust in Artificial Intelligence. The unwanted bias in the machine learning models can be caused due to the following reasons:

- The *data Collection* [20] may be biased, as certain minority groups of society, or people living in rural areas do not generate enough data. This leads to an unfair model because of unbalanced and biased datasets while training.
- The *training algorithm* may be subject to bias if one chooses an inappropriate model or training set. Additionally, the model may consider sensitive or discriminatory features while training, which leads to process unfairness.[3]

Till now, the notions of fairness have focused on the outcomes of the decision process [21,22], with lesser attention given to the process leading to the outcome [9,10]. These are inspired by the application of anti-discrimination laws in various countries, which ensures that the people belonging to sensitive groups (e.g. race, color, sex etc.) should be treated fairly. This issue can be addressed through different points of views, which include:

- *Individual Fairness or Disparate Treatment* [21] considers individuals who belong to different sensitive groups, yet share similar non-sensitive attributes and require them to have same decision outcomes. For instance, during job applications, applicants having same educational qualifications must not be treated discriminately based on their sex or race.
- *Group Fairness or Disparate Impact* [21] states that people belonging to different sensitive attribute groups should receive beneficial outcomes in similar proportions. In other words, it states that "Different sensitive groups should be treated equally".
- *Disparate Mistreatment or Equal Opportunity* [22] proposes different sensitive groups to achieve similar rates of error in decision outcomes.
- *Process or Procedural fairness* [9,10] deals with the process leading to the prediction and keeps track of input features used by the decision model. In other words, the process fairness deals at the algorithmic level and ensures that the algorithm does not use any sensitive features while making a prediction.

In this study, we aim to deliver a potential solution to deal with the process fairness in ML Models. The major problem while dealing with process fairness is

---

[1] https://www.zdnet.com/article/gdpr-an-executive-guide-to-what-you-need-to-know/.

[2] General Data Protection Regulation (GDPR): https://gdpr-info.eu/.

[3] Terms unfairness and bias are used interchangeably.

the opaqueness of ML models. Indeed, this black-box nature of ML models, such as in deep neural networks and ensemble architectures such as random forests (RF), makes it difficult to interpret and explain their outputs, and consequently for users and general public to trust their results. There are several proposals of explanatory models to make black-box models more interpretable and transparent. Due to the complexity of recent black-box models, it is unreasonable to ask for explanations that could represent the model as a whole. This fact, lead to local approaches to derive possible explanations.

The basic idea is to explain the model locally rather than globally. An ideal model explainer should contain the following desirable properties [18]:

- *Model-Interpretability*: The model should provide a qualitative understanding between features and targets. The explanations should be easy to understand.
- *Local Fidelity*: It is not possible to find an explanation that justifies the black-box's results on every single instance. But the explainer must at least be locally faithful to the instance being predicted.
- *Model Agnostic*: The explainer should be able to explain all kinds of models.
- *Global Perspective*: The explainer should explain a representative set to the user, such that the user has a global understanding of the explainer.

Such local explanatory methods include LIME, Anchors, SHAP and DeepSift [7,16,18,19]. These are based on "linear explanatory methods" that gained a lot of attention recently, due to their simplicity and applicability to various supervised ML scenarios.

In this study, we will mainly use LIME to derive local explanations of black box classification models. Given a black box model and a target instance, LIME learns a surrogate linear model to approximate the black-box model in a neighbourhood around the target instance. The coefficients of this linear model correspond to the features' contributions to the prediction of the target instance. Thus *LIME outputs top features used by the black box locally and their contributions.* In this paper, we propose LIME$_{Global}$, a method to derive global explanations from the locally important features obtained from LIME.

The LIME$_{Global}$ explanations can provide an insight into process fairness. This naturally raises the question of how to guarantee a fairer model given these explanations, while ensuring minimal impact in accuracy [23]. This motivated us to seek models M^{final} in which (i) their dependence on sensitive features is reduced, as compared to the original model, and (ii) their accuracy is improved (or, at least, maintained).

To achieve both goals, we propose LimeOut[4], a framework that relies on *feature dropout* to produce a pool of classifiers that are then combined through an ensemble approach. Feature drop out receives a classifier and a feature a as input, and produces a classifier that does not take a into account. Essentially, feature a is removed in both the training and the testing phases.

---

[4] The name comes from drop-out techniques [5,6] in neural networks. The github repository of LimeOut can be found here:
https://github.com/vaishnavi026/LimeOut.

LimeOut's workflow can be described as follows. Given the classifier provided by the user, LimeOut uses LIME$_{Global}$ to assess the fairness of the given classifier by looking into the contribution of each feature to the classifier's outcomes. If the most important features include sensitive ones, the model is unfairly biased. Otherwise, the model is considered as unbiased. In the former case, LimeOut applies dropout of these sensitive features, thus producing a pool of classifiers (as explained earlier). These are then combined into an ensemble classifier M_{final}. Our empirical study was performed on two families of classifiers (logistic regression and random forests) and carried out on real-life datasets (Adult and German Credit Score), and it shows that both families of models become less dependent on sensitive features (such as sex, race, marital status, foreign worker, etc.) and show improvements or no impact on accuracy.

The paper is organised as follows. In Sect. 2 we will discuss some substantial work related to explainability and fairness. We will briefly recall LIME (Local Interpretable Model Agnostic Explanations) in two distinct settings (for textual and tabular data) in Subsect. 2.1, and briefly discuss different fairness issues, some measures proposed in the literature, as well as the main motivation of our work in Subsect. 2.2. We will then present our approach (LimeOut) in Sect. 3, and two empirical studies are carried out in Sect. 4 that indicate the feasibility of LimeOut. Despite the promising results, this preliminary study deserves further investigations, and in Sect. 5 we will discuss several potential improvements to be carried out in future work.

2   Related Work

In this section, we briefly recall LIME and discuss some issues related to model fairness. There has been substantial work done in the field of "Interpretable Machine Learning" and "Fairness". LIME [18] and Anchors [19] are prominently being used to obtain the explanations of the black box ML models. These methods provide the top important features that are used by the black box to predict a particular instance. LIME and Anchors do not provide human like explanations (they provide "feature importance" or contributions), and they have some limitations [7]. In Sect. 3 we will use LIME to tackle fairness issues based on relative importance of the features.

2.1   LIME - Explanatory Method

LIME (Local Interpretable Model Agostic Explanations) takes the form of surrogate linear model, which is interpretable and mimics locally the behavior of a black box. The feature space used by LIME does not need to be the same as the feature space used by a black box. Examples of representations used by LIME include [18]: (i) the binary vector representation of textual data that indicates presence/absence of a word, and (ii) the binary vector which represents presence/absence of contiguous patch of similar pixels, in case of images.

LIME can be described as follows [18]. Let $f : \mathbb{R}^d \to \mathbb{R}$ be the function learned by a classification or regression model over training samples. No further information about this function f is assumed. Now, let $x \in \mathbb{R}^d$ be an instance, and consider its prediction $f(x)$. LIME aims to explain the prediction $f(x)$ locally. Note that the feature space of LIME need not be the same as the input space of f. For example, in case of text data interpretable space is used as vectors representing presence/absence of words, whereas the original space might be the word embeddings or word2vec representations. Indeed, LIME uses discretized features of smaller dimension $\hat{d}$ to build the local model, and aims to learn an explanatory model $g : \mathbb{R}^{\hat{d}} \to \mathbb{R}$, which approximates f in the neighborhood of $x \in \mathbb{R}^d$. To get a local explanation, LIME generates neighbourhood points around an instance x to be explained and assigns a weight vector to these points. The weight is assigned using $\pi_x(z)$, which denotes the proximity measure of z w.r.t. x. It then learns the weighted linear surrogate model g by solving the following optimisation problem:

$$g = argmin_{g \in \mathcal{G}} \ \mathcal{L}(f, g, \pi_x(z)) + \Omega(g)$$

where $\mathcal{L}(f, g, \pi_x(z))$ is a measure of how unfaithful g is in approximating f in the locality defined by $\pi_x(z)$, and where $\Omega(g)$ measures the complexity of g (LIME uses the regularization term to measure complexity). In order to ensure both interpretability and local fidelity, LIME minimizes $\mathcal{L}(f, g, \pi_x(z))$ while enforcing $\Omega(g)$ to be small in order to be interpretable by humans. The coefficients of g correspond to the contribution of each feature to the prediction $f(x)$ of x. LIME uses the following weighting function

$$\pi_x(z) = e^{\left(\frac{-D(x,z)^2}{\sigma^2}\right)}, \tag{1}$$

where $D(x, z)$ is the Euclidean distance between x and z, and σ is the hyper parameter (kernel-width). The value of σ impacts the fidelity of explanation [14].

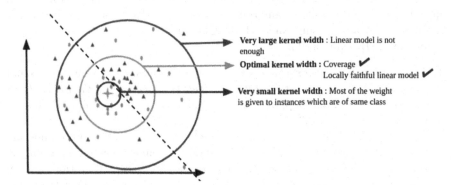

Fig. 1. Depicts the σ's selection and data distribution, where the red triangles are negative examples, whereas yellow dots constitute positive examples. (Color figure online)

For instance, when σ is too large, all instances are given equal weight, and it is impossible to derive a linear model which can explain all of them. Similarly if σ is too small, only a few points are assigned considerable weight and even a constant model will be able to explain these points, this will result in lower coverage. Thus we need to choose an optimal σ to ensure coverage as well as local fidelity (faithfulness). This is illustrated in Fig. 1: it displays the impact of σ on the explanations. The tuned value used by LIME [18] for tabular data is $\sigma = 0.75 * n$ for n columns, whereas for textual data it is $\sigma = 25$.

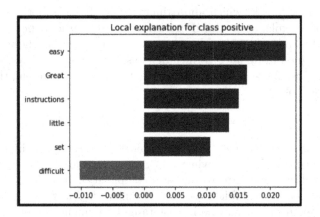

Fig. 2. The explanation for the classification of *Great easy to set up. Little difficult to navigate and the instructions are non-existent*, which indicates the contribution of each word (in red is the contribution to the negative feedback class, and in green to the positive feedback class). (Color figure online)

LIME for Textual Data [18]. Consider the text classification problem, in which the goal is to classify an amazon review into positive or negative feedback[5]. The model is trained using Naive Bayes Classifier. Let's discuss the procedure to get the LIME explanation:

1. *Take any instance x for which you need an explanation.* Consider the textual instance *Great easy to set up. Little difficult to navigate and the instructions are non-existent*, and suppose that the Naive Bayes prediction is $P(pos.) = 0.68$ and $P(neg.) = 0.32$.
2. *Perturb your dataset and get their black box predictions.* For finding the perturbation of this example, LIME randomly removes each word from the original instance (i.e., changes '1' to '0' in the binary representation) one by one, and considers all thus obtained neighborhood points. LIME then gets the black box prediction of these neighbour instances.

---

[5] https://www.kaggle.com/bittlingmayer/amazonreviews

3. *Weight the new samples based on their proximity to the original instance.* LIME assigns weights to the neighbourhood instances z based on their proximity to the original instance x using 1.
4. *Fit a weighted, interpretable (surrogate) model on the dataset with the variations.* LIME trains a linear weighted model that fits the original and the obtained neighbourhood instances.
5. *Get the explanations by interpreting the local model.* The output of LIME is the list of explanations, reflecting the contribution of each feature to the prediction of the sample. The resulting explanation is illustrated in Fig. 2.

LIME for Tabular Data [7]. The workflow of LIME on tabular data is similar to that on textual data. However, unlike LIME for textual data, it needs a training set (user defined) to generate neighbourhood points. The following statistics are computed for each feature depending on their type: (i) for categorical features it computes the frequency of each value, (ii) for numerical features, it computes the mean and the standard deviation, which are then discretized into quartiles.

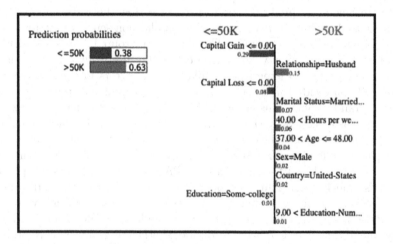

Fig. 3. Local explanation in case of Adult dataset. The orange bar represents the contribution of feature, to predict salary $\geq$ 50k dollars and blue bar is for the features which contributes to the negative class (salary $<$ 50k dollars) (Color figure online)

Suppose that f is the black-box function, and that we want to explain the prediction $f(x)$ of $x = (x_1, x_2, \ldots, x_i., x_n)$, where each x_i may be a categorical or a numerical value. Each categorical value is mapped to an integer using LabelEncoder[6]. Note that the values of each feature in the training set is divided

---

[6] LableEncoder Class is given in the sklearn preprocessing library
https://scikit-learn.org/stable/modules/generated/sklearn.preprocessing.
LabelEncoder.html.

into p quantiles. These quantile intervals are used for discretizing the original instance. If x_i lies between quantile q_j and q_{j+1}, it gets the value j. This is done for all the features to get the quantile boxes for all $x_i, i \in \{1, \ldots, n\}$.

To get the perturbation $\hat{y}$ in the neighbourhood of $\hat{x}$, LIME samples discrete values from $\{1, \ldots, p\}$, n times. To get the continuous representation y of $\hat{y}$, LIME Tabular uses a normal distribution and the quantile values. The neighbourhood instance $\hat{y}$ is represented as binary tuple with the i-th component equal to 1 if $\hat{x}_i = \hat{y}_i$, and 0 if $\hat{x}_i \neq \hat{y}_i$. In this way LIME Tabular generates all the neighbourhood points. The following steps are similar to LIME for textual data. These points are assigned weights using the exponential kernel (1), and a weighted linear function is learned over the neighbourhood permutations. To illustrate, consider an example of the Adult dataset (see Subsect. 4.1). The task is to predict if a salary of a person is $\geq$50k dollars. We have trained the model using Random Forest Classifier. An example of local explanation is given in Fig. 3.

2.2   Model Fairness

Several notions of model fairness have been proposed [3,9,10,21,22] based on decision outcomes as well as on process fairness. Individual fairness [2] (or disparate treatment, or predictive parity) imposes that the instances/individuals belonging to different sensitive groups, but similar non-sensitive attributes must receive equal decision outcomes. The notion of group fairness (or disparate impact or statistical parity [4]) is rooted in the desire for different sensitive demographic groups to experience similar rates of errors in decision outcomes. COMPAS[7] is a recidivism detection tool, where the goal is to predict whether a criminal would re-offend his crime based on a long questionnaire. The popular algorithm was designed by the commercial company, Northpointe (now Equivant). A study by ProPublica[8] showed that COMPAS has a strong ethnic bias. Among non-reoffenders, COMPAS is almost twice more likely to signal black people as high risk. Furthermore in COMPAS, white reoffenders are predicted as low risk much often than black offenders. In other words, this indicates that COMPAS has considerable high false positive and lower true negative rates for black defendants when compared to white defendants. COMPAS is used across US by judges and parole officers to decide whether to grant or deny probation to offenders; hence, it is very important to understand how this model reaches its conclusion and ensure it is fair. If we focus on the decision outcomes, the fair algorithm in case of COMPAS (if we consider only Race as sensitive feature) should be such that: (i) black and whites with the same features get the same output (no disparate treatment and thus non-discriminatory), and (ii) the proportion of individuals classified as high-risk should be same across both the groups (statistical parity).

We can deal with this bias during training (see [22]) by: (i) excluding all features that may cause the model to create bias, e.g. race, gender etc., or (ii)

---

[7] https://en.wikipedia.org/wiki/COMPAS_(software).

[8] https://www.propublica.org/article/machine-bias-risk-assessments-in-criminal-sentencing.

including discrimination measures as learning constraints, i.e., the model should be trained to minimize $P(y_{pred} \neq y_{true})$ such that

$$P(y_{pred} \neq y_{true} | race = Black) = P(y_{pred} \neq y_{true} | race = White),$$

where y_{pred} is the risk predicted by trained ML model (e.g., COMPAS) and y_{true} is the true risk value. This constraint is motivated by the fact that 'race' is a sensitive feature. Such constraints are applied to different sensitive attributes separately (e.g. sex, race, nationality etc.), it might lead to unfairness for the groups which lie at the intersection of multiple kinds of discrimination (e.g. black women), also known as *fairness gerrymandering* [13]. To avoid this, [25] proposed constraints for multiple combinations of sensitive features. However, constraints for multiple combinations of sensitive attributes render model training highly complex and may lead to overfitting.

Earlier studies in fair ML [23,24] consider individual and group fairness as conflicting measures, and some studies tried to find an optimal trade-off between them. In [1] the author argue that, although apparently conflicting, they correspond to the same underlying moral concept. In fact, the author provides a broader perspective and advocates an individual treatment and assessment on a case-by-case basis. In [9,10] the author provides another noteworthy perspective to measure fairness, namely, *process fairness*. Rather than focusing on the outcome, it deals with the process leading to the outcome. In [10] the author provides a key insight to rely on *human's moral judgement or intuition* about the fairness of using an input feature in algorithmic decision making. He also assesses the impact of removing certain input features on the accuracy of the classifier, and designs an optimal trade-off between accuracy and the process fairness for the classifier. However, humans may have different perspectives on whether it is fair to use a input feature in decision making process. In [8] the authors propose a framework to understand why people perceive certain features as fair or unfair. They introduce seven factors on which a user evaluates a feature in terms of reliability, relevance, privacy, volitionality, causes outcome, causes vicious cycle, causes disparity in outcomes, caused by sensitive group membership.

We are inspired by the idea of using a combination of classifiers instead of a single one. For instance, in [9] the authors explore the benefits of replacing a single classifier with a diverse ensemble of random classifies, regarding the accuracy as well as individual and group fairness. In this paper, we further explore this idea and propose a method, that we call *LimeOut*, to ensure process fairness while improving (or, at least, maintaining) the model's accuracy.

3   LimeOut Workflow

In this section, we describe in detail the framework of LimeOut that consists of two main components: $LIME_{Global}$ and $ENSEMBLE_{Out}$. It receives as input both a classifier[9] and a dataset. The first component then checks whether the

---

[9] Here we focus on binary classifiers that output the probability for each class label.

classifier is biased on the dataset in the sense that the predictions depend on sensitive features. To do this, we make use of LIME$_{Global}$ [18] (see Subsect. 3.1). This will output the most important features (globally). If sensitive features are among the most important, then the classifier is considered unfair and the second component of LimeOut is employed. Otherwise, the classifier is considered fair and no action is taken. The second component is the core of LimeOut (see Subsect. 3.2). Given the most important features, ENSEMBLE$_{Out}$ produces a pool of classifiers using feature-drop. Each of these classifiers does not depend on the corresponding sensitive features. It then constructs an ensemble using this pool of classifiers. Following a human and context-centered approach, the choice of sensitive features is left to the user within the given context. This framework will be illustrated in Sect. 4.

3.1 LIME$_{Global}$

LIME is prevalent to get local explanations for the instances. These explanations can be combined to provide insights into the global process of the classifier [15, 18]. First, LIME$_{Global}$ chooses instances using *submodular pick* method [18]. The choice of instances can impact the reliability of the global explanation. The method submodular pick provides a set of instances for which explanations are diverse and non-redundant. To obtain a global insight into the classifier's inner process, we use the instances obtained from submodular pick[10]. LIME$_{Global}$ obtains the local explanations (important features and their contributions) for all these instances. This results in a list of top important features used by the model globally.

3.2 ENSEMBLE$_{Out}$

LimeOut uses the globally important features obtained by LIME$_{Global}$ to assess process fairness of any given ML model. In this way, we can check whether the model's predictions depend on sensitive features and measure its dependence. If sensitive features are ranked within the top 10^{11} globally important features, then it is deemed unfair or biased. If the model is deemed unfair, then one easy solution would be to remove all the sensitive features from the dataset before training. However, these sensitive features may be highly correlated to non-sensitive features, thus keeping the undesired bias. To mitigate this drawback, LimeOut also removes all such correlated features.

Now this could entail a decrease in performance since, after removing all the sensitive features, the model could become less accurate due to the lack of training data. To overcome this limitation, LimeOut constructs a pool of

---

[10] In [18] the authors argue that the submodular pick is a better method than random pick. We still experimented random pick on the datasets of Sect. 4, but the relative importance of features remained similar.

[11] In this study we focused on the top 10 features. However this parameter can be set by the user and changed according to his use case.

classifiers each of which corresponding to the removal of a subset of sensitive features. To avoid the exponential number of such classifiers, in this paper we only consider those obtained by removing either *one* or *all* sensitive features. LimeOut constructs an ensemble classifier M_{final} through a linear combination of the pool's classifiers.

More precisely, given an input (M, D), where M is a classifier and D is the dataset. Suppose that the globally important features given by $\text{LIME}_{\text{Global}}$ are $a_1, a_2, \ldots, a_n$, in which $a_{j_1}, a_{j_2}, \ldots, a_{j_i}$ are sensitive. LimeOut thus trains $i + 1$ classifiers: M_k after removing a_{j_k} from the dataset, for $k = 1, \ldots, i$, and M_{i+1} after removing all sensitive features $a_{j_1}, a_{j_2}, \ldots, a_{j_i}$. In this preliminary implementation of LimeOut, the ensemble classifier M^{final} is defined as the "average" of these $i + 1$ classifiers. More precisely, for an instance x and a class C,

$$P_{M_{final}}(x \in C) = \frac{\sum_{k=1}^{k=i+1} P_{M_k}(x \in C)}{i + 1}.$$

As we will see empirically in Sect. 4 over different datasets and classifiers, the dependence of M_{final} on sensitive features decreases, whereas its accuracy is maintained and, in some cases, it even improves.

4 Empirical Study

To validate our approach, we applied LimeOut on two different families of classifiers (Logistic regression and Random Forests) over different datasets. In each case, the ensemble classifier obtained by LimeOut is fairer than the original classifiers. The datasets we use, Adult and German credit score, are known to be biased. These experiments illustrate different possible scenarios, namely, the case of unfair process (see Subsect. 4.1) and of a fair process (see Subsect. 4.2 for Random Forests).

4.1 Adult Dataset

This dataset comes from the UCI repository of machine learning databases[12]. The task is to predict if an individual's annual income exceeds 50,000 dollars based on census data. An individual's annual income is the result of various features such as "Age", "Workclass", "fnlwgt", "Education", "Education-Num", "Marital Status", "Occupation", "Relationship", "Race", "Sex", "Capital Gain", "Capital Loss", "Hours per week" and "Country". Intuitively, the income of a person should get influenced by the individual's education level, age, occupation, number of hours he works, company etc. But it would be unfair if our model considers race, sex or the marital status of the individual while making any prediction.

This dataset has 14 features out of which 6 are continuous and 8 are nominal, and it comprises 45,255 instances. We partitioned the dataset randomly into 80%

---

[12] Adult Dataset: http://archive.ics.uci.edu/ml/datasets/Adult.

for training and 20% for testing. However, the class distribution of Adult dataset is extremely unbalanced and majority of the dataset consists of individuals with annual income <50,000 dollars. To balance this, we used Synthetic Minority Oversampling Technique (SMOTE[13]) over training data. SMOTE generates new samples from the minority class and includes them in the training set, resulting to a balanced training dataset. We then perform training on the augmented (balanced) dataset using: Logistic Regression and Random Forest.

Table 1. Top 10 important features used by M_{LR} (left) and $(M_{LR})_{final}$ (right).

Features	Contribution	Features	Contribution
Capital Gain	−23.792107	Capital Gain	−23.543842
Capital Loss	−6.469338	Capital Loss	−5.767617
Hours per week	−2.496092	Education-Num	−1.673827
Marital Status	2.116016	Hours per week	−1.541263
Race	1.927533	Country	0.802061
Sex	1.804058	Education	0.547427
Education-Num	−1.573597	**Sex**	0.477145
Age	0.698024	Workclass	0.426351
Education	0.667795	Age	−0.242858
Relationship	0.235550	Relationship	0.065351

Logistic Regression: We trained a logistic regression model over the obtained training set. In binary classification problems, logistic regression often uses a default threshold value of 0.5, i.e. if predicted value ≥0.5, then the predicted class will be positive, and negative, otherwise. However, this threshold may lead to poor results, especially, in the case of unbalanced datasets. We used threshold tuning[14] in order to improve the performance of our classifier. The threshold is chosen to be optimal for Precision Recall Curve and the ROC Curve (to ensure maximum F1-score). The classifier M obtained after threshold tuning had an accuracy of 82.65%. To assess the process fairness of M, we used LIME$_{Global}$ to get the 10 most important features used by M.

From Table 1, it is evident that Race, sex and marital status are among the top 10 features used by model M with contributions 1.93, 1.80 and 2.11 respectively. We know that it's unfair to use these features while predicting

---

[13] https://imbalanced-learn.readthedocs.io/en/stable/generated/imblearn.over-sampling.SMOTE.html.

[14] https://machinelearningmastery.com/threshold-moving-for-imbalanced-classification/.

someone's income. And as these are among the top 10 features, we can deem the model to be unfair. Now we train four models by dropping out sensitive features: Race, Sex and Marital status. Note that all the classifiers are trained using Logistic Regression with threshold tuning. Through feature dropout, we thus obtain 4 classifiers: $M1$ trained without "Sex", $M2$ trained without "Race", $M3$ trained without "Marital Status", and $M4$ trained without the 3 (Accuracy = 81.97%).

We can infer that $M4$ is fairer because it has not used any sensitive feature while training. But the accuracy is reduced from 82.65% to 81.9%. The ensemble M^{final} of models $M1$, $M2$, $M3$ and $M4$ achieved an accuracy of 84.18%. The statistical test[15] showed that this improved accuracy is significant. The global impact of the sensitive features is also reduced (see the explanations in Table 1).

Table 2. Top 10 important features used by M_{RF} (left) and $(M_{RF})_{final}$ (right).

Features	Contribution	Features	Contribution
Capital Gain	−10.218573	Capital Gain	−10.304901
Capital Loss	−3.109039	Capital Loss	−3.436587
Hours per week	−1.332370	Hours per week	−1.362630
Sex	1.244931	Education-Num	0.574524
Marital Status	0.744446	Relationship	0.413276
Race	0.456074	**Sex**	0.306334
Occupation	−0.256388	**Marital Status**	0.243644
Age	−0.249529	Workclass	0.137123
Country	0.249083	Country	0.091939
Relationship	0.215706	Occupation	0.078968

Random Forest: We also used Random Forest and checked its fairness. This model M_{RF} has accuracy = 83.49%. The global explanations for M_{RF} LimeOut's ensemble model $(M_{RF})_{final}$ are given in Table 2. From the Table 2 we see that the impact of sensitive features decreased for $(M_{RF})_{final}$, and that its accuracy increased to 83.86%. While when we removed all three sensitive features Race, Sex and Marital status, the accuracy was 81.6%. Again we observe a significant improvement in the accuracy of the LimeOut's ensemble classifier, while ensuring a fairer model.

---

[15] We performed the t-test.

488 V. Bhargava et al.

4.2 German Credit Score Dataset

The data was initially prepared by Prof. Hoffman and is available publicly as 'german.data' on UCI Machine Learning Repository[16]. If a bank receives a loan application based on the applicant's profile it can decide whether it can approve the loan. Two types of risk are associated with the bank's decision: (i) if an applicant is at *good credit risk*, he is likely to pay back his loan, and (ii) if an applicant is at *bad credit risk*, he is unlikely to pay back.

The dataset set has information about 1000 individuals on the basis of which they have been classified as good or bad risk. The goal is to use applicant's demographic and socio-economic profiles to assess the risk of lending loan to the customer. The dataset consists of 20 features and a classification label (1: Good Risk, 2: Bad Risk). We split the dataset into 80% training set and 20% testing. As the dataset is highly imbalanced, we used SMOTE Oversampling to generate the samples synthetically.

Table 3. Top 10 important features used by M_{LR} (left) and $(M_{LR})_{final}$ (right).

Features	Contribution	Features	Contribution
peopleliable	−6.410473	peopleliable	−5.210576
foreignworker	5.398807	foreignworker	2.586505
otherinstallmentplans	−1.769830	otherinstallmentplans	−1.858603
savings	1.769533	credithistory	1.418544
telephone	1.349587	installmentrate	1.185539
statussex	−1.263993	savings	1.087709
creditamount	0.899089	purpose	0.570004
existingchecking	0.798037	duration	−0.427534
duration	0.691543	employmentsince	−0.385297
employmentsince	−0.619419	creditamount	0.354635

Logistic Regression: For training we used Logistic Regression along with threshold tuning. The obtained accuracy of M was 74.67% with the explanations from LIME$_{\text{Global}}$ given in Table 3. Here, we see the sensitive features "statussex" (sex of the customer), "telephone[17]" and "foreign worker" appear in the top 10, thus showing that M is process unfair. Hence, LimeOut trains $M1$, $M2$ and $M3$

---

[16] https://archive.ics.uci.edu/ml/datasets/statlog+(german+credit+data).
[17] It depicts if a person gave aphone number. Due to privacy reasons, the number may not be given. Thus it should not be considered important.

by removing each one of them, and $M4$ after removing all 3. Despite being fairer, $M4$ suffered a drastic accuracy decrease to 69%.

LimeOut then trained the ensemble M^{final} and output the explanations given in Table 3. Again, the impact of sensitive features decreased in case of M^{final}. In addition, the accuracy of M_{final} is 74.67%, same as M. Again, a fairer classifier without compromising accuracy.

Random Forest: We trained the model using Random Forest, and the accuracy was found to be 59%. In this case, $LIME_{Global}$ showed a single sensitive feature in the top 10 and no action was taken[18]. We will further discuss this case below.

5 Conclusion and Future Work

We demonstrated the idea of using LIME to determine model fairness, and integrated it in LimeOut that receives as input a pair (M, D) of a classifier M and a dataset D, and outputs a classifier M_{final} less dependent on sensitive features without compromising accuracy.

This preliminary study shows the feasibility and the flexibility of the simple idea of feature dropout followed by an ensemble approach. This opens into several potential improvements and further investigations. First, we only experimented LimeOut on two classes of classifiers, but LimeOut can be easily adapted to different ML models and data types, as well as different explanatory models. An improvised approach to get the global explanation like [15] can be used, and this should be thoroughly explored.

Also, the workflow can be further improved, e.g., the classifier ensembles could take into account classifier weighting and other classifiers resulting from the removal of different subsets of sensitive features (here we only considered the removal of one or all features). In this study, we took a human and context-centered approach that requires domain expertise (for identifying sensitive features in a given use-case). However, there is room for automating this task, possibly through a metric or utility-based approach to assess sensitivity that takes into account domain knowledge.

We also identified some limitations as that illustrated in the last scenario. Indeed, despite providing insights on process fairness, LimeOut seems of little use when only one sensitive feature is detected in the top k important features. In this case, an alternative method should be employed, for instance, to consider the model obtained by removing this feature. These are some of the issues to be tackled in future work.

References

1. Binns, R.: On the apparent conflict between individual and group fairness. In: Conference on Fairness, Accountability, and Transparency (FAT20), pp. 514–524 (2020)

---

[18] Interestingly, there is an accuracy increase when that variable is dropped. However, the current implementation of LimeOut does not take action in these cases.

2. Chouldechova, A.: Fair prediction with disparate impact: a study of bias in recidivism prediction instruments. Big Data **5**(2), 153–163 (2017)
3. Dressel, J., Farid, H.: The accuracy, fairness, and limits of predicting recidivism. Sci. Adv. **4**(eaao5580), 1 (2018)
4. Dwork, C., Hardt, M., Pitassi, T., Reingold, O., Zemel, R.S.: Fairness through awareness. In: Goldwasser, S. (ed.) Innovations in Theoretical Computer Science 2012, Cambridge, MA, USA, January 8–10, 2012, pp. 214–226. ACM (2012)
5. Gal, Y., Ghahramani, Z.: Dropout as a Bayesian approximation: representing model uncertainty in deep learning. In: Balcan, M., Weinberger, K.Q. (eds.) International Conference on Machine Learning, ICML16. JMLR Workshop and Conference Proceedings, vol. 48, pp. 1050–1059 (2016)
6. Gal, Y., Ghahramani, Z.: A theoretically grounded application of dropout in recurrent neural networks. In: Lee, D.D., Sugiyama, M., von Luxburg, U., Guyon, I., Garnett, R. (eds.) Neural Information Processing Systems (NIPS16), pp. 1019–1027 (2016)
7. Garreau, D., von Luxburg, U.: Explaining the explainer: a first theoretical analysis of LIME. CoRR abs/2001.03447 (2020)
8. Grgic-Hlaca, N., Redmiles, E.M., Gummadi, K.P., Weller, A.: Human perceptions of fairness in algorithmic decision making: a case study of criminal risk prediction. In: World Wide Web (WWW18), pp. 903–912 (2018)
9. Grgic-Hlaca, N., Zafar, M.B., Gummadi, K.P., Weller, A.: The case for process fairness in learning: feature selection for fair decision making. In: NIPS Symposium on Machine Learning and the Law, vol. 1, p. 2 (2016)
10. Grgić-Hlača, N., Zafar, M.B., Gummadi, K.P., Weller, A.: Beyond distributive fairness in algorithmic decision making: feature selection for procedurally fair learning. In: Proceedings of the Conference on Artificial Intelligence (AAAI18), pp. 51–60 (2018)
11. Guegan, D., Addo, P.M., Hassani, B.: Credit risk analysis using machine and deep learning models. Risks **6**(2), 38 (2018)
12. Iskandar, B.: Terrorism detection based on sentiment analysis using machine learning. J. Eng. Appl. Sci. **12**(3), 691–698 (2017)
13. Kearns, M., Neel, S., Roth, A., Wu, Z.S.: Preventing fairness gerrymandering: auditing and learning for subgroup fairness. In: International Conference on Machine Learning (ICML18), pp. 2564–2572 (2018)
14. Laugel, T., Renard, X., Lesot, M.J., Marsala, C., Detyniecki, M.: Defining locality for surrogates in post-hoc interpretablity. arXiv preprint arXiv:1806.07498 (2018)
15. van der Linden, I., Haned, H., Kanoulas, E.: Global aggregations of local explanations for black box models. arXiv abs/1907.03039 (2019)
16. Lundberg, S.M., Lee, S.: A unified approach to interpreting model predictions. In: Conference on Neural Information Processing Systems (NIPS17), pp. 4765–4774 (2017)
17. Maes, S., Tuyls, K., Vanschoenwinkel, B., Manderick, B.: Credit card fraud detection using Bayesian and neural networks. In: NAISO Congress on Neuro Fuzzy Technologies, pp. 261–270 (2002)
18. Ribeiro, M.T., Singh, S., Guestrin, C.: "Why should i trust you?": explaining the predictions of any classifier. In: International Conference on Knowledge Discovery and Data Mining (SIGKDD16), pp. 1135–1144 (2016)
19. Ribeiro, M.T., Singh, S., Guestrin, C.: Anchors: high-precision model-agnostic explanations. In: AAAI Conference on Artificial Intelligence, AAAI18, pp. 1527–1535 (2018)

20. Roh, Y., Heo, G., Whang, S.E.: A survey on data collection for machine learning: a big data - AI integration perspective. arXiv abs/1811.03402 (2018)
21. Speicher, T., et al.: A unified approach to quantifying algorithmic unfairness: measuring individual & group unfairness via inequality indices. In: International Conference on Knowledge Discovery & Data Mining (SIGKDD18), pp. 2239–2248 (2018)
22. Zafar, M.B., Valera, I., Gomez Rodriguez, M., Gummadi, K.P.: Fairness beyond disparate treatment & disparate impact: learning classification without disparate mistreatment. In: World Wide Web (WWW17), pp. 1171–1180 (2017)
23. Zafar, M.B., Valera, I., Rodriguez, M.G., Gummadi, K.P.: Fairness constraints: mechanisms for fair classification. In: Artificial Intelligence and Statistics (AIS-TATS17), pp. 962–970 (2017)
24. Zemel, R., Wu, Y., Swersky, K., Pitassi, T., Dwork, C.: Learning fair representations. In: International Conference on Machine Learning (ICML13), pp. 325–333 (2013)
25. Zhang, Z., Neill, D.B.: Identifying significant predictive bias in classifiers. CoRR abs/1611.08292 (2016)

Interpretable Privacy with Optimizable Utility

Jan Ramon$^{(\boxtimes)}$ and Moitree Basu

Inria, Lille, France
jan.ramon@inria.fr

Abstract. In this position paper, we discuss the problem of specifying privacy requirements for machine learning based systems, in an interpretable yet operational way. Explaining privacy-improving technology is a challenging problem, especially when the goal is to construct a system which at the same time is interpretable and has a high performance. In order to address this challenge, we propose to specify privacy requirements as constraints, leaving several options for the concrete implementation of the system open, followed by a constraint optimization approach to achieve an efficient implementation also, next to the interpretable privacy guarantees.

Keywords: Privacy · Explainability · Constraint optimization

1 Introduction

Over recent years, one has seen an increasing interest in privacy, as the awareness of privacy risks of data processing systems increased. Legislation was introduced to protect data, and sufficient data and insights became available to create technology capable to realize several tasks while preserving the privacy of participants. One of the most popular notions of privacy, which we will also adopt in this paper, is differential privacy [3] and its extensions, e.g., [4,10].

An important aspect of this evolution concerns informing users of what are the privacy guarantees a system offers. Some legislation, such as Europe's GDPR [1], requires transparency, i.e., users have the right to know how their data are used and how their sensitive data are protected. Explaining privacy protection strategies is also important to increase trust among the users of a system. Finally, being able to explain what privacy guarantees a system offers is also helpful in the sometimes challenging communication between computer scientists who develop solutions and legal experts who are interested in understanding the guarantees without the burden of having to investigate many technical details.

While a large number of papers in the machine learning community studies a single machine learning problem and strategies to perform that machine learning task in a privacy-preserving way, real-world systems are often complex, consisting of several machine learning, preprocessing, prediction or inference

© Springer Nature Switzerland AG 2020
I. Koprinska et al. (Eds.): ECML PKDD 2020 Workshops, CCIS 1323, pp. 492–500, 2020.
https://doi.org/10.1007/978-3-030-65965-3_33

steps, user interactions, and data transfers. The privacy requirements of interest
to a user are requirements on the system as a whole, combining the behavior of
its many components including their privacy guarantees. While some researches
have focused on analyzing privacy guarantees of complete systems, the literature
on that topic is still rather limited.

Such large systems combine heterogeneous components, each having their
own characteristics for what concerns their effects on the privacy of the data.
There is an increasing need for systems allowing one to specify and explain
the privacy guarantees for a complete system. However, next to interpretability,
performance, e.g., in terms of precision of computation, communication, and
storage cost, is also required. In this paper, we study strategies to achieve both
interpretability and good performance.

In particular, we argue that composition rules for differential privacy, which
start from the building blocks and combine them bottom-up, may not offer
sufficient flexibility. We suggest an alternative approach, where privacy requirements are specified top-down and implementation choices, such as the allocation of "privacy budget" to several components or the choice between more
costly multi-party computing and less accurate noisy data sharing, are optimized
afterward.

We start in Sect. 2 with a brief review of relevant literature and a discussion
of the advantages and drawbacks of several strategies. We then sketch our ideas
in Sect. 3 and provide a number of examples to illustrate them.

2 Existing Approaches

An important notion of privacy is differential privacy [3]:

Definition 1 (Differential privacy). *Let $\varepsilon > 0, \delta \geq 0$. A (randomized) protocol $\mathcal{A}$ is (ε, δ)-differentially private if for all neighboring datasets X, X', i.e.,
datasets differing only in a single data point, and for all sets of possible outputs
$\mathcal{O}$, we have:*

$$Pr(\mathcal{A}(X) \in \mathcal{O}) \leq e^{\varepsilon} Pr(\mathcal{A}(X') \in \mathcal{O}) + \delta. \tag{1}$$

Several variants and generalizations of differential privacy have been proposed,
including proposals focusing on the adversarial model [4] and proposals allowing
for more refined secret definitions [10]. In this paper, we will sometimes adopt the
term 'secret' from Pufferfish privacy [10] to refer to variables that are private but
are not necessary on the level of a single individual in a database of individuals
(classic differential privacy).

A wide variety of languages have been proposed to describe privacy properties
of systems. Some are aimed at compilers or circuit evaluators [6], others are not
necessarily aimed at privacy-preserving technology but rather at trust or consent
[8]. In the sequel, we will focus our discussion on languages aimed at specifying
privacy properties of systems using privacy-preserving technology.

A classical approach to study the privacy of a compound system is to take the
different components as input and to analyze the behavior of the compound system. One basic strategy is to apply composition rules for differential privacy. The

basic rule states that if data is queried twice, once with an (ϵ_1, δ_1)-differentially private algorithm and once with a (ϵ_2, δ_2)-differentially private algorithm, then the combination is $(\epsilon_1 + \epsilon_2, \delta_1 + \delta_2)$-differentially private. Even though this always holds, this is usually not a tight bound on the privacy of the combination. A number of improved bounds have been proposed, e.g., [5], but even those are often not immediately practical. One issue is that the order of steps to be performed in a system may not be known a priori, e.g., a system could branch due to an if-then-else decision, or parts could be repeated.

To address this problem and at the same time have a more uniform way to represent privacy properties, many authors have proposed languages to specify privacy properties, together with associated techniques to verify whether these properties are satisfied when a number of rules can be applied [7,9,11]. The advantage is that next to a language there is a system which can attempt to verify whether a given system satisfies the described privacy properties. However, several problems remain. First, theorem proving style techniques usually only work for a limited set of rules or reasoning primitives and they don't scale very well with increasing problem size. Second, while verifying that a property holds is interesting, optimizing the performance would be even better. In such theorem proving settings, it remains the task of the human expert to design the characteristics of the individual components of the system and combine them such that they collaborate efficiently.

3   Privacy Constraint Optimization

Similar to earlier work discussed in the previous section, our approach starts from a language to describe privacy constraints. However, rather than aiming at verification, we aim at optimization. We propose to first formulate the problem and its privacy requirements in a systematic way, and then to treat these privacy requirements as the constraints of an optimization problem where the objective function is the utility, or conversely the loss. The loss function can incorporate various types of costs, such as the expected error on the output, the computational cost of the resulting system, or its storage cost.

Below, we first sketch at a high level, how problems can be specified. Next, we provide examples of this idea applied to different types of problems. In this position paper, our goal is not to improve some quantifiable performance measures or to solve more difficult problems than before, but rather to illustrate that the idea of constraint programming with privacy requirements has several potentially interesting applications.

3.1   Problem Specification

For the purpose of this paper, our main aim is not to develop a complete language allowing for representing as many as possible privacy properties (languages to describe privacy properties have been proposed in the literature to some extent), our main objective is to open the discussion on how to optimize the performance of a system given fixed global privacy requirements.

Therefore, we will use here only a basic language sufficient for our examples. In particular, we distinguish the following components in a specification:

- **Declaring relevant variables.** We will treat both data and models as random variables: data may be public or private and may be drawn jointly with other data variables from some distribution. According to the definition of differential privacy, a differentially private learning algorithm must be a randomized algorithm that outputs a model which follows some probability distribution conditioned on the training data.
- **Specifying relations between variables (background knowledge).** After specifying the relevant random variables, we can specify the conditional dependencies between these variables using a probabilistic model, e.g., a Bayesian network or a Markov random field.
- **Privacy requirements.** Then, we can specify the required privacy properties. This typically involves specifying that the several possible values of a secret can't be distinguished with significant probability by parties not authorized to know the secret.

Below, we present a number of example scenarios where we can apply the proposed technique of compiling privacy requirements to constraint programs.

3.2 Optimizing Differential Privacy Noise as a Function of the Desired Output

Assume we have n sensitive input variables and we want to answer m queries over these sensitive variables. For the simplicity of our presentation, we will assume that the answer to each query is a linear combination of the sensitive variables. We can specify our problem as follows:

Variables:
- $x \in [0,1]^n$: input
- $y \in \mathbb{R}^m$: intermediate variable
- $A \in \mathbb{R}^{m \times n}$: constant
- $b \in \mathbb{R}^m$: constant
- $\mathcal{O}$: output

Background knowledge:
- $y = Ax + b$
- Loss function: $L = \|\mathcal{O} - y\|_2^2$

Privacy requirements:
- $\mathcal{O}$ is (ϵ, δ)-DP w.r.t. x.

Here, we organize our specification as outlined in Sect. 3.1. It is clear that revealing the exact answers to the queries y_i is unacceptable, resulting in some approximation of the original answers to the queries. So, we specify a loss function representing the cost of the approximation errors.

There are two classic approaches. First, one can use Local Differential Privacy (LDP) [2]. This means that to every input variable x_i sufficient noise is added to obtain a fully private version $\hat{x}_i$. Next, any query can be answered starting from these noisy versions, so, the output can be computed as $\mathcal{O} = A\hat{x} + b$. A major drawback of this approach is that this requires a lot of noise and hence the expected loss will be high. For the simplicity of our analysis, we use the Gaussian mechanism throughout this example. We get

$$\mathbb{E}\left[L_{LDP}\right] = tr(A^\top A) \left(\frac{2\log(1.25/\delta)}{\epsilon^2}\right).$$

Second, one can use classic differential privacy for each query y_i separately, adding noise to every y_i to obtain a noisy version $\hat{y}_i$. If multiple queries are obtained, the realized loss may be still high, and if $m > n$, even higher than in the LDP case above:

$$L_{DP} = \left(\sum_{j=1}^{m}\left(\sum_{i=1}^{n}|A_{i,j}|\right)^2\right)\left(\frac{2\log(1.25/\delta)}{\epsilon^2}\right).$$

In contrast, given the specifications above, we propose to (semi-automatically) generate options to address the privacy requirements, not committing to adding noise to input (as in LDP) or output (as in classic DP), but to address the possibility to add noise at meaningful points in the computation. This could result in the following constraint optimization program:

Minimize

$$\mathbb{E}_{\eta,\xi}\left[L\left(\sigma_{(\eta)}, \sigma_{(\xi)}\right)\right] = \mathbb{E}_{\eta,\xi}\left[\|\mathcal{O} - (Ax + b)\|_2^2\right]$$

Subject to
- $\hat{x} = x + \eta$
- $\mathcal{O} = \hat{y} = A\hat{x} + b + \xi$
- $\eta_i \sim \mathcal{N}\left(0, \sigma_{(\eta),i}^2\right)$
- $\xi_i \sim \mathcal{N}\left(0, \sigma_{(\xi),i}^2\right)$
- $\mathcal{O}$ is (ϵ, δ)-DP w.r.t. x.

For one query ($m = 1$), the optimal solution to this problem will correspond with classic differential privacy, in the case the number of queries m is large, the solution of the optimization problem will converge to the local differential privacy case. Between the two extremes, we expect a loss that is lower than either of both classic strategies.

The constraint program we consider is easy to solve numerically, and if some approximations are made which are commonly used for the Gaussian mechanism, we get a relaxed constraint optimization problem only involving quadratic functions.

We hence distinguish four steps to address problems with privacy requirements:

1. Specifying the problem and the privacy requirements
2. Adding options to realize the privacy requirements and casting it into a constraint optimization problem
3. Solving the constraint optimization problem
4. Executing the algorithm with the obtained solutions and parameters.

3.3 Shaping Differential Privacy Noise

In a number of situations, the classic additive noise mechanisms don't provide an adequate solution. Consider for example the following problem. Suppose that we have a finite domain $\mathcal{X}$ of positive numbers. Consider n parties numbered from 1 to n. Each party i has a sensitive value $x_i \in \mathcal{X}$ which it doesn't want to be revealed. At the same time, the parties collectively would like to compute $k \geq 2$ means of their private values, including the arithmetic mean m_1 and harmonic mean m_{-1} where

$$m_p = \left(\frac{1}{n} \sum_{i=1}^{n} x_i^p \right)^{1/p}.$$

This gives us the following problem:

Variables:
- $x \in [0,1]^n$: input
- $p \in \mathbb{R}^k$: constant
- $\mathcal{O}$: output

Background knowledge:
- Loss function: $L = \sum_{i=1}^{k} \left(\mathcal{O}_i - m_{p_i}(x) \right)^2$

Privacy requirements:
- $\mathcal{O}$ is (ϵ, δ)-DP w.r.t. x.

The several parties don't trust a common curator and therefore decide they will all share noisy versions $\hat{x}_i$ of their private values x_i and perform the computation on these noisy values. This is also the setting considered by local differential privacy.

Classic additive noise mechanisms such as the Laplace mechanism and the Gaussian mechanism have the drawback that the noise distribution has an infinite domain. So, for every value x_i, especially if x_i is one of the smallest elements of $\mathcal{X}$, there is a probability that $\hat{x}_i$ is close to 0 or negative, which would make the estimation of m_{-1} very difficult.

Several solutions are conceivable. First, for every i we could approximate the p_i-mean $m_{p_i}(x)$ using a separate noisy version of x^{p_i}. Averaging over values of x^{p_i} with additive zero-mean (Laplacian or Gaussian) error would give an unbiased estimate. Still, this would imply that the k means to be computed should share the available privacy budget. We could follow an approach similar to the one in Sect. 3.2 to optimally spread the privacy budget.

Another option is to use the full privacy budget for a single noisy version $\hat{x}_i$ of x_i for every i. As we can't use classical additive noise mechanisms, we consider an arbitrary parameterized distribution, and aim at estimating optimal parameters for it subject to a number of desirable properties. We should take into account that if the smallest (respectively largest) possible noisy versions of the x_i can't be much smaller (resp. larger) than the smallest (resp. largest) possible value of $\mathcal{X}$ (in our case to avoid zero or negative noisy versions which may harm the approximation of $m_{-1}(x)$), then we can't use zero-mean additive noise. A common solution is to choose for $\hat{x}_i$ with probability α an unbiased estimator of x and with probability $1 - \alpha$ some background distribution B.

In particular, we consider a distribution over a domain $\mathcal{Y} \supseteq \mathcal{X}$. For $(x, y) \in \mathcal{X} \times \mathcal{Y}$, let $f_{x,y} = P(\hat{x}_i = y \mid x)$, i.e., $f_{x,y}$ is the probability, given that a private value is x, that the noisy version is y. This naturally leads to the following quadratic program:

Minimize

$$\sum_{x \in \mathcal{X}, y \in \mathcal{Y}} f_{x,y}(x - y)^2$$

Subject to

- $\forall x, \sum_{y \in \mathcal{Y}} f_{x,y} y = \alpha x + (1 - \alpha)\mathbb{E}[B]$
- $\forall x, \sum_{y \in \mathcal{Y}} f_{x,y} y^{-1} = \alpha x^{-1} + (1 - \alpha)\mathbb{E}[B^{-1}]$
- $\forall x, \sum_{y \in \mathcal{Y}} f_{x,y} = 1$
- $\mathcal{O}$ is (ϵ, δ)-DP w.r.t. x, i.e., $\forall x_1, x_2, y : f_{x_1,y} \leq e^\epsilon f_{x_2,y} + \frac{\delta}{|\mathcal{X}|}$

3.4   Combining Building Blocks

The examples in Sects. 3.2 and 3.3 focused on isolated problems. Practical systems are often large and consist of many steps. Even if for each of these steps a privacy-preserving solution is available, these still need to be combined into a global solution.

Classic approaches to differential privacy often use combination rules, e.g., the combination of an (ϵ_1, δ_1)-differentially private step and an (ϵ_2, δ_2)-differentially private step is $(\epsilon_1 + \epsilon_2, \delta_1 + \delta_2)$-differentially private. The disadvantage is that the privacy budget is not recycled and therefore is exhausted quickly.

The same approach can be taken using constraint programs. However, additionally, we can attempt to obtain globally better solutions. First, we can combine two constraint programs, which share variables and/or constraints. An optimal solution for the combined program may be globally more optimal than the combination of the solutions of the individual programs. Second, it becomes easier to program design choices. Often, several possible solution strategies exist, especially when considering in distributed settings the trade-off between encryption (which is more expensive in terms of computational cost) or adding noise (which decreases the utility of the output). In such situations, we can introduce both solution strategies as separate sub-programs of the larger constraint program, and introduce an additional variable π which is 0 when the first solution is used and 1 if the other solution is used. While constraint optimization typically works with real-valued variables, if the constraint programs corresponding to the two solutions don't share parameters then the design choice variable π will be either 0 or 1 in the optimum of the constraint program. In this way, in several cases, the user can focus on specifying requirements and possible solution strategies, while the optimization algorithm computes the value of the alternatives and selects the best solution.

4 Discussion and Conclusions

In this position paper, we argue that the explainability of privacy-preserving systems can be helped by clearly specifying the privacy guarantees satisfied by the systems, and we propose to see these privacy requirements as constraints in an optimization problem.

First, during the design and development phase, this methodology helps the developer to focus on the requirements rather than on implementation choices. In fact, the constraint optimization problem represents the space of all possible high-level implementations, and the solver accordingly finds the most interesting implementation strategy.

Second, in the deployment phase, such an explicit representation of the privacy guarantees facilitates answering user queries about exactly to what extent sensitive data is protected.

We presented a few examples showing that in several cases the translation of privacy requirements to constraint optimization problems is reasonably easy, and often yields constraint optimization problems which can be solved efficiently. Of course, this doesn't constitute a proof that such a methodology will deliver good results in all cases. An interesting line of future work is to explore more different situations and analyze whether the obtained constraint optimization problems remain tractable and scale well with the problem complexity.

Another idea for future work may be to explore whether this methodology also allows us to translate interpretable fairness requirements to efficiently solvable constraint optimization problems. However, a number of additional challenges that may arise there, e.g., there is no widespread consensus on a single good notion of fairness (as is the case with differential privacy in the privacy domain). Second, while in the current paper on privacy we rely on the relation between uncertainty (e.g., variance) and privacy strength, which often leads to efficiently solvable constraints, it is not immediately clear whether we could rely on a similar relation in the fairness domain.

References

1. European General Data Protection Regulation. https://gdpr-info.eu/
2. Duchi, J.C., Jordan, M.I., Wainwright, M.J.: Local privacy and statistical minimax rates. In: FOCS (2013)
3. Dwork, C.: Differential privacy: a survey of results. In: Agrawal, M., Du, D., Duan, Z., Li, A. (eds.) TAMC 2008. LNCS, vol. 4978, pp. 1–19. Springer, Heidelberg (2008). https://doi.org/10.1007/978-3-540-79228-4_1
4. Erlingsson, U., Feldman, V., Mironov, I., Raghunathan, A., Talwar, K.: Amplification by shuffling: from local to central differential privacy via anonymity. In: SODA (2019)
5. Kairouz, P., Oh, S., Viswanath, P.: The composition theorem for differential privacy. In: Proceedings of the 32nd International Conference on Machine Learning, Lille, France (2015)
6. Kreuter, B., shelat, A.: Lessons learned with PCF: scaling secure computation. In: Proceedings of the First ACM Workshop on Language Support for Privacy-Enhancing Technologies, PETShop 2013, pp. 7–10. Association for Computing Machinery, New York (2013). https://doi.org/10.1145/2517872.2517877
7. Near, J.P., et al.: Duet: an expressive higher-order language and linear type system for statically enforcing differential privacy. Proc. ACM Program. Lang. 3(OOPSLA), 172:1–172:30 (2019). https://doi.org/10.1145/3360598
8. Pardo, R., Le Métayer, D.: Analysis of privacy policies to enhance informed consent. In: Foley, S.N. (ed.) DBSec 2019. LNCS, vol. 11559, pp. 177–198. Springer, Cham (2019). https://doi.org/10.1007/978-3-030-22479-0_10
9. Paverd, A.J., Martin, A., Brown, I.: Modelling and automatically analysing privacy properties for honest-but-curious adversaries. Tech. rep. (2014). https://www.cs.ox.ac.uk/people/andrew.paverd/casper/casper-privacy-report.pdf
10. Song, S., Wang, Y., Chaudhuri, K.: Pufferfish privacy mechanisms for correlated data. In: Proceedings of the 2017 ACM International Conference on Management of Data, SIGMOD 2017. Association for Computing Machinery (2017)
11. Xu, L.: Modular reasoning about differential privacy in a probabilistic process calculus. In: Palamidessi, C., Ryan, M.D. (eds.) TGC 2012. LNCS, vol. 8191, pp. 198–212. Springer, Heidelberg (2013). https://doi.org/10.1007/978-3-642-41157-1_13

Prediction and Explanation of Privacy Risk on Mobility Data with Neural Networks

Francesca Naretto[1], Roberto Pellungrini[2]([✉]), Franco Maria Nardini[3], and Fosca Giannotti[3]

[1] Scuola Normale Superiore, Pisa, Italy
francesca.naretto@sns.it
[2] University of Pisa, Pisa, Italy
roberto.pellungrini@di.unipi.it
[3] ISTI-CNR, Pisa, Italy
{franco.nardini,fosca.giannotti}@isti.cnr.it

Abstract. The analysis of privacy risk for mobility data is a fundamental part of any privacy-aware process based on such data. Mobility data are highly sensitive. Therefore, the correct identification of the privacy risk before releasing the data to the public is of utmost importance. However, existing privacy risk assessment frameworks have high computational complexity. To tackle these issues, some recent work proposed a solution based on classification approaches to predict privacy risk using mobility features extracted from the data. In this paper, we propose an improvement of this approach by applying long short-term memory (LSTM) neural networks to predict the privacy risk directly from original mobility data. We empirically evaluate privacy risk on real data by applying our LSTM-based approach. Results show that our proposed method based on a LSTM network is effective in predicting the privacy risk with results in terms of F1 of up to 0.91. Moreover, to explain the predictions of our model, we employ a state-of-the-art explanation algorithm, SHAP. We explore the resulting explanation, showing how it is possible to provide effective predictions while explaining them to the end-user.

Keywords: Privacy risk assessment · Privacy risk prediction · Privacy risk explanation · Machine learning sequence-based algorithms

1 Introduction

Mobility data analysis is one of the key activities for the development of new services and innovations. Applications vary from location based services to urban planning, from sociology to automation. Naturally, with the use of these kinds of data comes the problem of dealing with possible privacy violations for the people represented in the data. It has been shown that almost all individual in a mobility dataset are re-identifiable just by knowing four points of their

© Springer Nature Switzerland AG 2020
I. Koprinska et al. (Eds.): ECML PKDD 2020 Workshops, CCIS 1323, pp. 501–516, 2020.
https://doi.org/10.1007/978-3-030-65965-3_34

trajectories [16]. To quantitatively assess privacy risk, Pratesi et al. proposed PRUDEnce, a privacy risk assessment framework able to evaluate privacy risk on any kind of data in a systematic way [18]. Assuming a worst-case scenario, PRUDEnce assesses privacy risk by evaluating all the possible combinations of background knowledge that a potential adversary may use in an attack. However, the evaluation of privacy risk assessment with PRUDEnce comes at the price of a high computational complexity.

Pellungrini et al. propose a data mining approach to overcome this limitation [17]. This approach is based on classification models, specifically random forest classifiers, used to predict privacy risk without the need of re-computing it when new data becomes available. Such approach requires the extraction of individual mobility features from the data to train the classifier. Therefore, the approach is bounded by the domain-knowledge of the user: the more appropriate and descriptive the features selected, the better the results.

In this paper, we propose a predictive approach based on Recurrent Neural Network, in particular Long Short-Term Memory networks (LSTM). LSTM are specifically designed to handle prediction tasks on sequential data such as trajectories. With LSTM we can bypass the need to compute individual features from the data by directly predicting privacy risk from the original data. Moreover, Pellungrini et al. propose possible ways of partially interpreting the results of their model by using feature importance [17]. We improve on this by using SHAP [12], an explanation algorithm that is able to give to the end-user information about the reason behind our model's predictions. In particular, the application of SHAP to our predictive approach based on LSTM can give important information about which locations in an individual's trajectory where crucial for the prediction of results. Using this information, users can understand which places in their movement put them at risk of re-identification. We evaluate our approach on real-world mobility data showing good results both in terms of accuracy and precision/recall. We also show how SHAP can be applied to obtain local explanations and show the kind of insights that can be gathered from the results.

The paper is organized as follows. Section 2 discusses related work. In Sect. 3, we briefly discuss the necessary definitions and the framework we used for the privacy risk assessment. Section 4 presents our approach. In Sect. 5, we report the results of our experimental evaluation on real mobility data. Finally, Sect. 6 concludes the work and discusses future work.

2   Related Work

Privacy is a fundamental aspect to consider when designing data-driven services [4]. A comprehensive summary of existing methodologies used for privacy risk assessment can be found in [26]. There are many privacy risk assessment frameworks proposed in the literature. A line of research propose an evaluation methodology for privacy risk based on the actual number of records that are uniquely identified inside the data [20,25]. Armando et al. propose a risk-aware framework to allow data-access based on the actual disclosure risk associated with the data that is being accessed [3]. Other existing risk management systems, e.g., Microsoft's DREAD [13], do not consider the risk evaluation as they simply include privacy considerations when assessing the impact of possible threats. In this paper, we use PRUDEnce [18], a privacy risk assessment framework that allows for the systematic computation of empirical privacy risk for any kind of data. PRUDEnce allows us to produce a data-driven computation of privacy risk that is flexible and that allows for the simulation of different kinds of attacks. The main drawback with many privacy risk assessment frameworks, such as PRU-DEnce, is the computational complexity. We overcome this issue by employing machine learning techniques to predict the privacy risk. This idea has been previously explored by Pellungrini et al. in the context of human mobility data [17], where the authors implement a prediction model based on both individual and collective mobility features extracted from the data.

In this work, we propose to predict privacy risk by applying neural networks directly on mobility data. We use Long Short-Term Memory networks (LSTM) [11], a specific architecture belonging to Recurrent Neural Network (RNN), that are able to overcome some of the shortcomings of RNN, e.g., vanishing gradient in fully connected RNN. LSTM have been applied to human mobility data in many works [7,27].

Song et al. use a LSTM network to develop a system for simulating and predicting human mobility and transportation model at a citywide level [24], while Altché et al. use a LSTM to model vehicular movement on highways [1]. Recently, LSTMS have been also applied to model other kinds of trajectories, such as airplane traces [22].

This paper also deals with providing explanations of the predictions produced with a LSTM. Interpretability is one of the most important modern fields of research in AI. Recently, Guidotti et al. provide a comprehensive overview of existing techniques for interpretability in machine learning [10]. They identify two main types of explaination models: *global* and *local* explainers. Local explainers focus on explaining the results of predictions on single records [9,12,19] while global explainers explain the logic of the whole machine learning model [5,6,8]. Here, we provide explanations by using SHAP [21], a well-known explainer based on *Shapely values* that is commonly used for its stability and robustness of results.

3   Background

A mobility dataset is a collection of records that describes the movements of a set of individuals in a given time window. This kind of data is usually collected in the form of raw trajectories. A raw trajectory is composed of a sequence of points that identifies the movements of an individual during a period of observation ordered with respect to time. Each point of a trajectory is made up of a geographic location, expressed in the form of coordinates such as latitude and longitude, and a timestamp that represents the time at which the user stopped in that location or went through that location.

Definition 1 *Trajectory.* *A human mobility trajectory* T_u *is a temporally ordered sequence of tuples that represent the locations visited by the user u.* $T_u = \langle (l_1, t_1), (l_2, t_2), ..., (l_n, t_n) \rangle$, *where* l_i *represents the location visited at the time* t_i, $t_i < t_j$ *iff* $i < j$. *Each location is in the form* $l_i = (x_i, y_i)$, *where* x_i *represents its latitude and* y_i *its longitude.*

From the definition of trajectory, we now define the concept of *mobility dataset.*

Definition 2 *Mobility dataset.* *A mobility dataset is a set of trajectories* $D = \{T_1, T_2, ... T_n\}$ *where* n *represents the number of users in the dataset and* T_u *represents the trajectory of the individual u with* $1 \le u \le n$.

Without loss of generality, from now on we assume that an individual is represented by a single trajectory collecting all her chronologically-sorted movements done within the period of analysis.

3.1 Privacy Risk Assessment

In this paper, we use PRUDEnce [18], a privacy risk assessment framework that allows for a systematic assessment of the privacy risk via simulation of background knowledge-based attacks. The framework allows a Data Provider to assess the privacy risk associated with the individuals represented in the data before sharing them, thus complying with the responsibility of guaranteeing privacy. After a proper risk assessment has been done, the Data Provider can choose the most suitable privacy-preserving technique to apply to the data before releasing them. Taking into consideration possible data requirements from subjects or stakeholders interested in the data, the Data Provider aggregates, selects, and filters the dataset $\mathcal{D}$ and then performs privacy risk assessment. First, the risk assessment requires the definition of possible attacks that an adversary might conduct on the data, and, second, the simulation of these attacks on the data.

An individual's privacy risk is related to her probability of re-identification in a dataset w.r.t. the defined set of re-identification attacks. An attack assumes that an adversary gets access to a dataset and, then, using some background knowledge, i.e., a portion of an individual's mobility data, the adversary tries to re-identify all the records in the dataset regarding that individual. An attack is defined by a matching function that represents the process with which an adversary uses the background knowledge to find the corresponding individual in the data. PRUDEnce is based on the notions of background knowledge category, configuration and instance. The first indicates the type of information known by the adversary about a specific set of dimensions of an individual's mobility data. Examples of background knowledge are a subset of the locations visited by an individual (spatial dimension) or the specific times an individual visited those locations (spatial and temporal dimensions). The number of the elements known by the adversary, we refer to it with h, is called background knowledge configuration. For example $h = 2$ indicates an adversary knowledge of two locations visited by an individual.

Finally, an instance of background knowledge is the specific information known by the adversary, such as a visit in a specific location. Therefore, the background knowledge configuration includes all possible instances of length h.

The assessment of privacy risk requires the analysis of the probability of re-identification associated with each instance of background knowledge, defined as:

Definition 3.1. *Let h be the number of locations of an individual known by the adversary. Given an attack and its function, matching(T, b), indicating whether or not a record $T \in \mathcal{D}$ matches the instance of background knowledge configuration $b \in B_h$, let $M(\mathcal{D}, b) = \{T \in \mathcal{D} \mid matching(T, b) = True\}$. We define the probability of re-identification of an individual u in dataset $\mathcal{D}$ as: $PR_{\mathcal{D}}(T = u|b) = \frac{1}{|M(\mathcal{D}, b)|}$ that is the probability to associate a record $T \in \mathcal{D}$ to an individual u, given instance $b \in B_h$.*

Since each instance $b \in B_h$ has its own probability of re-identification, the risk of re-identification of an individual is defined as the maximum probability of re-identification over the set of instances of a background knowledge configuration:

Definition 3.2. *The risk of re-identification (or privacy risk) of an individual u given a background knowledge configuration B_h is her maximum probability of re-identification $Risk(u, \mathcal{D}) = \max PR_{\mathcal{D}}(T = u|b)$ for each $b \in B_h$.*

By specifying a matching function, we can thus apply the framework with any background knowledge-based attack. In this paper, we will focus on a specific attack introduced by Mohammed *et al.* [14] and Monreale *et al.* [15], where the adversary knows a subset of the locations visited by the individual and the temporal ordering of the visits. We apply this attack on the trajectories of individuals, as defined in Sect. 3.

Definition 3.3 *Location Sequence Background Knowledge*. *Let h be the number of locations l_i of an individual u known by the adversary and let $L(T_u)$ to be the sequence of locations $l_i \in T_u$ visited by u.*

The location sequence background knowledge is a set of configurations based on h locations, defined as $B_h = L(T_u)^{[h]}$, where $L(T_u)^{[h]}$ denotes the set of all the possible k-subsequences of the elements in the set $L(T_u)$.

In this setting, therefore, each instance $b \in B_h$ is a subset of locations $X_u \subseteq L(T_u)$ of length h. The matching function for this privacy attack is then defined as:

$$matching(T_u, b) = \begin{cases} true, & \text{if } b \subseteq L(T_u) \\ false, & \text{otherwise} \end{cases} \tag{1}$$

in which $T_v \in D$ is a trajectory in the dataset under analysis.

4 Predicting and Explaining Privacy Risk

The PRUDEnce framework evaluates risk on a worst-case scenario: out of all the possible background knowledge instances, the risk is computed based on the one producing the highest risk, i.e., the probability of re-identification is evaluated for every possible combination and then the maximum out of all computed probabilities is chosen as the risk for that individual. However, we do not know such best combination in advance. This means that we have to evaluate all possible background-knowledge instances, i.e., all possible combinations. As a consequence, the risk assessment is computationally demanding as, given h, we need to compute all possible h-combinations of points an adversary could know and then match each combination against the entire dataset to find the individual that has that combination in their data. The overall computational complexity is $\mathcal{O}(\binom{len}{h} \times N)$, where len is the length of the trajectory from which we are generating the background knowledge, h is the length of the background knowledge instances that we are generating and N is the number of trajectories in the dataset. This is motivated by the framework generating $\binom{len}{h}$ background knowledge instances and, for each instance, executing N matching operations by applying the matching function introduced in Eq. 1. Moreover, the process of risk assessment depends on the specific dataset to which it is applied, and therefore, it has to be performed every time new data becomes available.

Recently, Pellungrini *et al.* propose a data mining approach to overcome the computational complexity of the PRUDEnce framework by predicting privacy risk with a feature-based classifier [17]. The idea is to extract some mobility features from the data and use them to train a classifier that estimate the privacy risk without having to re-assess privacy risk each time new data becomes available. The proposed approach leads to good results. However, it requires the computation of an array of mobility features that must be selected beforehand. Moreover, the classification approach used by Pellungrini *et al.* allows the user to have some insights about the prediction by looking at the importance of the features used by the classifier. Our goal is to improve on the proposed solution by overcoming the necessity to select and compute the mobility features required for the training process. We do this by using a Long Short-Term Memory neural network (LSTM) that can learn directly from the original trajectories in the dataset. LSTM networks are often used with sequential data for their ability to capture recurring trends. We employ LSTM to solve a classification task, i.e., to distinguish risk in *high* or *low*, with the aim of providing an estimation of which individuals are at risk in a dataset. We also want to motivate our prediction to the user by providing her with an explanation of why a specific risk has been predicted. To this aim, we apply a state-of-the-art explainability algorithm: SHAP. SHAP (SHapley Additive exPlanations) is a local explainer that assigns to each feature an importance value for a particular prediction. It is a unified approach, able to interpret any kind of black-box model. Overall, our proposed approach can be summarized as follows:

(i) Privacy Risk Computation: For each individual u, a privacy risk value is computed by simulating an attack with background knowledge configuration B_h on the mobility dataset $\mathcal{D}$. We thus obtain a privacy risk vector Γ for all individuals in the data.

(ii) The privacy risk vector is discretized to get a set of risk classes. In our experiments, we discretize the risk in two main classes: low risk (privacy risk ≤ 0.5) and high risk (privacy risk > 0.5).

(iii) We use $\langle \mathcal{D}, \Gamma \rangle$ as training set for a LSTM network that can estimate the privacy risk for each new individual that is added to the data.

(iv) For each individual, we explain the prediction obtained with the LSTM using SHAP.

The prediction of privacy risk has some peculiar characteristics: similarly to prediction of diseases, we want our model to be "conservative", i.e., in case of misclassification, we want to avoid misclassifying a high risk individual as a low risk one. Therefore, we are interested in a predictive model that is able to achieve high recall and precision on the high risk and low risk classes. This would indicate that the probability of misclassifying a high-risk individual as a low-risk one is negligible and also that low-risk individuals are mostly classified as such.

5 Experiments

5.1 Privacy Risk Prediction

We validate our methodology by analyzing the performance of: *i)* the prediction of the privacy risk using Long Short-Term Memory networks; and *ii)* the local explanation that we want to present to the user.

Data. For our experiments we use GPS tracks of private vehicles traveling in Tuscany (Italy). This data were provided by Octo Telematics, an insurance company. We selected trajectories of private vehicles from a single area comprising two urban centers, Prato and Pistoia, covering the period from 1st May to 31st May 2011. We end up with a total of 8651 distinct vehicles. We recall that in our context, each user is represented by a single Trajectory as defined in Definition 2. Each trajectory contains all the points visited by the user in temporal order. We performed two different transformations on the original data to experiments on two variants of the dataset. The first transformation gave as result a dataset that we call istat. It is composed by trajectory points that are generalized according to the geographical tessellation provided by the Italian National Statistics Bureau (ISTAT): each point is substituted with the centroid of the geographical cell to which it belongs. We then remove redundant points, i.e., points mapped to the same cell at the same time, obtaining 2274 different locations with an average length of 31.9 points per trajectory. Regarding the second dataset, called voronoi, we first apply a data-driven Voronoi tessellation of the territory [2], taking into consideration the traffic density of an area, and then we used the cells of this tessellation to generalize the original trajectories. The algorithm

Table 1. Class distribution for the two datasets

Dataset	$h = 2$		$h = 3$		$h = 4$		$h = 5$	
	high	low	high	low	high	low	high	low
istat	77%	23%	93%	7%	95%	5%	96%	4%
voronoi	28%	72%	55%	45%	57%	43%	62%	38%

applies interpolation between non adjacent points[1]. With this methodology, the total number of different locations is 1473 with an average length of 240.2 points per trajectory. To obtain a labelled dataset, we computed the privacy risk for each user employing the simulation of the privacy attack presented in Sect. 3.1. For our experiments we considered four background knowledge configurations B_h using $h = 2, 3, 4, 5$ obtaining four different risk datasets, $\Gamma_{h=2,3,4,5}$. We discretized the risk values in two classes: *low risk*, when the privacy risk is in the interval $[0, 0.5]$ and *high risk* for the interval $]0.5, 1]$. At this point, we merged the privacy risk data with the trajectories to obtain the classification datasets for our supervised learning task, following the methodology explained in Sect. 4. Hence, we obtained 8 different datasets for our experiments.

Privacy Risk Prediction. We validate the effectiveness of the privacy risk prediction for trajectory data by using the Long Short Term Memory (LSTM) [11]. The code for the experiments was written in Python 3.6 with Tensorflow 2.0 and Keras 2.2.5[2].

This prediction task has two challenges: firstly, the two risk classes are strongly imbalanced. Table 1 reports the distribution of the two classes for each dataset. It is possible to notice that for the istat dataset there is a strong imbalance between the classes: the *high risk* class is always the majority, while the *low risk* class is under-represented. In particular, the imbalance grows as h: this is due to the fact that for the attacker it is easier to identify a user if she has more information about her.

For what regards the voronoi dataset, we observe less imbalance between the classes. Interestingly, $h = 2$ shows the higher imbalance but it is the opposite of the istat case: for voronoi, the least represented class is the *high risk* one. Another challenge of these dataset is in the length of the trajectories, as presented in Fig. 1: especially for voronoi the trajectories are long.

In this setting our main goal is to obtain a "conservative" classifier from the point of view of users with high privacy risk (as mentioned in Sect. 4).

In practice, we aim at predicting correctly the users that have a high privacy risk to avoid to release highly sensitive data. At the same time, we want to give the possibility of sharing the data of people that have a low privacy risk. Hence, we also want to reduce the probability to classify low risk users as risky ones. For these reasons, we focused on obtaining classifiers that have a good precision and recall on the two classes.

---

[1] Voronoi tessellation obtained using http://geoanalytics.net/V-Analytics.

[2] Code available on https://github.com/francescanaretto/Privacy-Risk-onMobility-Data-with-LSTMs.

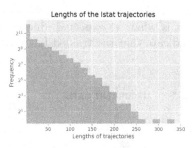
Lengths of the Istat trajectories

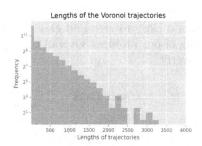
Lengths of the Voronoi trajectories

(a) Distribution of the lengths of the trajectories for the `istat` dataset.

(b) Distribution of the lengths of the trajectories for the `voronoi` dataset.

Fig. 1. These two plot shows the log-scale frequency distribution of the lengths of the trajectories for the two variants of the dataset.

Fig. 2. The structure of our neural network. We choose two LSTM layers with a Dropout layer in between, to avoid overfitting.

For the evaluation of our models we applied the following procedure: i) we padded the trajectories so to have a dataset with sequences of the same length; ii) we selected the network structure proposed in Fig. 2: there are 2 layers of LSTM neurons, with 35 neurons in the first LSTM layer and 20 in the second layer. Each layer has a recurrent dropout of 0.3 and the layer of dropout is 0.2. With this architecture, we executed a hyper-parameter tuning by performing grid search in the parameter space. We considered as parameters the number of epochs, the size of the batch and the optimizer. The results obtained from the grid searches are reported in Table 2. iii) We applied 5-fold cross validation with stratified sampling to validate our methodology. For our experimentation we used a small dataset (8651 trajectories) and we show in Table 1 that it is also suffers from class imbalance. For these reasons, during the training of our models, we found several cases of overfitting, which are typical in this setting. We solved the overfitting problem for all models by introducing an early stopping criterion driven by a validation set, with patience of 4, i.e., the training of the neural network stops if no gain on validation is observed for 4 consecutive epochs. Moreover, we added dropout, both internally in the LSTM layers (0.3 for each layer) and externally, between layers (0.2). Finally, we decreased the neurons for each layer (obtaining 35 and 20 neurons, respectively) and limited the neural network complexity to two layers of LSTM (as presented in Fig. 2). These measures allows us to avoid the overfitting of the LSTMS. To further analyze the resulting models, we plot the neural network: in Fig. 3 we presented the histograms of the weight distributions per kernel, and within each kernel, per gate. The shapes of the weights distributions in the kernel layer show a homogeneous distribution, while for the recurrent layer the gates have a Gaussian-like shape. Lastly, the bias can be found close to zero and close to one, that is what we expected, due to the setting of our problem. Overall these plots indicate that the trained LSTM does not overfit[3].

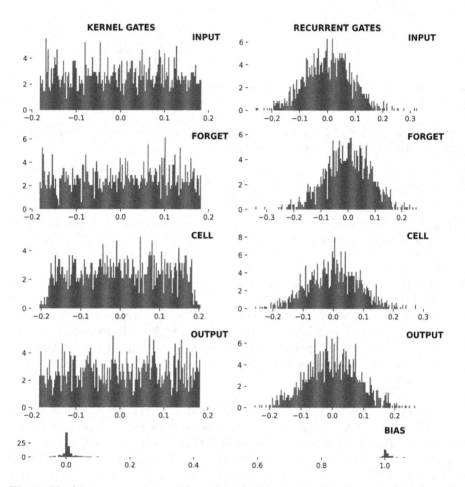

Fig. 3. The histograms represent the weight distributions on the LSTM per kernel, and within each kernel, per gate.

Given the particularity of the setting under analysis, for the evaluation of the performance of the LSTMS, we present: i) the *accuracy* (Acc) to give a general idea of how good the predictor is; ii) the *precision* on both high and low risk classes (P_{high} and P_{low}); iii) the *recall* on both high the low risk class (R_{low} and R_{high}) and iv) the F1-score to summarize the performance of the predictor

---

[3] The analysis of the LSTM has been performed with the see-rnn package: https://github.com/OverLordGoldDragon/see-rnn.

Table 2. The results obtained from the grid search of each model.

B_h	Parameter	istat	voronoi
h = 2	Batch	64	64
	Epoch	20	100
	Optimizer	Adadelta	Adamax
h = 3	Batch	64	32
	Epoch	20	100
	Optimizer	Adamax	Adadelta
h = 4	Batch	64	64
	Epoch	40	80
	Optimizer	Adadelta	SGD
h = 5	Batch	64	32
	Epoch	40	20
	Optimizer	Adadelta	Adamax

with respect to the "conservative" behavior we are aiming at. The results of the experiments are shown in Table 3. We have assessed the performance of the LSTMS by first analyzing the *accuracy*: we achieve good results both for the istat and the voronoi dataset. Due to the peculiarity of our setting, we aim at having predictors with a "conservative" behavior: for this reason, we focused on the *precision* and *recall* for both the classes. Overall, the recall is good, indicating that our predictors capture most of the correct individuals in each class. We also note that the P_{low} for the istat dataset and the P_{high} for the voronoi show lower percentage points w.r.t. the other metrics. This is due to the extreme imbalance of the data. However, in all these cases we surpass the baseline. In summary, for both data we achieve good results for all our metrics, overcoming the high class imbalance. This result is also highlighted by the F1-score: we range from a minimum of 0.76 to 0.91, indicating good performances overall.

5.2 Explanation of the Predictions

The goal of our methodology is to provide the end-user with her privacy risk and an explanation about the reasons that lead her to be classified with a certain privacy risk by our model. Therefore, we want to provide a *local* explanation for the end user.

For our experiments, we employed SHAP [12], a feature importance explanator. We used DeepExplainer, that is one of the explainers available in the SHAP library. It approximates SHAP values for deep learning models. It is based on an enhanced version of *DeepLIFT* algorithm [23]. In particular, it approximates the conditional expectations of SHAP values exploiting background samples. In our setting, the data is limited to the locations that compose the trajectory of the user. Therefore, to provide the end-user with an explanation, we considered each element of the trajectory as a feature.

In the following, we report the results obtained by applying SHAP to the LSTM model trained with the istat dataset with background knowledge $h = 2$.

Table 3. Evaluation performance of the LSTM on the `istat` (right) and `voronoi` (left) datasets for each adversarial attack ($h = 2, 3, 4, 5$). Each metric is averaged over the 5-fold cross validation.

B_h	Class balance	Metric	LSTM	B_h	Class balance	Metric	LSTM
h = 2	High = 77 Low = 23	Acc	0.83 (0.00)	h = 2	High = 28 Low = 72	Acc	0.80 (0.02)
		P_{low}	0.70 (0.01)			P_{low}	0.90 (0.02)
		P_{high}	0.88 (0.01)			P_{high}	0.62 (0.03)
		R_{low}	0.70 (0.02)			R_{low}	0.81 (0.02)
		R_{high}	0.88 (0.00)			R_{high}	0.76 (0.06)
		$F1$	0.79 (0.01)			$F1$	0.76 (0.03)
h = 3	High = 93 Low = 7	Acc	0.89 (0.04)	h = 3	High = 55 Low = 45	Acc	0.88 (0.00)
		P_{low}	0.70 (0.03)			P_{low}	0.90 (0.02)
		P_{high}	0.80 (0.02)			P_{high}	0.88 (0.00)
		R_{low}	0.78 (0.03)			R_{low}	0.84 (0.01)
		R_{high}	0.92 (0.04)			R_{high}	0.92 (0.02)
		$F1$	0.81 (0.03)			$F1$	0.88 (0.00)
h = 4	High = 95 Low = 5	Acc	0.90 (0.01)	h = 4	High = 57 Low = 43	Acc	0.89 (0.01)
		P_{low}	0.69 (0.01)			P_{low}	0.90 (0.02)
		P_{high}	0.93 (0.01)			P_{high}	0.89 (0.01)
		R_{low}	0.80 (0.04)			R_{low}	0.84 (0.01)
		R_{high}	0.92 (0.01)			R_{high}	0.92 (0.02)
		$F1$	0.80 (0.01)			$F1$	0.89 (0.01)
h = 5	High = 96 Low = 4	Acc	0.87 (0.00)	h = 5	High = 62 Low = 38	Acc	0.92 (0.07)
		P_{low}	0.66 (0.01)			P_{low}	0.89 (0.01)
		P_{high}	0.92 (0.01)			P_{high}	0.94 (0.01)
		R_{low}	0.68 (0.04)			R_{low}	0.89 (0.01)
		R_{high}	0.92 (0.01)			R_{high}	0.93 (0.01)
		$F1$	0.80 (0.01)			$F1$	0.91 (0.01)

In particular, we trained the explainer on the same training set employed for the training of the LSTM model. Then, we tested it on the test set on which we also tested our LSTM model. We remark that the same locations can be found multiple times in a trajectory and hence in SHAP since it considers each point of the trajectory as a feature.

We present our results by anonymizing the names for the different locations. This is due to privacy issues: we trained our models on real human mobility data, and presenting the real explanation provided by SHAP could reveal some sensitive information such as home and work address.

A first result we obtained from the application of SHAP confirmed our expectations from the LSTM: SHAP do not consider as important the padding added to normalize the trajectories. In Fig. 4, we report the result obtained by the application of SHAP on a record that the LSTM classified as *high risk*. In Fig. 5, we also report the explanation of a record that was classified as *low risk*. For each record, we plot the *expected value* and the *shap values* of the actual class predicted by the black-box model.

To analyze the results obtained, we look at the locations suggested by SHAP. For each local explanation, we look at the top 3 most important locations for the prediction, as indicated by SHAP. Then, we considered the top 3 most frequent

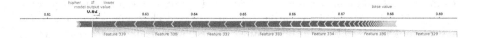

Fig. 4. The local explanation obtained employing SHAP. This record was classified as *high risk* with high probability.

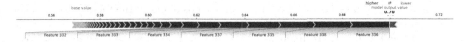

Fig. 5. The local explanation obtained employing SHAP. This record was classified as *low risk* with high probability.

locations of the same trajectory. Thus, we investigate how many users have one of their 3 most frequently visited locations as their top 3 most important locations for prediction. The results obtained are shown in Table 4. It is interesting to note that for the *low risk* class the top 3 locations that SHAP considers most important are the most frequent ones in the trajectory of the user under analysis (the first and the second most frequent locations cover more of the 90% of the records). For the *high risk* class, the distribution is smoother, but the majority of the locations under analysis are among the first and the second most frequent locations. Theoretically, if the attacker knows information such as the most frequent locations (home address and the workplace), she has an advantage in the process of identity discovery. However, we discover that both for the *high risk* and the *low risk* class, the majority of the locations that SHAP considered important, are among the top-2 most frequent locations of the user under analysis. Analyzing this result further, we found another interesting evidence: the *relative frequency*, presented in Table 4. At the beginning of the section we mentioned that SHAP considers each location in the trajectory as a variable and hence it assigns to each of it an importance value. For each user, we first sorted, in decreasing order, the locations by their SHAP values and selected the top-3 locations with the highest SHAP values. These locations are the most important for the classification of that individual as indicated by SHAP. For each of these 3 locations, we computed the frequency of visits of the user under analysis. Regarding the user, we are also able to compute the total number of visits she made during the period of observation. We then calculated the ratio between the frequency of visits of the top 3 locations and the total number of visits for that individual. Finally, we averaged it over the total number of users, obtaining an averaged normalized relative frequency. For the *low risk* class, the frequencies are quite high, while for the *high risk* class they are lower. This result suggests that for the people that are in the *low risk* class, the most important location for the prediction of their privacy risk is a location that they tend to visit often. In contrast, for the *high risk* class, we can see that the most important location is, on average, one visited less often. An example of this phenomenon is reported in Fig. 5, that is an explanation of a record labeled as *low risk*: here Feature 336,

Table 4. Exploration of the locations highlighted by SHAP. We considered separately users classified as *high risk* from the ones that are *low risk*. The column *Shap Rank* refers to the locations ranked by importance values: for each user, we first sorted, in decreasing order, the locations by their SHAP values and selected the top-3 locations with the highest SHAP values. The *relative frequency* column reports the average frequency of all the top-3 locations for each user, as explained in details above. The columns *Loc* and *User* have to be considered together: for each user, given the location that SHAP has identified as top $i - th$, we report if it corresponds to one of the top-3 most frequent places of the user. In the table, we show the percentage of users who have SHAP's top $i - th$ location as the $j - th$ frequency of visits. As an example, for the *low risk* case, almost 65% of the users have the top-1 location of SHAP that is also her most frequently visited location.

Shap rank	Class high			Class low		
	Relative freq.	Loc.	Users	Relative freq.	Loc.	Users
top 1	0.350 (0.261)	f_1	0.493	0.605 (0.273)	f_1	0.649
		f_2	0.200		f_2	0.273
		f_3	0.082		f_3	0.013
top 2	0.344 (0.26)	f_1	0.477	0.609 (0.27)	f_1	0.640
		f_2	0.196		f_2	0.264
		f_3	0.089		f_3	0.0176
top 3	0.349 (0.26)	f_1	0.501	0.554 (0.28)	f_1	0.635
		f_2	0.183		f_2	0.252
		f_3	0.088		f_3	0.018

indicated by SHAP as the most important location for the prediction of the subject, is the second most frequent location (work address) in the trajectory of the subject. Moreover, Feature 338, indicated by SHAP as the second most important location for the prediction of the subject, is the most frequent location (home address) in the trajectory of the subject. A similar situation can bee seen for the record in Fig. 4. In this case the top seven Features for the prediction are all the most frequent location for that user. These preliminary results suggest a connection between privacy risk (and consequently the explanation given by SHAP), and the individual movement behavior of users. Moreover, the explanation of SHAP indicates that the frequency of visit is a much more determining factor for the lower class of risk, suggesting, as expected, that visiting more frequently the same location may hide one user's movement in the crowd.

6   Conclusions

In this work we presented a methodology for the privacy risk prediction and explanation for mobility data. Traditionally, the privacy risk evaluation for this kind of data is done by extracting some features which are dependent on the type of data under analysis. Our methodology, instead, exploits Recurrent Neural Networks to predict the privacy risk directly on the "raw" mobility data. In this way, we avoid the feature definition and the feature extraction steps. Our experiments empirically demonstrated that the performance of the prediction task are very good, especially considering our aim of maintaining a "conservative" approach for our prediction model. Our objective is to provide the end user with her privacy risk correlated by an explanation about the reasons that lead the black-box algorithm to predict it. For our experiments we employed SHAP. We correlated the local explanations provided by SHAP with some statistical information on the dataset under analysis. This comparison highlighted interesting insights on the data under analysis. For this reason, it would be interesting as a future work to develop a methodology that merges the local explanations with other analysis on the dataset to provide to the end-user a comprehensive and clear explanation.

Acknowledgments. This work has been partially funded by the European projects SoBigData-PlusPlus (Grant Agreement 871042), XAI (Grant Agreement 834756) and HumanE-AI-Net (Grant Agreement 952026).

References

1. Altché, F., de La Fortelle, A.: An LSTM network for highway trajectory prediction. In: 2017 IEEE 20th International Conference on Intelligent Transportation Systems (ITSC), pp. 353–359 (2017)
2. Andrienko, N.V., Andrienko, G.L.: Spatial generalization and aggregation of massive movement data. IEEE Trans. Vis. Comput. Graph. **17**(2), 205–219 (2011)
3. Armando, A., Bezzi, M., Metoui, N., Sabetta, A.: Risk-based privacy-aware information disclosure. Int. J. Secur. Softw. Eng. **6**(2), 70–89 (2015)
4. Cavoukian, A., Emam, K.: Dispelling the myths surrounding de-identification: anonymization remains a strong tool for protecting privacy. DesLibris: Documents collection, Information and Privacy Commissioner of Ontario, Canada (2011)
5. Craven, M., Shavlik, J.W.: Extracting tree-structured representations of trained networks. In: NIPS, pp. 24–30 (1996)
6. Craven, M.W., Shavlik, J.W.: Using sampling and queries to extract rules from trained neural networks. In: JMLR, pp. 37–45. Elsevier (1994)
7. Crivellari, A., Beinat, E.: LSTM-based deep learning model for predicting individual mobility traces of short-term foreign tourists. Sustainability **12**, 349 (2020). https://doi.org/10.3390/su12010349
8. Deng, H.: Interpreting tree ensembles with intrees. Int. J. Data Sci. Anal. **7**(4), 277–287 (2019)
9. Guidotti, R., Monreale, A., Giannotti, F., Pedreschi, D., Ruggieri, S., Turini, F.: Factual and counterfactual explanations for black box decision making. IEEE Intell. Syst. **34**(6), 14–23 (2019)
10. Guidotti, R., Monreale, A., Ruggieri, S., Turini, F., Giannotti, F., Pedreschi, D.: A survey of methods for explaining black box models. ACM Comput. Surv. **51**, 1–42 (2019)
11. Hochreiter, S., Schmidhuber, J.: Long short-term memory. Neural Comput. **9**(8), 1735–1780 (1997)
12. Lundberg, S.M., Lee, S.I.: A unified approach to interpreting model predictions. In: NIPS, pp. 4765–4774 (2017)
13. Meier, J., Corporation, M.: Improving Web Application Security: Threats and Countermeasures. Patterns & Practices. Microsoft, Redmond (2003)

14. Mohammed, N., Fung, B.C., Debbabi, M.: Walking in the crowd: anonymizing trajectory data for pattern analysis. In: CIKM, pp. 1441–1444. ACM (2009)
15. Monreale, A., et al.: Movement data anonymity through generalization. TDP **3**(2), 91–121 (2010)
16. de Montjoye, Y.A., Hidalgo, C.A., Verleysen, M., Blondel, V.D.: Unique in the crowd: the privacy bounds of human mobility. Sci. Rep. **3**, 1376 (2013)
17. Pellungrini, R., Pappalardo, L., Pratesi, F., Monreale, A.: A data mining approach to assess privacy risk in human mobility data. ACM TIST **9**(3), 31:1–31:27 (2018)
18. Pratesi, F., Monreale, A., Trasarti, R., Giannotti, F., Pedreschi, D., Yanagihara, T.: Prudence: a system for assessing privacy risk vs utility in data sharing ecosystems. Trans. Data Priv. **11**(2), 139–167 (2018)
19. Ribeiro, M.T., Singh, S., Guestrin, C.: "Why should I trust you?": explaining the predictions of any classifier. In: ACM SIGKDD, pp. 1135–1144 (2016)
20. Rossi, L., Musolesi, M.: It's the way you check-in: identifying users in location-based social networks. In: COSN, pp. 215–226. ACM (2014)
21. Shapley, L.S.: A value for n-person games. Contrib. Theory Games **2**(28), 307–317 (1953)
22. Shi, Z., Xu, M., Pan, Q., Yan, B., Zhang, H.: LSTM-based flight trajectory prediction. In: 2018 International Joint Conference on Neural Networks (IJCNN), pp. 1–8 (2018)
23. Shrikumar, A., Greenside, P., Kundaje, A.: Learning important features through propagating activation differences. In: Proceedings of the 34th International Conference on Machine Learning, ICML 2017, vol. 70 (2017)
24. Song, X., Kanasugi, H., Shibasaki, R.: Deeptransport: prediction and simulation of human mobility and transportation mode at a citywide level. In: Proceedings of the Twenty-Fifth International Joint Conference on Artificial Intelligence, IJCAI 2016, pp. 2618–2624. AAAI Press (2016)
25. Song, Y., Dahlmeier, D., Bressan, S.: Not so unique in the crowd: a simple and effective algorithm for anonymizing location data. In: International Workshop on Privacy-Preserving IR: When Information Retrieval Meets Privacy and Security, pp. 19–24 (2014)
26. Torra, V.: Data Privacy: Foundations, New Developments and the Big Data Challenge. SBD, vol. 28. Springer, Cham (2017). https://doi.org/10.1007/978-3-319-57358-8
27. Wu, F., Fu, K., Wang, Y., Xiao, Z., Fu, X.: A spatial-temporal-semantic neural network algorithm for location prediction on moving objects. Algorithms **10**(2), 37 (2017). https://doi.org/10.3390/a10020037

Approximate Explanations for Classification of Histopathology Patches

Iam Palatnik de Sousa$^{(\boxtimes)}$ ⓘ, Marley M. B. R. Vellasco ⓘ,
and Eduardo Costa da Silva ⓘ

Department of Electrical Engineering, Pontifical Catholic University
of Rio de Janeiro, Rio de Janeiro, Brazil
iam.palat@gmail.com

Abstract. An approximation method for faster generation of explanations in medical imaging classifications is presented. Previous results in literature show that generating detailed explanations with LIME, especially when fine tuning parameters, is very computationally and time demanding. This is true both for manual and automatic parameter tuning. The alternative here presented can decrease computation times by several orders of magnitude, while still identifying the most relevant regions in images. The approximated explanations are compared to previous results in literature and medical expert segmentations for a dataset of histopathology images used in a binary classification task. The classifications of a convolutional neural network trained on this dataset are explained by means of heatmap visualizations. The results show that it seems to be possible to achieve much faster computation times by trading off finer detail in the explanations. This could give more options for users of artificial intelligence black box systems in the context of medical imaging tasks, in regards to generating insight or auditing decision systems.

Keywords: Explainable artificial intelligence · Local interpretable model agnostic explanations · Medical imaging

1 Introduction

In an attempt to increase the transparency of black box models in Artificial Intelligence (AI) application, recent research has increasingly focused on the explainability of opaque classifiers such as Neural Networks [1,4].

The potential benefits of this transparency have been frequently discussed in literature, for areas of application ranging from social good and fairness to legal use [7].

These developments are especially crucial for Medicine related applications, where auditing Machine Learning (ML) and Deep Learning (DL) systems is

© Springer Nature Switzerland AG 2020
I. Koprinska et al. (Eds.): ECML PKDD 2020 Workshops, CCIS 1323, pp. 517–526, 2020.
https://doi.org/10.1007/978-3-030-65965-3_35

518 I. P. de Sousa et al.

seen as essential. Requiring blind trust of these models would be an obstacle for greater application in clinical settings [4].

Among the explainable AI (XAI) approaches, a frequently applied one involves training interpretable surrogate models that approximate the more complex black-box model studied. Among these the most known and used method is that of the Local Explainable Model Agnostic Explanations (LIME), developed by Ribeiro et al. in 2016 [6].

Such a technique can generate human understandable explanations, and its model-agnostic nature means it can be applied to any number of classifier systems, from various neural network architectures to other complex ensembles.

LIME can further be used for various data types, from Natural Language Processing problems to Image Classifications. The main idea of this technique, described in greater detail within the next sections, is to explain individual instances by locally perturbing them. For images, this means generating images where parts are covered, training a simpler more interpretable model to identify how much each region contributes to a given classification.

More recently, Palatnik-de-Sousa et al. [8] have employed LIME to generate explanations for a dataset of lymph-node metastasis images, used in a binary classification task for presence/absence of metastatic tissue. The explanations of a Convolutional Neural Network's (CNN) classifications were then compared to medical expert segmentations, showing agreement between both.

A recent survey of the state of the art for XAI in digital pathology [5] mentions two additional related works dealing with XAI for medical imaging. Tang et al. [10] developed interpretable classifications of Alzheimer's disease pathologies, and Huang and Chung [2] describe a method for weakly supervised learning that can effectively pinpoint cancerous tissue in cancer detection tasks.

However, after the results in [8] some key issues became apparent and highlighted potential problems of directly applying LIME without fine tuning. Namely, using this technique with standard parameters might not generate the best results. The segmentation of the image into meaningful contextual subregions (often called segments or superpixels) is controlled by certain parameters that were shown to influence the results.

In the case of [8] these parameters were manually tuned. However this demonstrated other two possible issues. The first is related to computational times. Since LIME depends on generating sets of perturbed images, and each of these must be evaluated by the black-box model studied, this can and does create a computational bottleneck, especially for large CNN models that might take more time to evaluate each image. This makes the task of fine tuning parameters more time consuming. Also, due to the random nature of how these perturbed images are generated, the results of a given LIME explanation could, and generally do vary, if repeated multiple times for the same instance.

Aiming to solve these issues, Palatnik-de-Sousa et al. [9] developed a novel explainable methodology, modular in nature, that uses Multi-Objective-Optimization (MOO) combined with an explainable algorithm (in this case LIME) to automate parameter fine tuning, and consequently find the best explanations. The explanations generated by their EvEx model shows it's possible to find explanations that are robust against the random nature of LIME, improving upon their previous results.

However, although this seems to remedy the reproducibility problem, it still generates a large computational cost, with the runs of this explainable model taking between 4 and 8 h for each patch studied. The goal in this manuscript is to present an alternative solution to this problem, that dramatically reduces the computation times from the order of magnitude of hours, to minutes.

In order to do this, the detail and quality of the explanations is traded off. By using very simple square divisions on the image, the idea is to test whether this simple approach can find the most relevant parts of an image quickly, whenever this might be necessary or enough for a given image classification problem, or auditing.

2   Materials and Methods

In this section the main aspects of the methodology are briefly described. A summary of how LIME and EvEx work, as well as the dataset used for this study are presented. Then, the proposed approximated model is described.

The experiments here described largely follow the same methodology discussed in greater detail on [9], with the main difference being the use of the approximated explanation generation, instead of the EvEx model.

2.1   Patch Camelyon

Patch Camelyon (P-CAM) [3,11] is a dataset derived from the Camelyon 16 Whole Slide Images (WSI). It consists in about 200 thousand 96 by 96 pixel patches of histopathology images. These images have a binary label representing the presence or absence (labels 1 or 0 respectively) of at least one pixel of metastasis in the 32 by 32 pixel center of the image. Furthermore the dataset is balanced so that the classes are divided in nearly equal splits.

A more detailed discussion of this dataset can be found in [8] and [9]. The patches selected for this study were true positives, to allow for comparison with medical expert manual segmentations contained in the dataset.

2.2   LIME

For the case of image classification problems, the computation of LIME explanations involves first separating the images into segments that hold some contextual information.

In general this means contiguous sub-regions of the image - often called super-pixels - that have colors or textures in common, and could reasonably represent a relevant pattern in a human understandable explanation. There are multiple algorithms that can be used to segment an image into such super-pixels, and it has been shown [8,9] that good segmentations can deeply affect the results of the explanation.

Once a given instance – meaning a given image whose classification is meant to be explained – is selected and segmented into superpixels, a set of perturbed images is then generated. This is accomplished by randomly covering superpixels (for instance, with a black color). Typically hundreds or thousands of such perturbed images are created, to generate a varied distribution compared to the original instance to be explained.

Each perturbed image is then passed through the model being studied, generating a prediction. From these predictions and the perturbed distribution a linear model is trained, which finds how much each particular superpixel in the original segmentation contribute in favor or against a given classification. The explanation can then be visualized as a heatmap showing how relevant each super-pixel is.

Additionally, to get a sense of how the linear model fits the perturbed data, a quantity termed 'explanation score' can be defined as the R-squared of the linear fit [6].

2.3   EvEx

The EvEx model proposed by Palatnik de Sousa et al. [9] essentially expands upon LIME by using a multi objective genetic algorithm to determine the instance segmentation parameters. It generates a set of best parameters (and subsequently best explanations) which are then averaged onto a final heatmap.

Since an MOO is used the best individuals form a Pareto Front of explanations. The model is described in greater length and detail in [9].

2.4   Convolutional Neural Network Model

The same CNN used in [8] and [9] was used in this manuscript to allow for better comparison. It is a typical convolutional network, consisting in three convolution blocks of increasing filter sizes with a dense block ending in a softmax output layer. It is a publically available model from a Kaggle competition, trained on the P-CAM version used in this paper [3].

2.5   Proposed Method

Instead of using complex segmentation algorithms, the approximation proposed in this manuscript simply divides the instance to be explained in two "segments" or regions. A square, and the area surrounding the square. It is clear that such a simple division typically will not hold as much contextual color/texture information as a more precise segmented superpixel, however using this approximation with only one square creates a simplification of the next step in the process.

Figure 1 shows an example of this square segmentation. Notably, it is immediately clear that for such a simple segmentation, there are only 4 possible options

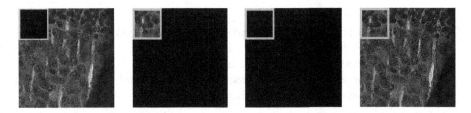

Fig. 1. Example of square segmentation and perturbed images. The yellow square is overlaid onto a P-CAM sample patch. The 4 images represent the original (on the right) and the three possible perturbations. (Color figure online)

regarding perturbed images. Either the image is left intact, as seen on the right-most part of Fig. 1, or there are three possible perturbations, where the square is covered, the area outside the square is covered, or the entire image is covered.

It is not immediately trivial whether using such a simple approximation could generate meaningful explanations with lime, especially since now the linear surrogate model is adjusted on only 4 images, rather than a large distribution of perturbations with hundreds or thousands of examples.

On the other hand, as seen later in the next section, the approximation potentially yields useful results while dramatically reducing the computational costs. The massive reduction in the number of perturbed images means the CNN also performs less evaluations. The key idea is that the approximation, despite leading to less detailed explanations, can compensate this trade-off by being faster by orders of magnitude.

However, to generate the most meaningful explanations possible with this approximation, it would be interesting to find the most explainable squares. Typically, making the squares too small would mean the area outside the square holds most of the contextual information and would yield larger explanation weights, as seen in similar scenarios where large superpixels dominate explanations [8,9]. As such, it is interesting to try to find the square, of a given size, that has the highest explanation weights.

It is also expected, by the same reasons, that larger squares will have larger explanation weights, since they cover a larger area of the image. However, smaller squares might be able to discern which smaller features in a given patch contribute more towards a given class.

As a preliminary test, all square sizes were tested, for all positions on the patch. This means that for a given P-CAM patch, explanations were generated using this square segmentation, using squares with sizes from 1×1 pixels to 95 $\times$ 95 pixels, in which these explanation squares are swept across the image from the top left corner down to the lower right corner.

Besides plotting the weights of each square, at each size, to analyze which ones best explain classifications, a strategy was also devised to create a visualization heatmap for each size of square:

- A given square size is selected
- The squares of that size with positive explanation weights (contributing in favor of the classification) are selected.
- They are added together to create a heatmap
- To compute the average of the added squares, each pixel of the heatmap is divided by the number of squares that are contributing to it.

In this sense, this visualization heatmap is the pixel-wise weighted average of the positive weight squares.

This emulates and approximates the final result of EvEx which is the averaged heatmap of the best explanations found. The expectation is that possibly this square approximation can find similar areas to those identified by EvEx, although with much less detail. On the other hand, the approximation might find them in minutes, compared to the 4 8 h it takes for an EvEx run to complete for one P-CAM patch.

For this initial experiment, 95 such heatmaps are generated for each P-CAM patch (one for each square size).

3 Results and Discussion

The preliminary tests described in the previous section, with varying square sizes, showed that in general the squares of high explanation weights tend to focus in on the same regions of the patch as the size decreases from 95 to 1.

Initially the squares are too large and take most of the patch, which causes them to have high explanation values. However as size decreases these values diminish until the point where the squares are too small to explain the full patch, causing the weights to be negligibly small (close to zero or slightly below zero).

This initial test seems to demonstrate that it is not necessary to generate all the heatmaps of all square sizes. Rather, for each particular patch one may generate a few heatmaps at different sizes and observe the regions to which they converge. Sizes below 30 often are too small to generate explanations, and sizes above 80 are generally too large. Figure 2 shows an example for two patches, including the medical segmentation and also the EvEx equivalent explanation.

Notably, the plots in Fig. 2 also highlight the similarities and differences between the square approximations and the much more detailed EvEx output. The latter seems to clearly delineate some regions, both within the medical segmentation, where the averaged explanation weights are much higher than the surroundings. These regions follow the shape, texture and color contours of certain cellular structures within the tissue.

However, one may note that these EvEx highlighted regions roughly coincide with the regions highlighted by the square approximation, as seen both by sub-panels E and F of Fig. 2, for both patches. Both the squares with highest explanation weights and heatmaps seem to be able to at least approximate the position of the most relevant areas of the patch.

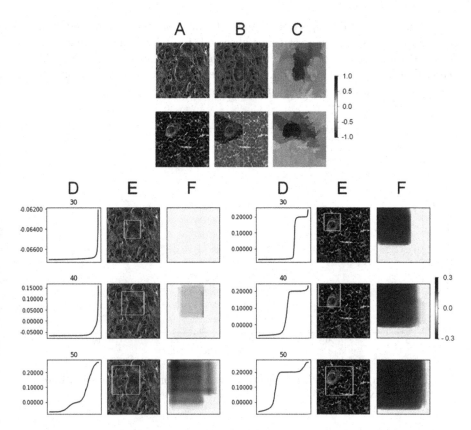

Fig. 2. Results for two different patches. (A) – original patches; (B) – medical segmentation as green overlay; (C) – EvEx heatmap; (D) weights of all squares generated, by size, sorted by increasing values. Sizes (30, 40, and 50) indicated above each plot; (E) – square with the largest weight overlaid on patch; (F) – averaged heatmap as described in Sect. 2. Note that the EvEx heatmaps have a color scale from −1 to 1, while the approximated square heatmaps range from −0.3 to 0.3. (Color figure online)

Another important difference is in regards to the absolute values of the explanation weights. Typically the highest weights found in the EvEx explanation reach values around 0.6 to 0.9, while the square approximation did not yield values above 0.3 in any of the patches studied. This is expected to a degree, as the squares hold much less contextual information than the more detailed EvEx optimized segments. It is also the reason why the color scale of the bottom panels in Fig. 2 was adjusted to a smaller range than the top panels. This seems to mean that lower explanation weights could be expected in the square approximation, but it still manages to roughly delineate relevant regions.

Another key difference, and perhaps the central one to this approach, is in computation times. Figure 3 shows the amount of time taken to generate heatmaps at each square size, in seconds. For the sizes of 30, 40 and 50 used in

Fig. 2, the times were respectively of about 5 min, of about 3 min and 42 s, and of 2 min and 31 s. The largest times observed, for 1 by 1 pixel squares, was of about 10 min. As a comparison, the top and bottom heatmaps of Fig. 2, sub-panel C, took about 4 h and 7 h, respectively. This constitutes a computation time decrease of many orders of magnitude.

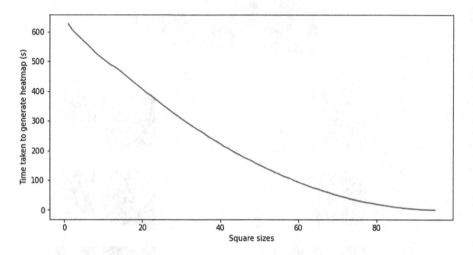

Fig. 3. Time, in seconds, taken to generate heatmaps for each square size, from 1 by 1 to 95 by 95 pixel squares.

Figure 4 shows a side by side comparison of two heatmaps. The first, to the left, corresponds to a high scoring EvEx Pareto front individual used to generate the averaged heatmap in Fig. 2, topmost row of column C. The second, to the right, corresponds to the approximated square of highest explanation weight, size 40, for the same image. Besides the already noted and discussed difference in weights, it seems the explanation score is also lower for the square approximation. As previously mentioned, this score corresponds to the R-squared of the surrogate linear model fit.

However it is worth remembering that the EvEx pareto front individual, in this case, is an explanation generated with 200 perturbations, whereas the square approximation only uses 4. This most likely affects the R-squared metric and contributes to the observed result. Importantly, despite these lower metrics, the heatmaps seem to highlight the same areas.

As such, these results seem to indicate that, while more computationally efficient versions of LIME and EvEx are created, these square approximations can be used to generate faster insights on what might be the key areas of an image the CNN is focusing on.

Future studies could also focus on developing criteria for selecting best square sizes in order to create combined heatmaps.

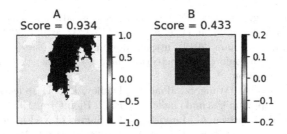

Fig. 4. Side by side comparison of heatmap explanations generated by both methods analyzed in this work, for the same patch (Fig. 2, topmost row of column A), with corresponding explanation scores. Panel A shows an EvEx Pareto Front Individual, while panel B shows the square approximation with highest explanation weight for squares of size 40.

4 Conclusion

In this manuscript an approximation method was presented, in order to generate faster explanations for a medical imaging classification task.

The trade-off between the level of detail of explanations (such as the ones generated with EvEx) and the time it takes to generate such explanations was highlighted. In this way, aiming at reaching much faster computational times and by accepting less detailed explanations, an alternative was presented where simple square segmentations are used.

This, in turn, means that the LIME explanations would be generated from only 4 perturbed images, which is a very rough approximation. However the results seem to show that this rough approximation can still be used to determine, even if with less detail, which areas of an image are most relevant. The gain of several orders of magnitude in computation times might be interesting for some applications, however. Furthermore, results showed that this new method reduce computational times from several hours [9] to a few minutes or less, depending on the square size.

Future projects might focus on further testing this concept in other medical imaging datasets, as well as datasets from other computer vision areas.

Acknowledgment. This study was financed in part by the Coordenação de Aperfeiçoamento de Pessoal do Nível Superior - Brasil (CAPES), Finance Code 001. The authors also acknowledge the Conselho Nacional de Desenvolvimento Científico e Tecnológico (CNPq) and Fundação de Amparo à Pesquisa do Rio de Janeiro (FAPERJ) for the funding to this research.

References

1. Adadi, A., Berrada, M.: Peeking inside the black-box: a survey on explainable artificial intelligence (XAI). IEEE Access **6**, 52138–52160 (2018)

526   I. P. de Sousa et al.

2. Huang, Y., Chung, A.C.S.: Evidence localization for pathology images using weakly supervised learning. In: Shen, D., et al. (eds.) MICCAI 2019. LNCS, vol. 11764, pp. 613–621. Springer, Cham (2019). https://doi.org/10.1007/978-3-030-32239-7_68
3. Kaggle: Histopathologic cancer detection. https://www.kaggle.com/c/histopatho logic-cancer-detection
4. Miotto, R., Wang, F., Wang, S., Jiang, X., Dudley, J.T.: Deep learning for healthcare: review, opportunities and challenges. Brief. Bioinform. **19**, 1236–1246 (2017)
5. Pocevičiūtė, M., Eilertsen, G., Lundström, C.: Survey of XAI in digital pathology. In: Holzinger, A., Goebel, R., Mengel, M., Müller, H. (eds.) Artificial Intelligence and Machine Learning for Digital Pathology. LNCS (LNAI), vol. 12090, pp. 56–88. Springer, Cham (2020). https://doi.org/10.1007/978-3-030-50402-1_4
6. Ribeiro, M.T., Singh, S., Guestrin, C.: Why should i trust you?: explaining the predictions of any classifier. In: Proceedings of the 22nd ACM SIGKDD International Conference on Knowledge Discovery and Data Mining, pp. 1135–1144 (2016)
7. Samek, W., Montavon, G., Vedaldi, A., Hansen, L.K., Müller, K.-R. (eds.): Explainable AI: Interpreting, Explaining and Visualizing Deep Learning. LNCS (LNAI), vol. 11700. Springer, Cham (2019). https://doi.org/10.1007/978-3-030-28954-6
8. Palatnik de Sousa, I., Maria Bernardes Rebuzzi Vellasco, E.: Local interpretable model-agnostic explanations for classification of lymph node metastases. Sensors **19**(13), 2969 (2019)
9. Palatnik de Sousa, I., Maria Bernardes Rebuzzi Vellasco, M., Costa da Silva, E.: Evolved explainable classifications for lymph node metastases. arXiv preprint arXiv:2005.07229 (2020)
10. Tang, Z., et al.: Interpretable classification of Alzheimer's disease pathologies with a convolutional neural network pipeline. Nat. Commun. **10**(1), 1–14 (2019)
11. Veeling, B.S., Linmans, J., Winkens, J., Cohen, T., Welling, M.: Rotation equivariant CNNs for digital pathology. In: Frangi, A.F., Schnabel, J.A., Davatzikos, C., Alberola-López, C., Fichtinger, G. (eds.) MICCAI 2018. LNCS, vol. 11071, pp. 210–218. Springer, Cham (2018). https://doi.org/10.1007/978-3-030-00934-2_24

Eighth International Workshop on News Recommendation and Analytics (INRA 2020)

Preface

Publishers increasingly automate content curation and personalization to present the most relevant stories to readers. This task is challenging due to the dynamics of the news eco-system and lack of information concerning readers' preferences and interests. Besides, ethical and legal issues emerge from recent trends such as deliberate misinformation campaigns and ignoring privacy regulations. Conversely, readers face information overload as more and more stories become easily accessible.

The Eighth International Workshop on News Recommendation and Analytics (INRA 2020)[1] addresses technical, societal, and ethical questions related to news recommendation and analytics. Even though the workshop has a technical focus, we welcome interdisciplinary contributions that shed light on legal, ethical, and societal ramifications of algorithmic news curation. The workshop introduces a more holistic view of news as a particular application domain of machine learning and knowledge discovery. Topics of interests include but are not limited to:

News Personalization

– Innovative algorithms for news personalization
– Reader Profiling
– News context and trend modelling
– Big data technologies for news streams
– Practical applications

News Analytics

– News semantics and ontologies
– News summarization, classification, and sentiment analysis
– Large-scale news mining and analytics
– News evolution and trends
– News from social media

Ethical Aspects of News Recommendation

– Detection and analysis of fake news and disinformation
– News diversity and filter bubbles
– Privacy and security in news recommender systems
– Spread mechanisms of disinformation

INRA 2020 has been held in conjunction with The European Conference on Machine Learning and Principles and Practice of Knowledge Discovery in Databases (ECML/PKDD 2020[2]) digitally on 14 September 2020 as a half day workshop.

---

[1] http://research.idi.ntnu.no/inra/.

[2] https://ecmlpkdd2020.net/.

We have received nine submissions. Each paper has been reviewed by at least three reviewers, in a single blind reviewing process. Thereof, seven papers have been accepted for presentations where three of them are long papers and four of them are short papers. The workshop program included of a keynote speech by Dr. Hiroto Nakajima who is the Chief Scientist at NIKKEI Lab, and a visiting researcher at Tokyo University. He directed several projects including "NIKKEI AI News" and "NIKKEI AR", and won the Japan Pressnet prize in 2019 for the contribution to data journalism. He contributed to INRA 2020 with his keynote speech titled "Practices of Data Analytics and Machine Learning in News Service".

The contributions to the workshop inspect different aspects of news recommendation and analytics. The contributions discuss technical aspects of news recommender systems such as multi-stakeholder news recommendation and automatic classification of news articles. In addition to the technical aspects, presented works include educational datasets in news recommender systems, media bias, diversity of news recommendations, and fake news detection. We believe that this diversity of presented papers in INRA 2020 complies well with the interdisciplinary nature of news recommender systems. We hope that the research community we try to establish around INRA workshop series will help researchers to develop better solutions with the help of different points of views from different disciplines.

Information about previous editions of INRA can be found on the web page http://research.idi.ntnu.no/inra.

October 2020   Özlem Özgöbek
                                                              Benjamin Kille
                                                        Andreas Lommatzsch
                                                              Jon Atle Gulla

Organization

General Chairs

Özlem Özgöbek   Norwegian Univ. of Science and Technology,
                         Norway
Benjamin Kille   Berlin Institute of Technology, Germany
Andreas Lommatzsch   Berlin Institute of Technology, Germany
Jon Atle Gulla   Norwegian Univ. of Science and Technology,
                         Norway

Program Committee

Felix Hamborg   University of Konstanz, Germany
Frank Hopfgartner   The University of Sheffield, UK
Dietmar Jannach   University of Klagenfurt, Germany
Mozhgan Karimi   University of Antwerp, Belgium
Benjamin Kille   Berlin Institute of Technology, Germany
Martha Larson   Radboud University, The Netherlands
Andreas Lommatzsch   Berlin Institute of Technology, Germany
Özlem Özgöbek   Norwegian Univ. of Science and Technology,
                         Norway
Yujie Xing   Norwegian Univ. of Science and Technology,
                         Norway
Lemei Zhang   Norwegian Univ. of Science and Technology,
                         Norway

Multi-stakeholder News Recommendation Using Hypergraph Learning

Alireza Gharahighehi[1,2]([✉]), Celine Vens[1,2], and Konstantinos Pliakos[1,2]

[1] Itec, imec research group at KU Leuven, Kortrijk, Belgium
[2] Faculty of Medicine, KU Leuven, Campus KULAK, Kortrijk, Belgium
{alireza.gharahighehi,celine.vens,konstantinos.pliakos}@kuleuven.be

Abstract. Recommender systems are meant to fulfil user preferences. Nevertheless, there are multiple examples where users are not the only stakeholder in a recommendation platform. For instance, in news aggregator websites apart from readers, one can consider magazines (news agencies) or authors as other stakeholders. A multi-stakeholder recommender system generates a ranked list of items taking into account the preferences of multiple stakeholders. In this study, news recommendation is handled as a hypergraph ranking task, where relations between multiple types of objects and stakeholders are modeled in a unified hypergraph. The obtained results indicate that ranking on hypergraphs can be utilized as a natural multi-stakeholder recommender system that is able to adapt recommendations based on the importance of stakeholders.

Keywords: News recommendation · Multi-stakeholder recommender system · Hypergraph learning

1 Introduction

Classic news recommender systems try to model user preferences based on users' previous interactions with articles. Such systems typically consist of only two types of objects, i.e. users and articles, taking into account only interactions between them [4]. Nevertheless, in many applications there are multiple types of objects and stakeholders. For example, Airbnb should take into account the preferences of both hosts and guests [1]. The same case holds in news aggregator platforms where recommender systems should take into account the preferences of their corresponding stakeholders (e.g., readers, journalists, magazines, etc.). It is therefore crucial that multi-stakeholder news recommender systems should include these different sets of objects and model the complex relations between them when generating lists of recommendations. Here, we show that the use of hypergraph ranking is a *natural* way to address multi-stakeholder news recommendation. A hypergraph is a generalization of a graph that consists of multiple node sets and hyperedges modeling high order relations between them.

© The Author(s) 2020
I. Koprinska et al. (Eds.): ECML PKDD 2020 Workshops, CCIS 1323, pp. 531–535, 2020.
https://doi.org/10.1007/978-3-030-65965-3_36

There have been some studies that have applied hypergraph learning for recommendation, especially in the field of multimedia. Indicatively, in [2] the task of music recommendation was addressed as a hypergraph ranking problem, while in [7], users, images, tags, and geo-tags were modeled in a unified hypergraph model, for tag recommendation. Moreover, the authors in [6] also modeled news recommendation as a hypergraph learning problem by defining hyperedges between users, news articles, news topics and named entities. Despite its capability in modeling relations between several types of objects/stakeholders, to the best of our knowledge, hypergraph learning has not been used in the context of multi-stakeholder recommender systems.

2   Methodology

Let $\mathbf{H}$ be the hypergraph incidence matrix of size $|N| \times |E|$, where N corresponds to nodes (users, articles, authors, topics, sources) and E to hyperedges. $H(n, e) = 1$, if $n \in e$ and 0 otherwise. Let $\mathbf{A} = \mathbf{D}_n^{-1/2}\mathbf{HWD}_e^{-1}\mathbf{H}^T\mathbf{D}_n^{-1/2}$ be a symmetric matrix with each item A_{ij} indicating the relatedness between nodes i and j. $\mathbf{D}_n$, $\mathbf{D}_e$, and $\mathbf{W}$ are the node degree, hyperedge degree, and weight matrix (here $\mathbf{W} = \mathbf{I}$), respectively. Although there are approaches to adjust or optimize the hyperedge weights (e.g. [8]), for the sake of simplicity, here we assign equal weights to all the hyperedges. We try to find a ranking vector $\mathbf{f} \in \mathbf{R}^{|N|}$ that minimizes $\Omega(\mathbf{f}) = \frac{1}{2}\mathbf{f}^T\mathbf{Lf}$, where $\mathbf{L}$ is the hypergraph Laplacian matrix and $\mathbf{R}$ represents the real numbers. This problem is extended with the ℓ_2 regularization norm between the ranking vector $\mathbf{f}$ and the query vector $\mathbf{y} \in \mathbf{R}^{|N|}$, resulting in $Q(\mathbf{f}) = \Omega(\mathbf{f}) + \vartheta||\mathbf{f} - \mathbf{y}||_2^2$, where ϑ is a regularizing parameter. The optimal ranking vector is $\mathbf{f}^* = \frac{\vartheta}{1+\vartheta}\left(\mathbf{I} - \frac{1}{1+\vartheta}\mathbf{A}\right)^{-1}\mathbf{y}$ [2]. To generate the recommendation list for user u in a regular recommendation task, one sets the corresponding value in the query vector to one ($\mathbf{y_u} = \mathbf{1}$) and all the other values to zero.

We used a dataset from a Flemish news content aggregator website (Roularta Media Group). It consists of 3194 users, 4685 news articles and 108 authors. Each article is accompanied by title, text, tags, topics, authors and source (publisher). We defined five types of hyperedges in the unified hypergraph that are presented in Table 1. E1 connects an author to the articles he/she has written. E2 and E3 model high-order relations between the articles and their metadata. E4 represents hyperedges that connect each article to its k (we used $k = 6$) most content-wise similar articles based on article embeddings. E5 models user-article interactions, connecting a user with the articles he/she has seen. To generate the article embeddings we used the CNN based deep neural network proposed by [3] based on title, text and tags of news articles.

In this dataset the majority of articles are related to a limited number of authors. This imbalanced distribution causes biased recommendations toward high frequency authors and high coverage of them in the recommendation lists. For instance, during the COVID-19 outbreak, the platform may be interested in covering more articles written by a specific author (e.g., a science journalist) or magazine in recommendation lists. This can be handled by considering a higher weight for that specific author or magazine in the query vectors. The main aim here is to demonstrate the potential and flexibility of hypergraph learning in considering different stakeholders in the model. In real cases, the platform owners should consider a trade-off between short-term utility and long-term utility. The exact weighting and strategy depend on the context and the policies of the platform owners.

Table 1. Hyper-edge definitions

Hyperedge	Definition
E1	Hyperedges for articles-authors
E2	Hyperedges for articles-topics
E3	Hyperedges for articles-sources
E4	Hyperedges for similar articles
E5	Hyperedges for users-articles

3 Results

Three scenarios are assessed in this section and their results are shown in Table 2. The obtained results are based on per-user queries hiding/testing for each user 25 related article-interactions. Therefore only train interactions are used to form E5. The accuracy measures (nDCG@10 and Precision@10) are calculated based on test interactions. In the first scenario (baseline), the hypergraph consists of E1, E2, E3 and E5. In the second scenario, the article embeddings (E4) are added to the baseline. This way we investigate whether employing article content embeddings boosts recommendation performance. In the third scenario, we consider a higher weight for a specific author (α) in the query vector ($\mathbf{y}$).

The obtained results show that exploiting article embeddings (E4) boosts the hypergraph ranking performance compared to the baseline. In the third scenario, adding a weight (β) for the specific author (α) to the queries ($y_a = \beta$) triples the coverage of the selected author in the recommendation lists. Here, coverage is defined as the percentage of recommendation lists that contain articles of the selected author. This strategy can be used to adapt the ranked lists based on the importance of stakeholders in a specific context. Furthermore, it is vital in order to avoid bias and maximize coverage in news recommendation. The recommender can provide fairer coverage over authors by adapting their weights. It is worth mentioning that this adaptation comes at the cost of reduced precision. The weight of selected stakeholders in the query vectors can be adjusted to balance precision and coverage based on the context.

Table 2. Results of news recommendation

Scenarios	nDCG@10	Precision@10	Coverage
baseline (b)	0.196	0.210	0.108
(b) + article embeddings	0.202	0.220	0.116
(b) + article embeddings + multi-stakeholder	0.152	0.155	0.383

4   Conclusion

In this study we showed that hypergraph ranking can naturally address multiple stakeholders in recommendations. We also showed that one can achieve better recommendation performance by adding article content embeddings. An interesting future research topic would be to dynamically adapt the queries to include more stakeholders balancing as well precision and coverage. Moreover, the trade-off between precision and coverage can be achieved by using the Pareto frontier [9]. Another interesting topic would be to diversify the recommendation lists based on the content of news articles [5]. Finally, a comprehensive evaluation study should be conducted to compare the proposed approach with other multi-stakeholder recommendation methods.

Acknowledgments. This work was executed within the imec.icon project NewsButler, a research project bringing together academic researchers (KU Leuven, VUB) and industry partners (Roularta Media Group, Bothrs, ML6). The NewsButler project is co-financed by imec and receives project support from Flanders Innovation & Entrepreneurship (project nr. HBC.2017.0628).

References

1. Abdollahpouri, H., Burke, R.: Multi-stakeholder recommendation and its connection to multi-sided fairness. arXiv preprint arXiv:1907.13158 (2019)
2. Bu, J., et al.: Music recommendation by unified hypergraph: combining social media information and music content. In: Proceedings of the 18th ACM International Conference on Multimedia, pp. 391–400 (2010)
3. Gabriel De Souza, P.M., Jannach, D., Da Cunha, A.M.: Contextual hybrid session-based news recommendation with recurrent neural networks. IEEE Access **7**, 169185–169203 (2019)
4. Gharahighehi, A., Vens, C.: Extended Bayesian personalized ranking based on consumption behavior. In: Postproceedings of the 31st Benelux Conference on Artificial Intelligence (BNAIC 2019) and the 28th Belgian Dutch Conference on Machine Learning (BENELEARN 2019). Springer (2020, to appear)
5. Gharahighehi, A., Vens, C.: Making session-based news recommenders diversity-aware. In: OHARS 2020: Workshop on Online Misinformation- and Harm-Aware Recommender Systems (2020, to appear)
6. Li, L., Li, T.: News recommendation via hypergraph learning: encapsulation of user behavior and news content. In: Proceedings of the Sixth ACM International Conference on Web Search and Data Mining, pp. 305–314 (2013)

7. Pliakos, K., Kotropoulos, C.: Simultaneous image tagging and geo-location prediction within hypergraph ranking framework. In: 2014 IEEE International Conference on Acoustics, Speech and Signal Processing (ICASSP), pp. 6894–6898 (2014)
8. Pliakos, K., Kotropoulos, C.: Weight estimation in hypergraph learning. In: 2015 IEEE International Conference on Acoustics, Speech and Signal Processing (ICASSP), pp. 1161–1165 (2015)
9. Ribeiro, M.T., Lacerda, A., Veloso, A., Ziviani, N.: Pareto-efficient hybridization for multi-objective recommender systems. In: Proceedings of the Sixth ACM Conference on Recommender Systems, pp. 19–26 (2012)

Monitoring Technoscientific Issues
in the News

Alberto Cammozzo[1], Emanuele Di Buccio[2,3]([✉]), and Federico Neresini[1]

[1] Department of Philosophy, Sociology, Education and Applied Psychology,
Section of Sociology University of Padova, Padova, Italy
{alberto.cammozzo,federico.neresini}@unipd.it
[2] Department of Information Engineering, University of Padova, Padova, Italy
emanuele.dibuccio@unipd.it
[3] Department of Statistical Sciences, University of Padova, Padova, Italy

Abstract. Research at the intersection between Science and Technology Studies (STS) and Public Communication of Science and Technology
(PCST) investigates the role of science in society and how it is publicly
perceived. An increasing attention has been paid to coverage of Science
and Technology (S&T) issues in newspapers. Because of the availability
of a huge amount of digitized news contents, the variety of the issues
and their dynamic nature, new opportunities are offered to carry out
STS and PCST investigations. The main contribution of this paper is a
methodology and a system called TIPS that was co-shaped by sociologists and computer scientists in order to monitor the coverage of S&T
issues in the news and to study how they are represented. The methodology relies on machine learning, information retrieval and data analytics
approaches which aim at supporting expert users, e.g. sociologists, in the
investigation of their research hypotheses.

Keywords: Media monitoring · News analytics · Computational social
science

1 Introduction

Science and Technology (S&T) have a promising role in the contemporary society: their contribution is often considered crucial to solve issues that are collectively acknowledged, such as climate change, energy supply or waste management. One problem is that when S&T issues become publicly relevant, the
way they are discussed or they are represented can be very different from the
"specialist" perspective. The study of these representations could be useful to
provide policy makers with insights on the public perception of some issues on
which they should or intend to take actions, or provide guidance on the way
these issues should be publicly discussed (e.g. on the use of "sensible" words or
aspects related to the issues).

The main contribution of this paper is a methodology and a system that were
co-shaped by sociologists and computer scientists to support the investigation

I. Koprinska et al. (Eds.): ECML PKDD 2020 Workshops, CCIS 1323, pp. 536–553, 2020.
https://doi.org/10.1007/978-3-030-65965-3_37

on this research direction at the intersection between Science and Technology Studies (STS) and Public Communication of Science and Technology (PCST). Previous interdisciplinary studies in PCST have been carried out, either adopting a content analysis perspective, e.g. [21], or following a network analysis, e.g. [10]. Differently from those works, this paper focuses on newspaper articles to investigate the perception of technoscientific issues in the public sphere. "Technoscience" is a useful neologism coniated by STS scholars in order to indicate the increasingly fusion of science and technology [11]. Even if a great deal of attention has been recently paid to social media, newspapers are still very attractive sources because they allow broader longitudinal studies, reach a wide audience, and their content can be regarded reasonably as a proxy of those spread by other media.

This work reports on the design and the implementation of a methodology allowing to monitor and analyse technoscience coverage in online newspapers.

2 Background and Methodological Problems

The work reported in this paper has been carried out as part of an interdisciplinary research project called TIPS: Technoscientific Issues in the Public Sphere. The project is interdisciplinary because it involves sociologists, computer scientists, linguists, psychologists and statisticians. The objective of the TIPS project is the analysis of the presence of technoscience in the mass media, which constitute a relevant part of the public sphere. These analyses are usually based on a limited portion of news coverage, within the traditional frame of content analysis. TIPS aims at extending this perspective, by making reference to the whole set of newspaper articles dealing with relevant technoscientific issues.

There are some methodological problems that need to be addressed:

- The longitudinal character of the observed phenomena.
- The importance of a comparative perspective both in diachronic and in synchronic terms.
- The "demarcation problem", that is what distinctive traits make science a specific object being studied; that allows the thematic domain of technoscience to be defined.

In order to address the first two problems, we designed a methodology and a system to collect, manage and provide access to newspaper articles published in diverse languages and over a long time span. With regard to the third problem, we opted for a "pragmatic" approach assuming the point of view of a hypothetical "typical newspaper reader", asking ourselves what this person may recognise as "science". That led us to a list of six features which should characterize a technoscience-related article:

- a scientist/engineer is mentioned;
- a research centre is mentioned;
- a scientific journal is mentioned;

- a scientific discipline is mentioned (excluding the humanities and social sciences);
- there is a generic reference to research processes and/or technological innovations;
- a discovery, an innovation, a scientific instrument or a medical apparatus is mentioned.

These features will be adopted to build a manually labeled corpus used to evaluate some of the methodology steps and gain insights on some research questions.

3   Methodology

The first step in the design of the methodology and the system was the analysis and the abstraction of (some) research methodologies adopted by the sociologists to investigate their research hypotheses. "Objects" used to carry out these investigations are generic informative resources (e.g. a newspaper article), hereafter named *documents*. Documents are organized in *sources*. With regard to on-line newspapers, a source can be a section of a newspaper, e.g. "Homepage", "Technology" or "Science" section. Sources can be organized in *source sets*: for instance, a newspaper is the source set constituted by all the sections in which the articles are published, or by a meaningful subset of these. Sources could be organized in a hierarchy of source sets; currently, source sets are grouped according to different national and cultural contexts, e.g. "English newspapers".

The analysis of the research methodologies allowed us to identify some common steps:

1. consider a theme, e.g. "science and technology" or "science";
2. identify (classify) documents pertinent to the theme;
3. consider a specific issue; an issue could be a sub-theme (a more specific theme within a theme, e.g. "nuclear power" in the "science and technology" theme) or can be another theme (e.g. "political debate on infrastructure").
4. identify documents pertinent to the theme and relevant to the considered issue; those documents constitute the sub-corpus of interest to investigate the research hypothesis;
5. perform analyses on the identified sub-corpus, e.g. how the presence of a theme in the corpus varies over time

The sub-corpus of interest could be also the entire document corpus – e.g. the entire set of articles gathered from the Italian newspapers; in that case, no specific issue is considered and steps 3–4 are not performed.

The analyses on the sub-corpus usually include:

- exploration of the sub-corpus, that could be completely manually or supported through unsupervised or supervised techniques;
- extraction of sub-themes and study of their evolution through time;

– study of the variation of the distribution of words, named entities or linguistic properties in the sub-corpus, eventually by the comparison with the overall corpus;
– computation of indicators trend.

Indicators are meant to provide a measure of the degree to which a certain concept/aspect is present in the considered (sub)corpus. Looking at the trends of the indicators the researcher can easily identify source sets, sources or periods with peculiar variations, e.g. peaks, and inspect the subsets of the corpus related to these variations in order to gain a deeper comprehension of their causes. The research methodologies are not necessarily linear – from step 1 to step 5 – but they can involve an iterative process where we can reconsider, for instance, the research question or the identification of the (sub)corpora of interest. The analysis of the indicators trends could be the step that leads to a new iteration.

The remainder of this section will describe the diverse methodology steps.

3.1 Source Set Selection

Setting up the source set required some crucial methodological choices: how to collect the articles and the choice of the newspapers.

Regarding the former, our aim was to start up a long-lasting monitoring platform which could provide a real-time automated monitoring system rather than a static document collection. In order to achieve durability and automatic real-time updating, we opted for the on-line version of newspapers, collecting the news-feeds through RSS.

As for the choice of the newspapers, we decided to follow two main criteria, defined as the *popularity* and the *spin* of the newspapers. Popularity has been operatively translated into the average number of daily readers, while the spin concerns the cultural and political orientation of the newspaper. When considering Italian newspapers, we relied on the Audipress 2010 data on popularity. We excluded the most popular newspaper, being almost exclusively a sport newspaper. We considered those ranked immediately below: "Il Corriere della Sera", "La Repubblica", "La Stampa" and "Il Sole 24 Ore". Then we added four additional newspapers considering two additional criteria: the cultural and political orientation and the geo-political location.

3.2 Document Collection

Once the newspapers of the source set are chosen, their RSS feeds are identified with manual inspection to their websites combined with an automated XML feeds survey through website crawling. This approach requires to periodically check the source collection coherence, in case some new RSS feed is published or some other is cancelled. It is known that paper and on-line editions might contain different sets of news; moreover, not all the news published on-line may be advertised. We have to accept these limitations, bearing in mind that following RSS feeds rather than performing a full website crawling responds to the (near) "real-time" collection requirement inherent in our main research purposes. The entire set of selected RSS feeds constitute our collection of sources. In case RSS feeds are absent or discontinued we shift to HTML website traversal, selecting newspaper main sections as a base for crawling.

The newspaper document harvesting process consists of three main phases: proper article collection, scraping, and de-duplication.

In the first phase, when the articles are downloaded, all RSS feeds in our source collection are continuously scanned several times a day, and feed items are collected along with their metadata. A single item consists of: newspaper name and feed, collection date, feed publishing date, feed content (usually a summary of the full newspaper article, or its first lines), URL of the full article and, sometimes, name of the author. Subsequently, the HTML page referenced by the feed URL is retrieved, along with its metadata.

The scraping process consists in extracting the relevant part of the article text from the HTML source, discarding ads, scripts, banners and any other content that is not within the boundaries of the article itself and out of our research scope. We explored several strategies; the currently adopted approach mainly relies on the `Newspaper3k` open source library.[1] As a complement and fallback, `html2text` scraping library is used.[2]

It may happen that an article is published in several different feeds. While its presence in multiple feeds adds significance to that article and represents a valuable information, we have to ensure that the article appears only once in the corpus. For this reason we scan for duplicate articles and retain only one version, keeping track of the different news-feeds involved. It may also happen that different newspapers share the same article. Another frequent case of duplicate item collection happens with articles being updated over time. In this case we keep the last version of the article, saving a record of the publication dates and times of each version. A refined version based on near-duplicates detection is currently being tested.

The source code of our collection, scraping and deduplicating platform is published with AGPL open source license.[3]

3.3 Document Classification

After de-duplication, articles are classified according to their pertinence to themes and sub-themes. For each theme, we investigated text classifiers that can be considered instances of Knowledge Engineering (KE) classifiers [19], where a set of rules encoding expert knowledge are manually defined.

Our classifiers rely on a list of weighted descriptors and a threshold θ; each descriptor can be either a single word or a set of words. A score is assigned to each document on the basis of the weight of those descriptors occurring in the document; if the score is equal or greater than θ, the document is labelled as

[1] https://newspaper.readthedocs.io/.
[2] https://github.com/Alir3z4/html2text/.
[3] https://gitlab.com/mmzz/hactar.

pertinent to the theme; otherwise, it is marked as not pertinent. Each classifier is characterized by two groups of descriptors: *keywords* and *multipliers*. Keywords are specific descriptors, i.e. words or sets of words that are determinant in distinguishing whether a document deals with a certain theme or not. In the specific case of the thematic area of technoscience, keywords have been manually identified according to the following criteria:

- Names of research institutions and scientific journals which are frequently cited by newspapers;
- Names of scientific disciplines;
- Words frequently associated to scientific research activities (such as those regarding discoveries, scientific achievements, features of the laboratory work and scientific instruments);
- Words frequently associated to technological innovations, including those which can be considered as consumer products, like smart-phones, PCs, the Internet, appliances, means of transport.

Differently from keywords, multipliers are descriptors related to the thematic area, but less specific than keywords. Some examples of multipliers we have considered for the field of "technoscience" are "research", "discovery', "environment". The multipliers only count when an article contain at least one keyword. More formally, if K and M denotes respectively the list of keywords and multipliers, and if w_k is the weight associated to keyword $k \in K$ and w_m is the weight associated to the multiplier $m \in M$, the score s_d of a document d is computed as:

$$s_d = \begin{cases} (\sum_{k \in K} t_{d,k} \cdot w_k) \cdot (\sum_{m \in M} t_{d,m} \cdot w_m) & \text{if } \sum_{m \in M} t_{d,m} > 0 \\ \sum_{k \in K} t_{d,k} \cdot w_k & \text{otherwise} \end{cases}$$

where $t_{d,k} = 1$ if the keyword k appears in the document d, $t_{d,k} = 0$ otherwise; similarly $t_{d,m} = 1$ if the multiplier m appears in the document d, $t_{d,m} = 0$ otherwise. The current technoscience classifier uses 218 keywords (with weights ranging from 2 to 15) and 17 multipliers (all weighting 2). Keywords and multipliers, as well as their weights, have been selected and applied after manually comparing the performances of many different versions of the classifier, by adding or dropping words, changing their weights and shifting words from the keyword to the multiplier group. The threshold has been identified by looking at the distribution of the scores obtained from the textual analysis, and choosing the value which could best distinguish between pertinent and non-pertinent articles; the currently adopted value is $\theta = 20$.

When no multipliers occur in the document, the classification function is a linear threshold function with threshold θ; when at least a multiplier occurs in the documents, the classification function corresponds to a *polynomial discriminator of order 2* [1]. Indeed, the above function can be described by a multinomial equation of degree 2 in the variables $x_1, \ldots, x_{|K|}, x_{|K|+1}, \ldots, x_{|K+M|}$ where

- $x_1, \ldots, x_{|K|}$ are the keywords, $t_{d,k}$'s
- $x_{|K|+1}, \ldots, x_{|K+M|}$ are the multipliers, $t_{d,m}$'s
- the weight associated to x_i^2 is always zero
- the weight associated to $x_i x_j$ is always zero if both i and j are in $\{1, \ldots, |K|\}$ (i.e. they correspond to keywords) or are in $\{|K|+1, \ldots, |K+M|\}$ (i.e. they correspond to multipliers).

In order to investigate the effectiveness of the proposed classifier, we manually labelled a sample of documents disjoint from that used to extract keywords and multipliers and to set the threshold θ. We extract all the articles published in the four most popular newspapers mentioned in Sect. 3.1 after 2008-01-01 and before or on 2014-09-04, satisfying the query "scienz*".[4] That led to 7779 possibly relevant articles; a random sample was extracted from this subset and manually labelled according to the features/criteria described in Sect. 2; documents were considered relevant if at least two criteria were met. That results in 1167 documents related to technoscience. Then, two random sets of articles with a score ranging from 1 to 19 – i.e. articles classified as non-related to the technoscientific theme, hereafter denoted as "non-relevant documents" – were selected from the corpus. The size of the first random sample was computed in order to maintain approximately the same size of the random sample of documents above the threshold. The second sample of non-relevant documents was obtained by augmenting the fixed non relevant sample by additional randomly selected documents with a score below the threshold of relevance; the number of added documents was computed in order to obtain a final sample where the proportion of documents above and below the threshold was approximately the same as in the entire corpus. Both non-relevant samples were labelled on the basis of the 6 criteria described in Sect. 2. In this way we obtained two datasets: one with 3814 documents (relevant sample + fixed non-relevant sample) and one with 5121 documents (relevant sample + proportional non-relevant sample).

As for the evaluation, we considered the KE classifier and two supervised learning approaches:

- **SVM:** Linear Support-Vector Machine (SVM) using all the terms occurring in the vocabulary of the training sets; each term was represented by TF·IDF, where TF is the *Term Frequency* and IDF the *Inverse Document Frequency*.
- **NB:** Naïve Bayes (NB) classifier using all the terms occurring in the vocabulary of the training sets; each term was represented by the TF.

We investigated also SVM and NB with document representation based only keywords and multipliers: **SVM-Vocab** and **NB-Vocab**. The former used IDF as term feature, while the latter the (binary) occurrence of the term in the document; the motivation was to use the same information of the KE classifier.

The SVM and the NB classifier implementation is that made available in Apache Spark (version 2.2.0). The evaluation was performed using a 60/40 split

---

[4] The word "scienza" is the Italian translation for "science"; the notation "scienz*" refers to all the words that begins with the string "scienz".

for the training/test set. As for the KE classifier, we used that trained by trial and error by the sociologists.

Table 1 reports the results in terms of F1 on the test set for the most effective combinations of methods and representations.

Table 1. F1 for the diverse classifiers and splits.

Method	Feature	F1			
		Random Split		Time Split	
		Fixed	Prop	Fixed	Prop
SVM	TFIDF	0.9153	0.9208	0.9098	0.8892
SVM-Vocab	IDF	0.9268	0.9297	0.9230	0.9226
NB	TF	0.9300	0.9227	0.9175	0.9074
NB-Vocab	Bin	0.9168	0.9020	0.8983	0.8941
KE	–	0.9286	0.9428	0.9298	0.9397

Automatic text classifiers can achieve an accuracy comparable to that of the KE classifier, whose development required a great effort by the sociologists; for this reason, we are currently relying on supervised learning approaches, e.g. SVM and Random Forests, to build additional classifiers, e.g. those for newspapers in other languages. The main issue with the previous experimental methodology is that articles in the corpus have a chronological order and, in principle, we should train the classifier on the past and predict categories in "future" documents. Following the approach reported in [12], we split the dataset chronologically; a 60/40 training/test split was adopted. The results are reported in the last two columns of Table 1: the KE classifier is still the most effective and it is less affected by the chronological split, thus suggesting that is capable to generalize through time. The curated vocabulary created for the KE classifier seems to be the reason for the robustness: indeed, also SVM-Vocab is only slightly affected by the use of a chronological split.

3.4 Indicators

Indicators are meant to provide a measure of the degree to which certain properties characterize a set of documents related to a theme or specific issue. The set of documents can be the entire corpus or a subset identified for the investigation of a specific research hypothesis. We defined several indicators; three of them are reported below:

- *salience*: ratio between the number of articles classified as relevant for a specific theme and the total of articles published over the same period by the source;
- *general framing*: distribution of the relevant articles across the various sections of the news websites;

– *risk*: presence in an article text of a set of words associated with the risk domain.

The first two indicators have been introduced in order to have two different measures of the coverage of technoscientific contents in the news. These indicators are normalized over the number of published articles – in the period or in the source – in order to obtain relative measures not affected by increments of articles published in absolute terms.

The last indicator, *risk*, is rooted in the "risk society" notion originally developed in the sociological field. The risk society refers to the idea that within contemporary society technoscientific issues are imbued with fears and preoccupations about unforeseen effects, calling for a precautionary approach on the side of policy making, society, and the public [2]. Diverse instantiations on the risk indicator have been proposed in [17] and [4]. The currently adopted version relies on term weight computed for keywords in a controlled vocabulary.

3.5 Information Access and Retrieval

All the collected newspaper articles are enriched with the scores assigned by the classifiers and some of the indicators, e.g. the risk indicator. All this information along with the extracted content and metadata, is stored using a NoSQL Database Management System, more specifically MongoDB; this technology has been selected because of its capability to scale and to handle replicas. All the information in the databases is indexed and made available through a Search Server implemented with Elasticsearch.[5] This search server relies on the Open Source library Apache Lucene and allows the user information need to be expressed through fulltext-search queries and, if needed, through the Lucene Query syntax which includes the specification of boolean constraints, fuzzy queries (e.g. "scienz*") or proximity queries. This component is crucial in our application domain where the users are researchers, mostly sociologists experts in the study of how technoscientific issues are discussed and represented in the mass media. The information retrieval functionalities are used:

– to get articles most pertinent (top-k) to themes, e.g. technoscience, on the basis of the classifier score and other metadata, e.g. a time range or the fact that the articles were published in Homepage;
– to identify subsets of the corpus pertinent to specific technoscientific issues, e.g. using *standing queries* [13];
– to perform fine-grained analysis of specific issues, looking at different perspectives/angles on the basis of complex queries devised by expert users.

Documents can be ranked according to several criteria, e.g. recency, classifier score, date range, newspaper, newspaper sections were they appeared, topicality "estimated" by BM25 [18].

---

[5] https://www.elastic.co/elasticsearch/.

4   The TIPS Architecture

The methodology has been implemented in an information system called TIPS[6]; a very concise description can be found in [4,8]. Since TIPS has been designed and developed for research purposes, it responds to several design criteria: modularity, open source components and languages, reproducibility of results, measurability of process, data and system reliability, data safety. A pictorial representation of the main modules constituting TIPS is reported in Fig. 1. The sources are RSS feeds of newspapers sections; however, we have recently extended the types of sources, e.g. including blogs and tweet streams. The collector module implements the procedures described in Sect. 3.2. The classifiers and indicators module performs the classification using the techniques described in Sect. 3.3 and computes some of the indicator values, most specifically those that can be computed for each document like the risk indicator [4]. The indexing module and the IR technology refer to the IAR functionalities discussed in Sect. 3.5. The last modules are those responsible to expose all the services as Web API – that can be access only through authentication – and the Web User Interface (Web UI).

TIPS has been designed to support reproducible research. Each researcher can work on a number of projects. A number of classifiers and predefined issues is associated to each project; a researcher can define its own issues, which are translated into structured queries that can consider both constraints on the full-content of the documents and/or their metadata. The researcher can then inspect trends of the indicators computed on the defined sub-corpus, and search the corpus in order to access the documents and carry out a more fine grained analysis. Several interactions with the system (task definition, search activities) are logged.

As mentioned above, TIPS functionalities are accessible through a Web UI. The UI has a dashboard section which is the page when a user is redirected after the login – see Fig. 2a. The dashboard allows the researchers to specify the classifiers and the specific issues to be used for their investigation. The specification of an issue determines the sub-corpus of interest (e.g. only documents topically relevant to "climate change"). The researcher must specify the document repository for the analysis. Currently, there are several repositories, e.g. that including all the Italian Newspapers, that including all the English Newspapers, diverse longitudinal samples or newspaper corpora spanning several decades and gathered through available archives.

Once the document repositories, classifiers and issues have been specified, the researcher can access charts that show indicators trends and/or indicator comparisons; charts are dynamically computed on the basis of the selected repository, classifiers and indicators. The currently available charts are displayed in Fig. 2b which is a screenshot of the "Charts" section of the TIPS Web UI; the first chart allows access to charts generated using the sub-corpus of documents relevant to a user-specified issue. In the following section we will discuss how the

---

[6] https://www.tipsproject.eu/tips.

TIPS Architecture allowed us to answer several research questions through the analysis of some indicators.

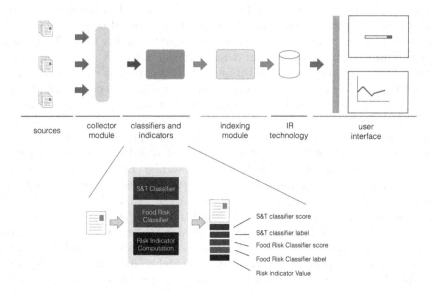

Fig. 1. TIPS Architecture.

5   Following Technoscience in the News

A first result that we obtained concerned with the trend of documents relevant to technoscientific issues. We considered a subset of the newspapers and look at the number of relevant documents over the years; the trend seems to suggests that the tendency on publishing articles on technoscience has become stronger over the years. However, because we gathered all the published articles, we were able to compute the *salience indicator* that showed how the coverage of technoscience is more stable and the increment is mostly due to the increasing number of articles published on-line over the years. This result is documented in [14].

Automatic classification of technoscientific content was investigated as an alternative to the classification performed by the newspaper editors, e.g. that derived by manually assigned tags, if any, or the section(s) where the articles were published. We could have classified as relevant all and only the articles published in "Science" or "Technology" sections of the newspapers. However, we are not aware of the criteria adopted by newspaper editors and we conjectured that content relevant to technoscience following our criteria is spread over all the section categories. In order to check if using newspaper-provided classification could have prevented us from identifying some relevant articles, we computed the *general framing* indicator. Seven different source categories were

(a) Dashboard

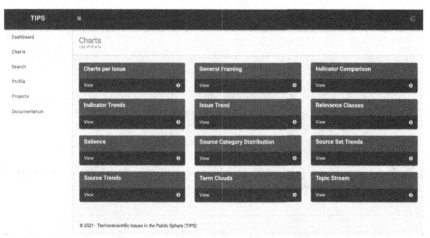

(b) Charts section

Fig. 2. TIPS Web UI

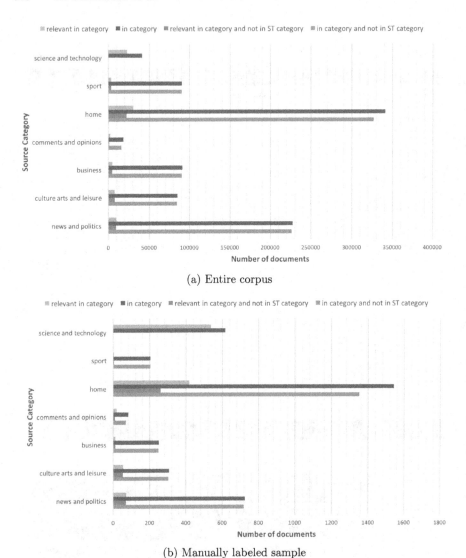

(a) Entire corpus

(b) Manually labeled sample

Fig. 3. Relevant articles per source category in the entire document corpus (Fig. 3a) and in the manually labeled sample (Fig. 3b).

manually defined by grouping newspaper feeds according to their content: "science and technology", "sport", "home" (homepage), "comments and opinions", "business", "culture, art and leisure", and "news and politics". Figure 3a reports the number of articles per source category, the number of those articles classified as relevant to technoscience; the indicator shows how technoscientific content is published also in sections not in the "science and technology" category. Since some articles could have been published both in a "science and technology" section and in other sections, we reported also the number of articles published in a given category but not published in a "science and technology" category; also in this case, the number of relevant articles in other source categories is positive. We performed the same analysis on the manually labeled sample described in Sect. 3.3—the "fixed" sample was used. The result of the analysis is reported in Fig. 3b and shows that also in this case there is a positive number of relevant documents published in feeds not in the 'science and technology" category. These results support our intuition of not relying on the newspaper classification.

Salience and *general framing* provide us with quantitative measures of the coverage of technoscience in the newspapers, and the distribution of techno-scientific content in different sections (categories). The latter could provide an indication on the thematic frames within which technoscientific issues are discussed—e.g. business, culture, politics. In order to gain additional insights on the thematic frames, we could follow one of the ways sociologists ordinarily use to analyse texts: "read texts and produce interpretations based on insights their readings [...] produce a set of themes, create a coding sheet, and then code texts by reading them [...] search texts for keywords and comparing subsets of texts with respect to the prevalence of those keywords" [5]. However, as suggested in that work, these approaches are impracticable for large number of documents or requires to restrict the scope of exploration a priori.

For this reason, we exploited the Topic Modelling algorithm Latent Dirichlet Allocation (LDA) [3]. We used the approached proposed in [22] and implemented in Mallet,[7] we extracted 20 topics from the articles classified as relevant in the entire dataset and we manually labelled them according to the top 100 words extracted for each topic.[8] Table 2 reports 3 of the 20 extracted topics; sixteen of these topics with the top 100 keywords have been made available online.[9] The first column of the table reports the manually assigned label, while the second column reports the topic proportion per year; topic proportion was computed counting the number of words in each topic published in a given year and then normalizing over the total number of words for that year.

The analysis of the trends of the topic proportions showed that the coverage of some thematic issues tend to be constant over the years. This is the case of research concerning with astronomy or space exploration. Peaks are present respectively in 2012 and 2014. The former can be explained by the involvement of the European Space Agency in multiple missions, e.g. the launch of Vega, or the discovery made through the Fermi Gamma-ray Space Telescope on the Extra-galactic Background Light. In 2014 there were multiple achievements in space exploration, e.g. the missions by India and Japan, the Lunar mission by China, the first landing on a comet (67P/Churyumov-Gerasimenko), or the observations provided by the NASA's Mars Curiosity rover; moreover, 2014 was the year of the first Italian woman in space. Other topics present more prominent peaks. This is, for instance, the case of topic labelled as "research policies" where a peak

[7] https://github.com/mimno/Mallet/releases/tag/v2.0.8RC3.
[8] We used 17 as random seed, 5000 iterations and 10 as optimization interval.
[9] http://www.dei.unipd.it/ dibuccio/tips/topics.html.

in term of topic proportion is present in the 2010. The peak can be explained by two controversial cases also evident from the top terms: the *stamina therapy* and the *university reform*. The first case refers to a controversial stem-cell therapy that had media and political repercussion; the second case refers to the reform concerning the reorganisation of universities in Italy.

Table 2. Three of the twenty topics extracted from technoscientific documents. The three charts use the same scale for the y axis.

Label	Proportion
research policies	
space exploration (research)	
astronomic research	

6   Related Works

Previous works on news search engines and media monitors are relevant to the work reported in this paper. In [9] the author described the architecture of a news search engine, *Velthune*; our system shares with Velthune the adoption of RSS and classifiers to complement the classification provided by the newspapers, e.g. the distribution among the newspaper sections. Differently from Velthune, our system was specifically designed to support expert users such as sociologists in the investigation of their research hypotheses. The Web UI has been designed in order to support research methodologies via diverse forms of interaction which include the creation of subcorpora on the basis of full-text and metadata, and the visualisation and the interaction with indicators and extracted topics. Even if also Velthune allows a private set of queries to be recorded, in TIPS the recorded queries are the basis for the analysis performed by the experts; all the indicators and visualisation are dynamically generated on the basis of the subcorpus determined by the query (issue). Our starting point was the methodological premises of our expert users, their methodology and how to support them in their exploration.

The Europe Media Monitor (EMM) [20] is a suite applications developed to monitor the media in order to update its users on relevant developments; EMM users include EU institutions, national organizations in the EU Member States and in some non-EU countries, international organizations, as well as the general public. The NewsBrief application is the most relevant to the work reported in this paper. One of the peculiar features of EMM is that supports Multilingual Information Access and Retrieval (IAR).

NOAM [6] and the system described in [7] are also relevant to our work. They were designed and developed in order to automate media content analysis for the social sciences. They rely on a modular architecture, allow diverse type of sources to be monitored, and are equipped with mood and topic detector, sentiment extractor and readability and popularity annotators.

TIPS shares with EMM part of the architecture components; with NOAM the focus on Social Science. However, TIPS is focused on the research areas of PCST and STS, is equipped also with classifiers that have been developed to fulfil specific theoretical principles underlying the study of S&T and provides diverse visualizations of the news corpora based on novel indicators. TIPS allows the information need to be described through a rich query language: this functionality is particularly useful to support expert users such as sociologists in the investigation of their research hypotheses. Moreover, TIPS supports also analysis and exploration of the information space by exploiting the thematic structure, e.g. through the adoption of topic modelling algorithms.

7   Final Remarks

In this paper we introduced a methodology that was co-shaped by sociologists and computer scientists to support the investigation on public perception of technoscience. We relied on a pragmatic approach based on six criteria to deal with the problem of demarcation. We showed how the existing newspaper categorizations are not sufficient to capture all the technoscientific content and how automatic classifiers can be adopted to obtain satisfactory results, even in evolving corpora. We defined several indicators and discuss how they can help us to avoid distorted interpretations of the prominence of technoscientific content in the news, e.g. through the salience indicator.

The adoption of machine learning algorithms to unveil the thematic structure, e.g. LDA, allowed us to rapidly obtain a general view of the public discourse on technoscience and its evolution; that would have been impossible (in reasonable time) through manual inspection.

The methodology and the TIPS system were the basis for carrying out other research activities, e.g. on the energy transition case in Italian daily newspapers [16] and to track biomedicalization in the media [15]; in the latter work, a comparative study between Italy and UK was performed and the proposed methodology relies both on topic analysis through time and the risk indicator.

Our current research directions include the study of heterogeneous sources, e.g. tweet streams, blogs, and forums, along with methods to study additional dimensions to characterize the public discourse on technoscientific issues in the media. Those methods include approaches to "measure" document readability and to characterize, e.g. through patterns of syntactic features, the language used for the communication of science and technology.

Moreover, we are exploring languages to support researchers, experts in domains other than computer science, in carrying out their research tasks, e.g. following the idea suggested in [23], where Zhai proposed to go beyond search and toward a general analysis engine that can support, for instance, decision making, learning or other tasks.

Acknowledgments. The authors would like to thank the Pa.S.T.I.S. research group of the University of Padova for the useful discussions and comments which helped to improve significantly the quality of the paper. The research of E. Di Buccio has partially been supported by the Quantum Access and Retrieval Theory (QUARTZ) project, which has received funding from the European Union's Horizon 2020 research and innovation programme under the Marie Skłodowska-Curie grant agreement No. 721321.

References

1. Anthony, M.: Classification by polynomial surfaces. Discret. Appl. Math. **61**(2), 91–103 (1995)
2. Beck, U.: Risikogesellschaft - Auf dem Weg in eine andere Moderne. Suhrkamp, Frankfurt/Main (1986)
3. Blei, D.M., Ng, A.Y., Jordan, M.I.: Latent Dirichlet allocation. J. Mach. Learn. Res. **3**, 993–1022 (2003)
4. Di Buccio, E., Lorenzet, A., Melucci, M., Neresini, F.: Unveiling latent states behind social indicators. In: Gavaldà, R., Zliobaite, I., Gama, J. (eds.) Proceedings of the SoGood@ECML-PKDD 2016, Riva del Garda, Italy, 19 September 2016. CEUR Workshop Proceedings, vol. 1831. CEUR-WS.org (2016)
5. DiMaggio, P., Nag, M., Blei, D.: Exploiting affinities between topic modeling and the sociological perspective on culture: application to newspaper coverage of U.S. government arts funding. Poetics **41**(6), 570–606 (2013)
6. Flaounas, I., et al.: NOAM: news outlets analysis and monitoring system. In: Proceedings of the 2011 ACM SIGMOD International Conference on Management of Data, SIGMOD 2011, Athens, Greece, pp. 1275–1278. Association for Computing Machinery, New York (2011). https://doi.org/10.1145/1989323.1989474. ISBN: 9781450306614
7. Flaounas, I., Lansdall-Welfare, T., Antonakaki, P., Cristianini, N.: The anatomy of a modular system for media content analysis. Arxiv - Social Media Intelligence (2014). arXiv:1402.6208v2
8. Giardullo, P., Lorenzet, A.: Techno-scientific issues in the public sphere (TIPS). EASST Rev. **35**(4), 14–17 (2016)
9. Gulli, A.: The anatomy of a news search engine. In: Special Interest Tracks and Posters of the 14th International Conference on World Wide Web, WWW 2005, pp. 880–881. Association for Computing Machinery, New York (2005). https://doi.org/10.1145/1062745.1062778
10. Kim, L.: Denotation and connotation in public representation: semantic network analysis of Hwang supporters' internet dialogues. Public Underst. Sci. **22**(3), 335–350 (2013)

11. Latour, B.: Science in Action: How to Follow Scientists and Engineers Through Society. Harvard University Press, Cambridge (1987)
12. Lewis, D.D., Yang, Y., Rose, T.G., Li, F.: RCV1: a new benchmark collection for text categorization research. J. Mach. Learn. Res. **5**, 361–397 (2004)
13. Manning, C.D., Raghavan, P., Schütze, H.: Introduction to Information Retrieval. Cambridge University Press, New York (2008)
14. Neresini, F.: Old media and new opportunities for a computational social science on PCST. J. Commun. **16**(2), C03 (2017)
15. Neresini, F., Crabu, S., Di Buccio, E.: Tracking biomedicalization in the media: public discourses on health and medicine in the UK and Italy, 1984–2017. Soc. Sci. Med. **243**, 112621 (2019). https://doi.org/10.1016/j.socscimed.2019.112621
16. Neresini, F., Giardullo, P., Di Buccio, E., Cammozzo, A.: Exploring socio-technical future scenarios in the media: the energy transition case in Italian daily newspapers. Qual. Quan. **54**, 147–168 (2020). https://doi.org/10.1007/s11135-019-00947-w
17. Neresini, F., Lorenzet, A.: Can media monitoring be a proxy for public opinion about technoscientific controversies? The case of the Italian public debate on nuclear power. Public Underst. Sci. (Bristol, England) (2014)
18. Robertson, S.: The probabilistic relevance framework: BM25 and beyond. Found. Trends® Inf. Retrieval **3**(4), 333–389 (2009). https://doi.org/10.1561/1500000019
19. Sebastiani, F.: Machine learning in automated text categorization. ACM Comput. Surv. **34**(1), 1–47 (2002)
20. Steinberger, R., Pouliquen, B., van der Goot, E.: An introduction to the Europe Media Monitor family of applications. In: Proceedings of the SIGIR 2009 Workshop on Information Access in a Multilingual World, vol. 43 (2009)
21. Veltri, G.A., Atanasova, D.: Climate change on twitter: content, media ecology and information sharing behaviour. Public Underst. Sci. (2015)
22. Wallach, H.M., Mimno, D., McCallum, A.: Rethinking LDA: why priors matter. In: Proceedings of the 22nd International Conference on Neural Information Processing Systems, NIPS 2009, pp. 1973–1981. Curran Associates Inc., USA (2009)
23. Zhai, C.: Beyond search: statistical topic models for text analysis. In: Ma, W., Nie, J., Baeza-Yates, R.A., Chua, T., Croft, W.B. (eds.) Proceeding of the 34th International ACM SIGIR Conference on Research and Development in Information Retrieval, SIGIR 2011, Beijing, China, 25–29 July 2011, pp. 3–4. ACM (2011). https://doi.org/10.1145/2009916.2009920

Pitch Proposal: Recommenders with a Mission - Assessing Diversity in News Recommendations

Sanne Vrijenhoek[(✉)] and Natali Helberger

University of Amsterdam, Amsterdam, The Netherlands
{s.vrijenhoek,n.helberger}@uva.nl

Abstract. By helping the user find relevant and important online content, news recommenders have the potential to fulfill a crucial role in a democratic society. Simultaneously, recent concerns about filter bubbles, fake news and selective exposure are symptomatic of the disruptive potential of these digital news recommenders. Recommender systems can make or break filter bubbles, and as such can be instrumental in creating either a more closed or a more open internet. This document details a pitch for an ongoing project that aims to bridge the gap between normative notions of diversity, rooted in democratic theory, and quantitative metrics necessary for evaluating the recommender system. Our aim is to get feedback on a set of proposed metrics grounded in social science interpretations of diversity.

1 Introduction

News recommender algorithms have the potential to fulfill a crucial role in democratic society. By filtering and sorting information and news, recommenders can help users to overcome maybe the greatest challenge of the online information environment: finding and selecting relevant online content. Informed by data on what people like to read, what their friends like to read, what content sells best, etc., recommenders use machine learning and AI techniques to make ever smarter suggestions to users [4,12,13,20]. With this comes the power to channel attention and shape individual reading agendas and thus new risks and responsibilities. Recommender systems can be pivotal in deciding what kind of news the public does and does not see. Depending on their design, recommenders can either unlock the diversity of online information [7,15] for their users, or lock them into boring routines of "more of the same", or in the worst case into so-called filter bubbles [16] and information sphericules. But what exactly is diverse? As central as diversity is to many debates about the optimal design of news recommenders, as unclear it is what diverse recommender design actually entails. In the growing literature about diverse recommender design, a growing gap between the computer science and the normative literature can be observed. For news recommenders to be truly able to unlock the abundance of information online and inform citizens better, it is imperative to find ways to overcome the

I. Koprinska et al. (Eds.): ECML PKDD 2020 Workshops, CCIS 1323, pp. 554–561, 2020.
https://doi.org/10.1007/978-3-030-65965-3_38

fundamental differences in approaching and conceptualizing diversity. There is a need to reconceptualise this central but also elusive concept in a way that both does justice to the goals and values that diversity must promote, as well as facilitates the translation of diversity into metrics that are concrete enough to inform algorithmic design. This pitch details the normative theory underlying our approach to evaluating diverse recommender systems, and five proposed metrics that follow from this theory. Our goal is to obtain feedback during the workshop on the applicability and explainability of these metrics, before we proceed with their operationalization in follow-up research.

2 Theory

Before we define more quantitative metrics to assess diversity in news recommendation, we first offer a conceptualization of diversity. Following the definition of the Council of Europe, diversity is not a goal in itself, it is a concept with a mission, and it has a pivotal role in promoting the values that define us as a democratic society. These values may differ according to different democratic approaches. This article builds on a conceptualisation of diversity in recommendations that have been developed by [7]. [7] combines the normative understanding of diversity, meaning what should diverse recommendations look like, with more empirical conceptions, meaning what is the impact of diverse exposure on users. There are many theories of democracy, but we concentrated on 4 of the most commonly used theories when talking about the democratic role of the media: *Liberal, Participatory, Deliberative* and *Critical* theories of democracy (see also [2,3,10,19]). It is important to note that no model is inherently better or worse than another. Which model is followed is something that should be decided by the media companies themselves, following their mission and dependent on the role they want to play in a democratic society.

2.1 The Liberal Model

In liberal democratic theory, individual freedom, including fundamental rights such as the right to privacy and freedom of expression, dispersion of power but also personal development and autonomy of citizens stands central. Under such liberal perspective, diversity would entail a user-driven approach to diversity that reflects citizens interests and preferences not only in terms of content, but also in terms of for example style, language and complexity. A liberal recommender is required to inform citizens about prominent issues, especially during key democratic moments such as election time, but else it is expected to take little distance from personal preferences. It is perfectly acceptable for citizens to be consuming primarily cat videos and celebrity news, as long as doing so is an expression of their autonomy.

2.2   The Participatory Model

An important difference between the liberal and the participatory model of democracy is what it means to be a good citizen. Under participatory conceptions, the role of (personal) freedom and autonomy is to further the common good, rather than personal self-development [8]. Accordingly, the media, and by extension news recommenders must do more than to give citizens 'what they want', and instead provide citizens with the information they need to play their role as active and engaged citizens [1,6,9,11], and further the participatory values, such as inclusiveness, equality, participation, tolerance. Here the challenge is to make a selection that gives a fair representation of different ideas and opinions in society, while also helping a user to gaining a deeper understanding, and feeling engaged, rather than confused. This means that diversity is not only a matter of the diversity of content, but also of communicative styles. What would then characterize diversity in a participatory recommender are, on the one hand, active editorial curation in the form of drawing attention to items that citizens 'should know', taking into account inclusive and proportional representation of main political/ideological viewpoints in society and a heterogeneity of styles and tones, possibly also emotional, empathetic, galvanizing, reconciliatory.

2.3   The Deliberative Model

The participatory and the deliberative models of democracy have much in common (compare [5]). Also in the deliberative or discursive conceptions of democracy, community and active participation of virtuous citizens stands central. One of the major differences is that the deliberative model operates on the premise that ideas and preferences are not a given, but that instead we must focus more on the process of identifying and negotiating and, ultimately, agreeing on different values and issues [5,10]. Diversity in the deliberative conception has the important task of confronting the audience with different and challenging viewpoints that they did not consider before, or not in this way [14]. Concretely, this means that a deliberative recommender (or recommendation) should include a higher share of articles presenting various perspectives, diversity of emotions, range of different sources; it should strive for equal representation, including content dedicated to different ethnic, linguistic, national groups, as well as on recommending items of balanced content, commentary, discussion formats, background information, as well as a preference for rational tone, consensus seeking, inviting commentary and reflection.

2.4   The Critical Model

A main thrust of criticism of the deliberative model is that it is too much focused on rational choice, on drawing an artificial line between public and private, on overvaluing agreement and disregarding the importance of conflict and disagreement as a form of democratic exercise [11]. The focus on reason and tolerance muffles away the stark, sometimes shrill contrasts and hidden inequalities that are present in society, or even discourage them from developing their identity in the first place. Good and diverse critical recommenders hence do not simply give people what they want. Instead, they actively nudge readers to experience otherness, and draw attention to the marginalised, invisible or less powerful ideas and opinions in societies. And again, it is not only the question of what kinds of content are presented but also the how: whereas in the deliberative and also the participatory model, much focus is on a rational, reconciling and measured tone, critical recommenders would also offer room for alternative forms of presentations: narratives that appeal to the 'normal' citizen because they tell an everyday life story, emotional and provocative content, even figurative and shrill tones - all with the objective to escape the standard of civility and the language of the stereotypical "middle-aged, educated, blank white man" [21].

3 Metrics

Table 1. Overview of the different models and expected value ranges for each metric. The column refer to Calibration (topic) (Cal t), Calibration (style) (Cal s), Fragmentation (Frag), Affect, Representation (Rep), and Inclusion (Inc).

	Cal t	Cal s	Frag	Affect	Rep	Inc
Liberal	High	High	High	–	–	–
Participatory	Low	High	Low	Medium	Reflective	Medium
Deliberative	–	–	Low	Low	Equal	–
Critical	–	–	–	High	Inverse	High

The democratic models described in the previous section lead to different expectations for recommender systems in terms of diversity. In this section, we propose five novel metrics for assessing diversity in news recommendations, that follow directly from these expectations: *Calibration, Fragmentation, Affect, Representation* and *Inclusion*. Table 1 provides an overview of the different models and their expected value ranges for each of the different metrics.

3.1 Calibration

The *Calibration* metric expresses to what extent the issued recommendations reflect the user's preferences, and is a well-known metric in traditional recommender system literature [18]. However, we extend our notion of Calibration to not only include topicality. News recommendations can also be tailored to the user in terms of article style and complexity, allowing the reader to receive content that is attuned to their information needs and processing preferences. This may be split up within different topics; a user may be an expert in the field of politics but less so in the field of medicine, and may want to receive more complex articles in case of the first, and less in case of the second.

In the Context of Democratic Recommenders. For the Liberal model we expect high Calibration, both in terms of style and topicality. For the Participatory model we expect low topic Calibration, but high style Calibration.

3.2 Fragmentation

News recommender systems create a recommendation by filtering from a large pool of available news items. By doing so they may stimulate a common public sphere, or create smaller and more specialized 'bubbles'. This may occur both in terms of topics recommended, which is the focus of the Fragmentation metric, and in terms of political orientation, which will be later explained in the Representation metric. Fragmentation specifically compares differences in recommended news stories *among* users; the smaller the difference, the more we can speak of a joint agenda. It is important here to focus on news story chains rather than individual articles, to account for sets of articles that may be written in a different style or from a different perspective, but that ultimately discuss the same issue.

In the Context of Democratic Recommenders. For both the Participatory and Deliberative models we expect low Fragmentation. For the Liberal model we expect a higher score.

3.3 Affect

The way in which an article is written may affect the reader in some way. An impartial article may foster understanding for different perspectives, whereas an emotional article may activate them to undertake action. The *Affect* metric aims to capture this by measuring the strength of emotions expressed in an article. In the context of democratic news recommenders a dimensional [17] approach is taken; what matters is the degree of 'activation' that is conveyed, not whether this happens in the positive or negative spectrum. It must be noted that it is less interesting what the feelings of the article's author are, and more how these feelings affect the reader. However since this is very difficult to measure or predict we hold to the assumption that a strongly emotional article will also cause strong emotions in a reader.

In the Context of Democratic Recommenders. In the Deliberative model we aim for neutrality, and therefore low Affect. In the Participatory model a slightly wider value range is expected; some affective content is acceptable, but nothing too extreme. The Critical model however focuses specifically on affective content, and high values should be expected.

3.4 Representation

One of the most intuitive interpretations of diversity focuses on its level of Representation, or the question whether the issued recommendations provide a good balance of different opinions and perspectives. Here we care more about what is being said than who says it, which is the goal of the last metric Inclusion.

In the Context of Democratic Recommenders. To define what it means to provide "a good balance" of opinions, one needs to refer back to the different models and their goals. The Participatory model aims to provide a good reflection of "the real world". The news recommendations therefore need to have a larger share in the Representation for the more prevalent opinions in society. On the other hand, the Deliberative model aims to provide a complete overview of all opinions without one being more prevalent than the other.

3.5 Inclusion

Where Representation is largely focused on the explicit content of a perspective (the *what*), Inclusion is more concerned with the person holding it (the *who*), and specifically whether this person or organisation is one of a minority group or an otherwise marginalised group that is more likely to be underrepresented in the mainstream media. What exactly entails a minority is about as vaguely defined as the concept of diversity itself: it may for example be related to ethnicity, gender, language group, religion, sexuality, disability.

In the Context of Democratic Recommenders. In the Critical model we aim for a high Inclusion score. The Participatory model fosters tolerance and empathy, and therefore we expect a slightly larger than average Inclusion.

4 Conclusion

At the basis of our work is that we believe diversity is not a single absolute, but rather an aggregate value with many aspects. In fact, we argue that what constitutes 'good' diversity in a recommender system is largely dependent on its goal, which type of content it aims to promote, and which model of the normative framework of democracy it aims to follow. As none of these models is inherently better or worse than the others, we believe that a media company should take a normative stance and evaluate their recommender systems accordingly.

References

1. Baker, E.C.: Media Concentration and Democracy: Why Ownership Matters. Cambridge University Press, New York (1998)

2. Christians, C., Glasser, T., McQuail, D., Nordenstreng, K., White, R.: Normative Theories of the Media: Journalism in Democratic Societies. University of Illinois Press, Champaign (2009)
3. Dahlberg, L.: Re-constructing digital democracy: an outline of four 'positions'. New Media Soc. **13**(6), 855–872 (2011). https://doi.org/10.1177/1461444810389569
4. Dörr, K.N.: Mapping the field of algorithmic journalism. Digit. Journal. **4**(6), 700–722 (2016). https://doi.org/10.1080/21670811.2015.1096748
5. Ferree, M.M., Gamson, W.A., Gerhards, J., Rucht, D.: Four models of the public sphere in modern democracies. Theory Soc. **31**(3), 289–324 (2002)
6. Ferrer-Conill, R., Tandoc Jr., E.C.: The audience-oriented editor. Digit. Journal. **6**(4), 436–453 (2018). https://doi.org/10.1080/21670811.2018.1440972
7. Helberger, N.: On the democratic role of news recommenders. Digit. Journal. **7**(8), 1–20 (2019). https://doi.org/10.1080/21670811.2019.1623700
8. Held, D.: Models of Democracy. Stanford University Press, Palo Alto (2006)
9. Tandoc Jr., E.C., Thomas, R.J.: The ethics of web analytics. Digit. Journal. **3**(2), 243–258 (2015). https://doi.org/10.1080/21670811.2014.909122
10. Karppinen, K.: Conceptions of democracy in media and communications studies (2011)
11. Karppinen, K.: Uses of democratic theory in media and communication studies. Observatorio **7**(3), 1–17 (2013)
12. Kunaver, M., Pozrl, T.: Diversity in recommender systems - a survey. Knowl.-Based Syst. **123**, 154–162 (2017). https://doi.org/10.1016/j.knosys.2017.02.009
13. Lewis, S.C., Westlund, O.: Big data and journalism. Digit. Journal. **3**(3), 447–466 (2015). https://doi.org/10.1080/21670811.2014.976418
14. Manin, B.: On legitimacy and political deliberation. Polit. Theory **15**(3), 338–368 (1987)
15. Nguyen, T.T., Hui, P.M., Harper, F.M., Terveen, L., Konstan, J.A.: Exploring the filter bubble: the effect of using recommender systems on content diversity. In: Proceedings of the 23rd International Conference on World Wide Web, pp. 677–686 (2014). https://doi.org/10.1145/2566486.2568012
16. Pariser, E.: The Filter Bubble: How the New Personalized Web is Changing What We Read and How We Think. Penguin, New York (2011)
17. Russell, J.A.: Core affect and the psychological construction of emotion. Psychol. Rev. **110**(1), 145 (2003)
18. Steck, H.: Calibrated recommendations. In: Proceedings of the 12th ACM Conference on Recommender Systems, RecSys 2018, pp. 154–162. Association for Computing Machinery, New York (2018). https://doi.org/10.1145/3240323.3240372
19. Strömbäck, J.: In search of a standard: four models of democracy and their normative implications for journalism. Journal. Stud. **6**(3), 331–345 (2005). https://doi.org/10.1080/14616700500131950
20. Thurman, N., Schifferes, S.: The future of personalisation at news websites: lessons from a longitudinal study. Journal. Stud. **13**(5–6), 775–790 (2012). https://doi.org/10.1080/1461670X.2012.664341
21. Young, I.M.: Communication and the other: beyond deliberative democracy. Democr. Differ.: Contest. Bound. Polit. **31**, 120–135 (1996)

An Educational News Dataset for Recommender Systems

Yujie Xing[✉], Itishree Mohallick, Jon Atle Gulla, Özlem Özgöbek, and Lemei Zhang

Norwegian University of Science and Technology, 7491 Trondheim, Norway
{yujie.xing,itishree.mohallick,jag,ozlem.ozgobek,
lemei.zhang}@ntnu.no

Abstract. Datasets are an integral part of contemporary research on recommender systems. However, few datasets are available for conventional recommender systems and even very limited datasets are available when it comes to contextualized (time and location-dependent) News Recommender Systems. In this paper, we introduce an educational news dataset for recommender systems. This dataset is the refined version of the earlier published Adressa dataset and intends to support the university students in the educational purpose. We discuss the structure and purpose of the refined dataset in this paper.

Keywords: Refined datasets · News recommender system · Machine learning

1 Introduction

The proliferation of online news creates the need for filtering and recommending specific news to focus on interesting articles. The past decade has seen a tremendous increase in the popularity of news recommender systems [1, 2]. Therefore, many online media houses have deployed news recommender systems for identifying interesting stories for its online readers and operates over a set of unlimited news sources.

With the ubiquity of access to instant news on online sources, the preference of users has changed over time from the traditional model of publishing news—from printed newspapers to online news. A large amount of news content availability on the web causes the information overload problem for online news readers. News recommender systems help these online readers in alleviating their effort in terms of time and choice by providing personalized lists of news articles. However, it is challenging for the media houses/online sources to recommend real-time news without any explicit user ratings from the users. Users are often seen moving from one news outlet to others for getting the most recent and relevant news [3]. Although controversies like filter bubbles and echo chambers remain associated with the recommender systems, most news readers prefer personalization features on news sites.

However, news recommender systems must deal with long-term user preferences and short-term trends. For instance, the long-term preference is driven by the professional activity of users, education, etc. and is best captured with content-based filtering

© The Author(s) 2020
I. Koprinska et al. (Eds.): ECML PKDD 2020 Workshops, CCIS 1323, pp. 562–570, 2020.
https://doi.org/10.1007/978-3-030-65965-3_39

methods. While the short-term user preference, such as popular stories, is captured using collaborative filtering methods in news recommender systems. The collaborative filtering approach tries to predict the utility of news articles for a particular user based on the news articles interacted with by other users in the past. In contrast, the content-based filtering approach tries to predict the utility of news articles for a particular user based on the new´s articles content in the past. More recent news recommender systems tend to be hybrid solutions, in which collaborative filtering and content-based recommendation are combined for news personalization.

News recommendation has a substantial practical relevance due to the specific challenges the news domain entails. Research in this area is still growing as the number of research papers increase since the last decades. The pioneers in the field of online news recommendations such as Google news have been using advanced recommendation strategies (novel scalable algorithms) for generating successful personalized news recommendation for the users of Google news [1, 2]. In recent decades, the traditional printed media like BBC, Washington Post, and New York times [4] have adopted news personalization as an attempted antidote for information overload. In Norway, the third-largest media house, Polaris media has deployed personalization features on its fully personalized first mobile news site "iTromsø". A significant growth-rates in both unique visitors and pageviews have been observed. In addition, readers spent 15% more time on reading recommended articles than regular articles, and there is a 28% increase in time spent on the front page of iTromsø [5].

The challenges associated with the news recommender systems are different from the conventional recommender systems. For instance, the unstructured format of the news stories, recency aspects, short item life time, large volume of available news, heterogeneous nature of the information sources, greater item churn, unavailability of user rating, unique user interaction style are some of the identified challenges in case of news recommender systems [6]. A recent survey paper reveals that [7] more researchers used a hybrid approach and combined content-based filtering and collaborative filtering methods for recommending news to overcome the above said challenges.

Methodologically this approach makes use of many techniques from information retrieval, like linguistic preprocessing of content data [8] and search queries expanded with profile models [9, 10]. Experiments indicate that users also appreciate additional strategies that boost fresh news, popular news and news that take place in their own neighborhood [11]. An earlier research paper demonstrates the architecture of an advanced news recommender system. It introduces the Adressa compact data set published within the RecTech Project at the Norwegian University of Science and Technology [12]. The paper later discussed how the Adressa dataset can be used in advanced news recommender systems. Research datasets are essential for training and evaluation to accommodate various recommendation strategies. For instance, Kaggle Dataset is used in the field of predictive modeling and machine learning whereas Sage research methods dataset is used for supporting in teaching and learning data analysis techniques [3]. As a follow-up research for the earlier compact Adressa dataset, this paper introduces the refined Adressa dataset. The refined dataset is different from the previously released dataset and can be utilized for the teaching/learning activities related to news recommendation in the university setting. The refined Adressa dataset is cleaner as a substantial amount of noise is reduced and requires less preprocessing time. This dataset is suitable for educational purposes because the students need less time to preprocess the raw news data.

This paper is organized as follows. In Sect. 2 we briefly discuss relevant datasets for news recommender systems. We present the structure of the Adressa refined dataset in Sect. 3. In Sect. 4 we show how the fields should be interpreted and used followed by the conclusions in Sect. 5.

2 Related Work

Evaluating recommender systems is an intricate issue and primarily recommender systems are evaluated using one of these three approaches: offline experimentation and simulation based on historical data, laboratory studies, or A/B (field) tests on real-world websites [7]. However, the research from the aforesaid paper states that offline evaluation approach is primarily used for evaluating news recommender systems as online studies are often difficult to carry out.

The types of evaluation in a recommendation setting is dependent on publicly available datasets (i.e., their size or the amount of user and item information). A dataset in this context is defined as collection of data that is used to train and test new systems under development. Some of the most used and recently published research dataset are as follows:

- *Yahoo's datasets* are specifically tailored for unbiased offline evaluation [14] and are used in several research activities concerning news recommendation. One of the datasets, Yahoo! Front Page, comprises clicks data of two weeks from the main page of Yahoo! News. Each visit to the page was described by a binary vector of features. The 182-item pool for recommendations always contains 20 items. The log consists of nearly 28M visits to a total of 653 items. Due to the limitation of the data collection period, research is piratically not possible for personalization based long term user models.
- Swiss dataset [15] comprises of the data from the websites of two daily SwissFrench newspapers called Tribune de Gen'eve (TDG) and 24 Heures (24H) from Nov. 2008 until May 2009. The aforesaid news sites contain news stories ranging from local news, national and international events, sports to culture and entertainment. The dataset contains all the news stories displayed and all the visits by anonymous users within the time period. Each time a user browses the website, a new visit is created even if she browsed the website before.
- *SmartMedia Adressa dataset* has recently been released [7, 12] which contains click logs of approximately 20 million-page visits from a Norwegian news portal as well as a sub-sample with 2.7 million clicks (referred to as "light version"). The dataset also contains some contextual information such as geographical location, time spent on reading an article and session boundaries for the users. The data set is published with the collaboration of Norwegian University of Science and Technology, Norway and Adresseavisen as part of the RecTech Project. The dataset is collected during a span of 10 weeks (from 1 January 2017 to 31 March 2017) and contains the click events of about 2 million users and about 13 thousand articles.

Details of datasets for recommendation such as Outbrain dataset, The Plista Dataset, The Netflix dataset, Movielens dataset are addressed in the research papers [7, 15, 16] where some of the datasets like Netflix and Movielens are used to develop solution concerning collaborative filtering. There are only a few datasets available publicly for the news recommendation such as Yahoo! dataset, Plista dataset, Adressa Dataset, Kaggle dataset from Globo.com, a news portal from Brazil [13]. Extensive use of proprietary and non-public datasets in news recommendation is addressed in [2, 15] while investigating the offline performance and online success of any news recommender systems. Offline performance in this context is measured in terms of accuracy metrics whereas the online success is measured in terms of click-through-rates. These non-public datasets such as Movielens and Netflix dataset are different from the conventional dataset due to sparsity aspect as there is no cold start problem associated. Therefore, the application of such datasets in the news domain is debatable [16].

3 Structure of Adressa Refined Dataset[1]

The Cxense platform[2], the recommendation platform provided by our partner Cxense for news recommendation and monitoring, was used to extract the dataset, which covers one week of web traffic from February 2017 on the www.adresseavisen.no web site. The details of the platform can be found in the earlier paper [12]. From the raw data extracted from the Cxense platform, we construct a refined dataset that contains reading events with 9 selected attributes. The three attributes–event ID, user ID, and document ID–give the index for each event. The remaining 6 attributes offer the most important information about the reading event.

The refined dataset includes anonymized user data from the local digital newspaper from 01.01.2017 to 31.03.2017 (3 months in total). To reduce sparsity, we filter 1000 most active users from the original dataset and select 9 attributes that we think most

Table 1. Fields of the refined adressa dataset.

Attribute	Description	Example
eventID	Id of Reading event	1082287123 (integer)
time	The time of the event	1487572383 (Unix time)
activeTime	The active time spent on a page	23 (s)
canonicalURL	URL of the visited page	"http://adressa.no"
documentID	Internal ID of page	"9757814edc2d346dfcf6f54e349f404c4e9775cf"
title	Title of the article	"Test av 19 grovbrød"
category	News category	"sport"
publishTime	Date of publication	"2017-02-20T09:45:47.000Z"
userID	The cross-site user identifier	"cx:i8i85z793m9j4yy0:cv8ghy3v45j8"

[1] The refined dataset can be downloaded using this link: http://Reclab.Idi.Ntnu.no/Active1000. Zip.
[2] https://www.cxense.com/.

relevant for the project. The attributes of the event table are listed in Table 1. Each reading event is given a unique ID, and the user (ID) and document (ID) that appear in these specific events are recorded, as well as the access time of the event. For each user, except for a unique user ID, the dataset also provides the active time during which the user spends on each document. For each document, the dataset provides the document ID, the title, the category, and the publish date. Also, the web page URL that the user visits (canonicalURL) is recorded.

There is no explicit rating of news stories, but there are implicit signals of interests in terms of click counts and time spent reading the articles that may be used to calculate scores.

As shown at the end of the table in Table 2, the refined Adressa dataset contains 20,344 news articles, 1,000 readers, and about 700 thousand events. Each of these events corresponds to a user reading a particular news article.

Table 2. Comparison of some well-known datasets.

Datasets	Items	Users	Ratings	Density (%)	Rating Scale
MovieLens 1 M	3,883 movies	6,040	1,000,209	4.26	[1–5]
MovieLens 10 M	10,682 movies	71,567	10,000,054	1.31	[1–5]
MovieLens 20 M	27,278 movies	138,493	20,000,263	0.53	[1–5]
Netflix	17,770 movies	480,189	100,480,507	1.18	[1–5]
MoviePilot	25,058 movies	105,137	4,544,409	0.17	[1–5]
Last.fm 360 K	294,015 artists	359,347	17,559,530	0.017	[1, 5]
Yahoo Music	624,961	1,000,990	262,810,175	0.042	[1, 5]
Jester	150 jokes	124,113	5,865,235	31.5	[−10, 10]
Book-crossing	271,379 books	92,107	1,031,175	0.004	[1, 10] + implicit
YOW	5,921 articles	28	10010	6.0	[1, 5] + implicit
Plista	70,353 articles	14,897,978	84,210,795	0.008	Click counts
Adressa 2 M compact	923 articles	15,514	2,717,915	0.19	Click counts, reading times
Refined Adressa	20344 articles	1,000	788,931	3.34	Click counts, reading times

As seen from Table 3, for the refined Adressa dataset, Nyheter (News) make up about 48% of the articles included in the dataset. There are also many Pluss (Paid content) and sports articles in the dataset. The total number of articles which has a category field is 12,748 out of 20,344 since some articles miss category inputs.

Table 3. Number of articles per news category for refined dataset.

Category	No. of articles	% of articles
"Nyheter" (news)	6,169	48.39
"Pluss" (paid content)	3,106	21.38
"100sport" (100sport)	2,726	24.36
"Meninger" (opinions)	240	1.88
"Bolig" (housing)	233	1.83
"Kultur" (culture)	104	0.82
"Forbruker" (consumer)	71	0.56
"Sport" (sport)	28	0.22
"Tema" (theme)	24	0.20
"Migration catalog"	21	0.16
"Tjenester" (services)	18	0.14
"Været" (weather)	4	0.03
"Bil" (car)	2	0.02
"omadresseavisen" (about Adresseavisen)	1	0.01
Average per category	910.6	7.1

In Fig. 1, we see how often the 20344 articles have been viewed by the users. Different from the compact dataset, a majority of articles-12906 articles (63.44%)-are viewed more than one time, and 2492 articles (12,25%) are viewed more than 100 times. This indicates that the refined dataset is less sparse.

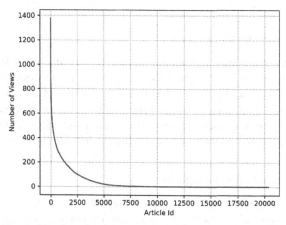

Fig. 1. Number of article views per article for refined dataset.

Table 3 and Fig. 1 indicate that the refined dataset is balanced on the article views. More than half of the articles have been viewed more than one time, and about 10% of articles are popular (viewed more than 100 times).

4 Dataset for Education

The refined dataset can be provided to students who take the recommender system course as a group project. The goal of the project is to recommend news to the users in the refined dataset, given the clicked documents, active time, publish time, access time, etc. The result is evaluated based on whether the recommended documents were clicked by the user through hit rate, click through rate, ARHR, and MSE. Students have the opportunity to compare results containing or not containing missing data, and to compare different methods of evaluation, which enables them a realistic prospective into the problem.

According to the students' feedback, the refined dataset is more suitable for a group project lasting one semester, since the data has a much higher density than the compact dataset. Previously, the students spent lots of time on filtering the dataset, while after changing to the refined dataset, students can spend more time on analyzing the dataset and implementing more algorithms. We introduce the different algorithms that the students can implement in the following subsections.

4.1 Collaborative Filtering

Collaborative Filtering (CF) is a widely adopted recommendation algorithm, and also an important part of the recommender system course. The fundamental assumption of CF is that if user X and Y rate n items similarly, or have similar behaviors (such as buying, rating, clicking, listening), and hence will rate or act on other items similarly. Given the access status and the active time, students can practice implementing collaborative filtering algorithms. We provide the Explicit Matrix Factorization (MF) as an example to the students.

4.2 Content-Based Recommendation

Content-based recommendation is another popularly used recommendation method. It makes recommendations by analyzing the content of textual information and finding regularities in the content. We provide the titles and categories of documents for students to practice content-based recommendation algorithms. The example codes that we offer adopt TF-IDF (Term Frequency – Inverse Document Frequency) for feature selection and Cosine similarity to find the most similar items with user clicking before.

4.3 Other Recommendation Algorithms

There are plenty of possibilities for students to create other algorithms. For example, they can use publish time and access time to implement temporal recommendation systems; or from collaborative filtering and content-based recommendation, they can create many different kinds of hybrid recommendation systems. Further, to improve performance, it is natural for them to utilize new technologies like deep learning.

5 Discussion and Conclusion

In this paper, we introduce a refined dataset from the original Adressa dataset for training and evaluating recommender systems for news. The refined dataset contains selected users with high activity rates, and it has a much higher density than the previous dataset. We kept 9 most important attributes in the dataset.

This smaller but denser dataset is suitable for teaching. It was provided to students of recommender system courses for their course project for several years. In the future, we look forward to seeing more utility of it on education or research.

Acknowledgement. This work was carried out as part of the industry-led research project RecTech, project number 245469, supported by the Research Council of Norway's BIA innovation research program. We would like to thank Peng Liu and Xiaomeng Su for their extended support for the refined dataset, as well as Adresseavisen for providing the data.

References

1. Liu, J., Dolan, P., Pedersen, E.R.: Personalized news recommendation based on click behavior. In: Proceedings of the 15th International Conference on Intelligent User Interfaces, pp. 21–40. Association for Computing Machinery, Hong Kong, China (2010)
2. Das, A.S., et al.: Google news personalization: scalable online collaborative filtering. In: Proceedings of the 16th international Conference on World Wide Web, pp. 271–280. Association for Computing Machinery, Banff, Alberta, Canada (2007)
3. Gulla, J., et al.: The Intricacies of time in news recommendation. In: UMAP (2016)
4. Doctor, K.: Newsonomics: The New York Times puts personalization front and center—just For You (2019). https://www.niemanlab.org/2019/06/newsonomics-the-new-york-times-puts-personalization-front-and-center-just-for-you/. Accessed 19 May 2020
5. Kvalheim, H.: Norway's first fully personalized mobile news site (2016)
6. Özgöbek, O., Gulla, J., Erdur, C.: A survey on challenges and methods in news recommendation. In: WEBIST 2014-Proceedings of the 10th International Conference on Web Information Systems and Technologies, vol. 2, pp. 278–285 (2014)
7. Karimi, M., Jannach, D., Jugovac, M.: News recommender systems–survey and roads ahead. Inf. Process. Manag. **54**(6), 1203–1227 (2018)
8. Atle Gulla, J., Gunnar Auran, P., Magne Risvik, K.: Linguistics in large-scale web search. In: Andersson, B., Bergholtz, M., Johannesson, P. (eds.) NLDB 2002. LNCS, vol. 2553, pp. 218–222. Springer, Heidelberg (2002). https://doi.org/10.1007/3-540-36271-1_21
9. Brasethvik, T., Gulla, J.A.: A conceptual modeling approach to semantic document retrieval. In: Pidduck, A.B., Ozsu, M.T., Mylopoulos, J., Woo, C.C. (eds.) CAiSE 2002. LNCS, vol. 2348, pp. 167–182. Springer, Heidelberg (2002). https://doi.org/10.1007/3-540-47961-9_14
10. Solskinnsbakk, G., Gulla, J.A.: Combining ontological profiles with context in information retrieval. Data Knowl. Eng. **69**(3), 251–260 (2010)
11. Ingvaldsen, J.E., Özgöbek, Ö., Gulla, J.A.: Context-aware userdriven news recommendation. In: INRA@RecSys (2015)
12. Gulla, J.A., et al.: The Adressa dataset for news recommendation. In: Proceedings of the International Conference on Web Intelligence, pp. 1042–1048. Association for Computing Machinery, Leipzig, Germany (2017)

13. Wu, F., et al.: Mind: a large-scale dataset for news recommendation. In: ACL (2020)
14. Li, L., et al.: Unbiased offline evaluation of contextual-bandit-based news article recommendation algorithms. In: Proceedings of the Fourth ACM International Conference on Web Search and Data Mining, pp. 297–306. Association for Computing Machinery, Hong Kong, China (2011)
15. Garcin, F., Zhou, K., Faltings, B., Schickel, V.: Personalized news recommendation based on collaborative filtering (2012)
16. Özgöbek, O., Shabib, N., Gulla, J.: Data sets and news recommendation. CEUR Workshop Proc. **1181**, 5–12 (2014)

Exploring Thematic Coherence in Fake News

Martins Samuel Dogo$^{(\boxtimes)}$, Deepak P., and Anna Jurek-Loughrey

Queen's University Belfast, Belfast, UK
{mdogo01,a.jurek}@qub.ac.uk, deepaksp@acm.org

Abstract. The spread of fake news remains a serious global issue; understanding and curtailing it is paramount. One way of differentiating between deceptive and truthful stories is by analyzing their coherence. This study explores the use of topic models to analyze the coherence of cross-domain news shared online. Experimental results on seven cross-domain datasets demonstrate that fake news shows a greater thematic deviation between its opening sentences and its remainder.

Keywords: Fake news · Topic modeling · Coherence

1 Introduction

The impact of news on our daily affairs is greater than it has ever been. Fabrication and dissemination of falsehood have become politically lucrative endeavors, thereby harming public discourse and worsening political polarization [1]. These motivations have led to a complex and continuously evolving phenomenon mainly characterized by dis- and misinformation, commonly collectively referred to as fake news [2]. This denotes various kinds of false or unverified information, which may vary based on their authenticity, intention, and format [3]. Shu et al. [4] define it as "a news article that is intentionally and verifiably false."

The dissemination of fake news is increasing, and because it appears in various forms and self-reinforces [1, 3], it is difficult to erode. Therefore, there is an urgent need for increased research in understanding and curbing it. This paper considers fake news that appears in the form of long online articles and explores the extent of internal consistency within fake news vis-à-vis legitimate news. In particular, we run experiments to determine whether thematic deviations—i.e., a measure of how dissimilar topics discussed in different parts of an article are—between the opening and remainder sections of texts can be used to distinguish between fake and real news across different news domains.

1.1 Motivation

A recent study suggests that some readers may skim through an article instead of reading the whole content because they overestimate their political knowledge, while others may hastily share news without reading it fully, for emotional affirmation [5]. This presents bad actors with the opportunity of deftly interspersing news content with falsity.

I. Koprinska et al. (Eds.): ECML PKDD 2020 Workshops, CCIS 1323, pp. 571–580, 2020.
https://doi.org/10.1007/978-3-030-65965-3_40

Moreover, the production of fake news typically involves the collation of disjoint content and lacks a thorough editorial process [6].

Topics discussed in news pieces can be studied to ascertain whether the article thematically deviates between its opening and the rest of the story, or if it remains coherent throughout. Thematic analysis is useful here for two reasons. First, previous studies show that the coherence between units of discourse (such as sentences) in a document is useful for determining its veracity [6, 7]. Second, analysis of thematic deviation can identify general characteristics of fake news that persist across multiple news domains.

Although topics have been employed as features [8–10], they have not been applied to study the unique characteristics of fake news. Research efforts in detecting fake news through thematic deviation have thus far focused on spotting incongruences between pairs of headlines and body texts [11–14]. Yet, thematic deviation can also exist within the body text of a news item. Our focus is to examine these deviations to distinguish fake from real news.

To the best of the authors' knowledge, this is the first work that explores thematic deviations in the body text of news articles to distinguish between fake and legitimate news.

2 Related Work

The coherence of a story may be indicative of its veracity. For example, [7] demonstrated this by applying Rhetorical Structure Theory [15] to study the discourse of deceptive stories posted online. They found that a major distinguishing characteristic of deceptive stories is that they are disjunctive. Also, while truthful stories provide evidence and restate information, deceptive ones do not. This suggests that false stories may tend to thematically deviate more due to disjunction, while truthful stories are likely to be more coherent due to restatement. Similarly, [6] investigated the coherence of fake and real news by learning hierarchical structures based on sentence-level dependency parsing. Their findings also suggest that fake news documents are less coherent.

Topic models are unsupervised algorithms that aid the identification of themes discussed in large corpora. One example is Latent Dirichlet Allocation (LDA), which is a generative probabilistic model that aids the discovery of latent themes or topics in a corpus [16]. Vosoughi et al. [17] used LDA to show that false rumor tweets tend to be more novel than true ones. Novelty was evaluated using three measures: Information Uniqueness, Bhattacharyya Distance, and Kullback-Leibler Divergence. Likewise, [18] used LDA to assess the credibility of Twitter users by analyzing the topical divergence of their tweets to those of other users. They also assessed the veracity of users' tweets by comparing the topic distributions of new tweets against historically discussed topics. Divergence was computed using the Jensen-Shannon Divergence, Root Mean Squared Error, and Squared Error. Our work primarily differs from these two in that we analyze full-length articles instead of tweets.

3 Research Goal and Contributions

This research aims to assess the importance of internal consistency within articles as a high-level feature to distinguish between fake and real news stories across different domains. We set out to explore whether the opening segments of fake news thematically deviates from the rest of it, significantly more than in authentic news. We experiment with seven datasets which collectively cover a wide variety of news domains, from business to celebrity, to warfare. Deviations are evaluated by calculating the distance between the topic distribution of the opening part of an article, to that of its remainder. We take the first five sentences of an article as its opening segment.

Our contributions are summarized as follows:

1. We present new insights towards understanding the underlying characteristics of fake news, based on thematic deviations between the opening and remainder parts of news body text.
2. We carry out experiments on five cross-domain datasets. The results demonstrate the effectiveness of thematic deviation for distinguishing fake from real news.

4 Experiments

We hypothesize the following: *the opening sentences of a false news article will tend to thematically deviate more from the rest of it, as compared to an authentic article.* To test this hypothesis, we carried out experiments in the manner shown in Algorithm 1. We use Python and open-source packages for all computations.

Procedure. All articles (S_{bg}) are split into two parts: its first x^1 sentences, and the remaining y. Next, N topics are obtained from x and y using an LDA model trained using Gensim[2] on the entire dataset. For $i = (1, ..., m)$ topics, let $p_x = (p_{x1}, ..., p_{xm})$ and $p_y = (p_{y1}, ..., p_{ym})$ be two vectors of topic distributions, which denote the prevalence of a topic i in the opening text x and remainder y of an article, respectively. The following are metrics used to measure the topical divergence between parts x and y of an article:

- Chebyshev (D_{Ch}):

$$D_{Ch}\left(p_{xi}, p_{yi}\right) = \max_i \left|p_{xi} - p_{yi}\right| \tag{1}$$

- Euclidean (D_E):

$$D_E\left(p_{xi}, p_{yi}\right) = \left\|p_{xi} - p_{yi}\right\| = \sqrt{\sum_{i=1}^{m}\left(p_{xi} - p_{yi}\right)^2} \tag{2}$$

- Squared Euclidean (D_{SE}):

$$D_{SE}\left(p_{xi}, p_{yi}\right) = \sum_{i=1}^{m}\left(p_{xi} - p_{yi}\right)^2 \tag{3}$$

---

[1] We used only articles with at least $x + 1$ sentences.

[2] https://radimrehurek.com/gensim/.

Intuitively, Chebyshev distance is the greatest difference found between any two topics in x and y. The Euclidean distance measures how "far" the two topic distributions are from one another, while the Squared Euclidean distance is simply the square of that "farness".

Finally, the average and median values of each distance are calculated across all fake (S_f) and real (S_r) articles. We repeated these steps with varying values of N (from 10 to 200 topics) and x (from 1 to 5 sentences).

Algorithm 1. Corpora comparison procedure.

Data: A corpus $S_{bg} = S_f \cup S_r$ of full-length fake ($S_f = \{d_1^f, d_2^f, ..., d_F^f\}$) and real ($S_r = \{d_1^r, d_2^r, ..., d_R^r\}$) documents

Input: Pairs of first $l = [1, 2, ..., 5]$ sentences and remainder y of each fake ($d_i^f = \langle d_{i_x}^f, d_{i_y}^f \rangle$; $\left| d_{i_x}^f \right| = l$) and real article ($d_i^r = \langle d_{i_x}^r, d_{i_y}^r \rangle$; $\left| d_{i_x}^r \right| = l$); LDA model $\mathcal{M}_{bg}$ generated using S_{bg}; the number of topics $N \in \{10, 20, 50, 100, 150, 200\}$; divergence functions $\mathcal{D} \in \{D_{Ch}, D_E, D_{SE}\}$.

1: **foreach** $l = [1, 2, ..., 5]$ **do**
2:    **foreach** article $\langle d_{i_x}^f, d_{i_y}^f \rangle$ **do**
3:      get the distribution of N topics in $d_{i_x}^f$ and $d_{i_y}^f$ using $\mathcal{M}_{bg}$
4:      $T_{i_x}^f = (p_i^x, ..., p_N^x)$; $T_{i_y}^f = (p_i^y, ..., p_N^y)$
5:      get the distribution of N topics in $d_{i_x}^r$ and $d_{i_y}^r$ using $\mathcal{M}_{bg}$
6:      $T_{i_x}^r = (p_i^x, ..., p_N^x)$; $T_{i_y}^r = (p_i^y, ..., p_N^y)$
7:      $D_i^f = \mathcal{D}\left(T_{i_x}^f, T_{i_y}^f\right)$; $D_i^r \ \mathcal{D}\left(T_{i_x}^r, T_{i_y}^r\right)$
8:    **end**
9:    $D_{avg}^f = \text{average}(D_i^f \mid i \in \{1, ..., F\})$; $D_{avg}^r = \text{average}(D_i^r \mid i \in \{1, ..., R\})$
10:   $D_{med}^f = \text{median}(D_i^f \mid i \in \{1, ..., F\})$; $D_{med}^r = \text{median}(D_i^r \mid i \in \{1, ..., R\})$
11:   **return** $\{D_{avg}^f, D_{avg}^r, D_{med}^f, D_{med}^r\}$
12: **end**

Pre-processing. Articles are split into sentences using the NTLK[3] package. Each sentence is tokenized and lowercased to form a list of words, from which stop words are removed. Bigrams are then formed and added to the vocabulary. Next, each document is lemmatized using spaCy[4], and only noun, adjective, verb, and adverb lemmas are retained. A dictionary is formed by applying these steps to S_{bg}. Each document is converted into a bag-of-words (BoW) format, which is used to create an LDA model ($\mathcal{M}_{bg}$). Fake and real articles are subsequently pre-processed likewise (i.e., from raw text data to BoW format) before topics are extracted from them.

We consider the opening sentences of articles to be sufficient for capturing the lead or "opening theme" of the story, which will likely fall within the first paragraph. The first paragraph may in some cases be either too short or long for this, especially for fake

---

[3] https://www.nltk.org/.
[4] https://spacy.io/models/en/.

articles that often lack a proper structure. Overly short or lengthy texts will influence the extraction of topics more adversely than if a set number of sentences are used.

Datasets. Table 1 summarizes the datasets (after pre-processing) used in this study and lists the domains (as stated by the dataset provider) covered by each. An article's length (Avg. length) is measured by the number of words that remain after pre-processing. The article maximum lengths (Max. length) is measured in terms of the number of sentences. We use the following datasets:

- BuzzFeed-Webis Fake News Corpus 2016[5] (BuzzFeed-Web) [19]
- BuzzFeed Political News Data[6] (BuzzFeed-Political) [20]
- FakeNewsAMT + Celebrity (AMT + C) [21]
- Falsified and Legitimate Political News Database[7] (POLIT)
- George McIntire's fake news dataset (GMI)[8]
- University of Victoria's Information Security and Object Technology (ISOT)[9] Research Lab [22]
- Syrian Violations Documentation Centre (SVDC)[10] [23]

Evaluation. We evaluate differences in coherence of fake and real articles using the T-test at 5% significance level. The null hypothesis is that the mean coherence of fake and real news is equal. The alternative hypothesis is that the mean coherence of real news is greater than that of fake news. We expect that there will be a greater topic deviation in fake news and thus, its coherence will be lesser than that of real news.

5 Results and Discussion

Results of the experimental evaluation using the different divergence measures are shown in Table 2. We observe that fake news is generally likely to show greater thematic deviation (lesser coherence) than real news in all datasets. Table 3 shows the mean D_{Ch} deviations of fake and real articles across N = {10, 20, 30, 40, 50, 100, 150, 200} topics. Although results for AMT+C and BuzzFeed-Web are not statistically significant according to the T-test and therefore, do not meet our expectations, results for all other datasets are. Nonetheless, the mean and median values for fake news are lower than those of real news for these datasets. Table 3, which shows mean and median D_{Ch} deviations of fake and real articles across all values of N. Figure 1 shows mean and median results for comparing topics in the first five and the remaining sentences. Results for values of N not shown are similar (with D_{Ch} gradually decreasing as N increases).

[5] https://zenodo.org/record/1239675.
[6] https://github.com/BenjaminDHorne/fakenewsdata1.
[7] http://victoriarubin.fims.uwo.ca/news-verification/access-polit-false-n-legit-news-db-2016-2017/.
[8] https://github.com/GeorgeMcIntire/fake_real_news_dataset (accessed 5 November 2018).
[9] https://www.uvic.ca/engineering/ece/isot/.
[10] https://zenodo.org/record/2532642.

Table 1. Summary of datasets after pre-processing (f – fake, r – real).

Dataset (domain)	No. of fake	No. of real	Avg. length of sentences in words (f)	Avg. length of sentences in words (r)	Max. length (f)	Max. length (r)
AMT+C (business, education, entertainment, politics, sports, tech)	324	317	14.7	23.2	64	1,059
BuzzFeed-Political (politics)	116	127	18.9	43.9	76	333
BuzzFeed-Web (politics)	331	1,214	21.7	26.4	117	211
GMI (politics)	2,695	2,852	33.9	42.8	1,344	406
ISOT (government, politics)	19,324	16,823	18.0	20.3	289	324
POLIT (politics)	122	134	19.2	34.9	96	210
SVDC (conflict, war)	312	352	14.0	14.6	62	49

Table 2. Results of T-test evaluation based on different measures of deviation used.

Dataset	p-value (D_{Ch})	p-value (D_E)	p-value (D_{SE})
AMT+C	0.144	0.126	0.116
BuzzFeed-Political	0.0450	0.0147	0.0287
BuzzFeed-Web	0.209	0.209	0.207
GMI	0.0480	0.00535	0.0106
ISOT	0.00319	0.000490	0.000727
POLIT	0.000660	0.0000792	0.0000664
SVDC	0.000684	0.0000112	0.0000789

We found that comparing the first five sentences to the rest of the article yielded the best results (i.e., greatest disparity between fake and real deviations) for most datasets and measures. This is likely due to the first five sentences containing more information. For example, five successive sentences are likely to entail one another and contribute more towards a topic than a single sentence.

It is worth highlighting the diversity of datasets used here, in terms of domain, size, and the nature of articles. For example, the fake and real news in the SVDC dataset have a very similar structure. Both types of news were mostly written with the motivation to inform the reader on conflict-related events that took across Syria. However, fake articles are labeled as such primarily because the reportage (e.g., on locations and number of casualties) in them is insufficiently accurate.

Table 3. Mean and median D_{Ch} deviations of N ={10, 20, 30, 40, 50, 100, 150, 200} topics combined for fake and real news (f – fake, r – real).

Dataset	Mean D_{Ch}(f)	Mean D_{Ch}(r)	Median D_{Ch}(f)	Median D_{Ch}(r)
AMT+C	0.2568	0.2379	0.2438	0.2285
BuzzFeed-Political	0.2373	0.2149	0.2345	0.2068
BuzzFeed-Web	0.2966	0.2812	0.2863	0.2637
GMI	0.4580	0.4241	0.4579	0.4222
ISOT	0.3372	0.2971	0.3369	0.2989
POLIT	0.2439	0.1939	0.2416	0.1894
SVDC	0.2975	0.2517	0.2934	0.2435

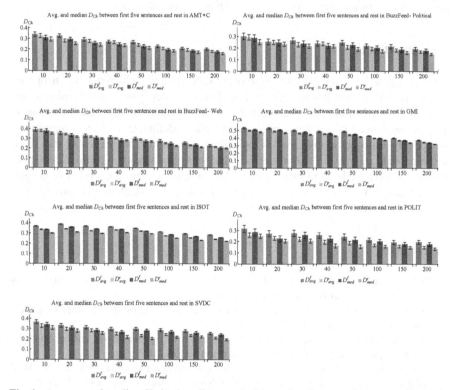

Fig. 1. Average and median Chebyshev distances in fake and real news, when comparing topics in the first five sentences to the rest of each article. Error bars show 95% confidence interval.

To gain insight into possible causes of greater deviation in fake news, we qualitatively inspected the five most and least diverging fake and real articles (according to D_{Ch}). We also compared a small set of low and high number of topics ($N \leq 30$ and $N \geq 100$). We observed that fake openings tend to be shorter, vaguer, and less congruent with the rest of the text. By contrast, real news openings generally give a better narrative background to the rest of the story.

Although the writing style in fake news is sometimes unprofessional, this is an unlikely reason for the higher deviations in fake news. Both fake and real news try to expand on the opening lead of the story, with more context and explanation. Indeed, we observed that real news tends to have longer sentences, which give more detailed information about a story, and are more narrative. It can be argued that the reason behind this is that fake articles are designed to get readers' attention, whereas legitimate ones are written to inform the reader. For instance, social media posts which include a link to an article are sometimes displayed with a short snippet of the article's opening text or its summary. This section can be designed to capture readers' attention.

It also conceivable that a bigger team of people working to produce a fake piece may contribute to its vagueness. They may input different perspectives that diversify the story and makes it less coherent. This may be compared to real news, whereby there typically are one or two professional writers and therefore, better coherence.

6   Conclusion

Fake news and deceptive stories tend to open with sentences which may be incoherent with the rest of the text. It is worth exploring if the consistency of fake and real news can distinguish between the two. Accordingly, we investigated the thematic deviations of seven cross-domain fake and real news using topic modeling. Our findings suggest that the opening sentences of fake articles topically deviate more from the rest of the article, as compared to real news. The next step is to find possible reasons behind these deviations through in-depth analyses of topics. In conclusion, this paper presents valuable insights into thematic differences between fake and authentic news, which may be exploited for fake news detection.

References

1. Waldman, A.E.: The marketplace of fake news. Univ. Pennsylvania J. Const. Law **20**, 846–869 (2018). https://scholarship.law.upenn.edu/jcl/vol20/iss4/3
2. Wardle, C.: Fake News. It's Complicated. First Draft (2017). https://firstdraftnews.org/fake-news-complicated/. Accessed 24 Jan 2019
3. Zhou, X., Zafarani, R.: Fake news: a survey of research, detection methods, and opportunities (2018). http://arxiv.org/abs/1812.00315. Accessed 10 Nov 2019
4. Shu, K., Sliva, A., Wang, S., Tang, J., Liu, H.: Fake news detection on social media. ACM SIGKDD Explor. Newsl. **19**(1), 22–36 (2017). https://doi.org/10.1145/3137597.3137600
5. Anspach, N.M., Jennings, J.T., Arceneaux, K.: A little bit of knowledge: facebook's news feed and self-perceptions of knowledge. Res. Polit. **6**(1) (2019). https://doi.org/10.1177/2053168018816189
6. Karimi, H., Tang, J.: Learning hierarchical discourse-level structure for fake news detection. In: Proceedings of the 2019 Conference of the North, pp. 3432–3442 (2019). https://doi.org/10.18653/v1/n19-1347
7. Rubin, V.L., Lukoianova, T.: Truth and deception at the rhetorical structure level. J. Assoc. Inf. Sci. Technol. **66**(5), 905–917 (2015). https://doi.org/10.1002/asi.23216

8. Das Bhattacharjee, S., Talukder, A., Balantrapu, B.V.: Active learning based news veracity detection with feature weighting and deep-shallow fusion. In: Proceedings - 2017 IEEE International Conference on Big Data, Big Data 2017, vol. Jan. 2018, pp. 556–565 (2018). https://doi.org/10.1109/bigdata.2017.8257971

9. Benamira, A., Devillers, B., Lesot, E., Ray, A.K., Saadi, M., Malliaros, F.D.: Semi-supervised learning and graph neural networks for fake news detection, pp. 568–569 (2019). https://hal.archives-ouvertes.fr/hal-02334445/. Accessed 29 Nov 2019

10. Li, S., et al.: Stacking-based ensemble learning on low dimensional features for fake news detection. In: Proceedings - 17th IEEE International Conference on Smart City and 5th IEEE International Conference on Data Science and Systems, HPCC/SmartCity/DSS 2019, pp. 2730–2735 (2019). https://doi.org/10.1109/hpcc/smartcity/dss.2019.00383

11. Chen, Y., Conroy, N.J., Rubin, V.L.: Misleading online content: recognizing clickbait as 'false news'. In: WMDD 2015 - Proceedings of the ACM Workshop on Multimodal Deception Detection, co-located with ICMI 2015, pp. 15–19 (2015). https://doi.org/10.1145/2823465.2823467

12. Sisodia, D.S.: Ensemble learning approach for clickbait detection using article headline features. Inf. Sci. **22**(2019), 31–44 (2019). https://doi.org/10.28945/4279

13. Ferreira, W., Vlachos, A.: Emergent: a novel data-set for stance classification. In: 2016 Conference of the North American Chapter of the Association for Computational Linguistics: Human Language Technologies, NAACL HLT 2016 - Proceedings of the Conference, pp. 1163–1168 (2016). https://doi.org/10.18653/v1/n16-1138

14. Yoon, S., et al.: Detecting incongruity between news headline and body text via a deep hierarchical encoder. In: Proceedings of AAAI Conference on Artificial Intelligence, vol. 33, pp. 791–800 (2019). https://doi.org/10.1609/aaai.v33i01.3301791

15. Mann, W.C., Thompson, S.A.: Rhetorical structure theory: toward a functional theory of text organization. Text – Interdiscip. J. Study Discourse **8**(3), 243–281 (1988). https://doi.org/10.1515/text.1.1988.8.3.243

16. Blei, D.M., Ng, A.Y., Jordan, M.I.: Latent Dirichlet allocation. J. Mach. Learn. Res. **3**(Jan), 993–1022 (2003). Accessed 01 Dec (2019). http://jmlr.csail.mit.edu/papers/v3/blei03a.html

17. Vosoughi, S., Roy, D., Aral, S.: The spread of true and false news online. Science **359**(6380), 1146–1151 (2018). https://doi.org/10.1126/science.aap9559

18. Ito, J., Toda, H., Koike, Y., Song, J., Oyama, S.: Assessment of tweet credibility with LDA features. In: WWW 2015 Companion - Proceedings of the 24th International Conference on World Wide Web, pp. 953–958 (2015). https://doi.org/10.1145/2740908.2742569

19. Potthast, M., Kiesel, J., Reinartz, K., Bevendorff, J., Stein, B.: A stylometric inquiry into hyperpartisan and fake news. In: ACL 2018 - 56th Annual Meeting of the Association for Computational Linguistics, Proceedings of the Conference (Long Papers), vol. 1, pp. 231–240 (2018). https://doi.org/10.18653/v1/p18-1022

20. Horne, B.D., Adali, S.: This just in: fake news packs a lot in title, uses simpler, repetitive content in text body, more similar to satire than real news (2017). http://arxiv.org/abs/1703.09398

21. Pérez-Rosas, V., Kleinberg, B., Lefevre, A., Mihalcea, R.: Automatic detection of fake news. In: Proceedings of the 27th International Conference on Computational Linguistics, pp. 3391–3401 (2018). https://www.aclweb.org/anthology/C18-1287/. Accessed 07 Dec 2019

22. Ahmed, H., Traore, I., Saad, S.: Detection of online fake news using n-gram analysis and machine learning techniques. In: Traore, I., Woungang, I., Awad, A. (eds.) ISDDC 2017. LNCS, vol. 10618, pp. 127–138. Springer, Cham (2017). https://doi.org/10.1007/978-3-319-69155-8_9

23. Abu Salem, F., Al Feel, R., Elbassuoni, S., Jaber, M., Farah, M.: Dataset for fake news and articles detection (2019). https://doi.org/10.5281/zenodo.2532642

Media Bias in German News Articles: A Combined Approach

Timo Spinde[1,2]([✉]) [iD], Felix Hamborg[1] [iD], and Bela Gipp[1,2] [iD]

[1] University of Konstanz, Konstanz, Germany
{timo.spinde,felix.hamborg,bela.gipp}@uni-konstanz.de
[2] University of Wuppertal, Wuppertal, Germany
{spinde,gipp}@uni-wuppertal.de

Abstract. Slanted news coverage, also called media bias, can heavily influence how news consumers interpret and react to the news. Models to identify and describe biases have been proposed across various scientific fields, focusing mostly on English media. In this paper, we propose a method for analyzing media bias in German media. We test different natural language processing techniques and combinations thereof. Specifically, we combine an IDF-based component, a specially created bias lexicon, and a linguistic lexicon. We also flexibly extend our lexica by the usage of word embeddings. We evaluate the system and methods in a survey (N = 46), comparing the bias words our system detected to human annotations. So far, the best component combination results in an F_1 score of 0.31 of words that were identified as biased by our system and our study participants. The low performance shows that the analysis of media bias is still a difficult task, but using fewer resources, we achieved the same performance on the same task than recent research on English. We summarize the next steps in improving the resources and the overall results.

Keywords: Media bias · News slant · News bias · Content analysis · Frame analysis

1 Introduction

Media bias, i.e., slanted news coverage, can change the public opinion on any topic heavily [5]. Many approaches to identify such bias exist, however, no automated methods aiming to identify bias in German news texts are available. The objective of this work is to propose, implement and evaluate a system capable of detecting bias words in German news articles. The key contribution of this poster is our media bias identification approach, which includes five components: (i) An IDF-based component, which utilizes word frequencies over a set of documents. (ii) A sentiment-based component using multiple dictionaries. (iii) A component that uses a dictionary of bias words based on semantic models. Two other components that have not yet been implemented are (iv) a component

© The Author(s) 2020
I. Koprinska et al. (Eds.): ECML PKDD 2020 Workshops, CCIS 1323, pp. 581–590, 2020.
https://doi.org/10.1007/978-3-030-65965-3_41

that uses SVM with cues of historical linguistic development, and (v) a network analysis component. Moreover, we provide a summary of characteristics of sentiment in German language and the cultural development of words in specific classes, such as pejorative derivatives, from a linguistic perspective.

The research described in this paper is based on a recent poster publication [17]. In contrast to the poster, the paper at hand elaborates in more detail on the methodology, results, especially considering the single components, and future improvements of our system.

The main shortcomings of prior work are a dependency on manually created resources, a small number of polarity categories and a focus on only specific topics. First, some of these methods identify media bias using predefined dictionaries, requiring manual and effortful creation and adaption. Second, the possible emotional influence of the detected bias words has not been analyzed on a computational scale. Third, limited research has been conducted on the combination of existing approaches. Except from component (v), all methods mentioned above have already been implemented in other research, but we are especially taking an attempt in combining them.

In Sect. 3, we describe the five components in further detail. Finally, we show the evaluation methodology and offer an outlook on future work.

2   Related Work

We first describe key concepts from linguistics, relevant in the context of media bias and framing. Then we give a brief overview of related methods that aim to identify media bias in news items.

2.1   Linguistics

Linguistic cues are important properties when identifying either framing (a particular point of view linked to subjective words or phrases) or epistemological bias (subtly focusing on the believability of a proposition) [16]. While a summary of cues is shown in [11], not all such resources are available in German.

Word embeddings can be used to find semantically similar words for any given word [6]. For example, in a word embeddings space, the vectors of the following words would typically be close to each other: *Flüchtling* (refugee), *Migrant* (migrant), *Asylant* (Asylum seeker) or *Geflüchteter* (displaced person). The words are, even though legally not completely synonymous, very similar.

2.2   Media Bias Detection Systems

In the following, we give a brief overview of relevant media bias detection systems. Linguistic cues are not the only way to solve the task: multiple approaches exist, mainly devised in computer science. A first way of identifying media bias is proposed by Ogawa et al., who use a stakeholder mining mechanism trying to analyze bias backgrounds [15]. The result of the analysis is a relationship graph which groups stakeholders who share mutual interests (and generally describes their interests), which can be especially interesting for another network analysis.

In 2013, Recasens et al. proposed an approach to identify bias words in Wikipedia [16]. They compiled a list of helpful linguistic resources and utilized them as features to detect the bias words from Wikipedias' revised sentence history. Baumer et al. developed a prototype to identify framing [2]. The linguistic components they classified as "dictionaries" are what Recasens et al. proposed, but extended by features of theoretical literature on framing. Hamborg et al. proposed an approach that aims to identify bias by word choice and labeling (see the example in Sect. 2.1) [6]. They used word embeddings to resolve broad coreferences across a set of news articles reporting on the same event.

Hube et al. addressed biased language statements in Wikipedia articles [8]. Their approach is mainly based on building a context-related set of word semantics, which identifies the relevant language in a certain topic sphere. For that, they utilized a right-leaning adaptation of Wikipedia, Conservapedia, to train word embeddings. With these, they manually selected 100 potential bias words and computed for every word the 20 most similar words, to create a certain bias word dictionary. With this resource, they then identified biased sentences by calculating bias word ratios and contexts. By furthermore adding the linguistic features by Recasens et al. [16], they achieved an F_1 score of 69%. Their findings also suggested that, on crowdsourced evaluation data, the bias words were only very helpful in finding the most biased sentences, which might be due to the Conservapedia database being rather extreme.

The main shortcomings of prior work are a dependency on manually created resources, a small number of polarity categories, a focus on only specific topics, or a non-scalable evaluation. First, some of these methods identify media bias using predefined dictionaries or grammatical features, requiring the manual and effortful creation and adaption of dictionaries. Second, the possible emotional influence of the detected bias words has not been analyzed on a computational scale. Common polarity features only consist of three categories positive, negative, and neutral. Third, limited research has been conducted on methods that combine existing approaches, leaving out one possibly huge way to further overall performance improvement. Lastly, a primary and well-surveyed common data set to address all of these word- and sentence-oriented bias types could make a more reliable evaluation possible. By addressing the previously mentioned issues, the analysis of media bias using other methods could benefit: e.g., network analysis provides promising practices to model and visualize the relations and underlying information of text documents, enabling statistical modeling of media bias [13]. Section 3 describes our approach, which addresses these four issues. It is not dependent on single topics or resources and will be scalable to any sort of related task.

3   Methodology

The methodology proposed in this paper consists of different steps, which are depicted as colored boxes in Fig. 1.

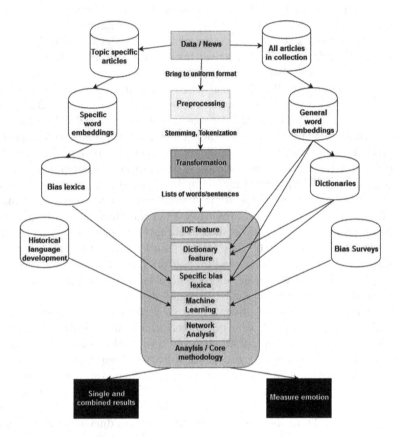

Fig. 1. System architecture (Color figure online)

We have collected news articles from four German news outlets, *Süddeutsche Zeitung* (65,000 articles), *TAZ* (500,000), *Südkurier* (286,700), and *BILD* (2,000 articles reporting on the refugee crisis). To enlarge the data set for the training of word embeddings, we used a collection of articles by Bojar et al. [3], which contains almost 90M sentences from over 40 sources, including the *Augsburger Allgemeine* and *Der Westen*. We preprocessed all files into a uniform format. To train our model of word embeddings, we used all articles and the collection of sentences and compared which words are more likely to appear.

The automated analysis workflow consists of five components, of which the following three are implemented in our prototype: an IDF-based component (based on the idea by Lim et al. [11]), a combined dictionary-based component (based on the idea by Recasens et al. [16]), and a component based on semantically created bias dictionary (based on the idea by Hube et al. [8]). We experimented with different combinations of these components, e.g., to determine if a word was identified as biased by one component but not by the other (if so, we classified it as bias word). One of the two components that are not yet implemented will use SVM to analyze historic linguistic cues. Apart from connotation, context and emotion, some words have developed linguistic patterns playing a role in gender discussions, but also in general sentiment. The German word *Flüchtlinge* is one example. Its general impression is influenced by the derivational component *-ling*, which frequently is and has been origin for ameliorating replacement constructions, e.g. *Sonderling, Schönling* or *Schwächling*. Official discussions, however, lead into the direction that such derivatives should generally be replaced by participle derivative constructions like *Geflüchtete*[7]. Our literature review yielded that no central collection of such rules or any large scale analysis of their real effects exists. Evaluating their impact and gathering similar rules will be a major future task. The second component that is not yet implemented relies on network analysis. Network structures can effectively represent not only the documents or news themselves but also model relations and correlations. A variety of nodes, edges, and attributes come to mind, such as newspapers, authors, emotional scores, bias words, content, year or time of publication and topic. With a sufficiently large data set and further reliable methodology to detect the actual values, topic- and context-dependent patterns could be modeled. Inherent characteristics would be centrality, clustering, and betweenness.

The first component uses IDF scores to measure whether a term is common or rare across the corpus. Thus, it serves as a dictionary-independent component to identify bias words. This way, we aim to find rare words in the collection of articles reporting on the same event. Lim et al. propose that, for such a set of news, words with high IDF scores are most likely to be biased words [11]. IDF scores were first calculated among the whole set of articles to be analyzed. We clustered the documents into the even more similar ones by using affinity propagation (which is a state-of-the-art clustering algorithm [20]), and analyzed again. This approach has not been applied in the media bias context within other literature. Therefore, we evaluated the first experimental results for both combinations of steps: IDF scores over all articles and of only the most similar ones due to different thresholds.

We based the second component mainly on a linguistic lexicon, containing factive and assertive verbs, entailments, hedges, subjective intensifiers, and one-sided terms [16]. We use the German Linguistic Inquiry and Word Count (LIWC) dictionary, published by Wolf et al. [22]. As especially slang and sociolect words are excluded, we include a separate dictionary by El-Assady et al. [9]. In a final step, we also extend the dictionary by assertive verbs, scraped from two sources: The *Online-Wortschatz-Informationssystem Deutsch* (OWID), a dictionary for corpus-based lexicography of contemporary German [14], and a collection by Edeltraud Winkler from 2007 [21].

With these resources, words were classified as bias words if they matched with any dictionary entry. To improve performance, words were also seen as biased if one of their two most similar terms, as modeled by the word embeddings described before, matched. The dictionary, primarily because it is based on the LIWC, gives an excellent opportunity to measure emotional, social, or psychological reactions to words [10].

The third component uses a topic-specific bias dictionary, based on a separate data set and word embeddings. To create such a dictionary, seed words are extracted and used to retrieve other bias words. The idea is, as shown in [8], to use word vectors from documents which "are expected to have a high density of bias words." For each 10-word batch in an initial manually selected list, the 20 most similar words are retrieved and again merged into one list, which hence contains 200 higher potential bias words. This process is then iterated a second time: the 200 words are used as new seed words to extract another 20 most similar words among batches of 10, which leads to an overall of 400 bias words. The full bias dictionary is then added to the dictionary described in the previous section. The overlap was 42%, so most of these bias terms were not previously included. The word embeddings for this first prototype were based on a 2000 article collection from the *Bild* news outlet, which uses rather strong language and is hence more likely to contain bias words than a more neutral medium [1]. A random 20 word sample of the lexicon can be seen in Fig. 2. The German words are all given in their stemmed version, with an English translation to give a better impression of the meaning. Even though there exist some exceptions, most of the words seem very plausible for inducing bias.

schaem* (to be ashamed), schlagzeil* (headline), schwerverbrech* (dangerous criminal), schwerwieg* (difficult), shishabar* (Shisha Bar), staatsregi* (government), straffaell* (delinquent), streng* (severe/strict), stroemt* (to swarm), toet* (to kill), tragisch* (tragic), ueberfordert* (overstrained), unbehelligt* (unmolested), ungebor* (unborn), unterstuetzt* (to support), unwahrschein* (unlikely), verbrech* (crime), verhind* (to prevent), verletzt* (to hurt), versteht* (to understand)

Fig. 2. Random sample of the newly built bias lexicon

4   Evaluation

To evaluate the approach, it was necessary to build a ground-truth data set which exhibits words that humans identify as bias words in a text with news characteristics. We conducted a test, in which we asked 46 participants (mostly students aged between 15–30 years, of balanced gender, from various study programs but without linguistic background, and consuming news daily while not intentionally comparing different media sources) to read two or three news articles, depending on the text length. The same group of articles has been shown to four persons.

For each text, we asked them to highlight bias words, i.e., words they "felt were inducing an assessment." We used a data set of 40 manually selected articles from *Bild, Junge Welt, Frankfurter Allgemeine Zeitung, Frankfurter Rundschau, Compact Online, PI-News, NachDenkSeiten* and *RT online*, all published from 2015 to the end of 2018. The participants made 718 annotations in total. Only words that were at least mentioned by 2 of the 4 persons in each group were kept, which reduced them to 432 bias words used in the evaluation. The data set was then used to determine the accuracy of the different components combined and individually. As baseline components, we used an IDF component and random guessing that selected every word as bias word with a 50% chance. The extended dictionary component, supplemented by the newly created bias dictionary, performed best ($F_1 = 0.31$). It outperformed the pure IDF component by 0.14 and random guessing by 0.26. In similar work by Recasens et al. [16], they achieved an overall F_1 score of 0.34, however using the more sophisticated dictionaries that are available for English language. On nouns, verbs, and adjectives, it correctly identified around half of the words, even though false positive rates for nouns and verbs were still relatively high. For adjectives, we achieved an F_1 score of over 0.40. General word embeddings mostly did not result in any improvement for all of the components and their combinations. It seems that the assumption that words similar to bias words are naturally also bias words did not hold. Overall F_1 score results are shown in Table 1. It will be a major future research direction to not only improve the components but also to create a larger and extensively tested evaluation data set.

Table 1. All evaluation results of the bias word detection, with precision/recall/F_1 score per cell

	Random guessing (average)	Pure IDF	IDF based on article clustering
Without word embeddings	0.04 / 0.04 / 0.04	0.09 / 0.69 / 0.17	0.24 / 0.35 / 0.25
	Pure Bias dictionary component (Only *Bild*)	Extended Dictionary + Bias Lexicon component	All combined
Without word embeddings	0.27 / 0.12 / 0.15	**0.26 / 0.43 / 0.31**	0.12 / 0.79 / 0.20
With word embeddings	0.20 / 0.21 / 0.18	0.23 / 0.45 / 0.30	0.12 / 0.79 / 0.20

We applied the best performing component in three small case studies to give insights into the potential of the overall approach. While analyzing newspapers within three topics (refugees in general, the 2018 Chemnitz protests [4] and the refugee politics of Viktor Orbán [19]), our proposed approach was able to identify general tendencies in political classifications of German news media [12].

From a qualitative perspective, some of the words in our lexicon were never identified as biased. The verb 'to understand', given in the lexicon sample in Fig. 2, is a good example. It appears that, even though we introduced many words that can be seen as potential bias words, this does not apply for all of them. As in the work by Hube et al. [8], we did not filter the words we added using the methodology in our third component. In the future, we plan to analyze the characteristics of each of the newly found potential bias word, to reduce the number of false positives.

5   Conclusion and Outlook

This paper proposed a work-in-progress approach to identify media bias words in German news texts. Moreover, the approach capably identifies emotion markers. The approach currently implements three components: an IDF-based component, selecting terms based on their frequency among a given corpus; a dictionary-based component, for which we merged and linked four sources of emotional and linguistic terms; and lastly a topic-dependent bias word dictionary that we created using word embeddings, calculated over a set of articles from the newspaper *Bild*. We plan to make our code and resources publicly available under an open-access license, but are currently verifying licenses of the included dictionaries.

We have compared the performance of our components with each other, based on an evaluation data set created using a bias word survey with 46 participants, each of them reading and highlighting words in up to three articles. We find that the dictionary component, combined with the topic-dependent bias word dictionary, performed best ($F_1 = 0.31$, $P = 0.43$, $R = 0.26$). When considering only adjectives, F_1 was 0.41. Integration of word embeddings did not lead to higher accuracy, i.e., $F_1 = 0.30$. Furthermore, we conducted a case study, which showed that the emotional detection function of the approach could already detect presumed differences between major German newspapers, such as *Bild*, *Frankfurter Rundschau* or *TAZ*. Despite the difficulty of detecting media bias, even for humans, we think our approach is a first step towards automatically analyzing bias in German media. Upcoming research will focus on improving the underlying model by enlarging the dictionary, adding more bias dictionaries for individual newspapers, training more reliable word embedding models, gathering a larger amount of data and especially integrating context. A more extensive evaluation, gathering a more precise ground truth, will also be essential. We will test two features for further improvements: machine learning using human bias classifications and historic rules of language development as well as a network analysis incorporating the context of documents. It could also be interesting to try to find out how we could show and visualize our results best [18]. Ultimately, our goal is to identify bias wording automatically and to understand the underlying emotions in a greater context.

Acknowledgments. This work was supported by the Hanns-Seidel-Foundation and the Federal Ministry of Education and Research of Germany.

References

1. Anhäuser, M.: Welche Medien stehen wo, welche sind verlässlich? (Update 22.2.) de-DE, February 2017. Accessed 26 Jan 2020
2. Baumer, E., et al.: Testing and comparing computational approaches for identifying the language of framing in political news. In: Proceedings of the 2015 Conference of the North American Chapter of the Association for Computational Linguistics: Human Language Technologies, pp. 1472–1482 (2015). https://doi.org/10.3115/v1/N15-1171
3. Bojar, O., et al.: Findings of the 2014 workshop on statistical machine translation. In: Proceedings of the Ninth Workshop on Statistical Machine Translation, pp. 12–58 (2014). https://doi.org/10.3115/v1/W14-3302
4. Grunert, J.: Chemnitz: Der Abend, an dem der Rechtsstaat aufgab. de- DE. In: Die Zeit, August 2018. Accessed 26 Jan 2020
5. Hamborg, F., Donnay, K., Gipp, B.: Automated identification of media bias in news articles: an interdisciplinary literature review. Int. J. Digit. Libr. **20**(4), 391–415 (2018). https://doi.org/10.1007/s00799-018-0261-y
6. Hamborg, F., Zhukova, A., Gipp, B.: Automated identification of media bias by word choice and labeling in news articles. In: Proceedings of the ACM/IEEE Joint Conference on Digital Libraries (JCDL), June 2019. https://doi.org/10.1109/JCDL.2019.00036
7. Harnisch, R.: Das generische Maskulinum schleicht zurück. Zur pragmatischen Remotivierung eines grammatischen Markers. In: Formen und Funktionen. Morphosemantik und grammatische Konstruktion, pp. 159–174 (2016)
8. Hube, C., Fetahu, B.: Detecting biased statements in Wikipedia. In: Companion of the the Web Conference 2018 on the Web Conference 2018. International World Wide Web Conferences Steering Committee, pp. 1779–1786 (2018). https://doi.org/10.1145/3184558.3191640
9. Jawale, M., et al.: Interactive visual analysis of transcribed multi-party discourse. In: The 55th Annual Meeting of the Association for Computational Linguistics, ACL 2017 pp. 49–54 (2017). https://doi.org/10.18653/v1/P17-4009
10. Kahn, J.H., et al.: Measuring emotional expression with the Linguistic Inquiry and Word Count. Am. J. Psychol. 263–286 (2007). https://doi.org/10.2307/20445398
11. Lim, S., Jatowt, A., Yoshikawa, M.: Towards bias inducing word detection by linguistic cue analysis in news. In: DEIM Forum 2018 C1-3 (2018)
12. Magazin, E.F.: Politisch meinungsbildende Zeitungen und Zeitschriften: Die Übersicht. de, July 2018. Accessed 26 Jan 2020
13. Martin, M.K., Pfeffer, J., Carley, K.M.: Network text analysis of conceptual overlap in interviews, newspaper articles and keywords. Soc. Netw. Anal. Min. **3**(4), 1165–1177 (2013). https://doi.org/10.1007/s13278-013-0129-5
14. Müller-Spitzer, C.: OWID - a dictionary net for corpus-based lexicography of contemporary German. In: Proceedings of the 14th EURALEX International Congress. In: Dykstra, A., Schoonheim, T. (eds.) Leeuwarden/Ljouwert, pp. 445–452. Fryske Akademy, The Netherlands, July 2010
15. Ogawa, T., Yoshikawa, M.: News bias analysis based on stakeholder mining. IEICE Trans. Inf. Syst. **94**(3), 578–586 (2011). https://doi.org/10.1587/transinf.E94.D.578
16. Recasens, M., Danescu-Niculescu-Mizil, C., Jurafsky, D.: Linguistic models for analyzing and detecting biased language. In: Proceedings of the 51st Annual Meeting of the Association for Computational Linguistics (Volume 1: Long Papers), vol. 1, pp. 1650–1659 (2013)

17. Spinde, T., Hamborg, F., Gipp, B.: An integrated approach to detect media bias in German news articles. In: Proceedings of the ACM/IEEE Joint Conference on Digital Libraries (JCDL), August 2020. https://doi.org/10.1145/3383583.3398585
18. Spinde, T., et al.: Enabling news consumers to view and understand biased news coverage: a study on the perception and visualization of media bias. In: Proceedings of the ACM/IEEE Joint Conference on Digital Libraries (JCDL), August 2020. https://doi.org/10.1145/3383583.3398619
19. Traynor, I.: Migration crisis: Hungary PM says Europe in grip of madness. en-GB. In: The Guardian, September 2015
20. Wang, L., et al.: Affinity propagation clustering algorithm based on largescale data-set. Int. J. Comput. Appl. 1–6 (2018). https://doi.org/10.1080/1206212X.2018.1425184
21. Winkler, E.: DerWortschatzausschnitt der deutschen Kommunikationsverben- eine empirische Bestandsaufnahme. In: Handbuch deutscher Kommunikationsverben, pp. 25–71 (2007)
22. Wolf, M., et al.: Computergestützte quantitative Textanalyse: Äquivalenz und Robustheit der deutschen Version des Linguistic Inquiry and Word Count. Diagnostica **54**(2), 85–98 (2008). https://doi.org/10.1026/0012-1924.54.2.85

On the Coherence of Fake News Articles

Iknoor Singh[1], Deepak P.[2(✉)], and Anoop K.[3]

[1] University of Sheffield, Sheffield, UK
iknoor.ai@gmail.com
[2] Queen's University Belfast, Belfast, UK
deepaksp@acm.org
[3] University of Calicut, Thenhipalam, India
anoopk_dcs@uoc.ac.in

Abstract. The generation and spread of fake news within new and online media sources is emerging as a phenomenon of high societal significance. Combating them using data-driven analytics has been attracting much recent scholarly interest. In this computational social science study, we analyze the textual coherence of fake news articles vis-a-vis legitimate ones. We develop three computational formulations of textual coherence drawing upon the state-of-the-art methods in natural language processing and data science. Two real-world datasets from widely different domains which have fake/legitimate article labellings are then analyzed with respect to textual coherence. We observe apparent differences in textual coherence across fake and legitimate news articles, with fake news articles consistently scoring lower on coherence as compared to legitimate news ones. While the relative coherence shortfall of fake news articles as compared to legitimate ones form the main observation from our study, we analyze several aspects of the differences and outline potential avenues of further inquiry.

1 Introduction

The spread of *fake news* is increasingly being recognized as a global issue of enormous significance. The phenomenon of fake news, or disinformation disguised as news, started gaining rampant attention around the 2016 US presidential elections [2]. While politics remains the domain which attracts most scholarly interest in studying the influence of fake news [7], the impact of alternative facts on economic [12] and healthcare [28] sectors are increasingly getting recognized. Of late, the news ecosystem has evolved from a small set of regulated and trusted sources to numerous online news sources and social media. Such new media sources come with limited liability for disinformation, and thus are easy vehicles for fake news. Data science methods for fake news detection within social media such as Twitter has largely focused on leveraging the social network and temporal propagation information such as response and retweet traces and their temporal build-up; the usage of the core content information within the tweet has been shallow. In fact, some recent techniques (e.g., [32]) achieve state-of-the-art performance without using any content features whatsoever. The

I. Koprinska et al. (Eds.): ECML PKDD 2020 Workshops, CCIS 1323, pp. 591–607, 2020.
https://doi.org/10.1007/978-3-030-65965-3_42

task landscape, however, changes significantly when one moves from the realm of tweets to online news sources (such as those in Wikipedia's list[1]); the latter form a large fraction of fake news that are debunked within popular debunking sites such as Snopes[2]. Fake news within online news sources (e.g., [31]) are characterized by scanty network and propagation information; this is so since they are typically posted as textual articles within websites (as against originating from social media accounts), and their propagation happens on external social media websites through link sharing. Further, it is often necessary to bank on exploiting text information in order to develop fake news detection methods for scenarios such as those of a narrow scope (e.g., a local council election, or regional soccer game) even for Twitter, since the narrow scope would yield sparse and unreliable propagation information. Accordingly, there has been some recent interest in characterizing fake news in terms of various aspects of textual content. Previous work along this direction has considered satirical cues [26], expression of stance [4], rhetorical structures [25] and topical novelty [30].

In this computational social science study, we evaluate the textual coherence of fake news articles vis-a-vis legitimate ones. While our definitions of textual coherence will follow in a later section, it is quite intimately related to the notion of *cohesion* and *coherence* in language studies [21]. We choose to use the term *coherence* due to being more familiar to the computing community. Cohesion has been considered as an important feature for assessing the structure of text [21] and has been argued to play a role in writing quality [3,6,17].

2   Related Work

With our study being on coherence on fake news as assessed using their textual content, we provide some background into two streams of literature. First, we briefly summarize some recent literature around fake news with particular emphasis to studies directed at their lexical properties and those directed at non-lexical integrity and coherence. Second, we outline some natural language processing (NLP) techniques that we will use as technical building blocks to assess textual coherence.

Characteristics of Fake News: In the recent years, there have been abundant explorations into understanding the phenomenon of fake news. We now briefly review some selected work in the area. In probably the first in-depth effort at characterizing text content, [25] make use of rhetorical structure theory to understand differences in distribution of rhetorical relations across fake and legitimate news. They identify that disjunction and restatement appear much more commonly within legitimate stories. Along similar lines, [24] perform a stylometric analysis inquiring into whether writing style can help distinguish hyperpartisan news from others, and fake news from legitimate ones (two separate tasks).

---

[1] https://en.wikipedia.org/wiki/List_of_fake_news_websites.
[2] http://www.snopes.com.

While they identify significant differences in style between hyperpartisan and non-hyperpartisan articles, they observe that such differences are much more subdued across fake and legitimate news and are less likely to be useful for the latter task. In an extensive longitudinal study [30] to understand the propagation of fake and legitimate news, the authors leverage topic models [29] to quantify the divergence in character between them. They find that human users have an inherent higher propensity to spread fake news and attribute that propensity to users perceiving fake news as more novel in comparison to what they have seen in the near past, novelty assessed using topic models. Conroy et al. [5] summarize the research into identification of *deception cues* (or tell-tale characteristics of fake news) into two streams; viz., linguistic and network. While they do not make concrete observations on the relative effectiveness of the two categories of cues, they illustrate the utility of external knowledge sources such as Wikipedia in order to evaluate veracity of claims. Moving outside the realm of text analysis, there has been work on quantifying the differences between fake and legitimate news datasets in terms of image features [14]. They observe that there are often images along with microblog posts in Twitter, and these may hold cues as to the veracity of the tweet. With most tweets containing only one image each, they analyze the statistical properties of the dataset of images collected from across fake tweets, and compare/contrast them with those from a dataset of images from across legitimate tweets. They observe that the average visual coherence, i.e., the average pairwise similarities between images, is roughly the same across fake and legitimate image datasets; however, the fake image dataset has a larger dispersion of coherence scores around the mean. In devising our lexical coherence scores that we use in our study, we were inspired by the formulation of visual coherence scores as aggregates of pairwise similarities.

NLP Building Blocks for Coherence Assessments: In our study, we quantify lexical coherence by building upon advancements in three different directions in natural language processing. We briefly outline them herein.

Text Embeddings. Leveraging a dataset of text documents to learn distributional/vector representations of words, phrases and sentences has been a recent trend in natural language processing literature, due to pioneering work such as word2vec [19] and GloVe [23]. Such techniques, called word embedding algorithms, map each word in the document corpus to a vector of pre-specified dimensionality by utilizing the lexical proximity of words within the documents in which they appear. Thus, words that appear close to each other often within documents in the corpus would get mapped to vectors that are proximal to each other. These vectors have been shown to yield themselves to meaningful algebraic manipulation [20]. While word embeddings are themselves useful for many practical applications, techniques for deriving a single embedding/vector for larger text fragments such as sentences, paragraphs and whole documents [16] have been devised. That said, sentence embeddings/vectors formed by simply averaging the vectors corresponding to their component words, often dubbed average word2vec (e.g., [8]), often are found to be competitive with more sophisticated embeddings for text fragments. In our first computational model for lexical coherence assessment, we will use average word2vec vectors to represent sentences.

Explicit Semantic Analysis. Structured knowledge sources such as Wikipedia encompass a wide variety of high-quality manually curated and continuously updated knowledge. Using them for deriving meaningful representations of text data has been a direction of extensive research. A notable technique [9] along this direction attempts to represent text as vectors in a high dimensional space formed by Wikipedia concepts. Owing to using Wikipedia concepts explicitly, it is called explicit semantic analysis. In addition to generating vector representations that is then useful for a variety of text analytics tasks, these vectors are intuitively meaningful and easy to interpret due to the dimensions mapping directly to Wikipedia articles. This operates by processing Wikipedia articles in order to derive an inverted index for words (as is common in information retrieval engines [22]); these inverted indexes are then used to convert a text into a vector in the space of Wikipedia dimensions. Explicit Semantic Analysis, or ESA as it is often referred to, has been used for a number of different applications including those relating to computing semantic relatedness [27]. In our second computation approach, we will estimate document lexical coherence using sentence-level ESA vectors.

Entity Linkings. In the realm of news articles, entities from knowledge bases such as Wikipedia often get directly referenced in the text. For example, the fragments *UK* and *European Union* in *'UK is due to leave the European Customs Union in 2020'* may be seen to be intuitively referencing the respective entities, i.e., *United Kingdom* and *European Union*, in a knowledge base. Entity Linking [11] (*aka* named entity disambiguation) methodologies target to identify such references, effectively establishing a method to directly link text to a set of entities in a knowledge base; Wikipedia is the most popular knowledge base used for entity linking (e.g., [18]). Wikipedia entities may be thought of as being connected in a graph, edges constructed using hyperlinks in respective Wikipedia articles. Wikipedia graphs have been used for estimating semantic relatedness of text in previous work [34]. In short, converting a text document to a set of Wikipedia entities referenced within them (using entity linking methods) provides a semantic grounding for the text within the Wikipedia graph. We use such Wikipedia-based semantic representations in order to devise our third computational technique for measuring lexical coherence.

3   Research Objective and Computational Framework

Research Objective: Our core research objective is to study whether fake news articles differ from legitimate news articles along the dimension of *coherence as estimated using their textual content* using computational methods. We use the term coherence to denote the overall consistency of the document in adhering to core focus theme(s) or topic(s). In a way, it may be seen as contrary to the notion of dispersion or scatter. A document that switches themes many times over may be considered as one that lacks coherence.

3.1 Computational Framework for Lexical Coherence

For the purposes of our study, we need a computational notion of coherence. Inspired by previous work within the realm of images where visual coherence is estimated using aggregate of pairwise similarities [14], we model the coherence of an article as the average/mean of pairwise similarities between 'elements' of the article. Depending on the computational technique, we model elements as either sentences or Wikipedia entities referenced in the article. For the sentence-level structuring, for a document D comprising d_n sentences $\{s_1, s_2, \ldots, s_{d_n}\}$, coherence is outlined as:

$$C_{sent}(D) = \text{mean}\left\{ \text{sim}(rep(s_i), rep(s_j)) | s_i, s_j \in D, i \neq j \right\} \tag{1}$$

where $rep(s)$ denotes the representation of the sentence s, and $\text{sim}(.,.)$ is a suitable similarity function over the chosen representation. Two of our computational approaches use sentence level coherence assessments; they differ in the kind of representation, and consequently the similarity measure, that they use. The third measure uses entity linking to identify Wikipedia entities that are used in the text document. For a document D comprising references to d_m entities $\{e_1, e_2, \ldots, e_{d_m}\}$, coherence is computed as:

$$C_{ent}(D) = \text{mean}\left\{ \text{sim}(e_i, e_j) | e_i, e_j \in D, i \neq j \right\} \tag{2}$$

where $\text{sim}(.,.)$ is a suitable similarity measure between pairs of Wikipedia entities. We consistently use numeric vectors as representations of sentences and entities, and employ cosine similarity[3], the popular vector similarity measure, to compute similarities between vectors.

3.2 Profiling Fake and Legitimate News Using Lexical Coherence

Having outlined our framework for computing document-specific lexical coherence, we now describe how we use it in order to understand differences between fake and legitimate news articles. Let $\mathcal{F} = \{\ldots, F, \ldots\}$ and $\mathcal{L} = \{\ldots, L, \ldots\}$ be separate datasets of fake news and legitimate news articles respectively. Each document in $\mathcal{F}$ and $\mathcal{L}$ is subjected to the coherence assessment, yielding a single document-specific score (for each computational approach for quantifying lexical coherence). These yield separate sets of lexical coherence values for $\mathcal{F}$ and $\mathcal{L}$:

$$C(\mathcal{F}) = \{\ldots, C(F), \ldots\} \qquad C(\mathcal{L}) = \{\ldots, C(L), \ldots\} \tag{3}$$

---

[3] https://en.wikipedia.org/wiki/Cosine_similarity.

where $C(.)$ is either of C_{sent} or C_{ent}. Aggregate statistics across the sets $C(\mathcal{F})$ and $C(\mathcal{L})$, such as mean and standard deviation, enable quantifying the relative differences in textual coherence between fake and legitimate news.

4   Computational Approaches

We now outline our three computational approaches to quantify coherence at the document level. The first and second approaches use sentence-level modelling, and leverage word embeddings and explicit semantic analysis respectively. The third uses entity linking to convert each document into a set of entities, followed by computing the coherence at the entity set level. Each coherence quantification method is fully specified with the specification of how the vector representation is derived for the elements (entities or sentences) of the document.

Coherence Using Word Embeddings. This is the first of our sentence-level coherence assessment methods. As outlined in the related work section, word2vec [19] is among the most popular word embedding methods. Word2vec uses a shallow, two-layer neural network that is trained to reconstruct linguistic contexts of words over a corpus of documents. Word2vec takes as its input a large corpus of text and produces a vector space, typically of several hundred dimensions, with each unique word in the corpus being assigned a corresponding vector in the space. We use a pre-trained word2vec vector dataset that was trained over a huge corpus[4] since they are likely to be better representations being learnt over a massive dataset. Each sentence s_i in document D is then represented as the average of the word2vec vectors of the words, denoted word2vec(w), it contains:

$$rep(s_i) = \text{mean}\{\text{word2vec}(w)|w \in s_i\} \qquad (4)$$

This completes the specification of coherence quantification using embeddings.

Coherence Using Explicit Semantic Analysis. Explicit Semantic Analysis (ESA) [9] forms the basis of our second sentence-level coherence quantification method. ESA starts with a collection of text articles sources from a knowledge base, typically Wikipedia; each article is turned into a *bag of words*. Each word may then be thought of as being represented as a vector over the set of Wikipedia articles, each element of the vector directly related to the number of times it appears in the respective article. The ESA representation for each sentence is then simply the average of the ESA vectors of the words that it contains.

$$rep(s_i) = \text{mean}\{\text{esa}(w)|w \in s_i\} \qquad (5)$$

where esa(w) is the vector representation of the word w under ESA.

---

[4] https://github.com/mmihaltz/word2vec-GoogleNews-vectors.

Coherence Using Entity Linking. Given a document, entity linking (EL) methods [10] identify mentions of entities within them. Identifying Wikipedia entities to associate references to, is often complex and depends on the context of the word. EL algorithms use a variety of different heuristics in order to accurately identify the set of entities referenced in the document. We would like to now convert each entity thus identified to a vector so that it may be used for document coherence quantification within our framework. Towards this, we use the Wikipedia2vec technique [33] which is inspired by Word2vec and forms vectors for Wikipedia entities by processing the corpus of Wikipedia articles. Thus, the representation of each entity is simply the Wikipedia2vec vector associated with that entity. That representation then feeds into Eq. 2 for coherence assessments.

5 Experimental Study

5.1 Datasets

In order to ensure the generalizability of the insights from our coherence study, we evaluate the coherence scores over two datasets. The first one, *ISOT fake news dataset*, is a publicly available dataset comprising 10k+ articles focused on politics. The second dataset is one sourced by ourselves comprising 1k articles on *health and well-being* (HWB) from various online sources. These datasets are very different both in terms of size and the kind of topics they deal with. It may be noted that the nature of our task makes datasets comprising long text articles more suitable. Most fake news datasets involve tweets, and are thus sparse with respect to text data[5], making them unsuitable for textual coherence studies such as ours. Thus, we limit our attention to the aforementioned two datasets both of which comprise textual articles. We describe them separately herein.

ISOT Fake News Dataset. The ISOT Fake News dataset[6] [1] is the largest public dataset of textual articles with fake and legitimate labellings that we have come across. The ISOT dataset comprises various categories of articles, of which the *politics* category is the only one that appears within both *fake* and *real/legitimate* labellings. Thus, we use the politics subset from both fake and legitimate categories for our study. The details of the dataset as well as the statistics from the sentence segmentation and entity linking appear in Table 1.

HWB Dataset. We believe that health and well-being is another domain that is often targeted by fake news sources. As an example, fake news on topics such as vaccinations has raised significant concerns [13] in recent times, not to mention the COVID-19 pandemic. Thus, we curated a set of articles with fake/legitimate labellings tailored to the health domain. For the legitimate news articles, we crawled 500 news documents on health and well-being from reputable sources

---

[5] Tweets are limited to a maximum of 280 characters.
[6] https://www.uvic.ca/engineering/ece/isot/datasets/index.php.

Table 1. Dataset Statistics (SD = Standard Deviation)

Dataset	Category	#Articles	#Sentences Per Article Mean (SD)	#Entities Per Article Mean (SD)
ISOT	Fake	5816	11.56 (10.54)	38.99 (30.17)
	Legitimate	11175	14.65 (10.71)	46.48 (27.31)
HWB	Fake	500	24.62 (18.04)	49.56 (28.67)
	Legitimate	500	28.24 (19.37)	62.91 (37.07)

such as CNN, NYTimes, Washington Post and New Indian Express. For fake news, we crawled 500 articles on similar topics from well-reported misinformation websites such as BeforeItsNews, Nephef and MadWorldNews. These were manually verified for category suitability, thus avoiding blind reliance on source level labellings. This dataset, which we will refer to as HWB, short for *health and well-being*, will be made available at https://dcs.uoc.ac.in/cida/resources/hwb.html. HWB dataset statistics also appear in Table 1.

On the Article Size Disparity. The disparity in article sizes between fake and legitimate news articles is important to reflect upon, in the context of our comparative study. In particular, it is important to note how coherence assessments may be influenced by the number of sentences and entity references within each article. It may be intuitively expected that coherence quantification would yield a lower value for longer documents than for shorter ones, given that all pairs of sentences/entities are used in the comparison. Our study stems from the hypothesis that fake articles may be *less* coherent; the article length disparity in the dataset suggests that the null hypothesis assumption (that coherence is similar across fake and legitimate news) being true would yield *higher* coherence score for the fake news documents (being shorter). *In a way, it may be observed that any empirical evidence illustrating lower coherence scores for fake articles, as we observe in our results, could be held to infer a stronger departure from the null hypothesis than in a dataset where fake and legitimate articles were of similar sizes.* Thus, the article length distribution trends only deepen the significance of our results that points to lower coherence among fake articles.

5.2 Experimental Setup

We now describe some details of the experimental setup we employed. The code was written in Python. NLTK[7], a popular natural language toolkit, was used for sentence splitting and further processing. The word embedding coherence assessments were performed using Google's pre-trained word2vec corpus[8], which was trained over news articles. Explicit Semantic Analysis (ESA) was run using the publicly available EasyESA[9] implementation. For the entity linking method,

[7] https://www.nltk.org/.
[8] https://code.google.com/archive/p/word2vec/.
[9] https://github.com/dscarvalho/easyesa.

Table 2. Coherence Results Summary (SD = Standard Deviation). Statistically significant results with $p < 0.05$ (two-tailed t-test) in bold. XE-Y is a commonly used mathematical abbreviation to stand for $X \times 10^{-Y}$

Dataset	Category	Word Embedding Coherence Mean (SD)	ESA Coherence Mean (SD)	Entity Linking Coherence Mean (SD)
ISOT	Fake	0.546518 (0.0070)	0.999218 (4.90E-05)	0.277454 (0.0010)
	Legitimate	0.567870 (0.0055)	0.999474 (2.45E-05)	0.286689 (0.0003)
	Difference in %	3.91%	0.03%	3.33%
	p-value	**6.29E-60**	**0.013341**	**1.90E-100**
HWB	Fake	0.468907 (0.0055)	0.995245 (0.0040)	0.307874 (0.0006)
	Legitimate	0.506322 (0.0059)	0.997276 (0.0020)	0.318574 (0.0008)
	Difference in %	7.98%	0.20%	3.48%
	p-value	**1.46E-14**	0.557432	**6.27E-10**

the named entities were identified using the NLTK toolkit, and their vectors were looked up on the Wikipedia2vec[10] pre-trained model[11].

5.3 Analysis of Text Coherence

We first analyze the mean and standard deviation of coherence scores of fake and legitimate news articles as assessed using each of our three methods. Higher coherence scores indicate higher textual coherence. Table 2 summarizes the results. *In each of the three coherence assessments across two datasets, thus six combinations overall, the fake news articles were found to be less coherent than the legitimate news ones on the average.* The difference was found to be statistically significant with $p < 0.05$ under the two-tailed t-test[12] in five of six combinations, recording very low p-values (i.e., strong difference) in many cases.

Trends Across Methods. The largest difference in means are observed for the word embedding coherence scores, with the legitimate news articles being around 4% and 8% more coherent than fake news articles in the ISOT and HWB datasets respectively. The lowest p-values are observed for the entity linking method, where the legitimate articles are 3+% more coherent than fake news articles across datasets for the ISOT dataset; the p-value being in the region of 1E-100 indicates the presence of consistent difference in coherence across fake and legitimate news articles. On the other hand, the coherence scores for ESA vary only slightly in magnitude across fake and legitimate news articles. This is likely because ESA is primarily intended to separate articles from different domains; articles within the same domain thus often get judged to be very close to each other, as we will see in a more detailed analysis in the later section. The smaller differences across fake and legitimate news articles are still statistically significant for the ISOT dataset (p-value < 0.05), whereas they are not so in the

---

[10] https://github.com/wikipedia2vec/wikipedia2vec.

[11] https://wikipedia2vec.github.io/wikipedia2vec/pretrained/.

[12] https://www.itl.nist.gov/div898/handbook/eda/section3/eda353.htm.

case of the much smaller HWB dataset. It may be appreciated that statistical significance assessments depend on degrees of freedom, roughly interpreted as the number of independent samples; this makes it harder to approach statistical significance in small datasets. Overall, these results also indicate that the word embedding perspective is best suited, among the three methods, to discern textual coherence differences between legitimate and fake news.

Coherence Spread. The spread of the coherence across articles was seen to be largely broader for fake news articles, as compared to legitimate ones. This is evident from the higher standard deviations exhibited by the coherence scores in the majority of cases. From observations over the dataset, we find that the coherence scores for legitimate articles generally form a unimodal distribution, whereas the distribution of coherence scores across fake news articles show some minor deviations from unimodality. In particular, we find a small number of scores clustered in the low range of the spectrum, and another much larger set of scores forming a unimodal distribution centered at a score lesser than that the respective centre for the legitimate news articles. This difference in character, of which more details follow in the next section, reflects in the higher standard deviation in coherence scores for the fake news documents.

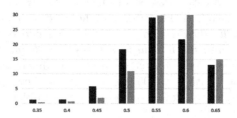

Fig. 1. ISOT Word Embedding Coherence Histogram (%articles vs. coherence scores): Legitimate and Fake articles' scores in green and red respectively. (Color figure online)

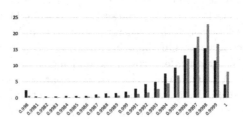

Fig. 2. ISOT ESA Coherence Histogram (%articles vs. coherence scores): Legitimate and Fake articles' scores in green and red respectively. (Color figure online)

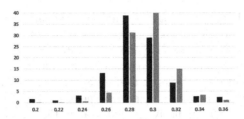

Fig. 3. ISOT Entity Linking Coherence Histogram (%articles vs. coherence scores): Legitimate and Fake articles' scores in green and red respectively. (Color figure online)

Coherence Score Histograms. We visualize the nature of the coherence score distributions for the various methods further by way of histogram plots in Figs. 1, 2 and 3 for the ISOT dataset. The corresponding histograms for the HWB dataset appear in Figs. 4, 5 and 6. We have set the histogram buckets in a way to amplify the region where most documents fall, density of scores being around different ranges for different methods. This happens to be around 0.5 for word embedding scores, 0.999 for ESA scores, and around 0.3 for entity linking scores. With the number of articles differing across the fake and legitimate subsets, we have set the Y-axis to indicate the percentage of articles in each of the ranges (as opposed to raw frequency counts), to aid meaningful visual comparison. All documents that fall outside the range in the histogram are incorporated into the leftmost or rightmost pillar in the histogram as appropriate.

The most striking high-level trend, across the six histograms is as follows. When one follows the histogram pillars from left to right, the red pillar (corresponding to fake news articles) is consistently taller than the green pillar (corresponding to legitimate news articles), until a point beyond which the trend reverses; from that point onwards the green pillar is consistently taller than the red pillar. Thus, the lower coherence scores have a larger fraction of fake articles than legitimate ones and vice versa. For example, this point of reversal is at 0.55 for Fig. 1, 0.9997 for Fig. 3 and 0.9996 for Fig. 5. There are only two histogram points that are not very aligned with this trend, both for the entity linking method, which are 0.36 in Fig. 3 and 0.34 in Fig. 6; even in those cases, the high-level trend is still consistent with our analysis.

The second observation, albeit unsurprising, is the largely single-peak (i.e., unimodal) distribution of the coherence score in each of the six charts for both fake and legitimate news articles; this also vindicates our choice of the statistical significance test statistic in the previous section, t-test being suited best for comparing unimodal distributions. A slight departure from that unimodality, as alluded to earlier, is visible for fake article coherence score. This is most expressed for the ESA method, with a the leftmost red pillar being quite tall in Figs. 2 and 5; it may be noted that the leftmost pillars count all documents below that score and thus, the small peak that exists in the lower end of the fake news scores is overemphasized in the graphs due to the nature of the plots.

Thirdly, the red-green reversal trend as observed earlier, may be interpreted as largely being an artifact of the relative positioning of the centres of the uni-modal score distribution across fake and legitimate news articles. The red peak appears to the left (i.e., at a lower coherence score) of the green peak; it is easy to observe this trend if one looks at the red and green distributions separately on the various charts. For example, the red peak for Fig. 1 is at 0.55, whereas the green peak is at 0.60. Similarly, the red peak in Fig. 3 is at 0.28, whereas the green peak is at 0.30. Similar trends are easier to observe for the HWB results.

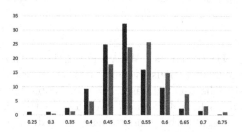

Fig. 4. HWB Word Embedding Coherence Histogram (%articles vs. coherence scores): Legitimate and Fake articles' scores in green and red respectively. (Color figure online)

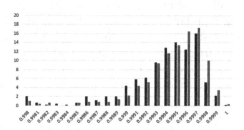

Fig. 5. HWB ESA Coherence Histogram (%articles vs. coherence scores): Legitimate and Fake articles' scores in green and red respectively. (Color figure online)

Summary. Main observations from our computational social science study are:

- *Fake news articles less coherent:* The trends across all the coherence scoring mechanisms over the two widely different datasets (different domains, different sizes) indicate that fake news articles are less coherent than legitimate news ones. The trends are statistically significant in all but one case.
- *Word embeddings most suited:* From across our results, we observe that word embedding based mechanism is most suited, among our methods, to help discern the difference in coherence between fake and legitimate news articles.

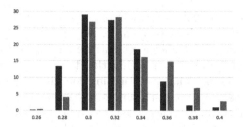

Fig. 6. HWB Entity Linking Coherence Histogram (%articles vs. coherence scores): Legitimate and Fake articles' scores in green and red respectively. (Color figure online)

- *Unimodal distributions with different peaks:* The high-level trend points to a unimodal distribution of coherence scores (slight departure observed for fake articles), with the score distribution for fake news peaking at a lower score.

6   Discussion

The relevance or importance of this computational social science study lies in what the observations and the insights from them point us to. We discuss some such aspects in this section.

6.1   Towards More Generic Fake News Detection

Fake news detection has been traditionally viewed as a classification problem by the data science community, with the early approaches relying on the availability of labelled training data. The text features employed were standard ones used within the text mining/NLP community, such as word-level ones and coarser lexical features. Standard text classification scenarios such as identifying the label to be associated with a scholarly article or determining disease severity from medical reports involve settings where the human actors involved in generating the text are largely passive to the classification task. On the other hand, data science based fake news identification methods stand between the fake news author and accomplishment of his/her objectives (which may be one of myriad possibilities such as influencing the reader's political or medical choices). Social networks regularly use fake news detection algorithms to aid prioritization of stories. Making use of low-level features such as words and lexical patterns in fake news detection makes it easier for the fake news author to circumvent the fake news filter and reach a broad audience. As an example, a fake news filter that is trained on US based political corpora using word-level features could be easily surpassed by using words and phrases that are not commonly used within US politics reporting (e.g., replacing *President* with *head of state*). On the other hand, moving from low-level lexical features (e.g., words) to higher level ones such as topical novelty (as investigated in a Science journal article [30]), emotions [15] and rhetorical structures [25] would yield more *'generic'* fake news identification methods that are more robust to being easily tricked by fake news peddlers. We observe that moving to higher-level features for fake news identification has not yet been a widespread trend within the data science community; this is likely to be due to the fact that investigating specific trends do not necessarily individually improve the state-of-the-art for fake news detection using conventional metrics such as empirical accuracy that are employed within data science. Nonetheless, such efforts yield insights which hold much promise in collectively leading to more generic fake news detection for the future. Techniques that use high-level features may also be better transferable across domains and geographies. We believe that our work investigates an important high-level feature, that of lexical coherence, and provides insights highly supported by datasets across widely varying domains, and would be valuable in contributing to a general fake news detection method less reliant on abundant training datasets.

6.2   Lexical Coherence and Other Disciplines

We now consider how our observations could lead to interesting research questions in other disciplinary domains.

News Media. The observation that fake news articles exhibit lower textual coherence could be translated into various questions when it comes to news media. It may be expected that fake news articles appear in media sources that are not as established, big or reputed as the ones that report only accurate news; these media houses may also have less experienced staff. If such an assumption is true, one could possibly consider various media-specific reasons for the relate coherence trends between fake and legitimate news:

- Is the lower coherence of fake news articles a reflection of less mature media quality control employed within smaller and less established media houses?
- Is the relative lack of coherence of fake news articles more reflective of amateurish authors with limited journalistic experience?

Linguistics. Yet another perspective to analyze our results is that of linguistics, or more specifically, cognitive linguistics[13]. The intent of fake news authors are likely more towards swaying the reader towards a particular perspective/stance/position; this is markedly different from just conveying accurate and informative news, as may be expected of more reputed media. Under the lens of cognitive linguistics, it would be interesting to analyze the following questions:

- Is the reduced coherence due to fake news generally delving into multiple topics within the same article?
- Could the reduced coherence be correlated with mixing of emotional and factual narratives?

---

[13] https://en.wikipedia.org/wiki/Cognitive_linguistics.

Besides the above, our results may spawn other questions based on perspectives that we are unable to view it from, given the limited breadth in our expertise.

7   Conclusions and Future Work

We studied the variation between fake and legitimate news articles in terms of the coherence of their textual content. Within the computational social science framework, we used state-of-the-art data science methodologies to formulate three different computational notions of textual coherence, in order to address our research question. The methods widely vary in character and use word embeddings, explicit semantic analysis and entity linking respectively. We empirically analyzed two datasets, one public dataset from politics, and another one comprising health and well-being articles, in terms of their textual coherence, and analyzed differences across their fake and legitimate news subsets. All the results across all six combinations (3 scoring methods, 2 datasets) unequivocally indicated that fake news article subset exhibits lower textual coherence as compared to the legitimate news subset. These results are despite the fact that fake news articles were found to be shorter, short articles intuitively having a higher propensity to be more coherent. In summary, our results suggest that fake news articles are less coherent than legitimate news articles in systematic and discernible ways when analyzed using simple textual coherence scoring methods such as the one we have devised.

Acknowledgements. Deepak P was supported by MHRD SPARC (P620).

References

1. Ahmed, H., Traore, I., Saad, S.: Detection of online fake news using N-gram analysis and machine learning techniques. In: Traore, I., Woungang, I., Awad, A. (eds.) ISDDC 2017. LNCS, vol. 10618, pp. 127–138. Springer, Cham (2017). https://doi.org/10.1007/978-3-319-69155-8_9
2. Allcott, H., Gentzkow, M.: Social media and fake news in the 2016 election. J. Econ. Perspect. **31**, 211–36 (2017)
3. Alotaibi, H.: The role of lexical cohesion in writing quality. Int. J. Appl. Linguist. Engl. Lit. **4**(1), 261–269 (2015)
4. Chopra, S., Jain, S., Sholar, J.M.: Towards automatic identification of fake news: headline-article stance detection with LSTM attention models (2017)
5. Conroy, N.J., Rubin, V.L., Chen, Y.: Automatic deception detection: methods for finding fake news. In: Proceedings of the 78th ASIS&T Annual Meeting, p. 82 (2015)
6. Crossley, S., McNamara, D.: Text coherence and judgments of essay quality: models of quality and coherence. In: Proceedings of the Annual Meeting of the Cognitive Science Society, vol. 33 (2011)
7. Davies, W.: The age of post-truth politics. The New York Times **24**, 2016 (2016)
8. Dilawar, N., et al.: Understanding citizen issues through reviews: a step towards data informed planning in smart cities. Appl. Sci. **8**, 1589 (2018)

9. Gabrilovich, E., Markovitch, S., et al.: Computing semantic relatedness using Wikipedia-based explicit semantic analysis. In: IJcAI, vol. 7, pp. 1606–1611 (2007)
10. Gupta, N., Singh, S., Roth, D.: Entity linking via joint encoding of types, descriptions, and context. In: Proceedings of the Conference on EMNLP, pp. 2681–2690 (2017)
11. Hoffart, J., et al.: Robust disambiguation of named entities in text. In: Proceedings of the Conference on EMNLP, pp. 782–792 (2011)
12. Hopkin, J., Rosamond, B.: Post-truth politics, bullshit and badideas: 'deficit fetishism' in the UK. New Polit. Econ. **23**, 641–655 (2018)
13. Iacobucci, G.: Vaccination: "fake news" on social media may be harming UK uptake, report warns. BMJ: Br. Med. J. (Online) **364** (2019)
14. Jin, Z., Cao, J., Zhang, Y., Zhou, J., Tian, Q.: Novel visual and statistical image features for microblogs news verification. IEEE Trans. Multimed. **19**, 598–608 (2017)
15. Anoop, K., Deepak, P., Lajish, V.L.: Emotion cognizance improves health fake news detection. In: 24th International Database Engineering & Applications Symposium (IDEAS 2020) (2020)
16. Le, Q., Mikolov, T.: Distributed representations of sentences and documents. In: International Conference on Machine Learning, pp. 1188–1196 (2014)
17. McCulley, G.A.: Writing quality, coherence, and cohesion. Res. Teach. Engl. 269–282 (1985)
18. Mihalcea, R., Csomai, A.: Wikify!: linking documents to encyclopedic knowledge. In: CIKM, pp. 233–242 (2007)
19. Mikolov, T., Sutskever, I., Chen, K., Corrado, G.S., Dean, J.: Distributed representations of words and phrases and their compositionality. In: NIPS (2013)
20. Mikolov, T., Yih, W., Zweig, G.: Linguistic regularities in continuous space word representations. In: NAACL, pp. 746–751 (2013)
21. Morris, J., Hirst, G.: Lexical cohesion computed by thesaural relations as an indicator of the structure of text. Comput. Linguist. **17**(1), 21–48 (1991)
22. Ounis, I., Amati, G., Plachouras, V., He, B., Macdonald, C., Johnson, D.: Terrier information retrieval platform. In: Losada, D.E., Fernández-Luna, J.M. (eds.) ECIR 2005. LNCS, vol. 3408, pp. 517–519. Springer, Heidelberg (2005). https://doi.org/10.1007/978-3-540-31865-1_37
23. Pennington, J., Socher, R., Manning, C.: Glove: global vectors for word representation. In: Proceedings of the Conference on EMLNP, pp. 1532–1543 (2014)
24. Potthast, M., Kiesel, J., Reinartz, K., Bevendorff, J., Stein, B.: A stylometric inquiry into hyperpartisan and fake news. arXiv:1702.05638 (2017)
25. Rubin, V.L., Conroy, N.J., Chen, Y.: Towards news verification: deception detection methods for news discourse. In: Hawaii International Conference on System Sciences (2015)
26. Rubin, V., Conroy, N., Chen, Y., Cornwell, S.: Fake news or truth? Using satirical cues to detect potentially misleading news. In: Proceedings of the 2nd Workshop on Computational Approaches to Deception Detection, pp. 7–17 (2016)
27. Scholl, P., Böhnstedt, D., Domínguez García, R., Rensing, C., Steinmetz, R.: Extended explicit semantic analysis for calculating semantic relatedness of web resources. In: Wolpers, M., Kirschner, P.A., Scheffel, M., Lindstaedt, S., Dimitrova, V. (eds.) EC-TEL 2010. LNCS, vol. 6383, pp. 324–339. Springer, Heidelberg (2010). https://doi.org/10.1007/978-3-642-16020-2_22
28. Speed, E., Mannion, R.: The rise of post-truth populism in pluralist liberal democracies: challenges for health policy. Int. J. Health Policy Manag. **6**, 249 (2017)
29. Steyvers, M., Griffiths, T.: Probabilistic topic models. Handb. Latent Semant. Anal. **427**, 424–440 (2007)

30. Vosoughi, S., Roy, D., Aral, S.: The spread of true and false news online. Science **359**, 1146–1151 (2018)
31. Wargadiredja, A.T.: Indonesian teens are getting 'drunk' off boiled bloody menstrual pads (2018). https://www.vice.com/en_asia/article/wj38gx/indonesian-teens-drinking-boiled-bloody-menstrual-pads. Accessed Apr 2020
32. Wu, L., Liu, H.: Tracing fake-news footprints: characterizing social media messages by how they propagate. In: WSDM, pp. 637–645 (2018)
33. Yamada, I., Asai, A., Shindo, H., Takeda, H., Takefuji, Y.: Wikipedia2vec: an optimized implementation for learning embeddings from wikipedia. arXiv:1812.06280 (2018)
34. Yeh, E., Ramage, D., Manning, C.D., Agirre, E., Soroa, A.: Wikiwalk: random walks on Wikipedia for semantic relatedness. In: Proceedings Workshop on Graph-based Methods for NLP, pp. 41–49. ACL (2009)

Short Paper – DINA 2020

Integrating Spreadsheets by Identifying and Solving Layout Constraints

Dirko Coetsee[1,2,3], McElory Hoffmann[1,3], and Luc De Raedt[2]

[1] Stellenbosch University, South Africa
[2] KU Leuven, Belgium
[3] Praelexis (Pty) Ltd, South Africa

Abstract. The integration of multiple spreadsheets is a time-consuming and tedious task for end users. We present a tool that semi-automatically helps non-programmers to merge different spreadsheets into a single spreadsheet, with particular emphasis on extending formulas to new data. Our work exploits the constraints that spreadsheets impose with respect to layout. The tool therefore identifies these layout constraints in input spreadsheets, generalizes them, and uses them to obtain a layout that is similar to the input sheets.

Unlike previous work to automatically merge spreadsheets, such as that of Chen et al. [2], who transform spreadsheets into first-normal form and then applies standard relational matching and mapping techniques, we do not assume or try to recover an underlying relational format. We rather work directly with layout constraints that we assume the user intended, and allow the user to interactively improve them.

We recognize three types of layout constraints: certain cells should be in the same row or column as certain other cells, below or to the right of certain cells, and certain formulas should be repeated over all cells of an implicit *type*. A formula constraint is recognized by grouping formula cells with the same *template representation*, a representation of the formula string where arguments are replaced with their position relative to the formula cell. The extent of a formula template group is assumed to be constrained by the extent of its arguments, and so the type of its arguments is identified and used to generalize to other cells of that type from other sheets.

We take the union of these layout constraints from different sheets and solve the resulting *constraint satisfaction problem*. To improve the run-time, we firstly note that the only necessary decision variables are the new output positions for each of the input rows and columns. Secondly, cells should not overlap. By grouping together input cells into *blocks*, we can encode the non-overlap constraint more efficiently.

Our preliminary result on a random sample of spreadsheets from the Fuse spreadsheet corpus [1], where each sheet was artificially split to produce mergeable sheets, is that most examples require less than 5 user suggestions to merge.

In the future, the performance can be improved by using machine learning techniques to reduce the number of human suggestions that is necessary, by recognizing more types of constraints, and ambiguous or contradictory constraints can be more gracefully resolved by assigning weights to the recognized constraints.

© Springer Nature Switzerland AG 2020
I. Koprinska et al. (Eds.): ECML PKDD 2020 Workshops, CCIS 1323, pp. 611–612, 2020.
https://doi.org/10.1007/978-3-030-65965-3

References

1. Barik, T., Lubick, K., Smith, J., Slankas, J., Murphy-Hill, E.: Fuse: a reproducible, extendable, internet-scale corpus of spreadsheets. In: 2015 IEEE/ACM 12th Working Conference on Mining Software Repositories, pp. 486–489 (2015)
2. Chen, Z., Cafarella, M.: Integrating spreadsheet data via accurate and low-effort extraction. In: Proceedings of the 20th ACM SIGKDD International Conference on Knowledge Discovery and Data Mining, KDD 2014, pp. 1126–1135. ACM, New York (2014)

Author Index

Printed in the United States
By Bookmasters